International Capital Markets

Developments, Prospects, and Key Policy Issues

By an IMF Staff Team
led by
David Folkerts-Landau with
Donald J. Mathieson and
Garry J. Schinasi

INTERNATIONAL MONETARY FUND
Washington, DC
November 1997

ISBN 1-55775-686-4
ISSN 0258-7440

Price: US$20.00
(US$12.00 to full-time faculty members and
students at universities and colleges)

Please send orders to:
International Monetary Fund, Publication Services
700 19th Street, N.W., Washington, D.C. 20431, U.S.A.
Tel.: (202) 623-7430   Telefax: (202) 623-7201
E-mail: publications@imf.org
Internet: http://www.imf.org

recycled paper

Contents

	Page
Preface	**xi**
List of Abbreviations	**xiii**
I. Introduction	**1**
II. Developments and Trends in the Mature Markets	**2**
Foreign Exchange Markets: Capital Flows and the Rise of the Dollar	2
Credit Markets: Spread Compression and Increased Volumes	7
Risks in Foreign Exchange and Credit Markets	12
Equity Markets	12
Expanding and Maturing Derivative Markets	17
Appendix: Market Surprised by Yen's Appreciation in May 1997	19
III. EMU: Systemic Implications and Challenges	**21**
Global Financial Adjustments After Introduction of the Euro	21
EMU and the Potential Benefits of Europe-Wide Securities Markets	22
Consolidation and Restructuring of European Banking Systems	24
Systemic Risk Management in EMU	25
IV. Developments and Prospects in Emerging Markets	**27**
Capital Flows to Emerging Markets	27
Performance of Emerging Debt and Equity Markets	31
Sustainability of Capital Flows and Speculative Attacks	33
Appendix 1: Sovereign Ratings and Fundamentals	35
Appendix 2: Mechanics of Speculative Attacks	37
V. External Liability Management	**39**
VI. Developments in International Banking	**43**
Industrial Countries	43
Banking System Developments in Emerging Markets	45
VII. Emerging Market Currency Crises of July 1997	**49**
VIII. Conclusions	**54**
Mature Markets	54
Structural Aspects of EMU	55
Emerging Markets	55
External Liability Management	57
Developments in International Banking	58

Page

Background Material—Part I
Recent Developments and Trends in Capital Markets and Banking Systems

Annexes

I. **Recent Developments in Emerging Capital Markets**   **61**
     Capital Flows, Reserves, and Foreign Exchange Markets   62
     Bond Markets   70
     Equity Markets   83
     Mutual Funds   88
     International Bank Lending   89

II. **Developments and Trends in the Mature Capital Markets**   **93**
     Exchange Rates   93
     Bond Markets   104
     International Syndicated Loan Markets   112
     Equity Markets   115
     Derivative Markets   120
     Developments in Systemic Risk Management   125
     Appendix 1: Extracting Information from Options Prices   127
     Appendix 2: Have Securities Markets Become More Volatile?   128
     Appendix 3: Current U.S. Equity Prices Compared with
         the 1987 U.S. and 1989 Japanese Bubbles   130

III. **Developments in International Banking**   **132**
     Restructuring and Consolidation of International Banking Systems   132
     Supervisory and Regulatory Developments   139
     Developments in Profitability and Asset Quality in
         Selected Industrial Countries   142
     Banking System Developments in Selected Emerging Markets   149
     Appendix 1: Credit Derivatives   158
     Appendix 2: Accounting for Nonperforming Loans   160

Background Material—Part II
Selected Issues

IV. **European Monetary Union: Institutional Framework for Financial Policies
     and Structural Implications**   **169**
     Potential Size of EMU Financial Markets   169
     Institutional Framework for Financial Markets   170
     Euro as a Catalyst: Incentives for Continued Structural Change   184
     Structural Implications for Securities Markets: Further Securitization of
         European Finance   188
     Structural Implications for Banking Systems   199
     Appendix: Remaining Impediments to Cross-Border Competition   209

V. **Risk Management of Sovereign Liabilities**   **214**
     Foreign Currency Exposure of Sovereign Liabilities   214
     Institutional Framework   218
     Strategic Management of Sovereign Liabilities   228
     Deviations from the Benchmark Portfolio   232
     Conclusion   232

VI. **Capital Flows to Emerging Markets—A Historical Perspective**   **234**
     Earlier Periods of High Capital Mobility   234
     International Capital Flows After the First Oil Shock   238

Page

Factors Stimulating Capital Flows and Renewed Market Access
in the 1990s   241
Appendix 1: Determinants of Balance of Payments and Banking Crises   245
Appendix 2: Speculative Attacks in the 1990s: Have
Economic Models Got It Right Yet?   249

Statistical Appendix   **252**

References   **261**

Boxes

Chapter

IV.   1. Building a Resilient Financial System in Hong Kong, China   34

Annexes

I.   2. The Brady Bond Market Comes of Age   75
             3. Repackaged Brady Bonds   80
             4. Emerging Market Currency Eurobonds: The Eurorand Market   81
II.   5. Trends in Fund Management   120
             6. Circuit Breakers   124
IV.   7. ERM 2   177
             8. Volatility and Correlation of Asset Returns in EMU   189
VI.   9. Liberalization of Capital Controls in Emerging Markets   242

Tables

Chapters

II.   1. Net Foreign Purchases of U.S. Bonds   4
             2. Net Purchases of Domestic Bonds by Nonresidents   5
             3. United States: International Transactions   5
             4. One-Year Interest Differentials with Germany, February 28,
                1995, January 30, 1997, and May 31, 1997   9
             5. Domestic and International Debt Securities: Amounts Outstanding
                and Net Issues   10
             6. Announced International Syndicated Credit Facilities by
                Nationality of Borrowers   11
             7. Average Spreads and Maturities on Eurocredits   12
             8. Major Industrial Countries: Equity Market Risk-Adjusted Returns
                in Local Currency (Sharpe Ratios)   16
             9. Markets for Selected Derivative Financial Instruments:
                Notional Principal Amounts Outstanding   17
            10. Notional Principal Value of Outstanding Interest Rate
                and Currency Swaps   18
III.   11. Total Foreign Exchange Reserves Minus Gold in Selected Countries
                and Regions   22
            12. European Union (EU), North America, and Japan: Selected
                Indicators of the Size of the Capital Markets, 1995   23
IV.   13. Private Capital Flows to Emerging Markets   28
            14. Emerging Market Total Return Equity and Debt Indices   31

Annexes

I.   15. Secondary Market Transactions in Debt Instruments of Emerging Markets 74
            16. Emerging Market Bond Issues, Equity Issues, and Syndicated
                Loan Commitments   77

		Page
	17. Emerging Market Bond Issues: Fixed-Rate, Floating-Rate, and Call Options	78
	18. Emerging Market International Bond Issues by Currency of Denomination	79
	19. Stock Market Turnover Ratio and Value of New Equity Issues in Selected Countries and Regions	87
	20. Emerging Market Medium- and Long-Term Syndicated Loan Commitments: Interest Margins and Refinancings	90
	21. Changes in Net Assets of BIS-Reporting Banks vis-à-vis Banks in Selected Countries and Regions	91
II.	22. United States: Selected External Account Variables	101
	23. Major Industrial Countries: Bond and Equity Index Returns	107
	24. One-Year and Seven-Year Interest Differentials with Germany, February 28, 1995, January 1, 1996, January 30, 1997, and May 31, 1997	108
	25. Outstanding Amounts of International Debt Securities	111
	26. Outstanding Amounts and Net Issues of International Debt Securities by Currency of Issue	111
	27. Changes in Net Assets of BIS-Reporting Banks vis-à-vis Banks in Selected Countries and Regions	114
	28. United States: Outstanding Repurchase Agreements (Repos)	114
	29. U.S. Mutual Funds: Net New Cash Flow and Total Assets	119
III.	30. Bank Financial Strength Ratings for Selected Countries, June 2, 1997	133
	31. Disintermediation in Selected Industrial Countries	135
	32. Japan and the United States: Summary of Prompt Corrective Action Provisions	141
	33. Major Industrial Countries: Commercial Bank Profitability	147
	34. Selected Asian Property Markets: Vacancy Rates and Changes in Rents	150
	35. Loan Classification in Selected Emerging Markets	161
IV.	36. Amounts Outstanding of International Debt Securities by Currency and Country of Nationality, March 1997	170
	37. Use of Selected Currencies on One Side of Foreign Exchange Transaction, April 1989, April 1992, and April 1995	171
	38. Notional Principal Value of Outstanding and New Interest Rate and Currency Swaps, 1995	172
	39. European System of Central Banks: Open Market Operations and Standing Facilities	175
	40. European System of Central Banks: Eligible Assets	176
	41. Key Monetary Policy Operating Procedures in Industrial Countries and in the European Central Bank	178
	42. Monetary and Supervisory Agencies	179
	43. Deposit Insurance Schemes for Commercial Banks in the European Union and G-10 Countries, 1995	182
	44. Permissible Banking Activities and Bank Ownership in the European Union and G-10 Countries, 1995	184
	45. List of Bank Activities Subject to Mutual Recognition in the European Union	185
	46. Components of Capital for Meeting the Capital Standards or Requirements in the European Union and G-10 Countries	186
	47. Commercial Bank Supervisory Practices in the European Union and G-10 Countries, 1995	187
	48. Mutual Funds, June 1996	188
	49. European Union: Cross-Border Interbank Assets	190
	50. European Union: Ratings of Foreign and Local Currency Debt of Sovereign Governments, May 29, 1997	192

Page

51. European Union Countries, North America, and Japan:
    Foreign Currency Debt, 1996 — 193
52. Estimates of Credit Spreads of EU Sovereigns, September 1996
    and June 1997 — 193
53. Interest Rate Spreads of Canadian Provinces — 194
54. Euro Benchmark Yield Curve: Germany vs. France — 195
55. Funds Raised in Capital Markets by Nonfinancial Enterprises
    in Selected Industrial Countries, 1990–95 — 196
56. European Union Countries, United States, and Japan:
    Equity Markets, 1996 — 198
57. Bank Restructuring: Number of Institutions and Size Concentration — 201
58. European Union Countries, North America, and Japan:
    Population per Bank Branch — 202
59. Mergers and Acquisition Activity in Banking — 203
60. European Union: Net Interest Margins — 204
61. European Union: Bank Profitability — 205
62. Implementation of the European Union Capital Adequacy and
    Investment Services Directives — 210
63. Regulatory Constraints on Portfolio Investment of Institutional
    Investors in Selected Industrial Countries — 211
V. 64. Long-Term Public and Publicly Guaranteed External Debt Outstanding
    and Reserves Excluding Gold in Selected Developing Countries, 1995 — 215
65. External Debt Profile of Selected Asian Countries, 1995 — 216
66. Institutional Structure of Debt Offices in OECD Countries:
    Debt Offices Within the Treasury — 222
67. Institutional Structure of Debt Offices in OECD Countries:
    Autonomous Debt Offices — 224
68. Institutional Structure of Debt Offices in OECD Countries:
    Debt Offices Within the Central Bank — 225
69. Institutional Structure of Debt Offices in OECD Countries:
    Debt Offices Within the Ministry of Finance — 226
VI. 70. Selected Crises, 1870–1914 — 238
71. External Financial Resources to Developing Countries — 239
72. Moody's Initial Ratings of Emerging Markets Countries — 244
73. Performance of Crises Indicators — 247

Statistical Appendix
A1. Merrill Lynch Global Investor Survey — 252
A2. Net Foreign Purchases of U.S. Bonds — 254
A3. Net Purchases of Securities in Major Industrial Countries — 255
A4. External Positions of Banks in Individual Reporting Countries — 256
A5. Annual Turnover in Derivative Financial Instruments Traded
    on Organized Exchanges Worldwide — 258
A6. New Interest Rate and Currency Swaps — 259
A7. Currency Composition of Notional Principal Value of
    Outstanding Interest Rate and Currency Swaps — 260

Figures

Chapters
II. 1. Spot Exchange Rates — 3
2. United States, Japan, and Germany: Interest Rate Differentials — 4
3. Major European Countries: Exchange Rates vs. Deutsche Mark — 6
4. Implied Volatility: Japanese Yen and Deutsche Mark
   Three-Month Forwards — 7
5. Selected European Long-Term Interest Rate Differentials with Germany — 8
6. United States: Yield Spreads of Corporate Bonds over U.S. Treasuries — 8

		Page
	7. Australia, Canada, and New Zealand: Yield Differentials on 10-Year Government Bonds	9
	8. Stock Market Indices: Major Industrial Countries	13
	9. Stock Market Indices: Smaller European Countries	14
	10. United States: Equity Market Performance	15
IV.	11. Distribution for Yen-Dollar Exchange Rate in Early September 1997 Implied by Options Prices on May 5, 9, and 19, 1997	20
	12. Private Market Financing for Emerging Markets	30
V.	13. Yield Spreads: Emerging Market and High-Yield U.S. Corporate Bonds	32
	14. Emerging Markets: Sovereign Ratings and Fundamentals	36
	15. Bank Receipts and Payments Arising from Forward Contract Operations	38
	16. External Long-Term Public and Publicly Guaranteed Debt Outstanding	39
VII.	17. Thailand: Selected Financial Indicators	50
	18. Financial Market Developments in Selected Asian Countries, 1997	51
	19. Financial Market Developments in Selected Latin American Countries, 1997	52
	20. Yield Curves in Selected Emerging Markets, July 1997	53

Annexes

I.	21. Net Private Capital Flows to Emerging Markets	62
	22. Total Reserves Minus Gold of Selected Emerging Markets, January 1990–May 1997	65
	23. Exchange Rates of Selected Emerging Markets, January 1990–May 1997	68
	24. Bond Markets: Selected Returns, Yields, and Spreads	71
	25. Yield Spreads for Selected Brady Bonds and U.S. Dollar-Denominated Eurobonds	72
	26. Emerging Market Debt: Volatility and Correlation of Returns with Mature Markets	73
	27. Brady and Eurobond Spreads	76
	28. Spreads and Maturities for Sovereign Borrowers	78
	29. Emerging Equity Markets: Selected Returns, Price-Earnings Ratios, and Expected Returns	83
	30. Emerging Equity Markets: Selected Volatilities, Return-Volatility Comparisons, and Correlations	85
	31. Emerging Market Mutual Funds	89
II.	32. Major Industrial Countries: Exchange Rates, January 1994–May 1997	94
	33. Major European Countries: Local Currency vs. Deutsche Mark, January 1994–May 1997	95
	34. Major Industrial Countries: Real Growth in Broad Money Supply and Claims on Private Sector	96
	35. Major Industrial Countries: Short-Term Interest Rates	97
	36. Major Industrial Countries: Long-Term Interest Rates	98
	37. Bilateral Exchange Rates and Short-Term and Long-Term Interest Differentials vis-à-vis the U.S. Dollar	99
	38. Foreign and International Holdings of U.S. Public Debt	100
	39. RiskMetrics Daily Price Volatility for U.S. Dollar Spot Exchange Rates, January 19, 1995–May 30, 1997	102
	40. Implied Volatility: Yen and Deutsche Mark Three-Month Forwards	103
	41. Selected European Long-Term Interest Rate Differentials with Germany	104
	42. Yield Differential for the 10-Year Government Bonds of Australia, Canada, and New Zealand	105
	43. United States: Yield Spreads of Corporate Bonds over U.S. Treasuries	106
	44. RiskMetrics Daily Price Volatility for 10-Year Government Bonds, January 19, 1995–May 30, 1997	110
	45. Spreads on Eurocredits	113
	46. Major Industrial Countries: Stock Market Indices	117

		Page
	47. United States: Corporate Profits and Market Capitalization	118
	48. United States: Corporate Profits Volatility	119
	49. Implied Volatility: S&P 500, Nikkei 225, and DAX Indices	122
	50. Distribution for Yen/Dollar Exchange Rate in Early September 1997 Implied by Options Prices on May 20, 1997	128
	51. Historical Stock and Bond Price Volatility in the United States, Japan, and Germany	129
	52. United States and Japan: Developments in Equity, Bond, and Money Markets Surrounding Significant Stock Market Increases	130
III.	53. Major Industrial Countries: Intemediation Spreads	148
IV.	54. Cross-Border TARGET Payment	173
	55. Labor Costs and Productivity in Banking, 1994	200
V.	56. External Long-Term Public and Publicly Guaranteed Debt Outstanding	215
VI.	57. Capital Mobility Index	235
	58. Net Capital Outflows, 1880–1913	235
	59. Net Capital Inflows, 1880–1913	236
	60. Contributions of Capital Flows to Investment, 1870–1914 versus 1980–90s	237

Box
9. Capital Controls in and Flows to Emerging Markets | 242

The following symbols have been used throughout this volume:

. . . to indicate that data are not available;

— to indicate that the figure is zero or less than half the final digit shown, or that the item does not exist;

– between years or months (for example, 1995–96 or January–June) to indicate the years or months covered, including the beginning and ending years or months;

/ between years (for example, 1995/96) to indicate a fiscal or financial year.

"Billion" means a thousand million; "trillion" means a thousand billion.

"Basis points" refer to hundredths of 1 percentage point (for example, 25 basis points are equivalent to ¼ of 1 percentage point).

"n.a." means not applicable.

Minor discrepancies between constituent figures and totals are due to rounding.

As used in this volume the term "country" does not in all cases refer to a territorial entity that is a state as understood by international law and practice. As used here, the term also covers some territorial entities that are not states but for which statistical data are maintained on a separate and independent basis.

Preface

The *International Capital Markets* report is an integral element of the IMF's surveillance of developments in international financial markets. The IMF has published the International Capital Markets report annually since 1980. The report draws, in part, on a series of informal discussions with commercial and investment banks, securities firms, stock and futures exchanges, regulatory and monetary authorities, and the staffs of the Bank for International Settlements, the Commission of the European Union, the International Swaps and Derivatives Association, the Japan Center for International Finance, and the Organization for Economic Cooperation and Development. The discussions leading up to the present report took place in Belgium, France, Germany, Indonesia, Italy, Japan, Korea, Singapore, South Africa, Switzerland, Turkey, the United Kingdom, the United States, and Hong Kong, China, between January and April 1997. The report reflects information available up to the end of May 1997; a special chapter provides an update of exchange market developments in the emerging markets through July 1997.

The *International Capital Markets* report is prepared in the Research Department. The International Capital Markets project is directed by David Folkerts-Landau, Assistant Director, together with Donald Mathieson, Chief of the Emerging Markets Studies Division, and Garry Schinasi, Chief of the Capital Markets and Financial Studies Division. Coauthors of the report from the Capital Markets and Financial Studies Division of the Research Department are Robert Flood, Senior Economist; Marcel Cassard, Peter Christoffersen, Laura Kodres, Alessandro Prati, and Todd Smith, all Economists; Charles Thomas, Visiting Scholar; and Subramanian Sriram, Senior Research Officer. Coauthors of the report from the Emerging Markets Studies Division of the Research Department are Bankim Chadha, Deputy Division Chief; Sunil Sharma, Senior Economist; Ilan Goldfajn, Jorge Roldos, and Michael Spencer, all Economists; and Anne Jansen, Senior Research Officer, and Peter Tran, Research Assistant. Sheila Kinsella, Adriana Vohden, Tammi Shear, and Ramanjeet Singh provided expert word processing assistance. J.R. Morrison of the External Affairs Department edited the manuscript and coordinated production of the publication.

This study has benefited from comments and suggestions from staff in other IMF departments, as well as from Executive Directors following their discussions of the International Capital Markets report on July 30, 1997. However, the analysis and policy considerations are those of the contributing staff and should not be attributed to Executive Directors, their national authorities, or the IMF.

List of Abbreviations

ABS	asset-backed securities
ADR	American Depository Receipt
ASB	Accounting Standards Board (U.K.)
ASEAN	Association of South-East Asian Nations
BAP	Bankers Association of the Philippines
BCCI	Bank of Credit and Commerce International
BIS	Bank for International Settlements
BOT	Bank of Thailand
BSP	Bangko Sentral ng Pilipinas
CAD	Capital Adequacy Directive
CBOE	Chicago Board Options Exchange
CBOT	Chicago Board of Trade
CCPC	Cooperative Credit Purchasing Company (Japan)
CFTC	Commodity Futures Trading Commission
CHAPS	Clearing House Association Payments System
CHIPS	Clearing House Interbank Payments System
CMBS	commercial-mortgage-backed securities
CME	Chicago Mercantile Exchange
CME-IMM	Chicago Mercantile Exchange—International Money Market
CSD	central securities depository
DTB	Deutsche Terminbörse
ECB	European Central Bank
ECU	European currency unit
EEA	European Economic Area
EFFAS	European Federation of Financial Analyst Societies
EMBI	Emerging Market Bond Index (J.P. Morgan)
EMI	European Monetary Institute
EMS	European Monetary System
EMU	Economic and Monetary Union
ERM	exchange rate mechanism
ESCB	European System of Central Banks
EU	European Union
FASB	Financial Accounting Standards Board (U.S.)
FCDU	Foreign Currency Deposit Unit (The Philippines)
FDI	foreign direct investment
FDIC	Federal Deposit Insurance Corporation (U.S.)
FOBAPROA	Fondo Bancario de Protección al Ahorro (Mexico)
FOGADE	Fondo de Garantiá de Depósitos y Protección Bancaria (Brazil)
G-7	Group of Seven (Canada, France, Germany, Italy, Japan, United Kingdom, United States)
G-10	Group of Ten (Belgium, Canada, France, Germany, Italy, Japan, the Netherlands, Sweden, United Kingdom, United States, Switzerland as honorary member)
GBI	Government Bond Index (J.P. Morgan)
GDP	gross domestic product
GDR	Global Depository Receipt
HKMA	Hong Kong Monetary Authority
HKSAR	Hong Kong Special Administrative Region

IASC	International Accounting Standards Committee
IFC	International Finance Corporation
IFCI	International Finance Corporation Investable index
IOSCO	International Organization of Securities Commissions
ISD	Investment Services Directive
ISDA	International Swaps and Derivatives Association
LIBOR	London interbank offered rate
LIFFE	London International Financial Futures Exchange
MAS	Monetary Authority of Singapore
MATIF	Marché à Terme International de France
MIDAM	Mid-America Commodity Exchange
MLHY	Merrill Lynch High-Yield
NASD	National Association of Securities Dealers (U.S.)
NASDAQ	National Association of Securities Dealers Automated Quotation (U.S.)
NBH	National Bank of Hungary
NDF	nondeliverable forward
NTMA	National Treasury Management Agency (Ireland)
NYFE	New York Futures Exchange
NYSE	New York Stock Exchange
NZDMO	New Zealand Debt Management Office
OECD	Organization for Economic Cooperation and Development
OTC	over the counter
PCA	prompt corrective action
PLMO	Property Loan Management Organization (Thailand)
RTGS	real-time gross settlement
SEC	Securities and Exchange Commission (U.S.)
SET	Stock Exchange of Thailand
SFE	Sydney Futures Exchange
SIMEX	Singapore International Monetary Exchange
SNDO	Swedish National Debt Office
S&P	Standard & Poor's
TARGET	Trans-European Automated Real-Time Gross Settlement Express Transfer System
TIFFE	Tokyo International Financial Futures Exchange
TSE	Tokyo Stock Exchange
VAR	value at risk
VVA	Valuación y Venta de Activos (Mexico)

I

Introduction

This year's capital markets report reviews developments and trends in the mature and emerging capital markets and banking systems and examines two important policy challenges—the implications of European Economic and Monetary Union (EMU) for financial markets and the management of external liabilities of emerging market countries. A key development in the mature markets was the continued appreciation of the dollar, owing mainly to large capital flows into the onshore and offshore dollar markets and to the relatively strong performance of the United States economy vis-à-vis Europe and Japan. Many of the mature equity markets also advanced further, reaching record highs. In an environment of low inflation and stable growth, investors entered into a broad spectrum of debt markets in search of higher yields, thus contributing to the compression of interest rate spreads that was a prominent feature of most markets. Against the backdrop of continuing globalization of financial markets, a record net inflow into the emerging markets reinforced the compression of borrowing spreads and contributed to surges of activity in domestic securities markets. But this generally favorable financial environment was not without problems, as markets challenged the ability of authorities in some emerging market countries to maintain currency stability in the presence of external imbalances.

The first of the two major international policy challenges discussed in the report concerns the European Union (EU). EU countries are entering into the most significant international financial arrangement since Bretton Woods, the establishment of EMU. It will create a stateless currency, the euro, and a multinational central bank to manage it. As a catalyst for change, the euro can provide impetus to existing initiatives for transforming the nationally segmented European financial markets into one of the largest single-currency financial markets in the world. Such an outcome would secure many of the benefits promised years ago by Europe's single-market initiatives. The opportunities are far reaching, but so too are the remaining institutional and financial challenges (see Chapter III).

The second policy challenge is the need for emerging and transition countries to better manage the risks associated with their external liabilities. The immediate cost savings of borrowing in foreign currencies at historically low interest rates has not always been met with an appropriate effort to assess and manage the currency and maturity risk of such borrowing. As more emerging market countries become closely integrated into the international financial system the problem of external debt management becomes more pressing (see Chapter V).

The report is followed by two groups of self-contained annexes that provide background material. In Part I, the first annex reviews recent developments in emerging capital markets and also examines recent pressures in selected foreign exchange markets. Annex II provides a survey of recent developments and trends in the mature international capital markets, including foreign exchange, credit, and derivative markets. Annex III is a survey of selected banking systems, focusing on the ongoing process of restructuring and consolidation, supervisory and regulatory developments, and banking system performance in both the mature and emerging market country banking systems.

Part II focuses on three issues. Annex IV examines the implications of EMU for capital markets. It first discusses the size of EU capital markets compared with those of the United States and Japan, and the potential international role of the euro. The annex also describes the institutional framework for cross-border payments, monetary policy, and banking supervision and market surveillance, and the potential implications of EMU for international securities markets and banking systems. Annex V discusses the problem of risk management of external sovereign liabilities. It draws on the experience of countries that have reformed debt management policies and outlines some broad principles for managing the risks inherent in sovereign liabilities, including currency, interest rate, and credit risks. Finally, Annex VI provides some historical perspective on capital flows to the emerging markets. It compares the nature and scale of recent capital flows with those of the gold standard period (1870–1914) and the 1920s, and examines factors that have influenced the scale, composition, and geographic distribution of capital flows to the emerging markets since the 1970s. This annex also reviews recent attempts to identify the key structural and cyclical developments and changes in international financial markets that best explain the resurgence of flows in the 1990s.

II

Developments and Trends in the Mature Markets

Since the last review of developments in international capital markets, the mature markets have been dominated by four related developments: large capital inflows into dollar fixed-income markets; the continued appreciation of the dollar; a convergence of interest rates at relatively low levels—and a compression of yield spreads—even in high-yield corporate and emerging markets; and further advances in the major equity markets. These developments occurred against a background of a stable macroeconomic environment, characterized by widespread convergence to low inflation rates and in some cases price stability, lingering disparities in growth rates, and continued fiscal consolidation. Intermittent periods of market tensions in currency and bond markets were associated with uncertainty about the sustainability of the appreciated value of the dollar, monetary policy, progress toward EMU, and the resolution of financial sector problems in Japan.

Foreign Exchange Markets: Capital Flows and the Rise of the Dollar

During the past twelve months, the key development in the major foreign exchange markets was the rise of the dollar against the deutsche mark and yen. The dollar's ascent occurred in relatively calm markets, interrupted only occasionally by increased market uncertainty about interest rates and U.S. equity prices. From its low of below ¥80 and DM1.35 in the spring of 1995, the dollar rose more than 50 percent against the Japanese yen and about 25 percent against the deutsche mark by May 1997 (Figures 1 and 2). In percentage terms, the dollar's ascent was one of the largest dollar-yen movements to occur over a two-year period. As was recognized in the communiqué of the meeting of G-7 Finance Ministers in April 1997, the movements in the dollar away from the low reached in the spring of 1995 generally brought currencies into better balance. Roughly 10 percent of the yen's decline against the dollar was reversed in May and June 1997.

The dollar's strength after early 1996 was to a large extent due to differences in the cyclical positions of the United States vis-à-vis Europe and Japan, as well as the related large inflows of foreign capital into dollar markets, in particular into the U.S. domestic fixed-income markets, and relatively attractive dollar yields.

Foreign net purchases of long-term U.S. government and corporate bonds reached a record high in 1996, almost 70 percent larger than the historical high reached in 1995 (Table 1). During these two record-setting years, foreign purchases of U.S. treasury bonds exceeded the cumulative net purchases over the previous 10 years (1985–94). Much of the flow into dollar fixed-income markets came from Germany, France, Spain, Japan, and China, and large dollar flows also originated in the major international financial centers—Hong Kong, China; Singapore; and the United Kingdom. By comparison, and despite the impressive performance of U.S. equity prices during the period under review, foreign investors accumulated less than $14 billion in U.S. equities in 1996.

The demand for dollar assets has been large not only in absolute terms, but also in relation to the U.S. current account deficit and to inflows into other mature markets. Net foreign purchases of U.S. bonds totaled about 5 percent of U.S. GDP in 1996, compared with a U.S. current account deficit of about 2 percent. On a bilateral basis, the magnitudes of capital flows into U.S. bond markets generally exceeded the current account surpluses of source countries (Germany and the United Kingdom had current account deficits). By comparison, foreign purchases of U.S. treasury bonds were 10 times foreign purchases of either German Bunds or Japanese domestic bonds (government and private) (Table 2).

Official reserve accumulation accounted for more than two-fifths of total foreign net purchases of U.S. treasury securities in 1996, half of which was the consequence of developing country efforts to manage exchange rates in the presence of substantial and volatile capital flows. During 1995–96, the Japanese monetary authorities accounted for the single largest accumulation of foreign exchange reserves, as total reserves (minus gold) reached $217 billion at end-1996, an increase of more than $90 billion since end-1994.

Private capital flows into U.S. markets totaling $425 billion were counterbalanced in 1996 by a substantial resurgence in U.S. investment abroad after the retrenchment from foreign markets in 1994; hence, official net capital inflows almost matched the U.S. current account deficit (Table 3). In 1995–96, the scale of these matching private flows were large relative to GDP. Increasing diversification of portfolios accounts for some of the two-way trade in financial assets, but

Figure 1. Spot Exchange Rates
(Local currency/U.S. dollar)

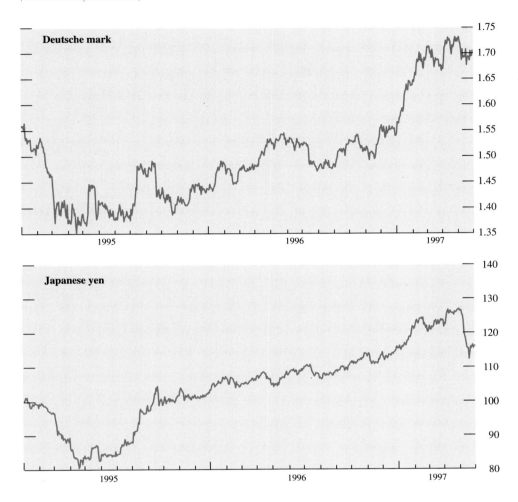

Source: Bloomberg Financial Markets L.P.

the scale of such flows is also consistent with the view that the United States is playing the role of a global intermediary: it attracts international capital by providing relatively safe, liquid instruments (U.S. government and high-grade corporate debt securities) at relatively high returns and then reinvests them through international markets in less liquid vehicles for higher returns.[1] A rationale for this role is that U.S.-based in-

---

[1] In the 1960s, Kindleberger (1965) argued the United States played the role of international banker, selling liquid, short-term obligations to nonresidents and buying longer-term claims against them. Triffin (1966) claimed U.S. short-term dollar liabilities to nonresidents were too large relative to the U.S. gold reserve, a view that led to the establishment of the SDR. It is also consistent with the view that capital markets have become more globally integrated. According to Feldstein and Horioka (1980), in an integrated global capital market, domestic savings and domestic investment will be uncorrelated. For a survey see Goldstein and Mussa (1993).

stitutional investors and global financial institutions are generally perceived as possessing advanced knowledge, expertise, and global reach in placing funds in the higher-yielding markets around the world.

Large differentials between U.S. and German and between U.S. and Japanese interest rates were a key factor driving the large flows into U.S. markets and in the dollar's strength. At the same time that interest rates remained low and even declined throughout Europe and Japan, monetary conditions began to tighten in the United States as market participants became concerned that economic activity continued to increase relative to estimates of U.S. capacity output. The Federal Reserve's 25 basis point increase in the federal funds rate in late March 1997 widened the differentials even further. In effect, the combination of asynchronous business cycles and divergent monetary conditions accounted for the relatively wide spreads

Figure 2. United States, Japan, and Germany: Interest Rate Differentials[1]

(In basis points)

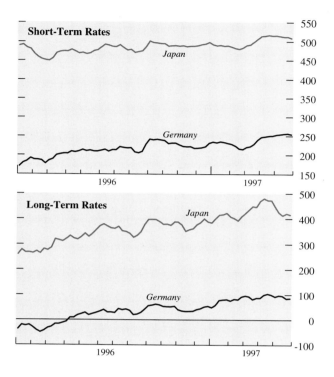

Source: International Monetary Fund.

[1]Interest rates in Japan and Germany are subtracted from U.S. interest rates.

(Figure 2). U.S. interest rate differentials with Germany have been most significant at the shorter end of the maturity spectrum: the spread on three-month

rates stood at 250 basis points at end-May 1997. Spreads between yen- and dollar-denominated bonds have been particularly large: long-term spreads have been in the range of 300–500 basis points since mid-1995, averaging about 420 basis points in May 1997, and short-term spreads have been in the range of 450–525 basis points, averaging about 510 basis points in May 1997.

Large global macro hedge funds viewed the relatively wide yen-dollar interest rate spread as a potentially lucrative trading opportunity. They presumed that the Bank of Japan did not want the yen to strengthen in 1996–97 and preferred not to raise interest rates in light of the continuing cyclical weakness as well as concerns over the loan books of Japanese banks and the banks' relatively large exposure to interest rate risk. If expectations about the yen-dollar rate and yen interest rates proved correct, then borrowing cheaply in yen, selling yen for dollars, and lending the proceeds to the U.S. Treasury would generate a net profit equal to the sizable interest rate differential. While Japanese banks reduced total cross-border positions by $20 billion in 1996, they increased lending to nonbank entities in the Cayman Islands—a home for some major hedge funds—by almost $19 billion. On the other side of the ledger, entities in the Cayman Islands accumulated $20 billion of U.S. long-term bonds in 1996.[2] These yen-carry trades were even more profitable than anticipated because the yen depreciated in 1996 and the first four months of 1997.

A second factor boosting flows into U.S. markets was a diversification out of instruments denominated in yen and deutsche mark, in part reflecting a precautionary move to avoid risks associated with uncer-

[2]These data are from the Bank for International Settlements and the U.S. Department of Treasury, *Treasury Bulletin.*

Table 1. Net Foreign Purchases of U.S. Bonds

(In millions of U.S. dollars)

	Government Bonds	Corporate Bonds	Total
1993	58,980	30,572	89,552
1994	100,481	37,992	138,473
1995	162,844	57,853	220,697
1996	293,685	77,978	371,663
Of which:			
Europe	137,148	56,194	193,342
Germany	19,297	3,514	22,811
United Kingdom	76,323	43,702	120,025
Spain	18,421	462	18,883
Asia	112,597	9,806	122,403
Japan	48,985	6,099	55,084
People's Republic of China	17,209	257	17,466
Hong Kong, China	15,281	1,737	17,018
1997:Q1	77,048	20,826	97,874

Source: U.S. Department of Treasury, *Treasury Bulletin.*

Table 2. Net Purchases of Domestic Bonds by Nonresidents

(In billions of U.S. dollars)

	United States	Japan	Germany Bunds[1]	Germany Other	France	United Kingdom	Canada
1993	89.55	−31.07	93.15	33.29	19.94	20.82	21.70
1994	138.47	−13.72	2.95	11.67	−36.15	1.85	10.83
1995	220.70	−8.46	35.38	25.35	2.84	5.26	21.78
1996	371.66	25.27	26.91	38.06	−31.29	15.75	13.58

Sources: BZW Securities Limited; and U.S. Department of Treasury, *Treasury Bulletin.*
[1]*Bundesanleihan* are German long-term federal bonds.

tainty about the likelihood, timing, and country composition of EMU[3] and about the resolution of financial system problems in Japan. This revealed preference for reducing yen and deutsche mark exposures

was also associated with the appreciation of the currencies of some of the higher-yielding EU and "dollar-bloc" countries, such as the United Kingdom, Australia, Canada, and New Zealand. A possible third interrelated factor was that Europe and Japan were net suppliers of international liquidity. In both locations, real money growth exceeded output growth, and domestic demand for funds fell short of domestic supplies.

In European currency markets, renewed optimism about the prospects for EMU and progress in reducing inflation and fiscal deficits led to the appreciation of

[3]The diversification away from Europe and toward the dollar can be seen as reflecting uncertainty about the initial strength or weakness of the euro once EMU begins. There were also occasions when the deutsche mark strengthened against the dollar and other European currencies, usually on the release of economic and financial data or on policy developments that called into question whether EMU would go ahead on time, in which case the deutsche mark could be seen as a "safe haven" within Europe.

Table 3. United States: International Transactions

	1990	1991	1992	1993	1994	1995	1996
	(In billions of U.S. dollars)						
Current account balance	−91.9	−5.7	−56.4	−90.8	−133.5	−129.1	−148.2
Foreign assets in the United States, net (increase/capital inflow (+))	141.0	109.6	168.8	279.7	297.3	451.2	547.6
Foreign official assets, net	33.9	17.4	40.5	71.8	40.4	110.7	122.4
Other foreign assets, net	107.1	92.3	128.3	207.9	256.0	340.5	425.2
Direct investment	47.9	22.0	17.9	49.0	45.7	67.5	77.0
Domestic securities	−0.9	53.0	67.2	104.5	91.2	195.9	289.4
U.S. liabilities to unaffiliated foreigners reported by U.S. nonbanking concerns	45.1	−3.1	13.6	10.5	−7.7	34.6	31.8
U.S. liabilities reported by U.S. banks, not included elsewhere	−3.8	4.0	16.2	25.1	104.3	30.2	9.8
U.S. currency flows	18.8	15.4	13.4	18.9	23.4	12.3	17.3
U.S. assets abroad, net (increase/capital outflow (−))	−74.0	−57.9	−68.8	−194.5	−160.5	−307.2	−352.4
U.S. official reserve assets plus government assets, net	0.1	8.7	2.2	−1.7	5.0	−10.3	6.0
U.S. private assets, net	−74.2	−66.6	−71.0	−192.8	−165.5	−296.9	−358.4
Direct investment	−30.0	−31.4	−42.6	−77.9	−69.3	−86.7	−87.8
Foreign securities	−28.8	−45.7	−49.2	−146.3	−60.3	−100.1	−108.2
U.S. claims on unaffiliated foreigners reported by U.S. nonbanking concerns	−27.8	11.1	−0.4	0.8	−31.7	−35.0	−64.2
U.S. claims reported by U.S. banks, not included elsewhere	12.4	−0.6	21.2	30.6	−4.2	−75.1	−98.2
Unrecorded outflows (statistical discrepancy)	24.9	−46.1	−43.6	5.6	−3.3	−14.9	−46.9
	(In percent of GDP)						
Memorandum items:							
Current account balance	−1.6	−0.1	−0.9	−1.4	−1.9	−1.8	−2.0
Foreign assets in the United States, net (increase/capital inflow (+))	2.5	1.9	2.7	4.3	4.3	6.2	7.2
U.S. assets abroad, net (increase/capital outflow (−))	−1.3	−1.0	−1.1	−3.0	−2.3	−4.2	−4.7

Sources: International Monetary Fund, *World Economic Outlook* database; and U.S. Department of Commerce, *Survey of Current Business.*

Figure 3. Major European Countries: Exchange Rates vs. Deutsche Mark
(Local currency/deutsche mark)

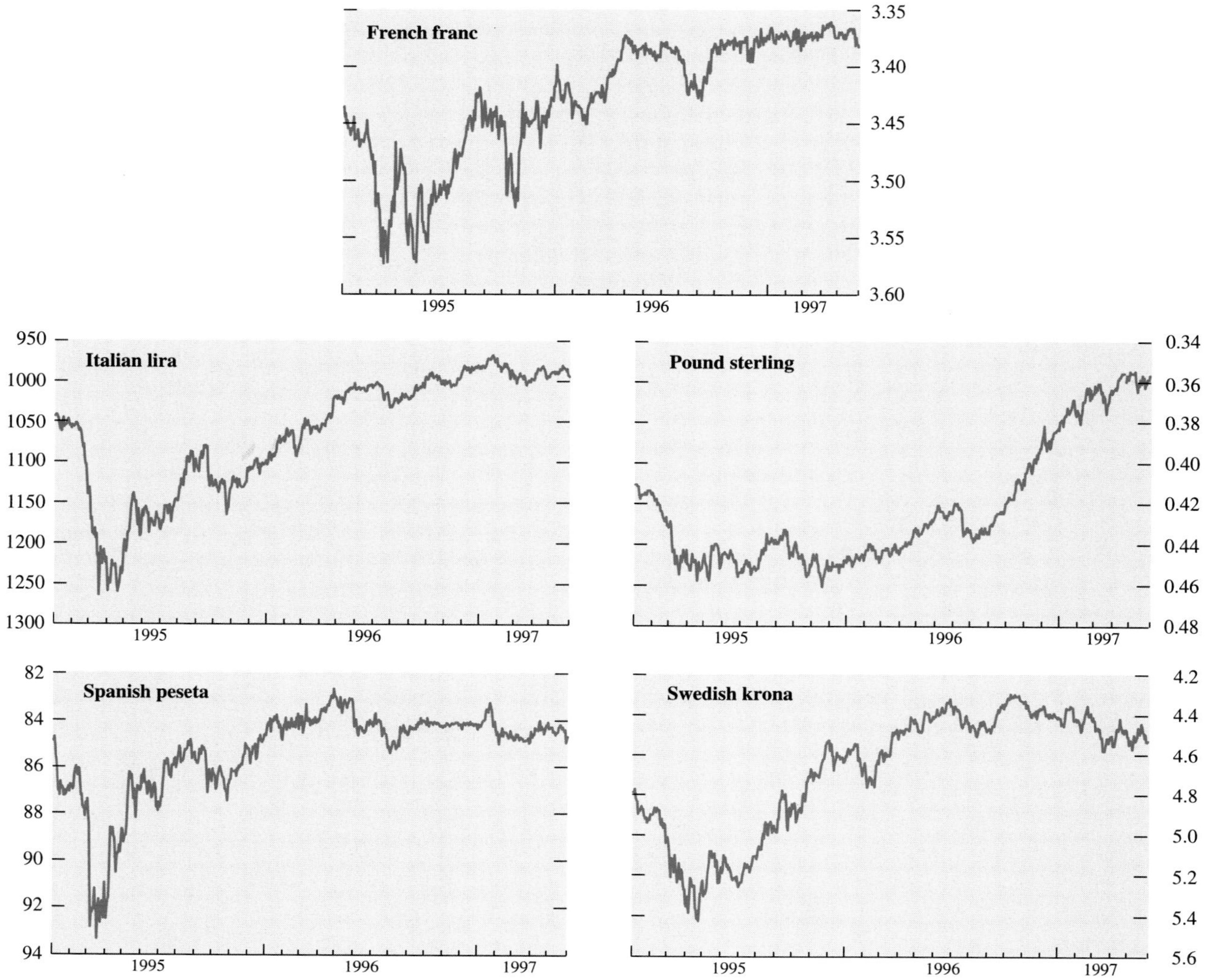

Source: Bloomberg Financial Markets L.P.

several EU currencies against the deutsche mark (Figure 3). The Finnish markka joined (October), and the Italian lira reentered (November), the exchange rate mechanism (ERM) of the European Monetary System in 1996. While both currencies strengthened upon entry, they have since lost these gains. The strongest currencies have been the pound sterling and the Irish pound, both of which have been supported by robust economic activity and expectations of rising interest rates. The Irish pound is the most appreciated currency in the ERM grid, having risen about 10 percent since mid-1996 above its central rate against the deustche mark, and the pound sterling was the only

major currency to appreciate against the dollar over the past 18 months.

Despite the large swings in the major currencies, month-to-month volatility in foreign exchange markets fell substantially in 1996, particularly for second-tier European currencies (Figure 4).[4] A tangible effect of the drop in volatility has been a sharp drop in turnover in currency spot markets, and both of

---

[4]Lower volatility has led to, and perhaps been supported by, increased activity in currency options (binary and range options), which allow investors to fine-tune exposures to the level, direction of change, and volatility of underlying asset prices.

Figure 4. Implied Volatility: Japanese Yen and Deutsche Mark
Three-Month Forwards

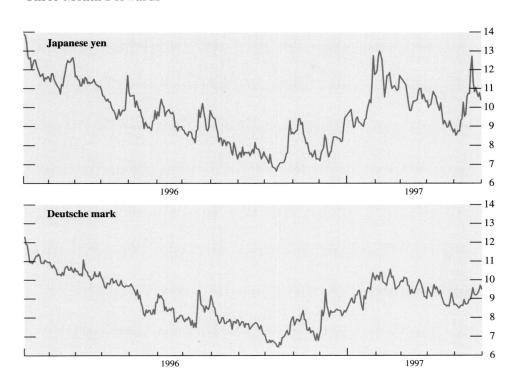

Source: Bloomberg Financial Markets L.P.
Note: Implied volatility is a measure of the expected future volatility of the currency based on market prices of the call options on forward contracts in the currency.

these developments were associated with a scaling back of European foreign exchange trading and dealing operations.

Credit Markets: Spread Compression and Increased Volumes

Bond Markets

During the past twelve months, low and declining inflation, fiscal consolidation, ample international liquidity, and a stable international environment supported a global compression of interest rate spreads (relative to benchmark yield curves) and record levels of new issuance in both domestic and international bond markets. Low interest rates in Europe and Japan, and the global search for yields, facilitated capital flows into the United States and higher-yielding mature domestic bond markets outside of Europe (Canada, Australia, and New Zealand), into corporate bonds (Figures 5–7), and into emerging markets (see Chapter IV). The demand for higher-yielding domes-

tic issues was broadly based geographically and included investors in the major European countries, Japan, and North America. In international markets, strong demand for dollar-denominated instruments raised the share of dollar issuance by more than 100 percent in 1996, whereas the shares of yen and deutsche mark issues dropped almost 80 percent and 40 percent, respectively.

Although substantial, the decline in interest rate spreads in the high-yield sectors stopped short of the low spreads reached as recently as 1994. Fears of a tightening of U.S. monetary policy caused periodic, temporary, retrenchments from U.S. bond markets (as with the large sell-off in early 1996). By late 1996, the extent of the narrowing of spreads in some segments of the higher-risk markets—notably the high-yield corporate sectors and selected emerging markets—raised concerns about spreads having narrowed beyond what was warranted by the fundamentals. In anticipation of a rise in U.S. interest rates, spreads widened modestly in most of the higher-yielding markets during the early months of 1997, and when the Federal Reserve eventually raised the federal funds

Figure 5. Selected European Long-Term Interest Rate Differentials with Germany
(In basis points)

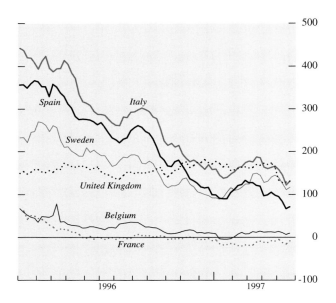

Source: International Monetary Fund.

Figure 6. United States: Yield Spreads of Corporate Bonds over U.S. Treasuries[1]
(In basis points)

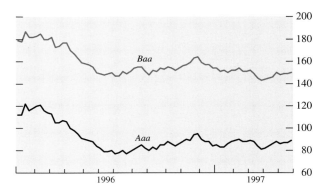

Source: Board of Governors of the Federal Reserve System, *Federal Reserve Bulletin.*
[1]Yields on 10-year U.S. treasury bonds of constant maturities are used for U.S. treasuries.

target rate by 25 basis points in late March 1997, the bond market reaction was muted.

In European bond markets, even though interest rate spreads have recently widened modestly, market participants have priced in a high probability of EMU going ahead in 1999 (Table 4). Spreads over deutsche mark yields peaked in early 1995 as a result of the flight-to-quality associated with the global bond market correction in 1994 and the Mexican crisis in 1994–95. The subsequent narrowing of intra-European spreads continued in 1996 as doubts about political and economic commitments to EMU dissipated, and monetary policy in Germany was further eased. In core Europe (Austria, Belgium, France, Germany, Luxembourg, and the Netherlands), where spreads were thin to begin with, French and Dutch long-term yields fell below deutsche mark yields by late 1996. Spreads in some other EU countries have been strongly influenced by fluctuations in the probability of EMU participation in 1999, displaying considerable sensitivity to news events. Against the German benchmark, the Italian 10-year yield spread narrowed about 350 basis points from early 1996 through the end of May 1997, Spanish spreads fell 300 basis points, and Swedish spreads fell 130 basis points. The United Kingdom is the notable exception to this convergence, a fact attributable to the unique U.K. cyclical position and perhaps to the uncertainty about U.K. participation in EMU.

In 1996, gains in total return indexes for European long-term bonds ranged from almost 50 percent in Italy to about 10–15 percent in core EU countries.[5] Returns on aggressive convergence plays have been even higher. Convergence plays in the early 1990s typically exploited yield differentials in cash markets, whereas convergence plays in 1996 were executed largely through interbank swap markets,[6] a tactic that avoids much of the capital outlay required to establish positions in cash markets. As a result, deutsche mark–denominated swap activity—the "pay side" of convergence plays—increased 44 percent in the first half of 1996 to $2.2 trillion. By late 1996, most of these convergence positions were reportedly unwound with the narrowing of spreads.

The compressed spreads in secondary markets created favorable conditions for issuance of debt securities in international and domestic markets in 1996. In international markets, the funds raised in debt securities markets slightly exceeded funds raised through newly announced syndicated lending facilities. Despite sluggish economic activity and fiscal consolidation in some advanced countries, record volumes of debt securities were issued in both international and

---

[5]Bloomberg/EFFAS (European Federation of Financial Analyst Societies) 10-year government bond Total Return Indexes (coupons reinvested).

[6]A simple example is a cross-currency interest rate swap in which the investor makes a stream of interest payments denominated in deutsche mark in exchange for a stream of interest payments denominated in a higher-yielding currency. If the interest rate spread narrows before the contract maturity date, the investor effectively books a profit equal to the change in the spread times the months to maturity (see Annex II of the Background Material for details).

**Figure 7. Australia, Canada, and New Zealand:
Yield Differentials on 10-Year Government Bonds**
(In basis points against the yield on 10-year U.S. government bonds)

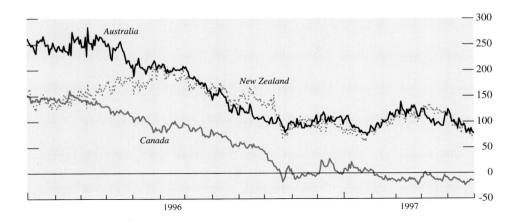

Source: Bloomberg Financial Markets L.P.

domestic markets. In international markets, issuance increased by nearly 100 percent on strong demand for funds by U.S. corporations and by Dutch, German, U.K., and U.S. financial institutions (Table 5). Financial institutions accounted for two-thirds of this sharp increase, and U.S. corporations accounted for more than half of all issuance by nonfinancial corporations. In domestic markets, private issuance rose 10 percent, half of which occurred in U.S. domestic markets; most of the remaining issuance occurred in Germany, Italy, Japan, and the United Kingdom. Public issuance declined slightly.

**Table 4. One-Year Interest Differentials with Germany, February 28, 1995,
January 30, 1997, and May 31, 1997[1]**

(In basis points)

	Spot	January 1, 1999[2]	January 1, 2000[2]	January 1, 2001[2]
February 28, 1995				
France	118	29	30	25
Italy	546	424	415	385
Spain	438	435	410	378
Sweden	319	. . .	. . .	. . .
United Kingdom	204	165	157	143
European currency unit (ECU)	132	91	70	56
January 30, 1997				
France	15	−22	−29	−26
Italy	342	154	105	81
Spain	231	86	54	33
Sweden	111	137	131	112
United Kingdom	370	293	211	146
ECU	87	6	10	−5
May 31, 1997				
France	39	−23	−28	−21
Italy	345	189	148	116
Spain	185	85	49	41
Sweden	144	173	158	130
United Kingdom	378	289	202	132
ECU	95	22	14	12

Source: Bloomberg Financial Markets L.P.
[1]Calculated based on the one-year forward rates embedded in the yield curve.
[2]Based on the data for the first available day of the year.

Table 5. Domestic and International Debt Securities: Amounts Outstanding and Net Issues
(In billions of U.S. dollars)

	Amounts Outstanding			1997	Net Issues				1997
					1996				
	1994	1995	1996	Q1	Q1	Q2	Q3	Q4	Q1
International debt securities									
Total issues	2,441.2	2,802.5	3,225.9	3,240.7	113.8	141.5	108.2	176.6	137.6
Bonds	2,035.2	2,208.7	2,391.8	2,354.0	57.4	65.9	60.1	91.7	54.6
Medium-term notes	292.0	461.3	662.5	711.9	47.5	58.1	51.9	66.4	75.9
Euro-commercial paper	81.5	87.0	102.9	110.2	6.7	10.4	−1.5	1.8	9.5
Other short-term notes	32.6	45.5	68.7	64.6	2.3	7.1	−2.4	16.7	−2.4
Private sector	1,559.1	1,804.2	2,150.7	2,178.2	91.7	106.4	83.9	134.5	105.5
Of which:									
United States	204.7	253.0	366.2	377.8	26.5	30.0	25.0	38.3	18.6
Japan	341.3	347.4	332.9	321.2	0.9	4.3	5.9	0.5	2.1
Germany	179.1	257.9	334.6	349.0	27.7	19.3	19.4	26.5	32.2
France	178.9	199.3	201.2	196.3	−0.3	8.5	5.2	−1.6	5.8
Italy	40.2	40.3	40.9	38.8	0.1	−0.4	−0.3	1.3	−0.1
United Kingdom	195.4	210.1	257.3	259.4	7.5	6.2	3.9	20.7	10.0
Canada	37.4	40.0	47.2	47.7	1.7	1.0	2.8	2.1	1.0
Public sector	598.7	689.3	756.0	751.8	18.6	27.3	21.4	31.4	23.7
Of which:									
United States	5.0	19.8	36.4	40.2	4.8	4.8	3.2	4.1	4.1
Japan	20.0	21.8	23.8	23.4	0.7	0.3	1.0	0.9	0.3
Germany	9.4	11.2	7.7	7.4	0.2	−0.2	0.0	−2.6	0.3
France	6.6	8.1	14.7	15.3	0.7	3.7	1.1	1.8	1.3
Italy	45.0	52.5	54.9	53.4	−0.2	3.0	1.3	0.9	0.8
United Kingdom	17.1	17.1	16.9	16.1	0.0	0.0	−2.0	2.0	−0.1
Canada	128.0	137.6	135.5	135.9	−1.4	−0.3	0.5	2.0	2.7
Domestic debt securities									
Total issues[1]	22,823.9	24,874.3	25,829.6	...	624.6	422.5	393.5	440.0	...
Bonds	18,336.2	19,923.6	20,541.9	...	329.6	400.2	347.9	330.9	...
Medium-term notes	530.9	612.4	664.1	...	23.2	19.8	20.1	8.0	...
Commercial paper	815.9	907.2	1,031.6	...	12.6	62.7	18.6	43.4	...
Treasury bills	1,876.9	1,998.3	1,964.3	...	106.1	−7.6	−37.9	−23.8	...
Other short-term notes	1,264.0	1,432.7	1,627.7	...	153.1	−52.6	44.8	81.6	...
Private sector[1]	8,335.0	9,195.4	9,624.9	...	255.4	121.8	165.6	245.8	...
Of which:									
United States	3,654.0	4,069.6	4,513.0	...	84.9	120.1	110.2	128.2	...
Japan	1,497.3	1,529.7	1,469.1	...	62.1	−40.9	15.9	79.5	...
Germany	863.9	1,026.6	1,024.6	...	38.5	13.9	18.8	9.5	...
France	572.7	601.9	549.5	...	4.3	−5.2	−2.3	−10.4	...
Italy	325.4	356.5	410.0	...	16.7	11.4	1.9	10.6	...
United Kingdom	170.0	186.2	258.6	...	18.5	2.1	7.9	23.1	...
Canada	47.2	53.1	65.9	...	0.2	4.1	0.9	7.8	...
Public sector[1]	14,488.9	15,678.9	16,204.7	...	369.2	300.7	227.9	194.2	...
Of which:									
United States	6,362.3	6,708.2	7,102.0	...	105.8	59.3	110.4	118.2	...
Japan	3,252.7	3,425.9	3,299.0	...	128.1	103.5	10.0	37.5	...
Germany	805.0	882.4	853.6	...	4.5	14.4	10.4	11.6	...
France	549.4	673.6	689.8	...	28.3	14.7	26.1	−8.6	...
Italy	1,074.0	1,169.5	1,277.8	...	16.4	26.1	22.2	4.2	...
United Kingdom	354.8	412.8	467.3	...	−6.6	17.8	6.9	−3.0	...
Canada	410.5	443.2	443.3	...	6.6	1.0	−0.6	−5.4	...
Memorandum items:									
International debt securities									
Financial institutions	835.9	1,037.5	1,344.4	...	78.1	78.0	72.6	113.9	89.8
Government and state agencies	603.1	689.1	755.8	...	18.5	27.3	21.4	31.3	23.6
Corporate issuers	718.5	766.7	806.4	...	13.6	28.3	11.3	20.6	15.7

Source: Bank for International Settlements.

[1]Organization for Economic Cooperation and Development countries plus major emerging markets.

Table 6. Announced International Syndicated Credit Facilities by Nationality of Borrowers
(In billions of U.S. dollars)

| | 1992 | 1993 | 1994 | 1995 | 1996 | 1996 | | | | 1997 |
						Q1	Q2	Q3	Q4	Q1
All countries	221.4	220.9	252.0	310.8	530.0	96.8	158.3	115.6	159.3	114.4
Industrial countries	165.2	168.3	199.4	244.1	448.1	77.0	140.3	93.5	137.1	93.7
Of which:										
United States	91.3	88.1	72.1	76.3	297.9	41.8	96.1	61.4	98.6	71.7
Japan	1.5	1.5	1.3	0.7	4.1	0.4	0.3	0.0	3.4	0.6
Germany	2.1	2.9	1.4	13.0	7.3	3.9	0.8	2.1	0.4	1.4
France	5.5	6.0	6.2	12.2	16.2	0.7	12.6	1.3	1.6	0.9
Italy	5.4	2.8	3.7	15.2	5.7	1.0	1.0	1.9	1.8	1.0
United Kingdom	25.5	17.0	34.2	54.6	59.4	11.1	17.2	17.6	13.5	11.6
Canada	3.5	9.4	16.0	11.9	12.2	1.4	3.0	0.5	7.2	1.1

Source: Bank for International Settlements.

Heightened investor concerns about the direction of interest rates during 1996–97 led to a shift in demand toward floating-rate and short-term paper and away from bonds. Between end-1994 and the end of the first quarter of 1997, issuance of medium-term notes, Euro commercial paper, and other short-term notes grew by 118 percent whereas international bond issuance grew by only 16 percent. The shift away from bonds is partly attributable to the growing sophistication of borrowers, who value the flexibility offered by note issuance facilities.

In search of higher yields, and in an attempt to economize on capital requirements, banks' issuance of asset-backed securities continued to expand briskly in the United States and in international markets. In 1996, issuance in the U.S. market—the largest asset-backed securities market in the world—expanded at double-digit rates, and the amount of outstanding asset-backed securities reached about $740 billion. In both the U.S. and international markets, some of the larger asset-backed securities issues included the securitization of loan portfolios and of various types of receivables from developing countries.

International Bank Loan Markets

The ample supply of funds in securities markets in 1996 intensified competition and maintained thin margins in international loan markets. Announced syndicated credits rose 68 percent in 1996, driven by refinancing operations, mergers and acquisitions, commercial paper and asset-backed securities backup facilities, and project financing. Most of the increase in borrowing was by entities located in the United States, the United Kingdom, the offshore centers, and developing countries (Table 6). The demand for syndicated loans by U.S. borrowers rose by $218 billion in 1996, an increase of almost 400 percent and greater than the increase in announced credits to all other countries.

Much of the increase in lending came from Benelux, British, Dutch, German, Italian, and Swiss banks, and EMU convergence plays provided a significant boost to the international lending activities of European banks. Cross-border activity by U.S. banks was buoyed by demand in the Eurodollar markets and by financing associated with the surge in foreign demand for U.S. bonds. Japanese banks are still the largest international lenders, but they continued to retreat, especially from international interbank markets, as their share of international lending dropped to the 13-year low of 22 percent.

Aggregate loan spreads over the London interbank offered rate (LIBOR) remained relatively constant in 1996–97, as banks in a relatively benign economic environment sought higher margins by expanding their lending into new geographic areas and to lesser-known names (Table 7). As competition has led investors to ratchet down the credit spectrum, spreads among prime and nonprime borrowers have narrowed.[7] These considerations once again prompted warnings from regulators that diligence must not be ignored in extending credits at razor-thin margins. U.S. regulators, in particular, expressed concern also with the lengthening of maturities and relaxation of covenants to higher-risk borrowers.

A notable development is the growing displacement of interbank lending by repurchase agreements (repos). At end-1996, international repos outstanding totaled about $1 trillion, and annual turnover is estimated to have reached between $40 trillion and $50 trillion. The increased use of repos reflects the greater emphasis on collateral in interbank funding, which is attributable to two factors. First, heightened credit-risk awareness, partly inspired by capital requirements, has encouraged the use of repos as banks have extended their funding activities into geographically

---

[7]For instance, in November 1996 a large commercial bank in the Czech Republic obtained financing from a group of European banks at a spread of 20 basis points over LIBOR for the first three years of the loan, which is within a few basis points of the cost of funds for any of the highest-rated borrowers.

Table 7. Average Spreads and Maturities on Eurocredits

	1991	1992	1993	1994	1995	1996
	(In basis points)					
Average spread[1]						
OECD countries	80	85	78	59	43	51
Non-OECD countries	78	87	103	113	117	99
All countries	79	85	81	64	50	56
	(In months)					
Average maturity						
OECD countries	62	56	51	61	64	64
Non-OECD countries	76	69	67	64	58	60
All countries	65	57	53	61	63	64

Source: Organization for Economic Cooperation and Development (OECD).
[1]Weighted average of spreads (over LIBOR) applied to Eurocredits signed during the period. Tax-sparing loans as well as facilities classified under "other debt facilities" are excluded.

less familiar markets and as concerns have increased about some major banks active in the international markets. Second, collateralization procedures and documentation are more standardized, which has facilitated the use of repos by banks.

Risks in Foreign Exchange and Credit Markets

Analysis of global currency markets suggests that the large volume of long dollar positions held by investors, speculators, and dynamic hedgers might have increased the sensitivity of international portfolios to downward movements in the dollar. An example of this increased risk is the mid-May 1997 sell-off of dollar assets in favor of yen assets and the sharp and unexpected rebound of the yen (see the appendix at the end of this chapter), which followed remarks about overshooting by Japanese officials and raised concerns that some of Japan's dollar reserves would be liquidated. The unwinding of yen-carry trades might have hastened the momentum of the yen's rebound as investors rushed to liquidate long dollar positions to cover their short yen positions. There are also market risks associated with the transition to EMU. In particular, market volatility could increase as investors rebalance their portfolios as decisions about the initial country composition and euro conversion rates are anticipated and made between now and January 1, 1999.

In credit markets, there is a risk that risk-adjusted spreads may have fallen below what is justified by fundamentals. Cyclical factors increasingly suggest that monetary policy is likely soon to be tightened in some major countries, and a key question is whether markets have fully priced in the risks of a further tightening and the associated credit risk. There appears to be significantly less leverage in credit markets than there was before the bond market turbulence in 1994. At a minimum, this would suggest a smaller likeli-

hood of overshooting if and when an adjustment in spreads occurs. In the event that growth continues to be sluggish in Japan and Europe, a further tightening of monetary policy in the United States could lead to a widening of interest rate differentials and an increased demand for dollar instruments.

Equity Markets

Equity prices in industrial countries have risen strongly over the past 18 months (Figures 8–9), with the increase in Japanese prices being somewhat less pronounced. Markets in 10 European countries ended 1996 at all-time highs, while North American, French, and German markets also reached record valuations in December. In local currencies, European markets comfortably outperformed the 20 percent advance in U.S. equity prices in 1996. Some of the momentum in European equity markets has been attributed to the improved prospects for their export sectors associated with the depreciation of most continental European currencies against the dollar. Also favorable has been the trend toward low interest rates, which have an important impact on the discounted value of future corporate earnings.

The U.S. equity market has clearly been the star performer in the 1990s (Figure 8). Although the rise in U.S. markets after early 1996 has been matched or exceeded by other advanced equity markets, U.S. markets have outperformed most other advanced equity markets since the beginning of the decade, in some cases by a factor of two or more. Remarkably, in the period 1992–96, the Dow Jones Industrial Average doubled in value, while historically the index has doubled every 17 years. Moreover, over the same period, U.S. equity market capitalization increased from 72 percent of GDP to 107 percent of GDP.

An important factor that has added significant momentum to U.S. equity prices during the past few

Figure 8. Stock Market Indices: Major Industrial Countries[1]
(Indices, January 1990 = 100)

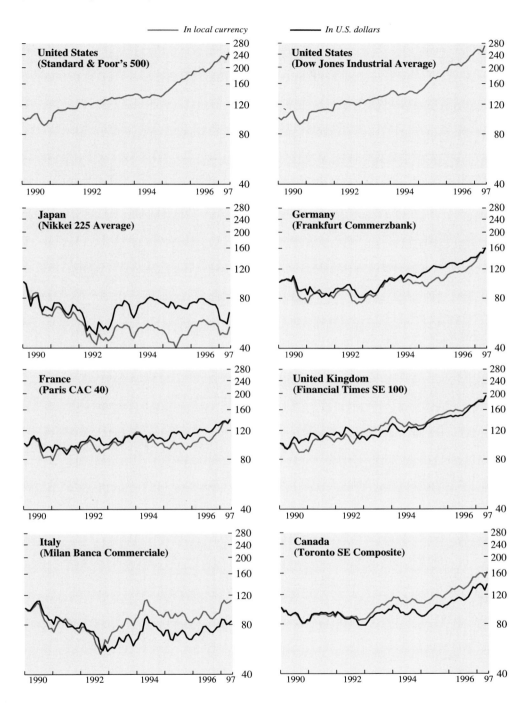

Source: International Monetary Fund.
[1]Monthly averages of daily observations, January 1990 through May 1997.

Figure 9. Stock Market Indices: Smaller European Countries[1]
(Indices, January 1990 = 100)

Sources: Bloomberg Financial Markets L.P.; Brussels Stock Exchange; International Monetary Fund; and The WEFA Group.

[1]Data for January 1990 through May 1997.

[2]January 1991 = 100.

Figure 10. United States: Equity Market Performance

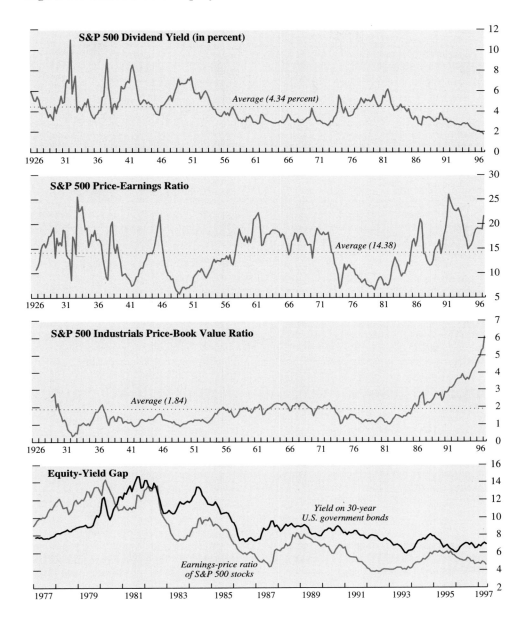

Sources: Board of Governors of the Federal Reserve System; Bloomberg Financial Markets L.P.; and Standard & Poor's.

years is the persistence of large inflows into U.S. equity mutual funds. Between January 1995 and April 1997, U.S. equity mutual funds were the recipients of $424 billion in new investments, and they currently manage $1.8 trillion. Mutual funds control 20 percent of the U.S. equity market capitalization, and they have a significant impact on prices, especially because they channel the bulk of new flows into U.S. equity markets.

Although improved profits help explain the rise in U.S. markets, price gains of the magnitude experienced in recent years have pushed some of the conventional valuation indicators into territory that has raised concerns of overvaluation (Figure 10). Dividend yields—currently about 2 percent—have fallen to historical lows and are about half their long-term average, and both the market-price-to-book ratio and the closely related Tobin's q ratio are deviating from

Table 8. Major Industrial Countries: Equity Market Risk-Adjusted Returns in Local Currency (Sharpe Ratios)[1]

Period	United States	Japan	Germany	France	Italy	United Kingdom	Canada
1983–87	0.42	1.03	0.36	0.61	0.53	0.60	0.23
1984–88	0.38	1.17	0.33	0.56	0.61	0.42	–0.04
1985–89	0.69	1.17	0.55	0.68	0.57	0.41	0.24
1986–90	0.27	0.23	–0.21	0.07	–0.30	0.05	–0.24
1987–91	0.39	–0.19	–0.23	–0.13	–0.84	–0.02	–0.22
1988–92	0.64	–0.46	0.12	0.27	–0.47	0.12	–0.49
1989–93	0.63	–0.59	0.17	0.07	–0.28	0.36	–0.17
1990–94	0.27	–0.61	–0.26	–0.37	–0.32	–0.03	–0.33
1991–95	1.16	–0.18	0.13	0.04	–0.05	0.60	0.28
1992–96	1.21	–0.16	0.39	0.21	0.03	0.69	0.63

Source: BZW Securities Limited.

[1]Sharpe reward-to-volatility ratios are calculated as the equity return minus three-month Euro deposit rates (i.e., portfolio excess return), divided by the standard deviation of equity returns, all measured over the previous five years.

their historical ranges. While these deviations can be explained by the shift away from capital-intensive industries to services, the rise in the ratio of equity prices to book value is still extraordinary. Moreover, the average price-earnings (P/E) ratio is clearly approaching the upper end of its normal range. On the other hand, given the favorable interest rate environment, the equity-yield gap, which measures the difference between long-term bond yields and the earnings-price ratio (inverse of the P/E ratio), remains within historical ranges and is still well below the levels reached prior to the 1987 stock market crash.

In assessing the sustainability of U.S. equity prices, a key question is whether U.S. equity valuations reflect expectations of further increases in earnings growth that may prove unrealistic. (This was emphasized by Federal Reserve Board Chairman Alan Greenspan in widely reported remarks before a meeting of the National Association of Business Economists on March 5, 1997.) In early 1997, S&P 500 earnings were about 15 percent above a year earlier, and a majority of companies' earnings exceeded market forecasts. Earnings growth averaged about 15 percent during the past five years, while average five-year real earnings growth since 1960 has been in the range of 2 percent. This suggests that the balance of risks would imply lower rather than higher earnings growth, especially because profit margins would be unlikely to improve in an environment of near-capacity economic activity and tight labor markets.

Despite these downside risks, U.S. equities do not appear to be as far out of line as they were in August 1987 or when compared with the Japanese market in 1989, when bond yields were high and rising, corporate earnings were weak, and monetary policy was stimulative. Nevertheless, equity prices are at levels that make them vulnerable to reductions in corporate earnings and to increases in interest rates. An additional concern is that the steady, high returns experienced in recent years might have created the illusion for small mutual fund investors that there are only limited risks associated with equity investments. It remains to be seen, therefore, how small investors (and the mutual funds they invest in) will behave in a more volatile environment in which equity investments are seen to be risky and to produce less-spectacular gains.[8]

The Japanese market has not performed as strongly as markets in some of the other main industrial countries (Table 8).[9] Japan's Nikkei 225 index declined 2.5 percent in 1996. There is little domestic demand for Japanese equities. Some major institutional investors (e.g., insurance companies) have negative cash flows, while others, such as banks, have weak balance sheets, and both groups have been forced to sell equities. Households also have been net sellers of domestic equities. Prior to the collapse of equity prices in 1990, investment trusts had more than half of their assets invested in Japanese equities; by the first quarter of 1997, this weighting was just over 20 percent. While this smaller weighting can be traced to lower equity prices, there also have been significant net redemptions in recent years. Public and foreign purchases have provided some support for Japanese equity prices. Continuing concerns about the nonperforming loan problem led bank stocks to underperform the market as a whole: between January 1996 and May 1997, the TOPIX index (a capitalization-weighted

---

[8]To bolster crisis management systems, in February 1997 U.S. and U.K. equity market regulators, exchanges, and clearinghouses held the first cross-border stress test involving a hypothetical default of a firm on a U.S. exchange that precipitated a corresponding default of a firm on a U.K. exchange. The test identified weaknesses ranging from incorrect emergency phone numbers to the inability to determine the amount of capital available to corporations with interlocking affiliates.

[9]Sharpe reward-to-volatility ratios indicate that Japanese equities have underperformed both equities in the other major industrial countries and the return on riskless yen assets.

Table 9. Markets for Selected Derivative Financial Instruments: Notional Principal Amounts Outstanding
(In billions of U.S. dollars)

	1986	1987	1988	1989	1990	1991	1992	1993	1994	1995	1996
Interest rate futures	370.0	487.7	895.4	1,200.8	1,454.5	2,156.7	2,913.0	4,958.7	5,777.6	5,863.4	5,931.1
Futures on short-term instruments	274.3	338.9	721.7	1,002.6	1,271.1	1,906.3	2,663.7	4,632.8	5,422.3	5,475.3	5,532.7
Three-month Eurodollar[1]	229.5	307.8	588.8	671.9	662.6	1,100.5	1,389.6	2,178.7	2,468.6	2,451.7	2,141.8
Three-month Euroyen[2]	0.0	0.0	0.0	109.5	243.5	254.5	431.8	1,080.1	1,467.4	1,400.7	1,445.6
Three-month Euro-deutsche mark[3]	0.0	0.0	0.0	14.4	47.7	110.0	229.2	421.9	425.7	654.6	526.2
Three-month PIBOR futures[4]	0.0	0.0	15.7	12.4	23.3	45.8	132.5	228.7	184.6	167.1	209.6
Futures on long-term instruments	95.7	148.8	173.7	198.2	183.4	250.4	249.3	325.9	355.3	388.1	398.5
U.S. Treasury bond[5]	23.0	26.5	39.9	33.2	23.0	29.8	31.3	32.6	36.1	39.9	45.7
Notional French government bond[4]	2.1	7.6	7.0	6.1	7.0	11.4	21.0	12.6	12.7	12.4	12.9
Ten-year Japanese government bond[6]	63.5	104.8	106.7	129.5	112.9	122.1	106.1	135.9	164.3	178.8	145.6
German government bond[7]	0.0	0.0	1.4	4.2	13.7	20.2	27.8	33.3	41.7	56.7	58.4
Interest rate options[8]	146.5	122.6	279.2	387.9	599.5	1,072.6	1,385.4	2,362.4	2,623.6	2,741.8	3,277.8
Currency futures	10.2	14.6	12.1	16.0	17.0	18.3	26.5	34.7	40.1	38.3	50.3
Currency options[8]	39.2	59.5	48.0	50.2	56.5	62.9	71.1	75.6	55.6	43.2	46.5
Stock market index futures	14.5	17.8	27.1	41.3	69.1	76.0	79.8	110.0	127.3	172.2	198.6
Stock market index options[8]	37.8	27.7	42.9	70.7	93.7	132.8	158.6	229.7	238.3	329.3	380.2
Total	618.3	729.9	1,304.8	1,766.9	2,290.4	3,519.3	4,634.4	7,771.1	8,862.5	9,188.2	9,884.6
North America	518.1	578.1	951.7	1,155.8	1,268.5	2,151.7	2,694.7	4,358.6	4,819.5	4,849.6	4,839.7
Europe	13.1	13.3	177.7	251.0	461.2	710.1	1,114.3	1,777.9	1,831.7	2,241.6	2,831.7
Asia-Pacific	87.0	138.5	175.4	360.0	560.5	657.0	823.5	1,606.0	2,171.8	1,990.1	2,154.0
Other	0.0	0.0	0.0	0.1	0.2	0.5	1.8	28.7	39.5	106.8	59.3

Source: Bank for International Settlements.

[1]Traded on the Chicago Mercantile Exchange-International Monetary Market (CME-IMM), Singapore International Monetary Exchange (SIMEX), London International Financial Futures Exchange (LIFFE), Tokyo, International Financial Futures Exchange (TIFFE), and Sydney Futures Exchange (SFE).

[2]Traded on the TIFFE and SIMEX.

[3]Traded on the Marché à Terme International de France (MATIF) and LIFFE.

[4]Traded on the MATIF.

[5]Traded on the Chicago Board of Trade (CBOT), LIFFE, Mid-America Commodity Exchange (MIDAM), New York Futures Exchange (NYFE), and Tokyo Stock Exchange (TSE).

[6]Traded on the TSE, LIFFE, and CBOT.

[7]Traded on the LIFFE and the Deutsche Terminbörse (DTB).

[8]Calls plus puts.

index of all companies listed on the Tokyo Stock Exchange First Section) recorded a drop of about 10 percent, whereas the TOPIX bank index fell nearly 30 percent.

A significant rebound in Japanese equity prices rests, therefore, on the resolution of several sources of uncertainty about the Japanese economy and the state of the financial system. The broader market is likely to be held back by weakness in financial sector equities and the weak local investor demand for equities. A resolution of the financial system problems in Japan would have significant benefits in terms of resolving uncertainty about the prospects for the Japanese economy and would help in reviving investor demand.

Expanding and Maturing Derivative Markets

Three general tendencies have shaped the evolution of global derivative markets. The first and most important tendency is that over-the-counter (OTC) derivative markets are increasingly becoming the hub of derivative trading. In 1987, the notional principal of outstanding OTC interest rate and currency swaps and interest rate options was 20 percent larger than the global exchange-traded derivative market, but by 1995 it was 90 percent larger. In 1995, turnover on the major North American, European, and Asia-Pacific derivative exchanges actually declined while OTC activity rose by 40 percent. A broad survey conducted by the Bank for International Settlements (BIS) estimated outstanding OTC contracts (foreign exchange, interest rate, equity, and commodity) at $47.5 trillion in early 1995 (after adjusting for double counting and including estimated gaps in reporting). The notional principal of outstanding OTC currency and interest rate swaps and interest rate options reported by the International Swaps and Derivatives Association (ISDA) in a less comprehensive survey was more than $24 trillion in 1996. Although the OTC markets continued to be the major sources of

17

Table 10. Notional Principal Value of Outstanding Interest Rate and Currency Swaps

(Of the members of the International Swaps and Derivatives Association; in billions of U.S. dollars)

	1987	1988	1989	1990	1991	1992	1993	1994	1995	June 1996
Interest rate swaps										
All counterparties	682.9	1,010.2	1,502.6	2,311.5	3,065.1	3,850.8	6,177.3	8,815.6	12,810.7	15,584.2
Interbank (ISDA member)	206.6	341.3	547.1	909.5	1,342.3	1,880.8	2,967.9	4,533.9	7,100.6	...
Other (end user and brokered)	476.2	668.9	955.5	1,402.0	1,722.8	1,970.1	3,209.4	4,281.7	5,710.1	...
End user	476.2	668.9	955.5	1,402.0	1,722.8	1,970.1	3,209.4	4,281.7	5,710.1	...
Financial institutions	300.0	421.3	579.2	817.1	985.7	1,061.1	1,715.7	2,144.4	3,435.0	...
Governments[1]	47.6	63.2	76.2	136.9	165.5	242.8	327.1	307.6	500.9	...
Corporations[2]	128.6	168.9	295.2	447.9	571.7	666.2	1,166.6	1,829.8	1,774.2	...
Unallocated	0	15.5	4.9	0	0	0	0	0	0	...
Brokered	0	0	0	0	0	0	0	0	0	...
Currency swaps										
All counterparties	365.6	639.1	898.2	1,155.1	1,614.3	1,720.7	1,799.2	1,829.7	2,394.8	2,589.4
(Adjusted for reporting of both sides)	(182.8)	(319.6)	(449.1)	(577.5)	(807.2)	(860.4)	(899.6)	(914.8)	(1,197.4)	(1,294.7)
Interbank (ISDA member)	71.0	165.2	230.1	310.1	449.8	477.7	437.0	422.5	619.9	...
Other (end user and brokered)	294.6	473.9	668.1	844.9	1,164.6	1,243.1	1,362.2	1,407.2	1,774.9	...
End user[3]	147.3	237.0	334.1	422.5	582.3	621.5	681.1	703.6	887.5	...
Financial institutions	61.9	102.7	141.7	148.2	246.7	228.7	221.9	227.1	378.5	...
Governments[1]	33.9	54.0	65.6	83.2	96.9	110.6	135.8	122.1	190.2	...
Corporations[2]	51.6	76.5	116.5	191.1	238.7	282.2	323.4	354.4	318.7	...
Unallocated	0	3.8	10.3	0	0	0	0	0	0	...
Brokered	0	0	0	0	0	0	0	0	0	...
Interest rate options[4]	0.0	327.3	537.3	561.3	577.2	634.5	1,397.6	1,572.8	3,704.5	4,190.1
Total (interest rate and currency swaps for all counterparties plus interest rate options)	865.6	1,657.1	2,489.0	3,450.3	4,449.5	5,345.7	8,474.5	11,303.2	17,712.6	21,068.9

Sources: Bank for International Settlements, *International Banking and Financial Market Developments;* and International Swaps and Derivatives Association, Inc. (ISDA).

[1]Including international institutions.

[2]Including others.

[3]Adjusted for double counting because each currency swap involves two currencies.

[4]Including caps, collars, floors, and swaptions.

growth in 1996, exchange activity increased on renewed interest in EMU. The volume of exchange-traded futures and options (currency, interest rate, equity) rose to 1.2 billion contracts at end-1996, and the total notional principal outstanding approached $10 trillion (Tables 9 and 10).[10]

Important reasons for the OTC markets' dominance are the flexible, customized nature of OTC contracts and regulatory advantages. These regulatory advantages may soon be reduced in the United States. Legislation pending in the U.S. Congress would amend the Commodity Exchange Act to recognize the distinction between "professional" and "retail" market segments, and to reduce the regulatory burden for

product innovation and reporting requirements in the professional segment. U.S. exchanges are hailing the legislation as contributing to a "truly more competitive industry world-wide."[11] In the medium term, exchanges could benefit from the activity in the new exchanges in emerging markets and by introducing new emerging-market products.

The second tendency in global derivatives markets has been consolidation, in both the exchange-traded and OTC market. In the U.S. OTC markets, the top eight banks account for about 94 percent (almost $19 trillion at end-1996) of the total notional principal outstanding. Consolidation in the exchange-traded markets is exemplified by the proliferation of trading links among exchanges. In Europe, consolidation has also occurred via mergers and closures, reflecting the

---

[10]Derivative markets are large relative to the size of cash markets: for example, outstanding debt securities in the EU, Japan, and North America totaled $25.8 trillion in 1995, whereas the notional principal of related derivatives amounted to $44.5 trillion.

[11]"Mixed Reactions to U.S. Regulatory Changes" (1997*)*.

increase in competition between exchanges as they seek to establish market shares before the introduction of the euro. For instance, the Swiss (Soffex) and German (Deutsche Terminbörse, or DTB) exchanges announced in late 1996 a strategic alliance that will create a common technical platform for trading derivatives and integrate the two clearing and settlement systems. In the United Kingdom the takeover of the London Commodity Exchange by the London International Financial Futures Exchange (LIFFE) expanded significantly the range of products traded, and in Ireland the Irish Futures and Options Exchange was closed in 1996.

The third tendency is commoditization (or standardization). The predominant derivative product, the swap contract, has become commoditized, and as a result swap margins have narrowed sharply as product volumes have risen. The tendency toward commoditization has been attributed to well-publicized losses incurred on derivative exposures some years ago, the riskiness of which may not have been fully understood. Although losses were not always associated with exotic products, they stimulated an awareness and reevaluation of the purposes and risks of derivative instruments. As a result, there was a sharp and widespread reduction in the demand for exotic, highly leveraged structures, and a shift toward well-understood structures—especially currency and interest rate swaps. Nonetheless, some structures that have traditionally been regarded as exotic (such as digital and barrier structures) have become mainstream, commoditized products.[12]

The continued expansion of derivatives has been fueled by structural changes, such as the trend toward securitization and the increased understanding of the capabilities of derivatives for unbundling, packaging, and reallocating cyclical and balance-sheet risks. A mark of their success is that derivatives are now an essential component of risk management in the major international banks and corporations. The growing use of derivatives has been aided by advances in analytical and information technology for evaluating and pricing the risks inherent in derivative contracts. Despite their rapid growth, there is still capacity for entities in a wide range of advanced and developing countries to take fuller advantage of them. One example is credit derivatives—one of the fastest-grow-

ing derivative product areas—which represent an unbundling of credit risk from various types of on-balance-sheet and off-balance-sheet items (see Annex III). Given the size and concentration of credit risk exposures, and the absence of an active secondary market for most of them, this market is likely to develop very rapidly.

Derivative markets present significant challenges for both private and public risk management, as demonstrated by the recent loss of about £85 million by a U.K.-based derivatives dealer due to its mispricing of interest rate options. In November 1996, the Basle Committee on Banking Supervision and the International Organization for Securities Commissions' Technical Committee released a joint survey on the trading and derivatives activities of international banks and securities firms. The study reported continuing improvements in disclosure practices but also noted that significant disparities in practices existed. The study urged banks and securities firms to strengthen further both their quantitative and qualitative disclosure. Market transparency will also be enhanced by the agreement of central banks to establish a system of regular derivatives reporting by major dealers, beginning in June 1998. Aggregate data on global trading activities will be collected in a manner that avoids double counting and publicly released to enable firms to assess their own activities in relation to the markets.

Appendix

Market Surprised by Yen's Appreciation in May 1997

Based on the information in options prices, the yen's sharp appreciation against the dollar during the second and third weeks of May 1997 was of a magnitude that market participants had considered quite unlikely, even as late as May 5 (see Figure 11). As the yen appreciated rapidly between May 5 and May 9, market-based price distributions began to reflect a significant probability of large further appreciations. By May 19, market expectations about the future value of the yen were very diffuse and assigned roughly equal probability to the yen-dollar rate in early September being anywhere within a seven-yen interval.

The evolution of market expectations over this period is illustrated in the figure, which plots market-based probability distributions for the yen-dollar exchange rate in early September. These distributions are derived from prices on the Chicago Mercantile Exchange's options on the September 1997 futures contract. Each day's distribution is based on prices for 50 options, offering protection over the range from ¥98 to ¥138 per dollar.

---

[12]A digital (or all-or-nothing) option is an option with a fixed, predetermined payoff if the underlying instrument is at or beyond the strike price at expiration; the value of the payoff is unaffected by the magnitude of the difference between the underlying and the strike price. Barrier options are path-dependent options for which both the payoff pattern and survival to the nominal expiration date depend not only on the final price of the underlying instrument but also on whether the instrument sells at or through a barrier price during the life of the option. Examples of barrier options include down-and-out and up-and-in puts and calls, early trigger CAPS options, and a variety of similar instruments.

Figure 11. Distribution for Yen/Dollar Exchange Rate in Early September 1997 Implied by Options Prices on May 5, 9, and 19, 1997

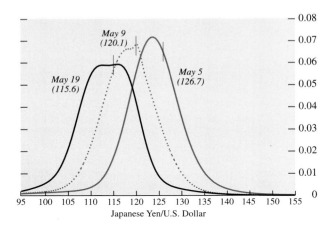

Sources: Bloomberg Financial Markets L.P.; and IMF staff calculations using data from the Chicago Mercantile Exchange.

Note: Spot exchange rates are shown in parentheses and indicated by vertical lines.

The distribution estimated from prices on May 5 was symmetric—indicating equal likelihood associated with appreciations and depreciations of similar magnitude—and assigned relatively little probability to appreciations of the size experienced over the next two weeks. On this day, the market assigned less than 6 percent probability to the yen-dollar spot rate being below 115 in early September. On May 6, the yen appreciated 1 percent against the dollar. Between May 5 and May 6, the distribution (not shown) shifted to the left and began to exhibit some leftward skew—associating somewhat larger probabilities with large appreciations of the yen. Nonetheless, on May 6, the probability assigned to the yen-dollar rate being below 115 in early September was still less than 9 percent. Between May 6 and May 9, the yen appreciated from 125 ¥/$ to 120 ¥/$. By May 9, the distribution had shifted down along with the spot rate, and the skew had become much more pronounced. At this point the market was pricing into the options a significant probability of further large appreciations in the months ahead. By May 19, after the rate had fallen to near 115, the distribution had returned to a near-symmetrical shape, but assigned roughly equal probability to yen-dollar rates within the range of 111 to 118.

III

EMU: Systemic Implications and Challenges

The creation of EMU is one of the most important international monetary developments in the post–Bretton Woods period. With the establishment of EMU, the euro will become the second most important official reserve currency in the world,[13] and the future European Central Bank (ECB) will assume its place as the supranational institution to manage a "multistate" currency. Although the political, cultural, and economic challenges are formidable, the euro has the potential to reshape European and international financial markets and to transform the multilateral international monetary system into a tripolar or even bipolar system.[14] At a minimum, the euro is likely to assume a more significant role in international trade, private financial transactions, and official reserves. Whether the euro will initially be a strong or a weak currency will depend in large part on the ability of EMU member countries to continue along the path of fiscal consolidation and structural reform and on the credibility of the ECB.

In addition to effective macroeconomic management, the international success of EMU will be influenced by the euro's ability to catalyze existing initiatives to enhance the efficiency and effectiveness of European capital markets (including early implementation of EU directives). The opportunities for beneficial structural changes are far reaching. They include the development of EMU-wide securities markets, the consolidation and restructuring of European banking systems, and the creation of a pan-European payments system. But the structural and institutional prerequisites for capturing these benefits are not all mandated by the Maastricht Treaty and may not evolve without the active participation of national and EU authorities and the confidence of market participants. The remaining challenges that could affect actual outcomes include the elimination of existing impediments to banking system consolidation and restructuring; the impact of the future European System of Central Banks (ESCB) operating procedures on the development of EMU-wide securities markets; access to the evolving European payments system; and the establishment of mechanisms for credible systemic risk management.

Global Financial Adjustments After Introduction of the Euro

Once markets absorb the decisions about the country composition and conversion rates of EMU, the introduction of the euro itself could raise the level of market volatility and cause shifts in the patterns of international capital flows. Various sources and motives have been identified that could produce an immediate and sharp sale of dollars for euros (and a depreciation of the dollar), including by EMU central banks and non-European central banks as they attempt to diversify into the euro. About 25 percent of EU reserves are held in core currencies and will be converted into euros at the start of Stage III. The bulk of remaining reserves are held in dollars, a portion of which would become redundant at the time of conversion. Market projections, which typically are based on trade flows, suggest that up to $50 billion could be sold.[15] However, the size and variability of EMU reserves would be determined primarily by capital flows and ECB exchange rate policies rather than trade flows. Moreover, if past behavior of the major central banks is any guide, the ECB is not likely to sell dollar reserves quickly. Central banks in other regions might wish to reduce the dollar share of their total reserves, either to achieve better portfolio diversification (Asia and the Middle East) or to peg to the euro (as in European developing countries or in some African countries), but they too are likely to shift out of dollars gradually (Table 11). Thus, official portfolio rebalancing is unlikely to be as large, or as concentrated in the near term, as is often suggested.[16]

In addition, as important as they are, official reserves (excluding gold) amounted to only about $1.4 trillion at end-1995, compared with private asset holdings of approximately $70 trillion in North America, Japan, and the EU alone; private portfolios are likely to be, therefore, the more important source of portfolio rebalancing (see Tables 11 and 12). As with official reserves, the direction and size of private capital flows into the euro zone will be influenced by the size,

[13]See Masson and others (1997) and Prati and Schinasi (1997).
[14]See Bergsten (1997).

[15]See several papers in Masson and others (1997) for detailed discussions of this issue.
[16]See, for example, J.P. Morgan (1997c) and Paribas Capital Markets (1997).

Table 11. Total Foreign Exchange Reserves Minus Gold in Selected Countries and Regions

(In billions of U.S. dollars)

	1995	1996
All countries	1,412.1	1,563.6
Industrial countries	725.0	789.2
Of which:		
United States	74.8	64.0
Japan	183.3	216.7
European Union	376.3	402.2
Developing countries	687.1	774.4
Africa	25.4	29.3
Asia	375.2	424.5
Europe	84.2	86.9
Middle East	73.7	78.5
Western Hemisphere	128.8	155.2

Source: International Monetary Fund, *International Financial Statistics* (May 1997).

depth, and liquidity of the euro sovereign bond markets and by the characteristics of private markets. Some of the pressures on the euro arising from inflows seeking higher returns could be offset by a rise in issuance of euro securities as the single-currency market evolves. Ultimately, the role of the euro in the international monetary system will turn on the future stability and strength of the euro vis-à-vis the dollar and yen, and will be defined by the shares of the euro in official and private portfolios, international financial transactions, and trade flows. For now, Asian and U.S. investors appear to have shifted out of the deutsche mark and into the dollar because of uncertainties surrounding EMU and the euro, but there could be a gradual rebalancing of portfolios toward EMU as both the euro and the credibility of the ECB become known and accepted and as euro markets acquire liquidity and depth.

EMU and the Potential Benefits of Europe-wide Securities Markets

By removing the volatile currency risk component of intra-EMU cross-border financing costs, the introduction of the euro may eventually create the largest single-currency financial market in the world. Viewed as a single set of markets, the value of EU bonds, equities, and bank loans circulating in European capital markets totaled more than $27 trillion at end-1995, compared with $23 trillion in U.S. capital markets and $16 trillion in Japan's (see Table 12). The potential benefits of establishing this kind of euro presence in international capital markets would be considerable in terms of market liquidity and depth, and lower funding costs for sovereign and private borrowers. Once the euro is introduced, borrowers and lenders will begin to seek lower costs and higher returns across na-

tional boundaries, European financial markets could become less segmented, and there could be more uniformity in market practices and more transparency in pricing. In addition, if continued efforts toward fiscal consolidation lead to the privatization of state-owned enterprises and of public pension, health, and other social insurance funds, the demand for, and supply of, capital could increase substantially, and this too would support the development of deep and liquid EMU-wide markets.

Major structural changes are required to bring this transformation about. The development of Europe-wide private securities markets has thus far been impeded by long-standing, inhibiting regulations for issuing, dealing, and trading securities, by elements of tax systems that encourage bank financing, and by differences in market practices and in securities clearance and settlement systems. Some progress has already been made in Europe to harmonize the regulations for issuing securities, the supervision of mutual investment funds and insurance companies, and the liberalization of services in those financial products. However, further progress in removing impediments would increase the pace of EMU-wide market integration.

Whether institutional arrangements and financial policies may also affect the pace of market integration and development is an open question. Two general paradigms and corresponding historical examples can be distinguished of how central bank operating procedures have affected the development of private securities markets.[17] In the United States, the central bank has played an active role by intervening daily in money and securities (repo) markets in order to smooth fluctuations in liquidity during the day and to provide stability to the pattern of interest rates on overnight funds; this paradigm applies also to Australia, Canada, the United Kingdom, and to some extent Japan. Financial institutions that operate within the U.S. markets (including European institutions) have come to expect this level of participation, and the structure of financial activities and balance sheets reflects this mode of central bank operations. It has been argued that this active participation has fostered the development of one of the most efficient money and securities markets in the world. By contrast, in Germany, the central bank's reliance on minimum reserve requirements, reserve averaging, other restrictions on instruments and market practices, and weekly market-smoothing interventions has tended, until recently, to discourage the development of a broad spectrum of deep and liquid money markets and to foster the predominance of bank-intermediated finance.

At this point in building the institutional structure of the ESCB, it is uncertain which paradigm will prevail over the next few years, but any solution would need

---

[17]See Folkerts-Landau and Garber (1992).

Table 12. European Union (EU), North America, and Japan: Selected Indicators of the Size of the Capital Markets, 1995

(In billions of U.S. dollars unless noted otherwise)

	Population (In millions)	GDP	Total Reserves Minus Gold	Stock Market Capitalization	Debt Securities[1] Public	Debt Securities[1] Private	Debt Securities[1] Total	Bank Assets[2]	Bonds, Equities, and Bank Assets[3]	Bonds, Equities, and Bank Assets[3] (In percent of GDP)
EU-15[4]	371.8	8,427.6	376.3	3,778.5	4,809.9	3,863.5	8,673.4	14,818.0	27,269.9	323.58
EU-11[5]	289.0	6,804.9	284.5	2,119.4	3,903.8	3,088.6	6,992.4	11,971.6	21,083.4	309.83
EU-8[6]	182.7	5,055.4	199.2	1,693.8	2,324.2	2,613.6	4,937.8	9,456.0	16,087.6	318.23
North America	383.1	8,105.7	106.7	7,314.7	7,339.5	4,439.2	11,778.7	5,652.4	24,745.7	305.29
Canada	29.6	565.6	15.0	366.3	580.8	93.1	673.9	515.8	1,556.0	275.11
Mexico	90.5	286.3	16.8	90.7	30.7	23.5	54.2	136.6	281.5	98.32
United States	263.0	7,253.8	74.8	6,857.6	6,728.0	4,322.6	11,050.6	5,000.0	22,908.2	315.81
Japan	125.2	5,134.3	183.3	3,667.3	3,447.7	1,877.1	5,324.8	7,382.2	16,374.2	318.92
Memorandum items:										
EU countries:										
Austria	8.5	233.2	18.7	32.5	105.9	105.7	211.6	457.7	701.9	300.97
Belgium	10.0	269.2	16.2	105.0	305.4	165.5	470.9	734.2	1,310.0	486.64
Denmark	5.2	172.7	11.0	56.2	142.1	188.6	330.7	155.5	542.4	314.07
Finland	5.1	125.0	10.0	44.1	94.6	49.5	144.1	143.5	331.8	265.46
France	58.0	1,538.8	26.9	522.1	681.7	801.2	1,482.9	2,923.0	4,927.9	320.25
Germany	81.6	2,412.5	85.0	577.4	893.6	1,284.5	2,178.1	3,752.4	6,507.8	269.76
Greece	10.5	114.3	14.8	17.1	100.1	5.8	105.9	63.9	186.8	163.41
Ireland	3.6	61.9	8.6	25.8	38.5	7.4	45.9	82.3	154.0	248.63
Italy	57.2	1,087.2	34.9	209.5	1,222.0	396.8	1,618.8	1,513.5	3,341.8	307.38
Luxembourg	0.4	19.3	0.1	30.4	1.0	15.9	16.9	555.0	602.3	3,125.08
Netherlands	15.5	395.5	33.7	356.5	203.5	183.9	387.4	808.0	1,551.9	392.39
Portugal	9.9	102.7	15.9	18.4	56.0	15.6	71.6	161.8	251.8	245.06
Spain	39.2	559.6	34.5	197.8	301.6	62.6	364.2	840.2	1,402.2	250.58
Sweden	8.8	230.6	24.1	178.0	234.0	184.2	418.2	202.8	799.0	346.49
United Kingdom	58.3	1,105.1	42.0	1,407.7	429.9	396.3	826.2	2,424.4	4,658.3	421.53

Sources: Bank for International Settlements; Bank of England, *Quarterly Bulletin* (November 1995); Bank of Japan, *Economic Statistics Monthly* (May 1996); Central Bank of Ireland, *Quarterly Bulletin* (Winter 1995); International Finance Corporation, *Emerging Stock Markets Factbook 1997*; Organization for Economic Cooperation and Development, *Bank Profitability: Financial Statements of Banks, 1985–1994*; and International Monetary Fund, *International Financial Statistics* and *World Economic Outlook* databases.

[1]Domestic and international debt securities shown by the nationality of the issuer.

[2]All bank data are for 1994. Category definition comprises all banks in each country except as follows: for Canada, comprises commercial banks consolidated worldwide; for Denmark, commercial banks and savings banks; for Greece, Luxembourg, and Mexico, commercial banks; for Japan, domestically licensed banks excluding trust accounts; for Sweden, commercial, savings, and cooperative banks; and for the United States, commercial banks, savings banks, and savings and loan associations.

[3]Sum of the Stock Market Capitalization, Debt Securities, and Bank Assets columns.

[4]Austria, Belgium, Denmark, Finland, France, Germany, Greece, Ireland, Italy, Luxembourg, the Netherlands, Portugal, Spain, Sweden, and the United Kingdom.

[5]Austria, Belgium, Finland, France, Germany, Ireland, Italy, Luxembourg, the Netherlands, Portugal, and Spain.

[6]Austria, Belgium, Finland, France, Germany, Ireland, Italy, Luxembourg, and the Netherlands.

to take into account the diversity of financial systems in Europe. Although final decisions have not been made, the current plan for monetary policy operating procedures is to rely on weekly repo operations that will be centrally controlled but decentrally implemented and on decentralized fine-tuning operations, while leaving open the possibility of a system of minimum reserve requirements, with reserve averaging acting as a liquidity buffer.[18] If the ECB is granted the authority to intervene more frequently and to issue its own paper, it remains to be seen if, when, and how the ECB would choose to centralize ESCB operations should the need arise. It is expected that leaving room for arbitrage by market participants, together with the European payments system, will provide the conditions that will encourage an active single money market. It has also been hypothesized by some officials that even if the ESCB chooses not to play an active role, a new breed of European financial institutions will emerge to manage the volatility that might be associated with deep and liquid European money and securities markets. However, there is market sentiment in Europe that the decentralized implementation of repo and fine-tuning operations would limit the ability of the ESCB to manage liquidity in money markets by way of active day-to-day operations in private interbank and repo markets.[19]

Another important aspect of EMU financial institutional arrangements is the safety and efficiency of the European payments systems. In order to implement an EMU monetary policy, to improve payments efficiency, and to reduce the potential for payments system problems, the EU is implementing a new European payments system, the Trans-European Automated Real-Time Gross Settlement Express Transfer (TARGET) system, that links the national real-time gross settlement payments systems that are already in place or being established in EU countries. The system is designed to process cross-border euro transactions after the start of Stage III on January 1, 1999. The system is still a work-in-progress, and if it is properly designed and successfully implemented it will support financial market integration within EMU.

Who has access to TARGET, and on what terms, could have important implications for the cost of transactions and for the safety and efficiency of the system. Because the euro will increase market integration, cross-border transactions between national payments systems are likely to increase significantly, even for European countries outside EMU. Although all credit institutions will have access to TARGET, still unresolved is the debate about access by non-EMU central banks to intraday credit in euros—not generally thought to have a monetary impact—which could turn into overnight overdrafts, which are thought to have a monetary impact. In practice, although limited access could affect the efficiency of TARGET, it might not affect the operation of euro money markets to the extent that banks in the non-EMU area have branches in the EMU area through which they can settle euro payments and access the ECB's liquidity facilities. However, by restricting intraday credit to EMU institutions and forcing banks outside the EMU area to delay their payments or to incur additional costs, it is likely that alternative settlement systems for euro transactions currently being developed, including private netting arrangements, will become increasingly attractive. This could reduce the number of payments across TARGET and slow down market integration as well as risk reduction in payment systems.

Consolidation and Restructuring of European Banking Systems

European finance has been dominated by bank intermediation, with EU bank loans accounting for 54 percent of outstanding financial instruments (bonds, equities, and loans). U.S. finance, by comparison, has been dominated by capital market intermediation, and bank loans account for only 22 percent of capital market activity. Indeed, the combined banking systems of the 15 EU countries would make up the largest banking system in the world, with bank loans totaling almost $15 trillion at end-1995. Europe currently has a core of internationally competitive financial institutions, most of which derive a considerable share of their revenues from providing wholesale banking and financial services. Some of these European universal banks are widely viewed as among the set of global wholesale banking institutions that will participate in, and probably prosper from, the consolidation and restructuring that is taking place in the international wholesale markets. By contrast, it is widely recognized that the retail banking industries in the majority of potential EMU countries still have considerable scope for enhancing efficiency. At the retail level, financial systems in Europe are relatively "over-banked," and a significant number of institutions are overstaffed. Complex ownership structures have pre-

---

[18]See European Monetary Institute (1997). This approach would preserve the now-decentralized credit-rating and discounting functions of some potential EMU countries, including Germany and France.

[19]Tools other than the ECB's regular repo and fine-tuning operations would include (1) other open market operations (main, longer-term, and structural refinancing operations) through instruments such as outright transactions, the issuance of debt certificates, and the collection of fixed-term deposits operations; (2) standing facilities; and (3) minimum reserve requirements. If relatively high and unremunerated, EMU reserve requirements could push a significant volume of euro transactions off shore, and into London and Switzerland, which would further inhibit the development of EMU-wide securities markets. See Background Material, Annex IV, for a more detailed discussion of ESCB operations.

vented free entry and exit and constrained management from responding to market incentives. Local market power has retarded innovation and perpetuated the mispricing of financial services, usually to the detriment of bank customers. Rigid labor laws have prevented private banks from shedding redundant labor to reduce operational costs. Although the introduction of the euro could temporarily aggravate the effect of these problems on retail bank performance, it will provide incentives for change.

The globalization of finance has been transforming financial institutions, banking systems, and securities markets worldwide for some time, and some countries are further along in the process of banking system restructuring and consolidation than others. Together with the ongoing changes related to EU banking and financial directives, the introduction of the single currency is likely to accelerate this transformation in Europe, in part by reducing, if not eliminating, the home currency advantages that EU banks currently have in their local retail deposit-taking and lending activities, and by encouraging bank customers to raise and lend funds directly in the EMU-wide markets. Such changes would increase cross-border competition for core businesses in European retail banking systems and increase the pace of disintermediation. If market forces are allowed to prevail in EMU, then European banking systems could experience some of the changes that have already taken place in other countries (e.g., in the United States), including a period of efficiency-enhancing structural changes, restructuring and consolidation (closures, mergers, and other alliances), and labor shedding. These structural changes would provide European borrowers and savers with competitively priced loans and deposits, allow more efficient financial services, and attract a more regional and international clientele to European financial and capital markets. In addition, such changes are likely to increase the flexibility and the diversity of financial markets in Europe, including enhancing the depth, breadth, and flexibility of European capital markets. These financial structural changes, in turn, could enhance the ability of European economies to create new firms and employment opportunities, in part by providing entrepreneurs with greater access to venture capital, as has been the experience in the United States.

Some European banking systems are likely to require greater adjustments and public support than others. The retail banking systems in Belgium, Luxembourg, Germany, and the Netherlands are thought to be in financial positions that will allow them to make some of the necessary adjustments without significant public funding. The banking systems in France and in Italy are viewed as more vulnerable, although the worst of the asset-quality problems may be over. Aggressively attacking existing problems would avoid a potential increase in the volume of nonperforming assets and the potential need for additional public funds for restructuring. Allowing market forces to contribute to the required adjustments through closures and mergers would help to some extent. The adjustment process would also be aided by changing ownership structures—in part, through privatization—and by liberalizing labor laws to allow inefficient financial institutions to better manage their costs.

Systemic Risk Management in EMU

As of August 1997, there was still considerable ambiguity about the mechanisms for resolving crises involving flows across the European payments system and about the coordination of systemic risk management functions. The Maastricht Treaty is silent about lender-of-last-resort responsibilities. Article 105 of the Maastricht Treaty does not provide for a general, direct involvement of the ECB in the supervision of financial intermediaries or institutions, and the subsidiarity principle applies, with national supervisors remaining fully competent. In addition, Article 105 (5) envisions only a supporting role for the ECB in ensuring the smooth functioning of European financial markets,[20] and it empowers the ESCB to promote the smooth operation of the European payments system. EMU national supervisory authorities, only in some cases the national central banks, will continue to have a mandate for banking supervision and for enforcing EU directives on capital adequacy, accounting standards, disclosure requirements, and other important aspects of financial supervision, regulation, and market surveillance. However, there is no central authority with the explicit mandate to ensure market stability over the EMU financial system in its entirety.

During a fast-breaking crisis, a central authority—usually the central bank—would require immediate access to information for assessing the financial condition of its counterparties, and in particular their liquidity and solvency. In some situations, problems could be resolved by the relevant national supervisory authorities and national central banks without the involvement of the ECB. But situations could arise in which the ECB would have to act decisively and quickly. This raises the issue of cooperation and information sharing between the ESCB/ECB and the relevant supervisors. Although the treaty establishes a clear institutional distinction between monetary and supervisory responsibilities, it does not prevent cooperation between banking supervisors and monetary authorities. Cooperation and information sharing be-

---

[20]The Maastricht Treaty empowers the ECB to "*contribute* to the smooth conduct of policies pursued by the competent authorities relating to the prudential supervision of credit institutions and the stability of the financial system" (italics added).

tween the ESCB and the ECB and the relevant supervisors have been discussed and work is in progress. In practice, Article 16 of the Second Banking Directive provides that banking supervisors are allowed to disclose to the national central banks, acting as monetary authorities, the information they may need. Conversely, the post-BCCI Directive (Directive 95/26/EC of June 29, 1995) stipulates that the national central banks are not prevented from communicating confidential information to the supervisory authorities, provided that this information is used exclusively for supervisory purposes. After the changeover to the euro, these procedures will be extended to the ECB in its capacity as monetary authority. By contrast, in some major countries it is viewed as desirable for central banks to have supervisory responsibility, shared with other agencies if necessary, for the wholesale or money center banking segment. Furthermore, the need

for money center banks to access central bank windows in an emergency also allows the central bank to exert informal but effective prudential influence over this banking segment.

There are alternative ways in which to organize and allocate supervisory and liquidity support responsibilities (see Background Material, Annex IV), but these would normally include mechanisms for determining when and if a problem exists, whether an institution that is experiencing difficulties in settling its payments obligation is liquidity constrained or fundamentally insolvent, and how to resolve the problem either by providing access to lender-of-last-resort facilities or by denying access to the payments system. The challenge in Europe is one of creating clear and easily implemented crisis management mechanisms for very low probability events that would impose potentially high costs on the payments system and its participants.

IV

Developments and Prospects in Emerging Markets

In rising to their highest peak to date, private capital flows to emerging markets during 1996 marked a new milestone in the ongoing integration of these economies into global financial markets. When measured relative to either GDP or domestic investment, the scale of capital inflows during the 1990s now exceeds that associated with the recycling of oil surpluses in the mid- to late 1970s. Moreover, this record level of flows was just one facet of the dramatic improvement in the terms and conditions under which emerging markets could access international financial markets: interest rate spreads fell sharply, average bond maturities more than doubled, lending covenants weakened, and four times as many countries now have access to international markets as in 1990. Nonetheless, not all regions have benefited equally. Flows continue to gravitate to Asian, Latin American, and certain transition economies, while some regions, notably Africa and the Middle East, have not shared fully in the expansion of private capital flows.

The record flows and sharp decline in yield spreads have been stimulated by three factors. First, the search for higher yields—a key feature of developments in mature markets—spilled over into emerging markets. As investors were forced to move down the credit spectrum in order to maintain yields, there was a strong increase in the demand for high-yield sovereign and corporate bonds issued by emerging market countries. Second, the continuing drive by institutional managers to increase their exposure to emerging markets and to achieve greater diversification of portfolios provided an important stimulus for flows to emerging markets. Institutional investors currently manage over $20 trillion in assets, only a small portion of which is invested in emerging markets. If institutional investors were to reallocate just 1 percent of total assets under management toward the emerging markets, this shift would constitute a capital flow of $200 billion. It has been estimated that institutional investors can continue to increase expected returns and reduce overall risks until the share of their portfolios allocated to emerging markets reaches a level that is three times as high as it is today.[21]

Third, the resurgence of capital flows has also reflected the clear recognition by investors that the economic fundamentals in most emerging markets in the 1990s have vastly improved over those that prevailed in the late 1970s. In the earlier period, many heavily indebted emerging market countries had pursued development strategies based on import substitution, which involved using capital inflows both to finance large fiscal imbalances and to offset the effects of capital flight. Fiscal imbalances often contributed to rapid inflation and a highly overvalued exchange rate. By contrast, in the 1990s a broad set of emerging markets pursued a strategy of opening their economies to international trade and capital transactions, fiscal consolidation, inflation stabilization, and extensive structural reforms designed to improve their economies' overall efficiency. Moreover, these changes took place against a background of a stable macroeconomic environment in the mature markets.

It is now evident that the Mexican crisis of 1994–95 had only a temporary and limited effect on the scale and geographic distribution of capital flows and the cost of external borrowing. Nonetheless, the spillover effects from Mexico in 1995 and, more recently, events in Thailand and in the Czech Republic have served as a reminder of how quickly international financial markets respond to perceived policy uncertainties and structural weaknesses, and the willingness of market participants to "test" the authorities' exchange rate commitment when weaknesses in policies are perceived.

Capital Flows to Emerging Markets

Private and Official Capital Flows

During 1996, net private capital flows to emerging markets surged to a record level of $235 billion—a 22 percent increase over 1995 (Table 13). The scale of the inflows and the broadening of market access provide evidence for the hypothesis that the 1990s represent a restoration of the trend toward global financial market integration that had been evident in the gold standard period and the 1920s but was disrupted by the Great Depression, World War II, and the capital controls systems of the postwar period.

---

[21]World Bank (1997).

Table 13. Private Capital Flows to Emerging Markets
(In billions of U.S. dollars)

	1990	1991	1992	1993	1994	1995	1996
Emerging markets							
Total net private capital inflows[1]	45.7	139.8	133.4	161.0	147.0	192.8	235.2
Net foreign direct investment	18.8	32.1	37.9	56.9	75.5	87.3	105.9
Net portfolio investment	17.0	39.7	59.2	106.8	97.2	31.6	58.7
Net other investment	9.9	68.0	36.3	−2.7	−25.7	73.9	70.6
Net external borrowing from official creditors	18.8	22.5	13.9	24.6	9.8	39.2	−13.2
Africa							
Total net private capital inflows[1]	2.9	5.5	5.7	4.7	12.7	13.6	9.0
Net foreign direct investment	1.4	2.4	1.9	1.2	3.4	2.3	5.1
Net portfolio investment	−1.6	−1.6	−0.7	0.9	0.4	1.9	0.7
Net other investment	3.1	4.7	4.5	2.5	8.8	9.4	3.2
Net external borrowing from official creditors	4.4	5.9	8.6	6.2	5.5	4.0	6.4
Asia							
Total net private capital inflows[1]	21.4	37.7	22.4	59.5	75.1	98.9	106.8
Net foreign direct investment	9.5	15.2	17.2	35.2	44.6	50.7	58.0
Net portfolio investment	−0.9	2.8	9.6	23.8	18.5	20.1	20.1
Net other investment	12.9	19.7	−4.5	0.5	12.0	28.1	28.8
Net external borrowing from official creditors	5.6	10.7	10.2	8.2	5.9	5.0	6.7
Middle East and Europe							
Total net private capital inflows[1]	7.0	73.3	42.8	24.1	−1.1	15.3	22.2
Net foreign direct investment	1.3	1.3	1.8	1.1	0.5	1.3	1.6
Net portfolio investment	2.0	23.2	20.5	17.4	14.7	13.8	9.3
Net other investment	3.7	48.8	20.5	5.5	−16.3	0.3	11.3
Net external borrowing from official creditors	−6.2	1.1	−2.7	5.9	10.3	−1.4	−5.9
Western Hemisphere							
Total net private capital inflows[1]	10.3	24.9	55.5	61.7	44.9	35.7	77.7
Net foreign direct investment	6.6	10.9	12.9	13.4	21.5	19.9	29.9
Net portfolio investment	17.5	14.5	30.6	61.1	60.8	−7.5	27.1
Net other investment	−13.8	−0.5	12.0	−12.8	−37.5	23.3	20.7
Net external borrowing from official creditors	8.3	3.2	−2.0	1.1	−1.7	22.7	−11.7
Countries in transition							
Total net private capital inflows[1]	4.2	−1.6	7.1	10.9	15.4	29.1	19.4
Net foreign direct investment	0.0	2.4	4.2	6.0	5.4	13.1	11.3
Net portfolio investment	. . .	0.8	−0.8	3.4	2.7	3.4	1.6
Net other investment	4.1	−4.8	3.8	1.5	7.3	12.6	6.6
Net external borrowing from official creditors	6.6	1.5	0.0	3.2	−10.3	8.8	−8.8
Memorandum items:							
Changes in reserve assets							
Emerging markets	66.2	75.1	31.7	83.9	90.5	122.9	104.8
Africa	4.6	3.7	−2.9	1.6	4.6	1.8	8.9
Asia	47.4	46.0	7.1	43.1	77.9	47.7	61.8
Middle East and Europe	−1.2	4.9	1.3	4.9	4.3	12.4	9.5
Western Hemisphere	14.7	18.0	23.0	20.2	−4.3	24.8	26.2
Countries in transition	0.7	2.6	3.3	14.2	8.1	36.2	−1.7

Sources: International Monetary Fund, *International Financial Statistics* and *World Economic Outlook* databases.
[1]Net foreign direct investment plus net portfolio investment plus net other investment.

In sharp contrast, in 1990–94, official flows declined significantly as a source of external finance for emerging markets, falling from 29 percent of total flows in 1990 to 6 percent in 1994. Official flows rose steeply during 1995 as assistance was extended to Mexico in the aftermath of the crisis. However, for the first time in the 1990s, total net official flows to emerging markets in 1996 were negative. Net official flows were negative not only to Latin America, reflecting the substantial repayments by Mexico of official assistance, but also to the Middle East, Europe,

and the transition economies. Still, for Africa, official flows have continued to be the largest source of flows, and in 1996 accounted for over 40 percent of total flows.

The regional distribution of private capital flows has been closely linked to the macroeconomic performance of countries in the various areas, reflecting an improved ability of investors to discriminate among countries according to the quality of policy and economic performance. While Asia remained the largest recipient of capital flows in 1996, Latin America experienced the sharpest increase in capital inflows. The relatively modest expansion of capital flows to Asia reflected the slowdown in the growth of both exports and output in the region, as well as the impact of uncertainties created by financial sector weaknesses in countries such as Korea and Thailand. The restoration of investor confidence in Latin America was brought about by the demonstrated willingness of many countries in the region to undertake extensive adjustments in the wake of the Mexican crisis, by the continued implementation of a strategy of opening their economies to international trade and capital flows, and by what is regarded by market participants as the successful management of the Mexican crisis and its immediate aftermath. In Africa and the transition economies in contrast, net private capital inflows declined during 1996. As a region, Africa has not shared in the expansion of private capital flows to emerging markets in the 1990s. Indeed, during the period 1990–96, Africa received negligible net portfolio flows. Another pattern that emerges is that private financing is still provided on a selective basis. These flows have been highly concentrated, with the top 10 countries receiving nearly three-quarters of capital inflows during the 1990s.[22]

Foreign direct investment and portfolio investment have grown strongly in importance relative to the share of commercial bank lending in private capital flows during the 1990s. Foreign direct investment has been the largest component of net private flows since 1995 and accounted for 45 percent of total private flows in 1996. While portfolio flows were negligible during the 1970s and 1980s, they became sizable in the early 1990s and represented the largest component of flows between 1992 and 1994. Foreign direct investment flows have been especially important in Asia, where they have been the key vehicle for the global reallocation of production activities to lower-cost sites.

Throughout the 1990s, a substantial proportion of the capital inflows into emerging markets has been accumulated as foreign exchange reserves (Table 13). Of the $1.2 trillion in net capital flows to emerging markets during 1990–96, $575 billion (49 percent of inflows) was accumulated as foreign exchange reserves. In Asia, 70 percent of the inflows were accumulated as foreign exchange reserves and in Latin America, 37 percent. This accumulation raised reserve assets in emerging market central banks to $822 billion by end-1996, a more than threefold increase since 1989, representing about half of the world's central bank foreign exchange reserves.

The buildup of foreign exchange reserves is a direct consequence of central bank intervention to prevent

nominal exchange rate appreciation in the face of substantial capital inflows. The accumulation of foreign exchange reserves also reflects a desire to build up a "buffer" against a sudden reversal of capital inflows. Many central bankers remember that Mexico lost $5 billion in only a few days in December 1994, and it is becoming apparent that, in the face of a high degree of capital mobility, traditional reserve-to-import ratios are no longer appropriate for judging the adequacy of the level of reserves. Moreover, a strong reserve position can also influence a country's credit rating and thereby its cost of funds. Indeed, reserve management must be seen as an integral part of a country's decision regarding its strategy for managing external asset and liability risk (see Chapter V).

While a large stock of foreign exchange reserves provides clear benefits for an individual country, the widespread and substantial accumulation of reserves by many emerging markets also has costs. Nearly half of the total capital flows undertaken in search of higher returns has ended up as foreign exchange reserves, which are typically composed of highly liquid and risk-free but relatively low-yielding assets, such as U.S. treasury bills. This sterilization of capital flows into emerging markets and their recycling through investment into mature market securities implies a significant fiscal cost for emerging market countries. In essence, residents of emerging market countries have to pay the equivalent of the differential between the cost of these external funds and the return on reserve assets multiplied by the stock of foreign exchange reserves. As discussed in Annex I of the Background Material, this fiscal cost currently amounts to approximately $10 billion a year.

Financial Instruments: Bonds, Equities, Bank Lending, and Derivatives

A remarkable development in the composition of external financing by emerging markets in the 1990s has been the increased reliance on bond issuance as opposed to bank lending. Indeed, international bond issues rose from $58 billion in 1995 to $102 billion in 1996 (Figure 12). The increased bond issuance reflected an across-the-board improvement in the terms and conditions under which borrowers in emerging markets could access global markets. The number of countries rated by international credit-rating agencies, often viewed as a prerequisite for the issuance of Eurobonds, has risen from 11 in 1989 to 49 in 1996 (see Appendix 1 to this chapter). Bond issuers from all regions except Africa increased their issuance during 1996. Yield spreads on sovereign issues declined from an average of 364 basis points in 1995 to 302 basis points in 1996, with more dramatic declines for the major Latin American sovereigns. For example, Mexico's spread at launch narrowed from 537 basis points in 1995 to 249 basis points in 1996. The average ma-

---

[22]The GDP of the top 10 recipient countries amounted to less than half of total emerging market GDP in 1996.

Figure 12. Private Market Financing for Emerging Markets[1]
(In billions of U.S. dollars)

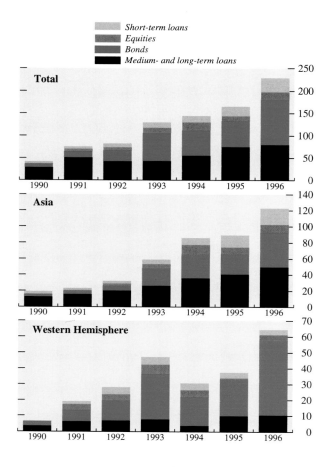

Source: Capital Data Loanware and Bondware.
[1]Gross primary market financing.

vember, Russia placed a $1 billion issue—the largest-ever debut sovereign issue—with booked demand reported to have exceeded $2 billion and priced well below expectations. In June 1997, Brazil sold $3 billion of 30-year bonds with $2.3 billion exchanged for Brady bonds. Moreover, several entities placed century (100-year maturity) bonds, including the People's Republic of China, the Israel Electric Corporation, India's Reliance Industries, and the Endesa Chile Overseas Company.

International placements of equity by emerging market entities rose during 1996 but remained subdued compared with the previous peak in 1993. American Depository Receipts (ADRs) and Global Depository Receipts (GDRs) continued to be the major instruments used to raise equity capital in the international markets, accounting for a little more than half the capital raised. Issuance by Asian entities rose slightly, to $9.8 billion, and continued to account for the major proportion of equity placements by emerging market countries.[23] Latin American placements rebounded to $3.7 billion in 1996 but remained modest compared with previous years. Placements by entities in the transition economies have continued to grow, and companies from the region doubled their 1995 equity placements to reach $1.3 billion in 1996.

Although the share of commercial bank lending in total flows to emerging markets has declined in importance, such lending continues to be a substantial source of syndicated and structured finance—trade finance, project finance, and bridge finance—and a particularly significant source of funds in some regions. In contrast to 1995, when syndicated bank lending rose by more than 35 percent as the cost of borrowing on international bond and equity markets increased sharply in the wake of the Mexican crisis, syndicated lending rose a modest 6 percent during 1996 to $79 billion. However, lending to Asian countries continued to grow robustly, increasing by 22 percent and accounting for the largest share of total syndicated bank lending—62 percent in 1996. The relatively higher reliance of the region on bank lending stems in part from the fact that many Asian borrowers are reportedly attracted to the syndicated loan markets because of the flexibility in structuring the drawdown, which is particularly useful in funding infrastructure investments. Lending to European emerging market countries also rose strongly, increasing by 9 percent, while loans extended to Latin America grew more modestly—by 5 percent—and declined for Africa and the Middle East. As interest rate margins on loans in industrial countries narrowed, competition between major international banks for higher-yielding loans to emerging markets intensified and resulted in smaller loan

---

[23]Convertible bond issuance by Asian entities continued to account for a quarter of the region's bond issuance during 1996, with Korean companies accounting for 40 percent of these issues.

turity for sovereign issuers, which had fallen sharply in the wake of the Mexican crisis to 3.9 years, rose dramatically in 1996 to 9.8 years.

The favorable environment for emerging market borrowers in global bond markets prompted several sovereigns to launch issues to restructure existing liabilities at improved terms (such as Brady bond buybacks and the repayment by Mexico of obligations to the United States and the partial repayment of its obligations to the IMF), to reduce refinancing risk through an extension of maturities, to diversify their investor bases, and to set benchmarks for their corporate borrowers. This situation has also facilitated the entry of several first-time sovereign and corporate borrowers. Large individual deals included the $6 billion of floating-rate notes arranged by Mexico in July 1996, the largest single-tranche Eurobond ever. In No-

Table 14. Emerging Market Total Return Equity and Debt Indices
(In percent unless otherwise noted)

	1990	1991	1992	1993	1994	1995	1996	1997:Q1
Emerging stock markets								
International Finance Corporation Investable (IFCI) indexes								
Composite[1]	−2.2	39.5	3.3	79.6	−12.0	−8.4	9.4	9.5
Latin America	9.1	139.3	3.5	60.8	−9.4	−16.9	17.2	15.1
Asia	−19.2	12.4	18.5	97.6	−12.8	−5.5	10.5	1.2
Europe, Middle East, and Africa	13.9	−29.2	−32.7	122.4	−27.1	22.5	−2.3	19.4
Memorandum item:								
S&P 500	−3.1	30.5	7.6	10.1	1.3	37.6	23.0	2.7
Emerging market debt								
J.P. Morgan Emerging Market Bond Index (EMBI)		38.8	7.0	44.2	−18.7	27.5	34.2	1.4
(Spreads in basis points)[2]	1,111	631	831	396	1,039	1,044	537	507

[1]The IFCI Composite Index comprised 1,224 stocks in 26 emerging markets at end-1996. It is widely used as a benchmark for international portfolio management.

[2]End of period.

spreads, with the average spread on new loans declining from 105 basis points in 1995 to 88 basis points in 1996. In addition, there was a weakening of loan covenants, such as restrictions on the double pledging of assets as collateral and limitations on the maximum leveraging of capital, particularly on loans to Latin American corporations.

Offshore derivative products in emerging market instruments have continued to proliferate. These products enhance the ability of investors to manage the risks associated with their emerging market investments and foster arbitrage between different instruments. Moreover, recent experience has again illustrated the ability of financial markets to innovate to manage risk exposures across markets and to circumvent official controls; it underscores the need for national authorities in emerging markets to understand the limited effectiveness of many restrictions that are being placed on financial transactions, lest institutions engage in a variety of unobserved, let alone unregulated, transactions. One new hedging product is the over-the-counter nondeliverable forward (NDF) foreign exchange contract, which allows investors to hedge foreign exchange risks on emerging market instruments when hedging transactions have been constrained by either underdeveloped local forward and futures foreign exchange markets or capital controls. While the price for the contract is linked to movements in a particular emerging market currency, settlement is made in U.S. dollars. The Asian segment of the market is particularly active, with banks and brokers in Singapore and Hong Kong, China, estimating daily volumes of between US$500 million and US$800 million; participants expect the market to continue to grow rapidly (by 30–50 percent) over the coming year. Other innovations include exchange-traded emerging market debt derivatives, for example,

futures and options on Brady bonds; structured notes; the development of emerging market index funds; growth of over-the-counter swaps and options on emerging market stocks and stock indices; and the creation of offshore exchange-traded equity derivative products, such as the stock index futures contracts on Mexico's and Taiwan Province of China's equity indices that are traded on the Chicago Mercantile Exchange. Since May 1995, futures exchanges in Chicago and New York have offered a variety of emerging market products including options on the Mexican peso and Brazilian real futures. Several new derivative products were also developed in emerging markets, including the launching of future and options contracts on the rand-dollar exchange rate on the South African Futures Exchange.

Performance of Emerging Debt and Equity Markets

The continued surge of capital flows into emerging markets during 1996 was an important contributor to the spectacular rally in emerging debt markets (Table 14 and Figure 13).[24] Spreads on new bond issues and in secondary markets, which had been declining since the peaks reached in the spring of 1995, continued to decline during 1996. Sovereign yield spreads, as measured by the J.P. Morgan Emerging Market Bond Index (EMBI), fell from 1,044 basis points at the end

---

[24]Traditionally, the bulk of trading activity by international investors in emerging market debt has been in instruments denominated in the major convertible currencies, which are issued and traded in the Eurobond, Yankee, Samurai, and other offshore markets. Foreign investment in domestic local currency debt has historically been limited, though it has been growing recently.

Figure 13. Yield Spreads: Emerging Market and High-Yield U.S. Corporate Bonds
(In percent)

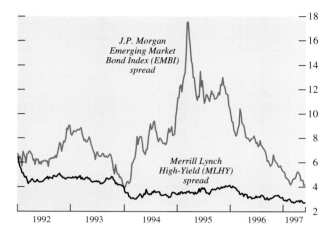

Source: Bloomberg Financial Markets L.P.

of 1995 to 537 basis points by end-1996.[25] Total returns on the EMBI reached 34 percent for 1996, compared with returns of 3 percent on the J.P. Morgan Government Bond Index for the United States. In early 1997, emerging market spreads continued to decline and by late February they had once again reached their historical lows of around 400 basis points. Since then yield spreads have fluctuated. As spreads on emerging market debt declined to their previous historical lows reached in late 1993 and early 1994, concern developed that the narrow spreads implied that risk was no longer being adequately priced. However, to put this concern in perspective, spreads on emerging market debt remained well above spreads on comparably rated corporates in the mature markets.

The growing volume of bond issuance by emerging market entities, matched by increased investor interest in emerging debt markets, led to a drastic increase in the turnover of such instruments which, after remaining relatively stable from 1994 to 1995, rose by 93 percent to $5.3 trillion in 1996. Brady bonds are the single most-traded emerging market debt instrument, with transactions during 1996 of $2.7 trillion. The sharp increases in turnover in Brady bonds (from $1 trillion in 1993 to $2.7 trillion in 1996) relative to a modest increase in the stock of such bonds suggests that there has been a substantial increase in their liquidity.

While the liquidity of emerging debt markets improved substantially during 1996, there still appear to be lingering market imperfections. For example, differential yield spreads between the Brady and Eurobond sectors endured, suggesting continued market segmentation. Spreads on Brady bonds have invariably exceeded those on Eurobonds and differentials have recently been of the order of 175–300 basis points. (See Annex I of the Background Material). While market participants have offered a number of explanations for these differentials, most are unconvincing. Some suggest a lack of investor sophistication and some a lack of liquidity.

While emerging equity markets have continued to recover since the 1995 Mexican crisis, 1996 was the first year since the boom of 1993 that these markets posted a collective positive annual return. Total dollar returns measured by the International Finance Corporation Investable (IFCI) Composite Index reached 9.4 percent.[26] Relative to the mature markets, however, emerging equity markets continued to perform modestly. Returns were substantially higher, for example, on the U.S. S&P 500 index (23 percent). The relatively modest overall performances of emerging equity markets during 1996 masked divergent performance between and within regions. While Latin American equity markets rose by 17.2 percent and Asian markets by 10.5 percent, European, Middle Eastern, and African markets fell by 2.3 percent.

Returns on emerging equity markets accelerated in early 1997, with the IFCI Composite Index rising by 9.5 percent during the first quarter. In contrast to 1996, this collective return was well in excess of the increase in the S&P 500 of 2.7 percent during the period. Returns in Latin American markets continued at robust levels (15.1 percent), while returns in Asian markets fell off (1.2 percent), and returns in the European, Middle Eastern, and African region rose sharply (19.4 percent). Market participants indicated a continuing shift of investor sentiment away from Asia toward Latin America. This shift reflected the perception that the regional slowdown in Asia represented a more permanent adjustment to a lower longer-term growth path as the economies matured and that economic fundamentals in Latin America had improved—projections for growth were revised upward and inflation continued to moderate. Despite the recovery in emerging equity markets during 1996 and early 1997, at their recent peaks they remained below the highs reached in September 1994 prior to the Mexican crisis.

---

[25]Since Brady bonds represent some of the most liquid emerging market bonds they are heavily weighted in the major emerging market bond indices. Furthermore, because Latin American issues represent a substantial proportion of outstanding Brady bonds, most of these indices largely reflect Latin American Brady debt. In the EMBI, for example, they receive a weight of 91 percent.

[26]The International Finance Corporation's Investable (IFCI) Composite Index, with 1,224 stocks in 26 emerging markets (at end-1996), is a broad index designed to measure returns on emerging market stocks that are legally and practically open to foreign portfolio investment. It is widely used as a benchmark for international portfolio management purposes and comprises regional indices for Asia (with a weight of 47 percent), Latin America (33 percent), and Europe, Middle East, and Africa (20 percent).

Sustainability of Capital Flows and Speculative Attacks

A key systemic issue is whether the high level of capital flows and recent improvements in the terms and conditions affecting market access are likely to be sustained or whether current market conditions are predominantly driven by cyclical developments in the major industrial countries that are prone to be reversed. There are several broad structural changes in international investment management that, when combined with the successful implementation of macroeconomic stabilization programs and structural economic reforms in emerging markets, suggest that a significant share of the favorable market conditions are likely to be permanent. In particular, the growing institutionalization of savings in the mature economies—by 1994, pension funds, insurance companies, and mutual funds in the OECD countries had grown to $20 trillion—and the continuing international diversification of these institutional funds are likely to provide a sustained source of flows in the foreseeable future (though mutual funds differ from other institutional investors in that they can face sudden fund outflows on a major scale).

However, this general optimism has to be tempered by two concerns. First, the terms and conditions governing market access could deteriorate suddenly should global monetary conditions tighten in response to changing cyclical conditions in mature markets or in response to a financial disturbance,[27] such as an abrupt downward movement in equity prices that could lead to a major redemption of mutual fund shares. Second, even if overall flows are sustained, a lack of flexibility in exchange rate arrangements puts individual emerging market countries increasingly at risk of being "tested" through a speculative attack on their exchange rate, combined with a potentially abrupt loss of market access, whenever there are uncertainties regarding the sustainability of macroeconomic policies and structural weaknesses.

Indeed, the rapid and continuing integration of emerging market countries into global financial markets during the 1990s has brought with it a number of currency crises, most recently involving the Thai baht and the Czech koruna. These events, like the Mexican peso crisis in late 1994, have raised a host of questions regarding the nature of speculative currency attacks, the appropriate defensive policies, the role of international financial support, and the degree of exchange rate flexibility (including exit strategies) appropriate to the evolving international financial environment.

The same structural changes that have improved the access of emerging market countries to international financial markets and that have internationalized financial markets have also increased the potential intensity and duration of speculative attacks. For example, the growing institutionalization of savings and the participation of institutional investors in international markets have been an important source of demand for emerging market securities, but they have also led to the growth of highly leveraged hedge funds and proprietary traders who are prepared to tolerate significant risk in their search for weaknesses in foreign exchange arrangements. It is evident that institutional investors now have the capacity to take substantial short positions in a weak currency through spot, forward, and currency options markets, and through the rapidly growing markets in structured products. (Structured foreign exchange products are leveraged debt or equity instruments with payoffs tied to an exchange rate.) It is estimated that the total assets of hedge funds, proprietary traders, and speculative-type mutual funds have grown to well above $100 billion, and these funds have at times undertaken investments that involved leveraging their capital by between 5 and 10 times. Hence, compared with earlier years, more international reserves and more complex intervention strategies are needed to offset these attacks (see Appendix 2 at the end of this chapter for a discussion of the mechanisms employed in a speculative attack).

These challenges are of course most pronounced in countries with little exchange rate flexibility. While many countries have found managed exchange rate arrangements useful as a means of providing a nominal anchor for their domestic price level and/or maintaining a competitive external position, managed exchange rate regimes demand that the macroeconomic policy stance be consistent with the exchange rate regime, and that the financial market structure be sufficiently strong and flexible to allow for an effective defense of the exchange rate (see Box 1 on the recent efforts of Hong Kong, China, to achieve such a policy mix). Market perceptions of inconsistencies or weakness in policies or in financial structure can readily precipitate speculative attacks on a country's exchange rate.[28]

---

[27]Despite all the structural changes that have occurred in the international financial system since the earlier periods of high capital mobility during 1870–1914 and in the 1920s, the potential sources of cyclical variability in capital flows remain the same, namely, divergent macroeconomic conditions in capital-exporting and capital-importing countries and crises in individual capital-importing countries (see Annex VI of the Background Material).

[28]Speculative attacks are not uniquely a feature of the current system. Indeed, an important feature of periods of high capital mobility and fixed exchange rates, such as the gold standard era and the 1920s, was that political and economic crises in individual countries led on occasion to speculative attacks on a country's gold reserves that sometimes forced a suspension of both gold convertibility and debt-service payments. Even in those periods, the response of investors and lenders to adverse "news" could be swift and abrupt (see Annex VI of the Background Material for a further discussion of this experience). The common element between earlier periods and the current one is that speculative attacks have taken place against countries with a fixed exchange rate when there was a high degree of capital mobility.

Box 1. Building a Resilient Financial System in Hong Kong, China

Under the Sino-British Joint Declaration of 1984, Hong Kong reverted to Chinese sovereignty on July 1, 1997, becoming the Hong Kong Special Administrative Region (HKSAR), governed by the Basic Law of 1990. In monetary and financial affairs, the relationship between mainland China and Hong Kong will follow the principle of "one country, two currencies, two monetary systems and two monetary authorities." Article 109 of the Basic Law protects the status of Hong Kong as an international financial center. Article 110 ensures the independent formulation of monetary and financial policies and of regulation and supervision by the government of the HKSAR. Article 111 stipulates that the Hong Kong dollar will be the legal tender, backed by a 100 percent reserve fund. Article 112 states that no foreign exchange controls will be applied. Article 113 specifies that the government of the HKSAR will manage the Exchange Fund, primarily to maintain the value of the Hong Kong dollar.

Current market sentiment appears strongly to support the view that over the medium term the transfer of sovereignty will not have any adverse effects on the Hong Kong dollar. Indeed, swapped into U.S. dollars, the yield curve of Hong Kong Monetary Authority (HKMA) bills and notes lies below the U.S. yield curve at maturities up to seven years. This sentiment reflects the generally positive assessment of the Hong Kong financial system and of the professional financial management practiced by the HKMA.

The cornerstone of the financial system is the currency board linking the Hong Kong dollar to the U.S. dollar, which the HKMA has successfully defended in the past, most recently in January 1995 in the wake of the Mexican financial crisis. The first line of defense of the linked exchange rate is a large stock of reserves—US$64 billion at end-April 1997, or 40 percent of 1996 GDP. The second line of defense is the ability of the HKMA to raise short-term interest rates to make it expensive for speculators to obtain Hong Kong dollar credit. The banking system is highly capitalized and liquid, with very low levels of nonperforming loans, and it can tolerate increases in short-term interest rates that may be necessary to defend the exchange rate. Moreover, in 1996 the HKMA put in place other features of the financial system that increase its robustness, implementing a real-time gross settlement system in December and establishing a Mortgage Corporation, which will help to isolate property finance from fluctuations in short-term interest rates.

In addition, the People's Bank of China, which has reiterated its support for the present exchange rate arrangements in Hong Kong, has stated that it would be prepared to use its own foreign exchange reserves to defend the Hong Kong dollar. The HKMA has also established a swap facility with the People's Bank to provide liquidity to its reserves in the event of an attack on the exchange rate, as it has with 10 other monetary authorities in the region.

A number of recent empirical studies have attempted to determine under what conditions a speculative attack will take place and when spillover effects are likely to be present (see Annex VI of the Background Material). A common set of factors tend to affect the likelihood that a country's currency will be attacked either directly or as a result of contagion. In particular, a country would most likely be attacked when it has a highly overvalued real exchange rate, a weak financial system (particularly when the problems arise following a very rapid expansion of credit), a weak fiscal position, an external debt position with a high proportion of short-term maturities, and limited international reserves.

Typically, the first line of defense has involved some form of sterilized intervention in the spot or forward foreign exchange market or both. When the intervention takes place in the spot market, the reduction in the monetary base resulting from central bank sales of foreign exchange would be balanced by actions designed to generate an offsetting rise in the supply of base money (such as through central bank purchases of government securities). While intervention in the forward market does not involve an immediate reduction in the monetary base, it would involve an offsetting action when the forward contract matures. The

authorities' ability to sustain a program of sterilized intervention is ultimately constrained by the quantity of the foreign exchange reserves and the resources they can obtain either from other official institutions or by borrowing on international markets.

Since a speculative attack requires that the speculator establish a net short position in the domestic currency, the authorities have employed a number of tactics to raise the cost of short positions (see Appendix 2 at the end of this chapter). When sterilized intervention has failed to stem the capital outflow, it has been necessary to allow short-term interest rates to rise, that is, to allow the monetary impact of the intervention to tighten conditions in financial markets and thereby make it more costly for the speculators to obtain a net short position by borrowing domestic currency. (Nonresidents borrow domestic currency in anticipation of a devaluation, as well as in order to deliver domestic currency when the forward contracts for sales of domestic currency against, say, dollars come due.) However, it is frequently found that such an increase in short-term money market rates is transmitted quickly to the rest of the economy and hence may be difficult to sustain for an extended period, especially if there are existing weaknesses in either the financial system or the nonfinancial sector.

In situations in which the authorities have regarded high short-term interest rates as imposing an unacceptable burden on domestic residents, they have attempted to "split" the market for domestic currency, by either requesting or instructing domestic financial institutions not to lend to those borrowers engaged in speculative activity. Foreign exchange transactions associated with trade flows, foreign direct investment, and usually equity investments are excluded from the restrictions. In essence, this two-tier system attempts to deny speculators the domestic credit needed to establish a net short domestic currency position, while allowing nonspeculative domestic credit demand to be substantially satisfied at normal market rates.

Most of these features were in evidence in the recent attacks on the Thai baht. Adverse economic news from Thailand, combined with concerns that Japanese interest rates would be raised, precipitated severe pressure on the baht starting on May 7, 1997. For the first time since the Mexican crisis, exchange rate pressures in one country spilled over to a number of other emerging market currencies. In Asia, the Indonesian rupiah, the Malaysian ringgit, and the Philippine peso all came under varying degrees of pressure. In Eastern Europe, the Czech koruna came under attack. There were no notable immediate spillover effects on Latin American currencies. The countries that were adversely affected by the run on the baht had, in the view of investors, a number of features in common with Thailand. Malaysia, Indonesia, and the Philippines had all been affected to varying degrees by the economic slowdown in the region. All had current account deficits, though of a smaller magnitude than that of Thailand, and most had accumulated debt rapidly during the 1990s. Furthermore, all had experienced a rapid appreciation in the property sector, and financial sectors in all were highly exposed to the property sector. The Czech Republic shared many of these features and had perhaps even more similarities with Thailand than its Asian neighbors did.

Central bank defenses in support of currencies under pressure included a combination of exchange market intervention and measures that increased the cost of short-term credit generally. As a result, interbank overnight interest rates rose by varying degrees and over differing time spans across countries: the rupiah rate rose from 14 percent on Friday, May 9 to 16 percent by Friday, May 16; the ringgit rate rose from 7 percent to 19 percent by Tuesday, May 20; the peso rate rose from 11 percent to 20 percent on Monday, May 19; koruna rates rose most substantially, reaching 200 percent on Thursday, May 22 (as discussed below, the 7.5 percent fluctuation band of the koruna was abolished as of May 27).

The Thai authorities found it necessary to employ selective capital controls—aimed at reducing foreign speculators' access to domestic currency credit but specifically excluding bona fide trade and investment transactions. Consequently, the sharpest increase in interest rates was not onshore but offshore, where rates shot up to 1,300 percent or over 0.7 percent a day. In response to official pressure, banks—the primary providers of baht—both onshore and offshore segmented the two markets by refusing to provide short-term credit to speculators.

The Bank of Thailand made extensive use of the forward foreign exchange market as part of its intervention strategy, purchasing forward contacts on baht. When these contracts came due, the foreign seller of baht needed to deliver baht in exchange for dollars. The limitation of baht credit then forced speculators to attempt to square positions through the spot market by selling dollars for baht, putting upward pressure on the exchange rate. To inflict further punitive costs on speculators, Thai authorities limited the sale of baht for dollars in the spot foreign exchange markets to nonresidents for speculative purposes. Furthermore, the authorities restricted the sale of foreign holdings of Thai stocks on the Stock Exchange of Thailand (SET) for baht, requiring instead that proceeds from sales be converted into dollars at the onshore rate, thus further restricting the supply of baht to speculators. In essence the authorities employed a strategy of cornering the baht available to nonresident speculators. Market sources report that the increased financing cost has resulted in losses of between $1 billion and $1.5 billion for the forward sellers of baht through end-June 1997. In the absence of extensive liquidation of baht positions by domestic wealth holders, Thai authorities were able to withstand the pressures on the baht by relying on extensive application of selective capital controls until early July.

Fear of wider contagion led to coordinated exchange market intervention among the Asian central banks, particularly in support of the baht. Since there are substantial offshore markets for these currencies—in Singapore and Hong Kong—some of the apparently coordinated intervention by the Monetary Authority of Singapore (MAS) and the Hong Kong Monetary Authority (HKMA) was mainly on behalf of other central banks. While the Thai baht withstood the initial attack, and the pressures on the other Asian currencies abated, the Czech National Bank was forced to abandon its policy of maintaining the koruna inside a trading band against a hard currency basket on May 26; it subsequently floated. See Chapter VII for emerging market foreign exchange developments through July 1997.

Appendix 1
Sovereign Ratings and Fundamentals

Figure 14 summarizes the performance of three groups of countries relative to a set of economic variables that have traditionally been identified by credit-rating agencies as important determinants of a coun-

Figure 14. Emerging Markets: Sovereign Ratings and Fundamentals[1]

Legend

YPC	GDP per capita growth rate, 5-year moving average
Y	GDP growth rate, 5-year moving average
INF	CPI inflation rate
I	Gross fixed capital formation as a percent of GDP
S	Gross saving as a percent of GDP
CGB	Central government balance as a percent of GDP
CA	Current account as a percent of GDP

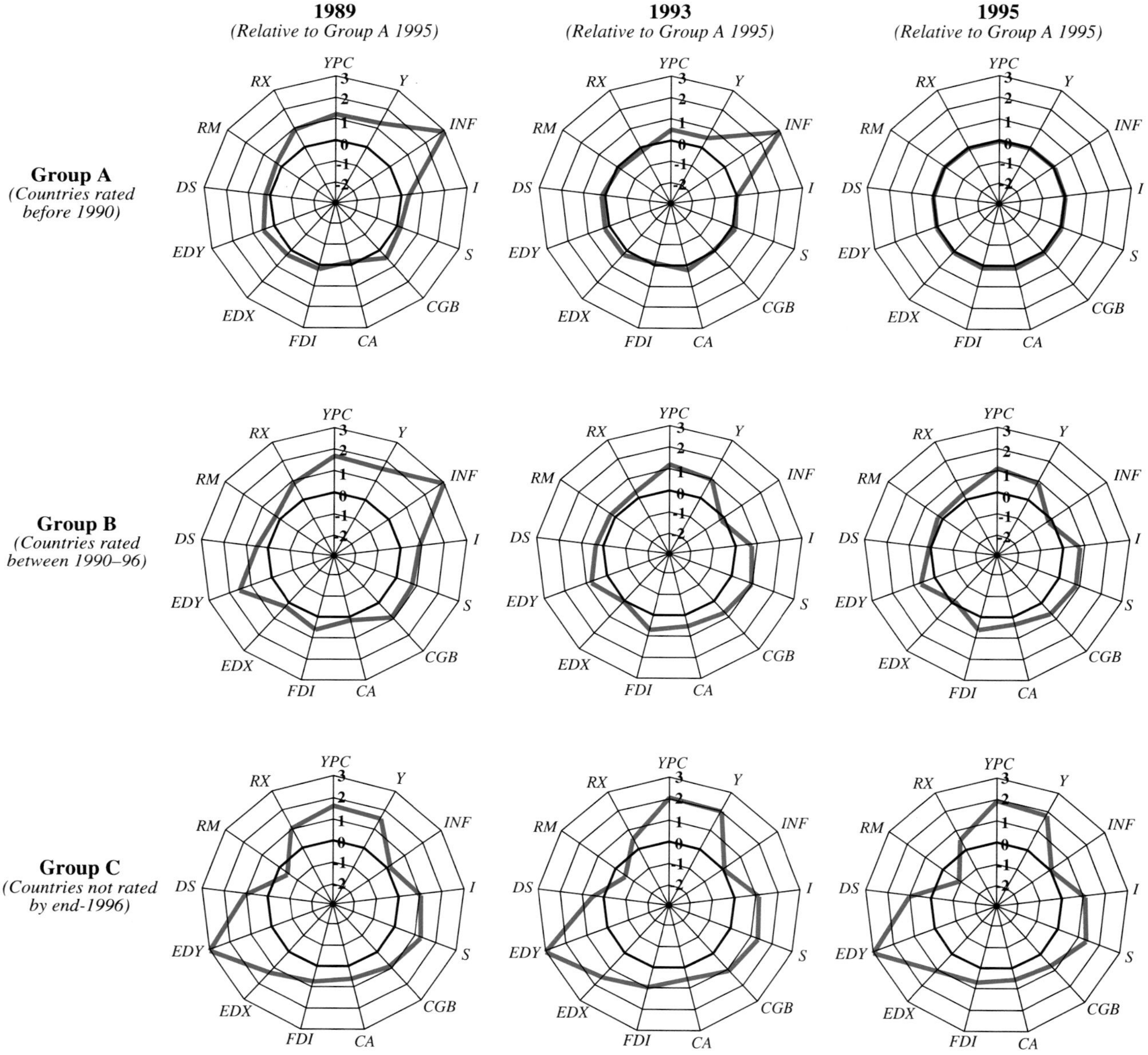

FDI	Foreign direct investment as a percent of GDP
EDX	Total external debt as a percent of exports
EDY	Total external debt as a percent of GDP
DS	Debt-service ratio
RM	Total foreign exchange reserves as a percent of broad money
RX	Total foreign exchange reserves as a percent of exports

Source: International Monetary Fund, *World Economic Outlook.*
[1]See text explanation.

try's credit rating. Group A comprises countries that had credit ratings from Moody's prior to 1990; Group B comprises countries that received credit ratings for the first time between 1990 and 1996; and Group C comprises countries that had not received a credit rating by end-1996.[29] The variables include growth in GDP per capita, GDP growth rate, inflation rate, investment and saving as a proportion of GDP, the fiscal balance, the current account, inward foreign direct investment flows, total external debt in relation to exports and GDP, the debt-service ratio, and foreign exchange reserves as a proportion of broad money and as a proportion of annual exports.

Figure 14 uses Group A's average performance in 1995 as the base for making comparisons over time and across groups. For a particular variable, the mean of each group at a specific point in time is normalized using the mean and standard deviation of Group A in 1995.[30] These standardized or normalized means are then plotted for each variable in the figures with a movement away from the origin signifying a deterioration and a movement toward the origin signifying an improvement. For example, the value of 2 assigned to the variable *YPC* for Group C in 1993 (bottom row, center) implies that the average growth rate in per capita GDP of Group B countries was 2 standard deviations below that of Group A countries in 1995.

These figures suggest three key conclusions. First, on average, Group A countries have improved their performance primarily through reducing inflation and raising their rate of GDP growth. Second, Group B's performance has improved during the 1990s both in absolute terms and relative to Group A. The largest improvements were in terms of lower inflation and, to a lesser extent, a stronger external debt position. Third, on average, Group C countries showed relatively little improvement in performance over the period 1990–95.

---

[29]These groups were constructed by starting with the set of all countries that were members of the IMF, adding Taiwan Province of China, and then deleting countries with the following characteristics: (1) OECD economies, except Korea, Mexico, and Turkey; (2) all transition economies (because of issues of data comparability); (3) countries with populations of less than 500,000; (4) economies with GDP of less than US$2.5 billion in 1991; (5) countries that experienced civil strife over the period under consideration. The countries in each group are as follows:

Group A: Argentina, Brazil, China, India, Korea, Malaysia, Singapore, Thailand, Venezuela.

Group B: Bahrain, Chile, Colombia, Egypt, Indonesia, Israel, Jordan, Mauritius, Mexico, Oman, Pakistan, Peru, the Philippines, Saudi Arabia, South Africa, Taiwan Province of China, Trinidad and Tobago, Tunisia, Turkey, United Arab Emirates, Uruguay.

Group C: Bangladesh, Bolivia, Botswana, Burkina Faso, Cameroon, Congo, Costa Rica, Côte d'Ivoire, Cyprus, Dominican Republic, Ecuador, Gabon, Ghana, Guinea, Jamaica, Kenya, Madagascar, Morocco, Nepal, Nigeria, Papua New Guinea, Paraguay, Senegal, Tanzania, Uganda, Zambia, Zimbabwe.

[30]For ease of exposition, the normalized variables for the plots have been truncated to lie between at +3 and −3.

Appendix 2
Mechanics of Speculative Attacks

While fixed exchange rate regimes have always been subject to speculative attack, the greater mobility of capital in the past five years—and the associated spectacular currency crises—have led to a profound rethinking of possible central bank defenses in this environment. All immediate defenses against attacks work through combinations of intervening in the exchange market and controlling the supply of domestic currency credit to short sellers.

Bank Covering Operations for Forward Contract Positions

Speculators attack a currency ("the domestic currency") through short sales, generally by selling the domestic currency under attack to a bank through relatively long-dated (at least one month) forward contracts. As standard practice, to balance the long domestic currency position that this transaction initiates, the bank will immediately sell the domestic currency on the spot market for, say, dollars for the conventional two-day settlement. While the bank will have balanced its currency mismatch, it still faces a maturity mismatch. To close this maturity mismatch, a bank typically will transact a foreign exchange swap, which entails a delivery of dollars for domestic currency in 2 days and a delivery of the domestic currency for dollars 30 days forward. Figure 15 presents a concrete example of such a forward transaction, which is a customary wholesale operation in both normal and speculative periods.

Central Bank Forward Intervention

The central bank may be a customer in the forward market. If its forward purchase of domestic currency matches a forward sale of some other customer of the banking system, its forward intervention will absorb the spot sale of domestic currency without the central bank having to intervene directly in the spot market. By entering into a forward contract, the central bank implicitly supplies domestic currency credit directly to the short seller of its currency.

Credit Provision in a Crisis

In a currency crisis with the potential for a one-sided bet, few private parties would be willing net suppliers of domestic credit. Nevertheless, to fuel a speculative attack, the banking system must in aggregate provide credit to the short sellers. This is evident in the first panel of Figure 15, where the bank's domestic currency receipts from the forward contract embody a one-month loan to the short seller. If the central bank does not supply the credit directly

Figure 15. Bank Receipts and Payments Arising from Forward Contract Operations[1]

Step 1. Forward Contract = Currency Mismatch

Receipt				Payment
Domestic currency (DC) in one month	2,500		100	U.S. dollars ($) in one month

Step 2. Forward Contract + Spot Sale = Maturity Mismatch

Receipt				Payment
DC in one month	2,500		2,500	DC in two days (spot)
$ in two days (spot)	100		100	$ in one month (forward)

Step 3. Forward + Spot + Swap = Balanced Position

Receipt				Payment
DC in one month (forward)	2,500		2,500	DC in one month (swap)
DC in two days (swap)	2,500		2,500	DC in two days (spot)
$ in one month (swap)	100		100	$ in one month (forward)
$ in two days (spot)	100		100	$ in two days (swap)

[1]Assuming a spot exchange rate of DC 25 = $1.

through forward intervention, the credit must come through either its money market operations or its standing facilities. In either case, the domestic currency provided by the banking system is a pass-through of credit from the central bank, which must be the ultimate counterparty in both legs of the position-balancing transactions of the banking system.

Interest Rate Defense

In a crisis, a standard defense for the central bank is to raise interest rates to impose a squeeze on short sellers. Nevertheless, to the extent that it continues to lend, the central bank partly finances the attack by providing funds at a ceiling interest rate, as the demand for domestic credit increases. This standard interest rate defense is designed to raise the finance cost to speculators, prior to a possible devaluation, above their anticipated capital gains in the event of a devaluation, a situation that might force an eventual closing of the short positions.

Derailing Speculative Attack Mechanics with Controls on Foreign Exchange Swaps

Unfortunately, the interest costs of a squeeze are imposed both on speculators and on agents who are short in the currency for commercial reasons; thus a squeeze may affect economic activity if prolonged. To mitigate this cost, a central bank may charge raised interest rates to those identified as speculators and concessionary rates to nonspeculators through credit controls. One way to do this is to identify as speculators those with foreign addresses who engage in foreign exchange swaps with domestic banks and either ban such swaps or insist that heavy forward discounts be imposed on the forward legs of such swaps. Similarly, domestic banks may be forbidden to provide on-balance-sheet overnight or longer maturity credit to foreign addresses. Such controls generate a spread between onshore and offshore interest rates on domestic currency loans, along with a strong incentive to circumvent the controls.

V

External Liability Management

Although greater access to international markets has been highly beneficial for emerging market countries, it has also exposed them to the vicissitudes and volatility of global financial markets. In addition to the macroeconomic challenges posed by relatively large and potentially volatile flows, the large external foreign currency debt of developing countries also makes them vulnerable to swings in international exchange rates and interest rates. The vulnerability of countries to speculative attacks is also often exacerbated by a weak external debt position. Indeed, the benefits of prudent macroeconomic policies have been compromised at times by the fiscal consequences of losses associated with these exposures.

In emerging market countries, sovereign exposures to currency risk can be broadly gauged by the amount of external public debt (Figure 16). In 1996, the outstanding stock of sovereign debt issued or guaranteed amounted to 25 percent of their combined GNP ($1.5 trillion) and three times their foreign currency reserves. Roughly half of the external debt of emerging markets was exposed to foreign interest rate risk: a fifth of that was short-term (less than one-year maturity), and two-fifths of the remaining long-term debt was at variable rates.

During the past two decades, a number of emerging markets have experienced the damaging consequences of adverse movements in international currencies and interest rates. In the early 1980s, the debt-servicing burdens of some Southeast Asian, Latin American, and African countries were severely affected by the appreciation of the dollar, the worldwide increase in interest rates, and the decline in commodity prices. In the first half of this decade, the debt burden of several Asian countries increased significantly owing to their large and unhedged exposure to the Japanese yen. A third of the increase in the dollar value of Indonesian external debt between 1993 and 1995, for example, was attributable to cross-currency movements, particularly the steep appreciation of the yen. The exposure of Indonesia to the yen has been especially costly as about 90 percent of its export revenues are denominated in dollars, while at the time 37 percent of its external debt was denominated in yen. In the Philippines, which has a third of its external debt denominated in yen, the appreciation of the yen accounted for about half of the increase in the dollar value of its ex-

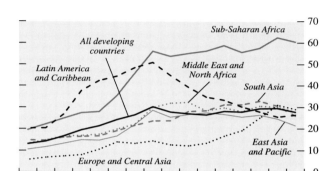

Figure 16. External Long-Term Public and Publicly Guaranteed Debt Outstanding
(In percent of GNP)

Source: World Bank, Global Development Finance database.
Note: The groupings are as shown in the source.

ternal debt in 1995. In China, the appreciation of the yen is estimated to have increased the servicing costs of the public debt by about $5 billion. The subsequent depreciation of the yen in 1996 offset some of the losses incurred by these countries.

The large foreign currency exposure of emerging market countries can be explained by a number of historical and structural factors, including the lack of domestic borrowing instruments, the large capital requirements of development and infrastructure projects, and a large share of official financing (multilateral and bilateral), which tends to be denominated in donor countries' currencies. More recently, as emerging market countries have gained greater access to international debt markets, the currency composition and the maturity structure of their external borrowing have tended to be driven to a large extent by a desire to reap the immediate fiscal benefits of borrowing in foreign markets with the lowest unhedged nominal interest rates. Several emerging markets (e.g., Argentina, Colombia, Mexico, Hungary, and Turkey) have issued foreign currency debt denominated in yen and deutsche mark in the last few years. Such borrowings often have been driven by the low coupon rates offered on these currencies, rather than by a debt strategy based on minimizing the exposure of the revenue of the sovereign or country to these currencies. Following the negative impact of the appreciation of the yen in 1994–95 on their debt burden, a few of these emerging markets (Hungary and Mexico) have reduced or hedged their exposure to the yen.

Furthermore, the lower cost of foreign currency debt vis-à-vis domestic currency debt does not just reflect the creditworthiness of sovereign borrowers, but also the presumption on the part of external creditors that their claims would have implicit seniority over domestic claims. Such implicit seniority arises from a covenant structure (e.g., cross-default and pari passu clauses) that allows for extensive legal recourse on the part of the external creditor. For example, cross-default clauses covering a wide array of lenders and instruments may deny the sovereign borrower the possibility of restructuring only a narrow, but particularly pressing, instrument, such as short-term note obligations falling due, without precipitating an advancing of the due dates of most other short- and long-term issues. Similarly, pari passu clauses make it difficult for sovereign borrowers to negotiate a bond restructuring unless the great majority of, if not all, bondholders are included. Furthermore, in the absence of an agreement, creditors have extensive rights under existing statutes to seek legal recourse in the relevant jurisdictions. Such recourse could result in a significant impairment of trade and financial flows involving the debtor countries, as well as impairment of its external debt. In addition, there is also a growing perception among external creditors that effective international and regional financial arrangements—such as the IMF's New Arrangements to Borrow and the new foreign exchange swap arrangements among some Asian countries—are evolving to reduce the risks of a systemic liquidity crisis. Indeed, the successful resolution of the Mexican crisis during the first half of 1995 is taken as tangible evidence that the risk of such a liquidity crisis has receded. It is unlikely that the cost of the macroeconomic adjustments needed to prevent an interruption in servicing external debt in the event of adverse economic developments is fully taken into consideration by a country when deciding on the size of external exposure.

The currency composition and maturity profile of the public debt contribute as much to the vulnerability to external shocks as the total volume of debt does, a fact demonstrated during the 1994 Mexican crisis.[31] Indeed, financial markets' concerns about Mexican risk were attributable primarily to the currency composition and maturity structure of the public debt rather than its size, which was relatively low by OECD standards—51 percent compared with an OECD average of 71 percent. The Mexican crisis underscored the dif-

ficulty and cost of refinancing a substantial volume of foreign currency debt maturing in turbulent foreign exchange markets.[32]

When foreign currency or interest rate exposures can be hedged in swap markets, emerging market countries can issue external debt into receptive international markets without being concerned about movements in exchange rates among other countries or in interest rates. The increasing sophistication of international derivative markets has greatly expanded the possibilities of hedging the risks associated with borrowing in foreign currencies. Thus, borrowers can respond to opportunities to exploit market niches and expand their investor base, say, to include Japanese retail investors, without bearing the cross yen-dollar exchange rate risk. Similarly, they can use the interest rate swap market to manage the maturity structure of their external debt. However, the sovereign credit exposure incurred by the external swap counterparty is usually counted against the counterparty's limit on exposures to a particular country.

The risks associated with a large net currency exposure, and the existence of deep and liquid domestic capital markets, are the main reasons why most industrial countries have negligible foreign currency debt. In recent years, several small advanced economies have significantly reduced their net foreign currency exposure. The New Zealand government decided in 1994 to eliminate its net foreign currency debt within three years, after concluding that foreign currency debt was adding significant variability to its net worth. Belgium and Denmark issue foreign currency government securities for replenishing foreign exchange reserves. Ireland restricts its gross foreign currency borrowing to the level of its maturing foreign currency debt. Others, like Spain and Sweden, issue foreign currency debt but use swaps or swap options to reduce or eliminate their foreign currency risk. Germany, Japan, and the United States do not issue foreign currency debt, while France and the United Kingdom issue most of their debt in domestic currencies and a small proportion in ECUs. In Italy, foreign currency debt represents about 6 percent of government debt. Canada's budget deficit is funded entirely in domestic currency, and its foreign currency debt—issued to finance foreign exchange reserves—represents about 3 percent of its total public debt.

Foreign currency debt may also be issued to signal the commitment of the sovereign authorities to a policy of stable exchange rates or prices. In a game theory framework, policymakers signal the credibility and time consistency of their policies to the public and

---

[31]See International Monetary Fund (1995).

[32]The vulnerability of the Mexican government to a financial crisis was exacerbated by the $29 billion of tesobonos maturing in 1995, in light of the low level of foreign reserves ($6.3 billion) as of end-1994.

financial markets by raising the cost of reneging on their commitment. Alternatively, policymakers could signal their commitment to stable prices by issuing inflation-indexed bonds.

The management of the risk associated with external exposures requires significant technical expertise, sophisticated information technology, and strictly controlled internal management procedures, with disciplined enforcement of internal trading and exposure limits. Such risk management requirements are difficult to meet in the best of circumstances, and they are particularly difficult to implement fully in many of the emerging market countries. For example, it has proven difficult for some emerging markets to attract qualified and experienced staff, to build adequate information and control systems, and to develop the administrative controls necessary to manage overall exposures.

In the past few years, the governments of several industrial countries, as well as some emerging market countries, have responded to the new realities of mobile and volatile capital flows and integrated capital markets by significantly revamping their debt management practices. Three principles emerge from their experiences. First, debt management should be shielded from political interference to ensure transparency and accountability in its conduct. Second, debt management should be entrusted to portfolio managers with sophisticated knowledge and experience in risk management techniques, and their performance should be measured against a set of criteria defined by the ministry of finance. Finally, sufficient resources should be allocated to hiring high-quality staff and to acquiring sophisticated systems to support the staff.

To achieve such objectives, a number of countries (e.g., Austria, Belgium, Ireland, New Zealand, Portugal, and Sweden) have concluded that debt agencies with some degree of autonomy from the political sphere should be set up, and that benchmarks for the public debt—specifying its currency composition and maturity structure, and the limits within which it may be exposed to market risks—should be established. Granting debt agencies a separate structure and an autonomous status enables the government to charge the agency with a clearly defined objective and to organize it to achieve such an objective without being hampered by either the management structure or pay scale of the public sector. Typically, debt agencies have been mandated to use modern risk management techniques, hire experienced portfolio managers, and provide incentives for their staff to lower borrowing costs.

In Ireland, the government delegated in 1990 the borrowing and debt management functions of the Irish Department of Finance and the domestic government bond market operations of the central bank to an autonomous debt agency, the National Treasury Man-

agement Agency (NTMA).[33] The decision to establish the NTMA was justified on the grounds that it could be given clearly defined performance objectives and a degree of independence from other government objectives, and that the concentration of resources and expertise would result in better risk management and lower debt-servicing costs. The main objective of the NTMA is cast with reference to a low-risk medium-term benchmark portfolio and aims at funding maturing government debt and annual borrowing requirements at a lower cost than that of the benchmark portfolio while containing the volatility of annual fiscal debt-service costs. The currency composition of the Irish foreign currency debt benchmark is not made public, but deviations of the actual portfolio from the benchmark tend to be small. As of December 1995, the currency composition of the Irish foreign currency debt was as follows: 38 percent in deutsche mark, Dutch guilder, and Swiss francs; 28 percent in pounds sterling and French francs; 20 percent in U.S. dollars; 7 percent in ECUs; and 7 percent in yen and other currencies.

In New Zealand, the country's debt management strategy is implemented through the New Zealand Debt Management Office (NZDMO), which has been responsible for managing the public debt since debt management policy became disentangled from monetary policy objectives in 1988. Although the NZDMO has been placed in a division of the New Zealand Treasury, it maintains some degree of autonomy from the rest of the government, and has its own advisory board. The objective of the NZDMO is "to identify a low risk portfolio of net liabilities consistent with the Government's aversion to risk, having regard for the expected costs of reducing risk, and to transact in an efficient manner to achieve and maintain that portfolio." To minimize its net risk exposure, the NZDMO has gradually set the duration and currency profile of its liabilities to match that of its assets. As most of the government assets are denominated in New Zealand dollars, this strategy has entailed a gradual elimination of the net public foreign currency debt—which was achieved in September 1996—and a lengthening of the duration of the domestic public debt.

In Sweden, the National Debt Office (SNDO), which was founded in the eighteenth century, was moved from under the authority of the Parliament to that of the Ministry of Finance in 1989 to improve debt management practices.[34] The primary objectives of the SNDO are to minimize the costs of borrowing within the limits imposed by monetary policy and to finance the day-to-day government budget deficit at the minimum possible long-term cost. The board of the SNDO establishes separate benchmark portfolios

---

[33]See Ireland, National Treasury Management Agency (1996).
[34]See Sweden, National Debt Office (1996).

for the domestic and foreign currency debt and sets the permitted deviations from the benchmark portfolios. Within these broad guidelines, the SNDO manages the currency allocation, the maturity structure, and the market risk of the overall debt portfolio. As of December 1996, the composition of the Swedish foreign currency debt benchmark was 26 percent deutsche mark, 16 percent French francs, 12 percent U.S. dollars, 6 percent yen, and the rest in ECUs and ECU-basket currencies. The duration of the foreign currency debt portfolio was around 2.2 years, and borrowing was diversified along the yield curve to reduce shocks to specific parts of the yield curve and to bunch risks.

In the past two years, a small number of emerging market countries have also reformed their debt management practices and introduced benchmarks for their external debt. In Colombia, the Ministry of Finance and Public Credit has recently authorized a substantial increase in the staff in charge of managing and hedging its external debt portfolio, modernized its data systems, and consolidated the external borrowing strategies of the central government and the parastatal companies. Particular attention has been paid to attracting staff with the appropriate knowledge and experience in portfolio analysis and to offering competitive remuneration to retain the staff. The main reform introduced by the authorities is to manage the sovereign liability portfolio with respect to a set of low-risk benchmark parameters specifying exchange rate, liquidity, and interest rate risks. The benchmarks are to be based on structural economic factors and the risk

tolerance of the government. The restructured portfolio will include a higher portion of dollar debt (80–85 percent instead of the current 72 percent), in line with the currency exposure of government revenues, and a lengthening of the maturity profile of the external debt.

In Hungary, the Ministry of Finance took over the cost of servicing Hungary's net foreign debt in early 1997. While the National Bank of Hungary (NBH) will remain formally responsible for the interest payments and amortization of the foreign loans issued under its name, it will receive transfers from the Hungarian Ministry of Finance broadly equivalent to the cost of servicing that part of external debt in excess of the foreign exchange reserves of the NBH at end-1996. The authorities also established benchmarks for external debt management and have aligned through hedging operations the currency composition of external debt with that of the currency basket to which the national currency is pegged (70 percent deutsche mark, 30 percent dollar). Particular emphasis is being placed on lengthening the maturity of the debt and evenly spreading debt redemptions to avoid a clustering of debt maturities.

While some other emerging market countries, including Argentina, Mexico, South Africa, and Turkey, are currently reviewing their debt management practices, in other developing countries there is no separate debt management office, debt management objectives are sometimes cast in general terms, and there are often no formal guidelines on the currency composition and the maturity structure of the public debt.

VI

Developments in International Banking

Industrial Countries

As was the case in 1995, the performance of commercial banks in industrial countries differed markedly in 1996 between countries, depending upon their relative position in the credit cycle. For banks in Canada, the United Kingdom, and the United States, which had resolved their asset-quality problems relatively quickly in the early 1990s, profitability and capitalization levels remained at or near historic highs, with nonperforming loan ratios at correspondingly low levels. For banks in France, Italy, and Japan, performance has lagged, although the worst of the asset-quality difficulties appears to be past. The overall condition of the banking systems in these countries has improved, but differences between stronger and weaker institutions have sharpened. Emphasis is increasingly placed on the resolution of serious problems in individual institutions and on the longer-term structural issues that confront the industry, such as the effects of EMU on competition within European banking systems, discussed in Chapter III.

Banks in *Canada,* the *United Kingdom,* and the *United States* again led the major industrial country banks in terms of profitability and asset quality in 1996.[35] Net income increased in all three banking systems, reaching an average return on equity of 15 percent in Canada, 19 percent in the United Kingdom, and 14 percent in the United States. These profits were earned despite a narrowing of net interest margins in each country and reflected an increase in noninterest earnings and a decline in loan loss provisions and write-offs. Asset quality remains strong, with the ratio of nonperforming loans to gross loans falling to historic lows in the United States (1 percent) and Canada (0.6 percent) and also to a very low level in the United Kingdom (2.5 percent). In addition, reserve coverage for current nonperforming loans appears to be more than adequate, with coverage ratios well in excess of 100 percent in Canada and the United States, and approaching that level for some of the banks in the

United Kingdom. The peak in asset quality, however, may have passed. Banks have expanded their consumer lending and other high-margin lending in order to compensate for declining margins on corporate loans, but in each country the quality of the consumer loan portfolio declined in 1996. Finally, the banks' capital ratios remain strong. At end-1996, Canadian banks had an average total risk-weighted capital ratio of 9 percent; U.K. banks' capital ratios averaged 11 percent; and U.S. banks' core capital ratio was almost 8 percent. These high capital levels were achieved despite significant volumes of share repurchases in all three countries, financed in part in the United States by issues of tax-exempt, trust-preferred securities that are eligible as Tier I capital under U.S. bank capital adequacy regulations.

The regulatory environment for banks in the United States has allowed a significant broadening of commercial banks' involvement in the securities and insurance businesses, and both the Federal Reserve Board and the U.S. Department of the Treasury have proposed repealing the Glass-Steagall Act's restrictions on affiliations between banks and securities dealers. The structure of financial supervision and regulation is also being reconsidered in the United Kingdom. The U.K. government has proposed to integrate all financial supervisory and regulatory authority, including that over banks currently exercised by the Bank of England, in the Securities and Investments Board. Such a consolidation of supervisory authority in one agency is occurring in response to the emergence of a unified financial services industry and is being incorporated in the regulatory structure in an increasing number of countries, including Japan.

Unlike banks in many other countries, *German* banks have not experienced a significant deterioration in asset quality in recent years. The five largest private banks reported a 19 percent increase in net income in 1996 (for a return on equity of 10 percent) due mainly to a sharp rise in noninterest income. The banking sectors in *France* and *Italy,* however, showed another year of moderate earnings on loan portfolios. For the first time in six years, all of the seven major banks in France reported positive net profits for 1996—earning a return on equity of 8 percent—owing mainly to exceptionally high income from capital market activities and from lower loan loss provisions. The same factors

---

[35]Banking system developments in these countries are based on the performance of the Schedule I banks in Canada, the six largest clearing banks in the United Kingdom, and the commercial banks insured by the Federal Deposit Insurance Corporation (FDIC) in the United States.

contributed to a 7 percent increase in operating profits for Italian banks. In both countries, banking operations continue to be affected by weak loan demand, narrowing interest margins due to aggressive competition and increasing disintermediation, and poor asset quality. The French and Italian authorities continue to provide support to individual institutions with serious asset-quality difficulties, which has translated into an increasingly large amount of contingent liabilities, albeit with limited immediate budgetary impact. Nevertheless, it is generally believed that the worst of the asset-quality difficulties in France and for the Italian banks in the center-north of the country are past. The banks are now reasonably well capitalized, with total risk-weighted capital ratios of between 8.7 percent and 11.4 percent for the major banks in France and 13 percent for banks in Italy. Several banks in southern Italy, however, continue to struggle with worsening asset quality. The ratio of bad loans to total loans in the region has been in excess of 20 percent with a rising fraction estimated to be irrecoverable. Countrywide, the stock of bad loans reached 10 percent of total loans at end-1996, up from 9 percent at end-1995, and the estimated loss rate increased to 38 percent from 33 percent at end-1995. However, the percentage of loans granted to firms considered to be at risk has decreased across sectors and regions, thus slowing down the growth in the ratio of bad loans to total loans.

The banking crisis in *Japan* continues to move toward a resolution. In the 1996/97 fiscal year, the 20 major banks again set aside loan loss provisions far in excess of operating profit, financed by realizing net gains on their equity investments. At the end of March 1997, aggregate nonperforming loans (loans to bankrupt borrowers and loans that were six months or more past due) were ¥13.2 trillion, essentially unchanged from a year earlier. However, total problem loans, including loans restructured at interest rates below the official discount rate and loans made to support customers, fell significantly, from ¥26 trillion to ¥19 trillion; net of specific reserves, problem loans fell from 4 percent of gross loans to 3 percent.

Although the definition of problem loans has been gradually widened in the last two years, it is still less comprehensive than, for example, U.S. bank supervisory definitions. The Japanese definition does not include loans that are past due for 90–180 days, loans that have been sold to the Cooperative Credit Purchasing Company (CCPC), special-purpose vehicles, or other affiliates, or loans restructured at interest rates above the official discount rate. Many of these loans would likely be considered nonperforming loans under U.S. practices. Applying a broader definition of nonperforming loans to the Japanese banks would yield an estimate for aggregate problem loans somewhat higher than the official estimate. Of course, the ultimate losses that the banks are likely to sustain are much smaller than the stock of problem loans, and depend upon the probability of default and the value of the collateral that is recovered.[36]

The decline in interest rates in Japan since 1995 has been beneficial to the banks. As interest rates fell, banks earned large returns on their bond portfolios, trading activities, and loan spreads, all of which contributed to very high pre-provision income. Furthermore, at current interest rates, the yield difference between a performing loan and a nonperforming loan is relatively small, so the bad loans have not depressed earnings or capital as much as they would have if interest rates were higher. The benefits to the banks of low interest rates are believed by many market participants to have been among the factors that have influenced the Bank of Japan's interest rate policy—since the banks have positioned themselves to benefit from a steep yield curve, an increase in short-term interest rates might reduce cash flows, with the magnitude and timing varying among banks depending upon the structure of their portfolios. This concern is reinforced by the banks' underlying weak profitability compared with banks in other industrial countries. During 1985–94, the average pre-provision return on assets for Japanese banks was 0.5 percent, compared with about 1.7 percent for Canadian, U.K., and U.S. banks. Even if all of their operating costs were eliminated, Japanese commercial banks would have earned a return on assets of only 1.4 percent.

During 1996, the Japanese authorities adopted a U.S.-style bank resolution framework built around (1) increased powers for regulators to intervene in problem banks, including declaring them insolvent; (2) prompt corrective action (PCA) measures for intervening in weak banks and maintaining a sound financial system; and (3) increased resources for the deposit insurance corporation, including a special premium to finance insurance coverage of deposits in excess of the statutory limit until end-March 2001. The prompt corrective action measures, which take effect April 1, 1998, require banks to classify their loan portfolios rigorously and to allow the authorities to force them to take corrective measures or ultimately to close them if their risk-weighted capital ratios fall below certain thresholds. A change in the structure of financial supervision has also been initiated. The Japanese Ministry of Finance's responsibilities in the area of bank supervision will be moved to an independent agency, the Supervisory Agency for Financial

---

[36]Adding the book value of loans sold to the CCPC increases total problem loans to ¥29 trillion. The 20 major banks began setting aside provisions against their contingent liabilities to the CCPC in 1996 because the collateral value on many of the loans they had sold to the CCPC has declined below the value at which they were sold, and the banks must make up this difference when the collateral is sold. IBCA Ltd. estimates that the total value of problem loans among the major banks at end-March 1997 was ¥40 trillion, of which the estimated uncovered loss was ¥4.5 trillion.

Entities, which will also exercise surveillance over securities firms, but the ministry will continue to be responsible for setting bank regulations, and the Bank of Japan will retain its bank examination powers.

A far-reaching set of financial reforms, described as Japan's "Big Bang," announced in November 1996, includes (1) the elimination of most remaining foreign exchange controls and ex ante reporting requirements, and the abolition of the authorized foreign exchange bank system; (2) the acceptance of financial holding companies; (3) the abolition of fixed commissions on securities transactions; and (4) the elimination of restrictions segregating securities, trust, and banking activities. The first measure is the central element of the reform plan, as increased foreign competition is expected to force domestic firms to be more innovative and more efficient and to provide better services and higher returns to retail investors, who are often perceived to be ill served under current financial market practices. The latter three measures are expected to lead to some restructuring and consolidation of the financial services industry, since they allow financial holding companies—combining all types of banking and securities activities—to be established, while at the same time making each type of activity more competitive and responsive to market forces.

Banking System Developments in Emerging Markets

Developments in the major emerging market banking systems were influenced in 1996 by the differing patterns of economic performance across regions. The economic recoveries in Latin America allowed banking systems to continue the necessary structural reforms and reorganizations in a less crisis-charged environment. In Asia, lower growth and exports, and weaknesses in property markets, had serious repercussions in some emerging market financial systems, because these conditions uncovered underlying problems—illiquidity and heavy net foreign currency liabilities of the corporate sectors—and directly affected banks' overall asset quality. In many emerging markets, existing measures of asset quality are based on weak accounting practices that do not provide accurate estimates of the true value of loan portfolios. In addition, off-balance-sheet operations, particularly in derivatives, often escape regulatory oversight and can substantially change banks' exposure to different risks.

The growing awareness that an unsound, inadequately regulated financial system can severely disrupt macroeconomic policy and performance led to a broad-based international effort to promote the soundness and stability of financial systems in emerging markets. The relevant international financial institutions and official groupings responded to these concerns by elucidating the general principles of a sound financial system. The Basle Committee on Banking Supervision published its consultative paper, *Core Principles for Effective Banking Supervision,* in April 1997, and the G-10 Working Party on Financial Stability in Emerging Market Economies also released its paper, *Financial Stability in Emerging Market Economies,* in the same month. The latter report called for a "concerted international strategy to promote the establishment, adoption and implementation of sound principles and practices needed for financial stability" in emerging markets and proposed a strategy in which, following the development of an international consensus on what constitutes a sound financial system, the IMF and other multilateral institutions would promote the adoption and implementation of these principles and practices. An early proponent of such an effort, Goldstein (1997), has called for the establishment of International Banking Standards, based on the principles developed by the international agencies, to which bank supervisors in emerging markets would voluntarily adhere.

Asia

Korea's membership in the OECD in 1996 and its commitment to further capital account liberalization lowered funding costs but also increased potential vulnerabilities from foreign competition and surges in capital flows. At present, however, the main risks to the banking system derive from the past practice of government intervention in banks' credit allocation decisions and the resulting large exposures to individual borrowers or high-risk sectors. The lack of a well-developed credit culture within banks and the emphasis on collateral, rather than credit evaluation, have also contributed to a worsening of asset quality as liquidity problems among the large corporations intensified in 1996.[37] While the official estimate of nonperforming loans (defined as loans that are unrecoverable and loans that are six months or more past due) is only about 1 percent of total loans, the Presidential Commission on Financial Reform estimated in April 1997 that under a broader definition, problem loans among the six largest commercial banks amounted to 5 percent of total loans. In addition to declining loan quality, the banks have had to deal with a decline in Korean equity prices in 1996, which produced large revaluation losses on their equity portfolios.

The authorities have responded to the declining asset quality and the losses on banks' equity portfolios in 1996 by tightening bank supervision, including a

---

[37]The 30 largest conglomerates (*chaebol*) have high gearing ratios by international standards. At end-1996, 19 of them had debt-equity ratios in excess of 400 percent. In early 1997, two of the large *chaebols* defaulted on their debts and are undergoing restructuring and/or liquidation.

recent proposal to create a Finance Supervisory Board, uniting supervision of banks, securities companies, and insurance companies in one agency. However, the authorities have also engaged in some regulatory forbearance. The loan loss provisioning requirement for doubtful loans was lowered to 75 percent from 100 percent, and the banks were allowed to provide for only 30 percent of the securities revaluation losses in 1996, rather than 50 percent as had previously been required. Despite these measures, the leading commercial banks reported a slight decline in net income in 1996.

A surge in capital inflows into the *Philippines* since 1991–92 has contributed to a sharp increase in equity and property prices and in liquidity in the banking system, which have fueled a rapid expansion in bank lending—42 percent a year during the last two years. These increases in asset prices and lending have raised concerns about asset quality, in part because a significant portion of the new lending has been to the consumer sector, which tends to have a relatively high loss rate, and because commercial banks in the Philippines have a high exposure to the property sector. The Central Bank of the Philippines estimated that commercial banks' property loans accounted for 10 percent of total loans at end-1996. However, the true exposure may be higher since property is a common form of loan collateral, and some of the banks have other stakes in property developers. In April 1997 the central bank limited real estate loans to 20 percent of a bank's total loans and lowered the allowed loan-to-value ratio, in an attempt to limit the system's exposure to that sector.

As is the case elsewhere in the region, foreign currency exposure has been increasing in the Philippines. Banks have borrowed in foreign currency to finance domestic lending, and their net foreign liabilities increased to $6 billion at end-1996 (9 percent of total liabilities plus capital) from a nearly balanced position at end-1995. Prudential regulations require banks to limit their foreign exchange exposure to 15 percent of capital. Foreign-currency-denominated lending from the banks' Foreign Currency Deposit Units (FCDUs) has also expanded rapidly—by 110 percent in 1996. While banks are required to maintain balanced FCDU books, the currency risk is borne by borrowers, some of whom may experience difficulties in servicing the loan if the peso depreciates or export revenues decline. To reduce the potential vulnerability of the banking system to foreign exchange risk, the central bank introduced a 30 percent liquidity requirement on foreign-currency-denominated assets in June 1997.

The exposure of the *Thai* corporate and financial sectors to foreign exchange risk is widely believed by market participants to have influenced the authorities' exchange rate policy. At the same time, the strength of the baht and the high interest rates needed to maintain the exchange rate, combined with a deteriorating

property market, contributed to an increase in nonperforming loans from 7 percent of loans at end-1995 to 8 percent at end-June 1996. While banks are believed to have hedged most of their net foreign liabilities, the opposite is believed to be true for the corporate sector. The combination of a stable exchange rate and a wide differential between foreign and (much higher) domestic interest rates provided a strong incentive for firms to take on foreign currency liabilities, until doubts about the sustainability of the exchange rate strengthened in July 1996. Hence, in addition to their own foreign exchange exposure, banks may have a large indirect exposure in the form of credit risk to firms that have borrowed in foreign currencies.

The property market in Thailand has been an important source of loan losses both because banks have lent to this sector and because property has often been used as collateral for loans. The vacancy rate on prime office space in Bangkok was 14 percent in March 1997, and the availability of office space is due to increase sharply in 1997–99. In addition, asset quality in the rapidly built-up consumer lending portfolio and in the general corporate lending business has deteriorated.

The official response to the latest concerns about the health of the financial system has focused on improving accounting and disclosure of asset quality and on rehabilitating the property market and the finance company sector. Banks are required to begin disclosing nonperforming loans and provisions with their June 1997 financial statements, and they are required to have set aside additional reserves equal to 15 percent of substandard loans by end-June 1999. The authorities have also introduced measures to support the property market, including the establishment in March 1997 of the Property Loan Management Organization (PLMO). The PLMO was capitalized with B 1 billion from the fiscal budget and authorized to borrow up to B 100 billion to finance the purchase of property-related loans from banks. The authorities have also established a secondary mortgage corporation and have permitted the securitization of financial assets.

The Thai authorities moved resolutely to deal with weak finance companies in late June 1997. The Ministry of Finance ordered 16 finance companies to suspend operations for 30 days and required them to submit, within 14 days, rehabilitation plans involving injections of capital from domestic or foreign investors. Five large and stable finance companies agreed to acquire the net assets of those of the 16 companies that are unable to recapitalize themselves. The Bank of Thailand will provide up to five new banking licenses to such merged entities subject to a minimum size requirement. Promissory notes issued by failed institutions will be rescheduled, while those of the 75 healthy finance companies can be converted to bank certificates of deposits at the investor's discretion. In addition, the Bank of Thailand has temporarily capped deposit rates of finance companies at 14 percent, and those of commercial banks at 12 percent.

Latin America

The economic recovery in *Argentina* continued in 1996 and resulted in a reflow of deposits back into the banking system, which allowed interest rates to ease and boosted lending activity. Nevertheless, net income for the 20 largest banks rose only marginally, and the return on average equity declined slightly to just below 7 percent. The restructuring of the banking system continued in 1996—three private banks were taken over and two others had their licenses revoked—and further consolidation is expected, including privatization and foreign investment in the banking system. This process is supported by the authorities, who modified the role of the deposit insurance fund in 1996 to allow it to assist in the acquisition or merger of banks.

Profitability continued to worsen among a sample including the 50 largest banks in *Brazil* because of a sharp decline in the net interest margin and a rise in administrative costs and despite an increase in noninterest income. With interest rates and margins declining, the banks included in the sample invested a greater share of their assets in investment and trading securities and less in loans—the ratio of securities and short-term investments to loans and advances exceeded 110 percent at end-1996, compared with 77 percent a year earlier. This move away from lending and toward securities investment and trading occurred while average asset quality in the banking system continued to decline. At end-1996, loans in arrears and nonperforming loans accounted for 14 percent of total loans of active commercial banks, up from 7 percent at end-1994.

In Argentina and Brazil, as well as elsewhere, the banking systems are segmented by performance and asset quality between government-owned banks and private banks. In Argentina, the ratio of loans past due more than 90 days to total loans was 19 percent for the federally owned banks at end-September 1996, 27 percent for the provincial banks, and 9 percent for the domestic private banks. The return on average equity for the government-owned banks was only 4 percent in 1996, compared with 11 percent for the large private banks. Similarly, in Brazil, while 14 percent of the financial system's loans were in arrears or liquidation at end-1996, the figure for the 21 largest private banks was only about 2 percent and that for 28 smaller private banks was about 5 percent, leaving the government-owned banks with the lion's share of bad loans. Such problems are illustrated by the R$12 billion in losses incurred by Banco do Brasil over 1995–96, due mainly to more rigorous criteria for classifying nonperforming loans, that led to increasing loan loss provision and weakening income. In April 1996, the government announced a recapitalization plan under which it eventually provided R$6.8 billion. In August 1996, the federal and state governments agreed to reschedule the states' debts in return for which the state banks would be privatized, liquidated, or transformed into development agencies.

Notwithstanding the improvement in the economy, banks in *Mexico* continued to struggle in 1996 with deteriorating asset quality. The commercial banking system, excluding banks that were under central bank intervention or in other special situations, recorded an aggregate net loss of MexN$7 billion (11 percent of equity) in 1996, after a profit of MexN$2.5 billion in 1995. The net interest margin fell to 4 percent from 6 percent in 1995, because of a decline in interest rates and an increase in nonperforming or low-yielding assets on the banks' balance sheets. Nonperforming loans increased by MexN$1.2 billion (2.5 percent) in 1996, despite the sale of MexN$124 billion in (mostly nonperforming) loans by the banks to FOBAPROA,[38] and at the end of the year they equaled 7 percent of loans, compared with 8 percent at end-1995. Since January 1, 1997, the accounting rules for asset quality have been significantly tightened with the application of accounting principles closer to those used in the United States. Under the new accounting principles, at the end of 1996, 12.2 percent of loans were nonperforming.

Despite the still-growing stock of nonperforming loans, the recapitalization commitments obtained in return for the loan sales to FOBAPROA have resulted in an increase in the ratio of equity to nonperforming loans to 149 percent at end-1996 from 137 percent a year earlier. However, of the total equity of MexN$70 billion at end-1996, only just under half (MexN$32 billion) was paid-up capital. Revaluation gains on equity and fixed assets contributed almost as much (MexN$25 billion), making the true capitalization of the system partially dependent upon asset market developments and property valuations.

The banking system in *Venezuela* began to recover in 1996 after two difficult years, in which 17 banks holding 54 percent of end-1993 deposits were closed or taken over by the deposit-guarantee fund, FOGADE,[39] at a total cost of 30 percent of 1994 GDP. The 13 largest Venezuelan banks' net income increased by a factor of three in 1996, owing mostly to higher net interest earnings from lending—loans increased by more than 80 percent in 1996—income from securities holdings, and profits from long dollar positions held at the time of the devaluation of the bolivar in April 1996. Asset quality also improved in 1996. At the end of the year, banks reported that 4 percent of gross loans were past due or in litigation, with a re-

---

[38]FOBAPROA is the deposit-guarantee fund (Fondo Bancario de Protección al Ahorro).

[39]FOGADE is the Fondo de Garantiá de Depósitos y Protección Bancaria.

serve coverage ratio of nearly 200 percent, compared with ratios of 10 percent and 121 percent, respectively, in 1995. The Venezuelan banks are similarly well capitalized. As a result of capital injections by FOGADE and bank shareholders, the equity-assets ratio has increased to 13 percent, from 8 percent at end-1994.

The immediate future for the Venezuelan banking system will be strongly influenced by the sudden emergence of foreign competition. After 1975 foreign banks were not permitted in Venezuela, but that ended in December 1996, when foreign financial institutions acquired controlling stakes in three of the four largest Venezuelan banks—two of which were acquired in privatizations. The foreign banks' more advanced practices (including technology), broader range of products, and deeper capital base will put pressure on the other Venezuelan banks to modernize and become more efficient and may lead to further consolidation in the industry.

Eastern Europe and Africa

In the *Czech Republic,* eight banks, including the fifth largest, were subject to intervention by the Czech National Bank in 1996, although in most cases the authorities had been preparing for this move for a number of years. At end-September 1996, 33 percent of credit was still classified below normal but the incidence of nonperforming loans actually declined over the previous year's figures. The larger banks especially have investment grade ratings and are generally believed to be fully reserved against their nonper-

forming loans, which are declining. Nevertheless, the provisioning needed to meet the required coverage ratio has consumed about a third of operating income in recent years.

Commercial banks in *South Africa* continued their recent pattern of high profitability and strong capitalization in 1996, with an aggregate risk-weighted capital ratio of about 10 percent. Although asset quality declined slightly, the incidence of nonperforming loans remains low and adequately reserved. Overdue loans rose by 17 percent in 1996 but represented only 3 percent of total loans at the end of the year, marginally lower than the previous year-end ratio. After more than a decade of near isolation, the South African banking system has become highly concentrated (the four largest banks hold about 85 percent of industry assets) and heavily exposed to the domestic corporate conglomerates (large credit exposures granted accounted for 1,033 percent of capital and reserves). Both forms of concentration have contributed to the relatively high profits of the banks, and both are likely to come under pressure from the liberalization of foreign capital flows, which will increase the level of competition from foreign banks and capital markets, a process that has already begun. In addition, the ongoing liberalization and development of domestic capital markets are likely to increase the pace of disintermediation. These two forces will induce South African banks to become more cost efficient and will require the bank supervision authorities to monitor the asset quality closely if banks increase their lending to riskier borrowers in search of higher yields.

VII

Emerging Market Currency Crises of July 1997

Following turbulence in emerging foreign exchange markets during May and June, pressures on emerging market currencies intensified in July. In Asia, several currencies depreciated sharply, while some of the European emerging market currencies and the South African rand were adversely affected by a variety of country-specific, possibly temporary factors. In the first signs of a potential spillover to Latin America, concerns that the turmoil in foreign exchange markets could lead to widespread foreign investment outflows from emerging markets had a negative impact on equity markets in the region.

On July 2, the Bank of Thailand abandoned the baht's peg to its traditional basket, and the baht immediately depreciated sharply against the U.S. dollar (Figure 17). Pressures then quickly intensified against the Philippine peso and the Malaysian ringgit, each of which received only limited support from its central bank (Figure 18). Bank Indonesia widened the trading band for the rupiah on July 11, which appeared to forestall a substantial buildup in pressures, although the rupiah depreciated to near the bottom of the new band by July 21. In Eastern Europe, the Czech koruna depreciated further during the period and the Polish zloty also fell. Local developments, including floods in the region, played an important role in affecting market sentiment in both cases. The South African rand also came under pressure, though again developments specific to South Africa, including a negative credit risk report and declines in the price of gold, appear to have played the major role. In Latin America, which had been relatively unaffected by the pressures in May and June, concerns about the deterioration in the Brazilian current account balance coincided with downward movements in equity prices, with the Bovespa index falling by 15 percent between July 11 and 18. Concerns then spread to other Latin American equity markets, particularly those with strong trade links to Brazil—Argentina and Mexico—though they soon recovered (Figure 19).

After the severe pressures in May, when intervention resulted in reserve losses of some $4 billion, followed by a period of relative calm in June, which was nonetheless accompanied by relatively high interest rates, the Thai baht was allowed to float on July 2. In the immediate aftermath of the baht's announced float, expectations of depreciation led the heavily in-debted domestic corporate sector to purchase foreign exchange in the spot market rapidly in an attempt to hedge their foreign exchange exposures. This move helped drive down the baht by 14 percent in onshore, and 19 percent in offshore, trading by the end of the day. Initial reactions to the float were favorable. The stock market index rose by 8 percent on July 3, and foreign investors were reported to be paying substantial premiums on the equity available to foreign residents. However, market sentiment subsequently deteriorated because of concerns about the impact of the devaluation on the financial sector. The baht was highly volatile, and interest rates remained high, suggesting a period of continued uncertainty for the exchange rate.

The Thai financial sector was particularly vulnerable to the interest rate increases traditionally employed in the defense of an exchange rate. After the bout of severe pressures on the baht in early May, the Thai authorities imposed controls on capital transactions in an effort to shield the domestic sector from interest rate increases, while at the same time making speculation costly to foreign entities.[40] Despite the floating of the baht, these controls remained in place. The combination of capital and exchange controls effectively drove a wedge between the onshore and offshore markets that was reflected in large interest rate and exchange rate differentials between the two markets. The segmentation, however, proved imperfect and attempts at circumventing restrictions led to escalating capital controls that became increasingly difficult to enforce. For example, foreign investors desiring baht to close out short positions or to arbitrage differentials between the two markets liquidated their equity positions for baht, putting downward pressure on equity prices. The authorities then moved to require foreign investors to liquidate their equity positions for dollars. They did not, however, impose similar restrictions on the fixed-income market, given the corporate and financial sectors' needs to roll over domestic debt and

---

[40]As noted in Chapter IV, these measures included restricting local banks (from May 15) from extending baht credit to offshore banks, restricting local banks (from May 16) from conducting foreign exchange swaps (baht for dollars), and restricting local banks (from May 16) from selling baht for dollars in the spot market to speculators in the offshore market.

Figure 17. Thailand: Selected Financial Indicators, 1997

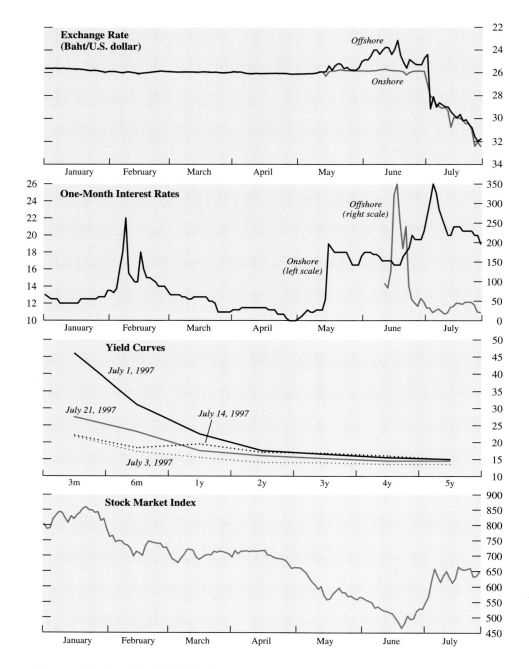

Sources: Bloomberg Financial Markets L.P.; Reuters; and IMF staff estimates.

maintain access to new financing. In spite of the segmentation of baht credit markets, onshore interest rates remained high. In addition, attempts to arbitrage the differential between onshore and offshore rates, for example through the purchase of bills of exchange at steep discounts, continued. The convergence of exchange rates and the reduction of interest rate differentials between the two markets suggest that the controls became progressively less effective (Figure 17).

The Philippine peso came under severe pressure in the immediate aftermath of the baht's depreciation on July 2. These pressures were largely confined to the

Figure 18. Financial Market Developments in Selected Asian Countries, 1997
(January 2, 1997 = 100)

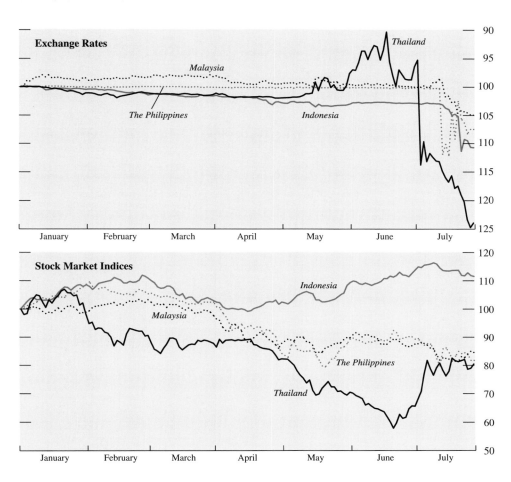

Source: Bloomberg Financial Markets L.P.

onshore spot market, given the absence of a liquid forward market in pesos. Attention has focused recently on the extent to which pressures on the peso originated in the offshore nondeliverable forward (NDF) market, and were subsequently transmitted to the spot market as participants attempted to arbitrage the differentials between the two markets. However, average volumes and liquidity in the NDF market are substantially lower than in the spot market. The small size of the NDF market suggests that it would be difficult for participants to build up substantial short positions through the market, and these pressures were largely channeled through the spot market. Nevertheless, on July 22, the central bank prohibited local banks—for a period of three months—from engaging in NDF contracts with offshore banks, reflecting the concern that the NDF market had contributed to speculation in the foreign exchange market.

The Bangko Sentral ng Pilipinas (BSP) responded to these pressures by raising interest rates and intervening in the spot market, and there were reports that local banks were also discouraged from making peso credit available for speculation (Figure 20). Overnight interest rates were raised in steps to 32 percent. It was estimated that between July 2 and July 10 the BSP lost more than $1.5 billion of reserves. It stopped intervening on July 11, allowing the peso to depreciate initially by 11.5 percent. The Bankers Association of the Philippines (BAP) unexpectedly invoked circuit breakers, imposing volatility caps on the Philippine Dealing System that shut down the spot foreign exchange market. On the following trading day the BAP eliminated this cap. Subsequently the peso mid-rate fluctuated in a wide range of some 8 percent. Liquidity in the spot market was extremely low and daily trading volume averaged $75 million between July 14

Figure 19. Financial Market Developments in Selected Latin American Countries, 1997

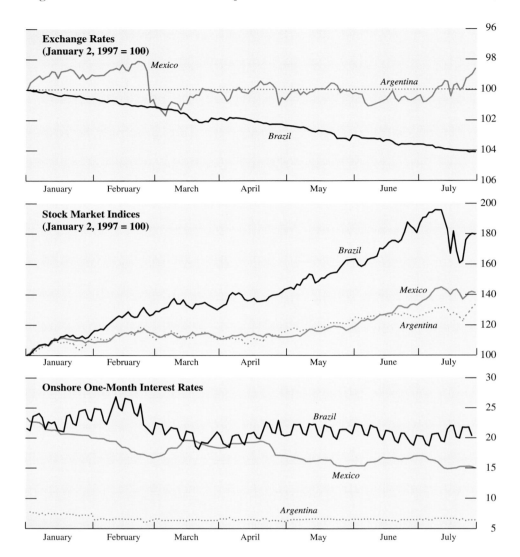

Source: Bloomberg Financial Markets L.P.

and 24 compared with an estimated $220 million over the previous six months. The low level of liquidity in the market, combined with uncertainty among market participants about the future value of the peso, resulted in reported bid-ask spreads of 5–10 percent.

Since the Malaysian ringgit was subject to pressures in the immediate aftermath of the baht's devaluation, Bank Negara Malaysia intervened heavily in support of the ringgit until July 11, when it abruptly withdrew from the foreign exchange market. The cessation of intervention allowed the ringgit to depreciate by 2.4 percent on July 11, before Bank Negara reentered the market and the exchange rate appreciated, thereby imposing a cost on speculators. Markets reacted with

nervousness to Bank Negara's intervention in support of the currency, and there was a perceived increase in the downside risks from shorting the ringgit. During the subsequent week, however, the central bank did not intervene in significant amounts, which gradually reduced perceived downside risks, triggering a sell-off, and the ringgit depreciated by 5 percent between July 11 and 18. Interest rates, which rose when pressures began, fell back substantially, leading to a fairly flat yield curve.

The intervention band for the Indonesian rupiah was widened from 8 to 12 percent on July 11 in a preemptive move designed to deter speculation. In the event, the rupiah depreciated by 8 percent by July 21,

Figure 20. Yield Curves in Selected Emerging Markets, July 1997

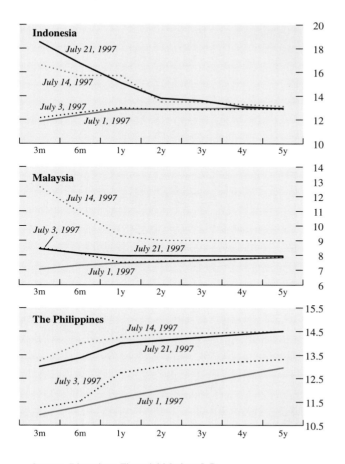

Source: Bloomberg Financial Markets L.P.

and as it fell toward the bottom of the band, some speculative pressures built up to test the floor. In response, Bank Indonesia raised interest rates from 12 percent to 13 percent on July 23, and reportedly intervened heavily in support of the currency.

In what was viewed as a spillover effect from the Asian emerging market currency depreciations, the Brazilian equity market fell by 15 percent during the week of July 11 to 18. This followed a spectacular rise in the market by over 90 percent from the beginning of the year, though, and was viewed by some market participants as representing perhaps a necessary correction. While there was no evidence of short selling of the real, concerns that speculative pressures could lead to a larger-than-expected depreciation, as they had in Asia, contributed to the sell-off in the equity market.

VIII

Conclusions

Mature Markets

A key development in the major foreign exchange markets during the past twelve months was the appreciation of the dollar against the other major currencies. The strong economic performance of the United States, combined with attractive interest differentials, contributed to a correction of the dollar's valuation vis-à-vis the deutsche mark and the yen. The sharp yen appreciation in mid-May 1997, which is partly attributable to official statements, demonstrated that exchange rates can react quickly to changes in perceptions about future policies and fundamentals.

The relatively favorable economic fundamentals in the advanced countries produced a compression of interest rate spreads across a broad range of credit markets, as investors searched for higher yields in a global environment of low and declining interest rates. Although spreads have narrowed considerably, they have remained above previous lows in most markets. The narrowing of sovereign spreads—against benchmark yields—is consistent with the convergence of inflation rates, fiscal policies, and other fundamentals experienced recently. Likewise, the narrowing of spreads across different risk classes (within and across countries) is broadly consistent with an increased tolerance for risk, reflecting a growing risk-seeking investor base and advances in risk management techniques that have improved the ability to manage market and credit risk. The main concern is whether credit markets have fully priced in the risks of a further tightening of monetary policy and the associated increase in credit risks. As in currency markets, unexpected events or policy changes could trigger a widening of spreads and a rebalancing of portfolios across domestic and international financial markets.

Equity markets in the majority of advanced countries are presently at or near record highs, and U.S. markets have continued to rise after doubling in value during 1992–96. While some indicators suggest that U.S. equities are optimistically priced, others suggest that U.S. markets are not as far out of line as they were in 1987. However, there is a consensus that a moderate correction in U.S. equity prices would not significantly affect the U.S. economy, because real spending was apparently not significantly bolstered by positive wealth effects during the run-up in equity prices. The present strength of the U.S. economy, the strong financial condition of banks, the development and widespread use of risk management systems, and recent improvements in the U.S. financial infrastructure all support this view and suggest that a correction would be manageable.

Increased optimism about EMU has fostered stability in European currency and credit markets, and forward interest rate spreads suggest that markets are continuing to price in a high probability of EMU starting on January 1, 1999. With currency valuations now largely anchored to a single event, the current environment of low volatility, appreciated peripheral currencies, and interest rate convergence is a delicate situation that could change markedly between now and the start of EMU. As decisions are made about initial EMU membership and euro conversion rates, and as portfolios are rebalanced in light of this new information, there could be periods of increased asset-price volatility and sizable cross-border capital flows in the run-up to 1999. However, unless there are major disruptive events—a delay of the start of EMU or substantive policy disagreements, for example, about which countries should make up the initial EMU or how to interpret the Maastricht criteria—the uncertainty about these decisions need not lead to significant and disruptive market turbulence, such as was experienced during the 1992–93 ERM crises.

The yet-to-be-defined intervention rules for managing parities between the euro and the currencies of EU countries not in the initial EMU but likely to join before 2002 could become a source of speculative activity and volatility beyond 1999. Currency stability requires that the arrangements should be based on objective evaluations of economic convergence and should be credibly and transparently implemented so as not to be perceived by markets as an unconditional commitment for intervention support. The potential for currency market instability could be contained by announcing the basic features of exchange rate arrangements with non-EMU countries well ahead of the decision on the choice of countries, which is currently set to take place in May 1998, and in particular the rules and conditions for providing support for such countries' exchange rate parities and the convergence criteria for entry into the union.

Structural Aspects of EMU

The potential benefits to European financial markets of EMU are far reaching and include the development of EMU-wide securities markets, more efficient banking systems, and the creation of a pan-European payments system. But none of these benefits are assured. There are remaining impediments, including regulatory restrictions and tax disincentives that could delay or even prevent the development of EMU-wide private securities markets.

One of the most pressing challenges is the restructuring and consolidation of continental European banking systems. By removing the home currency advantage in local retail banking markets for deposits and loans, the introduction of the euro will raise the level of cross-border competition and disintermediation. The required consolidation and restructuring can be accomplished through market mechanisms, such as mergers, acquisitions, alliances, and exits. But, unless structural reforms are implemented across European banking markets, there is a risk that local market power, rigidities in labor practices, public ownership structures, and other longstanding features could delay or prevent these pressures from having the desired effects. This could allow financial problems in troubled institutions to build up to the point where public intervention might be unavoidable.

Much remains to be done to transform the still highly segmented national securities markets into deep and liquid EMU-wide securities markets. Whether institutional arrangements and financial policies may also affect the pace of market integration and development is an open question. It has been argued that the active participation of the U.S. Federal Reserve has fostered the development of the extremely efficient U.S. money and securities markets. Although final decisions have not been made, the current plan for monetary policy operating procedures is to rely on infrequent (weekly) decentralized repo operations and on decentralized fine-tuning operations, while leaving open the possibility of a system of minimum reserve requirements, with reserve averaging acting as a liquidity buffer. Some expect that leaving room for arbitrage by market participants, together with the European payments system (TARGET), will lead to an active single money market. By contrast, others have argued that the decentralized implementation of repo and fine-tuning operations would limit the ability of the ESCB to manage liquidity in money markets by way of active day-to-day operations in private interbank and repo markets.

Plans for establishing mechanisms for managing systemic banking and payments crises are still evolving. A lender of last resort is not identified in the Maastricht Treaty, and the single central institution, the ECB, is assigned only a supporting role in financial market surveillance. Moreover, banking supervision will remain national, with national supervisors responsible for functions normally delegated to a central authority, and the immediate mechanisms for information sharing, coordination, and crisis management lack transparency. As EMU-wide markets evolve, the ECB may have to assume a greater independent supervisory capacity under the enabling articles of its statutes. This would help safeguard EMU financial markets from the consequences of incompatible incentives in the midst of a crisis: under existing plans, situations could arise in which national supervisory authorities would have information about the solvency of an institution that for practical reasons it may be unwilling or unable to provide to the ECB. Transparency about the supervisory framework and market surveillance would improve the ability to deal with these potential problems. Although constructive ambiguity about the conditions under which lender-of-last-resort facilities will be available is a necessary element in preventing moral hazard, there should be no ambiguity among policymakers about the mechanisms that can be used to manage crisis situations.

Emerging Markets

The record private capital flows into emerging markets observed in 1996 have been underpinned by sound economic fundamentals, reflecting both the efforts of large institutional investors to obtain the benefits associated with holding globally diversified portfolios, as well as the improved macroeconomic and structural policies of many recipient countries. Nonetheless, divergent macroeconomic conditions in capital-importing and capital-exporting countries are likely to impart a cyclical character to private capital flows even if the trend of further integration of emerging markets into the global financial system continues. Moreover, political and economic developments in individual countries and regions will undoubtedly lead to a highly uneven pace of capital inflows and outflows in individual emerging market countries. Strong and consistent macroeconomic, financial, and structural policies are the necessary conditions to ensure sustained market access.

The dramatic decline in emerging market spreads in an environment of low interest rates and ample liquidity in the mature markets raises the question of whether the compression in spreads has been excessive to the point where credit risk is underpriced. Some have suggested that abundant global "liquidity"—associated with low nominal interest rates in some of the major mature markets—has been a key factor in pushing down spreads on emerging market instruments, as the search for higher yields has generated high cyclical demand for emerging market obligations. If this is true, then a general tightening of global monetary conditions could produce a magnified response in the level of interest rate spreads on emerging market debt. When the Federal Reserve tightened monetary policy in early 1994 by initially raising the federal funds interest rate 25 basis points, spreads on the emerging market bond index rose from roughly 400 basis points in January 1994 to over 800 basis points by March 1994. Similarly, there was initially a sharp increase in spreads when the Federal Reserve announced a one-quarter increase in the federal funds interest rate in March 1997.

While markets will offer improved terms and conditions to countries whose economic performance is viewed as strong, recent experience indicates that they can impose large costs on countries where market participants perceive policy inconsistencies and structural weaknesses. The imposition of such "market discipline" can occur by way of a sudden speculative attack on a country's exchange rate arrangements. Authorities in many countries have increasingly relied on a graduated defense beginning with sterilized foreign exchange intervention. However, it has frequently been necessary to allow short-term domestic interest rates to rise, that is, to intervene without sterilizing. When the cost of maintaining high short-term interest rates has been viewed as excessive, temporary and selective capital controls have also been used to limit speculators' access to domestic credit, thereby denying them the possibility of establishing a net short position in the domestic currency. While such controls can at times be an effective means of limiting short-term speculative pressure, and may be justified when the attack is not warranted by underlying fundamentals, they soon begin to interfere with normal trade and finance. Moreover, the growing sophistication of financial markets has meant that "leakages" will quickly force authorities into casting ever-widening nets of administrative controls. In addition, the expectation that a country is likely to use capital controls during a crisis, thereby restricting the ability of investors to adjust their portfolio positions, could influence the cost and availability of external funds during normal periods. In contrast to imposing selective capital controls, the introduction of exchange controls—restricting the ability of market participants to exchange foreign for domestic currency—could have costly and disruptive effects on trade and finance and on market confidence.

A notable feature of several of the emerging market currencies that were subjected to speculative pressure—the Czech koruna, the Thai baht, the Philippine peso, and the Malaysian ringgit—was their rigidity prior to the recent crises. These currencies either were officially fixed or had fluctuated recently within very narrow bands. Taking a short position in a currency is like short selling in any asset market where investors expect prices to decline. However, typical short selling, for example of equities, entails not only the costs of borrowing the equities, but also the risk that equity

prices may actually rise. By contrast, in a general bear market for currencies created by a slowing of capital inflows, the fixity of the exchange rate limits the downside risks from shorting the currencies, and this downside limit tends to intensify speculative pressures. In fact the more rigid the exchange rate, the smaller the perceived downside risk to shorting the currency.

The recent episodes of foreign exchange market pressures illustrated some important interactions between central banks' defense of currencies and market perceptions of the costs and ability of sustaining such defenses. For one thing, the sharp increase in interest rates dictated by the arithmetic of discrete devaluations over short periods of time illustrated graphically the high level to which interest rates need to be raised to deter speculators from shorting a currency. Moreover, subsequent increases in the perceived likelihood of devaluation require successively higher interest rates. Market participants' perceptions of the costs of the cumulative increase in interest rates on the domestic corporate sector, real economic activity, and particularly the soundness of the domestic financial system appeared to play a key role in affecting expectations of an eventual devaluation. The experiences also illustrated that maintaining interest rates at a high level for a prolonged period of time—as in Thailand—can actually increase the market's belief in an eventual devaluation. It is also notable that while reserve levels declined in each of the emerging markets as the currencies came under pressure, they remained at relatively substantial levels. This fact suggests that the costs of defense in terms of higher interest rates may play a larger role than reserve levels—even with the prospects of enhanced regional cooperation of central banks—in affecting both market participants' expectations of eventual devaluation and the authorities' decisions whether or not to continue defending their currencies.

The small scale of emerging capital markets relative to the size of international capital flows has at times implied substantial movements in domestic asset prices, particularly for equities and real estate, in response to capital flows. Consequently, some countries have adopted or strengthened measures to reduce volatility in asset markets or to limit downside risks or both. Such policies include restrictions on margin purchases of securities and on short selling; prohibition of certain types of derivative products; limitations on foreign ownership; transactions taxes; and direct government intervention in equity and real estate markets. Such temporary prudential restrictions can, if applied selectively and sparingly, be helpful in maintaining market stability. However, price movements of equities and other assets in the face of changes in capital flows represent an important element of the adjustment mechanism. Restricting price movements can increase the adjustment in the quantity of flows as international investors attempt to alter their exposure to the country. For example, the loss of reserves in the event of an outflow is likely to be greater when prices do not fall. Furthermore, direct government intervention to prevent price declines can increase moral hazard since investors will come to expect that the government will provide at least partial protection against large losses. To improve the resilience of the economy to reversals in capital flows will need to become a key policy objective. In particular, policy needs to ensure that the financial sector adequately manages the risks to its balance sheets from sharp changes in asset prices.

Given the concerns about the potential cyclical nature of capital flows to emerging markets, as well as the recent experience with speculative attacks, a key issue for many market participants is *what role the IMF will play* in the new environment of increasingly integrated global capital markets. Investors are keenly aware of the role that the IMF, and other official institutions, played in the 1994–95 Mexican crisis and that the IMF's ability to address acute systemic crises will be augmented once the country ratification process for the New Arrangements to Borrow is completed. There appears to be a growing expectation that the IMF will use its own resources, as well as act as a catalyst for regional official balance of payments support for systemically important emerging market countries. It is, therefore, particularly important that the IMF's surveillance over the financial positions of its member countries be strengthened to compensate for a potential lack of market discipline over sovereign borrowers, and that the IMF's financial support be granted only in the context of rigorous adjustment programs.

The global financial developments discussed in this report can, and frequently do, exert an important impact on developments in the balance of payments and on the stock and composition of external liabilities of various IMF members, and these issues are being considered in the context of the periodic review of IMF surveillance. These discussions have, among other things, recognized that the management of the various risks associated with the financial sector and with foreign liabilities are key areas where IMF surveillance needs to be, and has already been, strengthened.

Beyond surveillance there is the question of the availability and use of IMF resources by countries experiencing balance of payments difficulties as a result of volatile international capital flows and speculative currency attacks. This important issue is under consideration.

External Liability Management

In a world of increasingly mobile capital flows and integrated capital markets, large and unhedged external sovereign liabilities could expose countries to risks that some of them are not fully prepared to man-

age. In the current environment, the sound management of sovereign liabilities has become an important element in safeguarding a country's economic stability. As a first step toward achieving a reduction in exposure to external shocks, countries should aim to improve the management of their net foreign exchange exposure. The choice of the currency denomination of external debt should not be driven by the level of nominal interest rates; instead, such borrowing costs should be calculated on a hedged or risk-adjusted basis. Reducing currency risk does not preclude sovereigns from tapping international markets to broaden their investor base, lengthen their maturity profile, or develop benchmark debt instruments. Rather, it implies that, unless governments have access to foreign currency revenues, sovereign foreign currency borrowing beyond a safe level should as far as possible be hedged against currency risks.

The relatively low spreads in the Eurobond markets have raised concerns about whether the pricing of external debt is efficient, or whether it reflects expectations on the part of the lenders of priority treatment in case the country experiences economic difficulties. Such priority treatment could arise through the aggressive use of legal instruments, or it might be based on assumptions about international financial rescues organized to support systemically important emerging markets. If the pricing of external debt does not reflect all economic costs of such debt, then countries may be led to exceed the optimal amount of external debt.

Limiting the sovereign currency exposure beyond what can be achieved through hedging should be viewed as a medium-term strategy and a gradual process. The more pressing issue confronting governments is to reform the institutional arrangements governing debt policy, so that the technical expertise and experience to risk-manage debt competently and transparently can be applied. The experience of the growing number of governments that have reformed their debt management practices suggests that such professionalism and accountability is best achieved when debt management is assigned to an agency that is separate and autonomous from the political process. Within this framework, the ministry of finance would formulate and publicly announce the strategy for debt management (e.g., composition and maturity of the public debt), while the debt office would implement that strategy and manage the daily risk exposure of the sovereign portfolio. Entrusting debt management to a separate and autonomous debt office signals to financial markets and to the general public the authorities' commitment to a transparent and accountable debt management policy. It also enables the authorities to assign a clearly defined objective to the debt agency, and to organize the agency to achieve such an objective, without being hampered by either the management structure or pay scale of the public sector.

Developments in International Banking

Performance of the industrial country banking systems has ranged from strong in the United Kingdom and the United States to broadly acceptable in continental Europe. By contrast, difficulties remain in the Japanese banking system. While problem loans among the 20 major banks are officially estimated at just under 5 percent of total loans, the true quantity of bad loans may be much higher. The current low interest rate environment has not been conducive to exposing potentially nonperforming borrowers, and it has boosted bank profitability. An increase in short-term interest rates could have a detrimental effect on net cash flow into the banking sector. The experience with resolving banking problems in a number of other industrial countries suggests that a timely resolution of bad loan problems serves to limit losses and restore the health of the banking system earlier than an approach based on forbearance. Furthermore, a timely writing down of bad loans, together with the sale of collateral assets, has the effect of restoring liquidity to the real estate market. As a case in point, Japanese experience during the last five years suggests that an earlier and more decisive and transparent approach to the resolution of the bad loan problem could have been less costly to the financial system and to the economy as a whole.

The restructuring of the international financial system toward a model in which financial conglomerates provide the full range of services requires a reexamination of the structure of financial supervision and regulation, as is currently under way in the United Kingdom, Japan, and elsewhere. Since financial institutions increasingly manage risk on a consolidated legal entity basis, a supervisory structure that combines the supervision of banking, securities, and perhaps insurance activities, would seem appropriate. At the same time, it is important to ensure that the central banks retain a role in the supervision of the money center banks, which are the key participants in the wholesale payments system, and which may at some time be the recipient of central bank liquidity support.

With international barriers to competition having been reduced significantly among the industrial countries, regulators need to reconsider policies that hinder competition between different segments of the domestic financial systems. Thus, both Japan and the United States have begun the process of lowering the barriers between commercial and investment banking. Similarly, the issue of assistance to government-owned banks and its effect on competition in the industry has been raised in France and Germany. There is broad international agreement that government-owned banks should be made to operate as purely commercial entities, and subsidization of their cost of capital is incompatible with that principle.

In emerging markets, banks and regulators in most countries continue to deal with the aftereffects of banking crises or with efforts to prevent new crises from developing. While asset quality in the Brazilian and Mexican systems is not yet showing much improvement, the other major Latin American banking systems appear to be recovering. In Asia, however, banking systems in a number of countries remain vulnerable to further deterioration in corporate liquidity, an exchange rate devaluation, or a correction in property prices. There are concerns about the banking systems in Korea, the Philippines, and Thailand, although regulators there and elsewhere are attempting to address the underlying problems of poor credit risk management, overcapacity, and excessive foreign exchange risk or other large exposures.

Background Material—Part I

Recent Developments and Trends in Capital Markets and Banking Systems

Annex I

Recent Developments in Emerging Capital Markets

As the effects of the Mexican peso crisis on investor sentiment continued to wane, a number of factors helped propel private capital flows to the emerging markets from $192.8 billion in 1995 to a new peak of $235.2 billion during 1996.[1] These factors included, first, the low level of interest rates in Japan and Germany and the compression of corporate bond spreads in the United States, which prompted fixed-income investors in the mature markets to move down the credit spectrum and search for higher yields on emerging market debt. Second, improved economic performance in many emerging markets reduced perceived credit risks. Third, institutional investors in the mature markets continued to seek the benefits of portfolio diversification in the emerging markets. Fourth, innovations in financial markets improved the ability of investors to manage exposures and risks to emerging markets, increasing the attractiveness of such investments. Fifth, continued financial and capital account liberalization in many emerging markets encouraged inflows. Finally, improvements in the availability and quality of information on emerging markets facilitated improved asset selection and assessment.

Underlying the surge of total private flows in 1996 were both strong foreign direct investment (FDI) and portfolio flows. FDI continued to grow rapidly, representing the largest component of flows, while portfolio flows almost doubled. As portfolio flows rebounded vigorously, bank lending flows fell off, though they continued to grow strongly to particular regions, such as Asia. Across the emerging markets, during 1996 and into 1997, investor sentiment shifted away from Asia in view of the regional slowdown, concerns about the current account deficits of some countries, and uneasiness about the state of the property and financial sectors, in favor of Latin America, where growth picked up, inflation slowed, and there

was visible progress in strengthening and restructuring banking systems. The growth of total flows to Asia moderated, while flows to Latin America more than doubled, rising above the previous highs of 1993. While flows to the Middle East and Europe grew strongly, flows to Africa and the transition economies declined. As through the first half of the decade, the aggregate reserves of the emerging market countries continued to grow during 1996, and almost half of the net inflows were accumulated as reserves. Compared with the turbulence during late 1994 and 1995, emerging foreign exchange markets were relatively calmer in 1996 and early 1997. Though certain systemically important emerging markets remained susceptible to speculative attack, these pressures remained localized. In mid-May 1997, however, as the Thai baht came under severe speculative attack, pressures spilled over to a number of other countries, both within and outside the region, where international investors saw parallels in economic circumstance and structure.

The surge in portfolio flows during 1996 was associated with a spectacular boom in emerging debt markets, while emerging equity markets continued to recover from the trough following the Mexican crisis. There were dramatic improvements in the liquidity of emerging debt markets and steep reductions in the volatility of returns on both debt and equity markets. The bond market rally sparked a sharp shift in the structure of emerging market primary external financing toward increased bond issuance and a reduced reliance on syndicated bank lending. Spreads on new bond issues fell across the board, while maturities lengthened. The favorable environment encouraged a number of new entrants into the market and led several borrowers to restructure existing liabilities at improved terms. By early 1997 spreads on emerging market debt had declined to their previous historic lows—of late 1993 and early 1994—leading to concerns that yields may have reached their lower limits in adequately compensating for risk. Although trading activity continued to increase, returns fell off sharply during the first quarter of 1997. Expected returns on emerging market equity—earnings-price ratios adjusted for growth—rose steadily during 1996 and into 1997, buoyed by upward revisions to forecasts of growth, while volatility declined. Adjusted for volatility, returns, particularly in Latin America, looked in-

---

[1]The term "emerging markets" is used in this report to describe the group of countries comprising "developing countries," "countries in transition," and the "advanced economies" of Hong Kong, China; Israel; the Republic of Korea; Singapore; and the Taiwan Province of China, as classified in the *World Economic Outlook.* This is a significantly broader interpretation of the term than is used in many other contexts. The review of developments in this annex is principally concerned with the period January 1996–May 1997. The cutoff date for charts and tables was May 31, 1997.

creasingly favorable relative to those in the mature markets. The increase in emerging market equity prices during 1996 accelerated in the first quarter of 1997, again particularly in Latin America. In the international syndicated loan market, a reduced demand for bank financing by emerging market borrowers coincided with rising supply, and strong competition among banks created considerable pressures on pricing and weakened loan structures, also raising concerns as to whether risks were being sufficiently priced. Refinancings accounted for almost a fifth of new syndications of medium- and long-term loans in 1996, and over a third in Latin America.

This annex discusses emerging market financing, with a focus on recent developments during 1996–97. The first section discusses net capital flows in the balance of payments, the behavior of international reserves, and developments in foreign exchange markets. The following sections discuss developments in emerging debt markets, equity markets, mutual funds dedicated to emerging markets, and international bank lending.

Capital Flows, Reserves, and Foreign Exchange Markets

Capital Flows in the Balance of Payments

In spite of several unfavorable developments, total private capital flows to emerging markets during the 1990s have proven remarkably resilient (Table 13 and Figure 21). Increases in interest rates in the mature markets during the course of 1994, the Mexican peso crisis and "Tequila" (contagion) effects that followed, and occasional high volatility in the mature assets markets all had only temporary and localized effects on these flows. Similarly, during 1996 the strong performance of many of the mature equity markets, uncertainties relating to the course of interest rates in the mature markets, and perceived vulnerabilities in some of the systemically important emerging market countries failed to deter the overall volume of private flows to emerging markets, which grew by 22 percent to a new record of $235.2 billion. For the first time in the 1990s, private capital flows to the emerging markets exceeded total (private plus official) capital flows in 1996, and $13.2 billion in net repayments of official flows meant that total capital flows actually declined from $232.0 billion in 1995 to $222.0 billion in 1996. Net official flows were negative not only to Latin America, reflecting the substantial repayments by Mexico of the official assistance extended in the aftermath of the crisis, but also to the Middle Eastern, European, and transition economies.

A key characteristic of the surge in private capital inflows to the emerging markets during the 1990s, and one that has been critical in underpinning the re-

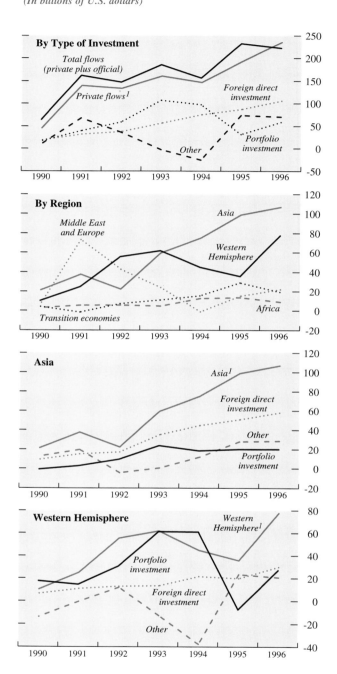

Figure 21. Net Private Capital Flows to Emerging Markets
(In billions of U.S. dollars)

Sources: International Monetary Fund, *World Economic Outlook*; and IMF staff estimates.
[1]Total net private capital inflows equal net foreign direct investment plus net portfolio investment plus net other investment.

silience of total private flows during the period, has been the steady growth of FDI flows. Encouraged by continued capital account liberalization and the easing of restrictions on FDI in emerging market countries, multinational corporations swiftly relocated and purchased existing production facilities in the relatively lower-labor-cost emerging market countries. FDI flows to emerging market countries expanded between 1991 and 1995 at an average annual rate of 37 percent and continued to grow robustly during 1996, increasing by 21 percent. Since 1995, net FDI flows have accounted for the largest proportion of flows, and in 1996, at $105.9 billion, accounted for some 45 percent of total private capital flows.

Unlike FDI flows, portfolio flows to the emerging markets have been volatile. After falling off sharply during 1994 and 1995 in the wake of the Mexican peso crisis, total portfolio flows to emerging markets recovered robustly, increasing by 86 percent, from $31.6 billion in 1995 to $58.7 billion in 1996, accounting for 25 percent of total private flows. Despite the rebound, however, portfolio flows remained well below—at just over half—the peak levels reached in 1993 when they accounted for 66 percent of private flows. "Other" flows, which largely reflect bank lending, after having risen sharply during 1995 as the increased costs of borrowing on international capital markets in the wake of the Mexican crisis caused emerging market borrowers to turn to bank financing, declined modestly during 1996 to $70.6 billion. As a proportion of total private flows, however, they declined from 38 percent in 1995 to 30 percent in 1996.

During the last few years, investors have displayed an increasing tendency to discriminate between regions and countries in response to changes in economic fundamentals, and this has been reflected relatively quickly in the behavior of capital flows. The Mexican peso crisis resulted in a reallocation of flows away from Latin America toward Asia and the transition economies. As total flows to Latin America fell off during 1994–95, flows to Asia continued to increase and flows to the transition countries rose steeply. During 1996, as investor sentiment turned away from Asia, the growth of flows to that region slowed and there was a sharp rebound in flows to Latin America. Portfolio flows have been more responsive than FDI flows, and in 1996 Latin American countries were the largest recipients of portfolio flows among the emerging markets.

Total private capital flows to Latin America more than doubled from their depressed levels in 1995 of $35.7 billion to $77.7 billion in 1996. The sharp rebound raised total flows to the region above the previous peak of 1993, completing the recovery of total flows from the effects of the Mexican crisis. FDI flows, which had declined only modestly during 1995, grew by 50 percent, to $29.9 billion in 1996. After net outflows of $7.5 billion during 1995, net portfolio inflows resumed, totaling $27.1 billion. Portfolio flows remained, however, well below half their peak of $61.1 billion in 1993. Reflecting the declining re-

liance on bank lending, "other" flows contracted by 11 percent to $20.7 billion in 1996. As a share of total net inflows, they contracted more sharply, falling from 65 percent in 1995 to 27 percent in 1996. While total flows to the region recovered during 1996, there was a drastic change in the composition of these flows relative to 1993. Net portfolio inflows, which equaled total net private inflows during 1993, represented only 35 percent of flows during 1996.[2] On the other hand, the share of FDI in total flows to the region rose from 22 percent in 1993 to 38 percent in 1996, and compared with net "other" capital outflows during 1993, there were net "other" inflows during 1996 representing 27 percent of total net inflows.

While total private flows to Asian emerging markets continued to grow during 1996, rising to $106.8 billion, the rate of growth decelerated sharply, from 32 percent in 1995 to 8 percent. The increase was due primarily to increased FDI flows, which grew by 14 percent, to $58.0 billion. Portfolio flows to Asia, after having declined modestly from their peak of $23.8 billion in 1993, remained steady at $20.1 billion during 1995 and 1996, while "other" net inflows increased modestly. In comparison with Latin America, FDI flows account for a substantially larger proportion of flows to Asia—54 percent in 1996—while portfolio flows account for substantially less—19 percent during 1996. Japan represents an important source of FDI flows to the Asian emerging markets, and the relocation of Japanese manufacturing to the region since the mid-1980s has been a major driving force behind the growth of FDI to the region.

Following a substantial increase in capital flows to the transition economies in 1995, inflows declined sharply in 1996. There were sharp declines to both the Czech Republic and Hungary, where all categories of flows declined, and a somewhat more modest decline in flows to Poland, where FDI continued to grow. Net flows of capital to the Middle East and Europe rose from $15.3 billion in 1995 to $22.2 billion in 1996, reflecting an increase in "other" flows, while FDI flows remained modest and steady, and portfolio flows declined. Private capital flows to Africa, which rose modestly during 1995, fell in 1996 to $9.0 billion. Africa is the only region that has not shared significantly in the resurgence of private capital flows to the emerging markets during the 1990s, not receiving any significant portfolio flows over the period, and during 1996, official flows accounted for over 40 percent of flows to the region.

The rapid and unfaltering growth of FDI flows to emerging markets during the 1990s and the steady increase in the share of FDI flows in total private flows have led many observers to conclude both that the

---

[2]"Other" flows to Latin America were negative in 1993, that is, there was an outflow, or net repayments of bank lending.

risks of a reversal of sentiment against the emerging markets have concomitantly diminished and that, were such a reversal to occur, the consequences would not be severe. Underlying this belief are several notions. First, that FDI flows, by their nature, tend to be "long-term," in that they are driven by positive longer-term sentiment in favor of emerging markets and, therefore, less likely to be reversed than relatively "short-term" portfolio flows. Second, since FDI entails physical investment in plant and equipment, it would, in fact, be difficult to reverse.

The events surrounding the Mexican crisis certainly help support this view. Even as portfolio flows to Latin America switched from a net inflow of $60.8 billion during 1994 to a net outflow of $7.5 billion in 1995, substantial net inflows of FDI continued, declining only modestly, from $21.5 billion to $19.9 billion. However, there are a number of features of both the data on FDI flows, and the historical behavior of FDI flows, that suggest caution in interpreting the growth in importance of such flows as imparting an enduring resilience to capital flows to emerging markets.

Several factors suggest that the proportion of FDI in total flows as measured by balance of payments data may overstate the importance of these flows. First, the balance of payments differentiation between FDI flows and portfolio flows is arbitrary. Foreign investment in the equity of a company above a critical proportion of outstanding equity is classified as FDI, whereas that below the critical threshold is classified as portfolio equity investment. In reality, small differences above the critical level are unlikely to represent any substantially longer-term intentions of the investor, as compared with those below. Second, if the foreign company undertaking the FDI borrows locally to finance the investment, say from a local bank, depending on the form of incorporation of the company locally, the setup of the plant may count as FDI while the bank lending could show up as a capital outflow, reducing the proportion of net bank lending in overall flows and raising the proportion of FDI flows. Finally, there are sometimes tax or regulatory advantages to rerouting domestic investment through offshore vehicles and these factors have likely overstated the growth of FDI in recent years. The most commonly cited example of such rerouting of domestic investment is that by Chinese enterprises through Hong Kong, because of the tax advantages of doing so. With regard to the reversibility of FDI flows, while it may, in principle, be more difficult and expensive to sell physical rather than portfolio assets, physical assets, nevertheless, can still be sold, albeit typically at a discount, and in the end the sentiment for reversal will be weighed against the discount. There is little reason to expect the discount to always be prohibitive. With regard to the predictability of FDI flows, the experience of the Mexican crisis discussed above notwithstand-

ing, research indicates that, historically, for both industrial and developing countries, FDI and other flows labeled "long-term" according to the traditional balance of payments definition have generally been as volatile as, and no more predictable than, flows labeled "short-term."[3]

Reserve Accumulation

As has consistently been the case throughout the 1990s, the aggregate reserves of the emerging markets continued to grow during 1996 (Table 13 and Figure 22). Of the $222.0 billion total capital flows to the emerging markets during 1996, $104.8 billion—47 percent—was accumulated as central bank foreign exchange reserve assets, while the remainder was used to finance current account deficits. The increase was larger in Asia ($61.8 billion—59 percent of total) than in Latin America ($26.2 billion—25 percent of total), though as a proportion of flows (54 percent in Asia and 40 percent in Latin America) it was substantial for both regions. Central bank reserve assets of the major Asian emerging market countries rose across the board, with the exception of the Taiwan Province of China, where reserves declined sharply early in the year but recovered most of these losses by year-end. The most rapid growth was in China, where reserves increased by $31.7 billion during the year. In Latin America, as capital inflows rebounded, reserves accumulated rapidly in Argentina, Brazil, and Venezuela, not only recovering from their losses during 1995, but rising well above previous levels. In Mexico, after recovering from their losses during the crisis by late 1995, reserves rose during the latter half of 1996 but remained below the levels of early 1994. In Eastern Europe, reserves declined modestly in both the Czech Republic and Hungary, though they remained at relatively high levels. In South Africa, which has persistently had perhaps the lowest level of reserves among the major emerging markets, reserves continued to fluctuate at low levels.

How large has the 1990s buildup of reserves been? Of the $1.2 trillion in total net flows to emerging markets during 1990–96, some $575 billion—49 percent—was accumulated as reserves. This raised emerging market central banks' reserve assets to $823 billion by end-1996, a more than threefold increase since end-1989 and representing about half of the stock of reserve assets of the world's central banks. Five of the world's 10 largest holders of reserves are now emerging market economies. These holdings are concentrated in Asia—China, Taiwan Province of China, Singapore, and Hong Kong, China. Growth in China's reserves has been the most dramatic—rising by $89 billion during the 1990s—making it the largest

---

[3]See Claessens, Dooley, and Warner (1995).

Figure 22. Total Reserves Minus Gold of Selected Emerging Markets, January 1990–May 1997
(In billions of U.S. dollars)

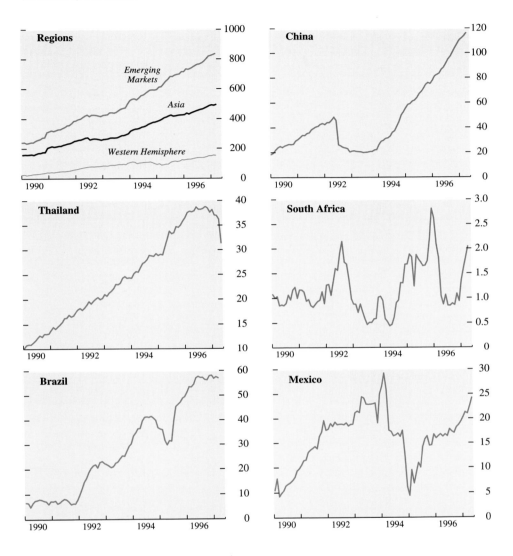

Source: International Monetary Fund, *International Financial Statistics.*

holder of reserves among the emerging market countries. Other notable increases over the period include Singapore ($56 billion), Brazil ($51 billion), and Thailand ($27 billion).

The large buildup in emerging market central bank reserve assets during the 1990s reflects in part direct central bank intervention to prevent nominal exchange rate appreciation in the face of the substantial capital inflows. It also reflects concerns about the risks of a sudden reversal of capital flows. Recent history, in particular the sharp loss of reserves during the reversal of capital flows to Mexico during 1994

when, within a few days in December, the central bank lost $5 billion in reserves, and portfolio management considerations in a world of increased capital mobility suggest that traditional import-cover measures are no longer appropriate for judging the adequacy of the level of reserves. Reserve coverage needs to be measured instead in relation to a broad range of monetary aggregates and banking system and government short-term liabilities. Relative to these aggregates, the buildup in reserves has been more modest. At end-1996, for example, while Thailand's reserves were sufficient to cover over six months' of imports, they represented only about a quarter of broad money.

The substantial accumulation of reserves by emerging market country central banks raises several issues about the efficiency of allocation of capital. First, reserve assets represent a component of national wealth but are typically held in low-yield (albeit liquid and credit-risk-free) assets such as government securities in the mature markets—particularly U.S. treasury securities; thus, excess holdings of reserves would imply an inefficient allocation of national wealth. (Asset-liability management at a national level is discussed in Annex V of the Background Material.) Second, it is ironic that some 49 percent of the $1.2 trillion of net capital flows into emerging markets in search of higher returns has ended up accumulated as reserves, a substantial proportion of which has then been reinvested back in low-yield instruments in the mature markets. This implies that the differential between the higher yield demanded and earned by investors from the mature markets in emerging markets, and that earned on reserves reinvested back into the mature markets, represent a cost that will ultimately be borne by residents of emerging markets. This flow cost could be substantial, and present yield spreads on emerging market debt suggest these costs could be of the order of $10 billion annually. These costs, of course, need to be weighed against the benefit of the liquidity provided by the reserves and the objective of alleviating downward pressures on the exchange rate in the event of a reversal of capital flows from emerging markets.

The large buildup of reserves also implies that emerging markets now have a bigger presence in world securities markets. As a measure of their importance, consider that the $823 billion of emerging market reserves represented over 20 percent of the stock of marketable U.S. government securities at the end of 1996.[4] The buildup of reserves also creates channels for the interaction and feedback of disturbances in financial markets among the emerging and mature markets. First, the recycling of capital inflows into emerging markets back into the mature markets means that disturbances in either could have multiplier effects. A disturbance that leads to a decline in interest rates in the mature markets, for example, and stimulates flows into the emerging markets, but results in almost half of it being reinvested back in the mature markets, is likely to place further downward pressure on interest rates in the mature markets, cause further outflows to emerging markets, and so on. Second, very similarly, a reversal of flows from the emerging markets, to the extent that it prompts a sell-off of reserve securities by emerging market central banks and puts upward pressure on interest rates in

the mature markets, is likely to exacerbate outflows from the emerging markets.

Foreign Exchange Markets

A cornerstone of macroeconomic management in most emerging markets in response to the surge in capital inflows during the 1990s has been sustained central bank intervention to prevent nominal exchange rate appreciation, and emerging market currencies have, with few exceptions, either been pegged or depreciated in nominal terms over the period (Figure 23). In response to episodes of reversals in flows, authorities have relied on their reserve holdings to resist downward pressures on nominal exchange rates. Since the adjustment of real exchange rates can take place through the adjustment of either nominal exchange rates or domestic prices, preventing nominal exchange rate adjustment shifts the pressure to domestic prices. Forcing adjustment through goods prices can—if goods prices are slow to adjust—reduce the volatility of real exchange rates in the event that the sources of pressure for change—capital flows—themselves tend to be reversed frequently. An important consideration, therefore, is the nature of the capital flows—whether they are temporary and likely to be reversed or they are of a more permanent nature. The substantial buildup of reserves during the 1990s, and the limiting of nominal exchange rate movements, suggests that capital inflows into the emerging markets have tended to be treated as short term. The strategy of intervention and of limiting nominal exchange rate movements has increasingly given rise to uncertainty on the part of market participants as to the sustainability and future course of exchange rate management.

Compared with the turbulence in foreign exchange markets during late 1994 and 1995 when several emerging market currencies came under attack in the aftermath of the Mexican peso crisis, exchange markets were relatively calmer in 1996 through April 1997. In Asia, the Indian rupee, after falling early in 1996, came under strong upward pressure, then stabilized during the latter half of the year. The depreciation of the Indonesian rupiah against the U.S. dollar slowed, while the volatility of the Philippine peso continued to decline, and it remained relatively stable against the U.S. dollar. The substantial appreciation of the yen against the U.S. dollar through mid-1995 and its subsequent reversal significantly affected some of the Asian emerging market currencies. In particular, the Korean won first appreciated through late 1995 and then depreciated substantially through 1996 and into 1997. The Thai baht followed a similar pattern, though within the much smaller bands set by the Bank of Thailand (BOT). The Malaysian ringgit and the Singapore dollar are the only major Asian emerging market currencies to have appreciated against the U.S. dollar over

---

[4]They are not, of course, all invested in U.S. treasuries.

the 1990–96 period. In Latin America, there was a marked reduction in the volatility of the Mexican new peso and the Brazilian real during 1996 through May 1997. The Mexican new peso depreciated modestly during the period, while the real depreciated steadily against the U.S. dollar. In April 1996, after the Venezuelan bolivar was floated, it depreciated by some 62 percent during the month, then remained relatively stable until a system of crawling bands was implemented in July. Elsewhere, in the transition economies, the Czech koruna was relatively stable until it came under attack in mid-May 1997 (discussed below), while the Hungarian forint and the Russian ruble continued to depreciate relatively steadily.

During 1996 through April 1997, among the larger emerging markets, the currencies that were subject to substantial pressures were the Thai baht and the South African rand. The Thai baht was subject to periodic bouts of speculative pressure amid a host of concerns: a slowdown in exports and growth, a current account deficit at 8 percent of GDP in 1996, a buildup in short-term debt, a glut in the property sector, and weaknesses in the domestic financial system. Such bouts of speculation were often driven by the possibility that the BOT would alter the basket of currencies against which it traditionally determines the value of the baht because of changes in trading patterns. As the BOT maintained interest rates at relatively high levels to relieve pressures on the currency, this further depressed economic activity and increased pressures on the domestic financial system. This policy conundrum caused speculative pressures to erupt periodically in the belief that eventually interest rates would have to be lowered out of concern for the state of the economy, and the baht devalued.

Market participants report that these speculative pressures were driven primarily by foreign investors. Several conditions facilitated the ability of foreign investors to speculate against the currency, relative to other emerging market currencies: specifically, Thailand maintains an open foreign exchange system, there are well-developed spot and forward foreign exchange markets, and foreign residents can obtain baht credit from domestic banks. The ability of speculators to obtain domestic currency credit, either implicitly or explicitly, is a key element in currency attacks. Speculation against the baht included directly taking positions on the forward market—selling baht forward—creating pressure on the forward rate to depreciate. When the speculator enters into a forward contract, typically with a domestic bank, the bank bears the investor's credit risk, and the forward contract represents an implicit extension of credit. If the domestic bank enters into an offsetting transaction with the central bank to hedge its position—say, by the central bank buying baht forward—this implicit extension of credit ultimately reverts to the central bank (see Chapter IV, Appendix 2). Settlement of forward sales of

baht by a foreign speculator also typically involves the extension of credit. Speculation against the baht also included the use of explicit baht credits, which, when converted into foreign currency, created a short position on the baht. The conversion of baht credit into foreign currency represented a capital outflow, placing downward pressure on the spot exchange rate and, to the extent that these pressures were offset by central bank intervention, they resulted in a loss of reserves.

In South Africa, the predominant source of pressure in the foreign exchange market between late February and early May 1996, when the rand plunged by 18 percent, was political uncertainty. While the pressure originally began with rumors about the health of President Mandela, as these rumors proved unfounded, attention focused on other political concerns. Unlike Thailand, South Africa, with a long history of capital controls on domestic residents, has much less developed spot and forward foreign exchange markets. In addition, foreign residents are not permitted to obtain rand credit from domestic banks without an underlying transaction. These features make it, in principle, more difficult to short the rand. Despite the fact that Thailand had a substantial stock of reserves, and South Africa did not, a common feature of the central banks' defense of their currencies was intervention in the forward foreign exchange market.

Amid widespread concerns that Japanese interest rates were likely to be raised with negative consequences for capital flows to emerging markets, and following adverse economic news, starting May 7, 1997, the Thai baht once again came under severe speculative pressure. For the first time since the contagion in the form of Tequila effects following the Mexican crisis, these pressures quickly spilled over to a number of other emerging market currencies. In Asia, the Indonesian rupiah, the Malaysian ringgit, and the Philippine peso all came under pressure. In Eastern Europe, the Czech and Slovak currencies came under attack. There were no notable immediate spillover effects to Latin America. Central bank defenses in support of the currencies included a combination of exchange market intervention, interest rate hikes, and measures aimed specifically at reducing foreign investors' access to domestic currency credit. Interbank overnight interest rates rose to varying degrees and over differing time spans across countries: the rupiah rate rose from 14 percent on Friday, May 9, to 16 percent by Friday, May 16; the ringgit rate rose from 7 percent to 19 percent by Tuesday, May 20; the peso rate rose from 11 percent to 20 percent on Monday, May 19; koruna rates reached 200 percent on Thursday, May 22.[5] On baht, the sharpest increase in interest rates was not onshore but in the offshore market,

---

[5]As discussed below, the ±7½ percent fluctuation band of the koruna was abandoned on May 26.

Figure 23. Exchange Rates of Selected Emerging Markets, January 1990–May 1997
(Local currency/U.S. dollar)

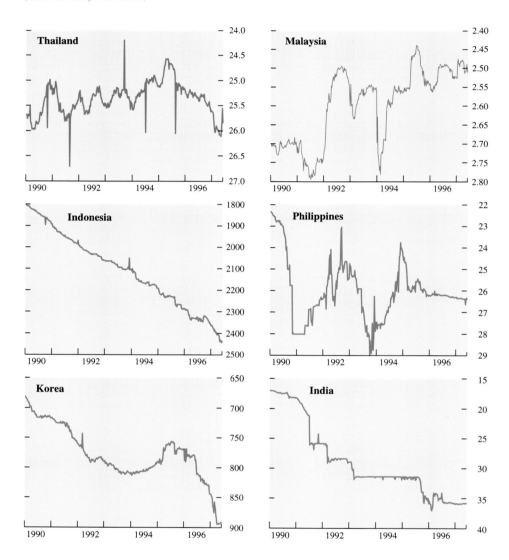

where rates shot up to 1,300 percent. The Bank of Thailand directed banks, usually the primary providers of baht, both onshore and offshore, to segment the two markets. The limitation of baht credit offshore drove up interest rates substantially more than onshore, causing speculators to settle their forward positions through the spot market, which put upward pressure on the exchange rate. Domestic banks also segmented the customer base by restricting baht lending to foreign clients, or charged them prohibitive swap rates, and stopped buying back baht-denominated commercial paper from offshore. Similar pressures were reported, though to a lesser extent, on both ringgit and rupiah offshore rates, and Malaysian and Philippine banks restricted the lending of local currency to for-

eign customers. The Czech National Bank limited access by nonresidents to the domestic money market.

In Asia, market participants widely reported coordinated exchange market intervention among the Asian central banks, particularly in support of the baht, and though it was unclear as to whether the recently established network of regional bilateral repurchase agreements had been utilized, the perception that they could be appeared to deter speculation. Since there are substantial offshore markets for these currencies—in Singapore and Hong Kong, China—some of the apparently coordinated intervention by the Monetary Authority of Singapore and the Hong Kong Monetary Authority was simply on behalf of other central banks. Some market participants reported pressures on U.S.

Figure 23 *(concluded)*

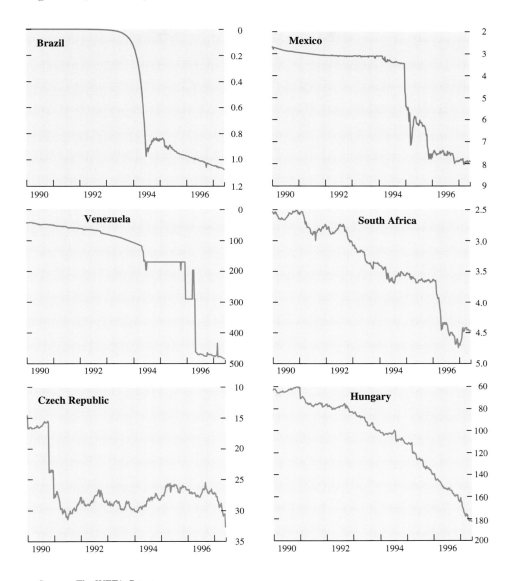

Source: The WEFA Group.

bond markets during the period as Asian and Eastern European central banks sold treasuries. While the baht withstood the pressures in May, and the pressures on the other Asian currencies abated, on May 26 the Czech National Bank abandoned its policy of maintaining the currency inside a trading band against a hard currency basket.

The contagion of speculative pressures on emerging market currencies in May was selective. The countries to which the run on the baht spread had, in the view of investors, a number of features in common with Thailand. Within Asia, Malaysia, Indonesia, and the Philippines had all been affected by the slowdown in

the region, though to varying degrees. All had current account deficits, though of a smaller magnitude than that of Thailand, and most had accumulated debt rapidly during the 1990s, though again to a lesser extent. All had undergone booms in the property sector, and all had varying degrees of financial sector fragilities. The Czech Republic shared many of these features and had perhaps even more similarities with Thailand than the affected Asian countries did. Among currencies not affected by the contagion was the Korean won, even though there were many parallels in economic circumstance with Thailand. Several observers have noted that this was perhaps because

Korea's debt levels were lower, because the substantial depreciation of the won during the last year and a half had left it at a more appropriate level, or because the recent appreciation of the yen would have greater benefits for Korea than its neighbors. While these factors may have played a role, it should be noted that, unlike the Czech Republic and the Asian economies that were attacked, Korea restricts won credit to foreign residents, and the foreign exchange markets, particularly the forward market, are undeveloped. Simply put, this makes it difficult for foreign investors to speculate against the won.

In the wake of the volatility in emerging market currencies following the Mexican peso crisis in late 1994, a strong demand developed for products with which foreign investors could hedge exchange rate risk on emerging market investments. Such hedging has often been hindered by underdeveloped local forward and futures foreign exchange markets in these countries or by capital controls prohibiting or limiting such transactions, and this situation has led to the development of a number of products offshore. Since May 1995, futures exchanges in New York and Chicago have offered a variety of products including options on the Mexican new peso and Brazilian real futures. A particularly notable development has been the use of OTC nondeliverable forward (NDF) contracts in emerging market currencies. While markets exist for a variety of currencies in London and New York, the Asian segment of the NDF market has been particularly active. The market, which operates between banks and brokers in Singapore and Hong Kong, China, is estimated to have daily volumes of between $500 million and $800 million, and market participants expect it to continue to grow over the coming year. NDF contracts allow agents to take notional forward positions in currencies for which restrictions exist in the forward market or for which an established forward market is absent. NDFs in New Taiwan dollars, Korean won, Philippine pesos, Indian rupees, Chinese yuan, and Vietnamese dong trade actively in Singapore and Hong Kong, China. A typical contract works as follows. Counterparties establish a price for the contract at the start date. The contract is then settled at maturity based upon a rate indexed to the underlying currency. Settlement is made in U.S. dollars and no local currency is paid or received. Agents can, therefore, manage foreign exchange exposures without violating local exchange control restrictions.

Bond Markets

Several factors acted in concert to create a spectacular rally in emerging debt markets during 1996.[6] These included, first and perhaps foremost, the low-yield environment in the mature markets. While inter-

est rates remained at low levels in Japan and Germany, there was a compression of spreads on the U.S. corporate bond market as improved business prospects lowered perceived corporate credit risk. This spurred fixed-income investors from the mature markets to search for higher yields on emerging debt markets during 1996 and into 1997. Second, improvements in underlying fundamentals in many emerging markets resulted in both formal upgrades of sovereign credit ratings and in perceptions of reduced credit risks. Third, the continued diversification of the portfolios of institutional investors from the mature markets into the emerging markets boosted the ongoing process of securitization in international capital markets. Fourth, Japanese and European retail interest in emerging market debt continued to be sustained at high levels.

The coincidence of these factors interacted to reinforce interest in emerging debt markets. First, as lower perceived credit risks narrowed spreads, one of the ways investors sought to pick up yield was to seek out longer-maturity issues. This favorable environment prompted several sovereign borrowers to launch new issues to restructure existing liabilities at improved terms and reduce refinancing risk by extending the maturity profile of their external debt. This further lowered perceived credit risks, reinforcing demand and narrowing spreads. By creating more comprehensive yield curves for emerging market debt, the new, longer-term sovereign issues improved the ability of international investors to manage, diversify, and hedge their exposures, enhancing the desirability of these instruments. These issues also set benchmarks for domestic corporate bonds, thereby increasing the access of these entities to international bond markets. Second, the decline in spreads also led investors to move down the credit spectrum in search of higher yields, facilitating the entrance of several new—that is, first-time—borrowers, both sovereign and corporate, hence increasing the size and breadth of the market. Finally, increased investor interest was associated with dramatic improvements in the liquidity of emerging debt markets, enhancing the attractiveness of these instruments.

While the liquidity of emerging debt markets improved substantially during 1996, two characteristics suggest lingering market imperfections. First, yield spread differentials between the Brady and Eurobond sectors endured, suggesting continued market segmentation. Second, the dramatic decline in emerging market spreads in an environment of low interest rates in the mature markets raised questions about whether the compression of spreads had been excessive.

Secondary Markets

Spreads and Returns

Spreads on emerging market debt, which have been declining since the peak reached in the spring of 1995 in the aftermath of the Mexican crisis, continued to

---

[6]See footnote 24 in Chapter IV above.

Figure 24. Bond Markets: Selected Returns, Yields, and Spreads

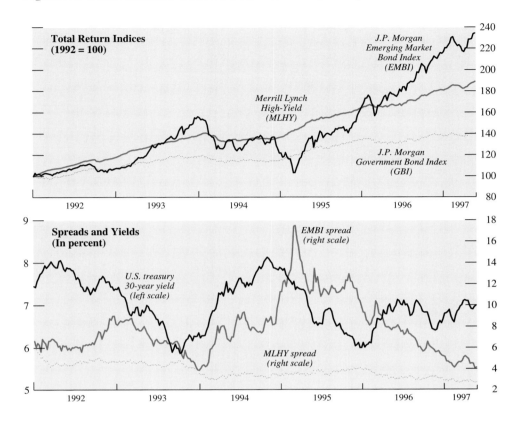

Source: Bloomberg Financial Markets L.P.

decline during 1996 (Figure 24).[7] Sovereign yield spreads, for example, in the J.P. Morgan Emerging Market Bond Index (EMBI), fell from their peak of 1752 basis points in March 1995 to 1044 basis points at the end of 1995, then to 537 basis points by the end of December 1996.[8] Total returns on the EMBI rose from a robust 27 percent in 1995, to 34 percent during 1996. These returns were in contrast to sharp declines in returns in the mature markets, with returns on the J.P. Morgan Government Bond Index for the United States (GBI) dropping to 3.4 percent in 1996 from 17 percent in 1995, and returns on the Merrill Lynch High-Yield (MLHY) index of U.S. corporate bonds dropping to 11 percent from 20 percent.[9]

In early 1997, emerging market spreads continued to decline, falling by the third week of February to about their previous historic lows of around 400 basis points, last reached in late 1993 and early 1994. As spreads had last reached their historic lows in the period preceding the run-up in U.S. interest rates during 1994 that ushered in the Mexican crisis, these levels gave rise to concerns that yields had reached their lower limits in adequately compensating for risk. Spreads then fluctuated, widening at first, then narrowing again, and returns on the EMBI dropped off to 2.6 percent during the first quarter of 1997, though they continued to exceed those of the GBI, with losses of 1.1 percent, and the MLHY, with returns of 1.4 percent. Starting in the last week of February 1997 there was a sharp correction, and by the time the U.S. federal funds rate was raised in the third week of March, emerging market spreads had risen by around 60 basis points. Following the 25 basis point hike in the U.S. federal funds rate, emerging market spreads widened by an additional 60 basis points through mid-April, having risen a total of 120 basis points over a two-month period. Spreads then fell by about 75 basis points through May 1997, to around 450 basis points,

[7]*Spreads* refer to yield differentials relative to comparable government securities in that currency. Spreads in the J.P. Morgan Emerging Market Bond Index (EMBI) are relative to U.S. treasuries.

[8]Most emerging market bond indices heavily weight Latin American Brady debt. (In the EMBI, for example, they receive a weight of 91 percent.) As discussed below, Brady bonds are among the most liquid emerging market debt instruments.

[9]The MLHY is an index of high-yield U.S. corporate bonds that are rated below investment grade. All of the sovereigns in the EMBI were rated below investment grade during 1996.

Figure 25. Yield Spreads for Selected Brady Bonds and U.S. Dollar-Denominated Eurobonds[1]
(In basis points)

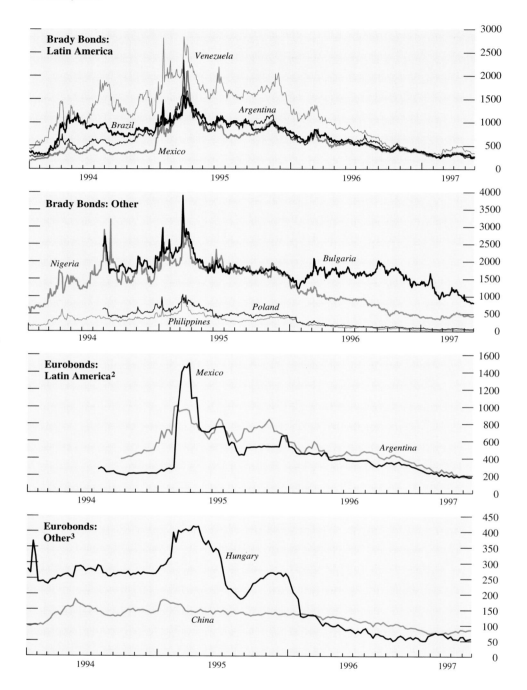

Sources: Bloomberg Financial Markets L.P.; Salomon Brothers; and IMF staff estimates.
[1]Yield spreads on Brady bonds are "stripped" yields.
[2]Latin America: Republic of Argentina bond due 12/03 and United Mexican States bond due 9/02.
[3]Other: National Bank of Hungary bond due 6/98 and People's Republic of China bond due 11/03.

some 50 basis points above their historical lows. (Factors driving the compression of emerging market spreads over the recent period are discussed at the end of this section.)

Figure 25 shows that the decline in spreads on emerging market debt during 1996 and early 1997 and the subsequent correction were, with few exceptions, across the board. In the Brady market, the decline in stripped yield spreads for each of the major Latin countries brought them below precrisis levels by mid-1996. While Mexico had enjoyed a spread substantially below the other major Latin countries prior to the crisis, it has not done so since. Bulgaria was a notable exception to the broad-based decline in spreads during 1996, with the stripped yield spread on its Bradys widening early in the year, and then declining sharply in early 1997 with the announcement of plans to proceed with a currency board. On the secondary market for Eurobonds, Hungarian spreads fell by more than 100 basis points over the period, to 70 basis points, while those for China fell by 50 basis points.

Reflecting both changes in perceptions of credit risk and the relatively lower liquidity of emerging debt markets, returns on emerging market debt have been considerably more volatile than those on mature market debt (Figure 26, top panel). The volatility of returns on the EMBI rose steadily, from about 1 percent in early 1993 through the Mexican crisis, peaking in mid-1995 at 3 percent. Volatility has since declined steadily, falling by May 1997 to 1.5 percent. The close correspondence between the level and volatility of spreads—both rising and falling together—indicates that while the rise in yields during 1994–95 and the subsequent period of turnaround tended to be erratic, suggesting increased uncertainty of credit risk, the subsequent decline in spreads was accompanied by diminishing uncertainty.[10] Despite the reversals in yields during the early part of 1997, volatility continued to diminish. Throughout the period, the volatility of returns on the GBI and the MLHY have remained relatively stable around 0.5 percent and 0.4 percent, respectively.

An important consideration for investors from the mature markets in emerging market debt is the gains from diversification of their portfolios. These gains depend on the correlation of returns between the emerging and mature markets. The bottom panel of Figure 26 presents the correlation of returns on the

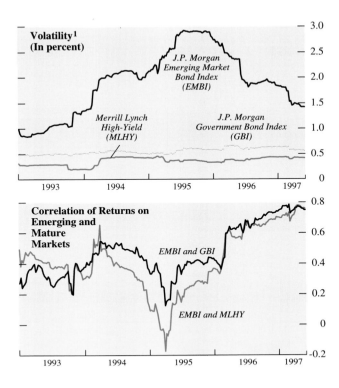

Figure 26. Emerging Market Debt: Volatility and Correlation of Returns with Mature Markets

Sources: Bloomberg Financial Markets L.P.; and IMF staff estimates.
[1]Computed as the standard deviation of weekly changes in (the logarithm of) the total return index over the preceding year.

EMBI and the mature markets.[11] It shows that after a low in early 1995 following the Mexican crisis, returns on emerging market debt and both U.S. treasuries and high-yield U.S. corporate bonds have tended to be highly positively correlated, with the correlation of returns recently reaching almost 0.8. This suggests that the benefits of diversification among the emerging and mature debt markets have been diminishing.

Turnover

The surge of investor interest combined with the growing volume of new issuance resulted in a tremendous growth of trading in all types of emerging market debt instruments and derivatives. After remaining unchanged in 1995, transactions in emerging market debt instruments increased by 93 percent, to $5,296 billion in 1996 (Table 15).[12] Brady bonds remained

---

[10]As both spreads and volatility of emerging market debt declined, movements in the ratio of yields to volatility (not presented) have been more modest. After declining in early 1995, the ratio has fluctuated around a little less than one. It is important to note, however, that the ex post volatility of returns captures only market risk, and though this includes volatility in returns induced by *changes* in perceptions of credit risk, it does not capture the *level* of credit risk. The behavior of such ratios for bonds with default risk can, therefore, be misleading.

[11]The reported correlations are computed for weekly changes over the preceding year.
[12]See Emerging Markets Traders Association (1997).

**Table 15. Secondary Market Transactions in Debt Instruments
of Emerging Markets**

(In billions of U.S. dollars)

	1993	1994	1995	1996	1997:Q1
Total turnover	1,978.9	2,766.2	2,738.8	5,296.9	1,620.6
By region					
Africa	78.8	110.0	108.8	222.4	53.4
Asia	16.4	23.5	26.3	165.8	30.7
Eastern Europe	104.5	172.3	314.2	612.7	161.5
Middle East	2.8	2.6	5.3	21.2	6.6
Western Hemisphere	1,621.6	2,259.3	2,284.2	4,265.9	1,366.8
Unspecified	154.8	198.5	. . .	8.9	1.6
By instrument					
Loans	273.6	244.4	175.1	248.6	68.9
Brady bonds	1,021.3	1,684.0	1,580.1	2,686.0	671.4
Corporate and non-Brady sovereign bonds	176.6	164.9	233.3	658.1	361.4
Local market instruments[1]	361.9	518.9	571.1	1,187.9	427.4
Options and warrants on debt	57.4	142.4	179.2	471.0	90.8
Unspecified	88.1	11.6	. . .	45.3	0.7

Source: Emerging Markets Traders Association.

[1]Data for 1993 do not include trading in short-term local market instruments.

the most traded instrument, with transactions increasing by 70 percent to $2,686 billion. Despite the sharp increases in turnover of Brady bonds, their share in total trading has continued to decline steadily, falling from 61 percent in 1994 to 58 percent in 1995, and 51 percent in 1996. Similarly, the share of loans traded in the market has continued to decline as the stock of loans traded has fallen, and in 1996 accounted for 4 percent of activity, compared with a third of all activity in 1992. These declines have been offset by robust increases in the trading of corporate and non-Brady sovereign bonds, of local market instruments, and of derivative instruments on emerging market debt. With the rapid increase in primary issuance, turnover of corporate and non-Brady sovereign bonds rose almost threefold to $658.1 billion, and their market share expanded from 8.5 percent in 1995 to 12 percent in 1996. Trading of local emerging market instruments doubled during 1996 to $1,187.9 billion.[13] The steady growth of this segment of the market, which in 1996 accounted for 22 percent, is a particularly significant development since it suggests the increasing acceptance of emerging market debt into the mainstream. Reflecting the growing maturity of the secondary market for emerging market debt, trading in options and warrants also continued to grow rapidly, contributing 9 percent to total turnover in 1996.

Trading in Latin American instruments continued to dominate the market, accounting for 80 percent of total trading in 1996, while the debt of four coun-

tries—Brazil, Argentina, Mexico, and Venezuela—accounted for 77 percent of all trading activity. Brazilian instruments were the most commonly traded ($1,441 billion—27 percent), followed closely by Argentine ($1,292 billion—25 percent) and Mexican ($946 billion—18 percent) instruments. There was a significant increase in the volume of trading in several Asian instruments. In particular, trading in Indonesian, Thai, and Malaysian debt totaled $75 billion, compared with negligible amounts in 1995. In other segments, there was also tremendous growth in volumes of South African instruments, which rose fourfold to $170 billion, and in Russian instruments, which grew by 160 percent to $380 billion.

Trading volumes surged again in the first quarter of 1997, reaching $1,620 billion, with all of the major trends evident in 1996 continuing. As increases in turnover have exceeded new issuance, there have been substantial improvements in the liquidity of emerging market debt instruments. The turnover on Brady bonds, for example, increased from $1,580 billion in 1995 to $2,686 billion in 1996, while the outstanding stock of Brady bonds increased only modestly over the period, from around $148 billion to $156 billion (these figures should be viewed as only broadly indicative as there are wide disparities in turnover across Brady bonds). This implies that, on average, each dollar face value of Brady bonds turned over 17 times in 1996 compared with 11 times in 1993. While such improvements in liquidity helped further stimulate demand for the instruments, these markets remain small relative to the mature debt markets. The U.S. government bond market, for example, with a marketable stock of around $3.5 trillion, is estimated to have a daily turnover of $200 billion—more than the

---

[13]The coverage of transactions in local instruments is limited to external trading of local instruments, that is, purchases and sales of local instruments arranged with counterparties outside of the jurisdiction of the issuer.

Box 2. The Brady Bond Market Comes of Age

Since the first restructuring of Mexico's defaulted sovereign loans into Brady bonds in 1990, the Brady market has grown to become the largest and most liquid emerging debt market. The investor base, composed originally of commercial and investment banks, gradually widened to include mutual funds, insurance companies, and other institutional investors. The number of distinct issuers and diverse characteristics of the different classes of Brady bonds—fixed- and floating-rate, collateralized and uncollateralized—and more recently the availability of derivatives, facilitated a rich set of sovereign and interest rate investment strategies. However, seven years after Mexico turned its defaulted sovereign loans into the first Bradys, some market participants are forecasting a rapid demise of the market. With the conclusion of a debt restructuring deal in March 1997 for Peru, the stock of outstanding dollar-denominated Brady bonds reached a peak of around $156 billion and has been declining following a series of buybacks and exchanges for uncollateralized global and Eurobonds. Côte d'Ivoire and Vietnam are expected to be the last significant entrants to the market, but their additions to the stock of Bradys is unlikely to offset the amounts recently retired by Brazil, Ecuador, Panama, and Poland.

As in previous Brady deals, Peru's debt restructuring operation offered a menu of options to creditors, with the government repurchasing $2.6 billion of principal and past-due interest and issuing $4.8 billion of Brady bonds.

Creditor preferences determined the issuance of $2.4 billion in past-due interest bonds (PDIs), $1.7 billion in front-loaded interest reduction bonds (FLIRBs), $560 million in discount bonds, and $182 million in par bonds. The PDI bonds and FLIRBs carry below-market interest rates for the first 10 years, paying LIBOR plus $13/16$ percent thereafter, and have a graduated amortization schedule to maturity in 2017. The discount and the par bonds are collateralized and mature in 2027.

Improved conditions in emerging debt markets following the sustained rally since the Mexican crisis have led several countries to buy back and/or exchange their outstanding Brady bonds, mainly the collateralized instruments, at significantly lower spreads. Following the high-profile exchange in April 1996, Mexico used the proceeds of a 20-year global bond to retire $1.2 billion of discount bonds in September and called the remaining $1.1 billion of Aztec bonds in early 1997. In a deal that mimicked the Mexican swap, the Philippines exchanged one-third of its par bonds for a $690 million 20-year uncollateralized Eurobond in September 1996. The exchange freed up $183 million of collateral in U.S. treasury bonds. Ecuador, Panama, and Poland also followed this strategy and bought back some $250 million, $600 million, and $1.7 billion of Brady bonds, respectively. More recently, Brazil—the largest Brady country, with almost $50 billion in bonds outstanding—exchanged $2.7 billion of Brady bonds for a 30-year uncollateralized global bond.

---

entire stock of outstanding Brady bonds. As discussed below, the small size of emerging debt markets, and the potential ability of large trades to move the market, have contributed to inefficiencies and arbitrage opportunities between segments of the markets. In particular, persistent spread differentials between Brady bonds and Eurobonds with equivalent sovereign risk have raised questions as to whether these securities are priced appropriately and why these differentials have not been arbitraged. Since several countries have recently retired their Brady bonds, and others are expected to do so in the near future, this has raised further concerns about the size and liquidity of emerging debt markets as the stock of Brady bonds diminishes (see Box 2).

Market Segmentation: The Brady-Eurobond Differential

Figure 25 suggests that yields on Eurobonds have typically been lower than on Brady bonds. (Note the differences in scale for the Latin Brady bonds and Eurobonds.) The reported differential, however, reflects in part the fact that these bonds have different maturities, and the yields are not directly comparable. Moreover, many Brady bonds are partially collateralized by

U.S. treasury discount bonds, while the more recently issued Eurobonds are not. The yield spreads reported on those Bradys that are collateralized are "stripped" yields, that is, yields after the value of the collateral has been subtracted from the value of the bond.[14] Since the Bradys and Eurobonds have very different cash-flow patterns, rather than comparing yields and maturities, Figure 27 compares yields relative to duration.[15] It is apparent that spreads on Brady bonds exceed those on Eurobonds, and the differentials can be substantial. On the date shown (April 11, 1997), for example, the Argentine floating-rate bond was some 175 basis points above the comparable Eurobond, while the par bond was some 285 basis points above. The yield differential between the Mexican par and discount Bradys and the Eurobond yield spreads was some 210 basis points.

Market participants have offered various explanations for the persistence of these yield differentials.

---

[14]In practice, different approaches (assumptions in the event of default) have been used to value the rolling interest guarantees, resulting in a range of stripped yield estimates.

[15]*Duration* is defined as the weighted average term to maturity of the cash flows from a bond, where the weights represent the present value of the cash flow relative to the price of the bond.

Figure 27. Brady and Eurobond Spreads[1]
(In basis points)

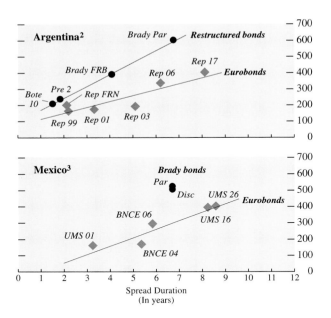

Source: J.P. Morgan.
[1]As on April 11, 1997.
[2]Restructured bonds: Brady Par = Brady par bonds due 2023; Brady FRB = floating rate bond due 2005; Pre 2 = U.S. Pensioner I due 2001; and Bote 10 = 10-year U.S. dollar-denominated domestic government debt due 2000. Eurobonds: Rep 99, etc. = Republic of Argentina bond due 1999; and Rep FRN = floating-rate note due 1999.
[3]Brady bonds: Par = par bond and Disc = discount bond due 2019. Eurobonds: UMS 01, etc. = United Mexican States bond due 2001; and BNCE 04, etc. = Banco Nacional de Comercio Exterior bond due 2004.

Many of the explanations put forward are unconvincing. Some suggest a lack of investor sophistication, and some a lack of liquidity. First, it has been argued that since Brady bonds represent restructured loans, they carry the stigma of prior defaults, whereas Eurobonds are original-issue debt. For such aspects of debt to affect yield requires that investors perceive that there is a greater risk of default on the Brady bonds than on Eurobonds, despite the fact that rating agencies assign identical ratings to sovereigns' Brady and other foreign currency debt.[16] Second, the actual "stripping" of the Brady bonds of their collateral to earn the stripped yield—which requires shorting the collateral, U.S. treasury discount bonds, in a portfolio—entails costs. Market participants place these costs at 40–80 basis points, and they cannot, therefore, provide a complete explanation of the 175–300 basis point differentials. Third, the unusual cash-flow patterns—such as below-market coupons—of Brady

[16]See Standard & Poor's (1996).

bonds may have prompted investors to demand higher yields on Brady bonds. Durations are employed in Figure 27 precisely to make different cash flows comparable. Fourth, since many of the Eurobonds are bearer securities, some investors may be willing to pay a premium—give up yield—for anonymity that allows them to forgo registering the securities. Fifth, Eurobonds have lower volatilities than Brady bonds, and so investors may require a lower yield. While this may be true, it may reflect the fact that Eurobonds trade less frequently than Bradys. The relative magnitudes of turnover discussed above suggest that the Bradys are more liquid than Eurobonds. Sixth, all Brady bonds are callable at par while most of the more recently issued Eurobonds are not. As the prices of emerging market debt have risen rapidly over the past two years with, for example, the Mexican discount bond trading in the low 90s recently, the value of the call feature on Brady bonds has become a consideration. (The value of the call option is also a consideration across different Bradys—with, for example, the Mexican par bond trading recently in the high 70s compared with the discount bond trading recently in the 90s.) For most of the period since their inception, however, the call option has been so far out-of-the-money that its value has been insignificant.[17] Finally, carrying out an arbitrage trade of buying Bradys and selling Eurobonds, which requires carrying out a repo, is expensive. As the size of particular Eurobond issues has been relatively small, and some are often traded infrequently, many of the Eurobonds trade "special" in the repo market, rendering arbitrage prohibitively expensive. Any sizable transaction would, therefore, be likely to move the market.

Primary Issues

The rally in emerging debt markets provoked a sharp shift in the structure of external financing for emerging markets toward bond issuance. International bond placements by emerging market entities soared in 1996 to $102 billion, far exceeding the previous record of $63 billion in 1993 (Table 16 and Figure 12). Issuance from all regions—with the exception of Africa—rose sharply. The increase was particularly marked for Latin America, where issuance more than

[17]In early 1990, for example, the Mexican discounts were trading in the mid-50s, and though prices rose relatively steadily through late 1993, they rose above 90 only very briefly—three months during end-1993 and early 1994—so that the value of the call option has been insignificant for much of the period since their issue.

In addition, certain Brady bonds—of oil-exporting countries such as Mexico—contain embedded options called Value Recovery Rights (VRR) that provide cash flows when oil prices hit a trigger level. Once the stripped yield on Brady bonds is adjusted for the VRR, the yield differential between Brady bonds and Eurobonds—for example for Mexico, whose bonds have such an option—would be even larger than in Figure 27.

Table 16. Emerging Market Bond Issues, Equity Issues, and Syndicated Loan Commitments

(In millions of U.S. dollars)

	1990	1991	1992	1993	1994	1995	1996	1997:Q1
Bond issues[1]								
Emerging markets	7,789	13,945	24,394	62,672	56,540	57,619	101,926	27,723
Africa	0	311	724	170	2,116	1,947	1,648	0
Asia	2,604	4,072	5,908	21,998	29,897	25,307	43,144	12,748
Europe	2,335	2,077	4,829	9,658	3,543	6,583	7,408	2,824
Middle East	0	400	0	2,052	2,993	710	2,570	275
Western Hemisphere	2,850	7,085	12,933	28,794	17,990	23,071	47,157	11,876
Equity issues								
Emerging markets	1,166	5,574	7,247	11,915	18,038	11,193	16,414	3,203
Africa	0	143	154	215	574	542	781	0
Asia	900	952	2,914	5,156	12,130	8,864	9,789	2,873
Europe	97	81	21	186	641	570	1,289	157
Middle East	70	506	281	336	89	256	894	93
Western Hemisphere	98	3,891	3,876	6,022	4,604	962	3,661	80
Syndicated loan commitments								
Emerging markets	28,377	50,669	42,488	43,015	55,156	74,933	79,737	21,367
Africa	2,127	6,426	6,214	2,327	569	6,929	2,658	932
Asia	12,541	15,613	20,069	26,130	35,502	40,402	49,488	13,638
Europe	9,139	10,257	5,753	4,484	8,361	10,511	11,457	1,473
Middle East	1,089	12,119	3,602	2,456	6,995	7,323	5,836	1,436
Western Hemisphere	3,480	6,255	6,851	7,618	3,729	9,768	10,297	3,888
Short-term commitments[2]								
Emerging markets	4,423	5,247	8,245	11,868	14,312	21,565	30,458	7,352
Africa	83	494	96	155	449	2,237	3,701	99
Asia	3,116	2,417	3,090	5,733	8,272	14,628	20,374	5,252
Europe	775	522	336	1,177	1,245	1,198	3,136	1,611
Middle East	350	44	369	25	52	14	0	0
Western Hemisphere	100	1,770	4,355	4,778	4,295	3,487	3,248	390
Total								
Emerging markets	41,755	75,435	82,374	129,470	144,046	165,310	228,535	59,645
Africa	2,210	7,374	7,188	2,867	3,708	11,655	8,788	1,031
Asia	19,161	23,054	31,981	59,017	85,801	89,201	122,795	34,511
Europe	12,346	12,937	10,939	15,505	13,790	18,862	23,290	6,065
Middle East	1,509	13,069	4,252	4,869	10,129	8,303	9,300	1,804
Western Hemisphere	6,528	19,001	28,015	47,212	30,618	37,288	64,363	16,234

Sources: Capital Data Bondware and Loanware.

[1]Including note issues under Euro medium-term note (EMTN) programs.

[2]Commercial paper, certificates of deposit, revolving credits, and trade finance.

doubled, from $23.1 billion in 1995 to $47.2 billion in 1996, while its share in total issuance rose from 40 percent to 47 percent. The three largest borrowers—Mexico, Argentina, and Brazil—raised $18 billion, $14 billion, and $11 billion, respectively, accounting for over 90 percent of issuance from the region. Asian issuance rose from $25.3 billion in 1995 to $43.1 billion in 1996, while the share in total issuance remained steady at 43 percent. Following the liberalization of external borrowing restrictions, Korean entities were the most active issuers, raising $16 billion, accounting for 38 percent of issues from the region, while Hong Kong, China, Indonesia, and Thailand each raised about $4 billion. While issuance from the European emerging markets rose, their share in total issuance fell to 7 percent, as increases from Russia and Romania were offset by declines from Hungary. Issuance from the Middle East rose to account for

some 3 percent of the total, while that from Africa continued to decline, accounting for 1½ percent.

Sovereign issuance, which had risen sharply in 1995 in the aftermath of the Mexican crisis, as private sector issuance fell off, continued to rise, accounting for 37 percent of issuance in 1996 and 40 percent in the first quarter of 1997. The growth of sovereign issuance was driven by, as noted earlier, the restructuring of previous liabilities at improved terms, the entrance of several new sovereign credits, and the establishment of benchmarks for domestic corporate bonds. In a number of headline deals, several sovereigns bought back or swapped existing Brady bonds for uncollateralized Eurobonds with lower sovereign risk spreads and relatively long maturities, and freed up the collateral on the Brady bonds. With strong demand for the new Eurobond issues, many of the placements were heavily oversubscribed. In September

Figure 28. Spreads and Maturities for Sovereign Borrowers[1]

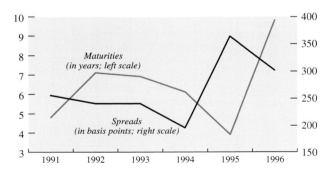

Source: Capital Data Bondware.
[1]Unenhanced U.S. dollar-denominated bonds.

1996, Mexico followed up its April exchange of Brady bonds for $1.8 billion uncollateralized dollar-denominated 30-year global bonds, by using the proceeds of a $1 billion issue to retire a further $1.2 billion of discount bonds. In the same month, the Philippines launched a $690 million 20-year bond in exchange for Brady bonds. The Mexican and Philippine transactions were widely viewed as forerunners for other such exchanges and as heralding the eventual demise of the Brady market. More recently, in June 1997, Brazil swapped a 30-year $3 billion global bond for $2.7 billion (face value) of Brady bonds and $750 million of new money. Among the newly rated sovereign credits, in November 1996, Russia placed a $1 billion five-year issue, its first since 1917 and the largest-ever debut issue by an emerging market sovereign.

There was a broad-based improvement in the terms of issuance for borrowers (Figure 28 and Table 17). Spreads declined, maturities lengthened, the proportion of fixed-rate issues increased, and the proportion

of callable bonds rose. While the average spread for unenhanced dollar issues actually increased from 218 basis points in 1995 to 244 basis points in 1996, this reflected higher average spreads on private sector issues as the spectrum of borrowing entities expanded and maturities lengthened. For sovereign issues, spreads declined from an average of 383 basis points in 1995 to 307 basis points in 1996. There was an impressive lengthening of yield curves as several issuers placed 10-, 20-, 30-, and even some 100-year bonds. During 1996 and the first quarter of 1997, some 175 issues, or almost a quarter of all issues by emerging market entities, had maturities of 10 or more years, while six entities issued 100-year bonds.[18] The average maturity of new issues in the dollar sector rose from 6.6 years in 1995 to 7.7 years in 1996, while sovereign maturities, after having shortened to 4.5 years in 1995, rose dramatically to 9.5 years during 1996. The search for higher yields also appeared to shift issuance in favor of fixed-rate issues, as investors traded yield for interest rate risk. The proportion of fixed-rate issues rose from 67 percent in 1995 to 70 percent in 1996, and to 72 percent in the first quarter of 1997. Similarly, bonds with call options, offering a pickup in yield for the risk of the call being exercised, rose from 13 percent in 1995 to 21 percent in 1996.

The U.S. dollar has traditionally been the primary currency in which international issues of emerging market debt have been denominated, accounting for some 70 percent during 1990–94 (Table 18). A remarkable change in the last two years has been the growing diversity of currencies of issuance. The currency sectors targeted by issuers have not always corresponded to the pattern of their export earnings, as issuers have sought to take advantage of pockets of strong local investor—often retail—interest, some-

---

[18]These were the People's Republic of China, the Endesa Chile Overseas Company, India's Reliance Industries, the Israel Electric Corporation, the Korean Electric Power Company, and Malaysia's Tenaga Nasional Berhad.

Table 17. Emerging Market Bond Issues: Fixed-Rate, Floating-Rate, and Call Options[1]
(In percent)

	1990	1991	1992	1993	1994	1995	1996	1997:Q1
Fixed-rate issues as a percentage of total issues								
Number of issues	61.3	48.9	69.5	67.7	43.4	52.3	57.4	54.8
Issue amount	69.4	64.5	75.0	74.2	48.3	67.1	69.6	73.6
Floating-rate issues as a percentage of total issues								
Number of issues	13.3	13.5	10.8	10.8	29.7	32.7	27.6	31.5
Issue amount	8.9	6.9	7.9	8.2	26.5	27.0	22.5	18.0
Callable as a percentage of total issues								
Number of issues	20.0	30.8	11.2	18.5	30.4	25.1	27.8	21.0
Issue amount	11.3	18.4	8.5	15.5	25.1	12.8	21.1	13.7

Source: Capital Data Bondware.
[1]The combined total for fixed- and floating-rate bonds may not add to 100 percent because convertible and unclassified bonds are excluded.

Table 18. Emerging Market International Bond Issues by Currency of Denomination

(In percent)

	1990	1991	1992	1993	1994	1995	1996	1997:Q1
Share in total issues by emerging markets								
U.S. dollar	60	68	70	74	75	57	69	68
Deutsche mark	26	12	9	7	3	10	11	16
Yen	10	13	16	13	13	26	14	8
Other	4	7	5	6	9	7	6	8
Asia								
U.S. dollar	65	62	70	81	72	70	79	83
Deutsche mark	11	2	2	1	1	3	1	4
Yen	19	30	22	14	16	19	16	11
Other	5	6	6	4	11	8	4	2
Western Hemisphere								
U.S. dollar	85	88	92	88	89	56	64	63
Deutsche mark	12	5	5	4	5	18	17	20
Yen	0	0	0	3	4	22	11	4
Other	3	7	3	5	4	4	8	13
Europe								
U.S. dollar	24	14	22	12	31	18	44	21
Deutsche mark	60	49	21	34	12	14	29	58
Yen	11	25	52	45	44	61	25	15
Other	5	12	5	9	13	7	2	6
Share in total issues in global bond markets								
U.S. dollar	35	31	37	39	41	40	43	43
Deutsche mark	7	7	10	11	7	14	11	9
Yen	13	13	13	12	18	18	13	8
Other	45	49	40	38	34	28	33	40

Sources: Capital Data Bondware; and IMF staff estimates.

times tailoring issues to investor preferences, and suggesting that primary markets for emerging market debt remain segmented. The spate of issues in a host of currencies has continued to raise concerns about pricing in nontraditional sectors—that investors may be underpricing credit risk and issuers underestimating exchange rate risk. Little information is available on the extent to which the proceeds from emerging market borrowing have been swapped into currencies matching their export earnings patterns and, therefore, on their exposure to exchange rate movements among the major currencies.

Following the surge in yen issuance after the liberalization of rating requirements on the Samurai market in 1995, the value of yen issuance (in yen) remained steady in 1996, though the share in total issuance (measured in dollars) fell from 26 percent to 14 percent. Retail investor demand in Japan remained strong and is estimated to have accounted for about half of the purchases. Emerging market issues also continued to receive positive receptions in the deutsche mark sector, and the share of deutsche mark issuance remained steady at around 10 percent in 1996. Strong retail investor interest was evidenced by the successful repackaging by investment banks of

outstanding Latin American Brady bonds and other bonds into deutsche mark–denominated bonds that were predominantly sold to German retail investors (see Box 3). Although the proportion of "other" currencies of issuance remained unchanged, there was a shift to new and largely untapped currency sectors as borrowers sought new niches. The lira sector was particularly active, with an unprecedented $3.7 billion of issuance since the beginning of 1996, with large sovereign issues by Argentina and Mexico. With the decline of Italian interest rates prompting a strong interest in these issues, the authorities limited emerging market issues in the sector to two a month. Moreover, there were a number of issues in French francs, Dutch guilders, Australian dollars, and pounds sterling.

The share of dollar issuance by all emerging market borrowers rose from 57 percent in 1995 to 69 percent in 1996—about its level during 1990–94. While the share of total dollar issuance returned to its historical level, there remained some notable shifts in currency composition across regions. The most notable shift has been the increase of the nondollar segment for Latin America, where dollar issues, which had accounted for almost 90 percent of issuance during 1990–94, represented only 64 percent during 1996.

Box 3. Repackaged Brady Bonds

"Repackaged" or "synthetic" Brady bonds are structured asset-backed securities in which the underlying asset is a portfolio of Brady bonds and the structure is provided by a credit derivative providing for a reduction, or suspension, of payment if a credit event involving the issuer of the Brady bond occurs (see Appendix 1, "Credit Derivatives," to Annex III). These credit-linked notes are issued by an offshore trust or special purpose vehicle that holds the underlying Brady bonds, usually with a significant degree of overcollateralization. Most repackaged Brady bonds are sold to retail investors in Germany and are denominated in deutsche mark at fixed interest rates, so the issuer will, if necessary, swap the income from the Brady bonds into fixed-rate deutsche mark. Hence, the investor acquires a hedged exposure to emerging market credit that earns a significant premium over German government bonds.

The first public repackagings of Brady bonds in 1992 involved Venezuelan Debt Conversion Bonds, but the market for Brady repackagings really only developed in 1996—in 1993–94 there had been a large number of repackagings of Mexican tesobonos and some other non-Brady debt. Since 1992 there have been at least 76 public repackagings of emerging market debt with a total value of $6.6 billion. Repackaged Brady bonds have accounted for $2.1 billion—most of the remainder was composed of Brazil Multi-Year Deposit Facility Agreement bonds ($1.3 billion) and repackaged Mexican tesobonos ($1.1 billion). The most common sovereign risks identified in the repackagings were Brazil ($2 billion in repackaged bonds), Mexico ($1.2 billion), Venezuela ($737 million), and Argentina ($513 million). Other countries whose bonds have been repackaged include Ecuador, Mexico, Russia, and Turkey.

These bonds provide a means of arbitraging yield differentials between different investor bases—a comparatively high demand in Germany for deutsche mark–denominated emerging market credit—and between different classes of bonds (Eurobonds versus Bradys). However, if such transactions increase in popularity, credit-linked bonds may have a detrimental effect on liquidity in the markets for emerging market debt—since the Brady bonds are stored in trusts and replaced by relatively illiquid Eurobonds. Also, credit-linked bonds are issued by private firms but provide exposure to sovereign credit risk, and therefore compete for investor interest against new sovereign debt, possibly increasing the borrowing costs for emerging market issuers.

The proportion of dollar issuance by Asian entities on the other hand was some 10 percentage points higher in 1996 than it has been historically.

International issuance of emerging market debt has traditionally been in the major convertible currencies, requiring issuers to bear or manage the inherent exchange rate risk. While investment in domestic currency debt has represented a viable alternative to foreign investors in many emerging debt markets, this channel has been relatively limited.[19] By avoiding domestic currency instruments and thus avoiding exchange rate risk, however, given the typically higher interest rates in emerging markets, they sacrificed yield. With investors searching for higher yields, and in another sign of the coming of age of emerging market debt as an international asset class, the last two years have seen the international issuance of debt—by entities from both the emerging and mature markets—in previously untapped emerging market currency sectors. Many of these markets were created by inaugural issues by supranationals (including the European Bank for Reconstruction and Development, the European Investment Bank, the Inter-American Development Bank, the International Bank for Reconstruction and Development, and the International Finance Corporation), and some have grown rapidly to include sovereign, bank, and corporate borrowers. Since the development of these sectors, many supranationals have continued to find them attractive sources of funding, tapping them repeatedly as investors have traded higher yields for emerging market currency risk.

Among the Asian currencies, the New Taiwan dollar, the Philippine peso, and the Korean won sectors have been quite small, with issuance of under $1 billion each. In Eastern Europe, the Polish zloty and the Slovak koruna have also featured among the smaller markets. The Czech koruna market, on the other hand, has been very popular, growing quickly to reach $3.4 billion. The market has largely been tapped by supranationals through short-dated bonds at high yields with the supranationals accounting for about a third of issuance, and Austrian, German, and Dutch banks accounting for the remainder. The Argentine peso ($650 million) market generated considerable interest following the issue in January 1997 of a 10-year Arg$500 million bond that focused attention on relatively cheap peso debt and extended the local currency yield curve from 2 to 10 years. The most active emerging market currency sector has been the South African rand, growing from its inception in 1995 to $17.9 billion of issuance by end-May 1997 (see Box 4).

The favorable environment facing potential issuers in emerging debt markets caused a frenzy of first-time

---

[19]Foreign investment in domestic currency debt instruments has been hindered in some emerging markets by the lack of well-developed domestic markets, and sometimes by capital controls preventing foreign investment in them. Traditionally, Latin America has had better-developed and more accessible domestic bond markets than Asia.

Box 4. Emerging Market Currency Eurobonds: The Eurorand Market

Recently, offshore issuance and trading in South African rand-denominated debt have grown rapidly. Following its inception in September 1995, issuance activity in the Eurorand market remained relatively modest, with issuance of around $1 billion annually in 1995–96. During the first half of 1997, issuance surged to over $15 billion, while the yield curve was extended out to first 10 and then 30 years. The sector has been particularly popular with supranational issuers, who have accounted for about half of the issues. While a wide range of other entities have been active in the sector, including international banks and corporations, these have been almost exclusively from the mature markets. By May 1997, only two South African entities had tapped the sector. It is estimated that less than 10 percent of the funds raised in the sector have been for use in South Africa.

For *investors,* the attraction of Eurorand debt has been the combination of high yields and highly rated issuers. Investors have, therefore, been able to earn rand interest rates, but at lower perceived credit risks than if they invested directly in South Africa, where entities are bound by the sovereign ceiling. By permitting the separation of exchange rate and (sovereign) credit risk, Eurorand debt has been extremely popular with retail investors—particularly in Europe—willing to accept rand exchange rate risk but preferring the lower credit risk of an investment grade issuer, and with institutional investors bound by fund management rules to investment grade issues. The attraction for *issuers* to the Eurorand market has been the low cost of funding. By offering rand exposure without sovereign risk, triple-A-rated issuers have been able to price primary deals typically

some 75 basis points below the South African gilts yield curve. The fact that investors have been willing to accept lower yields from the more highly rated issuers than is available on South African gilts has created a yield gap that has allowed issuers to swap the proceeds with, for example, a highly rated international investment bank or a South African counterparty, to obtain dollar funding rates of 35–40 basis points below LIBOR.

The fact that a majority of the funds raised have not been intended for use in South Africa raises the question of what effect the Eurorand market has on capital flows to South Africa and on the value of the rand. In the first instance, when the rand required for purchase of a Eurorand issue is obtained on the domestic spot market by surrendering dollars, there is a capital inflow into South Africa. There are then a variety of possibilities, and the net effect could be neutral or positive for capital flows and foreign exchange markets. First, the issuer could exchange the rand raised for dollars on the domestic spot market, implying a capital outflow that offsets the original inflow, and the net effect is zero. Second, the issuer could invest the proceeds in South Africa. In this case there is a net capital inflow equal to the value of the issue. Third, after exchanging the proceeds into dollars, the issuer could enter into a swap to buy rand forward from a domestic South African counterparty, and this would reduce pressure on the forward rand exchange rate. If the issuer enters into a swap with an international investment bank, the investment bank in turn could hedge its risk by, for example, making a leveraged purchase of gilts. In this case, there would be some net inflow, but less than the value of issue.

---

ratings by the major international credit-rating agencies. During 1996, 16 sovereigns, primarily from Eastern Europe and the Middle East (7 from each), were assigned ratings by at least one of the two major international credit-rating agencies. By comparison, only five new sovereigns were assigned ratings in 1995. By May 1997, an additional five countries had received ratings. The number of countries with sovereign ratings from at least one of the major ratings agencies has grown rapidly from 11 in 1989 to 58 in 1996. In addition to the increase in the number of sovereigns rated, there has been a rapid increase in the number of nonsovereign entities in emerging markets that have been rated. This latest round of ratings has more or less completed the waves of regional ratings through the major emerging market regions, again with the exception of Africa.[20] The fact that a major-

ity of the new ratings have been in the investment grade category, coupled with upgrades of existing ratings over the last few years, has resulted in a steadily increasing proportion of investment grade emerging market sovereigns. Compared with 44 percent in 1993, the proportion had risen to 55 percent by May 1997 (based on Moody's ratings). Systematic regional differences among the emerging markets persist, however, as a majority of the Asian emerging markets are rated investment grade, while in Latin America, though ratings have been improving, the majority are still rated below investment grade. The European emerging markets are somewhat evenly split.

Spread Compression in Emerging Debt Markets

Numerous market participants and observers have argued that the low level of interest rates in the mature markets caused investors to substitute risk for increased returns, and that the resulting increase in demand pushed down spreads on riskier securities. This is evidenced, it is argued, not only by the decline in

---

[20]Many of the Asian economies were assigned ratings in the late 1980s, followed by Latin America in the early 1990s, and now the Middle East and Europe.

spreads on emerging market debt instruments but also on other risky assets, such as U.S. corporate bonds. Several market participants have also argued that spreads on sovereign emerging market debt instruments can be expected to decline further, to levels comparable with similarly rated U.S. corporate bonds.

Looking back at Figure 24, it is apparent that sovereign spreads moved closely in line with U.S. interest rates from early 1993 through early 1996, albeit with a lag of three to four months, suggesting that the level of interest rates in the mature markets has played a role in affecting spreads. The historic low in emerging market spreads reached in January 1994 closely followed the bottoming out of U.S. interest rates in October 1993, while the peak in spreads in March 1995 followed the peak in the U.S. interest rate cycle in November 1994. Subsequently, as U.S. interest rates continued to decline through 1995, sovereign spreads also fell, but then continued doing so even as U.S. rates began to rise in February 1996 and then remained at a relatively higher level. The behavior of high-yield U.S. corporate bond spreads, on the other hand, appears to have been relatively independent of the behavior of the level of U.S. interest rates. What is evident is a persistent and substantial decline in MLHY yields over the period, from around 6 percent in early 1992 to 2.8 percent in May 1997, while U.S. interest rates fluctuated considerably over the period.

The differential between sovereign spreads and high-yield U.S. corporate spreads has fluctuated considerably over the period. At the start of 1992, for instance, average yield spreads on the EMBI and the MLHY were equal. Then, after moving apart in early 1992, they converged briefly again in December 1993, before diverging substantially as sovereign spreads widened in the period leading up to and following the Mexican crisis. As both yields fell during 1996, with sovereign spreads declining by more, the differential has once again narrowed, though sovereign yields remained 140 basis points above high-yield U.S. corporate spreads in May 1997.

In a liquid and efficient bond market, such as the U.S. corporate bond market, yields on (straight) corporate bonds relative to a (credit) risk-free benchmark of the same duration should depend on premiums for default risk, market risk, and the correlation of returns with other assets (the market portfolio). Therefore, unless movements in the level of the (credit) risk-free interest rate directly have an impact on the creditworthiness of corporate borrowers, on volatility, or on their correlation with returns on other assets, there is no reason to expect changes in corporate bond spreads to be related to the general level of interest rates. There are a number of features of emerging debt markets, however, that suggest that in contrast to the U.S. corporate bond market, investors would demand additional premiums for holding these instruments. These include the liquidity problems discussed above which,

for example, resulted in persistent yield differentials between Bradys and Eurobonds, incomplete yield curves in emerging market debt instruments, and the lack of a well-developed or liquid derivatives market. Spreads on emerging market debt can in general, therefore, be thought of as representing a combination of premiums for default risk; market risk from volatility due in part to changes in perceptions of default risk; the correlation of returns with other assets; liquidity problems; and the availability—or lack thereof—of related instruments that could be used to manage or hedge market risks from the particular instrument.

Several factors suggest that there are reasons for each of these components to have declined recently. First, improved economic performance in many emerging market countries, including improved prospects for growth, particularly in Latin America, and declines in inflation, lowered perceptions of default risk. The tremendous increase in emerging market holdings of reserves has probably also contributed to declining investor perceptions of default risk on external borrowings. Second, the decline in interest rates in the mature markets directly lowered the required servicing of existing external floating-rate debt for emerging market borrowers, thus lowering overall debt-servicing requirements and improving creditworthiness. In addition, as noted above, the favorable external financing environment allowed many emerging market borrowers to restructure existing liabilities at improved terms, lengthen the maturity profile of external debt, and further improve creditworthiness. Third, since the abatement of the Mexican crisis, the volatility of emerging market debt instruments has declined considerably, suggesting that the premium for volatility should have declined. Fourth, liquidity in emerging market debt instruments has been growing steadily with increases in both the size and turnover in these markets as discussed above. Fifth, the ability of investors to manage risks from holdings of emerging market debt instruments in their portfolios has steadily improved with the lengthening of yield curves on these instruments, permitting increased diversification across maturities, and a filling out of the spectrum of debt-issuing entities across geographic regions, sectors of economic activity, and different risk classes within countries. Risk management has also improved with the growth of derivative products in emerging market instruments.

Has the compression of emerging market spreads been excessive? As discussed above, the behavior of EMBI and MLHY yield spreads suggests that, relative to historical differentials, there remains some room for emerging market spreads to decline to U.S. corporate levels. However, history provides a limited guide to determining whether yield spreads are sufficient to compensate for the risk of future default. The question of whether yields are sufficient to compensate for default risk could be answered directly if the probability of default implicit in market spreads could be identified and compared with independent estimates of the probability of default. Market spreads would clearly be judged to have declined too far if they were insufficient to cover the probability of default—that is, if the spread were decomposed into (1) a premium estimated to be due to the probability of default and (2) a liquidity premium to encompass the variety of other factors potentially affecting demand, and the liquidity premium were found to be negative (since there is no obvious reason to expect that investors would be willing to pay a premium—give up yield—to hold emerging market debt). Estimating default risk for sovereigns requires simulating a country's balance sheet to do a financial risk exercise as is done for a bank or other enterprise. It would then be possible to calculate directly the probability distribution that a country would not be able to meet its payments and hence the probability of default. Few countries, however, publish such balance sheets. This is an important difference between sovereigns and corporates: debt-issuing corporations publish balance sheets and are subject to stricter disclosure requirements. Moreover, the legal framework in the event of corporate default is relatively clear. The volatility of perceived credit risk for emerging market sovereigns is, therefore, likely to be greater. Inherently higher volatility of perceptions of credit risk for sovereigns suggests that yields on sovereigns should exceed those for corporates.

Equity Markets

As several of the mature equity markets reached new highs in 1996, emerging equity markets continued to recover from the trough in early 1995, though cumulative returns since the peak in 1994 remained negative. The effects of the Mexican crisis continued to fade, and the volatility of equity prices—in both Latin America and Asia—subsided during 1996 and into 1997 to levels prior to the crisis, while the recovery of economic prospects in Latin America boosted forecasts of earnings growth. These factors combined to make emerging market equity look increasingly attractive relative to the mature markets, and price increases in Latin America accelerated in early 1997. The recovery in emerging equity markets in 1996 was accompanied by increased liquidity for most markets as turnover rose but new issuance remained subdued. While overall flotations of new equity by the emerging markets continued to decline, there were marked differences across regions, as placements by Latin American entities rebounded while those by Asian entities fell. There was an increased reliance on international issuance across regions, however, and the volume of international issuance increased.

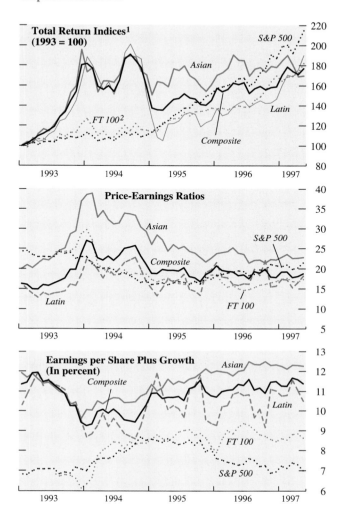

Figure 29. Emerging Equity Markets: Selected Returns, Price-Earnings Ratios, and Expected Returns

Sources: Bloomberg Financial Markets L.P.; International Finance Corporation (IFC), and Emerging Markets Data Base.
[1]All return indices are expressed in U.S. dollars.
[2]Price index.

Secondary Markets

During 1996 emerging equity markets posted their first collective positive return since the boom of 1993, with total dollar returns measured by the International Finance Corporation's Investable (IFCI) Composite Index rising by 9.4 percent (Figure 29).[21] Relative to the mature markets, however, emerging equity markets performed modestly. Returns were substantially higher on the S&P 500 index (23 percent) in the United States, for example. The relatively modest

---

[21]See footnote 26 in Chapter IV above.

overall performance of emerging equity markets during 1996 masked divergent performance across regions. While Latin American equity markets rose by 17 percent and Asian markets by 10 percent, European, Middle Eastern, and African markets fell by 2.3 percent. During the first half of 1996, emerging equity markets rose along with those in the mature markets, with the major regional component indices of the IFCI rising along with the S&P 500 index. In July, as U.S. share prices gyrated downward amid concerns about possible increases in U.S. and international interest rates, the S&P 500 fell by 4.4 percent. Concerns of a spillover into emerging markets, combined with domestic developments, led to a simultaneous decline in emerging stock markets, and the IFCI Composite Index fell by 6.6 percent, as both Asian and Latin equity prices declined sharply. While U.S. share prices recovered quickly and rose rapidly (17 percent) during the remainder of the year, the IFCI Composite Index recovered only somewhat, and was virtually unchanged by the end of the year.

The rise in emerging market equity prices during 1996 accelerated in early 1997, with the IFCI Composite Index rising by 9.5 percent during the first quarter. Latin American markets rose particularly sharply, increasing by 15 percent, while Asian markets rose by 1.2 percent. Again, as during the first seven months of 1996, the emerging and mature stock markets moved in tandem. The S&P 500, and the IFCI Asian and Latin American indices all rose during January and February, and fell in March. In contrast to 1996, however, the collective increase in emerging market equity prices of 9.5 percent during the quarter was well in excess of the increase in the S&P 500 of 2.7 percent. While Asian markets then recovered modestly through May 1997, returns in Latin America once again accelerated, with returns of 13 percent during April and May. Despite the recovery in emerging market equity prices during 1996 and 1997, at their recent peaks they remained below the previous highs of September 1994. While Asian markets in the aggregate regained their previous peak levels in February 1997, before falling again, Latin markets in May remained 5.5 percent below their peak in September 1994.

Price-earnings (P/E) ratios are the most commonly employed summary measures used to discern relative value in equity prices.[22] Figure 29 (middle panel) compares P/E ratios in emerging equity markets with those in the United States and the United Kingdom from January 1993 through May 1997. It is apparent that P/E ratios in emerging markets have not generally

been lower than those in the mature markets. P/E ratios for the Asian emerging markets, in fact, consistently exceeded those in all the other markets over the period, and sometimes substantially so. Latin American P/E ratios, on the other hand, starting from well below those in the mature markets in early 1993, rose steadily to the levels of mature markets as share prices in the region increased through early 1994 without a commensurate increase in earnings. Despite the sharp declines in share prices in early 1995, and their relatively lower level since, P/E ratios for the region have been in the same range as those in the mature markets.

Earnings-price ratios—the inverse of P/E ratios—provide a measure of the yield or expected return on equity in the event earnings are expected to remain constant. When earnings are expected to grow, however, current earnings per share underestimate expected returns. Since growth rates in the emerging markets exceed those in the mature markets—and those in Asia have been well above those in Latin America—a better comparison of expected returns is provided by actual earnings-price ratios plus expected earnings growth. Figure 29 (bottom panel) compares earnings-price ratios plus a proxy for expected earnings growth constructed using forecast GDP growth from the IMF's *World Economic Outlook*.[23] This comparison shows that expected returns on equity in the emerging markets, once adjusted for expected earnings growth, consistently exceeded those in the mature markets during the period. The differential in expected rates of return between the emerging and mature markets has fluctuated within 5 percentage points. From January 1996 through May 1997, the expected return on the composite of emerging market equity rose by about ½ of a percentage point to 11½ percent, while that on the S&P 500 fell by ¾ of a percentage point to 7 percent.

Among the emerging markets, expected returns in Asia have more or less consistently exceeded those in Latin America. Returns in the two regions have, however, tended to remain relatively close together, with changes in the differential among the two stemming largely from the volatility of Latin American returns. This volatility has implied that for brief periods the difference has been as high as 3 percentage points and at other times it has been negligible. There have also been extended periods, such as during much of 1993, when the differential was only ¼ of a percentage point to ½ of a percentage point. From January 1996 through May 1997, expected returns on Latin American equity edged up, albeit somewhat erratically, by 1½ percentage points to 10½ percent, of which some ½ of a percentage point is attributable to upward revi-

---

[22]In that fairly valued share prices should represent the present value of expected earnings, a low P/E ratio—for the same degree of risk—is often interpreted as representing a better value. In comparing equities with different degrees of risk, all else equal, one would expect a lower P/E ratio to be associated with the higher-risk equity, as compensation for the higher risk.

[23]Expected future GDP growth in each period is constructed from the prevailing *World Economic Outlook* forecast as the average GDP growth forecast over the ensuing five years. See IMF (1997).

sions to growth, while those on Asian equity rose modestly by ¼ of a percentage point to 12¼ percent.[24] Consequently, the differential of 3 percentage points at the start of 1996 narrowed to 1¾ percentage points by May 1997.

Higher expected returns on equity in emerging markets relative to the mature markets have been associated with generally higher price and return volatility (Figure 30, top panel), with that in Latin American markets exceeding that in the Asian emerging markets.[25] Volatility in emerging equity markets rose steadily during 1994 in the run-up to the Mexico crisis, plateauing at a considerably higher level during 1995. The rise was substantial in both Latin America and Asia. Volatility in Latin American markets rose from 2 percent in late 1993 to 5 percent by mid-1995, and in Asian markets from 1½ percent to 3 percent. Volatility then declined dramatically during the course of 1996 and continued doing so through May 1997, with that in Latin America falling below its previous low, to 1¾ percent, and that in Asia returning to its previous low of 1½ percent. The behavior of volatility in emerging equity markets was in contrast to that in the United States, where the volatility of the S&P 500 rose steadily during the course of 1996 and into 1997. In fact, by July of 1996, the volatility of the S&P 500 exceeded that of the composite of emerging markets, by October it exceeded that of the Asian emerging markets, and by early May 1997 it exceeded that of the Latin American markets. The middle panel of Figure 30 compares the ratio of expected returns to volatility. It shows that during 1996 and into 1997, as expected returns on emerging market equity rose and volatility declined, risk-adjusted rates of return rose dramatically for both Asian and Latin American markets. In the United States, on the other hand, the run-up in share prices and increase in volatility caused the S&P 500 to look less and less attractive, while in the United Kingdom, after declining during the first half of 1996, the ratio fell during the later part of the year and then stabilized in 1997.[26]

Market participants have pointed to the ongoing process of increased portfolio diversification by institutional investors in the mature markets as playing an important role in driving portfolio flows into emerg-

---

[24]The projected output growth numbers employed for 1997 are based on a forecast date of end-March 1996. Some observers have continued to revise their forecast for growth in Latin America upward and those for Asia downward. Figure 29 may, therefore, underestimate returns in Latin America and overestimate returns in Asia.

[25]Volatilities are computed as the standard deviation of weekly changes in the (logarithm of) prices over the preceding year. The volatility of total returns over the period was very similar.

[26]Besides the higher volatility of returns, however, there are a number of other sources of risk in investing in emerging equity markets. These include inadequate accounting and disclosure practices, limited information, settlement and legal risks, and limited liquidity in some emerging markets.

Figure 30. Emerging Equity Markets: Selected Volatilities, Return-Volatility Comparisons, and Correlations

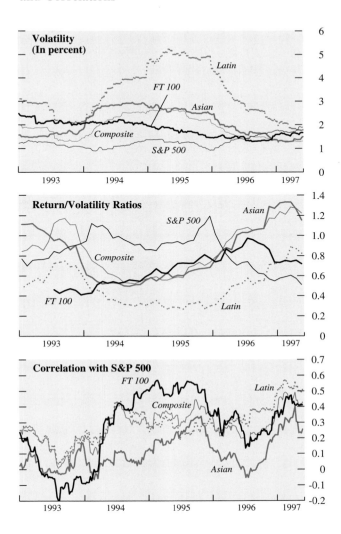

Sources: Bloomberg Financial Markets L.P.; and IMF staff estimates.

ing markets during the 1990s. The benefits of diversification into the emerging markets depend on the (lack of) correlation among returns between the emerging and mature markets. The correlation of price changes between the S&P 500 and the emerging markets, over the period 1992 through May 1997, were as follows: composite emerging 0.26, Latin American 0.27, and Asian 0.09. The correlations between the FT 100 and the emerging markets were as follows: composite emerging 0.32, Latin American 0.24, and Asian 0.21. The correlation between the Latin American and Asian emerging markets was 0.14, and that between the S&P 500 and the FT 100 was 0.29. All of these correlations are relatively small, suggesting considerable benefits from diversification. The weakest correlations, suggesting the greatest benefits from diversification, are between the United States and the Asian emerging markets, and between the Asian and Latin American emerging markets. It is notable that the correlations among the mature markets do not appear to be substantially greater than between the mature and emerging markets. Figure 30 (bottom panel) presents rolling correlations, calculated over the preceding year, and provides an indication of the evolution of co-movements between markets. The correlations of both the Asian and Latin American emerging markets with the S&P 500 increased during the latter half of 1996 through the first quarter of 1997, and were at their highest levels over the period by the spring of 1997.

The aggregate regional indices mask substantial diversity in individual country returns within regions.[27] In Asia, there was a wide range of returns during 1996–97. At one end of the spectrum, stock markets in China, in Taiwan Province of China, and in Hong Kong, China, performed very strongly. The dissipation of tensions between China and Taiwan Province of China helped raise cumulative returns in Taiwan Province of China to 51 percent during 1996 through May 1997, while China's stock market posted returns of 57 percent, driven by a sharp increase in retail interest with the abolition of inflation subsidies on bank deposits. As concern over the return of Hong Kong to China diminished, returns in Hong Kong increased to 50 percent. Returns in Indonesia (21 percent), India (19 percent), and Malaysia (12 percent) were more moderate, while there were modest losses in the Philippines (–2.3 percent). At the other end of the spectrum, stock markets in Korea and Thailand were some of the worst performers in the world. Losses on the Korean stock market reached 32 percent, as the effects of economic slowdown were exacerbated by financial scandals, bankruptcies of large conglomerates, and labor unrest. Despite the government's repeated easing of restrictions on foreign ownership limits, the Korean stock market failed to revive through much of the period, doing so only modestly in mid-1997. The Thai stock market registered a cumulative loss of 58 percent over the period, reflecting the host of concerns noted earlier.

In Latin America, performance was almost uniformly positive. All the major countries in the region showed substantial gains. The most spectacular increase was in Venezuela, where dollar returns rose to 144 percent during 1996 through May 1997, as confidence surged following the adoption of a macroeconomic adjustment program in early 1996, a return of flight capital, strong oil prices, and some large privatizations. Brazil (94 percent) was not far behind, while·

Argentina (46 percent) and Mexico (39 percent) recorded robust returns. The Mexican total return index remains—in dollars—well below (60 percent at the end of May 1997) its high in January 1994. Eastern European equity markets registered tremendous gains from January 1996 through May 1997. Notable among them was Hungary, where total returns reached 166 percent, and Poland with 67 percent, both experiencing strong foreign investor interest. Elsewhere, in South Africa, dollar returns were –8.1 percent, reflecting the depreciation of the rand.

As emerging equity markets recovered, liquidity, measured by the turnover ratio of shares traded to market capitalization, rose from 54 percent in 1995 to 76 percent in 1996, but remained well below the high of 94 percent in 1994 (Table 19). The increase in liquidity in emerging markets was similar to that in the mature markets, where the turnover ratio rose to 71 percent from 63 percent. Liquidity generally improved in Asia, with the exception of the Thai market, where turnover declined to 37 percent from 42 percent, continuing the decline begun in 1993. By contrast, turnover in China rose threefold to above 300 percent, leading the world's equity markets. The dramatic increase has been ascribed to increased retail participation in the stock market—estimated at 25–30 million individuals in 1996 and expected to continue growing. Latin markets showed mixed results, as turnover increased in Brazil (to 61 percent from 47 percent) and Mexico (to 44 percent from 31 percent), while it declined in Argentina and Chile. In Europe, stellar returns were associated with improved liquidity in Hungary (to 42 percent from 17 percent) and Poland (to 86 percent from 73 percent).

Primary Markets

As emerging market equity prices remained below their previous highs, total equity flotations by companies, including both domestic and international placements, declined by 21 percent in 1996 to reach $42 billion for the year (Table 19). Again, however, this figure masks diverse regional trends, as Asian issuance plummeted some 42 percent while Latin issuance rebounded 173 percent. Nevertheless, Asian equity placements continued to account for the major proportion of overall issuance, though to a considerably lesser extent, and the region's share fell from 75 percent in 1995 to 55 percent in 1996. The decline in overall equity issuance by Asian companies was largely due to lower amounts of equity capital being raised in India, Indonesia, and Korea as other countries in the region continued to issue at the previous year's pace. In Latin America, the level of equity placements surged largely owing to massive privatization issues in Brazil, which accounted for some $6 billion of placements. In Europe, issuance dropped off sharply, by $3.2 billion, as companies failed to take

---

[27]There have been notable performances in some emerging equity markets that do not—as yet—receive any weighting in the major equity market indices. Russia and Egypt, for example, were only recently added to the IFCI index.

Table 19. Stock Market Turnover Ratio and Value of New Equity Issues in Selected Countries and Regions

	1990	1991	1992	1993	1994	1995	1996
				(In percent)			
Annual stock market turnover ratios[1]							
Developed markets	47.0	46.0	41.0	55.0	56.0	63.0	71.0
All emerging markets[2]	132.0	83.0	72.0	86.0	94.0	54.0	76.0
Africa							
South Africa	...	...	...	...	13.9	6.7	10.4
Asia							
China	...	...	...	131.3	235.0	116.6	328.9
India	66.3	53.6	36.7	20.8	24.2	8.8	17.4
Indonesia	77.1	39.9	41.3	40.6	29.4	25.3	40.7
Korea	60.4	82.2	114.0	171.6	173.4	99.3	110.6
Malaysia	24.6	19.8	28.6	94.2	58.8	36.5	65.5
Philippines	13.7	18.7	26.0	24.9	29.6	25.7	36.6
Taiwan Province of China	425.4	322.5	213.4	234.0	321.8	176.6	204.1
Thailand	92.4	100.8	153.2	84.9	61.3	41.9	36.8
Europe							
Czech Republic	...	...	...	...	...	46.7	49.9
Hungary	...	...	7.1	13.7	22.4	17.4	42.1
Poland	...	13.5	87.4	135.7	180.3	72.9	85.6
Western Hemisphere							
Argentina	20.6	42.7	84.4	33.0	28.1	12.3	10.6
Brazil	20.3	37.1	51.6	55.0	67.9	46.9	61.2
Chile	6.7	9.1	7.1	7.5	9.4	15.7	12.2
Mexico	44.0	48.1	37.6	37.5	50.0	30.6	43.6
Venezuela	43.0	32.4	28.6	25.8	20.0	11.8	18.2
				(In millions of U.S. dollars)			
Value of new equity issues[3]							
Emerging markets[2]	19,364.1	16,712.1	16,856.2	35,377.9	52,903.5	53,077.8	41,631.1
Africa	...	...	...	...	851.7	1,903.3	2,178.4
South Africa	...	...	...	...	851.7	1,903.3	2,178.4
Asia	18,856.8	13,177.8	12,977.7	21,283.8	41,209.1	41,040.5	23,722.6
China	...	...	0.0	0.0	0.0	804.5	550.6
India	1,796.5	2,849.8	4,267.8	7,421.4	12,242.3	10,516.3	3,691.5
Indonesia	0.0	178.2	734.8	3,509.8	11,255.5	9,284.8	1,584.7
Korea	4,039.5	3,648.3	2,269.5	3,512.3	6,805.7	7,323.3	4,285.4
Malaysia	3,488.5	1,896.2	2,378.8	2,738.9	2,684.0	4,572.7	4,824.8
Philippines	339.4	381.1	124.5	413.7	1,387.7	1,493.3	1,198.0
Taiwan Province of China	7,444.6	1,688.0	1,044.6	2,526.9	3,676.9	3,878.0	3,983.1
Thailand	1,748.2	2,536.3	2,157.7	1,160.8	3,157.0	3,167.0	3,604.6
Europe	...	0.0	399.0	117.6	1,175.6	5,538.2	2,373.3
Czech Republic	...	...	...	...	...	4,453.8	2,327.2
Hungary	...	0.0	274.1	93.8	387.9	959.0	29.2
Poland	...	0.0	125.0	23.9	787.7	125.4	17.0
Middle East	...	...	...	...	...	...	723.0
Egypt	...	...	...	...	...	...	723.0
Western Hemisphere	507.3	3,534.3	3,479.5	13,976.5	9,667.0	4,595.7	12,633.7
Argentina	4.8	182.5	107.5	9,439.7	2,058.7	236.3	0.0
Brazil	...	0.0	977.4	884.6	2,590.9	1,820.0	8,971.5
Chile	208.8	242.7	511.7	944.4	917.2	625.0	1,629.9
Mexico	293.7	3,091.9	1,812.2	2,698.8	4,011.9	1,899.1	2,009.5
Venezuela	0.0	17.2	70.6	9.0	88.3	15.3	22.8

Source: International Finance Corporation (IFC), Emerging Markets Data Base.
[1]Ratios for each market are calculated in dollar terms by dividing total value traded by average market capitalization.
[2]All emerging markets rather than the 30 countries for which the IFC compiles indices.
[3]Regional totals do not reflect individual countries shown.

advantage of soaring equity prices to raise capital. Companies in the emerging markets relied more heavily on international placements. As a share of total issuance, international placements accounted for 38 percent in 1996, double the share in 1995. Both Asian and Latin American companies exhibited this increased reliance on international markets, albeit to different degrees. The share of international placements by Asian companies rose to 41 percent from 22 percent, while that for Latin American companies rose to 29 percent from 21 percent.

International equity placements rose from $11 billion in 1995 to $16 billion in 1996, compared with a record of $18 billion in 1994 (Table 16 and Figure 11). Equity flotations by the telecommunications sector accounted for a quarter of the issuance during 1996, representing one of the largest concentrations ever in a single sector, while the proportion of equity placements by the financial sector—mostly bank issues—continued to rise steadily, reaching 14 percent in 1996. Issuance by Asian entities rose only slightly to $9.8 billion, though they continued to account for the major proportion of international placements by the emerging markets with companies in Hong Kong, China, placing more than a third of the issues. Latin American placements rebounded in 1996 with large telecommunications privatizations in Venezuela (CANTV) and Peru (Telefónica del Peru), but remained modest compared with previous years, reaching some $3.7 billion. After staying out of the market in 1995, entities from Argentina and Mexico placed modest amounts during 1996. Placements by entities in the transition economies have continued to grow, reaching $1.3 billion, double the level in 1995. Issuance by Russian entities accounted for some $800 million, most notably through a $429 million ADR placement by Gazprom, a gas and oil company. In the first quarter of 1997, international placements continued at about their pace in the first quarter of 1996. One of the more notable issues was that of VSNL, a telecommunications firm from India, which raised $526 million through a GDR placement in the country's largest share offering to date.

Mutual Funds

The increased delegation by individual investors of their portfolios to professional fund managers and the institutionalization of savings have dramatically increased the importance of institutional investors in international capital markets.[28] The importance of institutional investors in intermediating portfolio flows to emerging markets has been no exception. Some estimates place the proportion of total portfolio flows to emerging markets intermediated—either directly or indirectly—by fund managers as high as 90 percent.[29] The sheer size of institutional investor assets in the mature markets has meant that small changes in their portfolio allocations to emerging markets could have enormous effects on flows to these markets. The OECD reports the value of institutional investor assets in the G-7 countries in 1995 at $20.6 trillion. This compares with a total market capitalization of emerging equity markets at the end of 1996 of just $2.1 trillion, and cumulative net portfolio flows to the emerging markets during all of the 1990s of $410 billion, which amounts to just 2 percent of the value of institutional investor assets in the mature markets. Estimates of the portfolio shares of institutional investors in the mature markets dedicated to emerging markets vary considerably across types of institutions and countries. These estimates unanimously suggest, however, that in spite of the increased allocations during the 1990s, the share of institutional investor portfolios dedicated to emerging markets remains well below—by a factor of 3 to 5—that suggested by portfolio theory.[30] The pace at which this gap is closed will be an important determinant of flows to the emerging markets.

Data on emerging market investments for the spectrum of institutional investors are unavailable, but some indication of the rapid increase in institutional flows during the 1990s, their regional allocation, and portfolio composition is provided by the behavior of emerging market mutual funds, presented in Figure 31 for the aggregate of open- and closed-ended funds. (Note that mutual funds have represented a vehicle for investment into emerging markets not only for retail but also for institutional investors.) The net asset value of emerging market mutual funds rose rapidly during the 1990s from $6.8 billion in 1990 to $112.2 billion by the first quarter of 1997, and was remarkably resilient to the Mexican crisis. Among the region-specific funds, the distribution continues to favor Asian funds, which accounted for almost half of asset values in the first quarter of 1997, while those dedicated solely to Latin America accounted for some 15 percent. The broader "emerging markets" funds, which are not dedicated to a particular region, represent a significant proportion—some 30 percent in terms of

---

[29]Howell (1993).

[30]One rule of thumb from modern portfolio theory suggests that an optimally diversified portfolio for an individual investor should have country weights corresponding to the ratio of a country's market capitalization to the world market capitalization. This argues for a share of around 10 percent dedicated to emerging market equities. See International Monetary Fund (1994). Other estimates argue that the share should be some three to four times present levels. See World Bank (1997).

---

[28]See International Monetary Fund (1994). Institutional investors include mutual funds, hedge funds, funds managed by pension funds, insurance companies, trusts, foundations, endowments, and proprietary trading by investment banks, commercial banks, and securities companies.

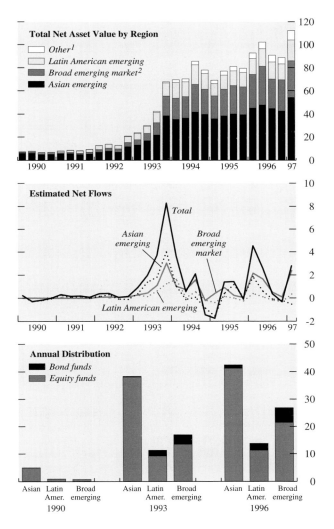

Figure 31. Emerging Market Mutual Funds
(In billions of U.S. dollars)

Source: Lipper Analytical Services, Inc.
[1]Africa, Europe, and Middle East.
[2]Non-region-specific funds dedicated to emerging markets.

Net flows into emerging market mutual funds rebounded from their low of $963 million in 1995 to reach $7.2 billion during 1996. There were particularly robust inflows of $4.5 billion in the first quarter of 1996, which subsequently declined through the year, culminating in an outflow of some $326 million in the fourth quarter, a pattern that was common across both region-specific and broad emerging market funds. In the first quarter of 1997, there was a strong recovery of flows with purchases reaching $2.7 billion, concentrated in the broad emerging market and Latin American funds, while there were net redemptions from Asian funds of $532 million. Generally, purchases and redemptions of individual country-specific funds also mirrored the performance of the local markets. The pattern of flows—both total volumes and regional allocations—corresponded relatively closely to the behavior of emerging market equity prices discussed above.

International Bank Lending

Syndicated Loans

The international syndicated loan market for emerging market borrowers during 1996 and the first quarter of 1997 was, albeit to differing extents across regional segments, characterized by moderating demand for bank lending that coincided with a rising supply of loanable funds. This mismatch created considerable downward pressure on pricing and caused loan structures to weaken. The favorable pricing of emerging market bonds caused borrowers increasingly to turn away from bank lending in favor of the longer maturities and less burdensome restrictions offered by fixed-income instruments, while favorable conditions in the loan market itself encouraged refinancing, which accounted for almost a fifth of new medium- and long-term syndications. On the other hand, the low level of interest rates in the mature markets and the tightening of interest margins on loans in these markets caused banks to look increasingly to the emerging markets for higher yields. The resulting intense competition among banks for lending to emerging market entities pushed down spreads, cut fees, increased tenor, and resulted in a weakening of loan covenants.

Following the sharp increase in syndicated bank lending to emerging markets during 1995 of over 36 percent due to the increased costs of borrowing on bond and equity markets in the aftermath of the Mexican crisis, the total volume of syndicated lending rose more modestly during 1996 by 6.4 percent to $79.7 billion (Table 16 and Figure 11). Lending to Asian countries continued to grow robustly, however, increasing by 22 percent and accounting for the largest share of bank lending, 62 percent in 1996, up from 54 percent in 1995. Lending to the European emerging

asset value—of all funds. Equity funds continue to represent the majority of funds, around 90 percent in 1996, though this share has declined steadily from an estimated 98 percent in 1990, while the share of bond funds, which account for almost all of the remainder, has steadily increased from 2 to 10 percent, and multi-asset funds have remained negligible. Bond funds have been more significant among the dedicated "emerging market" and Latin American funds, where their shares had risen to 19 and 17 percent, respectively. Among Asian funds, on the other hand, bond funds continue to represent a modest share, around 3 percent at end-1996.

Table 20. Emerging Market Medium- and Long-Term Syndicated Loan Commitments: Interest Margins and Refinancings

	1990	1991	1992	1993	1994	1995	1996	1997:Q1
	(In basis points)							
Interest margins[1]								
Emerging markets	56	80	103	90	100	105	88	92
Africa	84	119	106	53	126	91	46	37
Asia	56	88	99	84	94	85	85	104
Europe	47	106	112	105	162	131	88	73
Middle East	98	51	86	109	91	60	83	72
Western Hemisphere	74	88	113	127	58	181	109	98
	(In percent)							
Refinancings								
Emerging markets	3.1	10.5	4.1	4.9	7.5	16.6	18.5	18.4
Africa	—	37.3	—	—	5.6	48.5	19.8	51.9
Asia	2.3	4.3	6.6	5.6	7.7	16.0	16.5	17.4
Europe	4.4	3.6	3.4	2.2	2.4	3.7	13.0	3.9
Middle East	—	0.8	—	13.4	4.3	0.9	14.7	—
Western Hemisphere	5.8	28.4	2.9	2.7	24.0	22.5	36.3	26.5

Source: Capital Data Loanware.

[1]On unenhanced loans.

markets also rose strongly, increasing by 9.0 percent, while the volume of loans extended to Latin America grew more modestly, by 5.4 percent, and declined to Africa and the Middle East. In the first quarter of 1997, the total volume of syndicated lending to the emerging markets dropped off by 2.4 percent relative to the average quarterly pace during 1996. Lending to the European emerging markets fell sharply, to half its pace during 1996, while lending to Asia (–2.4 percent) and the Middle East (–1.6 percent) declined moderately. By contrast, loan volumes to Latin America picked up, growing by a strong 38 percent, and lending to Africa recovered. The proportion of refinancings in new syndications for emerging market entities grew from the unusually high level of 17 percent in 1995 to 19 percent in 1996 (Table 20), with particularly strong increases to Latin America, Europe, and the Middle East. Average interest margins on new loans to the emerging markets as a whole, after having risen modestly in 1995, declined from 105 basis points to 88 basis points in 1996 (Table 20). The rise in spreads during 1995 had been localized to loans to Latin American entities, while average spreads on loans to the other emerging market regions had narrowed. The compression of spreads during 1996 was most evident in the Latin American and European emerging markets, where margins sometimes fell to levels close to those of the most highly rated international borrowers, again raising concerns as to whether risks were being mispriced.

During 1996, refinancings accounted for around 36 percent of new medium- and long-term syndications to Latin America, while average margins on loans declined steeply, from 181 basis points in 1995 to 109 basis points. An example of the levels to which competition pushed spreads was provided in Septem-

ber by the five-year $500 million refinancing loan by Codelco, a Chilean copper conglomerate, which priced at LIBOR plus 22.5 basis points. The proportion of refinancings in new syndications to Latin America moderated in the first quarter of 1997 to 27 percent, margins appeared to bottom out, and average margins remained unchanged. The deterioration in loan covenants, such as restrictions on the gearing ratio of the borrower and the double pledging of assets as collateral, was most evident in mid-1996 when three unsecured loans by Argentine companies were put up for syndication without financial covenants. In another unprecedented deal, in December 1996 the Central Bank of Argentina arranged a collateralized $6.1 billion contingent repo facility with international private sector banks to provide liquidity to the domestic banking system.[31]

Average margins on loans to the European emerging markets fell from 131 basis points in 1995 to 88 basis points in 1996, and further to 73 basis points in the first quarter of 1997. The National Bank of Hungary pushed pricing to an all-time low for the region by refinancing a $350 million loan, priced at LIBOR plus 50 basis points signed in August 1996, at LIBOR plus 20 basis points in December. This rapid decline, also enjoyed by other Hungarian borrowers, coincided with the country's membership in the OECD, which reduced capital requirements for lenders against loans to various Hungarian entities. The keen competition among banks for high-yielding loans was evidenced in April 1997 by the $2.5 billion syndication for Gazprom, the Russian gas and oil

---

[31]The convertibility plan limits the extent to which the central bank can provide liquidity to the domestic banking system.

Table 21. Changes in Net Assets of BIS-Reporting Banks vis-à-vis Banks in Selected Countries and Regions[1]
(In millions of U.S. dollars)

	1993	1994	1995	1996	1996 Q1	1996 Q2	1996 Q3	1996 Q4	Net Outstanding Credit at End-1996
Africa									
South Africa	−323	842	267	1,104	−195	471	−63	891	6,706
Asia									
China	5,146	−4,990	12,120	1,874	3,989	2,082	986	−5,183	−1,888
Hong Kong	15,629	10,846	40,246	26,049	6,507	10,267	2,083	7,192	216,866
India	−2,524	−292	−1,433	−4,002	−1,793	−455	−628	−1,126	−4,947
Indonesia	5,252	3,443	2,920	−1,254	330	−682	91	−993	11,105
Korea	2,634	8,287	14,899	14,442	898	3,700	4,902	4,942	58,190
Malaysia	−2,680	8,363	208	935	−2,274	1,495	3,141	−1,427	4,208
Singapore	10,406	8,136	18,021	7,713	−4,890	5,296	3,321	3,986	116,290
Thailand	8,816	17,188	31,705	9,632	2,544	3,073	3,019	996	77,439
Europe									
Czech Republic	−770	497	818	−395	−366	−1,633	1,674	−70	472
Hungary	−767	227	−795	−323	−402	−399	157	321	3,357
Poland	−55	−8,022	−3,541	1,997	−1,857	1,808	959	1,087	−7,963
Russia	2,222	−3,286	−1,461	1,150	2,472	228	−1,832	282	33,272
Turkey	3,282	−8,230	−750	4,296	−830	−972	3,822	2,276	−3,868
Middle East									
Algeria	266	−1,090	−1,096	−2,994	−575	−425	−1,170	−824	3,438
Egypt	−3,333	−2,246	1,390	2,741	2,401	191	−111	260	−17,252
Iran	−81	1,004	−1,108	−3,152	−894	−284	−1,204	−770	1,496
Kuwait	822	870	−441	−371	−464	−58	790	−639	−4,670
Saudi Arabia	1,910	3,256	−3,520	−1,053	−6,258	3,541	7,036	−5,372	−27,415
United Arab Emirates	6,338	1,430	−4,479	−5,149	−3,086	492	−1,340	−1,215	−16,937
Western Hemisphere									
Argentina	−4,895	2,859	−2,244	2,857	−658	−2,130	3,677	1,968	4,154
Brazil	2,681	−20,826	−15,104	−435	2,145	−9,083	1,592	4,911	−10,043
Chile	−2,404	−2,144	−181	−744	−535	−658	−136	585	−3,789
Colombia	768	−21	922	307	94	−54	499	−232	−995
Mexico	−2,854	9,404	−11,297	−3,481	−233	−2,001	−1,880	633	1,676

Source: Bank for International Settlements (BIS).
[1]BIS-reporting banks comprise banks in the Group of Ten countries (Belgium, Canada, France, Germany, Italy, Japan, the Netherlands, Sweden, the United Kingdom, and the United States) plus Austria, Denmark, Finland, Ireland, Luxembourg, Norway, and Spain, and foreign affiliates of these banks.

company, which priced at LIBOR plus 200 basis points and was three times oversubscribed.

The robust growth of syndicated lending to the Asian emerging markets was underpinned by the continued expansion of lending to the financial and property sectors and for infrastructure financing. Infrastructure financing increasingly took the form of project finance which, by allowing for a separation of risks specific to the project from the overall balance sheet of the parent company, can provide higher yields. Project finance accounted for 32 percent of medium- and long-term syndications to the region during 1996. In terms of the number of project financing arrangements worldwide, the emerging markets of Indonesia, Thailand, China, India, and Hong Kong, China, have been among the top 10 most active countries in the world. These have included projects in power, telecommunications, water, and transport. Project financing has been particularly popular in Hong Kong, China, with the largest number of deals outside the United States, driven by the surge in building ahead of the territory's handover to China this year. Compared with the sharp pickups in the share of refinancings in total syndications to Latin America and the European emerging markets during 1996, the share in Asia remained steady at around 16 percent and was essentially unchanged in the first quarter of 1997. Average interest margins on syndicated lending to Asia remained unchanged in 1996 at 85 basis points, then rose to 103 basis points in the first quarter of 1997.

Interbank Market

In addition to syndicated lending, interbank loans account for an important share of bank lending to emerging markets. Table 21 documents the recent evolution of interbank credit from BIS-reporting banks to banks in several emerging market countries.[32] In Asia, while the stock of net interbank loans to Singapore and Hong Kong, China, has historically been high because of their roles as regional financial centers, net interbank lending flows during 1994–95 to Thailand ($48.9 billion) and Korea ($23.2 billion) were very high, with net credits outstanding by the end of 1995 of $69.9 billion and $43.8 billion, respectively. International banks' reassessment in the face of unfavorable economic developments and measures by the authorities aimed at reducing reliance on international short-term bank borrowing caused a sharp slowdown in lending to Thailand in 1996. The flow of interbank lending to Thailand declined from $31.7 billion in 1995 to $9.6 billion in 1996, with flows in the last quarter dropping off to below $1 billion. The flow of interbank lending to Korea moderated during the early part of 1996 but, as membership in the OECD approached, picked up again, and for the year as a whole reached $14.4 billion, barely below that of $14.9 billion in 1995. Considerable attention has been focused on the buildup of interbank debt by the Asian economies, in particular in Thailand and Korea, and the fact that a substantial proportion of this debt is

short term and needs to be rolled over frequently. The progressive liberalization of financial systems, in an environment of relatively undeveloped local equity and bond markets, combined with rapid economic growth and restrictive monetary policies that have kept interest rates high, has created strong incentives for lending to these countries.

The situation is very different among the Latin American countries where Brazilian, Chilean, and Colombian banks, for example, were net lenders to BIS-reporting banks, with outstanding credits of $10 billion, $3.8 billion, and $1 billion, respectively, at the end of 1996. Similarly, Argentine banks have not been significant borrowers, with $4.1 billion in loans outstanding at the end of 1996. Mexican banks made substantial net repayments during 1995 and the first three quarters of 1996, totaling $15.4 billion, and had a modest outstanding debt of $1.7 billion at end-1996. Among the European countries, Russian banks are the largest debtors to BIS-reporting banks, with an outstanding amount of $33.3 billion at the end of 1996, while Polish banks have been net lenders with a net stock of claims of $7.9 billion at the end of 1996. In the Middle East, Egyptian banks were the main recipients of funds in 1996, and they, along with banks in Kuwait and the United Arab Emirates, remain net lenders.

---

[32]See note 1 to Table 21 for definitions.

Annex II

Developments and Trends in the Mature Capital Markets

During the period under review, prices and volumes in the mature international capital markets responded favorably to low or declining inflation rates, efforts toward fiscal consolidation, continued strong growth in the United States and the United Kingdom, and the expected strengthening of economic activity in most other countries. An improved macroeconomic environment—along with ample liquidity—also curtailed volatility in the major markets. Equity prices in most advanced countries surged as corporate earnings forecasts were progressively marked up. Large yield spreads among the three largest economies—favoring dollar-denominated securities—attracted unprecedented capital inflows to U.S. securities markets, which were a key factor behind the dollar's sharp rise against the yen and deutsche mark during the past two years. The first section of this annex discusses developments since early 1996 in foreign exchange markets. The second and third sections summarize recent developments in bond and syndicated loan markets, respectively, and the next section reviews developments in international equity markets. The fifth section reviews developments in global derivative markets, and the final section discusses supervisory and regulatory developments.

Exchange Rates

Overview

The dollar appreciated sharply against the deutsche mark and yen in 1996 and through May 1997, in large part because of record-high capital inflows into U.S. securities markets and the relatively strong performance of the U.S. economy vis-à-vis Europe and Japan. From its all-time low of ¥80 and DM1.35 in the spring of 1995, the dollar rose fairly steadily over the subsequent two years, peaking in May 1997 at a level that amounted to a cumulative appreciation of about 60 percent against the Japanese yen and about 30 percent against the deutsche mark (Figure 32). The dollar has since reversed some of its gains against the yen in anticipation of higher Japanese interest rates as well as concerns that the Japanese monetary authorities might sell some of their dollar reserves, though it remains more than 40 percent above its low in early 1995.

In percentage terms, the movement in the dollar–deutsche mark rate over the past two years has been large but not unprecedented over similar time frames during the past two decades. By comparison, the movement in the dollar-yen rate from the spring of 1995 to its peak in May 1997 was one of the largest moves ever for this exchange rate. The dollar's depreciation from ¥260 at the end of February 1985 to below ¥122 in November 1988 was the same order of magnitude in percentage terms as the recent experience (although opposite in sign), but it occurred over a longer period of time. The 42 percent depreciation of the dollar from October 1978 through February 1980 is perhaps the only instance in the postwar period that rivals the magnitude and speed of the recent change in the dollar-yen rate.

The dollar's appreciation in 1995–97 occurred against the backdrop of relatively high yields on dollar assets. With interest rates low in Japan and core Europe, investors' search for higher yields produced large capital inflows not only into the U.S. markets but into higher-yielding markets globally. As a result, traditionally higher-yielding currencies—in Europe and in the dollar bloc—were supported by capital inflows, as well as improved macroeconomic fundamentals. Within Europe, lower inflation, efforts toward fiscal consolidation, and renewed optimism about European Economic and Monetary Union (EMU) were instrumental in the appreciation of most EU countries' currencies against the deutsche mark after early 1996 (Figure 33). Despite improved exchange rate fundamentals in Europe and in the dollar-bloc countries, however, record-high capital inflows to dollar markets prevented most currencies—the notable exception being the pound sterling—from strengthening appreciably against the U.S. dollar.

Interest Differentials, Capital Flows, and the Dollar's Rise

Market participants in the major financial centers attribute much of the dollar's momentum to abundant liquidity in international financial markets that has disproportionately been funneled into the dollar markets, especially dollar-denominated fixed-income markets. This concept of liquidity in international financial markets refers to both looser monetary policies in some

Figure 32. Major Industrial Countries: Exchange Rates, January 1994–May 1997
(Local currency/U.S. dollar)

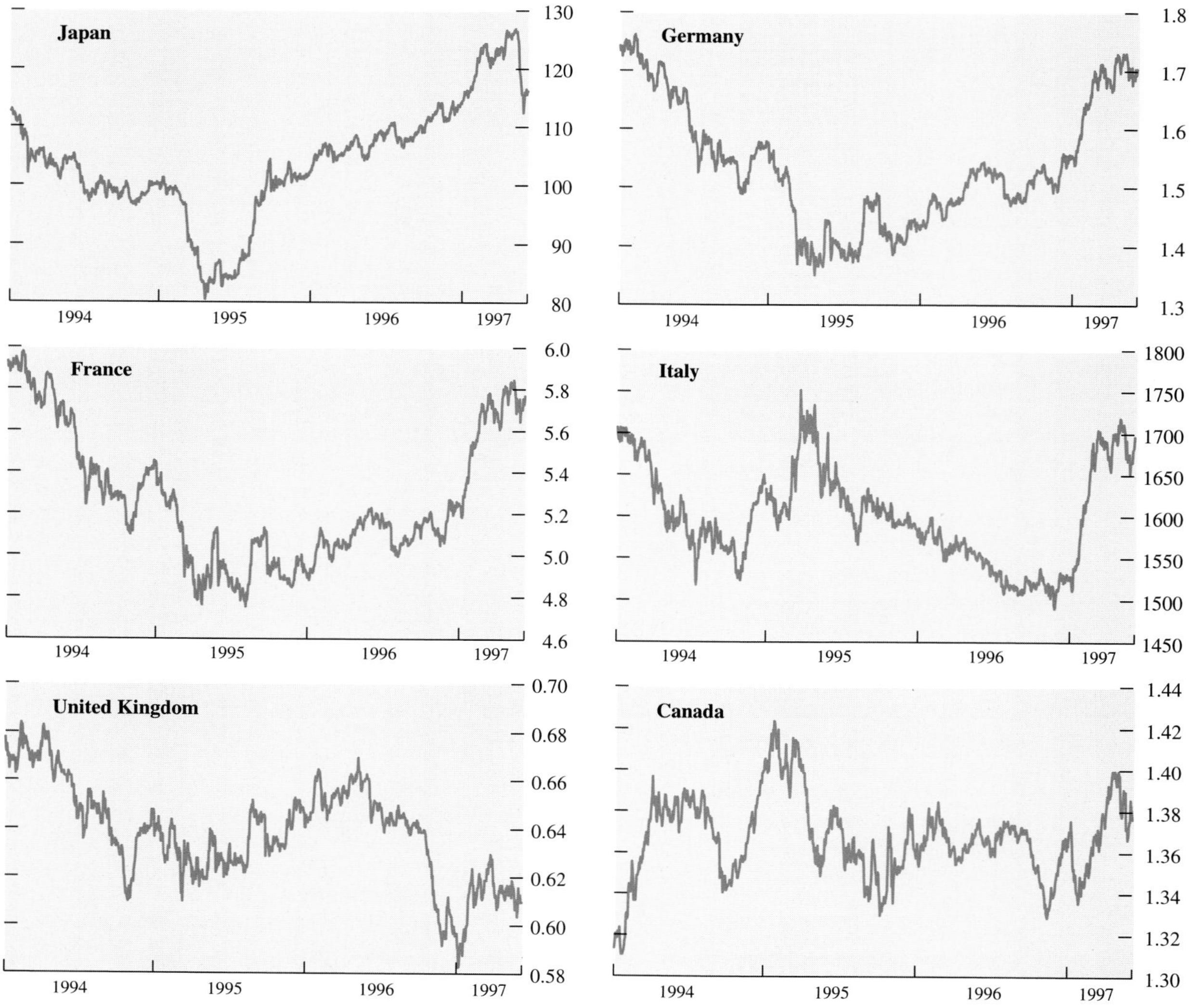

Source: Bloomberg Financial Markets L.P.

countries as well as simply large flows of capital internationally. Monetary stimulus in the major industrial countries has on balance shifted toward an easier stance since early 1996, with slightly tighter monetary conditions in the United States and the United Kingdom partially offsetting the monetary stimulus from Europe, Japan, and Canada (Figure 34). In addition, growth in firms' demand for bank financing in some of the major countries has been low in relation to monetary growth rates, and thus monetary easing may have significantly affected liquidity (see Figure 34).

The difference in cyclical positions and in the stances of monetary policies—which reflect the dif-

ference in cyclical conditions—among the major countries have created large interest differentials between countries. Of particular significance are the higher interest rates in the United States versus the two next-largest economies, Japan and Germany (Figures 35–37; see also Figure 2). The interest differential between yen- and dollar-denominated fixed-income securities has been especially large during the period under review. At the short end of the yield curve, the differential between three-month yen and dollar rates has been more than 4.5 percentage points since January 1996, and in May 1997 exceeded 5 percentage points. At the long end of the yield curve, the

Figure 33. Major European Countries: Local Currency vs. Deutsche Mark, January 1994–May 1997

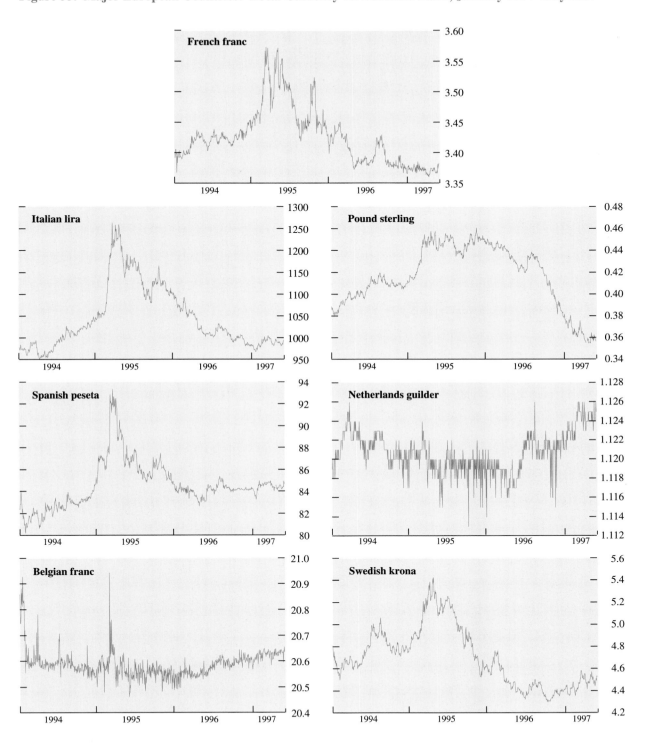

Source: Bloomberg Financial Markets L.P.

Figure 34.   Major Industrial Countries: Real Growth in Broad Money Supply and Claims on Private Sector[1]

(In percent from four quarters earlier)

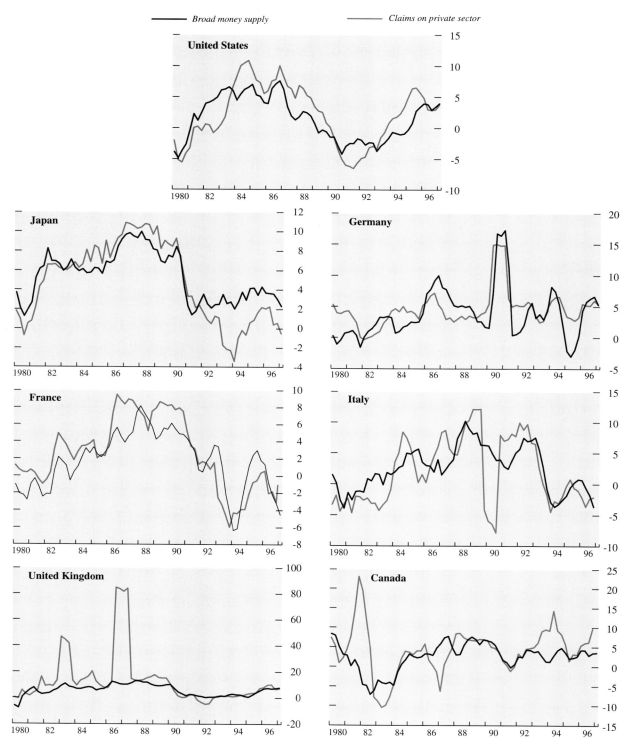

Sources: International Monetary Fund, *International Financial Statistics* database; and The WEFA Group.

[1]M3 for broad money supply for all countries except the United Kingdom, for which M4 is used. Claims on private sector are taken from International Monetary Fund, *International Financial Statistics* (line 32d). Data for 1980: Q1 through 1997: Q1.

Figure 35. Major Industrial Countries: Short-Term Interest Rates[1]
(In percent a year)

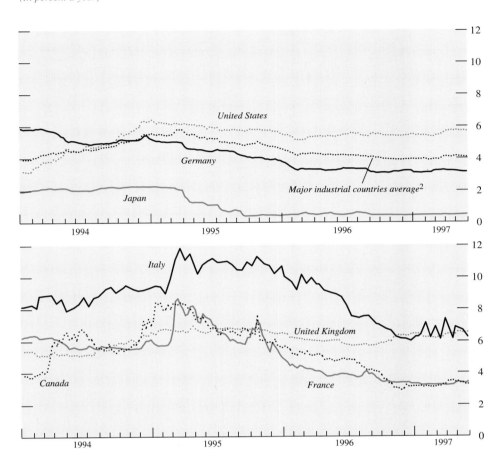

[1]Three-month certificate of deposit rates for the United States and Japan; three-month treasury bill rate for Italy; rate on three-month prime corporate paper for Canada; and three-month interbank deposit rates for other countries. Weekly averages of daily observations are plotted for all countries other than Italy and Canada. For Italy, results of fortnightly treasury bill auctions are shown. For Canada, weekly observations are plotted.
[2]1987 GDP weights.

spread on long-term yen and dollar government bonds rose steadily from early 1996, and in May 1997 stood at more than 4 percentage points. The spread between deutsche mark and dollar yields has increased steadily since early 1996, reaching about 2.5 percentage points in May 1997 for short-term rates and about 1 percentage point for long-term rates.

The relatively attractive yields on dollar investments encouraged Japanese and European investors to increase the weight of dollar bonds in their portfolios. This is reflected most clearly by survey data on currency exposures of investors: since early 1995, investors have clearly tilted their portfolios in favor of assets denominated in dollars, pounds sterling, and other high-yielding currencies (Statistical Appendix Table A1). The appreciation of many of the higher-

yielding EU countries' currencies, as well as currencies in the dollar bloc (Canada, Australia, New Zealand), against the deutsche mark and yen, is consistent with yield-seeking international capital flows. Further, the attractiveness of the relatively higher yields in the United States (and elsewhere) has been compounded by uncertainties about investing in core Europe and Japan, which might have caused risk-adjusted interest differentials to be even larger. Specifically, uncertainty about financial system problems in Japan and uncertainty about the future value of the euro—which has been highlighted by renewed optimism about EMU—might have further increased the relative attractiveness of dollar-denominated investments.

The available data on capital flows strongly suggest that investors have been seeking higher yields by in-

Figure 36. Major Industrial Countries: Long-Term Interest Rates[1]
(In percent a year)

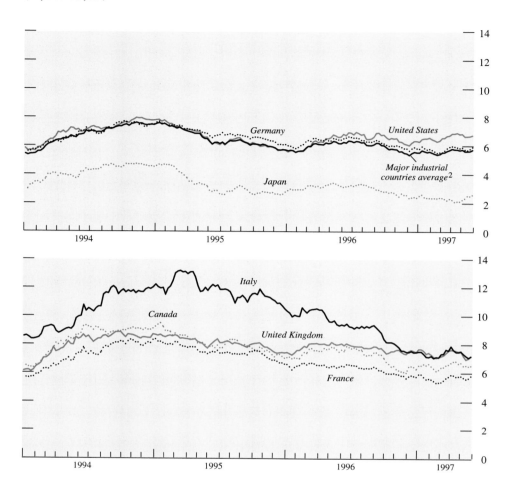

[1]Yields on government bonds with residual maturities of 10 years or nearest. Weekly averages of daily observations.
[2]1987 GDP weights.

vesting abroad. Outward portfolio flows during the past 18 months have been associated with aggressive buying of foreign securities by U.S., Japanese, French, Spanish, and German investors, as well as positions booked in the major international financial centers outside the United States—the United Kingdom, Singapore, and Hong Kong, China (Statistical Appendix Tables A2–A3). As for the recipients of these capital flows, the United States has clearly been a major target of non-U.S.-based investors. Foreign purchases of U.S. treasury and government agency bonds and notes reached $293.7 billion in 1996, and there was a further $78 billion of foreign purchases of U.S. corporate bonds. Similarly strong capital inflows to U.S. securities markets have been apparent in the first quarter of 1997: foreign purchases of government and corporate

bonds during the first quarter of 1997 were slightly above the quarterly average during 1996. In comparison, despite the sharp increase in U.S. equity prices in recent years, there were only $13.2 billion of foreign inflows into the U.S. equity market in 1996.

As noted in Chapter II of the report, particularly wide interest differentials between the United States and Japan, in conjunction with the belief that the Bank of Japan did not want the yen to strengthen in 1996–97, were viewed by some large global hedge funds as a potentially lucrative situation. These so-called yen-carry trades involved borrowing in yen, selling the yen for dollars, and investing the proceeds in relatively high-yielding U.S. fixed-income securities. In hindsight, these trades turned out to be considerably more profitable than simply the interest differ-

Figure 37. Bilateral Exchange Rates and Short-Term and Long-Term Interest Differentials vis-à-vis the U.S. Dollar[1]

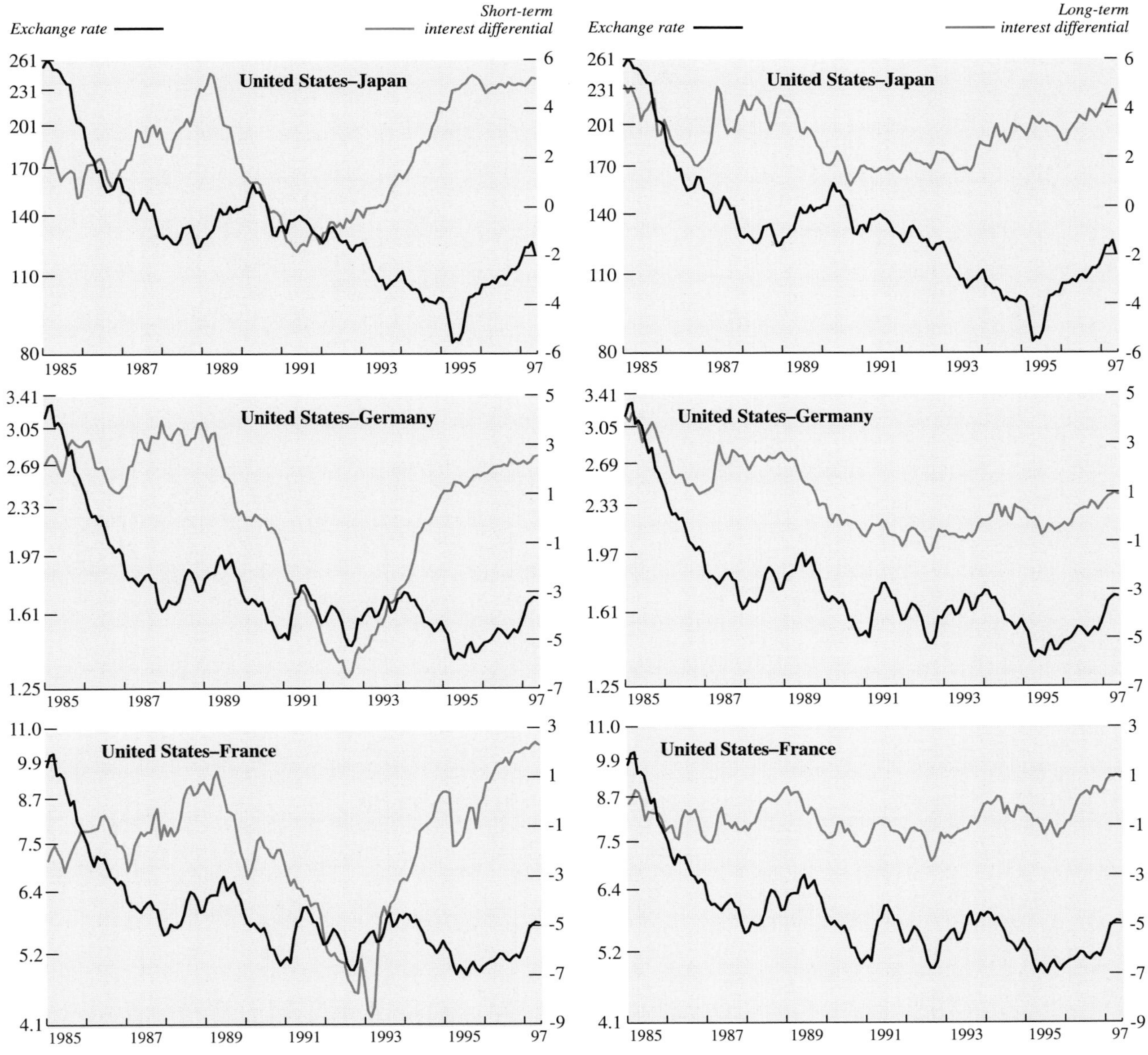

Source: International Monetary Fund.
[1]Interest differentials shown are U.S. interest rates minus domestic interest rates in percent a year. Exchange rates are drawn on logarithmic scales and are defined in terms of national currency units per U.S. dollar, except for the United Kingdom, where it is defined as U.S. dollars per pound sterling. The figures show monthly averages of daily data from January 1985 through May 1997.

ential, for the yen depreciated continuously over the two years from May 1995 through May 1997, which reduced the yen liability relative to the dollar investment that it financed.

With available data, it is difficult to determine the scale of yen-carry trades implemented over the past two years. It is noteworthy, however, that while Japan-

ese banks reduced total cross-border assets by $20 billion in 1996, they increased lending by almost $19 billion to nonbank entities located just in the Cayman Islands (British West Indies)—a home for some of the major hedge funds. Over the same period, entities located in the British West Indies accumulated $20 billion of U.S. long-term bonds. Further, lending by

Figure 38. Foreign and International Holdings of U.S. Public Debt[1]
(Percentage of gross marketable public debt)

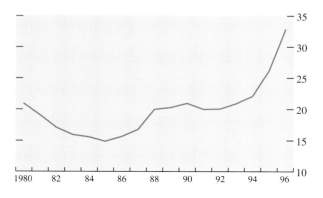

Source: Board of Governors of the Federal Reserve System, *Federal Reserve Bulletin.*

[1]Foreign and international holdings are U.S. Treasury estimates and consist of investments of foreign balances and international accounts in the United States.

Japanese banks to U.S. nonbank entities expanded by an additional $28.8 billion during 1996.[1] Viewed in light of the significant contraction in total cross-border assets of Japanese banks in 1996, the fact that Japanese banks increased their cross-border claims on nonbanks in the Cayman Islands and the United States by almost $48 billion is consistent with parties in these regions instituting significant yen-carry trades.

The volume of international inflows into U.S. bond markets in 1996 is by far the largest ever—70 percent larger than the previous record set in 1995. Net foreign purchases of U.S. government bonds alone ($294 billion) accounted for 250 percent of the increase in the stock of privately held public debt securities in 1996. This pushed the share of foreigners' total ownership to one-third of the stock of public debt securities, up from 26 percent in 1995 (Figure 38).

Yield-seeking by private investors accounted for much of the large capital inflows to dollar markets during the past eighteen months, but foreign exchange reserve accumulation by central banks was also an important source of inflows to dollar markets. Central banks accounted for 35 percent of total foreign net purchases of U.S. treasury bonds in 1996. Much of this official accumulation of U.S. treasury securities has been a consequence of efforts by developing countries to manage the impact of large inflows of foreign capital on their respective currencies, which required the accumulation of official reserves. Indeed, more

[1]Data on international bank lending from the Bank for International Settlements.

than half of reserve accumulation by all central banks in 1996 was by central banks in developing countries. Among industrial countries, the Japanese monetary authorities have been most aggressive in accumulating reserves during the past two years. During 1995–96, the Bank of Japan accumulated more than $90 billion in reserves, bringing the total in early 1997 to about $218 billion (14 percent of global official reserves). The Bank of Japan's reserve accumulation in 1996 was almost four times greater than that of the other six G-7 countries combined, and it represented 45 percent of reserve accumulation by central banks in all industrial countries (20 percent of global official reserve accumulation). By contrast, the G-7 countries excluding Japan were responsible for only 5.4 percent of total official reserve accumulation over the year, and about 12 percent of reserves accumulated by all industrial countries during the year.

The magnitude of capital inflows into the dollar markets has also been large relative to the U.S. current account position (Table 22). The U.S. current account deficit in 1996 was $148 billion (or about 1.9 percent of GDP). Capital inflows amounted to $547 billion, or 370 percent of the current account deficit. Accumulation of U.S. securities by foreign central banks alone was only $26 billion less than what was required to finance the current account deficit. Private security purchases by foreigners, however, contributed inflows of $289 billion. Thus, total accumulation of U.S. securities by foreigners amounted to 5.4 percent of GDP, or 275 percent of what was necessary to finance the current account balance. This record level of portfolio inflows—both in absolute value and as a percentage of GDP—was intermediated in U.S. financial markets and invested abroad through purchases of foreign securities by U.S. investors ($108 billion) and by net lending abroad by U.S. banks ($98 billion).

The aggressive purchase of foreign securities by U.S. investors is consistent with the continued international diversification of U.S. investors' portfolios. The relatively large net amount of cross-border bank lending by U.S. banks reflects two factors. First, U.S. banks have onlent to their foreign subsidiaries to meet strong demand in the Eurodollar market and to finance the demand for dollar securities by foreigners. Second, as discussed under "International Syndicated Loan Markets" below, the international interbank markets have increasingly used repurchase agreements for interbank funding, and U.S. treasury securities are the predominant form of collateral in these markets.

The volume of foreign purchases of U.S. bonds has also been large relative to current account positions in many of the other major countries. In Japan, residents accumulated foreign fixed-income securities in 1996 amounting to 142 percent of the current account surplus of Japan, with well above half of these purchases being bonds issued by the U.S. government and U.S. corporations. Similarly, the German current account

Table 22. United States: Selected External Account Variables

	U.S. Assets Abroad, Net[1]		Foreign Assets in the United States[2]		Current Account Balance	U.S. Assets Abroad, Net[1]		Foreign Assets in the United States[2]		Current Account Balance
	Total	Private	Total	Private		Total	Private	Total	Private	
	(In billions of U.S. dollars)					*(In percent of GDP)*				
1963	−7.27	5.99	3.22	1.23	4.41	−1.18	0.97	0.52	0.20	0.71
1964	−9.56	−8.05	3.64	1.98	6.82	−1.44	−1.21	0.55	0.30	1.03
1965	−5.72	−5.34	0.74	0.61	5.43	−0.79	−0.74	0.10	0.08	0.76
1966	−7.32	−6.35	3.66	4.33	3.03	−0.93	−0.81	0.46	0.55	0.38
1967	−9.76	−7.39	7.38	3.93	2.58	−1.17	−0.89	0.89	0.47	0.31
1968	−10.98	−7.83	9.93	10.70	0.61	−1.21	−0.86	1.09	1.18	0.07
1969	−11.59	−8.21	12.70	14.00	0.40	−1.18	−0.84	1.29	1.43	0.04
1970	−9.34	−10.23	6.36	−0.55	2.33	−0.90	−0.99	0.61	−0.05	0.23
1971	−12.48	−12.94	22.97	−3.91	−1.43	−1.11	−1.15	2.04	−0.35	−0.13
1972	−14.50	−12.93	21.46	10.99	−5.80	−1.17	−1.04	1.73	0.89	−0.47
1973	−22.87	−20.39	18.39	12.36	7.14	−1.65	−1.47	1.33	0.89	0.52
1974	−34.75	−33.64	35.34	24.80	1.96	−2.32	−2.25	2.36	1.66	0.13
1975	−39.70	−35.38	17.17	10.14	18.12	−2.43	−2.17	1.05	0.62	1.11
1976	−51.27	−44.50	38.02	20.33	4.30	−2.82	−2.45	2.09	1.12	0.24
1977	−34.79	−30.72	53.22	16.40	−14.34	−1.72	−1.52	2.63	0.81	−0.71
1978	−61.13	−57.20	67.04	33.36	−15.14	−2.67	−2.50	2.93	1.46	−0.66
1979	−66.05	−61.18	40.85	54.52	−0.29	−2.58	−2.39	1.60	2.13	−0.01
1980	−86.97	−73.65	62.61	47.12	2.32	−3.12	−2.65	2.25	1.69	0.08
1981	−114.15	−103.88	86.23	81.27	5.03	−3.66	−3.33	2.77	2.61	0.16
1982	−122.34	−111.24	96.42	92.83	−11.44	−3.77	−3.43	2.97	2.86	−0.35
1983	−61.57	−55.37	88.78	82.93	−43.99	−1.75	−1.58	2.53	2.36	−1.25
1984	−36.31	−27.69	118.03	114.89	−98.95	−0.93	−0.71	3.02	2.94	−2.54
1985	−39.89	−33.21	146.38	147.50	−123.99	−0.95	−0.79	3.50	3.53	−2.97
1986	−106.75	−105.04	230.21	194.56	−153.19	−2.41	−2.38	5.21	4.40	−3.46
1987	−72.62	−82.77	248.38	203.00	−168.05	−1.55	−1.76	5.29	4.33	−3.58
1988	−100.02	−99.28	246.07	206.31	−128.25	−1.98	−1.97	4.87	4.09	−2.54
1989	−168.74	−144.71	224.39	215.89	−104.23	−3.10	−2.66	4.13	3.97	−1.92
1990	−74.01	−74.16	140.99	107.08	−91.89	−1.29	−1.29	2.45	1.86	−1.60
1991	−57.88	−66.56	109.64	92.25	−5.66	−0.98	−1.12	1.85	1.56	−0.10
1992	−68.77	−71.02	168.78	128.30	−56.38	−1.10	−1.14	2.70	2.05	−0.90
1993	−194.54	−192.82	279.67	207.92	−90.77	−2.97	−2.94	4.27	3.17	−1.39
1994	−160.52	−165.51	297.34	256.95	−133.54	−2.31	−2.39	4.29	3.70	−1.93
1995	−307.21	−296.92	451.23	340.51	−129.10	−4.24	−4.09	6.22	4.69	−1.78
1996	−352.44	−358.42	547.56	425.20	−148.18	−4.65	−4.73	7.23	5.61	−1.96
Period averages										
1963–69	−8.88	−5.31	5.90	5.26	3.33	−1.13	−0.67	0.75	0.67	0.42
1970–74	−18.79	−18.03	20.90	8.74	0.84	−1.50	−1.44	1.66	0.70	0.07
1975–79	−50.59	−45.79	43.26	26.95	−1.47	−2.45	−2.22	2.09	1.31	−0.07
1980–84	−84.27	−74.37	90.41	83.81	−29.41	−2.54	−2.25	2.73	2.53	−0.89
1985–89	−97.60	−93.00	219.09	193.45	−135.54	−2.05	−1.96	4.61	4.07	−2.85
1990–96	−173.62	−175.06	285.03	222.60	−93.65	−2.63	−2.65	4.32	3.37	−1.42

Sources: International Monetary Fund, *World Economic Outlook* database; and U.S. Department of Commerce, *Survey of Current Business.*
[1]A negative value represents an increase in U.S. assets abroad, a capital outflow.
[2]A positive value indicates an increase in foreign assets in the United States, a capital inflow.

deficit was ¾ of a percent of GDP, but residents accumulated U.S. government and corporate bonds equivalent to 1 percent of GDP. And in France, purchases of U.S. government and corporate bonds were almost 3 percent of GDP, or more than double the current account surplus. Finally, although the U.K. current account was roughly in balance, net purchases of U.S. government and corporate bonds booked in the United Kingdom were equal to more than 10 percent of GDP.

In summary, there have been large inflows into dollar markets during the past two years, and these capital flows have been attributed to three factors: liquidity spilling over into international capital markets associated with a loosening of monetary policy in Europe and Japan, which has been facilitated by the weak demand for funds by firms in several European countries and in Japan; wide interest differentials among the three largest economies, which have favored dollar assets; and uncertainties associated with

Figure 39. RiskMetrics Daily Price Volatility for U.S. Dollar Spot Exchange Rates, January 19, 1995–May 30, 1997
(In percent)

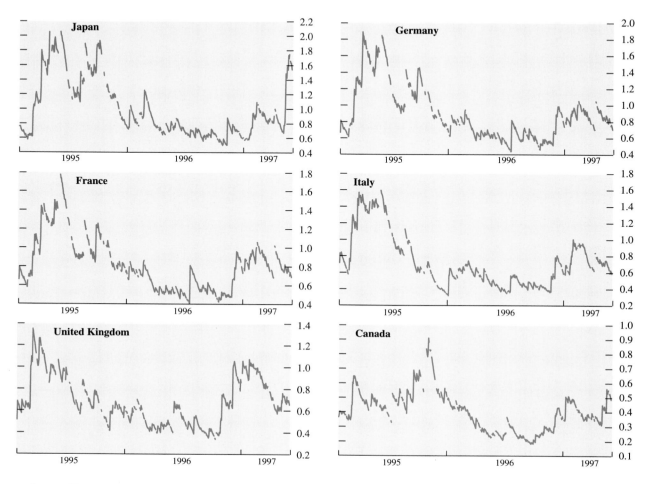

Source: J.P. Morgan.

EMU in Europe and with the financial system in Japan. It is difficult to quantify the role of these various factors in recent movements of the exchange rates among the major currencies. Perhaps the least tangible factor is that associated with uncertainties about EMU and banking problems in Japan. It is noteworthy, however, that recent analysis by some market participants attribute about half of the dollar's rally against the deutsche mark since mid-1996 specifically to EMU optimism.[2]

Volatility in Foreign Exchange Markets

Ample liquidity in the international financial markets and the lack of inflationary pressures helped to maintain low volatility in foreign exchange markets despite large movements in exchange rates among the major currencies (Figures 39–40). The absence of volatility has been especially marked for the currencies of the traditionally higher-yielding industrial countries, both because capital inflows to higher-yielding markets added liquidity to foreign exchange markets, and because the same factors that worked to strengthen many of these currencies also reduced risk premiums for holding these currencies. Specifically, a change in the stance of macroeconomic policy, which has emphasized low inflation and fiscal conservatism, contributed to a sharp reduction in uncertainty regarding the key currency market fundamentals—inflation and fiscal policy.

In the European Union, improved fundamentals have been closely tied with increased optimism that EMU would proceed in 1999. As a result, markets have

[2]See J.P. Morgan (1997a).

Figure 40. Implied Volatility: Yen and Deutsche Mark Three-Month Forwards

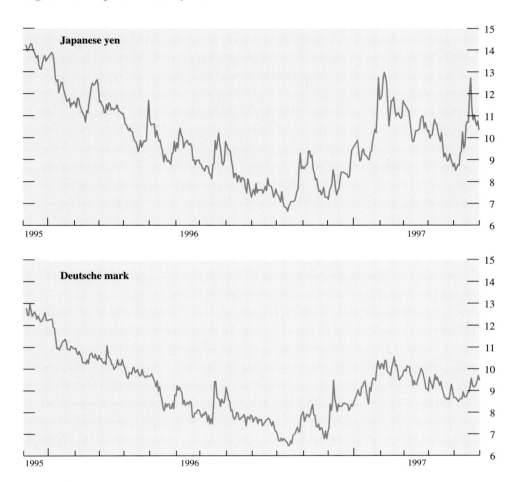

Source: Bloomberg Financial Markets L.P.
Note: Implied volatility is a measure of the expected future volatility of the currency based on market prices of the call options on forwards on the currency.

priced in not only observed improvements in fundamentals, but also an improved outlook for the future course of macroeconomic policy as EU countries seek to participate in EMU at an early stage. As a result, the currencies of most EU countries, and particularly those of the higher-yielding—or "non-core"—countries, have appreciated against the deutsche mark. This facilitated the reentry of the Italian lira, and the entry of the Finnish markka, into the ERM in late 1996. The strongest currencies in Europe since early 1996 have been the pound sterling and the Irish pound, both of which have received additional support from strong economic growth and expectations of rising interest rates. The strength of the Irish pound has attracted considerable attention because of its inclusion in the ERM and the fact that it has risen about 10 percent since mid-

1996 above its central rate against the deutsche mark. The market's interest in the Irish pound's strength within the ERM stems from concerns about what entry rate will be used for the pound when EMU begins.

Reduced volatility in foreign exchange markets in 1996 strongly affected turnover in spot foreign exchange markets, particularly European foreign exchange markets. Although recent data on turnover in the global foreign exchange market are not available, lower volatility has been widely pointed to as an explanation for the marked scaling back of European foreign exchange trading operations of the major market participants. Activity in currency derivative markets was unaffected by the absence of turbulence in the foreign exchange markets, as turnover continued to expand briskly. In the over-the-counter markets, the

Figure 41. Selected European Long-Term Interest Rate Differentials with Germany
(In basis points)

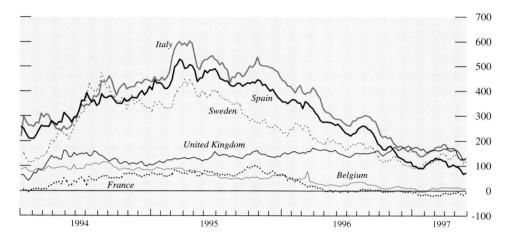

Source: International Monetary Fund.

notional principal of currency swaps rose 18 percent at an annual rate during the first half of 1996. On the exchanges, currency futures and options volumes rose 19 percent in 1996 over 1995, in part reflecting a rebound after the sharp drop in 1995. Reduced volatility and turnover in spot foreign exchange rates undoubtedly slowed the demand for currency derivatives, but the structural growth of derivative markets associated with the prevalence of risk management continues to expand derivative markets (see the "Derivative Markets" section below).

This increased use of foreign exchange derivatives for risk management is reflected by reportedly brisk activity in binary range options. These instruments are an effective tool for hedging volatility because their payoff structure is tied to whether or not the exchange rate stays within a specified range. Market participants report that positions of this type were widely used in the French franc–dollar, dollar-yen, deutsche mark–French franc, and many of the other European bilateral exchange rates in 1996. On the long side of these positions, U.S. hedge funds and other high net worth investors are reported to have placed large bets that EMU or official intervention by the Bank of Japan would ensure stable exchange markets in 1996 and early 1997. A notable instance occurred in the fall of 1996, when there were reportedly a large volume of dollar-yen range barriers issued with a range of ¥112–115. On October 29, the dollar reached ¥114.88, just below the knock-out level. Market participants reported that at the time the dollar was temporarily prevented from strengthening further on account of massive selling of dollars by dealers, hedge funds, and others with large long positions in dollar-yen range barriers.

One method of gaining some insight into the market's assessment of the direction of the major exchange rates in the future is to study information contained in asset prices. Distributions of the major exchange rates computed from foreign currency options premiums are a way to gauge the market's expectation about the range of possible future values for exchange rates (see Appendix 1 at the end of this annex). This technique reveals considerable dispersion in the market's assessment of future values for the yen-dollar rate.

Bond Markets

Overview

Low interest rates in core Europe and Japan (see Figures 35–36), as well as continued international diversification of U.S. investors' portfolios, led to substantial capital flows from the major industrial countries into the higher-yielding bond markets. In conjunction with low, and in some countries declining, inflation rates, these capital flows to the higher-yielding markets were instrumental in reducing yields relative to the major benchmark yield curves and in curtailing volatility in bond markets. The narrowing of spreads attracted considerable attention within the context of EMU as convergence plays were once again established in those markets, but the compression of spreads in Europe was a reflection of a global phenomenon that included the higher-yielding industrial countries outside of Europe—Canada, Australia, and New Zealand—the emerging markets, and corporate bond markets (Figures 41–43). This favor-

Figure 42. Yield Differential for the 10-Year Government Bonds of Australia, Canada, and New Zealand
(In basis points against the yield on 10-year U.S. government bonds)

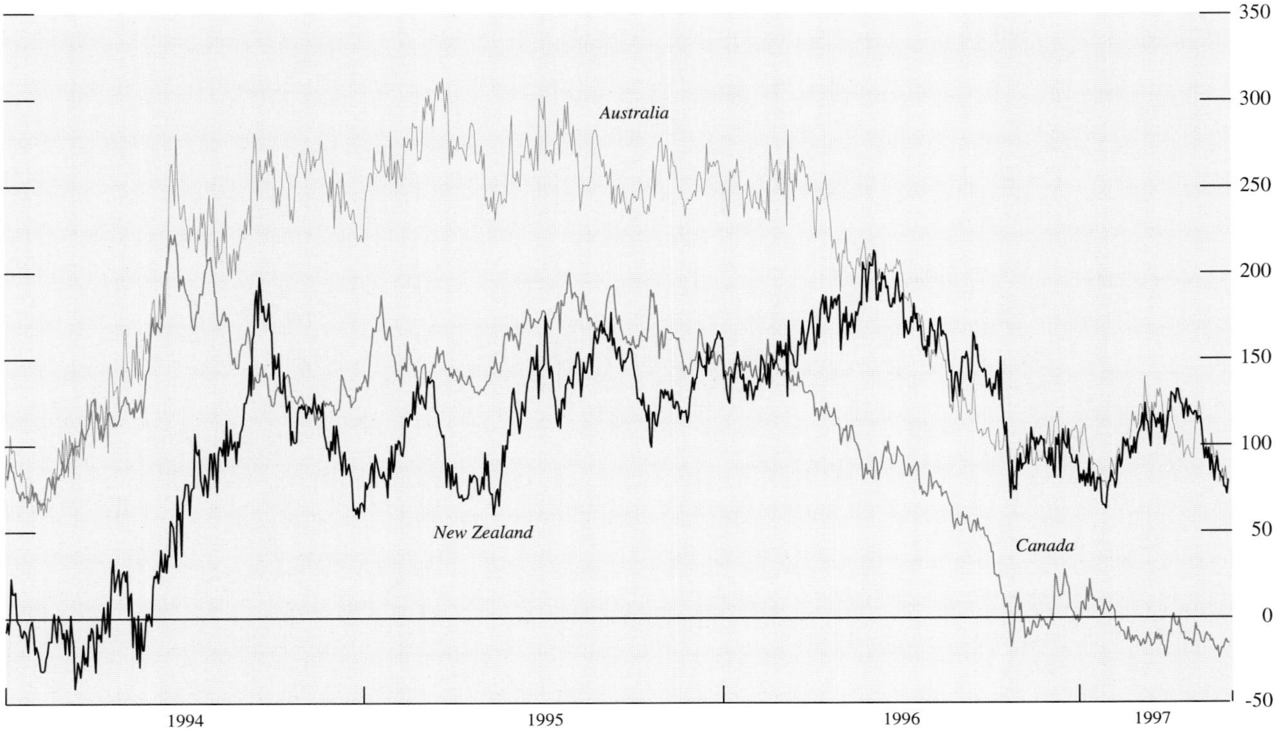

Source: Bloomberg Financial Markets L.P.

able environment for borrowers caused new issuance of fixed-income securities to reach record levels in the international markets and in most of the higher-yielding domestic bond markets. The yield-seeking behavior of investors was reflected also in international bond markets by the strong demand for dollar-denominated paper: the share of dollar-denominated bonds issued in the international markets more than doubled in 1996 over the previous year, whereas the share of yen bonds fell almost 80 percent and the share of deutsche mark issues fell close to 40 percent.

The narrowing of sovereign interest rate spreads globally has in large part been due to low inflation and progress toward fiscal consolidation. Nonetheless, the degree of spread compression may have been amplified by plentiful global liquidity in international financial markets and the related yield-seeking behavior of investors, which has accompanied the sharp decline in interest rates in Japan and core Europe. Additionally, capital inflows into U.S. securities markets were much greater than what was necessary to finance the current account deficit and may, therefore, have contributed to the narrowing in spreads as this capital was effectively

intermediated in the United States and reinvested in foreign bond markets (Table 22; see also Table 3).

European Monetary Union and Convergence Plays

Spreads in European fixed-income markets (relative to German benchmarks) peaked in early 1995 as a result of the flight to quality associated with the global bond market correction in 1994 as well as the Mexican crisis that developed later in the year. The subsequent narrowing of spreads continued in 1996 because of further easing of monetary policy in Europe and an improved outlook for EMU. The most notable narrowing of spreads occurred in those countries with high spreads at the start of the period. Specifically, the Italian 10-year yield spread narrowed by 350 basis points from early 1996 through end-May 1997, Spanish spreads fell 300 basis points, and Swedish spreads fell 130 basis points. In core EMU countries, where spreads were thin at the beginning of the period, they narrowed to the point that French and Dutch long-term yields traded below deutsche mark yields by late 1996. The United Kingdom is the notable exception to

Figure 43. United States: Yield Spreads of Corporate Bonds over U.S. Treasuries[1]
(In percent)

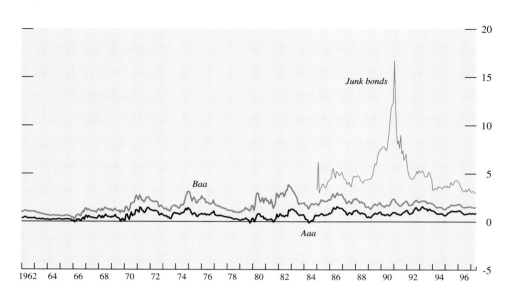

Sources: Bloomberg Financial Markets L.P.; Board of Governors of the Federal Reserve System, *Federal Reserve Bulletin*; and Merrill Lynch.

[1]Yields on 10-year U.S. treasury bonds of constant maturities are used for U.S. treasuries. Junk bonds are all high-yield bonds weighted by par value.

this latest round of convergence plays, a fact that has been attributed to the asynchronous cyclical position of the United Kingdom versus much of continental Europe, and to considerable uncertainty about when the United Kingdom will participate in EMU.

For the higher-yielding EU countries, from January 1996 to end-May 1997 yield spreads had narrowed by similar magnitudes at the short and long ends of the yield curves. Specifically, from January 1, 1996, through end-May 1997, the difference between rates paid on deutsche mark one-year deposits and Spanish peseta and Italian lira one-year deposits narrowed by 300–350 basis points, compared with the 270–285 basis point reduction in spreads on seven-year deposits for these currencies. Thus, the downward shift in yield curves relative to the deutsche mark curve was only slightly greater at the short end than at the long end of the curves.

The convergence of interest rates in Europe is often attributed to the improved fundamentals (inflation and fiscal accounts) in peripheral countries. The renewed focus on EMU, and the increased likelihood that it will begin on schedule, have shifted expectations of the future path of fundamentals in the higher-yielding EU countries in close alignment with the criteria of the Maastricht Treaty. As discussed below, there is considerable consensus among market participants that these improvements in current and expected fu-

ture fundamentals have been the primary driving force behind the convergence process, rather than extraneous factors such as excess liquidity.

The combination of monetary easing and convergence plays that narrowed interest rate spreads produced a favorable environment for fixed-income investors, especially for investors in the higher-yielding countries (again with the notable exception of the United Kingdom). Total returns on long-term bonds of maturities exceeding 10 years in 1996 amounted to almost 50 percent in Italy, 34 percent in Spain, 25 percent in Sweden, and on the order of 10–15 percent in core Europe. By comparison, with monetary policy leaning in the opposite direction, the total return on U.S. treasury bonds in 1996 was reduced by price depreciation (Table 23).

Statistics on "buy-and-hold" positions understate the (annualized) returns earned on aggressive convergence plays. Market participants report that these convergence plays were very different from those implemented in 1992. In the earlier episode, convergence plays typically exploited yield differentials in spot markets in an environment of managed exchange rates. These spot market convergence positions would involve funding a long position in the higher-yielding bond with a short position in German Bunds, or even more simply—but more capital intensive—establishing a long position in the higher-yielding bond. In either case, if the yield on

Table 23. Major Industrial Countries: Bond and Equity Index Returns
(In percent)

	1995		1996		January–May 1997	
	Local currency	U.S. dollars	Local currency	U.S. dollars	Local currency	U.S. dollars
Bond indices[1]						
United States	23.73	23.73	1.51	1.51	1.05	1.05
Japan	15.47	11.08	7.30	−4.42	1.10	1.01
Germany	18.91	28.15	8.45	0.25	2.23	−6.83
France	19.21	29.60	13.89	7.73	2.06	−8.24
Italy	19.83	22.40	30.46	35.58	2.84	−7.48
United Kingdom	18.69	17.53	7.55	18.96	4.80	0.20
Canada	22.73	26.10	13.10	12.61	2.07	1.59
Equity indices						
United States (S&P 500)	34.11	34.11	20.26	20.26	14.52	14.52
Japan (Nikkei 225)	0.74	−3.09	−2.55	−13.20	3.65	3.56
Germany (Commerzbank)	5.26	13.43	22.51	13.26	23.25	12.33
France (CAC 40)	−0.49	8.19	23.71	17.01	11.58	0.32
Italy (Banca Commerciale)	−6.78	−4.78	12.38	16.79	14.34	2.85
United Kingdom (FT-SE 100)	20.35	19.18	11.64	23.48	12.21	7.28
Canada (TSE-300)	11.86	14.93	25.74	25.19	7.68	7.17

Source: Bloomberg Financial Markets L.P.

[1] For government bonds with maturities of 7–10 years.

the long position fell in relation to German Bunds, then the capital gains on the position represented the excess return to the convergence position.

By contrast, in the recent episode, convergence plays were more sophisticated in that the capital cost associated with establishing positions in cash markets was circumvented to a large extent by taking spread positions in the interbank swaps market. This was reflected in the sharp expansion in swap market activity in 1996: according to the International Swaps and Derivatives Association (ISDA), swaps activity denominated in deutsche mark—the "pay side" associated with convergence positions in the swaps market—soared by 44 percent in the first half of 1996.

To illustrate how convergence plays are executed in swap markets, consider the following simple example. Suppose an investor believes that the spread between five-year lira and deutsche mark rates will narrow from its "current" level of, say, 300 basis points. The investor enters into a swap contract in which he or she agrees to pay a stream of deutsche mark fixed interest payments (calculated based on a given underlying notional sum) in exchange for a stream of lira fixed interest payments. One year later, suppose the spread on four-year lira and deutsche mark rates is 100 basis points, and to simplify things also assume that the lira-DM exchange rate has not changed—alternatively, the investor could have swapped out the currency risk of the original position. The investor could then unwind his position by entering into an offsetting swap in which he or she pays fixed lira rates for four years and receives fixed deutsche mark rates. In sum, the swap portfolio has no open currency position. However, the investor is receiving net lira income of 200 basis points guaranteed for the next four years.

With substantial convergence in interest rates having occurred by late 1996, there was a measure of consensus in financial markets that, based on current fundamentals (including the available information on which countries would participate in EMU in 1999), the convergence process had largely run its course. Convergence positions were, therefore, largely unwound by late 1996. This does not imply that it was unlikely that there would be further narrowing of some spreads in the run-up to EMU, but rather that any further narrowing of spreads would hinge on new information about entry into EMU or further improvements in fundamentals.

The most widely watched indicator of the "maturity" of the convergence process is the difference between current yield spreads and forward yield spreads after 1998 (as implied by current deposit and swap rate curves). For core EMU countries, spreads (over deutsche mark) on seven-year swaps at end-May 1997 were within 20 basis points of implied forward spreads in early 1999, and the levels of these spreads were small (Table 24). In other words, there is little room for further convergence in core Europe in the run-up to the introduction of the single currency in 1999, as the markets have effectively priced in participation in EMU by all core European countries in 1999.

In Italy and Spain, spreads on seven-year swaps at end-May 1997 were about 40–50 basis points above spreads on implied forward swaps in early 1999. As current long-term interest rates are a function of short-term rates in the run-up to EMU and beyond, one can interpret the difference between current and implied forward long-term interest rate spreads as a gauge of the maturity of convergence only by first separating out the (possibly large) component of these spreads that is

Table 24. One-Year and Seven-Year Interest Differentials with Germany, February 28, 1995, January 1, 1996, January 30, 1997, and May 31, 1997[1]

(*In basis points*)

	One-Year Interest Differential				Seven-Year Interest Differential			
	February 28, 1995	January 1, 1996	January 30, 1997	May 31, 1997	February 28, 1995	January 1, 1996	January 30, 1997	May 31, 1997
France								
Spot	118	132	15	39	53	50	−20	−13
January 1, 1999[2]	29	15	−22	−23	. . .	. . .	−25	−27
January 1, 2000[2]	30	−4	−29	−28	. . .	. . .	−26	−29
January 1, 2001[2]	25	4	−26	−21	. . .	. . .	. . .	−25
Italy								
Spot	546	648	342	345	464	439	150	168
January 1, 1999[2]	424	398	154	189	. . .	. . .	92	116
January 1, 2000[2]	415	334	105	148	. . .	. . .	78	98
January 1, 2001[2]	385	322	81	116	. . .	. . .	. . .	. . .
Spain								
Spot	438	532	231	185	467	356	87	73
January 1, 1999[2]	435	310	86	85	. . .	. . .	46	33
January 1, 2000[2]	410	269	54	49	. . .	. . .	37	30
January 1, 2001[2]	378	254	33	41	. . .	. . .	. . .	34
Sweden								
Spot	319	449	111	144	. . .	241	112	122
January 1, 1999[2]	. . .	206	137	173	. . .	. . .	100	123
January 1, 2000[2]	. . .	155	131	158	. . .	. . .	98	111
January 1, 2001[2]	. . .	95	112	130	. . .	. . .	. . .	. . .
United Kingdom								
Spot	204	269	370	378	149	133	201	171
January 1, 1999[2]	165	122	293	289	. . .	. . .	132	103
January 1, 2000[2]	157	94	211	202	. . .	. . .	99	63
January 1, 2001[2]	143	86	146	132	. . .	. . .	. . .	. . .
European currency unit								
Spot	132	135	87	95	103	73	20	28
January 1, 1999[2]	91	79	6	22	. . .	. . .	5	14
January 1, 2000[2]	70	12	10	14	. . .	. . .	4	12
January 1, 2001[2]	56	18	−5	12	. . .	. . .	. . .	. . .

Source: Bloomberg Financial Markets L.P.

[1]Calculated based on the one-year and seven-year forward rates embedded in the yield curve.

[2]Based on the data for the first available day of the year.

attributable to the convergence that has yet to take place in short-term rates in the run-up to EMU. There is, in general, substantial room for convergence in short-term rates for the peripheral countries because risk premiums for credit and currency risks have become concentrated to a considerable degree at the short end of yield curves. Specifically, spreads over deutsche mark one-year deposits were less than 100 basis points for core EMU countries in May 1997 as well as for implied one-year swaps in 1999 and beyond, but were several hundred basis points for lira and peseta deposits in May 1997, and the implied forward spreads narrow by early 1999 by roughly 50 percent for Spain and Italy. Thus, the fact that the difference between current and forward swap spreads suggests that there will be considerable further convergence in the interest rates of the non-core EMU countries reflects to a considerable degree the fact that short-term rates are expected to converge sharply over the next few years.

Trading positions in European fixed-income markets have most recently focused either on the prospects of participation in EMU by the various countries and exploiting what is considered to be overly optimistic or pessimistic pricing, or else on buying insurance (for spot positions) against an unraveling of the convergence process.[3] A particularly

---

[3]To varying degrees investors have sought to combine positions in derivative markets with spot positions in European bond markets with the objective of having some measure of insurance against adverse shocks to the EMU process. Some of the more common strategies in this regard involve combining long positions in call options on deutsche mark–lira spreads (for example) and short put option positions on the same spread at a lower strike price (so that the cost of the option position is negligible). In this example, if the spread were to widen, the option positions' value would offset the decline in the cash position in bonds. More simply, combining long positions in put options on lira bonds, say, with short positions on deutsche mark puts provides a qualitatively similar hedge.

notable instance of the former was the negative spread between French and German rates prevailing in late 1996 and early 1997. Strong domestic demand (especially by insurance firms) for French government bonds—caused by a large shift of funds from money market mutual funds into insurance products and administered savings products—reportedly was instrumental in pushing the French yield curve below the German yield curve.[4] Market participants report that this caused a massive deconvergence position taking: these convergence and subsequent deconvergence trades are estimated to be among the largest speculative positions ever taken in the international capital markets—some estimates put U.S. hedge funds' and proprietary trading desks' positioning in the French franc–deutsche mark sector at end-1996 in excess of $50 billion. U.S. hedge funds in particular amassed considerable positions in forward swaps designed to profit from a narrowing in the negative spread of French franc forward rates to deutsche mark.

Spreads in Dollar-Bloc Countries and Corporate Markets

The terms "spread compression" and "convergence" also well describe developments in the bond markets of industrial countries outside Europe, in the corporate bond markets, and in the emerging markets. As discussed in Chapter II, the narrowing of spreads on emerging market credits in 1996 was no less impressive than that which occurred in the context of EMU. Spreads in the U.S. corporate bond market fell sharply for all credit qualities, and there was compression in spreads across credit ratings—high-yield ("junk") bond spreads neared the all-time lows of the mid-1980s (see Figure 43). Spreads on Canadian, Australian, and New Zealand credits also narrowed dramatically (Figure 42), as reflected most clearly by the fact that the Canadian government yield curve through 10-year maturities slipped below the U.S. curve for the first time in two decades, and 30-year Canadian bonds traded at par with U.S. 30-year treasury bonds for the first time ever.

This spread tightening in global bond markets occurred in an environment of low volatility in both foreign exchange markets and bond markets (see Figures 39 and 44, and Appendix 2 at the end of this annex). As discussed above under "Exchange Rates," this should not be surprising, for the same factors that led to improved exchange rate fundamentals—low inflation and efforts toward fiscal consolidation—had similar consequences in fixed-income markets—as well as on volatility in these markets—as risk premiums decreased. A notable exception to this is Japan, in

which volatility in fixed-income markets has been high in recent years (see Appendix 2). In the United States, although anticipation of a tightening of monetary policy caused periodic retrenchment from U.S. fixed-income markets and caused volatility to rise—as with the massive sell-off in early 1996—these concerns subsequently dissipated in the absence of compelling signs of inflationary pressures. When the Federal Reserve finally did raise the federal funds target rate by 25 basis points in late March, the markets had little reaction as the action had already been discounted in asset markets.

Fund-Raising in Fixed-Income Markets

Stability in the major bond markets and convergence in the higher-yielding markets provided favorable conditions for issuance of debt securities by private sector institutions in the domestic and international markets. Issuance was strongest by private sector entities from the dollar-bloc countries and from the higher-yielding EU countries—particularly those that experienced the sharpest narrowing in interest rate spreads. Issuance from Japan and from core Europe was less robust. In addition, efforts toward fiscal consolidation had the effect of dampening overall new issuance activity in most domestic debt securities markets.

In the international securities markets, net new issues grew by 73 percent in 1996, setting a new record (Tables 5, 25, 26). Dollar issues accounted for almost half of all new issues in 1996—compared with less than a quarter the previous year—and this trend has continued in 1997. In terms of growth rates, dollar-denominated issues rose 353 percent in 1996, compared with a decrease in the amount of new issues denominated in yen and deutsche mark. To some degree, the surge in new issues of dollar-denominated securities reflects the strong demand for funds by U.S. corporations and financial institutions, as issues by private sector entities from the United States rose 164 percent in 1996 and accounted for 25 percent of total new issues in 1996, compared with 19 percent in 1995. This suggests, however, that the strong surge in dollar issues reflects also issuance of dollar-denominated bonds by entities located outside the United States. It seems plausible that this is attributable to the demand by investors for dollar issues, as discussed above.

Much of the growth in new issues in the international markets came from entities located in the United States and the United Kingdom. Issuance by other industrial countries generally increased as well, but at much slower rates. The strong demand for funds in the United States derived from both corporations and financial institutions, whereas in most other countries the demand for funds came mostly from financial institutions. This points to a more general develop-

---

[4]See J.P. Morgan (1997b).

Figure 44. RiskMetrics Daily Price Volatility for 10-Year Government Bonds, January 19, 1995–May 30, 1997
(In percent)

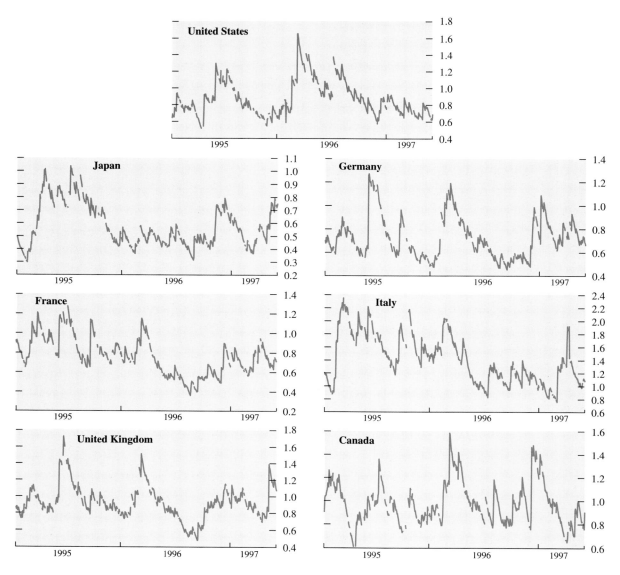

Source: J.P. Morgan.

ment in the international securities markets: financial institutions are accounting for a larger percentage of new issues by industrial countries in these markets. Indeed, currently almost three-quarters of issuance in the international markets by industrial countries is attributable to financial institution fund-raising.

In domestic debt securities markets, issuance grew at a much more moderate pace, just over 3 percent in

1996. Private sector issuance grew somewhat faster at about 11 percent, whereas public sector issuance fell in all of the major countries except Germany, Italy, Spain, and the United States. Among the major countries, private sector issuance was particularly strong in most dollar-bloc countries—Canada, Australia, the United Kingdom, and the United States. By contrast, issuance actually fell by private sector entities from

Table 25. Outstanding Amounts of International Debt Securities

(In billions of U.S. dollars)

	1993	1994	1995	1996	1997:Q1
All countries	2,037.8	2,441.2	2,802.5	3,225.9	3,240.7
Industrial countries	1,650.3	1,977.6	2,282.1	2,594.3	2,600.9
Of which:					
United States	176.9	209.6	272.8	402.6	418.1
Japan	340.1	361.3	369.2	356.7	344.6
Germany	120.1	188.6	269.1	342.4	356.4
France	153.1	185.5	207.4	215.9	211.6
Italy	70.2	85.2	92.8	95.8	92.2
United Kingdom	186.7	212.5	227.2	274.2	275.5
Canada	146.9	165.4	177.6	182.6	183.7
Developing countries	121.8	161.9	192.1	276.3	289.7
Offshore centers[1]	11.3	18.3	19.4	36.3	39.4

Source: Bank for International Settlements.

[1]The Bahamas, Bahrain, Bermuda, the Cayman Islands, Hong Kong, China, the Netherlands Antilles, Singapore, and other offshore centers.

most of the EU countries, although there was some modest increase in new issuance by entities in the higher-yielding EU countries.

Risks in Fixed-Income Markets

Low, and in many cases declining, inflation in the major countries, progress on the fiscal front, and low volatility in foreign exchange markets have created a favorable environment for fixed-income investors as well as lower borrowing costs for issuers. The bond market rally in 1996–97 rests on some assumptions about the future, which could change.

First, the markets have priced in an improved outlook for macroeconomic fundamentals—most important, low inflation—in all the major markets. The bal-

ance of risks points to accelerating economic activity and thus a tightening of monetary policy in at least some of the major countries. In the United States, capacity constraints evidently have little slack, and economic growth in Japan and several European countries appears to be gathering momentum. The main risk to the compression of yield spreads—in Europe, in the U.S. high-yield market, in emerging markets, and in smaller industrial countries—is that cyclical factors will increasingly imply a significant global tightening of monetary policy. If, however, growth does not accelerate in Japan and the major continental European economies, a further tightening of monetary policy in the United States will result in a further reallocation of global fixed-income funds toward the dollar markets.

Table 26. Outstanding Amounts and Net Issues of International Debt Securities by Currency of Issue

(In billions of U.S. dollars)

	Amounts Outstanding				Net Issues						
	1993	1994	1995	1996	1993	1994	1995	1996	1996 Q3	1996 Q4	1997 Q1
U.S. dollar	836.4	910.1	983.7	1,245.9	31.5	73.4	74.2	262.1	46.7	86.5	55.5
Japanese yen	272.3	412.6	496.7	517.6	33.8	106.8	108.3	81.2	24.5	19.0	14.1
Deutsche mark	192.8	244.0	318.8	347.1	31.2	27.5	55.1	54.8	10.6	12.6	13.9
French franc	92.7	131.6	149.0	168.1	34.5	27.0	5.2	29.1	7.0	7.1	7.2
Italian lira	37.7	57.5	69.7	99.7	13.0	18.4	10.4	27.3	3.7	11.7	12.1
Pound sterling	154.8	178.2	186.7	237.3	31.7	14.5	10.1	30.8	3.7	17.2	22.9
Canadian dollar	81.7	83.5	83.7	77.0	20.5	6.7	−2.1	−6.3	−2.6	−2.9	−0.2
Spanish peseta	10.6	10.7	13.2	17.9	3.5	−0.7	1.4	5.7	1.2	1.9	1.2
Netherlands guilder	44.9	65.9	84.5	95.3	7.9	14.8	13.5	18.1	3.8	6.3	4.0
Swedish krona	3.5	5.1	5.3	5.2	0.6	1.0	−0.4	0.0	−0.2	−0.2	−0.4
Swiss franc	149.1	161.2	189.0	165.7	−2.3	−6.4	4.4	4.2	0.4	0.3	0.2
Belgian franc	2.2	2.3	4.3	13.4	−0.4	−0.3	2.0	9.3	0.2	8.0	0.1
Other	159.1	179.0	217.9	235.7	−8.0	2.7	29.5	23.8	9.2	9.1	7.0
Total	2,037.8	2,441.7	2,802.5	3,225.9	197.5	285.4	311.6	540.1	108.2	176.6	137.6

Source: Bank for International Settlements.

In early 1994 the tightening of policy by the Federal Reserve Board was associated with one of the greatest corrections in global bond markets in history. Increased interest rates in the major industrial countries caused portfolio rebalancing in fixed-income markets away from the riskier markets, in part because of expectations of slower economic activity and thus a weakened ability of riskier credits to service their debts. In 1994, the correction was exacerbated by the unwinding of highly leveraged positions along the then very steep U.S. yield curve—when the Federal Reserve tightened monetary policy in February 1994, the rush to cover these short positions hastened and steepened the correction in bond markets. By contrast, market participants report that currently there is not a lot of leverage in the fixed-income markets. As noted above, there have been leveraged positions associated with the yen-carry trades, but these positions appear to have been unwound in 1997 because of the yen's strengthening and concern that interest rates may soon rise in Japan.

Markets have largely priced in the supposition that EMU will go ahead on time and that there is a high probability that many of the non-core countries will participate, if not in early 1999, then within the subsequent one to two years. It is widely believed that the major risk to EMU going ahead on time is that weak economic growth in Germany and France would prevent both countries from meeting the deficit criteria specified in the Maastricht Treaty. In such an event, proceeding with EMU by adopting a looser interpretation of the Maastricht criteria would open the door to a larger number of countries being eligible to participate in EMU from the start. The implications of continued weak growth and a larger number of initial participants in EMU could lead to increased volatility in European bond markets.

Spreads in Europe, whether current spot spreads or implied forward spreads, could in general reflect two factors: first, improved fundamentals—lower inflation, fiscal consolidation, and currency stability—and, second, the possibility that the conversion of currencies into a new (blended) currency has the effect of imputing value to fixed-income assets denominated in the weaker currencies. Short-term yield spreads are still quite large for the traditionally high-yield countries, and this, in tandem with the fact that yield curves for these countries are much flatter than for the core EMU countries, explains why implied forward yield spreads are projected to narrow significantly over the next few years. An important uncertainty is whether this expectation of further convergence is attributable to further improvements in economic fundamentals or to expectations that EMU will impute a direct benefit—in terms of lower yields—to the higher-yielding currencies.

Empirical studies have found that most convergence can be attributed to improved economic funda-mentals.[5] There is also a consensus among market participants that current spreads reflect improved inflation and fiscal outlooks in the higher-yielding countries, and by implication are not simply reflecting the expectation that some countries will benefit directly from a new currency that is supported by a firm monetary policy of the future European Central Bank (ECB). Nevertheless, concerns have been raised by market participants about two issues. First, it has been suggested that there is some risk that positions currently in place in European fixed-income markets could be sensitive to, say, a change in German monetary policy. In such a scenario, this could be associated with a sell-off in the U.S. markets to cover losses in the European swaps market. Second, market participants report that there exists a risk of the convergence plays on the high-yielding currencies unwinding if concerns arise in financial markets about the EMU process that call into question the future macroeconomic policies of peripheral countries. While an announcement of delayed entry for some of these countries is widely thought to imply some widening of spreads in these markets, such consequences could be managed so long as entry itself was not threatened.[6]

International Syndicated Loan Markets

Volumes and Margins

Keen competition from securities markets and from within loan markets maintained high volumes and slim margins in the international loan markets (Figure 45, and Table 6). Stimulative monetary policy in Europe boosted liquidity in European banking systems and, in tandem with sluggish growth in Japan and continental Europe, this liquidity spilled over to the international banking markets, and from there into those countries with buoyant economic activity (e.g., the United Kingdom, Australia, and the United States). Syndicated lending volumes have been spurred by refinancing operations, funding associated with mergers and acquisitions (particularly in the United Kingdom), backup facilities associated with commercial paper and asset-backed securities issues, and project financing—including loans arranged as components of financing packages involving securities and bank loans. Overall, announced syndicated credits rose 68 percent

---

[5]See, for example, Goldman Sachs International (1997a).

[6]As a major U.S. investment bank wrote in February 1997: "Our results suggest that the market valuation of Italian bonds has generally moved independently of the debates concerning the actual starting date for the EMU project and the timing of Italian participation in it. Unless the whole EMU project and/or Italy's eventual participation are put very seriously at risk, Italian assets would not necessarily suffer from Italy's delayed participation in EMU. Movements in economic fundamentals will continue to be the bond market's main driving forces." (Goldman Sachs International, 1997a, p. 1).

Figure 45. Spreads on Eurocredits[1]

(In basis points)

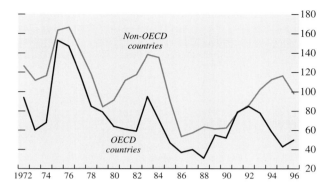

Source: Organization for Economic Cooperation and Development (OECD).

[1]Weighted average of spreads (over LIBOR) applied to Eurocredits signed during the period. Tax-sparing loans as well as facilities classified under "other debt facilities" are excluded.

in 1996 over 1995, or more than double the level in 1994. Syndicated loans to U.S. borrowers, however, soared 386 percent in 1996, an increase of $218.4 billion, which is more than the $213 billion increase in announced credits to all other countries combined.

Japanese banks continued their retreat from international lending markets in 1996, and this worked to hold back overall activity, especially in the interbank market: international lending by Japanese banks contracted by $20 billion in 1996, while fund-raising by Japanese banks in the international markets fell by $7.5 billion (Table 27 and Statistical Appendix Table A4). In terms of the share of international banking assets by nationality of banks, Japanese banks dropped 3 percentage points in 1996, which pushed their share to a 13-year low of 22 percent.[7] Activity by U.S. banks in the international markets was buoyed by increased demand in the Eurodollar market and financing associated with the increased demand by foreigners for U.S. bonds. Much of the activity in international banking markets was associated with the aggressive pursuit of foreign business by European banks, and especially German, Italian, Benelux, Swiss, and U.K. banks. Market participants report that convergence plays associated with EMU have been an important factor in the increased activity of European banks.

It has been widely reported that margins continued to come under pressure in 1996, but this is not reflected in data on weighted-average spreads for OECD countries (see Figure 45). These aggregate loan margins may mask the fact that lending activity

has expanded into new areas geographically as well as to new, lesser-known names with reportedly slim risk-adjusted margins. Indeed, the evidence is clear that margins on loans to non-OECD credits did narrow in 1996. In any case, these considerations prompted once again warnings from regulators that diligence must not be ignored in extending credits at razor-thin margins. U.S. regulators, in particular, expressed concerns also with the lengthening of maturities and relaxation of covenants to higher-risk borrowers.

Structural Developments

A notable development in cross-border banking is an increased displacement of traditional interbank credit by repurchase agreements (repos). There are many varieties of transactions that could be classified as repos, but they all consist of a contract that functions as a collateralized loan, and an agreement to repay the loan—repurchase the collateral—by a specified time (typically less than a week). The U.S. repo market is the oldest and also the largest such market, not least because most other countries have only recently introduced repo markets—most often owing to deregulation of money markets. For instance, repo markets opened in 1997 in Germany and in 1996 in the United Kingdom.

Only the international repo market comes close to the size of the U.S. repo market, a fact that reflects in large part the key role of U.S. institutions in the international markets and, thus, the integration of the U.S. domestic repo market with the international repo market. Recent estimates place outstanding repos at about $1 trillion in the international market—or roughly 10 percent of the stock of gross international bank lending—which is similar in magnitude to the U.S. market (Table 28).[8] Assuming an average life of about one week, this suggests annual turnover in the neighborhood of $40–$50 trillion. More important, the growth rates of repo markets have been high: the U.S. repo market has grown at about 20 percent annually in the 1990s, and during their first year of operation, repo markets in the United Kingdom and elsewhere have expanded very quickly.

The proliferation of repo agreements in interbank markets is attributable to several factors. First, there has been a heightened awareness of the credit risk associated with banks' expansion into less familiar geographic markets and also perhaps increased concern about the credit risk associated with advancing traditional lines to some of the major banks active in the international markets. Second, with banks increasingly active in securities markets, the repo market provides access to cheaper short-term funds than uncollateralized funds. Similarly, the other side of the

---

[7]Bank for International Settlements (1997).

[8]See Bank for International Settlements (1996b).

Table 27. Changes in Net Assets of BIS-Reporting Banks vis-à-vis Banks in Selected Countries and Regions[1]

(In billions of U.S. dollars)

	1990	1991	1992	1993	1994	1995	1996
All countries	−38.3	73.7	95.4	267.1	−299.0	206.8	. . .
Industrial countries	−22.7	87.1	22.2	179.9	−146.7	172.1	51.9
Of which							
United States	28.1	3.8	74.1	124.4	3.4	53.2	−21.3
Japan	47.0	−24.1	−59.9	−7.8	−6.3	−12.4	18.7
Germany	−21.5	13.1	55.2	−37.5	61.7	43.8	23.9
France	−17.0	−7.5	−52.1	0.8	12.0	−10.1	21.9
Italy	26.0	36.3	43.3	−18.0	1.7	−22.2	−9.3
United Kingdom	−32.1	44.4	27.4	116.0	−141.9	88.7	19.0
Canada	2.6	3.9	10.9	12.4	−5.8	−6.2	−10.9
Developing countries	−29.0	50.1	79.6	80.9	−115.3	112.0	54.5
Africa	−3.9	−3.7	−3.1	−1.0	−5.4	−3.9	−2.7
Asia	43.4	58.1	43.6	44.7	37.1	128.7	78.8
Europe	−1.8	−1.4	−8.2	−5.8	−29.4	−6.0	14.5
Middle East	−22.8	4.1	23.0	16.7	−0.9	−13.9	−19.4
Western Hemisphere	−43.9	−7.0	24.2	26.3	−116.8	7.1	−16.7

Source: Bank for International Settlements (BIS).

[1]BIS-reporting banks comprise banks in the Group of Ten countries (Belgium, Canada, France, Germany, Italy, Japan, the Netherlands, Sweden, the United Kingdom, and the United States) plus Austria, Denmark, Finland, Ireland, Luxembourg, Norway, and Spain, and foreign affiliates of these banks.

repo transaction—a "reverse repo" (a purchase with an agreement to resell at a specified price on a future date)—provides greater security because of the collateralization of the loan advanced. Third, (reverse) repo transactions are a more efficient use of a bank's capital than traditional interbank lines: capital requirements on banks' lending activities—including those of the Basle Capital Accord of 1988—provide for capital weights on collateralized loans corresponding to the weight attached to the collateral, which is zero for OECD government securities. Fourth, the increased emphasis on repos has fostered the development of standardized collateralization procedures and documentation which has, in turn, further facilitated the use of this method of interbank funding.

The rapid proliferation of repos in interbank markets has resulted in a closer integration of securities

Table 28. United States: Outstanding Repurchase Agreements (Repos)

(In billions of U.S. dollars)

	Overnight and Continuing Repos	Term Repos
1990	242.72	188.64
1991	276.80	237.57
1992	367.26	324.23
1993	438.66	372.86
1994[1]	441.94	344.27
1995	522.44	360.79
1996	571.03	428.55

Source: Board of Governors of the Federal Reserve System.

[1]Break in the series.

markets and banking markets. This integration has also been promoted by the participation of institutional investors and investment banks in the international loan markets. This is evidenced by the prevalence of securities structures such as note issuance facilities—including commercial paper facilities and medium-term notes programs—that have reduced the distinction between bank loans and securities issues. Further, financing packages that entail a blend of securities financing and bank loans have also become common. The distinction between loans and securities will undoubtedly narrow as new tools are developed for pricing (and thus trading) credit risk and as mergers between commercial and investment banks proceed.

The increased integration of securities markets and banking has also been facilitated by progress in securitizing loans, which has been fostered by the desire of many banks to economize on capital and thus pare loans from their balance sheets. The securitization of loans has proceeded along two dimensions. One dimension is establishing secondary markets for loans, which has already been implemented in the United States and is the objective of the recently formed Loan Markets Association in London. The second dimension is bundling portfolios of loans with the objective of securitizing the bundle. The issuance of these asset-backed securities (ABS) has grown rapidly in recent years. According to the Federal Reserve Board, in the United States asset-backed securities outstanding reached $738.1 billion in 1996. Although this represents less than 4 percent of all U.S. credit market debt—amounting to $19.9 trillion in 1996—its rate of growth has been two to three times that of overall credit market debt. Although asset-backed securities markets include the packaging of claims on bank loans to consumers and firms, credit card debt, and, in the international markets, the securitization of various types of receivables from developing countries, the market for securities-backed syndicated loans and junk bonds—collateralized loan obligations and collateralized bond obligations, respectively—are two segments of this market that have been particularly robust in the 1990s, after suffering a setback associated with the collapse of the high-yield bond market in the United States in the late 1980s.

Equity Markets

Recent Developments

Equity prices in industrial countries rose sharply in 1996 and this trend has continued in 1997. In local currencies, European markets have generally been the star performers, with most markets comfortably outperforming the 20 percent advance in U.S. equity prices in 1996 and the further 14 percent gain in U.S. equity prices during the first five months of 1997 (see Table 23 and Figures 8–9). Some of the momentum in European equity markets has been attributed to improved prospects for the exporting sector associated with the depreciation of most currencies in continental Europe against the dollar. This depreciation of local currencies against the dollar is clearly reflected by the fact that European equity prices rose substantially less when measured in U.S. dollar terms, although they still generally posted gains on a par with the U.S. market.

Underlying the strong performance of equity prices has been a downward trend in inflation and interest rates in the industrial countries, both of which are important for the discounted real value of future corporate earnings. In Japan, very low inflation and interest rates in 1996 were not sufficient to boost equity prices, largely because of lingering concerns about the health of the financial sector. On a risk-adjusted basis, the performance of Japanese equities relative to money market rates in recent years has lagged behind the performance of other major industrial country equities (Table 8 and Figure 8), although Japanese equity prices have shown evidence of strengthening in 1997.

Among the major industrial countries, the U.S. equity market has clearly been the star performer in the 1990s (see Figure 8). Canada has trailed the U.S. market somewhat, and Japan has followed a different course after the collapse of its asset-price bubble at the beginning of the decade. In Europe, the U.K. market has been the strongest performer, reflecting the relative performance of the U.K. economy and thus

corporate earnings. Equity prices have picked up recently in France and Germany, while following a more erratic course in Italy. The key questions that these very different performances raise are, first, whether there are indications of overvaluations in the United States given the duration of the market's rally and, second, why the Japanese equity market has languished.

Japanese equity prices have been weighed down by at least two factors. For one thing, there has been net selling pressure by important segments of the domestic investor base—life insurance companies, banks, nonfinancial companies, and equity investment trusts. Negative cash flow experienced by some of the major institutional investors in Japan (e.g., life insurance companies) has forced these investors to be net sellers of equities; in addition, weak balance sheets of other financial sector companies have led them to liquidate their equity holdings. Prior to the collapse of the asset-price bubble in 1989, investment trusts had more than half of their assets invested in Japanese equities. Since 1989, this share has fallen steadily, and by the first quarter of 1997 was just over 20 percent. This drop in portfolio allocation has been due in part to lower equity prices, but in recent years there have also been net redemptions from equity investment trusts. The large amount of liquidity in the nonfinancial corporate sector—which, as discussed above, has resulted in stagnant loan growth in the banking system—has not had the effect of supporting equity prices through share buybacks because of the current tax code. Indeed, if not for the net buying of Japanese equities by foreign investors and public institutions, Japanese equity valuations would have been even weaker.

Second, lower equity prices have raised concerns about their potentially damaging effects on business and consumer confidence as well as on bank balance sheets. The latter concern stems from banks' direct holdings of equities, their reduced ability to issue convertible bonds to raise capital, and the possible deterioration in both the quality of bank loans that weakness in equity prices might reflect as well as the value of the collateral underlying loans.[9] Reflecting these concerns, bank stocks have underperformed the broader market by a substantial margin: from the beginning of 1996 to May 1997, the TOPIX index recorded a drop of about 10 percent, whereas the TOPIX bank index fell about three times as much.[10]

A rebound in Japanese equity prices, therefore, rests on the resolution of some important sources of uncer-

---

[9]At end-1996, banks' direct holdings of equities were on average about 6 percent of total assets, although equity holdings vary considerably across banks (Bridgewater Associates (1997a)).

[10]The TOPIX is a capitalization-weighted index of all companies listed on the First Section of the Tokyo Stock Exchange. The TOPIX bank index represented 18 percent of the TOPIX index on July 10, 1997.

tainty. There can be little doubt about the positive prospects for Japan's exporters—automobile, machinery, and electrical equipment companies—in the current environment, but the overall index is likely to be held back by financial stocks and the lack of local investor support to the market. A resolution of the financial system problems in Japan would undoubtedly be an important positive development for Japanese equity prices.

In the United States, the rise in equity prices since early 1996 has been matched by stocks in many other industrial countries. However, this rise in the U.S. market came on top of larger and more sustained price gains in the first half of the 1990s. Indeed, since the beginning of the decade, U.S. equity markets have outperformed most other industrial country markets, in some cases by a factor of two or more. To some extent, these differences reflect the different stages of the economic cycle, with the U.S. expansion at a much more mature phase than that in Europe and Canada. It is also worth noting that over a longer historical period—going back to 1970—the performance of the U.S. market adjusted for exchange rate changes is quite similar to the performance of the French, German, and U.K. markets and still falls well short of the Japanese market (Figure 46). While the Japanese market has been particularly weak in the 1990s, it remains at relatively high levels given the very rapid price growth prior to the 1989 crash.

Although improved profits and lower interest rates may account for a large part of the rise in U.S. equity markets, the size and pace of the upswing, as well as its longevity, have raised questions about possible overshooting. The Dow Jones Industrial Average has taken just 4 years to double in value since 1992, compared with a previous historical average of 17 years. From 1900 through early 1997, the Dow Jones index has risen at an average annual growth rate of just under 5 percent (excluding dividends), but it rose more than 25 percent in 1995 and then again in 1996. Indeed, about two-thirds of the market's gain since 1970 has occurred in the 1990s, and about half since the beginning of 1995. Measured relative to GDP, U.S. market capitalization has increased from 69 percent in 1970 to about 107 percent in 1996.

To put the market's recent performance in context, it is helpful to compare it with the other great bull markets. Two previous periods of rapid increases in U.S. equity prices stand out. The first ran from October 30, 1923, through September 3, 1929, and the second great bull market ran from April 28, 1942, through January 18, 1966.[11] During the 1923–29 period the Dow Jones index rose by 343 percent, which translates into a 25 percent annual increase. During the 1942–66 period the index rose 969 percent, which

represents an annual growth rate of 10 percent. In comparison, the Dow has risen about 800 percent from August 1982 through early 1997, or about 15 percent annually. Focusing on a narrower window covering just the past two or three years would double this annual rate of increase. In any case, the current bull market is of the same order of magnitude as the two previous great bull markets. It should be borne in mind, however, that two of the greatest bear markets in the United States occurred after these two bull markets.

Improved fundamentals clearly underlie an important part of the rise in U.S. equity prices since the beginning of the decade. First, reductions in inflation and interest rates are generally correlated with movements in stock values—Japan is the lone, notable exception in recent years. Second, the rise in corporate profits, absolutely and as a share of national income, since early in the decade corresponds to an important part of the rise in market valuation relative to the size of the U.S. economy. The share of corporate profits in national income has reached its highest level in 20 years (Figure 47). But the key question is whether current market valuations also reflect expectations of further increases in the share of profits that may prove unrealistic.

On March 5, 1997, Federal Reserve Board Chairman Alan Greenspan addressed this question when he stated: "If you look at a normal pricing model for stocks, what you get is a not unreasonable level of prices if the earnings forecasts which the analysts are publishing are accurate."[12] These earnings forecasts are indeed high in a historical context, especially longer-term forecasts. In the mid- to late-1980s, five-year real earnings growth forecasts fluctuated between 5 and 6 percent. Since 1990, they have gone straight up and by the second quarter of 1997 they were about 10 percent.[13] An important reason for these unusually high earnings forecasts was noted above: actual earnings have been remarkable in the past five years or so, and thus earnings forecasts have simply been brought into line with recent experience. Earnings for the Standard & Poor 500 companies in the first quarter of 1997 grew by about 15 percent over the level a year earlier, and a majority of companies' actual earnings exceeded analysts' forecasts.

Risks to U.S. Equity Prices

Perhaps the key question in assessing the sustainability of U.S. equity prices is whether companies can continue to grow their earnings at double-digit rates. Average five-year real earnings growth since 1960 has been just over 2 percent; this raises the likelihood that

---

[11]See Emmons (1997).

[12]Quoted from Bloomberg Business News (1997).
[13]Bridgewater Associates (1997b).

Figure 46. Major Industrial Countries: Stock Market Indices[1]
(Indices, January 1970 = 100)

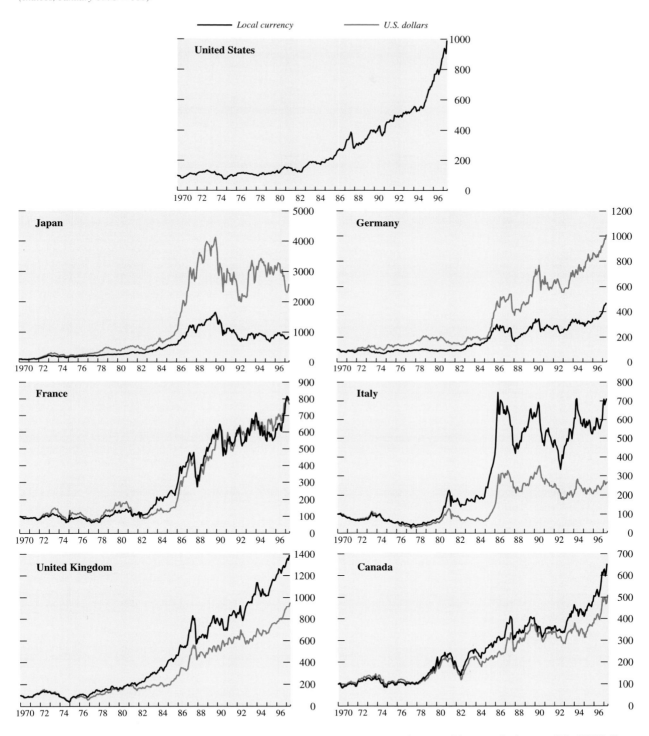

Sources: Bloomberg Financial Markets L.P.; International Monetary Fund, *International Financial Statistics* database; and The WEFA Group.
[1]Monthly averages of daily observations from January 1970 through May 1997.

Figure 47. United States: Corporate Profits and Market Capitalization[1]

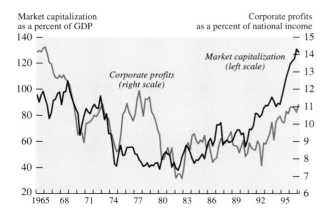

Source: The WEFA Group.

[1]Corporate profits are before deducting the federal, state, and local taxes. Data for 1965:Q1 to 1997:Q1.

the balance of risks to earnings is below analysts' forecasts. These risks derive from the observation that profit margins cannot continue to improve in an environment of near-capacity economic activity and tight labor markets. The unemployment rate in the United States reached a quarter-century low of 4.9 percent in April 1997.

There are other reasons to be cautious about current valuations of U.S. equities (see Figure 10). First, dividend yields at about 2 percent have fallen to historic lows and are about half their long-term average. This fact may be partly explained by changes in tax laws and an increasing share of tax-exposed investors. Moreover, current dividend yields are not unusual in an international perspective: dividend yields in 1996 were under 2.5 percent in Japan, Germany, Italy, Canada, Sweden, Switzerland, Austria, Denmark, Finland, and Norway, and above 3.5 percent only in the United Kingdom, Australia, Belgium, and New Zealand.[14] Second, the market-price-to-book ratio, and the closely related Tobin's q ratio, indicate substantial departures from their historical ranges. Although largely explained by the shift away from capital-intensive industries to services, the rise in the ratio of equity prices to book value is still extraordinary. And third, the average price-earnings ratio, while not yet outside its long-term range, is clearly approaching the upper end. On the other hand, given the favorable interest rate environment, the equity-yield gap, which measures the difference between long-term bond yields and the inverse of the P/E ratio, remains within

its historical range and, significantly, is still well below the levels reached prior to the 1987 stock market crash. Also, some analysts have argued that the dividend yield is now a less relevant indicator because many investors hold equities for capital gain rather than current income, and also that price-asset ratios have become less meaningful in view of the growing importance of service-based industries.

Some market commentators have suggested that it is inappropriate to judge current valuations by comparing standard valuation indicators to historical ranges. The argument put forward is that the U.S. business cycle has fundamentally changed insofar as the length of economic expansions has increased while the length of economic recessions has decreased.[15] Possible reasons for this structural change include just-in-time inventory management, trade liberalization, more flexible labor and capital markets, and financial market deregulation. Thus, the argument goes, corporate earnings have become less volatile, so the equity risk premium (over government bonds) has declined. Interpreting this argument in the context of the usual model for equity prices as representing the present discounted value of dividend payments, the associated decrease in the discount rate (from a drop in the risk premium component) can easily produce the conclusion that equity prices could increase sharply over a short period of time just owing to a modest decrease in the risk premium. Note that this hypothesis is equally applicable to explaining the narrowing in corporate bond yield spreads discussed under "Bond Markets" above. It is difficult to test this hypothesis as the risk premium is unobservable and estimates can vary widely. Nonetheless, although equity price volatility has shown some increase recently, earnings volatility has dropped sharply, which is consistent with this hypothesis (Figure 48).

On balance, it does not seem that U.S. equity markets are as far out of line as they were in 1987 or as Japanese markets were in 1989, when bond yields were high and rising, corporate earnings were much weaker, monetary policy was stimulative for several years leading up to the markets' corrections, and general asset-price inflation was apparent, especially in real estate markets (see Appendix 3 at the end of this annex). However, they clearly are at levels that make them vulnerable to negative shocks in the form of higher interest rates, which played an important role in the last two major stock market crashes (the 1987 U.S. and 1989 Japanese corrections), or lower corporate earnings. Also, market volatility has increased significantly in 1996, though this appears to represent a return to more normal levels after a period of unusual stability (see Appendix 2). Finally, the rapid run-up in

---

[14]BZW Securities Limited (1997).

[15]For instance, this view is advanced in Goldman Sachs International (1997b).

Figure 48. United States: Corporate Profits Volatility[1]

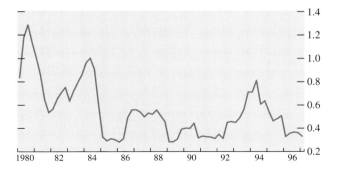

Source: IMF staff calculations using data from The WEFA Group.
[1]Calculated as standard deviation for the previous two years ending in the quarter shown of corporate profits (in percent of national income). Data for 1980:Q1 to 1997:Q1.

equity prices in late 1996 and into 1997—which seems more difficult to justify on the basis of improved fundamentals—also may suggest a cause for concern.

One of the factors that has helped propel the U.S. market upward has been significant net inflows from small investors, routed mostly through the conduit of equity mutual funds (Table 29 and Box 5). From 1989 to 1995, household (direct and indirect) holdings of

equities rose from 32 percent of all households to 41 percent, and equity holdings as a share of total financial assets of households rose from 26 percent to 40 percent.[16] The net inflow into U.S. equity mutual funds from January 1995 through April 1997 totaled $424 billion, almost $300 billion of which occurred since the start of 1996. To put the role of equity mutual funds into perspective, in April 1997 they managed $1.88 trillion in assets, which is equal to 20 percent of the market capitalization of the New York Stock Exchange, the American Stock Exchange, and NASDAQ (the over-the-counter market) combined.[17] The relative attractiveness of expected returns on equities, in comparison with other savings vehicles, has been at work here. But the historically low volatility of stock prices in recent years (see Appendix 2) may also have reassured investors. Recently, volatility, as reflected in options premiums, has been picking up (Figure 49). It remains to be seen how recent equity investors will react to an environment where equities appear more risky and turn in less spectacular gains.

There are reasons to expect that a sharp correction in equity prices—which would reduce price-earning ratios to near the long-term average—need not have serious consequences for the U.S. economy. Consumer spending has not been driven sharply upward

---

[16]See Board of Governors of the Federal Reserve System (1997).
[17]These data are from the Investment Company Institute.

Table 29. U.S. Mutual Funds: Net New Cash Flow and Total Assets
(In billions of U.S. dollars)

| | Net New Cash Flow | | | | | Assets | | | |
| | | To equity funds | | To bond and | To money | | Equity | Bond and | Money |
	Total	Total	Domestic	Foreign	income funds	market funds	Total	funds	income funds	market funds
1984	54.2	5.9	4.9	0.9	13.3	35.1	370.6	83.1	54.0	233.6
1985	68.3	8.5	7.7	0.8	65.2	−5.4	495.5	116.9	134.8	243.8
1986	164.4	21.9	17.7	4.2	108.6	33.9	716.2	161.5	262.6	292.2
1987	40.1	19.1	19.6	−0.6	10.9	10.2	769.9	180.7	273.2	316.1
1988	−23.1	−16.2	−13.8	−2.4	−7.0	0.1	810.3	194.8	277.5	338.0
1989	73.0	5.8	4.6	1.2	3.1	64.1	982.0	249.0	304.8	428.1
1990	44.5	12.8	6.3	6.5	8.5	23.2	1,066.8	245.8	322.7	498.4
1991	112.3	39.5	36.4	3.2	67.2	5.5	1,395.5	411.6	441.4	542.4
1992	156.5	79.2	72.1	7.0	93.7	−16.3	1,646.3	522.8	577.3	546.2
1993	229.2	129.6	91.1	38.5	113.7	−14.1	2,075.4	749.0	761.1	565.3
1994	84.6	119.3	75.4	43.9	−43.4	8.8	2,161.5	866.4	684.0	611.0
1995	212.8	128.2	116.5	11.7	−4.8	89.4	2,820.3	1,269.0	798.3	753.0
1996	323.7	221.6	175.3	46.3	12.6	89.4	3,539.2	1,750.9	886.5	901.8
1997										
January	53.9	29.1	23.0	6.1	3.6	21.2	3,687.0	1,854.7	897.6	934.7
February	40.9	16.1	13.7	2.4	2.3	22.5	3,731.1	1,865.5	907.2	958.4
March	10.1	10.7	8.1	2.7	−2.0	1.4	3,666.0	1,810.2	890.3	965.5
April	−5.8	15.7	10.6	5.1	0.8	−22.3	3,729.0	1,879.0	903.1	946.9
May[1]	. . .	18.5	. . .	. . .	2.5	. . .	. . .	. . .	. . .	. . .

Source: Investment Company Institute.
[1]Estimated.

Box 5. Trends in Funds Management

Large-scale shifts in households' saving behavior and deregulation of financial industries in many industrial countries have made the fund management industry one of the most dynamic segments of the financial industry in recent years. In 1985, the 10 largest institutional investors in the United States managed assets worth $969 billion (expressed in 1995 dollars). A decade later, the top 10 institutional investors managed assets of $2.4 trillion.[1] Growth has been especially marked in mutual funds. U.S. mutual fund assets have risen at double-digit growth rates since 1970 when they amounted to just $48 billion.[2] By the mid-1980s mutual fund assets had reached $495 billion, and by April 1997 they totaled $3,729 billion. Over the 1970–97 (April) period, the number of U.S. mutual funds increased from 361 to almost 6,500, and the number of individual accounts with mutual funds increased from about 11 million to 151 million. Although the institutionalization of savings, and especially the shift by households from bank accounts toward mutual funds, has not been as marked in most other industrial countries as it has in the United States, the trend is apparent in other countries also and this process is widely expected to gather momentum in coming years.

Demographic changes and the increased sophistication of small investors around the world, in tandem with the deregulation of financial markets, have intensified competition for savings among banks, mutual funds, insurance companies, and pension funds. In part because the fund management business is a low-overhead business, the response of the industry to intensified competition for funds has been consolidation. This consolidation activity has been evident in two main features of the fund management business.

First, in an increasingly global financial market, the importance of geographic presence has lessened, and thus fund management companies have responded to competitive pressures by consolidating their operations geographically. Global asset management companies are increasingly consolidating operations in one center, such as San Francisco, Boston, or London. For instance, Dresdner Bank, Germany's second-largest bank, and Barclays Bank, the largest bank in the United Kingdom, both announced in late 1996 that they were consolidating their global asset management operations in San Francisco. This geographic consolidation has been facilitated by the ability of fund management companies to contract out aspects essential to the business of fund management, but which are distinct from the management of funds per se. In particular, the development of mutual fund "supermarkets" that offer the services of a wide variety of fund management companies at the retail branch level has led to a geographic separation of the fund manager and the investor in those funds. Similarly, fund management companies have increasingly contracted out back-office functions to third parties, which themselves may be geographically far removed from the fund managers.

Second, there has been a great deal of merger and acquisition activity among fund management companies, particularly in the past few years. Fidelity Investments, the largest institutional investor in the United States, managed $426.7 billion in assets at end-1995, almost two-and-a-half times the assets (in 1995 dollars) of the largest institutional investor in 1985, Pru-

---

[1]*Institutional Investor* (July 1996).
[2]Data on U.S. mutual funds are from the Investment Company Institute.

---

by the rise of the market during 1996, and a market fall back would presumably not induce a sharp fall in final demand. Moreover, the strength of the economy and financial institutions along with an improved securities market infrastructure all suggest the consequences of a significant correction could be managed without having major consequences for the health of the economy. Such expectations are consistent with the experience after the 1987 crash (see Box 6 on Circuit Breakers).

Derivative Markets

Recent Developments

Growth of the global derivative markets during the past decade has been phenomenal both in the exchange-traded sector and in the over-the-counter markets (Statistical Appendix Tables A5–A7; see also Tables 9–10). During the period 1986–96, the annual trading volume of exchange-traded contracts—including interest rate futures and options, currency futures and options, and stock market index futures and options—nearly quadrupled, reaching 1.16 billion contracts at end-1996. The growth of these markets has been even larger when measured by outstanding notional principal: the average annual growth rate of outstanding notional principal of exchange-traded contracts has been 32 percent over the past decade and stood at $9.9 trillion at end-1996. The growth and the size of the over-the-counter markets is even more impressive: the notional principal of outstanding currency and interest rate swaps and interest rate options reported by members of the International Swaps and Derivatives Association (ISDA) rose from $0.9 trillion in 1987 to $24.2 trillion in 1996, representing an annual average growth rate of 45 percent.

More comprehensive surveys of the current size of global derivative markets paint an even more striking

dential.[3] In comparison, the 300th largest asset manager at the end of 1995 controlled $2.7 billion in assets, just slightly more than the $2.4 billion (in 1995 dollars) managed by the 300th-largest asset manager in 1985. This points clearly to a consolidation of assets, with the largest asset managers growing much more rapidly than the smaller asset managers. Although Fidelity's growth in total assets under management slowed in 1996—it received just 10 percent of net equity mutual fund inflows versus 20 percent in 1995—it is a very large player, with some estimates attributing 12–15 percent of turnover in U.S. equities to Fidelity alone. In Europe, too, consolidation in the fund management industry has taken hold in recent years. In late 1996, two French insurance groups, AXA and UAP, announced plans to merge to create one of the world's largest asset managers, with combined assets of $420 billion (end-1995 figures), rivaling Fidelity of the United States.

So, while it is clear that consolidation is having profound effects on the size of the larger asset managers, can one conclude that investment assets are concentrating in the hands of just a small number of mammoth asset managers? The evidence does suggest that consolidation is working in this direction, but the pace is not as fast as might be imagined, particularly in the United States. In 1985, the top 10 asset managers accounted for 23 percent of the assets of the largest 300 asset managers, and this share was the same five years

later.[4] By end-1995, however, this figure had increased modestly, to 27 percent. Moreover, the top 100 asset managers increased their share of the assets managed by the top 300 asset managers by 9 percentage points over 1985–95, accounting for 83 percent of assets at end-1995. Similarly, in Europe, the top 10 asset managers increased their share of assets managed by the top 100 asset managers by 7 percentage points over the period 1991–95, from 31 to 38 percent of the assets of the largest 100. Consolidation activity, therefore, seems to have increased the relative size of the largest asset managers much more in Europe than in the United States. In the United States, consolidation activity has been more broadly based, increasing the relative size of the largest hundred or so asset managers. However, it is noteworthy that classification of asset managers geographically is becoming increasingly meaningless—as mentioned above, recently some large European asset managers have consolidated global asset management activities in the United States. Moreover, consolidation activity has increasingly been across borders, reflecting a tendency toward the evolution of global asset managers.

In light of the forces affecting the fund management industry in recent years and the response of the industry to those forces, it is widely held that the outlook for the industry contains considerably more consolidation in the industry as well as geographically. An oft-painted scenario for the industry early in the next century is one in which there are a relatively small number of very large global companies each managing assets well in excess of $150 billion and a number of smaller management companies surviving in regional niche markets.

---

[3]The figures reported here and below on institutional investors are calculated from figures reported in *Institutional Investor* (various issues) and the IMF's *International Financial Statistics*.

---

[4]*Institutional Investor* (July 1996).

---

picture.[18] According to the survey conducted by the Bank for International Settlements in early 1995, the notional value of outstanding OTC foreign exchange, interest rate, equity, and commodity derivative contracts totaled $47.5 trillion (after adjusting for double counting and including estimated gaps in reporting) at the end of March 1995. About 98 percent of this total

is accounted for by interest rate ($28.85 trillion) and currency derivatives ($17.7 trillion). In addition to OTC derivatives, intermediaries that were involved in the survey coordinated by the BIS reported that they were engaged in a further $16.6 trillion of exchange-traded derivatives. In aggregate, therefore, respondents to this survey of users of derivatives in 26 countries revealed that (after adjusting for double counting) they were involved in about $64 trillion, by notional principal, of derivative contracts. To put this in perspective, the aggregate market value of all bonds, equities, and bank assets in Japan, North America, and the 15 European Union countries totaled $68.4 trillion at end-1995, which is about 7 percent larger than the size of derivative markets as measured by the above survey.

Considering the sheer size of the derivative markets, sustained growth rates of the magnitudes reported above are unprecedented in global financial markets. This fact clearly points beyond purely cycli-

---

[18]In April 1995, the Bank for International Settlements (BIS) coordinated the first survey by central banks in 26 countries of OTC and exchange-traded derivative markets in these countries, providing the most comprehensive survey to date and believed to capture about 90 percent of the intermediaries active in the derivative markets. The survey included swaps, forwards, and options for foreign exchange, interest rates, equities, and commodities, whereas the ISDA survey was limited to interest rate and foreign exchange swaps and options. Moreover, the BIS survey included many derivatives positions that were not recorded in the ISDA survey, not only because the BIS survey captured more market participants, but also because it reported many arm's-length derivatives contracts that are netted out in the ISDA survey.

Figure 49. Implied Volatility: S&P 500, Nikkei 225, and DAX Indices

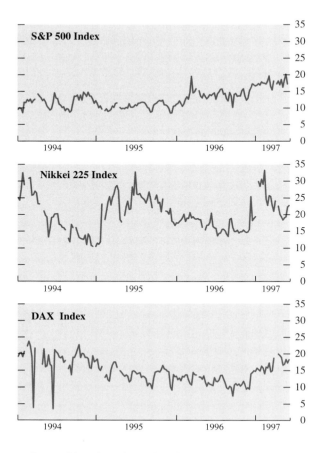

Source: Bloomberg Financial Markets L.P.
Note: Implied volatility is a measure of the expected future volatility of the index based on market prices of the call options on futures on the index. The annualized percent rate of change plotted in the figure is a weighted average of the estimates of the implied volatility of call option futures.

cal influences on derivative volumes, and in particular to the importance of structural factors fueling growth of these markets. Hedging and position taking associated with cyclical conditions are surely key motives for the use of derivative financial instruments to begin with—as reflected clearly in the sharp rise in the volume of interest rate products during the 1994 global bond market correction, for example—but the sustained growth of these markets does not derive from cyclical influences per se. Rather, the key structural factors influencing the growth of these markets are an increased understanding by financial and nonfinancial institutions of the capabilities these instruments offer for repackaging and reengineering major cyclical and balance-sheet risks, in tandem with technological, analytical, and numerical advances in pricing and evaluating the risks of derivative contracts.

Although the markets for derivative financial instruments, particularly in the major industrial countries but increasingly also in the developing world, are large by any measure, it is clear that sustained growth of the global derivative markets is not likely to abate soon. This momentum derives both from the major countries—where derivative markets for some of the largest risks, such as credit risk, are far from mature—as well as from the newer markets in the developing world—which have recorded the most dramatic growth in exchange-traded derivatives activity in the 1990s. Further growth in the global derivative market will present challenges to private risk management technologies and to supervision and regulation. Nonetheless, these markets, and the instruments traded in them, are increasingly better understood by dealers in the over-the-counter markets and by the financial and nonfinancial institutions that are the end users of derivative products.

Structural Changes in Derivative Markets

Three key structural changes have accompanied the rapid growth of derivative markets. First, derivatives have increasingly become a low-margin, high-volume business. This commoditization of derivative markets does not necessarily imply that the markets are becoming less personalized, or more centralized, but rather simply that the products traded in these markets have become familiar to market participants, and these markets have also become concentrated in well-understood, or "standard," instruments. Some have attributed this standardization of products to the huge losses incurred by financial and nonfinancial enterprises associated with large derivative positions—including Orange County, Procter & Gamble, MG Corporation, and Barings. Although these losses were not always associated with positions in exotic products, the magnitude of the losses provoked an awareness and reevaluation of the purposes and risks of derivatives in general. The immediate consequence was a widespread withdrawal of demand for exotic, highly leveraged structures and a shift toward simpler structures—especially currency and interest rate swaps—and a refocusing on the risks and benefits of using these instruments. Some structures that have traditionally been regarded as exotic—notably, digital and barrier structures—have become mainstream products. This category of derivative products has its payoff tied—often in a binary fashion—to whether an underlying asset price reaches some trigger level; it has become mainstream because it facilitates the trading of volatility of asset prices directly. Products in this category accounted for an important share of activity in the currency and interest rate segments of the over-the-counter markets in 1996 and 1997.[19]

---

[19]See, for example, *Euromoney* (1997).

Second, derivative markets are consolidating, planting the seeds for an integrated, concentrated global market. In the over-the-counter market, the concentration of activity is already large. For instance, U.S. commercial banks had $20 trillion notional principal of derivatives on their books at the end of 1996, of which 8 banks accounted for 94 percent and the top 25 banks accounted for 98 percent.[20] This concentration of derivatives activity among a small number of institutions in the United States mirrors the reality in global derivative markets, in which these same U.S. institutions account for a large share of OTC derivatives activity. Although it remains to be determined which, and how many, institutions are able to establish themselves as truly global financial institutions, it is clear that OTC derivatives activity has increasingly become concentrated among the handful of institutions that are best positioned to be global institutions, as these institutions are best able to intermediate risk management needs on a worldwide basis.

This globalization of derivative markets is also apparent in the exchange-traded segment of derivative markets. This is reflected most clearly by the proliferation of trading links among both major and smaller exchanges in all regions of the world. For example, the major U.S. derivatives exchanges—the Chicago Mercantile Exchange and the Chicago Board of Trade—have established links with foreign exchanges, and discussions continue between the two main U.S. exchanges over the possibility of a direct link between them. In 1996 alone, the Chicago Mercantile Exchange unveiled alliances with the Marché à Terme International de France (MATIF), London International Financial Futures Exchange (LIFFE), and Deutsche Terminbörse (DTB), the three major derivatives exchanges in Europe. For instance, the link between the Chicago Mercantile Exchange and the DTB permits DTB trading screens to be placed directly on the floor of the Mercantile Exchange for trading in German stock index (DAX) futures, while in the case of MATIF and LIFFE, the Chicago Mercantile Exchange is permitted to trade short-term European interest rate products after closing hours in Europe (an arrangement that mirrors the alliance between the Chicago Board of Trade and LIFFE for longer-term interest rate products).

Within Europe, consolidation of exchange-traded derivative markets has occurred as a result of trading links as well, but it has also been reflected in mergers and closures of exchanges. For instance, the Swiss (Soffex) and German (DTB) exchanges announced in late 1996 a strategic alliance that will create a common technical platform for trading derivatives and integrate the two clearing and settlement systems, and in 1997 the Danish and Swedish exchanges announced plans to merge their dealing systems. In London, LIFFE and the London Commodity Exchange have recently been merged, and in Ireland the Irish Futures and Options Exchange was closed in August 1996.

As discussed in Annex IV, EMU threatens to eliminate much of the trading in exchange-traded derivative products in Europe, and thus the three major derivatives exchanges—DTB, LIFFE, and MATIF—are aggressively trying to capture market share ahead of the introduction of the euro. Specifically, the major exchanges have accelerated the introduction of new products in an attempt to establish leadership in the interest rate instruments that are likely to be at the core of fixed-income markets with a single currency. On the heels of the launch in late 1996 of Euromark futures by LIFFE and DTB, a working party of MATIF members suggested in late 1996 that a three-month contract in euros should be introduced by April 1998 and suggested as well the introduction of one-month, 5-year, and even 30-year euro contracts in order to establish a position in a broad range of the euro yield curve.

A third structural change in derivative markets is that OTC markets are fast becoming the cornerstone of global derivative markets. In 1987, the notional principal of outstanding OTC interest rate and currency swaps was 44 percent larger than the global exchange-traded market. By 1990, the relatively faster growth of the OTC market pushed its size to 51 percent larger, and by 1995 it was 65 percent larger. In 1995, trading volume on the major North American, European, and Asia-Pacific derivative exchanges actually contracted, whereas in the OTC markets currency and interest rate swap activity soared—in terms of notional principal outstanding, it expanded by over 40 percent, reaching $15.2 trillion. The combination of renewed focus on EMU and intense focus on the direction of interest rates in several of the major countries contributed to a slight rebound in activity on exchanges in 1996—particularly in Europe—but the major arena of growth in global derivative markets in 1996 was once again the OTC markets.

There are at least four factors underlying the growth in the OTC markets' share of the derivative business. First, the flexible, personalized nature of the OTC market gives these markets natural advantages in terms of arranging suitable packages of products for customers. Second, the OTC markets have adopted those features of exchange-traded markets that are valuable. For example, in October 1996, 11 of the major players in the swaps market established a swaps collateral depository—the Chicago Mercantile Depository Trust Corporation—which will standardize and automate the process of managing collateral and manage payments netting, trade valuation and administration, and global reporting to dealers involved in OTC transactions. Third, the large risks for which derivative instruments have not yet been fully developed are

---

[20]United States, Office of the Comptroller of the Currency (1996).

Box 6. Circuit Breakers

As equity markets around the world continue their upward momentum, many of them reaching new heights, concerns about possible overshooting and a subsequent sudden drop in equity prices are beginning to emerge. Following the equity market crash of 1987, many countries instituted various forms of circuit breakers. Ten years later, these countries and others are taking a second look—deciding whether to reset the conditions for their use or whether to adopt some form of them for the first time. Despite their growing use, especially among emerging market countries, there continue to be misconceptions about the purpose and effectiveness of circuit breakers. Circuit breakers are only a temporary measure for reducing market volatility or unidirectional price movements.[1] If fundamental information is the basis for the price movement, and not features of destabilizing trading strategies or panics, then circuit breakers simply slow the eventual price movement: they do not reverse it.

The two most common circuit breakers are trading halts and price limits. Trading halts can be initiated in two ways: a specialist, or other exchange official, may have the authority to halt trading; or a trading halt may be imposed after a price change of a given amount or percentage. The length of the halt can be pre-established or can be discretionary. Price limits place bounds on the price change but do not limit the period of nontrading: if a price hits a limit, trading beyond that price limit cannot take place; only when prices fall back within the limits can trading resume. Another type of circuit breaker is a limitation on the types of trades or strategies that can be initiated during a period of high volatility, or even in a normal period. For example, some exchanges routinely disallow short sales unless the price has experienced an "uptick," that is, the price had to have moved up by the trading increment. Another example is that all index arbitrage trades must be executed through an electronic system that delays their execution by five minutes when price changes exceed a given amount.

To choose the circuit breaker mechanism that will be most effective, it is important to define the goals of the circuit breaker and to assess the surrounding environment. In most cases, the goal of circuit breakers is either to dampen price movements caused by speculative activity or to slow down the price effects of trading strategies that are thought to have destabilizing or overshooting effects (e.g., portfolio insurance, the dynamic hedging of options). Even when destabilizing speculative activities or trading strategies are absent, there is often a belief that sharp movements in prices, regardless of their cause, are likely to engender a panic mentality, causing investors to act irrationally, further reinforcing existing price movements. Similarly, even when price movements reflect underlying fundamentals, a limit on the maximum amount lost in a given period may allow participants who would not have been able to pay for their losses had the full price decline occurred to pay on a timely basis. Regardless of which type of circuit breaker is chosen, to operate effectively the market needs to be centralized, information needs to be disclosed during the halt, and there needs to be a well-known method for the resumption of trade.

Trading halts can only truly halt trading when trading is centralized. In the United States, for example, when trading halts were introduced after the 1987 market break, close coordination between the stock exchanges and the futures exchanges, on which associated futures contracts were traded, was required. In October 1996, the Dhaka Stock Exchange in Bangladesh instituted a circuit breaker to limit price movements to a daily 5 percent, only to have its effectiveness undermined by the unofficial curb market where no such impediment to trading could be maintained.

An integral element to using any circuit breaker mechanism is the disclosure of information. It is imperative

---

[1]In fact, some empirical studies find that circuit breakers may increase volatility (Lauterbach and Ben-Tsiyon, 1993; Lee, Ready, and Seguin, 1994).

---

most likely to be successful in OTC markets. Most important, the market for credit risk derivative contracts—in which banks in particular could trade loan credit risk—is inherently a highly heterogeneous product market (see Appendix 1 to Annex III), which exchanges are not conducive to handling efficiently. Finally, the OTC derivative markets have an important regulatory advantage over the exchange-traded markets. Specifically, whereas the Commodity Exchange Act of 1974 gives the Commodities Futures Trading Commission regulatory authority over the derivative exchanges, the so-called Treasury Amendment effectively exempted from CFTC oversight certain financial futures traded off of U.S. exchanges. There has been a great deal of uncertainty about the extent of the amendment's reach, which has in turn prompted numerous lawsuits and legal uncertainty. Legislation introduced in early 1997 would, among other things, limit the CFTC's oversight of OTC markets only with respect to foreign currency products[21] and would also permit the exchanges to establish separate, unregulated markets that are restricted to institutional investors. If passed into law, this latter feature would reduce the competitive advantage of the OTC markets, but the significance of this effect is unclear.

---

[21]If the proposed legislation is passed into law it would reverse the February 25, 1997, Supreme Court ruling that off-exchange trading in foreign currency options is exempt from CFTC regulation.

that market participants learn something during a trading halt that helps them determine the instrument's price: both fundamental information and order flow information are important. Depending on the trading mechanism, either indicative quotes or postings of bids and offers and the amounts underlying them should be given at intervals during the halt to provide information about order imbalances. If open outcry is used, market participants should freely announce their willingness to buy or sell at various prices.

In addition, there needs to be an established and well-known method for resuming trade. A single call auction, whereby a specialist gathers the bids and offers over a set period of time and establishes a market-clearing price at which all the existing orders receive the same execution price, is thought to be one of the most equitable. It helps to relieve an element found in most panics—the desire to get an order executed before the price falls farther.

In addition to the immediate microstructure issues surrounding the trading environment, there are also infrastructure issues that may require attention. When clearing and settlement procedures are not well established or take extended periods of time to operate, uncertainty regarding the solvency of the participants can arise, limiting liquidity and participation when it is most needed and, in some instances, inhibiting the use of the exchange entirely as a venue for trading.

As an alternative to circuit breakers, share repurchases by corporate issuers may help stem a dramatic price decline in equity markets. At some point, a firm may deem the price of its stock low enough to buy it back and reissue it at a later date for a profit, thereby obtaining additional equity from the market. Share repurchases signal to the market that the firm, with inside knowledge of its value, believes that the shares are undervalued. Similarly, purchases from a major participant in the market can show confidence and help inhibit further sales. To allow these mechanisms to operate, a country may need to relax or eliminate restrictions regarding corporate repurchases.

Other institutional features that may reduce the incidence of a crisis include (1) restrictions on bank lending for stock purchases by requiring various amounts of collateral;[2] (2) better audit trails to detect market-trading abuses, such as price manipulation that may start a panic; and (3) education of market participants, especially small retail investors, to enable them to understand the practices and procedures surrounding trading during normal times as well as the different procedures that may occur during stressful periods.

While certain types of circuit breakers may achieve some goals, they are all impediments to a freely functioning market—preventing buyers and sellers from executing trades at mutually agreed prices—and have some deleterious effects. Circuit breakers may limit trading by participants that are attracted only by large price moves, and hence eliminate a stabilizing factor. In most instances, the existence of circuit breakers is likely to alter participants' behavior around their imposition. For instance, a "magnet effect" may occur when participants recognize that as the price approaches a price limit they will be unable to execute their desired trades and so they execute early. Alternatively, an opposite "repelling effect" may occur when participants prevent the limit from being hit because they know their ability to trade will be impaired. While these behavioral trading effects are certainly present, the most basic criticism of circuit breakers is that when fundamental information implies a large price movement, circuit breakers merely lengthen the time involved in obtaining the new price level.

---

[2]The collateral should not be the same as the instrument being purchased because this would reinforce price movements. For example, if a bank loan is used to purchase equity and the collateral underlying the loan is also equity, a fall in equity prices means that, to maintain the collateral, the borrower needs to sell equity in an already falling market, adding further pressure on equity prices.

The increasingly central role of the OTC markets is reflected also by the approach that market participants took in establishing convergence positions in 1996 in Europe. As noted previously, these convergence positions were heavily concentrated in the swaps market, which pushed deutsche mark–denominated swaps activity up 44 percent in the first half of 1996. Earlier in 1996 these positions entailed paying deutsche mark and receiving a higher-yielding currency. Perhaps the most notable positioning in the context of EMU occurred later in 1996 and focused on the French franc versus the deutsche mark yield spread. Earlier in 1996, convergence positions in this market were mounted on the belief that this yield spread would narrow. However, the French forward curve actually traded below

deutsche mark's later in the year, which in turn caused very large deconvergence position taking—estimates and commentary from market participants suggest that the magnitude of these deconvergence trades made them some of the largest speculative positions ever mounted in international capital markets, with some estimates putting positions amassed by U.S. investors alone in excess of $50 billion at end-1996.

Developments in Systemic Risk Management

As financial markets become more integrated and increases in technology and telecommunications permit risks to be unbundled and managed on a more centralized basis, regulation will need to adapt to the changing environment of the institutions under its purview. This trend calls for a more centralized, or at least a more coordinated, form of regulation—or as Federal Reserve Board Chairman Greenspan put it, "regulation must fit the architecture of what is being regulated."[22]

A trend toward the removal of regulatory barriers separating financial institutions and toward more integrated regulatory structures is being considered in a number of countries. In the United States, the Treasury Department has proposed a financial sector restructuring that would permit further involvement of commercial banks in the securities and insurance businesses. The Federal Reserve Board has made it known that it would favor a repeal of the Glass-Steagall Act and has already relaxed a number of restrictions placed on commercial banks' Section 20 subsidiaries, the organizational structures originally permitted to carry out limited nonbanking businesses. In the United Kingdom, the new Labor government has proposed to house all financial institution regulation, including bank supervision, under one roof, within the Securities Investment Board. Japan, too, is introducing financial sector reforms that will allow linkages among banking and securities market activities and establish an independent agency, the Supervisory Agency for Financial Entities, charged with overseeing bank supervision as well as supervision of other financial institutions.

Along with proposals for consolidated new regulatory structures are efforts to increase the coordination among existing regulatory and supervisory entities. The number of bilateral memoranda of understanding (MOUs) signed by various regulatory agencies continues to increase dramatically. Recently a number of countries have signed multilateral MOUs assuring that their information sharing and emergency procedures are mutually consistent. Along these lines is the ongoing work of the Joint Forum, a group made up of bank, securities firm, and insurance regulators previously called the Tripartite Group. The Joint Forum is charged with the improved regulation of financial conglomerates in a global environment. While the forum has made some headway over the last year in facilitating the exchange of information among the groups of supervisors, the establishment of a definition for a "lead regulator" has eluded them so far. In many countries, the regulation of banks, securities firms, and insurance companies is executed in an isolated way and fears of losing influence in a merged regulatory entity or to another regulator have long dominated the political debates in these countries. The forum's latest progress was reported to the G-7 Summit Meeting in Denver.

As the international regulatory community attempts to find more efficient ways to ensure a systemically sound financial system, more reliance is being placed on self-regulation and market discipline. As public disclosure is the cornerstone for market discipline, efforts to harmonize accounting standards and increase meaningful disclosure are accelerating worldwide.[23] For instance, to enhance the functioning of market discipline by setting accounting and disclosure standards for all corporations, the International Accounting Standards Committee (IASC) has agreed to complete a core set of International Accounting Standards by March 1998, 15 months ahead of its scheduled release. If acceptable to the International Organization for Securities Commissions (IOSCO) and the various national regulatory bodies represented on its committees, this set of standards will pave the way for increased cross-border offerings and listings and other international capital flows. Note that IOSCO endorsement would permit companies outside of North America and Japan to have access to those capital markets without the cost or confusion caused by restating their accounts.

The U.S. Financial Accounting Standards Board (FASB) is pursuing a longer-term project that is devoted to studying the conceptual and measurement problems associated with establishing a "fair value" for all financial assets and liabilities appearing on the balance sheet. Although the United States usually leads developments, both the International Accounting Standards Committee and the United Kingdom's Accounting Standards Board (ASB) are hot on the heels of this development. By March 1998, the IASC intends to have in place, as part of its comprehensive set of standards, a standard that requires all financial instruments to be carried on the balance sheet at their current value. The ASB has also promulgated a discussion paper on the topic. The move toward fair value accounting, whereby financial instruments on the balance sheet will be carried at their current values, is now broadly based, with the FASB, the ASB, and IASC all on board. While it will not happen overnight, balance sheets are likely to provide a fuller picture of the financial health of corporations in the future.

Private sector financial institutions have already responded to increased pressure, both from regulators, but more important from other market participants, to publish additional information about their risk-taking activities. The Basle Committee and IOSCO jointly released a study in November 1996 examining the latest round of derivatives disclosures of banks and securities firms. Last year, for instance, a number of banks voluntarily disclosed more than is legally re-

---

[22]Greenspan (1997), p. 4.

[23]In recognition of the importance of harmonization, the Basle Committee has set up an Accounting Standards Subcommittee to do a cross-country comparison of current accounting and disclosure standards for banks.

quired of them. Financial institutions recognize that well-informed investors are more willing to provide funding and capital than poorly informed ones.

Of course, to report reliable information regarding earnings and the risks undertaken to obtain them, an institution must have the means to calculate the information. Information systems and risk measurement techniques are thus continuing to absorb an increasing share of the resources of most financial institutions. One U.S. accounting firm, utilizing the expertise of a number of private sector experts and regulators, has introduced a set of "Generally Accepted Risk Practices" to help coordinate an assessment of a firm's risk management system. The comprehensive framework comprises 89 core principles, grouped into the following categories: risk management strategy; risk management function; risk measurement, reporting, and control; operations; and risk management systems. The intention is to provide a robust risk management framework for banks, securities houses, and other financial institutions that will address the whole range of risks faced by these firms. The proposed practices could be used as a benchmark against which private sector auditors would judge firms' risk management systems, perhaps endorsing or certifying those that exceeded the benchmark. This is one type of self-regulation, potentially enhancing market discipline, that is part of a more general trend toward increased risk disclosure.

In sum, supervisory and regulatory developments mirror the trends occurring in global capital markets—increased consolidation of regulatory structures accompanied by increased coordination. Moreover, there is a movement toward more reliance on mechanisms and rules that are "market friendly," that is, ones that encourage self-regulation and reinforce market discipline.

Appendix 1
Extracting Information from Options Prices

Forward rates have long been used as indicators of market expectations. Adjusted for risk, these rates can be interpreted as the market's assessment of the mean of the distribution of possible future values for the underlying price. New techniques based on options prices offer a refinement on this information by providing market-based indications of the probabilities associated with different ranges for the future value of the underlying price, thus lending some context to the mean interpretation of the forward rate.

Options prices can reveal this added information because of the unique way their ultimate value depends on the price of the underlying security. An option has value at its expiration date (expiry) only if, on that date, the price of the underlying security (S) falls within a particular range. If S is outside this range at expiry, the option is worth nothing. The range of positive value is determined by the option's type—put (sell) or call (buy)—and its strike price. For a call option to have value at expiry, S must lie above the strike price. For a put to have value, S must lie below the strike price. If S is inside this range at expiry, the value of the option is always positive and equal to the difference between S and the strike price.

Prior to expiry, a call option's price will reflect the market's current assessment of the probability that S will lie above the call's strike price and the market's assessment of how far above the strike price S is likely to be, assuming that at expiry it does lie somewhere above the strike price. Analogously, a put's price is determined by the probability that S will lie below the put's strike price and the market's assessment of how far below the strike price S is likely to be, assuming that it is somewhere below the strike price.

There are now several techniques to extract market-based probabilities from options prices and they all rely on the fact that options with different strike prices reflect the probabilities associated with S falling within different ranges. By comparing the prices of several options that differ only in strike price, one can infer the probabilities associated with S being within these different ranges at the options' expiration date.[24]

When there are many options on a given instrument, so that the strikes are relatively close together and they range over a significant interval of the possible outcomes, the inferences one can draw about the distribution become quite detailed. Nonetheless, even when there are many options, the fact that the strikes do not range over all possible outcomes means that some a priori assumptions must be made about the distribution before it can be estimated from observed option prices. One such assumption is that the distribution comes from a particular family of distributions with unknown parameters. The unknown parameters are estimated by finding those that best explain the observed options prices—often by least squares.[25]

Figure 50 gives an example for the yen-dollar exchange rate for early September 1997 as estimated on May 20, 1997. It was estimated from options on the futures traded on the Chicago Mercantile Exchange, under the assumption that the distribution can be described by a weighted average of three lognormal distributions.[26] From this estimated distribution one can

---

[24]See Söderlind and Svensson (1997) for a review of these techniques.

[25]The familiar Black-Scholes formula and inferences based on it use one option price and the assumption that the distribution is lognormal. The example given below uses 50 options prices and a least-squares technique developed by Melick and Thomas (1997).

[26]This distribution has nine estimated parameters—a μ and σ for each of the three lognormal distributions and the three weights (π's) that mix them. It can be written as follows:

$$f(x) = \pi_1 \cdot lnd(x;\mu_1,\sigma_1) + \pi_2 \cdot lnd(x;\mu_2,\sigma_2) + \pi_3 \cdot lnd(x;\mu_3,\sigma_3);$$

$$0 \leq \pi_i \leq 1; \sum_{i=1}^{3} \pi_i = 1.$$

Figure 50. Distribution for Yen-Dollar Exchange Rate in Early September 1997 Implied by Options Prices on May 20, 1997

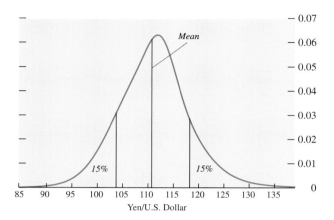

Source: Bloomberg Financial Markets L.P; and IMF staff calculations using data from the Chicago Mercantile Exchange.

compute market based probabilities associated with the exchange rate being within specific ranges. For example, on this day the market priced the options as though it assigned a 15 percent probability to the yen-dollar rate being below 104 in early September and an equal probability to the rate being above 118.3. The mean of the distribution, at 111.3, is below the peak of the distribution, reflecting a skew toward relatively large appreciations of the yen against the dollar.

There are two important caveats attached to any technique that extracts probabilities from options prices. The first concerns inferences about the shape of the distribution in the range above the highest strike price and below the lowest strike price. For the day plotted, the lowest available strike price was 98. The only information the options data provide about the distribution below 98 is the probability of S being below 98 and the mean of this portion of the distribution ($E[S \mid S \leq 98]$). If the mean of this portion of the distribution were 96, for example, then the options data alone could not distinguish between a distribution that assigned this probability evenly over the range from 95 to 97; a distribution that assigned this probability evenly over the range of 94 to 98; and any other distribution below 98 that has a mean of 96. For many purposes, such as the computation of the 15 percent confidence limits given above, the distinction between these "observationally equivalent" distributions is irrelevant. Nonetheless, it is important to note that the particular shape of the distribution above the highest strike and below the lowest strike is largely determined by the assumptions one makes about the functional form of the distribution.

The second caveat pertains to the interpretation of the estimated distribution. As noted above, the distribution implied by options prices can provide a context for the mean interpretation of the forward rate. As with forward rates, option prices incorporate market participants' preferences, or attitudes toward risk, as well as their beliefs about the possible future values of the underlying price. Thus, the probabilities calculated from options do not reflect market participants' beliefs alone. Instead, they reflect how much market participants are willing to pay to insure against certain outcomes, which incorporates both the probabilities attached to these outcomes as well as the costs associated with them. Without detailed information about the preferences and portfolio holdings of market participants, it is impossible to disentangle the influence of preferences and beliefs. (This difficulty arises with any inference made from financial market prices and is not confined to forwards and options.) Nonetheless, the information in options prices provides a glimpse at the range of possible outcomes that market participants consider possible and how much they are willing to pay to insure themselves against these various outcomes.

Appendix 2

Have Securities Markets Become More Volatile?

As a measure to dampen volatility in the U.S. equity market, the New York Stock Exchange begins to limit computer-guided trading once the Dow Jones Industrial Average moves by 50 points during the day. In 1996, the Dow Jones Industrial Average changed by more than 50 points from the previous day on 56 days. Compared with previous years, 1996 was truly unusual in that 50-point changes in the Dow Jones index were much more common. While this phenomenon is partly due to the rising index level, the large market moves along with worldwide financial market deregulation and the increase in international capital flows have fostered a widespread belief that volatility has increased in recent years. Critics have pointed to the introduction of derivative instruments with complex, nonlinear payoffs, and uncertain macroeconomic policies for additional causes of increasing securities market volatility.

Can one conclude that equity markets, and in particular, the U.S. equity market, have become more volatile recently? Similarly, the "bond market massacre" of 1994 has lead some observers to conclude that bond markets have become increasingly volatile in recent years. Is that a reasonable assessment?

Consider first the volatility of the U.S. equity market, as measured by the standard deviation of weekly percentage changes in the Standard & Poor 500 index

[27]For computational details, see figure note.

Figure 51. Historical Stock and Bond Price Volatility in the United States, Japan, and Germany[1]

(In percent)

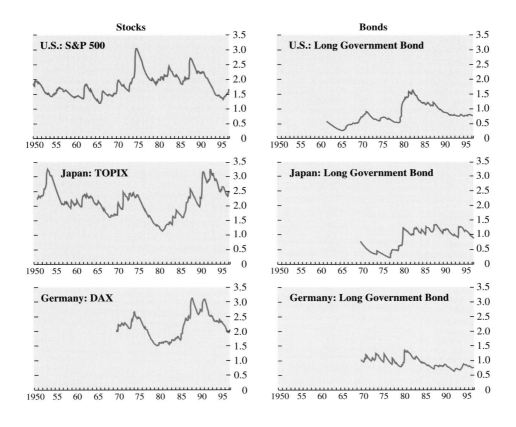

Sources: IMF staff calculations based on data from Bloomberg Financial Markets L.P.; and The WEFA Group.
[1]Weekly standard deviation in stock and bond price changes, computed as follows: standard deviations are calculated from a weighted moving average of past weekly squared returns. The weights decline exponentially starting with a coefficient of .01 producing relatively smooth curves designed to highlight long-run changes. Returns are weekly percentage changes in prices. Bond prices are calculated assuming a coupon rate equal to the yield.

(top left panel of Figure 51).[27] Comparing recent volatility levels to the postwar record clearly shows that current volatility by this measure is well within the historical range of variation. The U.S. stock market actually displays less volatility now than any time since the early 1970s, and the period following the first oil crisis remains the most volatile since the 1930s (not shown). Any long-lasting effects from the most recent upsurge in volatility following the 1987 crash seem to have all but vanished.

In Japan and Germany, current volatility in the equity markets is not large compared with historical levels, and in both countries the recent trend in volatility is downward sloping. The recent boom and bust of asset prices in Japan have increased volatility but only from a historical low in the early 1980s to a level now just slightly above the average for the last 45 years.

Stock market volatility in Germany peaked around the 1987 crash and again in the aftermath of the reunification and the Gulf War of 1990 but has clearly tapered off in recent years.

Next, consider bond markets, where volatility is generally lower. Events that change investors' beliefs about future inflation typically trigger bond market volatility; oil price shocks and changes in monetary policy are prominent examples. The volatility in weekly long-term U.S. government bonds (top right panel) topped around the shift in monetary policy in 1980, and bond price volatility has fallen markedly since. The bond market turbulence in 1994 associated with the tightening of policy by the Federal Reserve Board halted a further decrease in volatility. The subsequent bouts of turbulence in 1995 and 1996, associated in part with heightened uncertainty about the strength of the U.S. economy—and thus the possible course of Federal Reserve policy—have also kept volatility from decreasing to the pre-1980s level. This points to the key role of money market volatility in explaining recent bond market volatility, while conventional economic fundamentals such as inflation and economic growth seem to have played only minor roles.[28]

Comparing volatility of weekly long-term government bond yields across the United States, Japan, and Germany shows that the recent volatility has not been unusual in a historical context in any of the countries. The relatively high volatility in recent years in Japan reflects the fluctuating yen and money market rates, arising from heightened uncertainty about the collapse in asset prices, about the health of the financial system, and about the strength of economic growth. With zero inflation and short-term interest rates near zero, signs of a substantial strengthening of economic growth could have quantitatively important effects on expected inflation and official short-term interest rates, which would then filter into the long end of the yield curve. While bond market volatility in Japan is higher now than in the unusually tranquil 1970s, it is only slightly higher than in Germany and the United States, and the most recent trend in Japan seems to be downward sloping. In Germany, bond market volatility is now close to a historical low by the measure applied here.

The increased popular concern with securities market volatility is not warranted in general. Current stock and bond market volatilities are close to their historical averages in the major economies, and the folklore effects on volatility of the bond market sell-off in 1994 persisted only in the Japanese market and are dissipating now. The Japanese experience does illustrate that economic policies that successfully achieve stable goods prices do not necessarily accomplish the more difficult task of asset-price stability.[29]

Appendix 3

Current U.S. Equity Prices Compared with the 1987 U.S. and 1989 Japanese Bubbles

A natural approach to gauging whether stock prices are overvalued is to compare them with the theoretical price calculated from the discounted (expected) future stream of dividend payments that the stock has claim to. There are significant practical difficulties associated with this approach because of uncertainty about future dividends and the appropriate risk-adjusted discount rates. An alternative approach is simply to com-

---

[28]See Bank for International Settlements (1996c), and also IMF (1996).

[29]See Christoffersen, Lim, and Schinasi (1997).

Figure 52. United States and Japan: Developments in Equity, Bond, and Money Markets Surrounding Significant Stock Market Increases

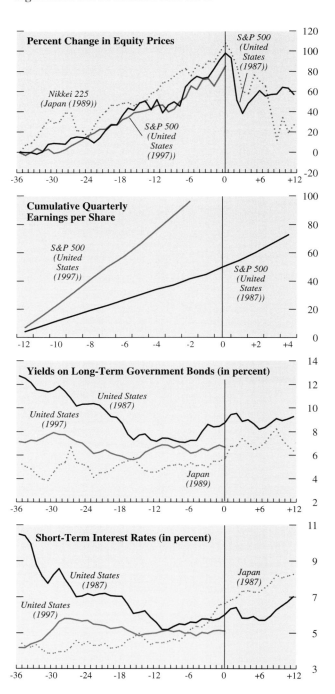

Sources: Bloomberg Financial Markets L.P.; and The WEFA Group.
Note: Stock markets peaked on August 25, 1987, in the United States and on December 29, 1989, in Japan. The figures show developments taking place in the respective markets 36 months prior to and 12 months after these dates. Earnings per share data for the United States are available only on a quarterly basis and are not available for Japan.

pare characteristics of equity price valuations with features of well-known bubbles in equity markets to determine whether there are clear differences between bubbles and current valuations. This appendix takes the latter approach by comparing some key aspects of the current U.S. equity price rally with the 1987 U.S. and the 1989 Japanese price bubbles.

Figure 52 shows the behavior of key variables for the three-year periods (−36 to 0 months) leading up to the 1987 U.S. and 1989 Japanese market crashes and the subsequent behavior for 12 months (0 to +12 months), compared with the behavior of the same indicator for the past three years in the United States. First, consider the behavior of equity prices themselves in the three cases. In the past three years U.S. equity prices have risen 95 percent, compared with about 100 percent in the United States over 1984–87 and in Japan over 1986–89. Thus, the current market rally is similar in magnitude to the earlier ones. It is noteworthy that the climb in equity prices recently has been much less volatile than in the two historical cases.

Second, consider earnings per share. Here there is clear evidence that the current market rally is much better supported by earnings. Earnings growth in the United States during 1984–87 provided no support for equity price gains. There is some indication that earnings are currently leveling off, however, and this raises concerns. Indeed, the recent upward pressure on the price-earnings ratio (as discussed in the text) reflects this fact.

Third, consider bond yields, which can be important for equity prices both because they are a competing asset and also because they are associated with the cost that firms must incur for servicing their debt. On this score, there is a rather marked difference between the current experience and the two historical experiences. Bond yields had been increasing sharply in the six months or so leading up to the 1987 U.S. and 1989 Japanese market corrections, whereas recently they have been trendless.

Finally, consider the tone of monetary policy in the three cases, as measured by short-term interest rates. The evidence is clear that monetary conditions had been loosened considerably in the earlier stages of the 1987 and 1989 market rallies, which differs from the current experience. Further, policy was tightened sharply beginning about 12 months prior to the U.S. and Japanese market corrections. By contrast, short-term interest rates have currently been trendless for over 24 months. The explanation for these differences in monetary policy across the three cases is easy to understand. Namely, real GDP growth was about 4 percent at the 1987 and 1989 markets' peaks, and inflation had increased sharply in the year leading up to the markets' peaks; by comparison, currently real GDP growth has been below the levels in the other episodes and inflation has not increased.

In summary, the doubling of U.S. equity prices in the past three years is of the same order of magnitude as in the United States prior to the crash in 1987 and in Japan prior to the collapse of asset prices in 1989. But, in contrast to these historical experiences, some of the critical underlying fundamentals—including corporate earnings and low volatility—provide considerably more justification for recent equity price gains. The key question in assessing the susceptibility of U.S. equity prices to sharp corrections—as occurred in 1987 in the United States and in Japan beginning in 1989—is whether corporate earnings can continue to grow well above the historical average. The answer to this question hinges on whether the recently high rates of corporate profitability derive primarily from possibly temporary cyclical influences or from more fundamental corporate restructuring.

Annex III
Developments in International Banking

The major international banking systems, including those in many emerging markets, have been engaged in a process of restructuring and consolidation in recent years that is profoundly changing the nature of the banking industry. Changes in regulation and technological developments have increased competition in traditional banking activities while simultaneously opening up new markets for expansion. In many countries, banking crises or the failure of important individual banks have provided additional impetus for restructuring. Continuing advances in information technology and the ongoing globalization of capital markets and the risk management business have resulted in consolidation in the investment banking industry. These issues are discussed with examples of recent important transactions in industrial countries and emerging markets in the first section of this annex.

Many of the catalysts of financial system restructuring have led to a reassessment of supervisory and regulatory practices. A consensus is emerging in policy circles that a functional approach must give way to supervision and regulation on a legal-entity basis to align the reporting requirements and inspection systems with the management structures of financial conglomerates. However, the most efficient method of implementing this approach remains undetermined. In many countries, the architecture of supervision itself would have to be changed, and the question of if or how to retain a role for the central bank in the supervision of money center banks considered. At the same time, bank supervision is moving away from the auditing of financial condition reports toward an emphasis on assessing the adequacy of systems, including those for risk management and internal controls. There is also increasing discussion of the role that could be played by disclosure and other market-based systems of supervision. Developments in supervision and regulation in industrial countries, and the international effort to improve financial supervision and regulation in emerging markets, are discussed in the second section.

These structural changes do not occur in isolation from the condition of the banking systems. Indeed, profitability and asset quality will affect the speed and nature of such developments. Banking systems that are dealing with the urgent resolution of asset-quality problems will have a restructuring dynamic that is very different from that in countries where such immediate pressures are less important, resulting in different patterns of mergers and acquisitions and perhaps a delay in responding to the longer-term structural issues. Recent developments in the banking systems of most of the systemically important industrial countries and emerging markets are discussed in the final two sections. Table 30 gives one indicator of relative strength of banking systems around the world, the Bank Financial Strength Ratings assigned by Moody's. The industrial country banking systems are deemed to be stronger on a stand-alone basis than those in the emerging markets, but there is considerable diversity of conditions within the two groups, with some of the emerging market banking systems faring well in comparison with the industrial country group, while some of the latter are considered to be in serious difficulty.

Restructuring and Consolidation of International Banking Systems

The restructuring and consolidation that are under way in international banking systems have been motivated by a number of developments in the past decade or so, among which four stand out: (1) the deregulation of international and domestic financial markets; (2) improvements in communications and computational technology; (3) significant asset-quality-driven problems in many banking systems; and (4) a growing recognition of the costs and distortions associated with official support for banking institutions. These mutually reinforcing developments have both provided the impetus for banking sector restructuring and in turn been affected by this restructuring.

Changes in the supervisory and regulatory framework have been an important source of pressure for industry consolidation and restructuring. Such changes include the liberalization of domestic and cross-border banking activities, the easing of segmentation barriers within national financial systems,[1] and the reorienta-

---

[1]For example, restrictions on the combination of commercial and investment banking activities in one institution or holding company have been eased in both Japan and the United States. Japanese commercial banks were permitted to open securities and trust subsidiaries in 1993, while U.S. bank holding companies were granted limited scope to deal in "ineligible" securities in 1987.

Table 30. Bank Financial Strength Ratings for Selected Countries, June 2, 1997[1]

	A	B+	B	C+	C	D+	D	E+	E	Average
Industrial countries										
Australia	0	0	4	0	6	2	0	0	0	C–C+
Austria	0	0	0	4	2	2	0	0	0	C
Belgium	0	2	2	2	1	0	0	0	0	B
Canada	0	1	5	4	0	0	0	0	0	B
Denmark	0	0	1	1	1	0	0	0	0	C+
Finland	0	0	0	0	0	3	0	0	1	D
France	0	2	5	6	4	6	2	1	1	C
Germany	1	4	4	9	8	3	0	0	0	C+
Greece	0	0	0	0	2	2	2	1	0	D+
Ireland	0	0	2	1	1	3	0	0	0	C
Italy	0	0	2	7	6	2	1	1	2	C
Japan	0	0	2	2	10	10	15	6	4	D+
Liechtenstein	0	0	1	0	0	0	0	0	0	B
Luxembourg	0	0	5	0	0	1	0	0	0	C+–B
Netherlands	3	1	1	1	1	0	0	0	0	B+
Norway	0	0	0	0	3	1	0	0	0	C
Portugal	0	0	0	1	3	1	0	0	0	C
Spain	1	3	5	1	2	0	0	0	0	B
Sweden	0	0	1	1	3	0	0	0	0	C–C+
Switzerland	1	1	2	2	1	0	0	0	0	B
United Kingdom	3	4	8	5	6	3	1	0	0	C+
United States	3	20	68	129	63	9	3	0	0	C+
Emerging markets										
Asia										
China	0	0	0	0	0	1	12	3	0	D
Hong Kong, China	0	0	2	0	7	2	0	0	0	C
India	0	0	0	0	0	2	3	0	1	D
Indonesia	0	0	0	0	0	3	5	2	2	D
Korea	0	0	0	1	1	4	7	4	1	D
Malaysia	0	0	0	1	1	0	0	0	0	C–C+
Philippines	0	0	0	1	1	5	2	0	0	D+
Singapore	0	3	0	1	2	0	0	0	0	B
Taiwan Province of China	0	0	0	1	4	4	0	0	0	C
Thailand	0	0	0	1	2	1	4	3	0	D–D+
Europe										
Croatia	0	0	0	0	0	0	1	0	0	D
Cyprus	0	0	0	0	2	0	0	0	0	C
Czech Republic	0	0	0	0	0	3	2	1	0	D
Hungary	0	0	0	0	0	3	3	0	0	D–D+
Israel	0	0	0	0	2	3	0	0	0	D+
Poland	0	0	0	0	0	3	3	1	0	D
Romania	0	0	0	0	0	0	2	1	1	E+
Slovak Republic	0	0	0	0	0	0	3	0	0	D
Slovenia	0	0	0	0	0	2	0	0	0	D+
Turkey	0	0	0	0	2	2	6	4	0	D
Latin America										
Argentina	0	0	0	0	2	3	4	1	0	D+
Brazil	0	0	0	3	5	10	4	1	2	D+
Chile	0	0	0	5	4	1	0	0	0	C
Colombia	0	0	0	1	3	0	2	0	0	D+–C
Mexico	0	0	0	0	0	0	3	4	2	E+
Panama	0	0	0	0	1	0	0	0	0	C
Peru	0	0	0	0	1	3	0	0	0	D+
Puerto Rico	0	0	0	0	0	1	1	0	0	D–D+
Uruguay	0	0	0	0	0	1	1	0	0	D–D+
Venezuela	0	0	0	0	0	2	3	0	0	D

Table 30 *(concluded)*

	A	B+	B	C+	C	D+	D	E+	E	Average
Middle East and Africa										
Bahrain	0	0	0	0	1	2	3	0	0	D+
Egypt	0	0	0	0	1	1	1	0	0	D+
Jordan	0	0	0	0	0	1	1	0	0	D–D+
Kuwait	0	0	0	1	1	1	3	2	0	D–D+
Oman	0	0	0	0	0	3	1	0	0	D+
Pakistan	0	0	0	0	0	0	0	2	2	E–E+
Qatar	0	0	0	0	0	1	2	0	0	D
Saudi Arabia	0	0	0	1	2	4	4	1	0	D+
South Africa	0	0	0	0	3	3	0	0	0	D+–C
United Arab Emirates	0	0	0	0	0	2	1	1	0	D

Source: Moody's Investors Service.

[1]The Bank Financial Strength Rating is Moody's assessment of whether a bank is likely to require financial support from shareholders, the government, or other institutions. The ratings range from A (highest) to E (lowest). Note that the coverage of banking systems is not generally complete, so that the ratings are not necessarily representative of the credit quality of the entire system.

tion of the emphasis of bank supervision toward capital adequacy. The deregulation of financial markets allowed for greater disintermediation from banking, as depositors searched for higher yields in investment funds and securities, and corporate borrowers found access to financing at competitive terms in the securities markets by selling bonds to institutional investors. Table 31 provides some evidence for these trends by presenting data on two indicators of disintermediation, the ratio of institutional investors' financial assets in total financial assets of domestic financial institutions, and the share of household assets represented by claims on institutional investors. Both ratios have increased sharply since the mid-1980s for most industrial countries. For example, in France the assets of institutional investors rose from 11 percent of total financial system assets in 1985 to 23 percent in 1995; the share of household assets held by institutional investors also rose, from 16 percent in 1985 to 27 percent in 1995. Disintermediation is most advanced in the United States, where in 1995 institutional investors accounted for 55 percent of financial system assets and held 45 percent of household assets. These indicators suggest the difficulties banks have faced in responding to the deregulation of financial markets.

The move toward risk-based capital requirements in the late 1980s marked a significant change in the supervision of banks and led to a reorientation of bank management objectives toward maximizing risk-adjusted returns on capital, rather than increasing gross measures of performance such as total revenues, profits, or market share. The need to increase capital as the scale of bank operations expands or as its activities become more risky reinforces the incentives to maximize shareholder value in order to maintain access to sources of capital. Mergers and acquisitions (M&A) have been viewed as one way to increase shareholder value, although it is notable that there is little evidence to support the existence of economies of scale or scope for banks or for improvements in efficiency resulting from mergers or takeovers.[2]

It may be, however, that recent technological developments will make improvements in shareholder value arising from M&A transactions more significant, even for so-called mega-mergers of very large banks. Developments in computational and communications technologies have been an important catalyst for restructuring both by possibly changing the scale and scope economies within banking and by increasing the effectiveness of competition from nonbank financial institutions. These developments have already revolutionized the products and services offered by banks, and the ways in which these are delivered. They have also increased the efficient scale of a number of operations, including check processing and other payment operations, the processing of loan applications (e.g., through the adoption of credit scoring models for mortgage loan applications), risk management and treasury operations, trading, and the centralization of most data back-office activities. More recently, and most visibly, the employment of electronic banking technology—automated teller machines, point-of-sale debit machines, telephone banking, and Internet banking—is more cost effective if the bank has a very large customer base. It is possible, therefore, that consolidation among very large banks can allow a more efficient adoption of these new technologies than is possible for smaller banks.

For many banks, the most effective incentive for restructuring has been a sudden decline in profitability, and this is true also for banking systems as a whole.

---

[2]See Berger and Humphrey (1997). Empirical studies have generally not found evidence of statistically significant economies of scale except for small banks. On average, mergers and acquisitions do not appear significantly to improve cost efficiency, but there is some evidence of increased profit efficiency arising from mergers of large banks in the United States.

Table 31. Distintermediation in Selected Industrial Countries

	Assets of Institutional Investors[1]		Institutionalization of Household Savings[2]	
	1985	1995	1985	1995
Canada	26.4	35.9	24.5	31.4
France[3]	11.4	23.4	15.7	27.3
Germany	12.8	19.0	19.6	28.9
Japan[4]	10.2	22.6	32.2	34.8
Norway[5]	13.0	21.9	25.1	37.5
Spain	3.2	15.0	2.9	24.4
United Kingdom[6]	26.7	31.6	. . .	52.0
United States	43.8	54.6	33.4	45.3

Source: Organization for Economic Cooperation and Development.

[1]Financial assets of insurance companies, pension funds, and investment companies as a proportion of total financial assets of domestic financial institutions.

[2]Outstanding claims of households on institutional investors as a proportion of total household financial assets.

[3]Data include financial assets of insurance companies and investment companies only.

[4]Earlier data are for 1990, not 1985. Data include financial assets of insurance companies, investment companies, and trust accounts of trust banks (excluding investment trusts) only.

[5]Later data are for 1993, not 1995.

[6]Earlier data are for 1988, not 1985.

The past decade or so has seen the emergence of serious banking difficulties in a large number of industrial countries and emerging markets, and their resolution has often provided an opportunity for consolidation or acquisitions by outside investors. Takeovers by strong banks of relatively weaker ones is a common pattern in bank mergers and acquisitions and can hasten the resolution of asset-quality problems by improving bank management, reducing the constraint on cash flow posed by nonperforming assets by combining them in a portfolio with a higher average quality, and providing greater income flows or capital with which to set aside loan loss reserves or to write off problem loans; for these reasons such takeovers are often encouraged by bank supervisors.[3]

Another factor that has contributed to the dynamics of restructuring in banking systems has been the declining role of the state in financial systems due, in part, to the growing pressure for fiscal consolidation and the allocation of scarce budgetary resources to other priorities, including pension finance, for example. As it becomes more difficult for governments to justify the expenditures necessary to bail out failed banks[4]—government owned or not—the direct ownership stake

that governments have had in individual institutions has gradually been withdrawn in many countries.

Banks have responded to these pressures with a variety of strategies, including concentrating on core activities in which they have a strong comparative advantage and expanding vertically (to exploit economies of scale) or horizontally (to capture economies of scope). The expansion strategy has been in many ways the most visible, as the past few years have seen a seemingly unprecedented wave of mergers and acquisitions within the international financial markets. One strategy that some large institutions appear to have adopted is to become a globally competitive actor. The liberalization of international financial transactions over the past two decades made most markets contestable to firms willing to expand geographically. With the asset-quality problems associated with the 1980s debt crisis and then the early 1990s real estate crisis behind them, many of the large banks in the major industrial countries have begun to compete for business on an international level.

The pace of consolidation in industrial country banking systems slowed slightly in 1996 after a hectic year. In the *United States,* where mergers and acquisitions are far more common than in other mature systems, activity slowed significantly in 1996 after a record volume of transactions in 1995. A total of 442 deals were announced in 1996, with a total value at announcement of $44 billion, compared with 537 deals for $73 billion in 1993.[5] More important than the volume of transactions, however, has been the types of deals announced. In the past two years, the five largest U.S. bank mergers ever arranged have been announced—Wells Fargo and First Interstate ($13.7 billion); Chemical Bank and Chase Manhattan Bank ($13.3 billion); NationsBank and Boatman's Bancshares ($9.5 billion); First Bank and U.S. Bancorp ($8.4 billion); and First Union and First Fidelity ($6.1 billion)—and a bid for the third-largest savings and loan institution (Great Western Financial Corp.) appears to have been won by the second-largest thrift (Washington Mutual) in a deal that might cost $6.7 billion. The banking industry has embarked on an almost unprecedented process of consolidation leading to the creation of a small number of institutions that are dominant on a national scale.

Most of this M&A activity has been truly consolidation of commercial banking within or between geographical areas as restrictions on interstate banking have been progressively relaxed, culminating in their widespread elimination under the Riegle-Neal Act of 1994. However, with the liberalization of banking regulations on sales of insurance and on securities underwriting and sales, the focus of attention has recently

---

[3]O'Keefe (1996) found, for example, that for unassisted bank acquisitions in the United States during 1984-94, target banks tended to have higher loan loss provisioning requirements, lower profitability, higher noninterest expenses, and higher liquidity (i.e., a smaller proportion of assets invested in loans) than the acquiring institutions.

[4]For estimates of the magnitude of such expenditures in recent years, see Lindgren, Garcia, and Saal (1996).

[5]Elstein (1997). First quarter 1997 data suggest that activity has picked up considerably, with a total of $22 billion in deals announced.

turned toward acquiring complementary skills as in, for example, the 1995 Mellon Bank acquisition of Dreyfuss, the $7.3 billion Bank One acquisition of First USA, or the more recent takeover of Alex. Brown by Bankers Trust. Increasingly, in response to the gradual relaxation of constraints on their non-banking activities, banks are expanding their securities and asset management capabilities. Nor has such activity been restricted to the banking industry, as reflected in the $10.2 billion merger between Dean Witter, Discover and Morgan Stanley (which had itself acquired Van Kempen America in 1996) creating the largest credit card issuer and fifth-largest asset manager in the world.

The *U.K.* banking system also saw some important repositioning by individual institutions in 1996, but of a more varied nature than is possible in the United States. Lloyds Bank and TSB Bank merged in 1996, creating the third-largest bank in the country. NatWest sold its U.S. and Australian banking subsidiaries, but acquired Gartmore, a U.K. asset management company. Three building societies (Alliance and Leicester, Halifax, and Woolwich) renounced their mutual status and took bank licenses, and Halifax also acquired a life insurance company. *Canadian* banks have been engaged in acquiring securities and trust subsidiaries since they were permitted to do so under the 1987 and 1992 revisions of the Bank Act. Similarly, some of the banks have acquired U.S. financial institutions: in 1996, the Bank of Montreal acquired a U.S. thrift, Household Bank, and Toronto Dominion Bank bought Waterhouse Securities in New York. In addition, Canadian banks continued to invest in emerging markets in 1996–97, as discussed below.

French banks also have responded to recent asset-quality difficulties and highly competitive markets in part by engaging in heightened merger and acquisition activity within the past year. This has included the mergers of Banque Française du Commerce Extérieure and Crédit National, and of Crédit Local and Crédit Communal de Belgique; the takeover of Banque Indosuez by Crédit Agricole; and the takeover of Banque Hydro-Energie by Crédit Commercial de France in 1996. In early 1997, Société Générale had acquired a majority stake in Crédit du Nord, which had last year acquired Banque Laydernier. Unlike mergers elsewhere, however, the elimination of redundancies is not usually a major objective in French bank mergers, since strict labor laws and high unionization within French banks make it difficult to reduce staff. M&A activity is geared more toward identifying complementary specializations or risk concentrations.

German banks have been perhaps the most active among continental banks recently in expanding into international investment banking and asset management (e.g., Deutsche Bank acquired Morgan Grenfell in 1989, and Dresdner Bank acquired Kleinwort Benson in 1995). This activity continued in 1996, as

Commerzbank acquired American Martingale Asset Management, and Bayerische Hypotheken-und Wechsel Bank acquired management control over U.K.-based Hypo Foreign & Colonial Management Holdings by increasing its equity stake to 65 percent, and entered into a cooperation agreement with a U.S.-based asset management company, Massachusetts Financial Services.

In *Italy,* bank restructuring has involved consolidation among the smaller institutions, often through mergers with larger banks, and through changes in bank ownership. Banco di Napoli was formerly 71 percent owned by a private charitable foundation. Such foundations had been important owners of banks in Italy, but under the Amato Law of 1990, incentives were given to these foundations to sell their stakes. This has been achieved gradually, most recently with the sale of 45 percent of the shares in Istituto Bancario San Paolo di Torino by its owners. Italy also has a large number of very small banks, many of which have low capital levels. While such institutions are gradually being merged with or taken over by larger banks, the labor laws and practices in Italy make it very difficult for banks to realize large efficiency gains from mergers. Banks still seem to view these mergers as mechanisms for increasing market share rather than increasing profits. It is not uncommon for merged banks to continue to operate under their own names in competition with each other, with almost no apparent effort to rationalize their structures or products.

Japan has seen a large number of bank takeovers in the last two years as this has been an integral element in the official response to asset-quality problems. Since the emergence of the current banking sector problems, at least 20 institutions, mostly credit unions and credit cooperatives, have been merged with healthier institutions, in many cases with assistance from the Deposit Insurance Corporation (DIC). The major institutions have not been left out of this process. In October 1994, Mitsubishi Bank took over Nippon Trust in an assisted transaction of the troubled bank, and in April 1997, Hokkaido Takushoku Bank and Hokkaido Bank agreed to merge. The only recent merger that does not appear to have been motivated by portfolio weakness in either of the participants was the merger between Bank of Tokyo and Mitsubishi Bank that took effect in 1996, creating the largest commercial bank in the world. By combining two banks with different traditional emphases—Bank of Tokyo had a relatively small branch network and did little domestic lending in Japan—this transaction appears to have been motivated more by international developments than by domestic asset-quality concerns.

The restructuring of the banking sectors in each of the *Nordic* countries continued in 1996. In Norway, Den Norske Bank acquired Vital Försikring, the second-largest life insurance company in the country, and Christiania Bank acquired Norgeskreditt. In Sweden,

Svenska Handelsbanken acquired 98 percent of the shares in Stadshypothek, a leading housing finance institution, and in February 1997, a merger of Swedbank and Föreningsbanken—the central banks of the cooperative bank system and the savings bank system respectively—was announced. Further consolidation is to be expected. The Nordic banks are experiencing the same increased competition, disintermediation, and narrower interest margins as the other banking systems in Europe.

The emerging market banking systems have also experienced an increase in the pace of restructuring and consolidation. In fact, banking crises have precipitated a remarkable restructuring of banking systems in some Latin American countries. Among most of the Asian emerging market countries, until very recently, the absence of a crisis atmosphere had prevented any sense of urgency about the need for restructuring, although many supervisory authorities had actively encouraged consolidation. An important element in the restructuring of Latin American and European emerging market banking systems has been the use of M&A transactions by foreign banks as a means of penetrating the market. Domestic shareholders, often lacking the means to recapitalize the banks, or seeking to reorganize the corporate structure of mixed financial/nonfinancial conglomerates, have increasingly been willing to sell controlling stakes to foreign financial institutions. Also, governments in many countries have reconsidered the benefits of public ownership of financial institutions and have privatized large proportions of financial sector assets. While most of the foreign purchasers have been from Europe (especially Spain) and North America, it is significant that there are a number of Latin American financial institutions that have regional ambitions (for example, Chile's Infisa group, and Argentina's Banco de Galicia). Foreign investment not only brings new competition, and therefore greater pressure for consolidation, but their more advanced practices and technology, broader range of products, and deeper capital base put pressure on the local banks to modernize and become more efficient.

The 1995 liquidity crisis and ongoing restructuring in response to the stabilization of inflation since the early 1990s have resulted in a significant reorganization of the *Argentine* banking system. Since the end of 1994, 11 government-owned banks and 36 privately owned banks and cooperatives have closed or been privatized or merged with other institutions.[6]

As in other countries in the region, there has been a surge in foreign investment in the banking system in recent months. In October 1996, Banco Bilbao Vizcaya acquired a controlling interest in Banco Frances del Rio de la Plata, and in May 1997 the latter took over Banco de Credito Argentino. Also in May 1997, Banco Santander acquired control over Banco Río, the Bank of Nova Scotia took control of Banco Quilmes, and a group of investors including Chile's Infisa, Chase Manhattan Bank, and National Bank of Canada was approved to take over Banco Union Comercial e Industrial, which had been experiencing capital adequacy problems, in December 1996. In June 1997, HSBC Holdings increased its 30 percent stake in the holding company of Banco Roberts to 100 percent. Further consolidation and foreign investment in the banking system are expected—including the privatization of more government-owned banks, among them the national mortgage bank, Banco Hipotecario Nacional.

The restructuring of the banking industry in *Brazil* is also well under way. Since July 1994, some 30 financial institutions have been closed, merged, or liquidated, including some quite large private and publicly owned banks (e.g., Banco Econômico, Banco Nacional, and Banerj). Foreign participation in the industry has increased, both in terms of new entry and in investment in existing banks. For example, in March 1997, HSBC Holdings bought the domestic banking operations of Banco Bamerindus, and Banco Santander acquired a controlling stake in Banco Geral do Comercio. These developments are likely to continue since a large number of small private banks are thought likely to need assistance or want to increase their chances of survival by merging or attracting new investors (six small commercial banks had been shut down by the central bank by end-July 1997). This process will likely be a costly one, as long as the central bank is prepared to make liquidity funding available and as long as the federal government is prepared to reschedule the state governments' debts as a means of ensuring that their banks are restructured.[7]

The *Mexican* banking system has also seen its share of foreign investment, associated with the sales of banks that were taken over by the central bank and efforts by the surviving banks to increase their capital and improve their management and product availability. Since early 1996, foreign banks have acquired important stakes in eight Mexican banks. In 1996, the Bank of Montreal acquired a 16 percent stake in Ban-

---

[6]In the first 10 months of 1996, 7 provincial banks (the provincial banks of Tucumán, Misiones, Salta, Río Negro, San Luis, Santiago del Estero, and Banco de Previsión Social in Mendoza) were privatized, 3 private banks were purchased by other banks (Banco Comercial de Tandil by Banco de Crédito Provincial, Banco Popular Argentino by Banco Roberts, and Banco Popular Financiero by Banco Sudecor Litoral), Chase Bank and Chemical Bank merged, and 2 other banks lost their licenses.

[7]Central bank financial assistance to government-owned banks has increased steadily since July 1994, reaching R$44 billion at end-January 1997. Assistance to private banks has likewise increased (but at a much faster rate, having started at negligible amounts) to R$27 billion over the same period. Both levels dipped slightly in February 1997.

comer, the Bank of Nova Scotia increased its stake in Inverlat, Banco Santander acquired Grupo Financiero Invermexico (the holding company of Banco Mexicano), Banco Bilbao Vizcaya took over Multibanco Mercantil Probursa and acquired the branch network of Banco Oriente, and Banco Comercial Portugues and Banco Central Hispanoamericano both invested in Banco Internacional. In 1997, this process has continued, with HSBC Holdings taking a 20 percent stake in Grupo Financiero Serfin and GE Capital acquiring Banco Alianza. Domestic banks have also recently taken an interest in growing by acquisition, especially as a means of diversifying into insurance and other nonbanking activities. For example, Grupo Financiero Banorte acquired two insurance subsidiaries of Banco Obrero and will participate in the auction for Banpais in July 1997.

The immediate future for *Venezuelan* banks is also strongly influenced by the sudden emergence of foreign competition. For the past two decades foreign banks have not been permitted in Venezuela, but that ended in December 1996 when foreign financial institutions were allowed to acquire controlling stakes in three of the four largest Venezuelan banks—two of which were acquired in privatizations. Banco Santander successfully bid for Banco de Venezuela when the latter was privatized in December 1996, and Banco Bilbao Vizcaya reached agreement to purchase 40 percent of Banco Provincial (including a 17.6 percent stake held by Crédit Lyonnais), the largest private bank. At the same time, a Chilean investment group, Infisa CA (which controls Chilean bank Banco Concepcion), won control over Banco Consolidado. Infisa plans to sell part of its 93 percent stake to a group of investors including Chase Manhattan Bank and National Bank of Canada. Most recently, Banco República was sold in June 1997 to a Colombian savings bank. With these sales, there remain two banks to be privatized: Banco Andino Venezolano and Banco Popular.

The *Czech* banking system has already undergone a fundamental restructuring in the transition from a highly centralized, exclusively government-owned system to a market-oriented system. However, this transformation is not complete. The industry is highly concentrated, and many banks rely heavily on the interbank market and on institutional funds for liquidity. Two new foreign banks were given licenses in 1996 (the first new banks of any kind since 1994), joining the 23 existing foreign banks and joint ventures. In addition, the privatization of two banks, Investicni a Postovni Banka and Ceskoslovenska Obchodni Banka, is under way.

Restructuring has also continued in the *Hungarian* and *Polish* banking systems, where privatization continues to dominate the structural changes. In Hungary, Magyar Hitel Bank, one of the three banks that were carved out of the National Bank of Hungary in

1987, was privatized, with 89 percent of its shares sold to ABN Amro, joining Budapest Bank, which was privatized in 1995. Both banks are being restructured by their foreign majority shareholders into retail-oriented banks, which will involve a significant reduction in size, especially for Magyar Hitel Bank, which has been dominant in lending to large enterprises. The state privatization agency (APV) has also announced plans to privatize the last of the government-owned banks, Kereskedelmi es Hitelbank (KHB), in a two-round sale in 1997. (KHB itself acquired a smaller Hungarian bank, Ibusz Bank, in 1996.) In the first round, a 25 percent stake will be sold, after which the remaining shares will be distributed to social security funds, management, employees, and small shareholders. In April 1996, the Deutsche Genossenschaftsbank received approval to purchase 61 percent of the shares of the central bank of the cooperative banks in Hungary, Takarekbank. Finally, the APV has announced that it will reduce its 25 percent ownership stake in the National Savings and Commercial Bank (OTP) to 10 percent in 1997, and the National Bank of Hungary has announced that it will seek to sell its 34 percent stake in Central European International Bank in 1997.

After a relatively slow start, in which only five of the *Polish* state-owned banks were privatized over as many years, the government in 1996 adopted a revised bank privatization strategy envisaging the consolidation and privatization of most remaining state-owned banks by the year 2000. As a first step, in late 1996 three of the remaining state-owned regional banks were merged into Bank PKO-SA, with a view to privatizing the consortium in 1998. In 1997, three banks are being privatized: first, in June, Bank Handlowy was sold in a complex transaction involving a public offer to individuals (29 percent of share capital), institutional investors (30 percent), three major "core shareholders" (foreign financial institutions expected mainly to strengthen the bank's know-how in different areas of financial services, 26 percent), employees (7 percent), and the Polish Treasury (8 percent). In addition, the bank is to issue so-called convertible bonds, initially to the treasury, for the equivalent of about 35 percent of its current share capital. These bonds are to be used later to help finance the reform of Poland's pension system. Second, the National Bank of Poland is finalizing the sale of its 100 percent stake in the Polish Investment Bank; and third, the government will shortly complete the sale of a 65 percent stake in the Warsaw-based Powszechny Bank Kredytowy SA (PBK). After that, the last of the nine state-owned regional banks (Bank Zachodni), the State Agricultural Bank (BGZ), and the Polish Development Bank are slated for sale in 1998–99. This would leave only two banks in state hands: the large domestic savings bank (PKO-SA), to be privatized eventually, and Bank Gospodarska

Komunalna (BGK), the only bank to remain government-owned in the future.

Supervisory and Regulatory Developments

Regulatory Structure

The technological advances noted above have allowed an increase in the sophistication of finance and the introduction of new products and innovative delivery mechanisms, and have also reinforced the blurring of divisions between different segments of the financial system in most countries. Improvements in risk management have allowed the portfolios of larger, more complex corporate organizations to be managed centrally. These trends call for a change in the structure of supervision over financial firms to reflect their changing internal organizations. Supervision along functional lines is not efficient in the presence of centralized risk management by financial conglomerates.

The problem of how best to organize supervision and regulation of financial conglomerates in a global marketplace is being examined by the Joint Forum, a group made up of bank, securities firm, and insurance regulators, previously called the Tripartite Group. The Joint Forum has made some headway over the last year in facilitating the exchange of information among the groups of supervisors and in outlining the responsibilities of a regulatory "coordinator" for conglomerates. A number of smaller countries, including Hungary, Norway, and Sweden, have implemented a centralized system of supervision, in which one agency, independent of the central bank, is responsible for supervising all types of financial institutions. Such a structure has been proposed too in Korea. This has not yet been implemented in any of the major industrial countries. However, in May 1997, the Chancellor of the Exchequer in the United Kingdom proposed a reorganization of financial supervision in which eventually all financial supervisory and regulatory authority will reside in the Securities and Investments Board (SIB). In addition to reducing the role of the self-regulatory organizations and their oversight agencies, the government proposes to remove responsibility over bank supervision and regulation from the Bank of England and transfer it to the SIB.

As the U.S. financial system evolves toward one in which there may be few restrictions on banks' activities in the securities and insurance businesses (and reciprocally for securities and insurance firms), there is now considerable debate on the need for a change in the regulatory structure. While a bid to consolidate the supervision of financial institutions in one agency did not win approval in 1996, banks' powers to sell insurance and to engage in the underwriting and trading of "ineligible" securities have been expanded.[8] The main issue being debated is the form of corporate organization that will be preferred. While in the European Union, for example, banks often have the choice of undertaking insurance or securities business in-house or through bank subsidiaries, the U.S. Federal Reserve Board has proposed allowing such activities only through bank holding company subsidiaries, suggesting that such a structure facilitates the supervision of insured deposit taking and related banking activities separately from other activities. The Office of the Comptroller of the Currency has argued that the holding company structure may not be the most efficient and that banks should have the option of engaging in securities dealing within the bank rather than through subsidiaries.

During 1996, the Japanese authorities announced a number of important policy initiatives. In June, three financial laws were passed by the Diet that implemented a U.S.-style bank resolution framework built around (1) increased powers for regulators to intervene in problem banks, including declaring them insolvent; (2) prompt corrective action (PCA) measures for intervening in weak banks; and (3) increased resources for the deposit insurance corporation to pay off depositors of failed banks, including a fourfold increase in deposit insurance premiums (to 0.048 percent of insured deposits), the temporary addition of a special premium of 0.036 percent, and a ¥2 trillion line of credit from the Bank of Japan. The special premium, implemented by a provisional amendment to the Deposit Insurance Act, was introduced to provide insurance for all deposits, including those in excess of the statutory ¥10 million limit. This additional guarantee, and an all-encompassing official guarantee that none of the banks with international activities would close, terminate at the end of the 2000/2001 fiscal year.

The PCA measures, which take effect April 1, 1998, require banks to classify their loan portfolios more rigorously by repayment risk and to set aside adequate reserves thereby providing a more accurate measure of economic capital in the bank; they also allow the authorities to intervene by forcing banks to take corrective measures or ultimately by closing them down based on their risk-weighted capital ratios. While these rules represent a move in the direction of market

---

[8]In December 1986, the Federal Reserve Board of Governors interpreted the Glass-Steagall Act's requirement that bank holding companies could not own subsidiaries that were "principally engaged" in underwriting and dealing in "ineligible" securities (i.e., corporate debt and equity) as restricting such activities to 5 percent or less of the revenue of the subsidiary. In 1989, the revenue ceiling was raised to 10 percent, and in December 1996 the ceiling was again raised, to 25 percent (effective March 1997). In March 1996, the U.S. Supreme Court ruled that states must allow nationally chartered banks to sell insurance as permitted under the National Bank Act.

discipline of the banking system, the measures prescribed for the supervisory authorities are less forceful, and allow for a greater deterioration of capital, than those implemented in the United States by the Federal Deposit Insurance Corporation (FDIC) Improvement Act of 1991 (Table 32). For example, while the FDIC is required to intervene in a bank by demanding recapitalization plans and restricting asset growth and new activities for banks once their total risk-weighted capital ratio falls below 8 percent, similar restrictions in the Japanese system would be introduced only after the capital ratio fell below 6 percent. Restrictions on deposit taking and managerial compensation are introduced in the U.S. system when the capital ratio falls below 6 percent, but under the Japanese regulations these are introduced only when the capital ratio falls below 4 percent. Finally, regulators have more discretion under the Japanese PCA rules than they do under the U.S. rules. For example, in Japan suspension of activities can be avoided if the bank's net income is expected to be positive as a result of implementing a restructuring plan, while in the U.S. system, once a bank is "critically undercapitalized" the regulators are required to close it down. More generally, in the U.S. PCA system, regulators have discretion to strengthen the required response to a decline in capitalization, while under the Japanese rules, they have discretion to scale down the required response.

A change in the structure of financial supervision has also been initiated in Japan. The responsibilities for bank, insurance, and securities supervision currently assigned to the Japanese Ministry of Finance will be transferred to a new agency, the Supervisory Agency for Financial Entities (provisional translation) in mid-1998 (the Bank of Japan will retain its bank examination powers). The ministry will retain responsibility for the formulation of bank regulation policy and will be consulted by the supervisory authorities in cases of systemic importance. The Securities Exchange Surveillance Commission will be merged into the new agency, creating a consolidated banking/securities supervisory agency.

A more far-reaching set of reforms was announced in November 1996. Described as Japan's "Big Bang" these measures include (1) the elimination of most foreign exchange controls and ex ante reporting requirements, and the abolition of the authorized foreign exchange bank system; (2) the acceptance of financial holding companies; (3) the abolition of fixed commissions on securities transactions; and (4) the elimination of restrictions segregating securities, trust, and banking activities. The latter three measures are expected to lead to a significant restructuring and consolidation of the financial services industry, as they allow financial holding companies to be established combining all types of banking, securities, and insurance activities, while at the same time making each type of activity more competitive and responsive to

market forces. It is the first measure, approved in May 1997 and to take effect in May 1998, however, that is potentially the most significant. Liberalization of the foreign exchange controls may allow foreign financial institutions to compete more effectively and to offer more services to Japanese customers. Indeed, this is the central element of the reform plan, as increased foreign competition is expected to force domestic firms to be more innovative and efficient and to provide better services and higher returns to retail investors.

Capital Requirements

Following a lengthy debate about the appropriate form of regulatory capital requirements for market risk, bank supervisors in the major industrial countries are taking a step back to evaluate the entire concept of regulatory capital. The Basle Committee on Banking Supervision ("Basle Committee") has formed a working group to examine the issue from a fresh perspective. Part of the impetus for doing so is a recognition that the complexities and interrelationships among the various sources of risk (credit, market, operational, legal, and so on) in bank portfolios makes it difficult to prescribe specific rules for the calculation of capital that appropriately capture the risks against which it is meant to insure. For example, even before the latest amendment to the Basle Capital Accord to incorporate market risks had been finalized, members of the Basle Committee were cognizant that even with fairly strict initial assumptions the use of a value-at-risk (VAR) model could result in different measures of regulatory capital for different banks. This "implementation risk" has important implications for regulators: clearly, it is insufficient for supervisors to vet the theoretical version of a bank's internal model, yet it would consume enormous resources if supervisors were to attempt to verify each bank's model by running a benchmark set of portfolios. Backtesting may emerge as the only way to gauge the effectiveness of a bank's VAR model.

Put forth as a possible solution to the problems associated with the inflexibility of the Basle Committee's rule-based approach to measuring market risk, the precommitment approach, in which each bank agrees not to violate its "precommitted" level of market risk capital, continues to elicit heated discussions. A one-year pilot study involving some 10 banks started on October 1, 1996, under the auspices of the New York Clearing House whereby these banks will, on paper, precommit to maintaining a certain minimum amount of capital and any violations will be recorded. Despite its potential lack of realism (there are no penalties applied to banks whose capital falls below their precommitted amount), the pilot study has at least forced those banks involved formally to allocate an amount of capital and to think carefully about whether to use their VAR model or some other technique for calculating that

Table 32. Japan and the United States: Summary of Prompt Corrective Action Provisions

Japan		United States		
			Actions	
Capital levels[1]	Actions	Capital levels[2]	Mandatory	Discretionary
n.a.	n.a.	"Well capitalized" Total ≥10 percent, and Tier 1 ≥6 percent, and Leverage ratio ≥5 percent.	None	None
n.a.	n.a.	"Adequately capitalized" Total ≥8 percent, and Tier 1 ≥4 percent, and Leverage ratio ≥4 percent.	Disallow brokered deposits, except with FDIC approval.	None
International capital ratio <8 percent; National capital ratio <4 percent.	Order formulation and implementation of management improvement plan.	"Undercapitalized" Total <8 percent, or Tier 1 <4 percent, or Leverage ratio <4 percent.	Suspend dividends and management fees. Require capital restoration plan. Restrict asset growth. Require approval for acquisitions, branching, and new activities. Disallow brokered deposits.	Order recapitalization. Restrict interaffiliate transactions. Restrict deposit interest rates. Order other measures necessary to carry out prompt corrective action.
International capital ratio <4 percent; National capital ratio <2 percent.	Order recapitalization plan. Impose restraints on asset growth. Impose ban on new activities and branches and limits on current activities. Impose ban on new subsidiaries and overseas affiliates and limits on the current activities of such entities. Limit payment of dividends. Limit payment of bonuses to directors and management. Limit deposits, interest rates.	"Significantly undercapitalized" Total <6 percent, or Tier 1 <3 percent, or Leverage ratio <3 percent.	Same as above. Order recapitalization. Restrict interaffiliate transactions. Restrict deposit interest rates. Restrict pay of officers.	Same as above. Order conservatorship or receivership if bank fails to submit or implement a plan to recapitalize. Impose any provision for "critically undercapitalized" banks if necessary.
International capital ratio <0 percent; National capital ratio <0 percent.	Suspend whole or part of banking business. This order can be replaced with lesser actions if: (1) the net value of assets, including unrealized gains, is positive; (2) the net value including unrealized gains is negative but expected to be positive after considering: (a) the implementation of management improvement plans and other specific measures; (b) business income and profitability; (c) the bad assets ratio. A business suspension order can be issued at any time when the net value of assets, including unrealized losses is, or is expected to be, negative.	"Critically undercapitalized" Tangible equity to total assets ratio of ≤2 percent.	Same as for "Significantly undercapitalized" banks. Order receivership/conservatorship within 90 days. Order receivership if critically undercapitalized for four quarters. Suspend payments on subordinated debt. Restrict certain other activities.	n.a.

Sources: Japan, Ministry of Finance; and United States, Federal Deposit Insurance Corporation.

[1]The international capital standards (BIS capital adequacy standards) apply to banks with international operations. The adjusted national capital standards apply to banks with purely domestic operations.

[2]The total capital ratio cited is the total risk-weighted capital; the leverage ratio is the ratio of Tier 1 capital to total assets.

amount. In fact, several banks have augmented their VAR number to take account of risks that are not included in their VAR models.

While a discussion of the management and measurement of market risk continues to dominate the lives of many regulators and practitioners, attempts to measure and manage other risks, most notably operational risk, are emerging as the next major issue. Banks are beginning to take a hard look at the operational risks in their business, and some of them are developing methods by which such risks can be measured and capital allocated against them. In the forefront is Bankers Trust which, after the collection and examination of appropriate data, discovered that their hierarchy of risks has been altered to first, credit risk, followed by operating risk, and lastly, market risk. Other banks have also found that unexpected losses can result from the application of sophisticated pricing systems, including recently NatWest Bank and Tokyo-Mitsubishi Derivative Products. The importance of internal controls and the measurement of risks incurred due to their failure is only now becoming fully appreciated.

Another important element in the discussion of capital and its purpose has been spurred by the development of credit derivatives (see Appendix 1 at the end of this annex) and the new progress achieved in analyzing credit risk. The international regulatory community has arrived at a consensus that these developments warrant a rethinking of credit risk capital requirements. The Bank of England has requested comments on a discussion paper regarding a possible supervisory approach to credit derivatives, and the Securities and Futures Authority has provided its first formal pronouncement regarding credit derivatives. In the United States, the three federal regulatory agencies have issued guidance notes on credit derivatives. However, all these documents stress the preliminary nature of the guidance regarding regulatory treatment and the quickly evolving characteristics of tradable credit risks. In addition to the impetus from credit derivatives, international regulators are also aware that the credit risk categories assigned within the original Basle Accord were based on relatively crude, qualitative assessments of relative risk and these should be reevaluated in light of the newer analysis.[9]

Supervision and Regulation in Emerging Markets

The soundness of the financial system, and especially the banking system, is increasingly recognized as an important part of any evaluation of the economic prospects of an emerging market. The role of the financial sector in propagating the crisis in Mexico illustrated the complicated implications for the conduct of macroeconomic policy that newly liberalized financial sectors raise. Investors in emerging markets are now provided with much more analysis of the health of the financial systems and of the potential relationships between financial fragility and macroeconomic performance in these countries.

In addition, the official international community has stepped up efforts to support improvements in financial infrastructure and to incorporate analysis of financial market developments in the monitoring of developing countries' macroeconomic performance. Thus, international attention has turned to the economic consequences of inadequate bank supervisory and regulatory capacity in emerging markets. Such concerns motivated a broad-based effort by the international financial community in 1996–97 to provide a basis for support for emerging market governments in this area. The Basle Committee released a set of *Core Principles for Effective Banking Supervision* (April 1997) and a G-10 Working Party on Financial Stability in Emerging Market Economies released its own paper (*Financial Stability in Emerging Market Economies*) the same month. The latter report called for a "concerted international strategy to promote the establishment, adoption and implementation of sound principles and practices needed for financial stability" in emerging markets, in which the IMF would promote the adoption and implementation of these principles and practices. An early proponent of this approach, Goldstein (1997), has called for the establishment of International Banking Standards, based on the principles developed by the international agencies, to which bank supervisors would voluntarily adhere.

Developments in Profitability and Asset Quality in Selected Industrial Countries

The banking systems in the major industrial countries performed strongly in 1996: most of the banks in the G-7 countries reported higher earnings and improved asset quality. The banks have benefited from a sustained period of declining interest rates and from an increase in economic growth rates that have raised loan volumes and provided the means to finance loan loss provisions and write-offs. Aside from a few individual institutions in certain countries, the problems that banks in these countries face are medium-term structural problems, not the immediate solvency threats they confronted in the early to mid-1990s.

Performance by Country

The performance of commercial banks in the industrial countries in 1996 differed markedly between

---

[9]One of the most obvious problems has arisen with the assignment of a zero credit risk weight within the weighted credit risk capital requirement for sovereign debt of OECD countries, requiring banks to allocate more capital to a loan to triple-A-rated Singapore than to Korea, which is rated AA⁻.

groups of countries depending upon their relative position in the credit cycle. For banks in Canada, Norway, Sweden, the United Kingdom, and the United States, which had resolved their asset-quality problems relatively quickly in the early 1990s, profitability and capitalization levels remained at or near historic high levels in 1996, with nonperforming loan ratios at correspondingly low levels. Asset quality may have peaked in these countries, and some deterioration can probably be expected. However, the banks have high loan loss reserves and are well capitalized, so they are generally well equipped to deal with such a development.

For banks in Finland and France, there is now reason to believe that the worst of their asset-quality problems are over. The overall condition of the banking systems in these countries has improved, and the emphasis is increasingly on the resolution of problems in individual institutions and in France on the longer-term structural issues that confront the industry, such as the effects of European monetary union on competition within European banking systems, as is discussed in Annex IV. The situation in Italy, however, remains difficult, especially for banks in the central and southern regions, while the Japanese banks continue to face serious asset-quality problems. The German banking system, alone it seems among the major industrial countries, has not experienced a serious decline in asset-quality due to real-estate-related loans, although some segments of the property market in Germany have weakened.

Supported by a strong increase in noninterest earnings and a 24 percent decline in provisions, the Schedule I banks in *Canada* reported a 22 percent increase in net income in the fiscal year ending October 1996, an average return on equity of 15 percent.[10] Canadian banks compensated for a tightening in net interest margins—the fifth consecutive year of tightening—by increasing the share of consumer lending and other relatively high-margin lending in their loan portfolios (including the contribution of some of the banks' Latin American subsidiaries). To date, this has not led to a deterioration of average loan quality. At the end of the fiscal year, only 0.6 percent of loans were nonperforming, down from 1.2 percent in 1995 and a peak of 3.2 percent in 1992. Reserve coverage is generally very high, in excess of 270 percent of nonperforming loans, although the ratio of reserves to gross loans fell to 1.6 percent, the lowest level in at least eight years. Canadian banks are also well capitalized by international

standards, with an average total risk-weighted capital ratio of 9.4 percent (a Tier I ratio of 6.8 percent) even after share repurchases by at least four of the banks.

Most banks in the *United Kingdom* also enjoyed record profits in 1996, bolstered by a sharp reduction in loan loss provisions, and despite a slight narrowing of the net interest margin. Aggregate net income for the five largest commercial banks rose 2 percent, for an average return on equity of 19 percent.[11] Banks compensated for declining interest margins on corporate loans by increasing both the volume of loans and the share of consumer loans and mortgages in their loan portfolios. After having peaked in 1992, asset-quality problems eased significantly, with the end-1996 incidence of impaired lending representing 2.5 percent of loans (compared with 9.8 percent at end-1992)[12] and loan loss reserves covering 85 percent of impaired lending. Capitalization remains high, with a total risk-weighted capital ratio of 10.9 percent, 7.26 percent of which was Tier I capital.

Banks in the *United States* continued their string of record earnings levels in 1996, as total net income of FDIC-insured commercial banks increased by more than 7 percent for a return on equity of 14 percent. Despite slightly lower net interest margins, net interest income increased by 5 percent, supported by strong loan growth. The diversification of banks' income sources continued in 1996, with noninterest income contributing 36 percent of gross operating income—the highest proportion ever for U.S. banks. While overall asset quality continued to improve in 1996—total noncurrent loans (i.e., loans that are 90 days or more past due or on nonaccrual status) fell to 1.05 percent of gross loans—consumer lending and domestic syndicated lending have been a source of concern. At end-1996, 3.6 percent of loans to individuals were past due, reflecting in particular a continuing deterioration of credit card loans.[13] Concerns about potential asset-quality problems were reflected in an increase in loan loss provisions for the second consecutive year. Overall, banks are well covered against potential losses on existing problem assets—loan loss reserves rose to 182 percent of noncurrent assets—although the ratio of reserves to total loans declined to 1.9 percent, the lowest ratio since 1986. While reserves may not provide a significant buffer against a sudden increase in loan losses, U.S. banks are well capitalized, with a core capital ratio of 7.6 percent at end-1996, its high-

---

[10]The Schedule I banks are Royal Bank of Canada, Canadian Imperial Bank of Commerce, Bank of Montreal, Bank of Nova Scotia, Toronto Dominion Bank, National Bank of Canada, and Canadian Western Bank. As is the case in all discussions of banking system developments in this annex, unless otherwise noted the description of the banks' performance is based on their financial statements as provided by IBCA Ltd.

[11]The banks included in this survey of recent developments are National Westminster Bank, Barclays Bank, Lloyds Bank, Abbey National, and Midland Bank.

[12]Impaired lending includes loans on nonaccrual status, doubtful loans, and potential problem loans, where disclosed. U.K. banks are not required to disclose nonperforming loans according to a uniform definition.

[13]Most consumer loans were only 30–89 days past due; only 1.7 percent of consumer loans were noncurrent, although this represents a deterioration from 1.2 percent at end-1995.

est level in at least nine years, despite a relatively high volume of share repurchases by many of the banks.[14]

For the first time in six years, all of the major banks in *France* reported positive net profits for 1996.[15] However, this outcome was due mainly to exceptionally high income from capital market activities and from lower loan loss provisions. The core banking operations continue to suffer from low loan demand, poor asset quality, and aggressive competition, which have limited net interest income and reduced the capitalization of the banks. Thus, while noninterest income rose by 23 percent in 1996, net interest income declined by 2 percent. A 10 percent reduction in loan loss provisions allowed net income to rise by 140 percent, albeit from a relatively low base, for a return on equity of 7.7 percent. Not all French banks disclose their nonperforming assets, but it is generally believed that the worst of the asset-quality difficulties is past. While a large number of loans to small and medium-sized firms are nonperforming, the banks are believed to have set aside sufficient reserves to cover anticipated loans. With the caveat in mind that it is difficult to judge the asset-quality position of the banks, the published figures on capitalization indicate that the leading banks are reasonably well capitalized, with total risk-weighted capital ratios of between 8.7 percent and 11.4 percent.[16]

Property markets, a key source of nonperforming loans in France, continued to deteriorate in 1996, with the vacancy rate on prime office space in the center of Paris, for example, rising to 9.2 percent at end-1996 from 8.4 percent a year earlier, and rents falling by 3.8 percent over the same period.[17] Since the market peaked in 1990–91, commercial real estate prices have declined by about 50 percent. As a result, some of the banks have had to seek assistance from their shareholders either to move real estate assets off their balance sheets or for capital injections.[18] Until

the end of 1995, these operations had not resulted in significant sales of real estate. However, in 1996, some of the French banks began in earnest to reduce their exposure to property markets after having opted in earlier years simply to increase provisions against potential losses. In 1996, sales of real estate by bank shareholders helped to boost the volume of property investment transactions to F 12 billion, more than twice the 1995 turnover. The banks also began selling off large portions of their real estate loan portfolios, much of it to U.S. investors. The process began with the sale of F 870 million in real estate loans by Barclays Bank in late 1995, followed in 1996 by Créditsuez (F 4.75 billion), and UAP (F 3.2 billion). Créditsuez has announced its intention to sell off a further F 4.9 billion in real estate loans by 2001, and the Consortium de Réalisation (CDR) has proposed to sell F 1 billion. The first securitization of real estate loans in France was accomplished in January 1997 with the sale of F 1.5 billion in commercial mortgage backed securities (CMBS) backed by mortgage loans of Banque SOFAL, a subsidiary of Union Industrielle de Crédit.[19]

The French government announced a three-point resolution plan for Credit Foncier de France (CFF) in July 1996: (1) the Caisse des Depots et Consignations (CDC) would launch a public offer on behalf of the government for a sale of at least two-thirds of CFF; (2) a new public entity, the Caisse National du Credit Foncier, wholly owned by the state, would be established and acquire these shares from the CDC and wind down CFF's business over the next 10 years; and (3) Credit Immobilier de France, a mutual institution, would take over the management of CFF's portfolio of F 110 billion in subsidized home loans as well as its branch network and 1,500 of its 3,300 employees.[20] The government has estimated the costs of this plan at F 2.5 billion. While the share issue went ahead as planned, with the government now owning more than 90 percent of CFF, the creation of Caisse National du Credit Foncier and the transfer of CFF assets to Credit Immobilier de France have not. CFF remains in business and reportedly earned F 1 billion in profit in 1996, but has virtually no capital (its total capital ade-

---

[14]In 1996, the Federal Reserve Board of Governors conferred Tier I capital-eligibility status on a class of tax-exempt trust-preferred subordinated securities known by various acronyms (e.g., TOPRs, MIPs, QUIPS, TRIPS). Banks are reported to have issued at least $30 billion of such securities, some of it used to repurchase shares, thereby leveraging up shareholder equity.

[15]This description of the results of the French banks is based on the financial statements of the seven largest commercial banks (Crédit Agricole, Crédit Lyonnais, Société Général, Banque National de Paris, Banque Paribas, Compagnie Financière de CIC et de l'Union Européenne, and Crédit Commercial de France).

[16]Not including Banque Paribas, whose capital ratios are assessed at the holding company level.

[17]Jones Lang Wootton (1997).

[18]In addition to the government support for Crédit Lyonnais, Banque Hervet, and Société Marseillaise de Crédit to cover mostly real-estate-related losses, banks have sought assistance from insurance companies that are major shareholders—Banque Worms from UAP, Union Industrielle de Crédit from GAN, and Comptoir des Entrepreneurs from AGF—and from other parent companies—Banque La Hénin from Groupe Suez, BRED from Banques Populaires, and Crédit du Nord from Groupe Paribas.

[19]Securitization of real estate loans was an important ingredient of the resolution of the savings and loans crisis in the United States and of the commercial banks' recent real-estate-related problems. Between 1989 and 1995, the Resolution Trust Corporation sold $17 billion in CMBS. Securitization has now become an accepted means of real estate finance in the United States. Total CMBS issuance in 1996 exceeded $30 billion, more than half of it to finance new construction. In the United Kingdom, securitization of loan portfolios has been undertaken since 1987, with a total of 94 CMBS issued representing a total volume of £18.7 billion. In 1997, NatWest Bank successfully securitized $5 billion worth of corporate loans and £1 billion in government housing association loans.

[20]The events leading up to the rescue of CFF are described in IMF (1996).

quacy ratio at end-1995 was 0.5 percent) and its loan portfolio has fallen by half.

The other institution that was forced to turn to the French government for assistance as a result of asset-quality problems, Crédit Lyonnais, returned to profitability in 1995 and improved on those results in 1996, earning a net profit of F 1.5 billion. However, this was possible only after the French Ministry of Finance agreed to neutralize the effect of the negative interest rate spread on a F 135 billion loan to the Etablissement Public de Financement et de Réstructuration—used to finance the purchase of loans from Crédit Lyonnais by the CDR. The carrying cost of the loan, estimated at F 3 billion in 1996, has been assumed by the government. As part of the EU approval for the recapitalization plan in 1996, Crédit Lyonnais has begun selling its domestic and foreign subsidiaries and investments, including Banque Laydernier, Crédit Lyonnais Bank Sverige, Woodchester Investments, Banco Portugues de Investimento, and Banco Provincial. The total cost of official support to Crédit Lyonnais was recently estimated by the ministry of finance at F 100 billion.

The largest private commercial banks in *Germany* reported substantially higher profits in 1996, owing mainly to strong trading profits and an increase in holdings of securities and other investments. Net income for the five largest commercial banks rose 19 percent (for a return on equity of 9.8 percent), as non-interest income rose by 25 percent.[21] German banks alone among those of the seven major industrial countries have not experienced a severe deterioration in asset quality in recent years, although data on nonperforming loans and specific loan loss provisions are not generally disclosed. Disclosed provisions—which include gains on securities held in the liquidity reserve—declined by 21 percent in 1996. Real estate may become more of a problem in 1997–98, however, with the removal of tax concessions on development in the eastern Länder and a softening of the office rental markets in some key markets, including Berlin and Hamburg.

The banking system in *Italy* continues to struggle with worsening asset quality, increasing labor costs, and an unfavorable tax regime that has contributed to weak profitability. However, the Italian Banking Association and trade unions have recently agreed to a reduction in labor costs to the EU average as measured by the ratio of labor costs to gross income. The costs associated with labor shedding will be borne by the banks without any support from the government. Furthermore, a recent reform of the corporate tax code and an increase in the deductability of loan loss provisions will lower the tax burden on banks. The contin-

uing weakness of the economy, particularly in the southern region, has slowed loan growth, while increasing competition has narrowed interest margins. The steady decline in the level of interest rates contributed to a resurgence of activity in the securities market, resulting in a 61 percent increase in noninterest income, which allowed operating profit to increase by 7 percent.[22] However, asset quality continued to deteriorate in 1996, albeit at a slower pace than in 1994 and 1995. The stock of bad loans (defined as *sofferenze* and protested bills) increased by 11 percent to Lit 128 trillion, or 10 percent of total loans, up from 9 percent at end-1995. The estimated loss rate on these loans also increased, to 38 percent from 33 percent at end-1995.

The relative severity of the economic recession in southern Italy has led to a higher concentration of bad loans in that part of the country,[23] with the result that a number of banks based in the south have experienced serious capital depletion because of loan losses. One of these, Banco di Napoli, incurred net losses of Lit 4.3 trillion during 1994–95. In the first half of 1996, the bank lost a further Lit 700 billion, and by the end of the year, it had lost Lit 1.6 trillion. In July 1996, the government announced a recapitalization package involving (1) the elimination of existing equity and the issue of Lit 2 trillion in new capital; (2) the transfer of about 30 percent of the loan portfolio to a special purpose company (Societa per la Gestione di Attivita); and (3) the sale of a 60 percent stake, which ultimately went in January 1997 to a combined offer from government-owned Banca Nazionale del Lavoro and a private insurer, Istituto Nazionale delle Assicurazioni. In addition, Banco di Napoli has sold much of its performing medium- and long-term loan portfolio; its largest subsidiary will be liquidated; 50 branches in the north have been sold; and agreement has been reached with trade unions to lower personnel costs. However, half of the capital increase obtained by the new share issue has already been drawn down to cover the losses incurred during 1996.

The provision of extensive government support for the *Finnish, Norwegian,* and *Swedish* banks in the early 1990s prevented what may have been the complete collapse of the banking systems in these countries. By the end of 1996, the recovery from the crisis was more or less complete in Norway and Sweden—marked by the removal of the government guarantee for Swedish banks in July 1996. Surging loan growth and plummeting loan loss provisions—indeed, many of the banks have been writing back significant amounts of provisions—and a supportive

---

[21]The banks are Deutsche Bank, Dresdner Bank, Commerzbank, Bayerische Vereinsbank, and Bayerische Hypotheken-und Wechsel-Bank.

[22]Data on the performance of Italian banks are from the Banca d'Italia and cover the entire industry.

[23]At end-1996, the proportion of *sofferenze* doubtful loans in the northern and central regions was 7.9 percent, while in the southern regions, including Sicily, it was 25.4 percent.

capital market environment have provided the stimulus for recovery. For the Finnish banks, however, important weaknesses remain, and the recovery has been uneven. The *Danish* banks, while avoiding an outright crisis, nevertheless endured a serious deterioration in asset quality and earnings in the early 1990s.

Net income for the four largest commercial banks in Denmark declined by 2 percent in 1996, for a return on equity of 16 percent.[24] The stock of nonperforming loans fell for the second consecutive year, by 31 percent, accounting for 1.5 percent of total loans. Despite a decline in provisioning, loan loss reserves at end-1996 equaled 207 percent of the stock of nonperforming loans. The banks in Finland, of all the Nordic banks, have experienced the slowest recovery. After five years of net losses, the three major banks[25] recorded a net profit in 1996 of FM 1.6 billion, a return on equity of 8 percent, due mostly to a 37 percent increase in noninterest income and a 23 percent decline in provisions. Net nonperforming loans declined by 41 percent to 2.5 percent of gross loans, or 26 percent of equity. The four major banks in Norway suffered an 11 percent decline in net income, but nevertheless recorded a return on equity of about 20 percent.[26] Net nonperforming loans declined by 20 percent, to 1.4 percent of total loans, or 20 percent of equity. The five largest commercial banks in Sweden reported sustained high income and lower nonperforming loans.[27] Aggregate operating profit rose 28 percent, owing mostly to strong noninterest income and a 43 percent decline in loan loss provisions and write-offs. Net problem loans fell by 30 percent, to 1.6 percent of aggregate loans. The extent of the recovery was highlighted by the removal on July 1, 1996, of the blanket guarantee that the government had established for the banks.

The resolution of asset-quality problems in *Japan* continued to dominate developments in the banking system. Net interest income rose by 9 percent owing mainly to special circumstances affecting the interest expenses of the long-term credit and trust banks;[28] the city banks' net interest income declined by 6 percent. Without the benefit of declining interest rates boosting the valuation of the banks' large investment bond portfolios, noninterest income declined by 31 percent, while commissions and trading income were flat overall. At the same time, the banks wrote off ¥2,267 billion in unrealized losses on their equity holdings, which offset much of the ¥3,488 billion they had realized in order to finance provisions. As a result, net profits on equity of ¥1,128 billion were used to offset part of the ¥5,555 billion in loan loss provisions and write-offs, leading to a net loss for the 20 banks of ¥146 billion.

At end-March 1997, the 20 major banks had ¥13,193 billion in core nonperforming loans (loans six months or more past due and loans to bankrupt borrowers), ¥3,247 billion in loans restructured at below the prevailing official discount rate, and ¥2,890 billion in loans made in support of customers. This total of ¥19,331 in problem loans represents a 25 percent decline over the previous year's ¥25,663 billion. Total problem loans represented 4.9 percent of gross loans at end-March 1997, compared with 5.4 percent at end-March 1996, but most of this decline was due to writing off loans to the housing loan corporations (*jusen),* which had been fully reserved but not written off in the previous year. Excluding the *jusen* loans, problem loans fell only 15 percent, while the core nonperforming loans remained unchanged.[29]

While the definition of problem loans has been gradually widened in the last two years it is still less encompassing than the U.S. model for example. The Japanese definition does not include loans that have been sold to the Cooperative Credit Purchasing Company (CCPC) or special purpose vehicles and excludes loans restructured at interest rates above the official discount rate.[30] Most, if not all, of these loans would likely be considered nonperforming loans of a bank under U.S. practices. Applying a broader definition of problem loans to the Japanese banks yields an estimated aggregate problem loan figure somewhat higher than the official estimate.[31]

Five depository institutions failed in 1996—including two regional banks, Taiheyo Bank and Hanwa Bank—some of which required intervention by the

---

[24]Den Danske Bank, Unibank, Bikuben Girobank, and Jyske Bank.

[25]Merita Bank, Postipankki Bank, and Okobank.

[26]Den Norske Bank, Christiania Bank, Union Bank, and Fokus Bank.

[27]Skandinavska Enskilda Banken, Svenska Handelsbanken, Nordbanken, Swedbank, and Foreningsbanken.

[28]The maximum permitted trust account special reserve was lowered from 3 percent to 0.5 percent, allowing the trust banks to release the ¥1 trillion excess, around half of which was used to charge off problem loans and half was written back to income. The long-term credit banks benefited from the redemption in late 1995 of high interest rate debentures that had been issued in 1990 and had depressed net interest revenue in 1995 as interest rates on assets declined.

[29]The ratio of core nonperforming loans to total loans at end-March 1997 was 3.3 percent, the same as at the end of the previous fiscal year. The same ratio was 3.5 percent at end-March 1995, 3.7 percent in 1994, and 3.4 percent in 1993. Under the broader definition of nonperforming loans that includes restructured loans, the ratio has declined steadily from 5.4 percent of total loans in September 1995 to 4.9 percent in March 1996 and 3.9 percent in March 1997.

[30]The CCPC has announced that it will stop purchasing loans after April 1998 and concentrate on liquidating its portfolio. Between March 1993 and March 1997, the CCPC paid ¥5.4 trillion to acquire loans with a book value of ¥13.6 trillion. By end-March 1997, however, the CCPC had recovered only ¥813 billion.

[31]IBCA estimates, for example, that total problem loans amounted to ¥40 trillion at end-March 1997, of which uncovered losses were ¥4.5 trillion.

Table 33. Major Industrial Countries: Commercial Bank Profitability

	Net Interest Income		Noninterest Income		Operating Expenses		Provisions		Real Return on Equity[1]	
	1985–89	1990–94	1985–89	1990–94	1985–89	1990–94	1985–89	1990–94	1985–89	1990–94
	(In percent of total assets)								*(In percent)*	
Canada	2.9	3.0	1.1	1.6	2.3	2.8	0.8	0.7	7.9	12.1
France[2]	1.9	1.2	0.5	0.8	1.6	1.4	0.5	0.5	…	–3.3
Germany	2.3	2.2	1.0	0.9	2.2	2.0	0.4	0.6	6.5	2.7
Italy	…	3.0	…	0.9	…	2.5	…	0.6	…	–1.2
Japan	1.2	1.0	0.3	0.1	0.9	0.9	…	0.1	10.4	1.5
United Kingdom	3.2	2.7	1.8	1.9	3.2	3.0	0.9	0.9	6.1	4.9
United States	3.5	3.7	1.5	2.0	3.3	3.7	0.9	0.7	5.0	8.5

Sources: International Monetary Fund, *World Economic Outlook* database; OECD (1996); and IMF staff estimates.
[1]Calculated as net income after taxes divided by capital and reserves at the end of the previous year, minus consumer price index for the year.
[2]Data for the first period cover 1988–89 only.

deposit insurance corporation. Also, 2 of the 20 major banks reported significant restructuring packages in April 1997. On April 1, 1997, Nippon Credit Bank (NCB) announced that it would: (1) write off ¥460 billion in nonperforming loans, which would result in a pretax loss of ¥350 billion; (2) cut salaries (by 10–30 percent for most personnel, and 50 percent for managers) and personnel (by 900, or 31 percent), and sell off all of its own real estate holdings, including its headquarters; (3) not pay dividends for the 1996/97 fiscal year; (4) cut assets by ¥6 trillion to ¥10 trillion (a 37 percent decline); (5) close its foreign branches and subsidiaries (five branches and seven representative offices); and (6) seek an injection of capital of ¥300 billion to prevent insolvency. This capital injection would come from shareholders and the other long-term credit banks (for a combined ¥70 billion), subordinated debt holders (mostly insurance companies, ¥140 billion), and the New Financial Stabilization Fund (¥80 billion), which was originally established to assist in the resolution of the *jusen* last year. It also announced that its three nonbank affiliates—Crown Leasing, Nippon Total Finance, and Nippon Assurance Finance Service—would file for bankruptcy rather than be bailed out by the NCB. These three institutions had total loans of ¥1.8 trillion, of which only ¥300 billion was owed to NCB. All other creditors would have to write off their loans to these nonbanks (it was reported that agricultural cooperatives had total loans to the nonbanks of ¥240 billion and the seven trust banks had lent a combined ¥430 billion). On April 10, 1997, NCB announced an agreement with Bankers Trust involving collaboration in securitization and international operations. Also on April 1, Hokkaido Takushoku Bank (HTB) announced that it would merge with Hokkaido Bank (the twenty-second largest of the first-tier regional banks) at the end of the 1997/98 fiscal year, forming a new institution, tentatively called the New Hokkaido Bank (NHB). HTB announced that it would also close or

transform to representative offices all of its 20 overseas branches and subsidiaries, and the merged entity would close 100 of its combined 340 branches. HTB will also cut 2,000 employees, resulting in expected cost savings equivalent to 30 percent of operating expenses.

The NCB resolution strategy combined elements of the old approach to bank failures—shareholder banks, the long-term credit banks, and the Bank of Japan (through the New Financial Stabilization Fund) are to provide capital for NCB—and some new ideas, and holders of subordinated debt were also asked to inject capital. More important, the bankruptcy of NCB's nonbank affiliates was a significant departure from the principle of parent responsibility. However, at end-March 1997, NCB had ¥1.3 trillion in problem loans, still 7 percent of total loans. In addition, NCB's total capital ratio has been reduced to 3 percent and its hidden reserves on listed and unlisted securities have been reduced by 86 percent, covering only 3 percent of problem loans. More fundamentally, NCB, like all of the long-term credit banks, suffers from a decline in franchise value. The market for long-term corporate loans has been eroded by competition from other banks, foreign institutions, and capital market funding.

The Next Challenge: Core Profitability

As the major banking systems recover from their asset-quality problems, the focus is turning toward their underlying strength and their ability to respond to the changes in the financial landscape outlined at the beginning of this annex by increasing noninterest income and yielding greater returns to equity holders. Table 33 shines some light on these issues by comparing the income generation and profitability of the banking systems of the major industrial countries over the 10-year period 1985–94. During that time, almost all of these countries have experienced a significant

147

Figure 53. Major Industrial Countries: Intermediation Spreads

(Average lending interest rate minus average deposit interest rate)

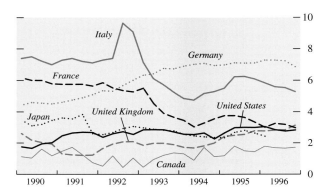

Source: International Monetary Fund, *International Financial Statistics.*

deterioration in asset quality and profitability at some time, which shows up in the reported returns on equity and pre-provision profits (banks with higher nonperforming loans incur greater expenses in managing their loan portfolios). Nevertheless, data reveal some major trends.

Over the 1985–94 period, the Canadian, U.K., and U.S. banking systems were consistently the most profitable in terms of core, pre-provision earnings among the G-7 countries. The average pre-provision return on assets over that period was 1.8 percent for U.S. banks, 1.7 percent for Canadian and U.K. banks, 1.1 percent for German banks, 0.6 percent for French banks, and 0.5 percent for Japanese banks (not shown). The relatively strong recent performance of the Canadian, U.K., and U.S. banks compared to those in, for example, France and Japan, is not, therefore, simply due to their having gone through the recent asset-quality cycle more quickly; banks in the three leading countries have simply been fundamentally more profitable. These profits, however, do not reflect relatively wide intermediation spreads.[32] As Figure 53 shows, loan rate spreads over deposits have tended to be higher in France, Germany, and Italy compared with Canada, the United Kingdom, and the United States. A relatively higher proportion of low-margin securities and

other assets, and relatively worse overall asset quality during the period, appear to explain most of the difference.

While most banks have responded to the increased competition in lending activities by expanding their noninterest earnings, banks in Germany and Japan have actually seen a decline in importance of such income. Noninterest income for the Japanese and three continental European banking systems, which is decreasing, remains a much less well developed source of income than it is for banks in Canada, the United Kingdom, and the United States. This lack of diversification in income has meant that the decline in asset quality was particularly costly, since these banks relied much more heavily on interest income. With increasing loan loss provisions and declining interest income, the banks' profitability dropped. The real return on equity, for example, has fallen sharply in Japan and in Germany, and less so in the United Kingdom, while it has risen significantly in Canada and the United States owing to a combination of increasing underlying profitability and declining provisions. As the data in Table 33 indicate, however, it is relatively weak earnings generation that hampers the French, German, Italian, and Japanese banking systems, and which has made their recovery from their asset-quality difficulties in some cases quite difficult.[33]

The issue of core profitability is inextricably linked to the structure of the banking system and, particularly, the advantages that certain types of institutions may have because of different regulatory regimes, subsidies, or ownership structures that place less emphasis on returns to capital. In an environment in which banks are encouraged by the regulatory regime to maximize returns to equity capital, such features of a financial system can make it more difficult for some banks to compete. To be sure, certain of these differences can be to the detriment of the special institutions—a contributing factor to the savings and loan (S&L) crisis in the United States was the more relaxed supervisory and regulatory environment in which they operated, which allowed the S&Ls to run up very large loan losses. Similarly, the lower level of official oversight over the credit unions and credit cooperatives in Japan contributed to difficulties in those sectors. However, often the special treatment of certain types of institutions works to the detriment of the larger, internationally active, commercial banks, in part by reducing the domestic profits on which they attempt to leverage their international activities. (For example, since profit margins on retail banking services tend to be wider than on

---

[32]Nor are lower costs the explanation, as is often argued. Operating expenses as a percentage of assets have been consistently higher in Canada, the United Kingdom, and the United States, and somewhat less so in Germany, compared with France and especially Japan, where annual operating costs amount to approximately 0.9 percent of assets, compared with about 3.5 percent in the United States over the same period.

---

[33]Note that the Japanese banks only began to make significant inroads on their nonperforming loans after pre-provision earnings soared to record levels in 1995/96.

wholesale transactions, restrictions on competition in retail markets can prevent access to profitable business by commercial banks.) While few, if any, countries have a perfectly level playing field—for instance, savings institutions often enjoy advantages over commercial banks—some of these distortions have been more prominent in recent years, including the government ownership or mutual ownership of banks in France, Germany, and Italy which, by apparently downplaying the incentive for maximizing shareholder returns, has arguably allowed these institutions to compete aggressively against the private commercial banks in the same countries. Private bankers from France and Germany have argued to the European Commission on Competition that government-owned banks in these countries have been unfairly subsidized by the manner in which they were recapitalized.

In France, a number of the largest commercial banks have criticized the terms of the official assistance given to Crédit Lyonnais. The EU Competition Commissioner approved the recapitalization only after it was agreed that Crédit Lyonnais would divest itself of 35 percent of its foreign affiliates. The private banks in Germany have also questioned the government support that had been extended to some of the Landesbanks in the late 1980s. More generally, the Landesbanks have received higher credit ratings than many of the private banks because they are guaranteed by the government. For example, Moody's rates the major commercial banks' long-term foreign currency debt between Aaa and Aa2 and nine Landesbanks' debt between Aaa and Aa1—with the average Landesbank rating slightly higher than that of the commercial banks—but the stand-alone Bank Financial Strength Ratings are much higher for the commercial banks (B+) compared with the Landesbanks (C+). This public guarantee allows the Landesbanks to raise funds domestically and on international markets at more favorable rates than private banks can. At the same time, the Landesbanks earn an interest margin approximately half of that of the major banks and earn a correspondingly small return on equity (averaging 4 percent over 1990–95).

The issue is not necessarily that government-owned or cooperative banks are less efficient than privately owned banks, although that is often the case, but that official guarantees, subsidies, or regulatory advantages that segregate markets—for example, by giving certain institutions exclusive rights to offer certain types of retail deposit instruments or bonds, or certain types of loans—are inherently inefficient. By restricting the scope of competition, such structures can end up supporting an inefficient allocation of capital in the financial system, and worse, allow the accumulation of large losses that ultimately become a claim on the official sector.

Banking System Developments in Selected Emerging Markets[34]

Developments in Asian Emerging Markets

Macroeconomic developments strongly influenced the performance of banking systems in Asian emerging markets. Growth slowed (and current account deficits worsened) partly because of cyclical factors but also because of longer-term fundamentals. Growth in countries such as India, Indonesia, Korea, Malaysia, and Thailand slowed in 1996 compared with 1995 and is forecast to slow further in 1997.[35] Granted that even these slower growth rates surpass all but the highest growth rates in Latin America, the slowdown, nonetheless, has had serious repercussions for the financial systems in some Asian emerging markets, because it has revealed the underlying illiquidity in the corporate sectors and the lack of preparedness among some financial institutions for the slowdown and the resulting worsening of asset quality. Unless growth and export performance improve in 1997 the banks in some Asian countries may face significant challenges to their profitability and possibly their solvency. Given the history in many Asian emerging markets of providing broad support to the financial system by ensuring the survival of individual financial institutions, this vulnerability of the banking sector to further deterioration of macroeconomic fundamentals may become an increasingly important constraint on fiscal and monetary policies.

Property market developments also figured prominently in Asian banking developments in 1996 as key real estate markets deteriorated. Table 34 shows the recent trends in vacancy rates and rents on prime office space in some of the key property markets in Asia. The well-publicized weakness in the Bangkok market appears in the table as a slight increase in the vacancy rate, from an already high 13.2 percent at end-1995 to 13.9 percent at end-1996, and virtually flat rents. Moreover, record amounts of commercial real estate and office space are due to become available in 1997–99, which will further depress values. In Jakarta, a significant increase in vacancy rates was offset at least partly by an increase in rents, but there

---

[34]This section discusses recent developments in the systemically important emerging markets' banking systems with a view toward assessing the vulnerabilities in these systems and their potential consequences for macroeconomic developments and policies. This analysis draws on publicly available material published by national authorities, banks, and rating agencies. Because of space and resource constraints, this section does not discuss developments in banking systems in all, or even most, emerging markets or even in all countries where there are significant banking problems. Instead, developments in a few of the more important emerging markets in Asia (Korea, the Philippines, and Thailand), Latin America (Argentina, Brazil, Chile, Mexico, and Venezuela) and Europe (Czech Republic, Hungary, and Poland) are discussed.

[35]See the projections in IMF (1997).

Table 34. Selected Asian Property Markets: Vacancy Rates and Changes in Rents[1]

(In percent)

	Vacancy Rate		Change in Rents[2]
	March 1996	March 1997	
Bangkok	13.2	13.9	0.3
Beijing[3]	1.0	22.9	-19.2
Hong Kong, China	4.7	5.1	6.3
Jakarta	10.8	12.4	3.9
Kuala Lumpur	2.8	2.9	0.0
Manila	2.1	2.0	1.9
Shanghai[3]	14.1	24.6	-24.0
Singapore	4.9	6.1	4.5

Source: Jones Lang Wooton (1997).

[1]Prime office space in central business locations.

[2]Change in contracted net rents denominated in local currency, except for Beijing, Jakarta, and Shanghai, which are changes in U.S. dollar values.

[3]The increase in vacancy rates and decline in rents for Beijing and Shanghai reflect both the small initial stock of office space and the comparatively large developments that were completed in 1996.

too the market has underlying weakness. In Kuala Lumpur and Manila (Makati), conversely, vacancy rates are extremely low.

Korea's accession to OECD membership in 1996 focused international attention on its banking system and in particular raised some concern that increasing competition from foreign banks and a surge in foreign capital inflows could put pressure on the system. However, foreign banks already have a presence in Korea and operate on an equal basis with domestic banks (there were 77 foreign branches at end-1995); and while capital account liberalization may have a more important effect, the gradual approach to liberalizing inflows provides an opportunity to strengthen the domestic financial sector. Instead, the vulnerabilities in the Korean banking system have their roots in past practices. Explicit government-directed lending (Industrial Rationalization Loans)[36] has given way to directed lending of a different kind—for example, banks are required to allocate a certain proportion of marginal loans to the small and medium-sized enterprise sector—while political influence on lending decisions appears to continue. Consequently, many Korean banks have not yet developed sophisticated internal credit evaluation systems, placing greater emphasis on collateral than on an analysis of the project being financed.

In the current environment, many banks have built up large exposures to individual corporate groups (*chaebols*), many of which are highly leveraged.[37] The

reduction in economic growth and export prices in 1996 heightened the illiquidity of many of these groups. In addition, many Korean firms have taken on increasing amounts of foreign-currency-denominated debt—both by borrowing in the international markets directly and by borrowing in foreign currencies from Korean banks. It is believed by many market analysts that very little of this currency exposure is hedged (the onshore forward foreign exchange market is very illiquid and would provide cover for only about 12 months in most cases), so that as the won depreciated these debts became more expensive to service. In the past year at least four large corporations or groups have defaulted on their debts, and other large companies are rumored to be in difficulty.

The growing liquidity problems among the large corporations have already put pressure on the banks' asset quality. At end-1995, nonperforming loans (those six months or more past due) among the eight largest commercial banks, for example, amounted to 6 percent of total loans.[38] By the end of 1996, the reported nonperforming loans had declined to 4.3 percent of loans for these eight banks, but if the exposures to Hanbo Iron and Steel Company and Sammi Steel are included, this ratio rises to 6.0 percent.[39] Net of reserves, these nonperforming loans equate to 68.9 percent of the banks' equity. However, since only loans six months past due are included, and restructured loans are not included at all, the true asset-quality situation of the Korean banks may be much worse (see Appendix 2 at the end of this annex for a description of asset-quality accounting practices in 20 emerging markets).

As is true among emerging markets elsewhere, much of the collateral that secures problem loans is real estate or specialized fixed capital that may be difficult to repossess or to sell at book value. Also, there are other potential sources of problems for the Korean banks in addition to the loans to the *chaebols*. Consumer loans, including credit cards, have been an important source of expansion for Korean banks in the past few years, and these have emerged as having high ratios of nonperforming loans. In addition to declining loan quality, the banks have had to deal with the collapse of Korean equity prices in 1996, which has imposed large revaluation losses on their extensive equity portfolios.

---

[36]The commercial banks still had W 4.5 trillion in policy loans on their books at end-1996, 56 percent of which were nonperforming.

[37]The 30 largest *chaebols* accounted for 16 percent of GDP in 1995. Among the 30 largest *chaebols,* 19 have debt-equity ratios greater than 400 percent, and 4 have ratios greater than 1,000 percent.

[38]These asset-quality data are reported by IBCA Ltd., which cites the Economic Research Institute of Korea as the source, and include substandard, doubtful, and loss loans. The Office of Bank Supervision in Korea reports nonperforming loans according to a narrower definition, which includes only doubtful and loss loans. According to this definition, bad loans in Korea average less than 1 percent of total loans. They report that substandard and precautionary loans are generally fully covered by collateral and that the historical loss rates are negligible.

[39]Hanbo Iron and Steel Company, the center of the Hanbo Group, the fourteenth largest *chaebol,* declared bankruptcy on January 23, 1997. Sammi Steel, the twenty-sixth largest *chaebol,* declared bankruptcy on March 20, 1997.

The Korean authorities have responded to the declining asset quality and the losses on banks' equity portfolios in part by engaging in regulatory forbearance. After raising the loan loss provisioning requirement for doubtful loans to 100 percent at the beginning of 1996, the requirement was later lowered to 75 percent. In addition, the banks were allowed to provision for only 30 percent of the securities revaluation losses in 1996, rather than 50 percent as would otherwise have been required. Despite these measures, the 15 largest commercial banks reported a 3.7 percent decline in net income in 1996.

The commercial banking system can be viewed as comprising three groups, the six large, older commercial banks, two government-owned banks, and a number of newer commercial banks.[40] Performance differs greatly between the first two groups and the third. The newer banks, with a shorter history of policy lending, generally have much better asset quality, are believed to have superior credit risk management skills, and are more efficient. The group of older banks have seen net income decline for two years in a row, with the return on equity falling from 5.9 percent in 1994 to 1.8 percent in 1996. With the share of loans at fixed low rates declining, net interest margins have increased slightly, but are still very low, at 2.3 percent in 1996. As an indicator of their relative inefficiency, the cost-to-income ratio for this group of banks rose from 82 percent in 1994 to 94 percent in 1996. Finally, 5.1 percent of their loans were nonperforming at end-1996 (6.9 percent with the exposures to the Hanbo and Sammi groups). For the group of newer banks, net income rose 34 percent in 1996 after a decline in 1995, for a return on equity of 8.8 percent. The net interest margin has fluctuated around an average of 3.1 percent since 1994, and the cost-to-income ratio in 1996 was 84 percent. On all of these measures, they outperform the older banks. Finally, for the two newer banks for which asset-quality data are available, nonperforming loans at end-1996 reached 2.4 percent of loans (only 2.5 percent with the loans to the Hanbo and Sammi groups), marginally higher than in 1995 (since they had fewer policy loans to begin with, and repayments on previously nonperforming policy loans were the main source of improvement in the asset quality of the older banks).

The *Philippines* has been the recipient of a surge in capital inflows since 1991–92 as foreign investor sentiment about the economic fundamentals—and expectations of ratings upgrades (S&P raised its rating for

the Philippines in February 1997, and Moody's followed suit in May 1997)—have led to increases both in foreign direct investment and in portfolio investment. The latter has partly fueled a rise in equity prices of almost 200 percent since early 1992. Also, in the last few years, property prices have surged, which has raised concern about the sustainability of asset prices, although as Table 34 indicates, at least some of the increase in prices was due to declining vacancy rates in office buildings.

Partly as a result of the inflows of capital, liquidity in the banking system has been high in recent years, fueling a rapid expansion in bank lending—up by 44 percent a year during the past two years. This doubling of loans in the past two years raises questions about asset quality in the future. While nonperforming assets accounted for only 3.3 percent of total bank assets in 1996, down from 3.6 percent in 1995, some analysts have raised concerns about the expansion in bank lending. The first concern is that, as in other countries in the region, commercial banks in the Philippines have a relatively high direct and indirect exposure to real estate. The central bank has estimated the direct exposure of commercial banks through real estate loans at about 10 percent in March 1997, up from 9 percent in March 1996. The true exposure may be higher since property is a common form of collateral, and the banks have other exposures through investments in property developers. In April 1997, the central bank imposed a limit on real estate loans of 20 percent of a bank's total loans and reduced the maximum loan-to-value ratio to 60 percent from 70 percent. Analysts have also expressed concern that consumer lending, including credit card debt, has increased as a share of total loans.

As is the case elsewhere in the region, foreign currency exposure, particularly of the corporate sector, has been expanding. Philippine banks' Foreign Currency Deposit Unit (FCDU) loans expanded by 110 percent in 1996 alone. Prudential regulations require banks to keep balanced FCDU books, so the direct foreign currency exposure should be small. Moreover, 74 percent of FCDU loans at end-1996 were extended to exporters, oil companies, and public utilities for whom currency risk is not thought to be significant. However, if the remaining borrowers are not hedged, their currency risk could be translated into credit risk for the banks. In addition, much of the expansion in peso-denominated lending has been financed by offshore foreign-currency-denominated borrowing by the banks, whose net foreign liabilities had increased to $6 billion at end-1996 from near zero at end-1995. In response, the central bank introduced a 30 percent liquidity requirement on foreign-currency-denominated assets in July 1997.

The condition of financial institutions in *Thailand* figured prominently in the exchange rate pressures in 1996 and 1997, as the financial system was seen as a

---

[40]The six older commercial banks are the Korea Exchange Bank, Cho Hung Bank, Hanil Bank, Korea First Bank, Commercial Bank of Korea, and Seoul Bank. The two government-owned banks are the Korea Development Bank and Industrial Bank of Korea. Finally, for reasons of data availability, seven newer commercial banks are grouped together: Kookmin Bank, Shinhan Bank, Daegu Bank, Boram Bank, Dongwha Bank, Hana Bank, and Koram Bank.

source of potential weakness by foreign investors. The banks were thought by some investors to be vulnerable to a depreciation of the baht as a consequence of their own net foreign-currency-denominated liabilities or those of their customers. At the same time, however, the strength of the baht and the high interest rates needed to maintain the exchange rate, combined with a heavily overbuilt Thai property market, have contributed to asset-quality problems for the banks.

In many respects, the performance of the major Thai commercial banks in recent years has been good.[41] While earnings, as measured by the return on equity, have dipped slightly, the return in 1996 was over 20 percent, and the decline has been due to an increase in equity rather than a decline in earnings. Net income has increased steadily for the last eight years, driven by average loan growth of more than 20 percent a year and a gradual widening of net interest margins, although there has been some retrenchment in margins in the past two years. The banks have, however, sharply increased their net foreign borrowing. The Bank of Thailand reports that all commercial banks' net foreign liability increased from B 51 billion (35 percent of capital) at end-1991 to B 1,035 billion (twice capital) in October 1996, but these are not necessarily the banks' true foreign currency positions. Some market participants report that the Thai banks had hedged most of their net foreign liabilities, so that the devaluation had perhaps relatively little direct effect on their balance sheets. The opposite is believed to be true for the Thai corporate sector: market participants report that until doubts about the sustainability of the exchange rate policy grew in late 1996, Thai firms had made little attempt to cover their foreign currency exposure. As a result, the depreciation of the baht could result in an increase in nonperforming foreign currency loans.

The incentive to borrow abroad over the past few years reflects the illiquidity in the domestic markets. The Thai banking system has grown at a very rapid pace in the past six years—the average annual growth rate of credit to the nonfinancial private sector over 1990–95 was more than 23 percent—and the loan-to-deposit ratio increased from 103 percent at end-1990 to 141 percent in October 1996. Liquidity concerns were exacerbated by the high interest rates used to prop up the baht, the inability to manage short-term liabilities in the domestic markets actively because these markets are illiquid or underdeveloped, and more recently, the emergence of wider spreads on Thai credit in international markets, including in the international interbank markets at times.

The illiquidity of the Thai corporate sector has created difficulties for the banks in terms of declining asset quality. The Bank of Thailand reported in December 1996 that total nonperforming (doubtful and substandard) loans amounted to 6.92 percent at end-1995 and 7.73 percent at end-June 1996.[42] The worsening nonperforming loan problem is frequently attributed to the weakness in the property market.[43] Developments in the property market in Thailand have been an important source of vulnerability both because the banks have lent to this sector—already this year two property developers have defaulted on debts—and because property has often been used as collateral for loans. While the official estimate is that 10 percent of bank loans are to the property sector, one private estimate puts the figure at 20 percent (equal to 33 percent of end-1996 equity). The Government Housing Bank has estimated that 40 percent of the housing stock built during 1992–96 was unoccupied at the beginning of this year. While property prices have not declined significantly, the data in Table 34 show that even the highest-quality office space in Bangkok has a relatively high vacancy rate and flat rents, and the supply of office space is projected to grow by 35 percent by the end of 1998. The excess supply is even worse for apartments and hotels.

A potentially greater danger to the banking system, however, is the possibility that the banks may be expected to supply financial support to affiliated finance companies, even if they are not majority shareholders. Many of the large commercial banks have invested in nonbank financial institutions, which are generally in weaker financial shape than the banks because of their much higher exposure to the property market. Since the Bank of Thailand has already stated its willingness to recapitalize nine very small unaffiliated finance companies through the Financial Institutions Development Fund (FIDF), some market participants suspect that the banks would be expected to do the same for the larger finance companies.

---

[41]This description is based on the financial statements of 10 commercial banks, including 7 of the 10 largest—Bangkok Bank, Krung Thai Bank, Thai Farmers Bank, Siam Commercial Bank, Thai Military Bank, First Bangkok City Bank, Bangkok Metropolitan Bank, Bank of Asia, Thai Danu Bank, and Union Bank of Bangkok.

[42]These figures do not include the $3 billion in nonperforming loans held by Bangkok Bank of Commerce, which is under special administration. The definition of doubtful loans varies across banks, but as generally applied it refers to loans that are 12 months past due but fully collateralized, or partially collateralized loans that are more than 6 months past due.

[43]The failure of Bangkok Bank of Commerce (BBC) in May 1996, however, was reportedly due to management failures resulting in unusually high loan concentrations and large trading losses rather than to property-related nonperforming loans. BBC was taken over by the Bank of Thailand, which has contracted with one of the large finance companies to manage the bank for seven years, during which time the nonperforming assets will be segregated and the bank will be prepared for privatization. The Bank of Thailand has already provided an estimated B 20 billion in liquidity assistance, underwritten B 50 billion in BBC commercial paper, purchased B 60 billion in nonperforming loans (at a price of B 48 billion), and, through the Financial Institutions Development Fund, provided B 65 billion in capital and B 25 billion in liquidity assistance—a total provision of B 178 billion of funds.

The Thai authorities' response to the latest concerns about the health of the financial system have focused on improving accounting and disclosure for asset quality and on rehabilitating the property market. On the first front, as of July 1997, banks are required to begin disclosing nonperforming loans and provisions and to report restructured loans as well. Also, by end-June 1999 the banks will be required to have set aside reserves equal to 15 percent of substandard loans. On the second front, the authorities have introduced a number of measures to try to support the property market including (1) the creation of a secondary mortgage market by the Government Housing Bank, which will also provide low-cost mortgages to government employees; (2) increases in the foreign-ownership limit on some types of property; (3) a reduction in the land transfer tax from 2 percent to 0.01 percent; (4) proposed legislative measures to allow the establishment of real estate investment trusts and the securitization of property related loans; and (5) the establishment in March 1997 of the Property Loan Management Organization (PLMO). With a mandate similar to that of the CCPC in Japan, the PLMO was capitalized with B 1 billion from the fiscal budget and authorized to borrow up to B 100 billion (the first B 1 billion bond has already been issued) to purchase bank loans to property developers (or the collateral) at fair market value and restructure the loan or the project.[44] The banks that sell the loans would have to write off any difference between the purchase price and the book value of the loan and guarantee repayment of 50 percent of the loan.

Finally, the Bank of Thailand is encouraging mergers among financial institutions, especially finance companies, as a way to weed out the weak and inefficient firms. In April, a group of seven finance companies announced plans to merge. However, merger talks between the largest finance company, Finance One, and Thai Danu Bank broke down in June 1997. Subsequently, in late June, the Thai Ministry of Finance ordered 16 finance companies to suspend operations and to draw up recapitalization plans within two weeks. Five large finance companies have agreed to take over the good assets of those of the 16 that are unable to comply.

Developments in Latin American Emerging Markets

The economic recovery in *Argentina* in the second half of 1995 continued in 1996 and allowed the banks to recover from the liquidity crisis that developed in the first quarter of 1995 and to proceed with the longer-term process of restructuring in a less crisis-charged atmosphere.[45] This recovery in economic activity was reflected in the growth of bank loans, particularly in the second half of 1996. After declining by just over 1 percent (in nominal terms) in 1995, and rising by less than half a percent through the first half of 1996, loan growth averaged 7 percent for the second half of the year.[46] Deposit growth was even more impressive: the stock of deposits grew by 21 percent in 1996 after falling by 4.5 percent in 1995. Moreover, the growth in deposits in 1996 has been evenly balanced between dollar deposits and peso deposits, and the "flight to quality" that was observed in 1995—wherein the larger banks' deposits actually increased while total banking system deposits declined—was not in evidence through most of 1996: deposits of the 20 largest banks grew only marginally faster than total systemic deposits.

The return to more normal levels of liquidity in the banking system allowed the level of interest rates to fall, fueling loan demand. At the same time, however, net interest margins declined on average, reaching 4.95 percent for 1996 compared with 5.75 percent in 1995. Despite a modest increase in lending, the narrower margins and higher loan loss provisions (which increased by 14 percent in 1996) resulted in only a marginal increase (0.4 percent) in net income for the 20 major banks, with a return on equity of only 6.8 percent compared with 7.3 percent in 1995.

However, a tiering of banks is observed in Argentina, consisting of (1) a group of large private banks that perform better than most other banks in terms of asset quality and profitability; (2) a group of smaller private banks and cooperative institutions; and (3) the government-owned banks (including the two largest banks) whose poor asset quality has necessitated high provisions and write-offs, resulting in poor profitability. The differences between these sectors are immediately apparent in their respective asset-quality data. At end-September 1996, the ratio of loans past due more than 90 days to total loans was 19 percent for the federally owned banks, 27 percent for the provincial banks, 9 percent for the domestic private banks, and 15 percent for the cooperative institu-

---

[44]Salomon Brothers estimates that B 100 billion could purchase 12.7 percent of the book value of outstanding real estate loans.

[45]The authorities' response to the liquidity crisis in 1995 was documented in IMF (1996). Subsequent developments include the modification of the role of the deposit insurance fund (the Fondo de Garantía de los Depósitos) to allow it to provide liquidity assistance to banks that are not insolvent and to assist in the acquisition or merger of banks by standing ready to purchase assets, and the establishment of a $6.1 billion facility (collateralized by Argentine bonds) from international banks to provide liquidity during a crisis.

[46]Because Argentine banks are not required to have the same fiscal year-end, aggregation and comparison across reporting periods is difficult. The discussion of the performance of Argentine banks here is based on data compiled by Salomon Brothers (1997b) from monthly reports to the central bank. Data from 1996 and 1995 are not perfectly comparable since inflation accounting was ended in September 1995.

tions.[47] Moreover, the return on average equity for the government-owned banks was only 3.9 percent in 1996, compared with 10.9 percent for the large private banks, and the respective overhead costs as a proportion of total revenues were 70 percent and 65 percent.

The banking system in *Brazil* came under pressure during the transition to a post-hyperinflationary economy under the Real Plan, which exposed weaknesses in asset quality and the regulatory and supervisory structures. The Real Plan succeeded in sharply reducing inflation but at the expense of a significant slowdown in economic growth—an outright contraction in activity for much of 1995. Loans in arrears and in liquidation increased from 7.25 percent at end-1994 to 13.4 percent at end-1995 and 14.4 percent at end-1996.[48] These developments have resulted in a number of bank failures and mergers under distress over the past two years, and more consolidation is expected.

The transformation of the economy after June 1994 has created a three-tiered commercial banking system in Brazil. There are, first, the publicly owned banks, including the banks owned by the state governments, which have in the past often been used simply as extensions of state treasuries. These banks did not develop a credit culture upon which to build franchise value from alternative lending, and they accumulated large stocks of nonperforming loans. A second group of institutions includes a large number of small, private commercial and multiple banks with limited branch networks and relatively undiversified product lines that tended to fill niches in the system—such as treasury operations and wholesale banking. Having relied upon "float income" for much of their profit, and lacking the economies of scale necessary to compete in a low-inflation environment, these institutions too have found it difficult to adapt to the new economic reality. Finally, there are a small, but growing, number of well-capitalized and well-run large private commercial banks that are expanding to fill the gaps left by the retreating government-owned banks.

Some insight into the condition of the government-owned banks can be gained by looking at the 12 state-owned banks for which balance sheets and income statements for 1995 and 1994 are available.[49] Between 1994 and 1995, net interest income declined by 24 percent and margins fell by more than half (to 10.4 percent), noninterest income declined by 52 percent, and loan loss provisions tripled, all of which contributed to a net loss of R\$862 million in 1995, after a net loss of R\$151 million in 1994. The weakest of this group, Banerj, had a negative net capital position at end-1995 of R\$1,859 million, or 79 percent of assets. For the seven banks that reported nonperforming loans to the private sector, these amounted to 10.8 percent of private sector loans and leases in 1995, up from 4.4 percent in 1994, and reserve coverage declined from 107 percent to 77 percent. Hence, even excluding nonperforming loans to the public sector (about 5 percent of total loans), asset quality deteriorated seriously in 1995.

The situation is similar among the four federally owned commercial banks. As a group, they earned a net loss in 1995 of R\$4.96 billion, although this was mostly owing to the loss incurred by Banco do Brasil. Excluding that bank, the three other federal banks for which data are available saw net interest income fall by 30 percent, interest margins fall to 13.1 percent, but noninterest income double, which compensated almost exactly for the shortfall. However, loan loss provisions rose to 13.7 percent of private sector loans and leases at end-1996 from 8.6 percent at end-1995.

A key development in the government-owned banking sector was the R\$12.3 billion loss by Banco do Brasil over 1995–96. In April 1996, the government announced a recapitalization plan for Banco do Brasil in which the government would underwrite a capital injection of R\$8 billion in new capital. In the event, the government itself injected R\$3.9 billion in new capital and transferred R\$2.9 billion in shares of state-owned companies, while the bank's pension fund injected R\$1.2 billion.

The group of small private banks is another source of stress in the Brazilian banking system, albeit perhaps less of a systemic threat. Aggregation of a sample of small banks' financial statements for 1994–96 reveals a pattern of declining profitability and capital and rising levels of nonperforming loans.[50] The return on average equity has declined for two successive years, from 42 percent in 1994 to 19 percent in 1996 (the return on assets has declined from 6 percent in 1994 to 3 percent in 1996), while the net interest margin has fallen from 13.7 percent to 8.6 percent.

---

[47]For the 14 largest private banks, nonperforming loans (C, D, and E loans) represented 6.7 percent of total loans (significantly higher than in 1994) at end-1996, but for the 6 government-owned banks, the ratio was 18.1 percent. The higher incidence of bad loans was combined with a slightly lower coverage ratio for loan loss reserves, resulting in a net exposure to bad loans equal to 32 percent of equity, compared with only 18 percent for the private banks. However, despite having more nonperforming loans, and a smaller revenue base (relative to assets), the state banks set aside only 18 percent of total revenues in loan loss provisions, compared with 25 percent for the private banks.

[48]Data published by the Central Bank of Brazil. These figures do not include the portfolios of the state banks of São Paulo and Río de Janeiro and of the federally owned savings bank, Caixa Economica Federal.

[49]Financial reports for the state banks of Río Grande do Sul, Minas Gerais (two), Paraña, Río de Janeiro, Bahía, Santa Catarina, Espirito Santo, Ceara, Pernambuco, Goias, and Maranhão, as provided by IBCA Ltd.

[50]This discussion of the performance of the smaller private banks is based on the financial statements of 28 banks with total assets below R\$1 billion and for which financial statements for the last three years are available from IBCA Ltd.

Net interest income has increased significantly since 1994, reflecting the banks' reorientation toward lending and away from the securities trading and interbank lending activities that were so profitable during the high-inflation period. However, operating expenses have also increased, and loan loss provisions have tripled, which contributed to a decline in net income in 1996. At the end of 1996, these banks had nonperforming loans equal to only about 5 percent of total loans (up from 2.8 percent in 1994). While these institutions are still well capitalized, with an equity-to-total-assets ratio of 15 percent at end-1996, they face growing competition from larger competitors, which have expanded to fill the niches these smaller institutions once occupied.

The third group of institutions in Brazil are the larger private banks. Overall, profitability improved slightly in 1996 despite a narrowing of the net interest margin (to 9.8 percent, from 12.3 percent in 1995).[51] Banks offset the declining margins by expanding loan volume by 12 percent and by increasing their noninterest earnings by 39 percent. However, a key source of improvement in the banks' earnings was a reduction in loan loss provisions made possible by a significant improvement in asset quality, after two years of high charge-offs. While differences clearly exist between the banks, asset quality appears at least to have stabilized. The ratio of private sector loans in arrears and liquidation to total gross loans fell from 5.1 percent to 3.7 percent. Improving asset quality allowed room for banks to make lower loan loss provisions, while still increasing reserve coverage to 233 percent of nonperforming loans. This improvement in asset quality may simply be due to the expansion in banks' loan books, but since much of this expansion reportedly went to consumer lending (almost all of it short term), where loan losses are usually relatively higher, it may only be temporary.

Since the inception of the Real Plan, a number of measures or programs have been implemented to improve the process of removing problem banks from operation and to restore confidence in the remaining banks. In August 1995, a private deposit insurance scheme, funded and operated by the larger banks, was established as a temporary mechanism until a formal deposit guarantee fund (FGC) could be established in November 1995. This fund—financed by premiums levied on all financial institutions, charges on returned checks, and the possibility of special levies (up to 50 percent of the ordinary premium) or advances from member financial institutions or the central bank—guarantees repayment of a maximum of R$20,000 to each depositor at each bank.

Also in November 1995, the government announced the PROER program to help promote consolidation in the banking sector by providing fiscal and financial incentives to banks that merge with or acquire all or part of another bank.[52] Funding through PROER has been used on a number of occasions (most notably in the cases of Bamerindus, Banco Economico, Banco Nacional, Banco Mercantil de Recife, Banorte, Banco United, and Banco Martinelli).

In August 1996, the federal and state governments agreed to a program to reschedule the state government's debt in return for the privatization, liquidation, or transformation (to development agencies that would not accept deposits) of the state-owned banks. The first to be privatized was Banco do Estado do Río de Janeiro, which was sold in June 1997. In 1996, the federal government established a program to restructure up to R$7 billion in debt of small agricultural producers (individual loans up to R$200,000).

The banking system in *Chile* is considered to be one of the strongest among the emerging markets. This is reflected mainly in the asset quality of Chilean banks. At end-1996, only 1.03 percent of the total loans of the major Chilean banks were nonperforming, somewhat below the 1992–95 average.[53] This low ratio is not thought to be due to lax accounting practices. On the contrary, the Chilean authorities have one of the most conservative accounting standards among all emerging markets regimes, and they are believed to cross-check the information they receive from the banks on loan performance against information from the tax authorities. On the issue of accounting for bad loans, therefore, the Chilean banks are widely considered to be among the most conservative banks in the world. Like their counterparts elsewhere in Latin America, Chilean banks maintain very high loan loss reserves relative to the stock of bad loans, although at 180 percent at end-1996, this ratio has declined rapidly since end-1993 (when it was almost twice as high).

Chilean banks' earnings have come under pressure from increasing competition in recent years. The net interest margin has declined gradually over the past four years to just over 3 percent, and this shrinkage is not due to a large stock of nonperforming assets. Rather, it reflects declining interest rates, increasing

---

[51]This discussion of the larger private banks' performance is based on the audited financial statements of 24 private banks with assets of at least R$2 billion and for which both 1996 and 1995 data are available from IBCA.

[52]Program of Incentives to the Restructuring and Strengthening of the National Financial System. In March 1996, PROER was expanded to allow a (solvent) bank to finance a restructuring of its assets and liabilities. Since the introduction of the PROER, liquidity lending (which includes lending under PROER) by the central bank to financial institutions has increased significantly, reaching a peak of R$20.6 billion at end-July 1996 (compared with R$4.3 billion at end-July 1995). As of end-February 1997, the outstanding balance had fallen back to R$5.2 billion.

[53]This discussion of Chilean banking developments is based on data of the Superintendencia de Bancos e Instituciones Financieras collected and published by Salomon Brothers (1997a). The measure of nonperforming loans used includes all past-due loans.

competition, and the concentration of the banks' activity in corporate lending. Only about 24 percent of end-1996 loans were to the consumer and mortgage sectors, where margins are higher than in the corporate sector. The banks are gradually changing this orientation—consumer loans grew at three times the overall growth rate in loans in 1996—and over time this reorientation will tend to boost net interest margins. Similarly, noninterest income has tended to be relatively unimportant for Chilean banks, but such income has increased significantly in the last few years. Faced as they are with relatively low income, Chilean banks are forced to be efficient providers of banking services, as indicated in the low overhead ratio (63 percent at end-1996).

While the Chilean banking sector is fairly efficient and free of the asset-quality problems that plague banking industries elsewhere, it is a relatively capital-poor industry. With the subordinated debt situation essentially resolved (the last bank has just announced an agreement with the central bank to repay its debt), the banks' capital levels have declined (subordinated debt was part of secondary capital). The average equity-assets ratio was only 5.3 percent at end-1996 and has declined steadily since at least 1992. Moreover, the ratio of liquid assets to total assets was only 8.9 percent at end-1996.

Notwithstanding the improvement in the underlying economic environment, banks in *Mexico* endured a very difficult year in 1996. Commercial banks, excluding banks that were under central bank intervention or in other special situations, recorded an aggregate net loss of MexN$6.9 billion in 1996, after a profit of MexN$2.5 billion in 1995.[54] The deterioration in net income stemmed mainly from a 27 percent decline in net interest revenue, reflected in a fall in the net interest margin to 3.83 percent from 6.54 percent in 1995. This contraction in interest income is attributable to the decline in interest rates and an increase in nonperforming or low-yielding assets on the banks' balance sheets. The bulk of the banks' total loans of MexN$698 billion were loans to FOBAPROA, UDI-restructured loans, loans to the government due to the ADE program, and nonperforming loans.[55] These assets, which more than doubled in 1996, earn relatively low yields, which drags down the banks' income.[56] Loan loss provisions, which had been mainly responsible for the deterioration in income in 1995 over 1994

levels, rose by only 20 percent in 1996, to MexN$30 billion.

After the serious disruption to the economy in 1995, asset quality remains a key concern for the Mexican financial system, and recent indications are that the situation has not improved. Nonperforming loans increased by 2.5 percent in 1996, to MexN$47.5 billion, despite the sale of MexN$124 billion in (mostly nonperforming) loans to FOBAPROA by virtually all of the important banks in Mexico in 1996.[57] At the end of the year, nonperforming loans represented 6.8 percent of total loans, compared with 7.8 percent at end-1995. (Of the total classified portfolio of MexN$495 billion, medium-risk, high-risk, and irrecoverable loans represented 17.5 percent at end-1996, compared with 13.8 percent at end-1995.)

The transfer of such a large stock of loans to FOBAPROA (approximately 39 percent of the end-1994 loan portfolio) and the associated recapitalization commitments have placed the system on what appears to be a much sounder footing.[58] At end-1996, the capital adequacy ratio calculated by Banco de México for the banking system was 13.1 percent, up from 12.1 percent at end-1996. However, most of the increase in capital has been in the form of revaluation gains. For example, of the total equity of MexN$70 billion at end-1996, only just under half (MexN$32 billion) was paid-up capital. Revaluation gains on equity and fixed assets contributed almost as much to equity (MexN$25 billion).

After two turbulent and difficult years—in which 17 banks holding 54 percent of end-1993 deposits were closed or taken over by the deposit guarantee fund, FOGADE, and official assistance to the banking sector amounted to Bs.1.6 trillion (18 percent of 1994 GDP)—the banking system in *Venezuela* recovered significantly in 1996. There were no further actions taken against any bank in 1996, and the authorities began toward the end of the year to privatize the banks that had been taken over. While important weaknesses and vulnerabilities remain, the crisis that began with the failure of Banco Latino in January 1994 appears to have eased.

The major Venezuelan banks' net income increased by more than a factor of three in 1996, resulting in a

---

[54]The discussion of developments in the Mexican banking system is based on the audited year-end financial statements of the 36 private domestic and foreign commercial banks for which both 1995 and 1996 results have been made available by IBCA Ltd.

[55]FOBAPROA is the Fondo Bancario de Protección al Ahorro; UDIs are Unidades de Inversión; the ADE program is the Programa de Apoyo Immediato a Dendores de la Banca.

[56]In addition to the interest income on UDI-restricted loans, the banks earn income from the UDI trust. In 1996, however, this amounted to only MexN$141 million.

[57]These purchases by FOBAPROA are financed by loans from the selling bank—hence, the operation effectively transforms nonperforming loans into performing loans to FOBAPROA. However, in most cases, the selling banks have retained a 20 percent (or thereabouts) stake in any future losses on the loans.

[58]In mid-1996, the Mexican government established a Resolution Trust-like company, Valuacion y Venta de Activos (VVA), to repackage and sell the loans purchased by FOBAPROA from the commercial banks. A competitive bidding process for the first package of 36 loans, valued at MexN$150 million, closed on June 23. At end-1996, FOBAPROA held approximately MexN$162 billion in loans, so this first auction represents a small fraction of the total to be sold.

return on average equity of 74 percent.[59] While this fell short of the average inflation rate for the year, much of the profit was earned in the second half of the year, during which inflation was considerably lower, which suggests that the banks have recently begun earning positive real profits. The three main sources of higher profits were net interest earnings from lending—loans increased by more than 80 percent in 1996—income from securities holdings, and extraordinary gains. The latter includes for some banks profits from long dollar positions (mostly in Brady bonds) that they had at the time of the devaluation of the bolivar in April 1996.

Asset quality also improved markedly in 1996. At the end of the year, the banks reported past-due loans and loans in litigation equal to 4 percent of the gross loan portfolio, down from 10 percent at end-1995. (If restructured loans are included, the figures are 6.5 percent of the gross loan portfolio, down from 13 percent.) The ratio of loan loss reserves to past-due loans and loans in litigation likewise rose from 121 percent to 196 percent during 1996. The Venezuelan banks are similarly well capitalized. As a result of capital injections by shareholders, the equity-assets ratio has increased to 13 percent, from 8 percent at end-1995.

All is not entirely well, however, with the Venezuelan banks. They continue to invest a large proportion (nearly 50 percent) of their earning assets in securities (mostly government bonds)—only 34 percent of total assets is represented by net loans, although lending has picked up significantly in 1997. Moreover, their current profitability is supported by still very wide net interest margins—19 percent in 1996, compared with 16 percent in 1995 and 14 percent in 1994. Finally, banks do not yet provide a reliable store of value for depositors, who are believed to keep only a small fraction of savings in Venezuelan banks.

Developments in European Emerging Markets

The banking system in the *Czech Republic* endured an eventful year in 1996, in which eight banks were intervened in by the Czech National Bank (CNB), including the fifth-largest bank, which has been supported by an irrevocable blanket guarantee of all liabilities by the CNB. At the end of the year, five banks, accounting for less than 4 percent of banking system assets, were under special CNB conservatorship and two had been liquidated—joining the four other banks that had failed since 1994.

The situation is not as bleak as these facts suggest, however, in part because the authorities had known of these banks' difficulties for a few years—this was not a situation in which a large number of banks suddenly became insolvent. Serious asset-quality problems began to emerge in 1993–94 among the newer private commercial banks that had been established in the Czech Republic during 1991–93 when licensing rules were fairly lax. Two banks were closed because of asset-quality problems in 1994 (and another because of alleged fraud). In 1995, similar problems emerged at a large number of the smaller banks, and the authorities responded by closing the worst affected, placing others under special monitoring, and ensuring that the CNB had sufficient powers to intervene in weak banks. When the financial results for 1995 revealed how weak these institutions were, the CNB exercised these powers in seven banks and closed them or placed them in receivership. An eighth bank required the support of the CNB, including a blanket guarantee for all domestic and foreign creditors, because it had a common shareholder with one of the failed banks and had therefore suffered a serious decline in liquidity. A scheme for restructuring small banks was announced in October 1996.

Although the share of impaired loans remains high, the official data on classified assets indicate a slight improvement in asset quality in 1996. Excluding the Consolidation Bank, classified loans declined from 33.4 percent at end-1995 to 30.1 percent at end-1996 and 29.7 percent at end-March 1997. In addition, the larger banks have seen a decline in nonperforming loans, are adequately (if not fully) reserved against nonperforming loans, and have investment grade ratings; foreign-owned or joint-venture banks are also in reasonably good condition.

However, poor asset quality is still a concern. Even after taking CzK 140 billion in nonperforming loans off the banks' balance sheets (by selling them to the Consolidation Bank) and transferring bonds worth CzK 57 billion to banks to boost their capital, some CzK 339 billion in classified assets remained on banks' balance sheets at end-September 1996. The ongoing provisioning requirements to meet the required coverage ratio and to maintain it as the stock of classified loans rises consumes a third of operating income (although this fraction is declining). The history of high loan loss provisioning and high nonperforming loan ratios has resulted in a system that is not highly profitable or capitalized. While most of the banks exceed the 8 percent minimum capital adequacy requirement, the average capital adequacy ratio at end-1996, excluding the Consolidation Bank, was 10.3 percent.

The banking systems in both *Hungary* and *Poland* continue to recover from the asset-quality problems that plagued them in the late 1980s and early 1990s. Improvements have been due in large part to extensive

---

[59]This discussion is based on the financial statements of the 13 largest commercial banks for which data are available for 1995 and 1996. This group of "major banks" includes three of the banks that were taken over by FOGADE: Banco Latino, Banco Consolidado, and Banco de Venezuela, which are, respectively, the third, fourth, and eighth largest banks in the country.

restructuring in the context of bank recapitalization and privatization. At end-1996, classified loans in Hungary represented 11.6 percent of total loans, down from a peak of 28.5 percent at end-1993. Similarly, in Poland, at the end of the first quarter of 1996, irregular loans represented 18 percent of the portfolio, compared with 31 percent at end-1993.

Hungarian bank regulations have gradually been brought up to EU standards, including the requirement that banks must publish their financial statements in both International Accounting Standards format and in Hungarian accounting format. The adjustments to the supervisory and regulatory structure accelerated in 1996, with a complete overhaul of the architecture of supervision and important changes to the content of bank regulations. The banking and securities supervisory agencies have been combined into a joint supervisory agency, and approval for banks to engage in securities activities was given in the new banking law implemented at the beginning of 1997. In addition, the new law doubled the minimum capital requirement to Ft 2 billion;[60] and tightened restrictions on ownership, related party transactions, and credit and market risk exposures.

Appendix 1

Credit Derivatives

While credit risk has vexed financial markets since money lending began, the ability to trade and transfer credit risks with ease is a new phenomenon. The first deals done with such structured products, called credit derivatives, were executed in 1992. Steady growth since then has brought the credit derivative market to what is viewed as a critical mass, catching the attention of potential customers and regulators alike. Although official statistics are not yet available, industry estimates put the size of the credit derivative market at about $40 billion of outstanding transactions.[61] While still only a drop in the bucket when measured against the $10 trillion of notional principal outstanding in the over-the-counter derivative market in 1996, the credit derivative market is expected to grow quite quickly.

Participants, Liquidity, Types of Products

Currently, the 10–15 dealers in credit derivatives consist of investment and commercial banks, which act as both intermediaries and end users. Investment banks, in particular, can be constrained by credit exposures obtained within the huge bond and derivatives portfolios they maintain, requiring them to free up credit lines. Large money center banks, with both their traditional expertise in evaluating and managing credit risks and their extensive customer bases, have been in the forefront of the development and pricing of credit derivatives.[62] Moreover, commercial banks are also large holders of credit risk (although it is typically more diversified) naturally leading them to consider altering their credit risk via derivative products.

To date, the end users in this market are predominantly banks. They have an appetite for over-the-counter products and understand credit evaluation, making them easily educated customers. Other institutions, such as corporate treasuries and hedge funds, are making their way into the market. The corporate entities are interested in trading their trade credit concentrations and in lowering their credit exposures to various derivative counterparties. Hedge funds are also interested since credit risk derivatives provide them with an efficient method of obtaining credit exposures. Institutional investors, such as pension funds and insurance companies, are expected to be interested in finding new types of credit exposures other than the ones they have traditionally undertaken through their predominantly fixed-income portfolios.

While the growth in the market has been led by U.S. entities, European institutions have recently become participants. Since European markets are heavily bank intermediated, and long-run client relationships are a large part of banks' franchise value, credit derivatives are likely to provide a particularly apropos method of unbundling credit risk from the client relationship. The Asian market is thought to be the next area of significant growth for credit derivatives as this market is now adopting more sophisticated credit risk extension policies and Asian institutions are becoming more conscious of the credit risks that characterize their balance sheets.

As yet, the market cannot claim to be liquid, as many of the transactions are "one-off" deals that are tailored to the specific needs of a customer. Despite the absence of a generic product, four or so of the most common product designs have been widely adopted, and most derivatives can be marked-to-market, or at least marked-to-model, providing at least some comfort as to their ability to be offset. The liquidity of the credit derivatives is higher for deriva-

---

[60]Hungarian banks must meet an 8 percent minimum risk-weighted capital adequacy ratio.

[61]A November 1996 survey by the British Bankers Association estimates the London market, about one-half the total market, covers loans worth $20 billion. Another estimate, by CIBC Wood Gundy, a Canadian investment bank, puts the number at $39.2 billion of outstanding transactions, half of which involve the credit risk of developing countries' debt. In the United States, where official data are now being collected on gross positions of U.S. banks, for the quarter ending March 31, 1997, there was a total of $19 billion notional principal worth of credit derivatives outstanding.

---

[62]J.P. Morgan introduced CreditMetrics™ on April 2, 1997, which provides transparent methodology, data, and software to evaluate credit risks individually or across an entire portfolio.

tives written on more liquid underlying instruments, such as Brady bonds, whose outstanding stock had reached $156 billion by the end of 1996.

There are four principal types of credit derivatives: credit default swaps, total rate of return (TROR) swaps, credit-linked notes, and credit spread options. All credit derivatives transfer credit risk between a credit-risk seller, interested in shifting the credit risk to another party in exchange for paying a premium, and a credit-risk purchaser, interested in obtaining credit risk along with receiving the premium for taking on such risk.

In a credit default swap the buyer of protection (the hedger) pays a fee, which effectively represents an option premium, in return for the right to receive a conditional payment if a specified "reference credit" defaults. The reference credit is the party whose credit performance determines whether payments are made. The amount to be paid is negotiated between the counterparties and may be determined prior to the default event or may be determined based on the observed prices of similar obligations after a default.

A total rate of return swap is structured so that the buyer swaps the "total return" on the reference asset for a regular floating-rate payment (in general based on LIBOR). For example, the buyer agrees to pay the total return on an emerging market Brady bond, consisting of all contractual payments as well as any appreciation in the market value of the bond; the seller agrees to pay the buyer LIBOR plus a spread and any depreciation in the value of the Brady bond. The TROR swap differs from the credit default swap in that a default event need not occur nor be verifiable: the TROR swap protects the buyer against a deterioration of credit quality, which can occur even without a default.

A credit-linked note is an on-balance-sheet structured note in which a credit derivative is embedded in the structure. Often these notes are issued by a special purpose trust vehicle, which is collateralized with high-quality assets to assure payment of the contractual payments due. A purchaser of a credit-linked note assumes the credit risk of the reference credit and the underlying collateral. To illustrate: a special purpose vehicle, rated AAA, issues a credit-linked note based on the credit risk of Corporation XYZ. If Corporation XYZ defaults on its debt, the credit-linked note is no longer redeemable at par value, but note holders receive, say, 60 percent of the par value.

A more recently developed credit derivative is the credit spread option. A credit spread option provides a payout to the buyer when the spread on two underlying assets exceeds a predetermined level. The buyer pays a premium for such protection and the seller pays out based on the spread. Since the credit risk of many fixed-income securities is often measured as a spread over a comparable-maturity "risk-free" security, this derivative product is highly sensitive to the market's

assessment of credit risk in these securities and is especially tailored to holders of emerging market debt and other high-yielding debt instruments.

Outstanding Issues

As yet, valuation and risk management methods for credit derivatives are not as analytically developed as those for other financial derivatives, in part, because the information required is more difficult to obtain. Generally, defaults are rare and severe—historical data are spotty, not fulfilling the normal preconditions for modeling: a continuous data series with few large observations. These data constraints are most severe for the relatively illiquid loan market: data are slightly more plentiful regarding the default experience on publicly issued debt for rated companies. However, these data focus on U.S. corporate entities, whereas about half the outstanding credit derivatives are written on emerging market Brady bonds, which have yet to experience a single default. The current paucity of data on the default experiences of emerging market debt instruments may be hindering accurate assessments of credit risk—and there may be a rude awakening for holders of such debt and the related credit derivatives if the economic environment changes for Brady bond countries.

Additionally, effective risk sharing is enhanced when adequate information about the reference credit is provided to the end user who is taking on the credit risk. Adequate information is more easily acquired for reference credits whose securities trade publicly and are subject to reporting requirements. But where no liquid security is traded and financial disclosures are absent, credit-risk purchasers may be at an informational disadvantage relative to the sellers. This may be especially true for credit derivatives related to bank loans, where the banks that originate such loans are thought to have superior information about the credit risk of the borrower. Further, there may be an incentive for a bank to rid itself of its more poorly performing loans when they cannot be easily distinguished from the better-performing loans. Moreover, once the credit risk of a loan has been transferred to a different party, the incentive for the bank to monitor the loan may be diminished, and the safety and soundness of banks may be negatively affected.

Some market participants believe the market's growth is hindered by the lack of regulatory clarity concerning the potential regulatory capital requirements and accounting treatment of credit derivatives. While many practitioners have strong views about the appropriate capital treatment, the debate so far can be characterized as one of intellectual exploration by both practitioners and the bank supervisory community. As of June 1997, regulators had offered little clear guidance regarding capital requirements, although some preliminary rules had been discussed in both the United States and the United Kingdom. The main issues are whether the hedging benefits of a credit derivative will lower the credit risk capital required on the combined position (derivative plus the underlying credit risk) and whether a credit derivative should be accounted for as product within a marked-to-market trading book or a "held to maturity" instrument within the so-called banking book, an issue that will take on added importance when market risk capital requirements are imposed on January 1, 1998.

At an industry level, issues regarding how the development of credit derivatives will affect banks' main business, the intermediation of savings by taking on credit risk, are yet unanswered. Will the credit derivative market overshadow the secondary loan market? If so, will this development mean more or less efficient credit risk sharing? Many dealers argue that the growth in credit derivatives allows those most willing and able to hold credit risk the opportunity to do so. Does this imply that the presumed special expertise within banks to measure and control credit risk will diminish relative to other institutions? Will bank loan products diminish in importance since increased information and pricing mechanisms for credit risk may permit bank customers direct access to public debt markets?

From a systemic point of view, the growth of credit derivatives could be expected to increase the diversification of credit risk across more types of institutions. This appears, at first glance, to be a net benefit since the cascading of defaults during a crisis period would appear less likely when credit risks are held more broadly. However, credit derivatives also permit more concentrated holdings of credit risk as well—and there is little transparency about the institutions that may be holding the risk. One could imagine a situation in which U.S. pension funds, for example, hold Latin American sovereign credit risk through the use of credit derivatives. How would a debt restructuring be implemented in such a situation, especially if the underlying reference instrument is not owned by those holding the credit risk? Alternatively, would end users

attempt to unload their credit derivative positions with the dealers in periods of stress and would this exacerbate an already turbulent period, putting dealers in a precarious position? Put another way, is it reasonable to assume the new participants in credit risk markets are as knowledgeable about the risks they are undertaking as the more seasoned banking institutions? While the answers to these questions depend on future developments in the market, a periodic appraisal of such issues is warranted as credit derivative markets expand.

Appendix 2
Accounting for Nonperforming Loans

Table 35 provides information on loan classification systems and exposure limits in 20 emerging markets. Clearly there is considerable diversity. While some countries have relatively strict classification and provisioning requirements, others have systems that allow for much more discretion on the part of banks to assess asset quality. What cannot be represented in such a table, however, is the monitoring of asset-quality accounting and provisioning regulations. In banking systems where the banks generally have sophisticated internal risk management systems, where these are monitored by auditors and bank examiners, and where there is no presumption of official support in the event of bank failure, it may be less important to have detailed requirements specifying how to classify loans and what level of provisions to hold. Even if banks are subject to rigorous auditing that verifies application of these prudential requirements, few of the systems described in Table 35 address issues such as recapitalization or "evergreening" of loans or the treatment of restructured loans. However, such conditions do not generally apply to most countries. Hence, in the absence of rigorous monitoring by bank supervisors, disclosed asset-quality figures may not accurately reflect the true extent of problem loans, and therefore the true capitalization of banking institutions.

Table 35. Loan Classification in Selected Emerging Markets

		Loan Classification System	Provisioning Requirements
Asia			
Hong Kong, China	Performing	Borrowers are current in meeting commitments and full repayment of interest and principal is not in doubt.	There are no requirements as to provisioning other than that individual banks have their own internal guidelines for maintaining adequate provisions. Interest must be accrued to a suspense account if loans are substandard and not fully secured or overdue by more than 6 months; interest accrual ceases altogether for substandard loans past due more than 12 months and for loans classified as doubtful or loss. Loans must be written off after they are deemed irrecoverable.
	Special mention	Borrowers are experiencing difficulties; ultimate loss is not expected but could occur.	
	Substandard	Borrowers displaying definable weakness; loan losses or rescheduling at concessional terms are possible.	
	Doubtful	Collection in full is improbable; loss of principal and/or interest is expected, taking account of collateral.	
	Loss	Uncollectible after exhausting all collection efforts, including realization of collateral.	
India	Nonperforming	Loans on which interest is overdue for at least six months.	None.
	Substandard	Loans that have been nonperforming for up to two years, term loans on which the principal has not been reduced for more than one year, and all rescheduled debts.	10 percent.
	Doubtful	Loans that have been nonperforming for two to three years and term loans on which the principal has not been reduced for more than two years.	100 percent of unsecured assets; for secured assets: 20 percent if doubtful for less than one year; 30 percent if doubtful for one to three years; 50 percent if doubtful for more than three years.
	Loss	All other assets deemed irrecoverable, where the loss has been identified by internal or external auditors or by the Reserve Bank of India inspectors, but where the amount has not been written off.	100 percent. Interest accrual stops once loans are nonperforming. For loans with balances below Rs 25,000, banks must set aside reserves equal to at least 10 percent of the balance.
Indonesia	Current	Installment credit with no arrears, other credit in arrears less than 90 days, overdrafts less than 15 days.	0.5 percent.
	Substandard	Generally, loans with payments in arrears between three and six months.	10 percent.
	Doubtful	Nonperforming loans that can be rescued and the value of collateral exceeds 75 percent of the loan, or loans that cannot be rescued, but are fully collateralized.	50 percent. 100 percent.
	Loss	Doubtful loans that have not been serviced for 21 months; credit in process of bankruptcy/liquidation.	Loans must be written off 21 months after litigation indicates the loan will not have to be repaid.
Korea	Current	Borrower's credit conditions (including collateral) are good and collectibility of interest and principal are certain.	0.5 percent.
	Special mention	Payments are past due for between three months and six months, but collection is certain.	1 percent.
	Substandard	Loans covered by collateral but borrower's credit conditions are deteriorating and payments are more than six months past due.	20 percent.
	Doubtful	Unsecured portion of the loans that are more than six months past due and losses are expected.	75 percent.
	Estimated loss	Unrecoverable amounts due net of collateral.	100 percent. Loans must be written off within six days of being declared unrecoverable; write-offs in excess of W500 million require Bank of Korea approval.

Table 35 (*continued*)

		Loan Classification System	Provisioning Requirements
Malaysia	Substandard	More than a normal risk of loss due to adverse factors; past due for between 6 and 12 months.	For loans less than RM 1 million: 0 percent.
	Doubtful	Collection in full is improbable and there is a high risk of default; past due for between 12 and 24 months.	50 percent of net (of collateral) outstanding value.
	Bad	Uncollectible; past due for more than 24 months.	100 percent of net outstanding value. Loans must be written off when bankruptcy hearings have finished and/or partial or full repayment is unlikely. A general provision of at least 1 percent of total loans net of interest in suspense and specific provisions is also required.
Philippines	Unclassified	Borrower has the apparent ability to satisfy obligations in full; no loss in collection is anticipated.	0 percent of net (of collateral) exposure.
	Special mention	Potentially weak due, for example, to inadequate collateral, credit information, or documentation.	0 percent.
	Substandard	Loans that involve a substantial degree of risk of future loss.	25 percent.
	Doubtful	Loans on which collection or liquidation in full is highly improbable, substantial losses are probable.	50 percent.
	Loss	Uncollectible or worthless.	100 percent. Interest is not accrued on past-due loans, which are loans or other credit not paid at the prescribed maturity date or, in the case of installment credit, in arrears by more than a prescribed amount depending upon the frequency of installments.
Singapore	Special mention	Accounts with evidence of potential weakness in creditworthiness, such as untimely repayment.	A provision of 50 percent of the loan value for defaults of over a year; for defaults of 3 to 6 months provision is the difference between the loan amount and 80 percent of collateral; for 6 to 12 months, the difference between the loan amount and 70 percent of the collateral. In aggregate, 100 percent of substandard, doubtful, and bad loans must be provided for, with those graded doubtful to have at least 50 percent provision.
	Substandard	Normal repayment may be jeopardized by continuing adverse trend of severe financial weakness.	
	Doubtful	Repayment of outstanding debt appears questionable; expectation of loss.	
	Bad	Outstanding debt is uncollectible.	Loans must be written off in the year that they are recognized as a loss. The Monetary Authority of Singapore has established a minimum (tax exempt) general provision of 2 percent of outstanding loans (including accrued interest) net of specific provisions.
Taiwan Province of China		Nonperforming loans (on which interest is not accrued) are: 1. Short-term loans with principal payments three months past due. 2. Loans with interest payments (or installments) six months past due. 3. Loans to companies for which legal proceedings by the bank have commenced.	Only provisions (general and specific combined) up to 1 percent of loan balance are tax deductible. Specific provisions in excess of that amount are made on a quarterly basis. Interest is no longer accrued after 180 days. Loans must be written off after all legal proceedings have finished.
Thailand		Loans are nonperforming (substandard or doubtful) if they are 12 months past due but fully collateralized or secured, or if they are 6 months past due but not fully secured.	
	Substandard	Loan is in arrears, but there is sufficient security to ensure that full recovery of the debt will be possible.	15 percent (by end-June 1999; at least 7.5 percent by end-June 1998).
	Doubtful	Loan is in arrears, but there is insufficient collateral.	100 percent.
	Irrecoverable	Legal enforcement has been initiated and has been unsuccessful.	100 percent.

162

Europe

Country	Classification	Description	Provision
Czech Republic	Watch	Accounts overdue by 30–90 days.	5 percent of net (after collateral) exposure.
	Substandard	Accounts overdue by 91–180 days.	20 percent of net exposure.
	Doubtful	Accounts overdue by 181–360 days.	50 percent of net exposure.
	Loss	Accounts have been overdue for more than a year, there is little likelihood of repayment, and assets are not adequately secured. Restructured loans must be classified as substandard for six months after restructuring and then as watch for three years.	100 percent of net exposure.
Hungary	Performing	Assumption that interest or principal will not be more than 15 days overdue.	0 percent.
	To be monitored	No loss is assumed, but management is of the opinion that the exposure requires separate monitoring.	0–10 percent.
	Substandard	Risks are higher than average or some loss may be assumed at the time of classification.	11–30 percent.
	Doubtful	A loss will be incurred but the size of the loss is uncertain or where payment is at least 90 days past due or payment delay becomes regular.	31–70 percent.
	Bad	The loss will exceed 70 percent or the company is in bankruptcy.	71–100 percent.
			General reserves (out of net income) must amount to 1.25 percent of the balance sheet total plus 1 percent of guarantees.
Poland	Standard	No arrears or doubts about the borrower's financial strength; receivables guaranteed by the state.	None.
	Substandard	Loans in arrears by more than a month, or loans to a borrower with weakened financial standing.	20 percent.
	Doubtful	Loans in arrears by more than three months, or loans to a borrower with deteriorating financial standing.	50 percent.
	Loss	Loans in arrears by more than six months or the subject of legal dispute, or loans to a borrower who is either in liquidation or whose location is unknown, or whose financial standing makes repayment impossible.	100 percent.
			Approval for lower provisions may be given if the loans are adequately collateralized. General reserves may be set up without limit, although reserves equal to only the first 1 percent of impaired loans are tax deductible.
Turkey	Special follow-up	Loans to uncreditworthy borrowers (defined as borrower whose capital is insufficient to pay the debt when due, or borrower lacks the ability to pay the debt, or the borrower's working capital is insufficient to meet its operating needs).	Initial 15 percent provision. Increased to 50 percent by the end of the first year, 100 percent after two years.
	Administrative follow-up	Loans classified as overdue or one month in arrears.	15 percent provision is required after two months (i.e., when 90 days past due).
	Legal follow-up	Loans in arrears for three months.	25 percent provision is required after 6 months, rising to 50 percent after one year, 75 percent after 18 months, and 100 percent after two years. Banks must cease accruing interest on loans in legal follow-up.
		Loans to state entities (including state-owned enterprises) are not included in the classification system, and provisions are not required for these loans.	

163

Table 35 *(concluded)*

		Loan Classification System		Provisioning Requirements		
Latin America		*Consumer loans*	*Commercial loans*			
Argentina				*Liquid guarantee*	*Preferred guarantee*	*Without guarantee*
	Normal	Less than 31 days overdue.	No doubt exists.	1 percent.	1 percent.	1 percent.
	Potential risk	31–89 days overdue.	Performing, but sensitive to changes; or more than 30 days overdue.	1 percent.	3 percent.	5 percent.
	Problem	90–179 days overdue.	Problems meeting obligations; or 90–179 days overdue.	1 percent.	12 percent.	25 percent.
	High risk	180–365 days overdue or subject to judicial proceedings for default.	Highly unlikely to meet obligations; or more than 180 days overdue.	1 percent.	25 percent.	50 percent.
	Irrecoverable	More than 365 days overdue.	Obligations cannot be met; more than 365 days overdue.	1 percent.	50 percent.	50 percent.
	Irrecoverable for technical decision	Bankruptcy/liquidation/insolvency.	Bankruptcy/liquidation/insolvency.	100 percent.	100 percent.	100 percent.
Brazil		*Consumer loans*	*Commercial loans*	*Unsecured*	*Partially/fully secured*	*Export/import*
		0–29 days overdue.	0–29 days overdue.	0 percent.	0/0 percent.	0/100 percent.
		30–59 days overdue.	30–59 days overdue.	0 percent.	0/0 percent.	100/100 percent.
		60–180 days overdue.	60–180 days overdue.	100 percent.	50/20 percent.	100/100 percent.
		181–360 days overdue.	181–360 days overdue.	100 percent.	100/20 percent.	100/100 percent.
		More than 360 days overdue.	More than 360 days overdue.	100 percent.	100/100 percent.	100/100 percent.
Chile		*Consumer loans*	*Commercial loans*	*Allowance*		
	A	Current	Probability of default: 0 percent.	0 percent.		
	B	1–29 days overdue.	Probability of default: less than 5 percent.	1 percent.		
	B–	30–59 days overdue.	Probability of default: 5–40 percent.	20 percent.		
	C	60–119 days overdue.	Probability of default: 40–80 percent.	60 percent.		
	D	More than 120 days overdue.	Probability of default: 80–100 percent.	90 percent.		
Colombia		*Consumer loans*	*Commercial loans*	*Unsecured principal*	*Interest*	*Secured principal*
	A (Normal)	Current.	Current.	0 percent.	0 percent.	0 percent.
	B (Subnormal)	30–59 days overdue.	30–119 days overdue.	1 percent.	1 percent.	0 percent.
	C (Deficient)	60–89 days overdue.	120–179 days overdue.	20 percent.	100 percent.	0 percent.
	D (Doubtful)	90–179 days overdue.	180–359 days overdue.	50 percent.	100 percent.	0 percent.
	E (Unrecoverable)	180–360 days overdue.	360–719 days overdue.	100 percent.	100 percent.	0 percent.
	E (Unrecoverable)	More than 360 days overdue.	More than 720 days overdue.	100 percent.	100 percent.	100 percent.
Mexico		*Consumer loans*	*Commercial loans*	*Allowance*		
	A	Minimal risk.	Minimal risk.	0 percent.		
	B	Low risk.	Low risk.	1 percent.		
	C	Moderate risk.	Moderate risk.	20 percent.		
	D	High risk.	High risk.	60 percent.		
	E	Noncollectible.	Noncollectible.	100 percent.		

Loan loss reserves should be at least equal to the greater of (1) reserves calculated according to the above classification; (2) 4 percent of total loans; or (3) 45 percent of past-due loans. The entire amount of an amortizing loan (including past-due interest)

Peru

	Consumer loans	Commercial loans	Unsecured consumer	Unsecured commercial
A (Normal)	Current.	Current with no doubts.	0 percent.	0 percent.
B (Potential problem)	10–29 days overdue.	Demonstrated difficulties.	3 (on total balance) percent.	1 (on total balance) percent.
C (Substandard)	30–59 days overdue.	Serious weaknesses.	30 percent.	25 percent.
D (Doubtful)	60–120 days overdue.	Making payments, but less than contracted.	60 percent.	50 percent.
E (Loss)	More than 120 days overdue.	Unrecoverable.	100 percent.	100 percent.

is considered past due if any payment is 90 days overdue (180 days for mortgages). Nonamortizing bullet loans are past due if more than 30 days overdue. Credit cards are past due when two minimum payments have been missed. Loans restructured into UDIs are transferred to trusts (consolidated into the bank's financial statements) and attract a 15 percent loan loss reserve.

Venezuela

	Consumer loans	Commercial loans	Allowance
A (Normal)	Fully performing.	Fully performing.	0 percent.
B (Potential risk)	1–3 monthly payments overdue.	Performing, but showing signs of potential future problems (e.g., deterioration of financial condition, inadequate documentation).	5 percent.
C (Real risk)	4–6 monthly payments overdue.	Experiencing delays in interest and/or principal payments with estimated losses.	10 percent.
D (High risk)	7–12 monthly payments overdue.	Interest and/or principal payments three months or more past due and where legal recovery proceedings have been initiated.	50 percent.
E (Irrecoverable)	More than 12 monthly payments overdue.	Interest and/or principal payments are 12 months past due or where legal proceedings indicate very scarce possibility of recovery.	100 percent.

Once a loan is 30 days past due it is placed on nonaccrual status, and a reserve equal to 100 percent of accrued interest must be created immediately. Loans must be written off after 36 months. Provisioning requirements do not apply to credits guaranteed by the Venezuelan public sector.

Consumer Loans
Provisioning based on the amount of principal overdue for A–D loans. For E loans, the reserve must take into account the entire outstanding balance.

Sources: IBCA Ltd.; ING Barings Securities; and J.P. Morgan.

Background Material—Part II

Selected Issues

Annex IV

European Monetary Union: Institutional Framework for Financial Policies and Structural Implications

This annex begins with a brief description of the potential size of the domestic euro capital markets in a European Economic and Monetary Union (EMU) and the role of existing European currencies in international capital markets. An analysis of the institutional framework for financial markets in EMU, including the payments system, the European System of Central Banks (ESCB), and the framework for other financial policies (financial supervision and regulation, lender-of-last-resort functions, and deposit insurance) follows. The next section discusses the catalytic role of the euro. The structural implications of EMU for European and international securities markets, including the possible evolution of EMU markets for repurchase agreements (repos), interbank funds, bonds, equities, and derivatives are then evaluated. The annex concludes by examining implications for wholesale and retail banking markets and the remaining impediments to cross-border competition in banking and financial services.[1]

Potential Size of EMU Financial Markets

In absolute terms, and compared with any reasonable benchmark, the introduction of the euro has the potential for creating the largest domestic financial market in the world. At end-1995, *the market value of bonds, equities, and bank assets* issued in EU countries amounted to more than $27 trillion (Table 12), roughly the same order of magnitude as world GDP (94 percent of world GDP).[2] By comparison, the market value of assets in North America—with roughly the same population and GDP as the European Union—amounted to about $25 trillion ($23 trillion in the United States). If the initial union includes only Austria, Belgium, France, Germany, Luxembourg, the Netherlands, Ireland, and Finland (the EU-8), the domestic euro market would equal the size of Japan's domestic market ($16 trillion). If the union includes in addition Italy, Portugal, and Spain (EU-11), it would

roughly equal the size of the U.S. domestic market. An interesting aside is that the value of bonds, equities, and bank assets is roughly three times the respective GDPs in the European Union, the United States, and Japan (about 320 percent in the European Union and Japan and about 315 percent in the United States).

EU private entities overwhelmingly have tended to finance their activities through bank loans rather than through bond and equity financing, and U.S. entities have relied more heavily on bond and equity financing. In the EU-11, bank assets represented 54 percent of all outstanding financial assets at end-1995. By contrast, U.S. bank assets accounted for only 22 percent of total assets outstanding.

In contrast to government securities markets, European private debt securities markets are segmented, with all but the largest firms borrowing solely from a domestic investor base. In the EU-11, for each dollar of bank borrowing, private firms borrowed, on average, only 50 cents through private securities issues. By contrast, in the United States, for each dollar of borrowing from banks, U.S. firms borrowed slightly more than two dollars through debt securities issues. Japanese private entities were much closer to their EU, than to their U.S., counterparts.

Although the amount of EU private bonds outstanding appears to be sizable enough to suggest a reasonably large market for corporate bonds (roughly three-fourths the size of the U.S. market), the bulk of these bonds were issued by European financial institutions. From the point of view of corporate balance sheets, as of end-1994, bonds accounted for a relatively small share of the total liabilities of nonfinancial firms in France (5.7 percent) and in Germany (less than 1 percent); by contrast, they accounted for 18.8 percent of the total liabilities of U.S. nonfinancial firms.[3] The low share of debt financing by European companies extends to the short end of the maturity spectrum as well, because European companies tend to rely on bank financing for short-term funds. U.S. corporate entities tend to rely more heavily on short-term financing because of their access to the very liquid and highly developed commercial paper market, which accounts for more than half of the world's outstanding

---

[1]This annex draws on the analysis in Prati and Schinasi (1997).

[2]This total is meant to be a measure of the size of net wealth stored in capital market instruments. It should be considered a proxy and may involve some double counting, as in the case of securities issued by banks. Consolidating the balance sheets of the financial institutions of each country would yield a more precise estimate.

[3]OECD and Deutsche Bundesbank.

Table 36. Amounts Outstanding of International Debt Securities by Currency and Country of Nationality, March 1997[1]

(In billions of U.S. dollars)

	Amounts Outstanding
By currency	
U.S. dollar	1,301.4
Japanese yen	499.6
Currencies of European Union (EU) countries[2]	1,107.9
Other[3]	331.8
Total	3,240.7
By country of nationality	
EU countries	1,478.2
Austria	64.4
Belgium	50.2
Denmark	32.0
Finland	53.8
France	211.6
Germany	356.4
Greece	20.0
Ireland	17.4
Italy	92.2
Luxembourg	11.8
Netherlands	124.4
Portugal	12.6
Spain	43.7
Sweden	116.3
United Kingdom	275.5
North America	647.2
Canada	183.7
Mexico	45.4
United States	418.1
Japan	344.6
Others	770.7
All countries	3,240.7

Source: Bank for International Settlements, *International Banking and Financial Market Developments* (May 1997).

[1]Euronotes and international bonds.

[2]Currencies of Austria, Belgium, Denmark, Finland, France, Germany, Ireland, Italy, Luxembourg, the Netherlands, Portugal, Spain, Sweden, and the United Kingdom; plus ECU.

[3]Currencies of Australia; Canada; Hong Kong, China; New Zealand; Norway; and Switzerland; plus other currencies.

commercial paper. These observations about the use of debt securities reflect the greater historical reliance by firms in the United States on direct intermediation through the corporate debt securities markets, the heavy reliance in Europe on bank financing, and the relatively undeveloped European corporate securities markets.

Another way of assessing the potential importance of the euro from a purely quantitative perspective is to examine the use of existing European currencies as currencies of denomination in *international financial transactions*. In international bond markets, 35 percent of the outstanding stock of international debt securities was denominated in EU currencies at end-September 1996 (Table 36). Although this is a

substantial share of international issues outstanding, and is a close second to the amount of dollar international issues outstanding, EU countries themselves issued more than 45 percent of all international bonds outstanding. In addition, in the five-year period ending in December 1995, only a minor share of developing country debt was issued internationally in EU currencies.

Still another way to gauge the potential role of the euro is to examine daily turnover in the global *foreign exchange markets*. According to the most recent Bank for International Settlements (BIS) survey, as of April 1995 the dollar was involved in at least one side of a transaction about 42 percent of the time, the deutsche mark 18.5 percent, the yen 12 percent, and the pound sterling 5 percent. EMS currencies combined were involved in at least one side of a transaction about 35 percent of the time, including European cross-currency trading (Table 37). In related derivative markets, the dollar, EU currencies, and the yen accounted for shares of trading that are roughly equivalent to the relative sizes of their economies (in terms of GDP), but most of this activity actually involved U.S. and U.K. financial institutions. Transactions involving currency swaps were clearly tilted toward the dollar, reflecting its now dominant position in international finance and as a reserve currency (Table 38).

In summary, although the EU currencies command a significant share of activity in international financial markets, they do not now command shares in line with either the size of the EU economy or the relative size of their domestic financial markets.

Institutional Framework for Financial Markets

Between now and the start of EMU, countries of the European Union will implement a new institutional framework for EMU financial policymaking. The main parts of this framework are the new EU-wide payments system, the institutional framework for conducting the single EMU monetary and exchange rate policy, and a still-evolving institutional framework for implementing and coordinating financial supervision and regulation across European financial markets, including the management of systemic risk. Each of these important elements of the new framework is discussed in this subsection.

TARGET Payments System

TARGET (Trans-European Automated Real-Time Gross Settlement Express Transfer) is a payments system designed to process cross-border transactions denominated in euros after the start of Stage III of EMU on January 1, 1999. TARGET has two main objectives. The first objective is to provide a safe payments

Table 37. Use of Selected Currencies on One Side of Foreign Exchange Transaction, April 1989, April 1992, and April 1995[1]

(As a percentage of global gross foreign exchange market turnover)

Currency	April 1989	April 1992	April 1995
U.S. dollar	90	82	83
Deutsche mark[2]	27	40	37
Japanese yen	27	23	24
Pound sterling	15	14	10
French franc	2	4	8
Swiss franc	10	9	7
Canadian dollar	1	3	3
Australian dollar	2	2	3
European currency unit (ECU)	1	3	2
Other European monetary system (EMS) currencies	3	9	13
Currencies of other reporting countries	3	3	2
Other currencies	19	8	8
All currencies	200	200	200
Memorandum item:			
EMS currencies including ECU	48	70	70

Source: Bank for International Settlements, *Central Bank Survey of Foreign Exchange and Derivatives Market Activity 1995* (May 1996).

[1]Numbers of reporting countries are 21 in 1989 and 26 in 1992 and 1995. Data for 1989 and data for Finland in 1992 include options and futures. Data for 1989 cover local currency trading only, except for the U.S. dollar, deutsche mark, Japanese yen, pound sterling, Swiss franc, and ECU. The figures relate to gross turnover because comparable data on a "net-gross" or "net-net" basis are not available for 1989.

[2]Data for April 1989 exclude domestic trading involving the deutsche mark in Germany.

mechanism within the euro area based on real-time gross settlement (RTGS) procedures that will insulate the payments system across Europe from the effects of liquidity and payment difficulties experienced by a single institution.[4] The second goal is to create an efficient system of cross-border payments that will integrate the money markets of the participating countries and support the implementation of the single monetary policy in Stage III.[5]

Participation

The TARGET system is composed of one RTGS system in each of the EMU countries and the payments mechanism of the European Central Bank (ECB) connected by common infrastructures and procedures forming the Interlinking system (a communications network) (Figure 54).[6] Only the ECB and national central banks (NCBs) will be allowed to use the Interlinking system, but any participant in any RTGS system connected to TARGET will be allowed to send payments via TARGET. Because TARGET is designed to process only euro transactions, RTGS systems of EU countries not in EMU will be allowed to connect to TARGET only if they are able to process euros. Remote access to domestic RTGS systems will be granted on a nondiscriminatory basis to credit institutions licensed in other EU states either through their local branches or directly from another EU country. (At the start of EMU, however, remote access to monetary operations will not be available.) To facilitate the operations of large-value net settlement systems working in euros through TARGET, net settlement systems will be allowed to open a special account with the ECB or a national central bank that must be used exclusively for settlement purposes and must have a zero balance at the beginning and at the end of the day.

[4]In RTGS systems, payments orders are processed one by one on a sequential basis. As long as there are sufficient funds or overdraft facilities available in the sending institution's account with the central bank, there will be immediate and final settlement of all payments. The receiving institution does not bear any credit or liquidity risk on the payments orders received since its account is credited only after the account of the sending institution is debited.

[5]Within TARGET the delay between the debiting of the account of the sending institution and the crediting of the account of the receiving institution should be a matter of seconds. Banks will then be able to move funds across borders immediately and at low cost, responding very rapidly to arbitrage opportunities. As a result, a single interbank rate is likely to prevail in all EMU countries and the liquidity impact of European Central Bank operations will be uniform across EMU.

[6]While the Interlinking procedures will be identical in all countries, the payments services for end users may differ reflecting local conditions under which RTGS systems have been developed in each country (e.g., some systems may include queuing facilities or cash management facilities).

Table 38. Notional Principal Value of Outstanding and New Interest Rate and Currency Swaps, 1995

(In billions of U.S. dollars)

	Amounts Outstanding	New Swaps
Interest rate swaps	12,810.7	8,698.8
U.S. dollar	4,371.7	2,856.5
Japanese yen	2,895.9	2,259.3
Currencies of European Union (EU) countries[1]	4,620.9	3,160.9
Of which:		
Deutsche mark	1,438.9	984.5
French franc	1,219.9	1,113.5
Italian lira	405.4	217.3
Netherlands guilder	101.8	62.3
Pound sterling	854.0	433.4
Spanish peseta	163.7	91.9
ECU	223.1	96.4
Other	922.4	422.1
Of which:		
Swiss franc	331.7	159.2
Currency swaps[2]	2,394.8	910.2
U.S. dollar	837.8	307.9
Japanese yen	400.0	164.5
Currencies of EU countries[1]	684.7	248.1
Of which:		
Deutsche mark	238.0	78.1
French franc	81.4	41.6
Italian lira	72.6	18.5
Netherlands guilder	28.1	13.0
Pound sterling	91.5	23.4
Spanish peseta	27.5	22.4
ECU	83.0	28.2
Other	472.3	189.8
Of which:		
Swiss franc	150.6	29.7

Source: Bank for International Settlements, *International Banking and Financial Market Developments* (November 1996).

[1]Includes the currencies of Belgium, Denmark, France, Germany, Italy, the Netherlands, Spain, Sweden, and the United Kingdom; plus ECU.

[2]Not adjusted for reporting on both sides.

Structure

TARGET is designed as a decentralized system in which payments messages are exchanged on a bilateral basis among national central banks, according to the "central banking correspondent model," without any central counterparty. It remains to be decided whether the ECB will have its own payments mechanism connected to TARGET. This may not be necessary because the national central banks will implement most monetary policy operations, in agreement with the principle of decentralization underlying monetary policy in EMU. Even if the Governing Council of the ECB decides to retain the execution of fine-tuning operations and foreign exchange intervention, the settlement of transactions for both operations may remain decentralized and the ECB may still not need to access the payments system.[7]

The ECB will neither monitor nor receive information on inter-NCB payments orders during the day. At the end of the day, the ECB will perform specific control operations with the aim of checking the correctness of cross-border payments exchanged during the day and the resulting inter-NCB balance positions. The European Monetary Institute (EMI) has not yet decided on the clearing and settlement modalities (frequency of settlement, degree of centralization, means of payment) of outstanding balances among national central banks.

In the U.S. Federal Reserve System, the Board of Governors, like the ECB, does not monitor the settlement positions of each federal reserve bank during the day. At the end of each business day, the reserve bank's Integrated Accounting System settles the cross-district financial transactions by debiting or crediting as appropriate each reserve bank's Interdistrict Settlement Account. This daily clearing process is known as the "gold wire process." The board coordinates once a year (in April) the settlement of the balances on the Interdistrict Settlement Accounts by means of transfer of Gold Certificate assets among reserve banks. The amount settled is equal to the daily average balance in the Interdistrict Settlement Account over the previous year. No such clearing process has been decided upon in the European System of Central Banks, and this opens up the possibility of one national central bank accumulating large claims against another national central bank with no mechanism for settling them.[8]

Transactions Processed

In accordance with the objective of facilitating the implementation of a single monetary policy, credit institutions will be required to use TARGET for payments directly connected with monetary policy operations. Furthermore, large-value net settlement systems are likely to use TARGET to perform their settlement operations because they are bound to settle in central bank money[9] and therefore in euros. Credit institutions will decide whether to use TARGET for other categories of payments, and there will be no upper or lower limits to the amounts transferred besides those in the domestic RTGS systems. Nevertheless, the European Monetary Institute has indicated that TARGET is expected to process mainly large-value payments

---

[7]There are only two other instances in which the ECB may need to connect its own payment system to TARGET. First, a net settlement system may open a special account with the ECB. Second, international organizations may keep their accounts at the ECB.

[8]See the papers by Bishop (1997), Dooley (1997), Garber (1997), and Kenen (1997).

[9]According to Principle 5 of the report on "Minimum Common Features for Domestic Payments Systems" released by the Committee of Governors in November 1993.

Figure 54. Cross-Border TARGET Payment

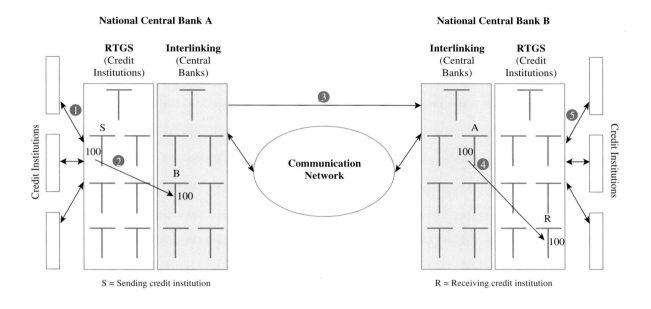

S = Sending credit institution

R = Receiving credit institution

Source: European Monetary Institute (1997).

between credit institutions, whereas private systems are expected to process small-value payments.[10]

Intraday Liquidity

Participants in RTGS systems may experience a liquidity shortfall whenever they need to send a payments order before receiving one. In this instance, payments may be blocked or queued until sufficient funds become available either through incoming payments or by borrowing in the market; in the limit, settlement may be delayed and gridlock may take place with systemic implications (i.e., payments cannot be processed because of a lack of sufficient funds). To avoid such events, EMU national central banks will allow intraday mobilization of reserve requirements and will provide participants in their RTGS systems with fully collateralized intraday credit in the form of daily overdrafts or repurchase agreements.

No decision has been made on whether non-EMU national central banks will be allowed to grant intraday credit in euros to participants in their RTGS systems linked to TARGET. The Governing Council of the ECB will have to choose one of the three mechanisms currently being prepared by the European Mon-

etary Institute with the aim of preventing intraday credit granted by non-EMU national central banks from spilling over into overnight credit and thus from having a monetary impact. The first mechanism would set a limit—possibly zero—to the intraday credit in euros that the ECB would provide to non-EMU national central banks (for participants in their RTGS systems) and would impose penalty rates on spillovers. The second would just impose penalty rates. The third would require non-EMU participants to complete their operations before the closing time of TARGET, so that they would have time to avoid spillovers by borrowing euros in the money market.

If non-EMU national central banks are not granted access to intraday credit or are penalized, institutions making cross-border payments to the euro area could adapt their behavior in a number of ways. In some instances they would still channel payments through the TARGET system; in others they would not. First, non-EMU national central banks could borrow euros in the market to provide intraday credit to participants in domestic RTGS systems for cross-border payments to the euro area; in this instance, systemic risks could be reduced as much as they would be reduced with direct access to ECB's intraday credit. Second, non-EMU banks could channel cross-border payments in euros through branches and subsidiaries in the euro area that have access to both intraday and overnight credit; the

[10]See European Monetary Institute (1996), p. 7.

potential risk reductions associated with TARGET would be fully captured in this second instance. Third, non-EMU institutions could decide to make cross-border payments to the euro area through private net settlement systems, thus reducing the number of transactions across TARGET; in this instance, some of the systemic risk reductions that could be achieved through TARGET would not be realized.

Operating Hours and Pricing Policies

The operating hours of TARGET will be from 7:00 a.m. to 6:00 p.m. and domestic RTGS systems will be allowed to open earlier to process domestic payments. One hour before closing time, participants in RTGS systems will stop processing customers' payments in euros and only interbank payments will be allowed. These hours will allow for a longer overlap between TARGET and the payments systems in North America and the Far East in an effort to reduce cross-currency settlement risk.

TARGET pricing policy will be directed at cost recovery but also at (1) maintaining a level playing field between participants; (2) contributing to risk-reduction policies by preventing institutions from using a less secure payments mechanism; and (3) avoiding transaction charges that would discourage interest rate arbitrage and hinder the integration of the money market.

Framework for EMU Monetary Policy

Decentralization is the key principle underlying the operational framework for monetary policy in Stage III. According to the European Monetary Institute, "the ECB should have recourse to the NCBs to carry out operations 'to the extent deemed possible and appropriate'" in accordance with Article 12 of the statute of the ESCB. The agreed goal is to "rely as much as possible on the existing infrastructure and on the NCBs' experience, provided that the application of this principle does not conflict with the other guiding principles." The latter include operational efficiency; conformity to market principles; equal treatment to all financial institutions accessing the ESCB's facilities; simplicity, transparency, and cost efficiency; conformity with the decision-making process of the ESCB, which requires the Governing Council of the ECB to be able to control the overall stance of monetary policy at all times; and harmonization of the instruments across countries to the extent necessary "to ensure a single monetary policy stance across the euro area, as well as the equal treatment of counterparties and the avoidance of regulatory arbitrage."[11]

Monetary Policy Instruments and Procedures

Open market operations will be the main monetary policy instrument of the ESCB. In addition, there will be standing facilities, and in particular a marginal lending and a marginal deposit facility. The option has been left open to rely on minimum reserve requirements, and a final decision on this will be taken by the ECB.

Open market operations are expected to take mainly the form of reverse transactions (repos), but four other instruments are envisaged: outright transactions, issuance of debt certificates, foreign exchange swaps, and collection of fixed-term deposits. To conduct open market operations, the ECB will be able to choose between three procedures: standard tenders, quick tenders, and bilateral procedures. These operations will be executed by the national central banks, which—in the case of tenders—will collect all the bids and transmit them to the ECB; the latter will then sum them up and select the winning bids. Most refinancing to the financial sector will be provided through regular weekly reverse transactions (repos) with a maturity of two weeks (Table 39).

To steer interest rates in the event of unexpected liquidity fluctuations, the ESCB will use fine-tuning operations. These will be executed primarily as reverse transactions but they may also take the form of outright transactions, foreign exchange swaps, or collection of fixed-term deposits. The European Monetary Institute established that "fine-tuning operations will normally be executed by the NCBs through quick tenders or bilateral procedures. The ECB Governing Council will decide if, under exceptional circumstances, fine-tuning operations may be executed in a centralized or decentralized manner by the ECB."[12]

Longer-term refinancing operations with a monthly frequency and a maturity of three months are also foreseen, but they would not be used to send signals to the market. Finally, reverse or outright transactions and debt certificates will allow the ECB to affect the structural liquidity position of the system.

Standing facilities (a marginal lending and a marginal deposit facility) will allow counterparties to obtain overnight liquidity or make overnight deposits with EMU national central banks. The interest rates on these two facilities should determine the ceiling and the floor of a corridor within which overnight rates are expected to fluctuate. Under normal circumstances, the access to these two facilities will not be restricted so that any eligible counterparty will be able to obtain an unlimited credit from the lending facility as long as it has enough eligible collateral.

The European Monetary Institute has indicated three possible rationales for the introduction of minimum average reserve requirements. First, average requirements would help to stabilize short-term in-

---

[11]European Monetary Institute (1997), p. 18.

[12]European Monetary Institute (1997), p. 19.

Table 39. European System of Central Banks: Open Market Operations and Standing Facilities

Monetary Policy Operations	Types of Transactions		Maturity	Frequency	Procedure
	Provision of liquidity	Absorption of liquidity			
Open market operations					
Main refinancing operations	Reverse transactions (repos)	n.a.	Two weeks	Weekly	Standard tenders
Longer-term refinancing operations	Reverse transactions (repos)	n.a.	Three months	Monthly	Standard tenders
Fine-tuning operations	Reverse transactions (repos)	Reverse transactions (repos)	Nonstandardized	Nonregular	Quick tenders
	Foreign exchange swaps	Foreign exchange swaps			
		Collection of fixed-term deposits			Bilateral procedures
	Outright purchases	Outright sales	n.a.	Nonregular	Bilateral procedures
Structural operations	Reverse transactions (repos)	Issuance of debt certificates	Standardized/ nonstandardized	Regular and nonregular	Standard tenders
	Outright purchases	Outright sales	n.a.	Nonregular	Bilateral procedures
Standing facilities					
Marginal lending facility	Reverse transactions (repos)	n.a.	Overnight	Access at the discretion of counterparties	Access at the discretion of counterparties
Deposit facility	n.a.	Deposits	Overnight	Access at the discretion of counterparties	Access at the discretion of counterparties

Source: European Monetary Institute (1997).

terest rates. Second, reserve requirements could be used to create or enlarge a structural liquidity shortage in the money market. Third, they could help to stabilize monetary aggregates. By stabilizing short-term rates, average reserve requirements would reduce the amount and frequency of fine-tuning operations, which in a decentralized operational framework could become cumbersome. The institute indicated that terms and conditions for reserve requirements would be harmonized in the euro zone, but it did not specify whether reserve requirements would be remunerated.

Eligible *counterparties* of the ESCB for monetary policy operations will be either institutions established in the euro area subject to at least one form of EU supervision or branches of non-EMU institutions that have their head office in an EU or European Economic Area (EEA) country. These institutions must be financially sound and the ESCB will have the authority to suspend temporarily or permanently their access to monetary policy instruments on prudential grounds. Branches of institutions from third countries could be counterparties only in bilateral outright operations involving purchases or sales of securities.

All ESCB liquidity-providing operations will be based on adequate *collateral* as required by Article 18.1 of the statute of the ESCB. Both public and private assets denominated in euros will be eligible as collateral. Tier I collateral will include assets that fulfill eligibility criteria specified by the ECB for the

whole euro area; Tier II collateral will include other assets that EMU national central banks may consider eligible in accordance with ECB guidelines (Table 40). Both Tier I and Tier II assets will be eligible in the whole euro area, but, whereas the default risk related to Tier I paper will be borne by the ESCB as a whole, default risk related to Tier II paper will be borne by the EMU national central bank that proposed it.[13] To avoid the "cheapest to deliver" problem (counterparts delivering the lowest-quality collateral), the ECB could impose margins ("haircuts") or additional guarantees on Tier II assets with a lower credit standing. A list of Tier II assets was deemed necessary because several national central banks have traditionally accepted sizable amounts of nonmarketable private bills and loans as collateral; to assess the related counterparty risk, some national central banks employ a considerable number of people (about 500 in France, 300 in Germany, and 100 in Austria).

The ESCB will have the capacity to conduct *foreign exchange intervention* from the start of Stage III by

---

[13]Cross-border use of collateral (i.e., the possibility of a counterparty located in one country of the euro area receiving credit from its national central bank using assets located in another country of the euro area) is envisaged. Given the incomplete coverage of international linkages between central securities depositories for this purpose, the European Monetary Institute is implementing a scheme that would allow the relevant transfer of information to take place across the ESCB itself.

Table 40. European System of Central Banks: Eligible Assets

Criteria	Tier I	Tier II
Type of asset	European System of Central Banks debt certificates. Other marketable financial obligations.	Marketable financial obligations. Nonmarketable financial obligations. Equities traded on a regulated market.
Settlement procedures	Assets must be centrally deposited in book-entry form with a national central bank or a Central Securities Deposit fulfilling European Central Bank minimum standards.	Assets must be easily accessible to the national central bank that has included them in its Tier II list.
Type of issuer	European System of Central Banks. Public sector. Private sector. International and supranational institutions.	Public sector. Private sector.
Financial soundness	The issuer (guarantor) must be financially sound.	The issuer/debtor (guarantor) must be financially sound.
Location of issuer	European Economic Area	Euro area. Location in other European Economic Area countries can be accepted subject to European Central Bank approval.
Location of asset	Euro area	Euro area. Location in other European Economic Area countries can be accepted subject to European Central Bank approval.
Currency of denomination	Euro	Euro. Other European Economic Area or widely traded currencies can be accepted subject to European Central Bank approval.
Memorandum item: Cross-border use	Yes	For "domestic" assets: yes. For "foreign" assets: possibly restricted.

Source: European Monetary Institute (1997).

means of reserves transferred from the EMU national central banks to the ECB, totaling a maximum amount of 50 billion euros (Article 30 of the statute of the ESCB). The management of foreign reserves that remain with the EMU national central banks will be subject to guidelines issued by the ECB (Article 31.3) to ensure that such operations will not interfere with the monetary and exchange rate policies of the ECB. Exchange rate policy cooperation between the euro area and other EU countries is envisaged within the framework of a new exchange rate mechanism called ERM2 (see Box 7). The ECB will make decisions related to foreign exchange intervention, but it has not yet been decided whether the ECB or the EMU national central banks will implement them; this decision is left to the Governing Council of the ECB. Counterparties for foreign exchange intervention will need to satisfy a number of prudential and efficiency criteria.

Monetary Policy Operating Procedures in Other Industrial Countries

Monetary policy operating procedures in industrial countries seem to be guided by two alternative para-digms (Table 41).[14] On the one hand, the central banks of the United States, Japan, the United Kingdom, Canada, and Australia play an active role in their domestic money markets by intervening daily. This reflects a relatively volatile demand for liquidity, owing in part to their more developed securities markets. On the other hand, most continental European central banks intervene infrequently, relying mainly on average reserve requirements to smooth liquidity shocks.[15]

Like the ECB, most central banks use reverse transactions, in the form of repos or reverse repos, as their main monetary policy instrument. Only in Canada are reverse transactions not the main monetary policy instrument; there the central bank transfers government deposits between its balance sheet and that of clearing banks. In the United Kingdom, since 1994 the Bank of England has increasingly used repos alongside the traditional outright purchases of commercial bills; this trend has continued with the opening of the private repo market in January 1996.

---

[14]See Borio (1997), pp. 286–368.
[15]In the United States, the growing use of so-called sweep accounts is increasingly reducing the buffer role of reserve requirements.

Box 7. ERM2

The Treaty of Maastricht does not specify the exchange rate arrangement between EMU and the EU countries that are not initial members. To eliminate this uncertainty, in December 1995, the European Council in Madrid announced that the current ERM will be replaced by a new exchange rate mechanism, called ERM2, whose main features were agreed on in the Resolution of the Amsterdam European Council in June 1997.

The main objective of ERM2 will be to support the single market by avoiding the disruption of trade flows resulting from real exchange rate misalignments or excessive nominal exchange rate volatility. Participation will be voluntary but expected, especially by countries planning to join EMU with a delay. To allow for different degrees and strategies of convergence, the structure of ERM2 will be flexible. Target fluctuation bands vis-à-vis the euro will be wide: plus or minus 15 percent. Narrower bands between the ECB and non-EMU national central banks are foreseen, but they will be "without prejudice to the interpretation of the exchange-rate criterion" of the Maastricht Treaty Also, bilateral fluctuation bands and intervention arrangements between two non-EMU national central banks will be possible. Intervention at the margin should be automatic and unlimited, but the ECB and the EMU national central banks will be entitled to suspend intervention if the primary objective of price stability is threatened. Intramarginal intervention will remain discretionary. The Very Short Term Financing Facility (VSTF) of the current ERM will be available also in ERM2 "broadly on the basis of the present arrangements."

The main uncertainty about the functioning of ERM2 regards the commitment of the ECB to support a currency of the system under attack. This commitment seems to be limited by the provision that intervention could be suspended "if this were to conflict with the primary objective of price stability." Threats to price stability, however, are likely to be much rarer than in the present ERM because the large scale of EMU will allow easier sterilization of any ERM2-related intervention; in addition, the latter will have a much more limited impact on the liquidity of the euro area. At the same time, intervention by a non-EMU national central bank will not be very effective in stabilizing its parity with the much larger euro zone. Thus, non-EMU countries can reasonably be expected to exercise their obligation for stabilizing ERM2 parities primarily through the maintenance of appropriate monetary, fiscal, and structural policies, rather than through foreign exchange market intervention.

The two-week maturity and the weekly frequency selected for the ECB's operations are identical to those of the reverse transactions in Germany. The maturity of reverse transactions is shorter in most other countries. There is a clear-cut distinction between the higher frequencies of intervention (up to three times a day in the United Kingdom) in the United States, the United Kingdom, Canada, Australia, and Japan, and the lower (generally weekly) frequencies in all other countries, especially those that are likely to be inaugural members of EMU. Additional irregular fine-tuning operations are used in every country with the exceptions of Germany and Austria. Also fairly common are long-term refinancing operations, though these are not used in Canada, Australia, Spain, and Sweden.

Most countries also have marginal lending and marginal deposit facilities. Where a formal standing facility does not exist, similar arrangements are in place. In the United Kingdom, there are several facilities charging escalating rates aimed at limiting the rise in the overnight rate. In Canada, discretionary reverse transactions operate as quasi-standing facilities. In Germany, issuance of short-term paper plays the role of a deposit facility. Although some countries still maintain a subsidized below-market facility (discount window), it has generally not been used in recent years for liquidity management purposes.

Average reserve requirements exist in Australia, Austria, Canada, France, Germany, Italy, Japan, the Netherlands, Spain, Switzerland, and the United States, but they are remunerated only in Australia, Italy, the Netherlands, and Switzerland. To reduce the volatility of the overnight rates, some countries without reserve requirements have introduced averaging provisions. In Canada, for example, there is a "zero" reserve requirement with averaging and banks are penalized when they have negative average settlement balances on a one-month period. In the United Kingdom, reserve requirements have been replaced by a small cash deposit ratio, but without averaging.

Although frequent interventions have not been ruled out, the announced framework for the ECB's monetary policy appears much closer to the continental European model than to that of one of the other industrial countries. Key decisions remain, however, and events could force the ECB to play a more active role.

Framework for General Financial Policies

Banking Supervision and Functions of Lender of Last Resort

Among the industrial countries, there is no clear tendency to combine banking supervision functions with monetary policy functions (Table 42). About half of the countries combine the two functions within the central bank. The other countries separate these func-

Table 41. Key Monetary Policy Operating Procedures in Industrial Countries and in the European Central Bank

	European Central Bank	Austria	Belgium	France	Germany	Italy	Netherlands	Spain	Sweden	United Kingdom	Australia	Canada	Japan	Switzerland	United States
Main operation	RT	RP	RP[1]	RP	RP	RT	CL	RP	RT	OT	RT	RT	RT	FXS	RT
Maturity (days)	14	7	7–15	7	14	≤30	2–8	10	7	1–33	av. 7	1	1–90	80–120	1–15
Frequency	1/wk	1/wk	1/wk	2/wk	1/wk	≥1/wk	1/4d	1/10d	1/wk	≤3/d	1/d	1/d	≤3/d	≈1/wk	≈1/d
Fine-tuning operations	Yes	No	Yes	Yes	No	Yes	Yes	Yes	Yes	Yes	Yes	Yes	Yes	Yes	Yes
Long-term refinancing operations	Yes	Yes	Yes	Yes	Yes	Yes	Yes	No	No	Yes	No	No	Yes	Yes	Yes
Standing facility															
Lending	Yes	Yes	Yes	Yes	Yes	Yes	No	No	Yes	2	Yes	Yes[3]	No	Yes	No
Deposit	Yes	Yes	Yes	No	No[4]	No	No	No	Yes	No	Yes	3	No	No	No
Below market	No	Yes	Yes	No	Yes	Yes	Yes	No	No	No	No	No	Yes[5]	No	Yes
Reserve requirements	6	Yes	No	Yes	Yes	Yes	Yes	Yes	No	7	Yes	Yes[8]	Yes	Yes	Yes
Remuneration	6	No	No	No	No	Yes	Yes	No	No	No	Yes	No	No	Yes	No

Source: Borio (1997).

Notes: RT = reverse transaction (repo or reversed repo); RP = repo (reversed purchase); OT = outright transaction, secondary market; CL = collateralized loan; FXS = foreign exchange swap (purchase or sale).

[1] Or collateralized loans, depending on assets backing the transaction.

[2] A number of facilities aimed at limiting the rise in the overnight rate.

[3] Mainly overdraft loans. In addition, discretionary reversed transactions operated on occasions as a quasi-standing facility.

[4] Discretionary issuance of short-term paper operated on occasions as a standing facility.

[5] Inactive since July 1995.

[6] Not yet decided.

[7] Cash ratio deposit.

[8] Requirement that average settlement balances before overdrafts be non-negative.

Table 42. Monetary and Supervisory Agencies

	Monetary Agency	Supervisory Agency	Notes
Australia	Reserve Bank of Australia (CB)	Reserve Bank of Australia (CB)	C
Austria	National Bank of Austria (CB)	(Federal) Ministry of Finance (MF)	S
Belgium	National Bank of Belgium (CB)	Bank and Finance Commission	S
Canada	Bank of Canada (CB)	Office of the Superintendent of Financial Institutions (MF)	
Denmark	Danmarks Nationalbank (CB)	Financial Supervisory Agency (MEA)	S
Finland	Bank of Finland (CB)	Financial Supervision Authority (CB) Bank of Finland (CB)	S
France	Bank of France (CB)	Bank of France (CB) Banking Commission	C
Germany	Deutsche Bundesbank (CB)	Federal Banking Supervisory Office Deutsche Bundesbank (CB)	S
Greece	Bank of Greece (CB)	Bank of Greece (CB)	C
Hong Kong, China	Hong Kong Monetary Authority (CB)	Hong Kong Monetary Authority (CB)	C
Ireland	Central Bank of Ireland (CB)	Central Bank of Ireland (CB)	C
Italy	Banca d'Italia (CB)	Banca d'Italia (CB)	C
Japan	Bank of Japan (CB)	Ministry of Finance (MF)	S
Luxembourg	Luxembourg Monetary Institute (CB)	Luxembourg Monetary Institute (CB)	C
Netherlands	De Nederlandsche Bank (CB)	De Nederlandsche Bank (CB)	C
New Zealand	Reserve Bank of New Zealand (CB)	Reserve Bank of New Zealand (CB)	C
Norway	Norges Bank (CB)	Banking, Insurance and Securities Commission (MF)	S
Portugal	Banco de Portugal (CB)	Banco de Portugal (CB)	C
Spain	Banco de Espana (CB)	Banco de Espana (CB)	C
Sweden	Sveriges Riksbank (CB)	Swedish Financial Supervisory Authority	S
Switzerland	Swiss National Bank (CB)	Federal Banking Commission	S
United Kingdom	Bank of England (CB)	Bank of England (CB)	C[1]
United States	Federal Reserve Board (CB)	Office of the Comptroller of the Currency (MF) Federal Reserve Board (CB) State governments Federal Deposit Insurance Corporation	S
Venezuela	Banco Central de Venezuela (CB)	Superintendency of Banks	S

Source: Goodhart and Schoenmaker (1995).

Note: The sample covers all industrialized countries (OECD); Hong Kong, China; and Venezuela. C = combined; CB = Central Bank; MEA = Ministry of Economic Affairs; MF = Ministry of Finance; and S = separated.

[1]In May 1997, the U.K. government announced plans to move responsibility for banking supervision from the Bank of England to the Securities and Investments Board.

tions and assign supervisory responsibilities to another agency, usually under the control of the ministry of finance. In some instances the distinction is blurred. In France, for example, the Banking Commission (Commission Bancaire) is chaired by the Governor of the Bank of France with representatives of the French Treasury; the commission supervises compliance with regulations, but the Bank of France carries out inspections on behalf of the commission.[16]

There does not seem to be any clear-cut correspondence between monetary operating procedures and banking supervision models. Industrial countries outside continental Europe do not share the same model. Some countries (Australia, New Zealand, the United Kingdom,[17] to some extent the United States) combine monetary and supervisory functions within the central bank, whereas other countries (Canada, to some extent the United States) separate them. Continental European countries are also split as to how to allocate these responsibilities. Germany, some of its close neighbors (Austria, Switzerland, Belgium, Denmark), and three Scandinavian countries (Sweden, Norway, and Finland) separate the two functions, whereas the other EU countries combine them.

Current plans suggest that EMU is likely to follow the German model of separating monetary and supervisory responsibilities. The Treaty of Maastricht limits the role of the ECB in the area of prudential supervision to "specific tasks" that the EU Council may confer to it on a proposal of the European Commission. Specifically, Article 105(6) of the treaty states: "The Council may, acting unanimously on a proposal from the Commission and after consulting the ECB and after receiving the assent of the European Parliament, confer upon the ECB specific tasks concerning policies relating to the prudential supervision of credit institutions and other financial institutions with the exception of insurance undertakings." The commission has not yet taken any initiative in this direction.

---

[16]These cases were classified following Goodhart and Schoenmaker (1995).

[17]The United Kingdom is about to adopt the alternative model of banking supervision. In May 1997, the government announced plans to move responsibility for banking supervision from the Bank of England to the Securities and Investments Board.

The treaty makes clear that the role of the European System of Central Banks is subordinate to that of the competent supervisory authorities by indicating that the ESCB is expected "to contribute to the smooth conduct of policies pursued by the competent authorities relating to the prudential supervision of credit institutions and the stability of the financial system" (Article 105(5)). Accordingly, the statute of the ESCB assigns the ECB only an advisory function by indicating that "the ECB may offer advice to and be consulted by the Council, the Commission and the competent authorities of the Member States on the scope and implementation of Community legislation relating to the prudential supervision of credit institutions and to the stability of the financial system" (Article 25(1)).

Central banks of industrial countries with highly securitized and liquid financial markets, such as the United States and the United Kingdom, have acted as lender of last resort in order to satisfy their respective mandates to ensure financial market stability.[18] In contrast, central banks of countries where credit is mainly intermediated by banks, such as Germany and other continental EU countries, have generally not taken up the role of lender of last resort for which they rarely have a statutory mandate.[19]

The treaty follows the German model in not attributing any lender-of-last-resort role to the ESCB. In fact, no mention is made of this function in either the treaty or in the statute of the ESCB. This implies that the ECB is not expected to inject liquidity into the system to deal with liquidity or insolvency crises of the banking system. In addition, it is yet to be determined how crises of this nature will be detected, monitored, and resolved. Although this arrangement may reduce moral hazard and enhance the credibility of the ECB, which would be less influenced by considerations of financial system stability when deciding monetary policy, it may be at odds with other functions assigned to the ECB by the Treaty of Maastricht, such as promoting "the smooth operation of payments systems" (Article 105(2)). Given that a central bank usually remains the only immediate source of funding in the system, close coordination between the ECB and supervisory agencies in participating countries will be essential for the ECB to have enough information to carry out its refinancing operations.

Clear and unambiguous mechanisms for managing liquidity crises are crucial to the smooth functioning of TARGET. There may be situations in which the ECB will have to extend a sizable credit within hours of being presented with an institution unable to meet its payments obligations. In this instance, the ECB should have all the supervisory information needed to assess whether it is facing a liquidity crisis or a solvency crisis. As the U.S. experience shows, the likelihood and the systemic consequences of liquidity crises are bound to increase as the volume of transactions in securities markets grows. Given that the rapid expansion of these markets is a widely anticipated consequence of EMU, it is of concern that no clear EMU-wide mechanism to deal with a liquidity crisis has been agreed upon in a context in which supervisory functions are decentralized nor has the ECB been given any supervisory or lender-of-last-resort role.

No additional agreement has yet been announced on the flows of supervisory information between the ECB and the competent authorities—not even in the event of a banking crisis. Information sharing is likely to be regulated by the so-called BCCI Directive (Directive 95/26/EC of June 29, 1995), which removes all legal obstacles to the exchange of information between the authorities supervising credit institutions, investment firms, or insurance companies and the staff of central banks or "other bodies with a similar function in their capacity as monetary authorities"—including the ECB. The implementation of this directive remains ambiguous, however, because it neither specifies the information that could be exchanged nor creates an obligation to provide it. Further arrangements between supervisory authorities and the ECB will be needed to make sure that the relevant information for the smooth functioning of the payments system and the conduct of monetary policy operations will be exchanged in a timely manner in the event of a crisis.

Deposit Insurance Schemes

The Directive on Deposit-Guarantee Schemes (May 1994) required all EU countries to introduce a deposit insurance scheme by July 1995 with the following main features: (1) a minimum coverage of ECU 20,000 for each depositor (ECU 15,000 until December 31, 1999); (2) insurance of deposits at foreign branches according to the home country scheme,[20] unless the foreign branch joins a more favorable host country scheme; (3) a possibility of excluding from coverage the deposits of financial institutions and insurance companies, as well as bonds issued by banks.

The directive notwithstanding, the structure of deposit insurance schemes in the EU is far from being

---

[18]See Folkerts-Landau and Garber (1992).

[19]In both groups of countries, however, banks in difficulties were rarely allowed to fail. In their sample of 104 banking crises from all industrial countries, Goodhart and Schoenmaker (1995) find that in only one-third of the cases were banks in difficulties liquidated; in the other instances, they were rescued with funds provided, often jointly, by central banks, commercial banks, deposit insurance schemes, and governments. Interestingly, there were only two cases in which a central bank acting alone rescued a bank.

---

[20]Until December 31, 1999, however, home country coverage of deposits at foreign branches of domestic banks cannot exceed the level of host country coverage.

harmonized (Table 43). Deposit insurance administration is the responsibility of the government in five EU countries, of the banking system in six, and of both in the remaining four. Funding is provided ex ante (i.e., a reserve fund is established before the occurrence of a bank failure) in two-thirds of the countries and ex post (i.e., funds are obtained after the occurrence of a bank failure) in the remaining ones, but no country seems to make explicit the source of funding for catastrophic losses; among ex ante funding schemes, only those of Denmark and the United Kingdom specify a minimum reserve level for the fund. Deposit insurance premiums are risk based only in Italy, Portugal, and Sweden, and the basis on which the premium is calculated varies considerably across the European Union. The extent of coverage is uneven, ranging from a low of about $12,000 in Spain to a high of some $118,000 in Italy. In Finland, each depositor is insured in full; full insurance exists in Germany but only up to 30 percent of the bank's capital per depositor. Coinsurance schemes, in which depositors share part of the losses, exist in the United Kingdom and Ireland and to some extent in Portugal, where depositors are fully covered up to a limit and only partially for additional amounts.

The lack of harmonization of deposit insurance schemes may become a source of concern. Various degrees of deposit insurance protection could trigger regulatory competition between banking systems in the European Union, with funds flowing toward countries offering the most protection. Furthermore, given that foreign branches can join a host country scheme, situations may arise in which foreign branches obtain "insurance coverage in a country even though that country has no authority to regulate the risk-taking behavior of those branches because of mutual recognition."[21]

Financial Regulation, Capital Standards, and Supervisory Practices

There are considerable differences in the regulation of banks' activities and their ownership structure across EU countries. Table 44 classifies EU and G-10 countries according to the extent to which they are allowed to engage in securities, insurance, and real estate activities, and to own or be owned by nonbanks.[22] Unless further harmonization takes place, banking regulations grant considerably different powers to banks in each country, ranging from the "very wide powers" given to British, French, Dutch, and Austrian banks to the "somewhat restricted powers" of Italian, Swedish, Belgian, and Greek banks; the banks in the remaining EU countries (Germany, Spain, Portugal, Ireland, Denmark, Finland, and Lux-

embourg) fall in an intermediate group with "wide powers."

Of all these possible banking activities, securities operations are the most uniformly regulated across the European Union: they are "unrestricted" in all EU countries except Belgium (where a bank may not underwrite stock issues) and Greece (where dealing and brokerage must be conducted through subsidiaries).[23] Firewalls (i.e., restrictions designed to maintain securities and insurance operations separate from affiliated banks) are mandated only in Italy, Denmark, and Greece. Insurance activities by banks are also "permitted" in most countries if they are conducted through subsidiaries, but they are "restricted" in Germany, Finland, and Greece (i.e., less than a full range of activities can be conducted in the bank or subsidiaries), and they are "prohibited" in Ireland. Real estate activities are restricted in more than one-third of the EU countries; permitted in Germany, France, the Netherlands, Denmark, and Finland; and unrestricted only in the United Kingdom, Ireland, Austria, and Luxembourg. Commercial bank investment in nonfinancial firms is unrestricted in two-thirds of the EU countries, permitted in Portugal, and restricted in Denmark, Italy, Sweden, and Belgium. Similarly, nonfinancial firm investment in commercial banks is unrestricted in 11 EU countries, permitted in Spain, and restricted in Italy and Luxembourg.

Most securities activities are on the list of bank activities subject to mutual recognition in the European Union, included in the Second Banking Directive, which took effect on January 1, 1993 (Table 45). This means that the single EU passport will allow any EU bank to follow its home country regulations on securities activities when it operates in another EU country even if the host country regulations are different. As a result, lack of harmonization of the regulations on securities activities may hamper the competitive position of some banking systems by causing outflows of funds toward countries permitting the widest range of activities, but it cannot be an obstacle to cross-border competition. This may explain the greater harmonization of securities regulations. In contrast, insurance and real estate activities are not included in the list of activities subject to mutual recognition so that whether banks are allowed to engage in them depends on both home country and host country regulations. Differences in these regulations can create opportunities for regulatory arbitrage and be an obstacle to cross-border competition.

---

[21]See Barth, Nolle, and Rice (1997), p. 25.
[22]The classification follows Barth, Nolle, and Rice (1997).

[23]Definitions: *Unrestricted:* a full range of activities in the given category can be conducted directly in the bank. *Permitted:* a full range of activities can be conducted, but all or some must be conducted in subsidiaries. *Restricted:* less than a full range of activities can be conducted in the bank or subsidiaries. *Prohibited:* the activity cannot be conducted in either the bank or subsidiaries. See Barth, Nolle, and Rice (1997).

Table 43. Deposit Insurance Schemes for Commercial Banks in the European Union and G-10 Countries, 1995

	Administration of System: Government or Industry	Extent or Amount of Coverage	Ex Ante or Ex Post Funding	Fund Minimum Reserve Level	Base for Premium	Risk-Based Premiums
Austria	Industry	S 260,000 (per physical person depositor)	Ex post; system organized as an incident-related guarantee facility	n.a.	The deposit guarantee system shall obligate its member institutions, in case of paying out of guaranteed deposits, to pay without delay pro rata amounts that shall be computed according to the share of the remaining member institution at the preceding balance sheet data as compared to the sum of such guaranteed deposits of the deposit guarantee system	n.a.
Belgium	Government/industry (joint)	ECU 15,000 until Dec. 1999, ECU 20,000 thereafter	Ex ante, but in case of insufficient reserves, banks may be asked to pay, each year if necessary, an exceptional additional contribution up to 0.04 percent	No	Total amount of customer's deposits that qualify for reimbursement and that are expressed either in BF, ECU, or another EU currency	No
Canada	Government (Crown Corporation)	Can$60,000 (per depositor)	Ex ante	No	Insured deposits	No
Denmark	Government	DKr 300,000 or ECU 42,000 (per depositor)	Ex ante	Yes, 3 billion DKr	Deposits	No
Finland	Industry	100 percent (per depositor)	Ex ante	No	Total assets	No
France	Industry	F 400,000 (per depositor)	Ex post	n.a.	The contribution consists of two parts: (1) A fixed part, irrespective of the size of the bank, equal to 0.1 percent of any claim settled and with a F 200,000 ceiling; and (2) a proportional part, varying according to a regressive scale relative to the size of the bank contributing, based on deposits and one-third credits.	n.a.
Germany	Industry	100 percent up to a limit of 30 percent of the bank's liable capital (per deposit)	Ex ante; however, additional assessments may be made if necessary to discharge the fund's responsibilities. These contributions are limited to twice the annual contribution	No	Balance sheet item "Liabilities to Customers"	No
Greece	Government/industry (joint)	ECU 20,000 (per depositor)	Ex ante	No	Total deposits	No
Ireland	Government	90 percent of deposits; maximum compensation is ECU 15,000	Ex ante	No, but minimum Premium Rate of £20,000	Total deposits excluding interbank deposits and deposits represented by negotiable certificates of deposit	No
Italy	Industry	100 percent of first Lit 200 million (per depositor)	Ex post; banks commit ex ante; however, contributions are ex post	No	Maximum limit for funding the whole system: Lit 4,000 billion. Contributions are distributed among participants on the basis of deposits plus loans minus own funds with a correction mechanism linked to deposit growth.	Yes
Japan	Government/industry (joint)	¥10 million yen (per depositor)	Ex ante	No	Insured deposits	No

182

Country	Administration	Funding	Coverage	Fund	Coverage base	
Luxembourg	Industry	Ex post	Lux F 500,000 (per depositor), only natural persons	n.a.	Banks' premiums based on percentage of loss to be met	n.a.
Netherlands	Government/industry (joint)	Ex post	ECU 20,000 (per depositor); compensation paid in guilders	n.a.	Amount repaid in compensation to insured is apportioned among participating institutions. However, the contribution in any one year shall not exceed 5 percent per an institution's own funds and per all institutions' own funds	n.a.
Portugal	Government	Ex ante. However, the payment of the annual contributions may be partly replaced, with a legal maximum of 75 percent, by the commitment to deliver the amount due to the Fund, at any moment it proves necessary	100 percent up to 15,000 ECU; 75 percent: 15,000–30,000 ECU; 50 percent: 30,000–45,000 ECU (per depositor)	No	Guaranteed deposits	Yes
Spain	Government/industry (joint)	Ex ante	Ptas 1.5 million (per depositor); to be increased to ECU 20,000	No	Deposits	No
Sweden	Government	Ex ante	SKr 250,000 (per depositor)	No	Covered deposits	Yes
Switzerland	Industry	Ex post	SwF 30,000 (per depositor)	n.a.	Two components: fixed fee in relation to gross profit; variable fee depending on share of total protected deposits of an individual bank	n.a.
United Kingdom	Government	Ex ante; banks make initial contributions of £10,000 when a bank is first authorized, further contributions if the fund falls below £3 million, not exceeding £300,000 per bank based on the insured deposit base of the banks involved, and special contributions, again based on the insured deposit base of the banks involved, but with no contribution limit	90 percent of protected deposits, with the maximum amount of deposits protected for each depositor being £20,000 (unless the sterling equivalent of ECU 22,222 is greater). Thus, the most an individual can collect in a bank failure is £18,000 (per depositor) or ECU 20,000 if greater	Yes, the fund is required by law to maintain a level of £5 million to £6 million, but the Deposit Protection Board can decide to borrow to meet its needs	All deposits in European Economic Area currencies less deposits by credit institutions; financial institutions, insurance undertakings, directors, controllers and managers, secured deposits, CDs, deposits by other group companies and deposits that are part of the bank's own funds	No
United States	Government	Ex ante	$100,000 (per depositor)	Yes, 1.25 percent of insured deposits	Domestic deposits	Yes
European Union (EC Directive on Deposit-Guarantee Schemes)	Only directs that each member state shall ensure within its territory one or more deposit guarantee schemes are introduced and officially recognized	Determined within each member state	The aggregate deposits of each depositor must be covered up to ECU 20,000. Until Dec. 31, 1999, member states in which deposits are not covered up to ECU 20,000 may retain the maximum amount laid down on their guarantee schemes, provided that this amount is not less than ECU 15,000 (per depositor)	Determined within each member state	Determined within each member state	Determined within each member state

Sources: IMF country desks; and Barth, Nolle, and Rice (1997).

183

Table 44. Permissible Banking Activities and Bank Ownership in the European Union and G-10 Countries, 1995

	Securities[1]	Insurance[2]	Real Estate[3]	Commercial Bank Investment in Nonfinancial Firms	Nonfinancial Firm Investment in Commercial Banks
Banks given very wide powers					
Austria	Unrestricted	Permitted	Unrestricted	Unrestricted	Unrestricted
Switzerland	Unrestricted	Permitted	Unrestricted	Unrestricted	Unrestricted
United Kingdom	Unrestricted	Permitted	Unrestricted	Unrestricted	Unrestricted
France	Unrestricted	Permitted	Permitted	Unrestricted	Unrestricted
Netherlands	Unrestricted	Permitted	Permitted	Unrestricted	Unrestricted
Banks given wide powers					
Denmark	Unrestricted	Permitted	Permitted	Restricted	Unrestricted
Finland	Unrestricted	Restricted	Permitted	Unrestricted	Unrestricted
Germany	Unrestricted	Restricted	Permitted	Unrestricted	Unrestricted
Ireland	Unrestricted	Prohibited	Unrestricted	Unrestricted	Unrestricted
Luxembourg	Unrestricted	Permitted	Unrestricted	Unrestricted	Restricted
Portugal	Unrestricted	Permitted	Restricted	Permitted	Unrestricted
Spain	Unrestricted	Permitted	Restricted	Unrestricted	Permitted
Banks given somewhat restricted powers					
Italy	Unrestricted	Permitted	Restricted	Restricted	Restricted
Sweden	Unrestricted	Permitted	Restricted	Restricted	Restricted
Belgium	Permitted	Permitted	Restricted	Restricted	Unrestricted
Canada	Permitted	Permitted	Permitted	Restricted	Restricted
Greece	Permitted	Restricted	Restricted	Unrestricted	Unrestricted
Banks given restricted powers					
Japan	Restricted	Prohibited	Restricted	Restricted	Restricted
United States	Restricted	Restricted	Restricted	Restricted	Restricted

Source: Barth, Nolle, and Rice (1997).

Definitions: *Unrestricted*: a full range of activities in the given category can be conducted directly in the bank. *Permitted*: a full range of activities can be conducted, but all or some must be conducted in subsidiaries. *Restricted*: less than a full range of activities can be conducted in the bank or subsidiaries. *Prohibited*: the activity cannot be conducted in either the bank or subsidiaries.

[1]Securities activities include underwriting, dealing, and brokering all kinds of securities and all aspects of the mutual fund business.

[2]Insurance activities include underwriting and selling insurance products/services as principal and as agent.

[3]Real estate activities include investment, development, and management.

The implementation of several EU directives[24] and of the Basle Accord has not fully harmonized capital standards, which still differ somewhat across EU countries owing to the different lists of items that banks can use to meet capital requirements (Table 46). Likewise, supervisory practices vary in terms of procedures for examinations and inspections, disclosure of regulatory information, lending limits (on borrowers, sectors, countries, and large exposures), and limits on bank activities abroad (Table 47). Whereas a single currency will increase pressures for harmonization, decentralized supervisory functions may well allow these differences to persist long enough to affect the location of the banking industry within EMU.

---

[24]The two main EU directives concerning capital standards are the EC Own Funds Directive (April 1989) and the EC Solvency Directive (December 1989). By January 1, 1993, EU banks had to satisfy a minimum 8 percent risk-weighted total capital ratio in line with the Basle Accord. A third directive, the EC Capital Adequacy Directive (June 1993), set capital requirements for the market risk resulting from trading in securities, derivatives, and foreign exchange.

Euro as a Catalyst: Incentives for Continued Structural Change

Driven by financial deregulation, changing opportunities for investment, and bank disintermediation, European securities markets have become more highly integrated and liquid. These changes have been associated with the placement of large sovereign debt issues, which provided strong incentives to develop liquid and efficient secondary bond markets, and with the accumulation of large stocks of public debt, which raised yields on government securities thereby making them an attractive alternative to bank deposits. Facilitated by the recent convergence of macroeconomic policies, greater capital mobility has contributed to market integration by linking national securities markets, reducing bond spreads, and increasing co-movements in bond and equity returns across EU countries.[25]

---

[25]See Artis and Taylor (1990), Frankel, Phillips, and Chinn (1993), and Eijffinger and Lemmen (1995).

Table 45. List of Bank Activities Subject to Mutual Recognition in the European Union[1]

Acceptance of deposits and other repayable funds from the public.

Lending.[2]

Financing leasing.

Money transmission services.

Issuing and administering means of payment (e.g., credit cards, traveler's checks and banker's drafts).

Guarantees and commitments.

Trading for own account or for account of customers in:
    Money market instruments (checks, bills, certificates of deposit)
    Foreign exchange
    Financial futures and options
    Exchange and interest rate instruments
    Transferable securities.

Participation in share issues and the provision of services related to such issues.

Advice to undertakings on capital structure, industrial strategy, and related questions and advice and services relating to mergers and the purchase of undertakings.

Money brokering.

Portfolio management and advice.

Safekeeping and administration of securities.

Credit reference services.

Safe custody services.

Source: Barth, Nolle, and Rice (1997).

[1]The Second Banking Directive specifies that an EU bank or "credit institution" (i.e., deposit-taking and lending institution) may conduct directly or through branches the listed activities throughout the EU so long as its home country authorizes the activities. Subsidiaries of credit institutions governed by the law of the same member state may also conduct the activities, subject to conditions that include 90 percent ownership and a guarantee of commitments by the parent credit institutions. Insurance and real estate activities are not on the list and are therefore determined by both home and host country regulations. The Second Banking Directive took effect January 1, 1993.

[2]Including among other things consumer credit; mortgage credit; factoring, with or without recourse; financing of commercial transactions (including forfaiting).

Against the background of these ongoing structural changes, the introduction of the euro will alter incentives in such a way so as to encourage the further securitization[26] of European finance, greater uniformity in market practices, more transparency of pricing, and increased market integration.[27] *First,* by eliminating separate currencies, the introduction of the euro reduces the direct cost of spot transactions and eliminates a relatively volatile element of market risk—foreign exchange risk—in longer-dated real and financial contracts between entities in EMU member countries. While foreign exchange risk between some ERM currencies may have diminished recently (as measured by implied volatilities, for example), the costs incurred by market participants—including central banks—during the violent disruptions in the ERM crisis in 1992–93 will long be remembered as will the frequent realignments, often preceded by speculative attacks, in the early years of the EMS and in the less formal exchange rate arrangements before the EMS.

Second, the elimination of currency risk increases the relative importance of other elements of risk, including credit, liquidity, settlement, legal, and event risks. Credit risk is likely to be the most important component of securities pricing within EMU, with the implication that the "relative value" of underlying credits rather than judgments about the stability and volatility of currency values will drive securities prices.

Increased attention will be paid to other elements of risk. Bond issues of two otherwise identical credit risks—say, a German company and a French one producing the same goods and having similar balance sheets—may be priced differently if issuing techniques, clearing and settlement procedures, and legal procedures are different in the respective countries. The impact of these remaining and less volatile components of risk on the cost of raising funds will provide incentives to suppliers of securities to narrow further their interest rate spreads by increasing transparency and by improving issuing techniques and financial infrastructures to attract investors. This competitive process, if allowed to run its course, could lead to the sufficient harmonization of market practices within the euro zone to eliminate the advantages a particular geographical market may now have. In this way, the elimination of currency risk could lead to greater uniformity and transparency of market practices, with the benefits of more uniform pricing and a breakdown of market segments within Europe.

The elimination of currency risk and its costs, the convergence of credit spreads, and more uniformity in market practices together can be expected to increase the depth and liquidity of European securities markets. In short-term markets (money, swap, and short-term

---

[26]*Securitization* refers to the creation of any credit, ownership, or derivative claims that are publicly tradable, either in organized exchanges or over the counter, and whose prices are determined at frequent intervals in an open market. The popular press has used this term, almost exclusively, to describe asset-backed securities (the creation of high-quality, negotiable, liquid securities that are funded by setting aside illiquid separate claims, such as mortgage obligations, consumer receivables, and other classes of assets).

[27]Even without the euro, full implementation of the EU Investment Services Directive (ISD), which creates a single passport for securities firms (brokers and dealers), portfolio managers, and investment advisories, would provide renewed stimulus for the creation of an EU single market in financial services, although some impediments to cross-border competition remain. The euro is likely to enhance the impact of the ISD.

Table 46. Components of Capital for Meeting the Capital Standards or Requirements in the European Union and G-10 Countries

	Noncumulative Perpetual Preferred Stock	Current Year Profit Added (or Loss Deducted)	Intangible Assets Other than Goodwill	Goodwill	Undisclosed Reserves	Hybrid Capital Instruments (Including Cumulative Perpetual Preferred Stock)	Subordinated Term Debt	Limited Life Redeemable Preference Shares	Fixed-Asset Revaluation Reserves	Latent, or Hidden, Revaluation Reserves	General Loan/Loss Reserves	Investment in the Capital of Other Banks and Financial Institutions
Austria	Yes	Yes	No	No	Yes, but limits	Yes, but limits	Yes, but limits	No	Yes, but limits	No	Yes	No
Belgium	Yes	Yes	No	No	Yes, but limits	Yes, but limits	Yes, but limits	Yes, but limits	Yes, but limits	No	Yes	No
Denmark	No, does not exist	Yes	No	No	No	Yes, but limits	No	No, does not exist	No, does not exist	No, does not exist	No, does not exist	No
Finland	Yes	Yes	No	No	No	Yes	Yes	Not applicable	Yes	No	Yes	No
France	No, issues not permitted in domestic markets	Yes	No, except lease renewal rights	No	No	Yes	Yes	Yes, but not issued	Yes	No	Yes	Yes, but limits
Germany	Yes	No	No	No	Yes, but limits	Yes, but limits	Yes, but limits	No	No	Yes, with limits	Yes, with limits	No
Greece	Yes	Yes	Yes	Yes	No	Yes, but limits	Yes, but limits	Yes, but not utilized at present	Yes, but limits	No	Yes	No
Ireland	Yes, no limits	Yes	No	No	No	Yes, but limits	Yes, but limits	Yes, but limits	Yes, but limits	No	Yes, but limits	No
Italy	Yes, but limits	Yes	Yes	Yes	No	Yes, but limits	Yes, but limits	No, does not exist	Yes, but limits	No	Yes, but limits	No
Luxembourg	Yes	Yes	No	No	Yes	Yes	Yes	Yes	No	No	Yes	No
Netherlands	Yes	Yes	Yes	Yes	Yes	Yes	Yes	Yes	Yes	Yes	Yes	Yes
Portugal	Yes	Yes	Yes	Yes	No information	Yes	Yes, but limits	No information	Yes	No information	Yes	No
Spain	Yes	No	No	No	No	Yes, but limits	Yes, but limits	Yes, but limits	Yes, but limits	No	No	No
Sweden	Yes	Yes	No	No	No	Yes with approval	Yes	No	Yes, with approval	No	No	No
United Kingdom	Yes	Yes	No	No	n.a.	Yes, but limits	Yes, but limits	Yes	Yes, with caution	n.a.	Yes, but limits	No
Canada	Yes	Yes	Yes	No	No	Yes	Yes	Yes	No	No	No	Yes, but back-to-back issues are deducted
Japan	Yes	Yes	Yes	No	No	Yes, but not prevalent	Yes	Yes, but not issued	No	Yes	Yes	No, if sole purpose is to raise capital ratio
Switzerland	Yes, no limits	Yes	No	No	Yes, but limits	Yes, but limits and not including cumulative perpetual preferred stock	Yes, but limits	No	Yes, but limits	Yes, but limits	Yes, no limits	No
United States	Yes	Yes	No, with limited exceptions	No	No	Yes, but limits	Yes, but limits	Yes, but limits	No	No	Yes, but limits	No

Source: Barth, Nolle, and Rice (1997).

Table 47. Commercial Bank Supervisory Practices in the European Union and G-10 Countries, 1995

	Examinations and/or Inspections		Required External Audits	Information Publicly Disclosed		Domestic Bank Activities Abroad		Lending Limits on:				
	On-site	Banks pay exam		Bank examinations or inspections	Enforcement actions	Specific authorization required	Limits or restrictions placed on domestic bank's foreign activities	A single borrower	Persons connected with the bank	Particular sectors	Country risk exposure	Large exposures
Austria	Yes	Yes	Yes	No	No	No	No	Yes	Yes	No	No	Yes
Belgium	Yes	No	Yes	No	Yes	No, only notification	No, only notification	Yes	Yes	No	No	Yes
Denmark	Yes, usually every 3 years	Yes	Yes	No	No	No	No	Yes	No	No	No	Yes
Finland	Yes, not regularly	Yes	Yes	No	No	No	No	Yes	Yes	Yes	Yes	Yes
France	Yes	No information	Yes	No information	No information	No	No	No information	No information	No information	No information	No information
Germany	Yes	Yes	Yes	No	No	No	No	Yes	No	No	No	Yes
Greece	Yes, generally every 2–3 years	No	Yes	No	No	Yes	No	Yes	Yes	No	No	Yes
Ireland	Yes, usually every 18–24 months	No	Yes	No	No	Yes	No	Yes	Yes	No	No	Yes
Italy	Yes, usually every 4–8 years	No	Yes, for banks quoted on the stock exchange	No	Yes	Yes	No	Yes	Yes	Yes	No	Yes
Luxembourg	Yes, on an ad hoc basis	Yes	Yes	No	No	No	No	Yes	Yes	No	No	Yes
Netherlands	Yes, depends on size/risk profile	No	Yes	No	No	No	Yes	Yes	Yes	Yes	Yes	Yes
Portugal	Yes, usually annually	No	Yes	No	Yes	Yes	No	Yes	Yes	No	No	Yes
Spain	Yes	No	Yes	No	No	Yes, but only branches outside EU	No	Yes	Yes	No	No	No
Sweden	Yes	No	Yes	No	No	No	No	Yes	No	Yes	No	Yes
United Kingdom	Yes, but limited and usually biennially	No, not directly	Yes	No	Yes, but not explicitly naming institutions	No	No	Yes	Yes	No	No	Yes
Canada	Yes, annually	Yes	Yes	No	No	No	No	Yes	Yes	No	No	Yes
Japan	Yes	No information	No information	No information	No information	No information	No information	No information	No information	No information	No information	No information
Switzerland	No	Yes	Yes, official part of supervisory system	No	No	No, only notification	No	Yes	Yes	No	No, but provision requirements per country	Yes
United States	Yes	Yes	Yes, for banks with assets exceeding $500 million	No	Yes	No	Yes	Yes	Yes	No	No	No

Source: Barth, Nolle, and Rice (1997).

Table 48. Mutual Funds, June 1996

	Equity	Bond	Money Market	Total
Net assets (in billions of U.S. dollars)				
European Union[1]	366.74	533.94	496.32	1,396.99
United States	1,532.46	741.78	817.75	3,091.99
Japan	119.12	189.39	102.22	410.73
Number of funds (in units)[2]				
European Union[1]	7,136	4,436	1,912	13,484
United States	2,611	2,390	995	5,996
Japan	4,118	2,060	15	6,193

Source: Investment Company Institute.

[1]Does not include Ireland and the Netherlands for equity and bond funds; does not include Austria, Denmark, Ireland, and the Netherlands for money market funds.

[2]The equity funds also include balanced funds and "other" funds.

treasury bill markets, for example), contracts denominated in individual currencies will be redenominated in euros and could be traded across national markets, even if small credit spreads remain. For securities with multiple exchange listings, competition among exchanges could lead to a consolidation of trading in a single location. Even in markets that remain somewhat segmented (because of higher credit spreads or restrictions), lower transaction costs (elimination of commissions on foreign exchange transactions and costs of hedging exchange rate risk) and the removal of trading restrictions (e.g., on institutional investors) will add liquidity. Moreover, competition among issuers—no longer based on the strength of the currency—will encourage sovereign borrowers to introduce market reforms.

Third, the euro will directly reduce the number of existing barriers to cross-border investment and eliminate some restrictions on currency exposures of various pools of capital (pension funds, insurance companies, other asset managers). To begin with, all intra-EMU foreign exchange restrictions on the investments of pension funds and insurance companies will become irrelevant within the EMU area (see the appendix at the end of this annex). The EU matching rule (liabilities in a foreign currency must be 80 percent matched by assets in that same currency) for insurance companies, which has been extended to pension funds in some countries, will also cease to be binding within EMU since insurance companies will be able to invest their assets in any country of the euro area as long as their liabilities are denominated in euros. The size and country diversification of assets managed by institutional investors in the European Union, say mutual funds—still far smaller than in the United States— could rapidly increase together with their share of foreign investments (Table 48). Finally, the "anchoring" principle, restricting lead managers of issues to full subsidiaries domiciled in the issuing country, will become irrelevant and will thereby increase the potential for intra-EMU market penetration.

Fourth, portfolio diversification will change along with volatilities and correlations of assets in the EMU area, although some "home bias" could remain (see Box 8). Moreover, the advantages of currency diversification will be lost to the extent that business cycles have been asynchronous and shocks asymmetric. This will encourage investors and financial institutions to search for, and find, new opportunities for portfolio diversification within EMU repo, government securities, and corporate securities markets, but it may also encourage them to seek diversification outside the euro area as well.

European securities markets will also be shaped by other important factors. Technological progress will soon make fully integrated EU-wide securities and derivative markets unavoidable, by making the location of trading, clearing, and settlement largely irrelevant. Continued fiscal consolidation—as part of the Stability and Growth Pact—is likely to reduce the volume of new government bond issues, providing room for private entities to issue new equity shares and debt securities. Finally, if the role of the unfunded social security system diminishes, the stepped-up activities of institutional investors (e.g., insurance companies and private pension funds) will increase the demand for public and private paper of various maturities and types, perhaps including corporate bonds.

Structural Implications for Securities Markets: Further Securitization of European Finance

As just discussed, the euro has the potential for catalyzing and enhancing the impact of EU financial directives, increasing transparency in credit evaluation, accelerating the processes of financial market integration, and further expanding Europe's institutional investor base. This section examines prospects for the development of EMU-wide securities markets, includ-

Box 8. Volatility and Correlation of Asset Returns in EMU

The relation between exchange rate stability and the volatility of asset prices has been one of the most debated issues in the economic literature. One view is that a fixed exchange rate regime—hence EMU—increases the volatility of securities prices. According to this view, when the exchange rate is not allowed to change, shocks to productivity, consumer preferences, or other real shocks of domestic origin will be reflected to a larger extent in securities prices ("volatility transfer hypothesis").

Several arguments have been put forward to counter or qualify this view. First, the volatility transfer hypothesis holds unambiguously only when real domestic shocks prevail; if domestic or foreign money demand shocks prevail, a fixed exchange rate regime would have, instead, an opposite, dampening, effect on the volatility of securities prices. Furthermore, for foreign real shocks, the consequences of fixing the exchange rate become ambiguous. Second, if the volatility of the exchange rate is created by uninformed "noise traders" or "chartists" responding to nonfundamental factors, then credibly fixing the exchange rate would eliminate the excess volatility without transferring it to other sectors of the economy. Finally, if the fixed exchange rate regime is imperfectly credible and stochastic shocks may trigger a speculative attack, then the volatility of interest rates is higher than it would be with a perfectly credible parity or a single currency, as in EMU; in this case, the impact of a fixed-rate regime on the volatility of interest rates provides no indication of what would happen with a perfectly credible fixed exchange rate regime or EMU.

The question can only be settled empirically. A recent study by Flood and Rose (1995) of various episodes of fixed and flexible exchange rates over the 1960–91 period for OECD countries concludes that there is little evidence that "reducing exchange rate volatility compromises the stability of other macroeconomic variables" (p. 36). Similar results are obtained for EMS countries by Artis and Taylor (1994) and Fratianni and von Hagen (1990). Following a methodology similar to Mussa (1988), Bodart and Reding (1996) compare the volatility of bond and equity market returns across different exchange rate regimes. They use high-frequency data (daily returns between January 1989 and December 1994) for Belgium, France, Germany, Italy, Sweden, the United Kingdom, and the United States. They find that the countries with the lowest foreign exchange volatility (Germany, France, and Belgium) have the lowest volatility of bond returns also. In these countries, the volatility of equity prices is also lower than in Sweden and Italy. Furthermore, after breaking up the sample into subperiods, they find that, as long as the EMS regime was credible, the low volatility in foreign exchange markets was associated with a low volatility in bond markets. When foreign exchange volatility increased, bond market volatility did also. Analogous—although weaker—results were obtained for equity prices. Frankel (1996) conducts a similar experiment on stock prices and reaches similar conclusions. This evidence suggests that lower—not

higher—volatility of securities prices is associated with lower exchange rate variability.

There are two main reasons why securities prices could be correlated across countries: a common fundamental factor or contagion effects. In both instances, the correlation is likely to be affected by EMU. First, if EU securities prices share a common fundamental, EMU can increase their correlation because it reduces the variance of idiosyncratic shocks due to independent monetary policies. EMU might also reduce the correlation of securities prices by increasing the variance of the credit risk component. In the government bond market, this may happen because EMU eliminates the possibility of using the inflation tax to resolve country-specific budgetary difficulties. Similarly, in the corporate bond market, EMU eliminates the possibility of using the exchange rate instrument to compensate for real idiosyncratic shocks. In stock markets, EMU is expected to have a lower impact on price correlations because of the much higher potential for idiosyncratic shocks. A higher cross-country correlation of equity prices should, however, also be expected because EMU eliminates idiosyncratic monetary policy shocks and is likely to increase the correlation of business cycles.

Second, international correlations of securities prices can also be explained by contagion effects due to noise trading or herd behavior unrelated to fundamentals. In this case, cross-country correlations should be higher in periods of high market volatility, when there is a large dispersion of expectations about fundamentals. As long as fixing exchange rates or introducing a single currency reduces the uncertainty about monetary policy, periods of high market volatility should become less frequent and contagion and correlation of securities prices should fall. Thus, if international correlations of securities prices stemmed mainly from contagion effects, EMU would not increase the correlation—as suggested by the fundamental approach—but reduce it.

Two studies on the effects of exchange rate regimes on the cross-country correlation of securities prices suggest that a smaller exchange rate volatility, and thus EMU, should increase cross-country correlations. Bodart and Reding (1996) find that correlations of both bond and equity prices were stronger for the countries with the lowest exchange rate volatility. Moreover, correlations weakened in the turbulent period of the ERM. Interestingly, the correlation between German and U.K. bond markets was higher during the short period in which the British pound was part of the ERM. Frankel (1996) conducts a similar experiment on Irish stock market data and obtains similar results. The existing empirical evidence suggests that the exchange rate regime matters and that exchange rate stability tends to increase cross-country correlations of securities prices. EMU may then be expected to have a similar effect. These results should, however, be interpreted with caution because they do not rule out the possibility that changes in the volatility of idiosyncratic fiscal and political shocks—affecting simultaneously foreign exchange markets and securities markets—could account for the observed changes in correlations.

Table 49. European Union: Cross-Border Interbank Assets

(In percent of GDP)

	1992	1993	1994	1995	1996
European Union countries					
Austria	17.71	16.72	17.77	17.89	21.16
Belgium	56.01	60.33	59.20	58.29	58.03
France	17.81	18.22	20.12	18.80	18.51
Germany	8.60	10.21	12.64	13.08	12.67
Ireland	26.26	35.66	38.82	50.80	55.90
Italy	15.81	17.74	18.22	16.71	16.25
Luxembourg	914.54	921.38	937.81	908.43	840.15
Netherlands	26.45	26.54	27.39	27.04	31.24
Portugal	7.63	13.50	20.36	22.17	20.75
Spain	7.38	9.14	10.85	9.61	10.24
United Kingdom	58.14	74.71	74.59	81.59	79.99
Memorandum items:					
North America					
Canada	8.27	9.27	10.10	9.92	10.41
Mexico	6.07	5.07	6.57	7.88	6.18
United States	9.36	8.96	9.49	9.65	8.89
Japan	16.97	13.85	13.49	12.78	12.67

Sources: Bank for International Settlements; and International Monetary Fund, *World Economic Outlook* database.

ing repo, bond (public and private), equity, and derivative markets.

EMU-Wide Repo and Interbank Markets

The decision that the ECB will use reverse transactions (repos) as the main instrument for implementing monetary policy could fuel the development of an EMU-wide market for repurchase agreements (repo market). Although private repo markets currently exist in some countries, with a few exceptions they are not highly developed and lack the liquidity and depth of the repo markets in the United States.

In the United States, repo markets are an important alternative money market instrument. By providing ready access to secured borrowing, and by enhancing liquidity in the securities markets, repos facilitate portfolio financing and the ability to short the market. Banks also can use repurchase agreements for extending credits to securities dealers collateralized by a zero-risk-weighted central government bond. In Europe, only France has a transparent and liquid repo market (20 primary dealers are required to post prices on Reuters). The United Kingdom recently introduced a gilt repo market, while other countries, notably Germany, discouraged them until the end of 1996 by subjecting repo transactions with nonbanks to reserve requirements, with the result that a large share of the German repo business migrated to London. In Italy, legal, taxation, and settlement obstacles have prevented the development of a liquid repo market.

Whether the different market structures characterizing the interbank markets in each member country will survive or whether market pressures—acting through price differentials—will lead to a single EMU-wide interbank market is an open question. Integration has already increased somewhat, with growing shares of foreign interbank deposits (Table 49) and smaller discrepancies between interest rates on euro and domestic markets. On short-maturity transactions, especially shorter than one month, interest rate arbitrage is still imperfect, in part because of differences in taxation and regulation. With the euro, the elimination of European cross-currency risk, the establishment of ECB repo operations, and the provision of intraday liquidity for settlement purposes, there would be few, if any, impediments preventing first-, second-, and third-tier European banks from dealing directly with each other for supplying or accessing overnight funds. This overnight borrowing and lending could quickly lead to the creation of an efficient EMU-wide interbank market with total volumes at least equal to the sum of those of current domestic interbank markets. In this scenario, domestic interbank rates would be harmonized across EMU with residual differences reflecting only the different credit standings of second- or third-tier banks.

It is a possible next step, although by no means certain, for a private repo market to develop in all EMU countries, in which a private yield curve will offer instruments ranging in maturity from overnight to long-term contracts. In such a market, financial and nonfinancial entities alike can engage in short-term collateralized refinancing operations for conducting day-to-day treasury operations in supporting their real economic activities. Many European multinationals now conduct such refinancing in New York, London, Tokyo, and other international financial centers.

With the development of an EMU repo market, collateralized borrowing and lending will enable financial institutions to refinance their operations at interest rates below those in the interbank deposit market. The development of this Europe-wide market could help set the tone for the development of other capital markets in Europe. It would also open up opportunities for large global financial institutions to participate more fully and actively in short-term EMU markets for liquidity management, in much the same way they participate in the markets in New York and London. European capital markets would benefit significantly from the participation of these large global players in terms of added depth, liquidity, and efficiency to European capital markets.

Possible remaining impediments to the establishment of EMU-wide repo markets would be reserve requirements on repo operations (remunerated at below-market interest), other long-standing legal and settlement obstacles, and elements of tax systems. In addition, interest rates in the repo market might not become fully uniform across Europe if different margins ("haircuts") are applied to Tier I and Tier II collateral for repurchase transactions with the ECB. Alternatively, if the ECB does not discriminate between the quality of collateral, the distinction between issuers at the short end of the curve may become blurred and lead to a "race to the bottom" in quality in providing collateral.

EMU Bond Markets: New Focus on Credit Risk

Government Bond Market

By eliminating currency risk on European cross-country transactions, and by directly reducing transactions costs, the introduction of the euro reduces the cost of issuing and investing in government securities. The increased transparency of costs and benefits is likely to influence both demand and supply and to provide strong incentives for the harmonization of market practices (e.g., auctioning techniques, issue calendars, maturity spectrums) toward the most transparent and cost-effective practices for both issuers and investors. As investors and issuers become familiar with these transactions, investors will search throughout EMU sovereign markets for their preferred risk-return profiles among the sovereign issuers in the union, and it is reasonable to expect market segmentation to diminish. EMU member governments can therefore no longer take for granted their "home currency" market, and will try to appeal to a broader investor base. Whether or not this harmonization of market practices and market desegmentation occurs in full, market participants who in the past focused on the relatively volatile currency risk will now focus attention on the other, less volatile risks, including credit (sovereign), liquidity, settlement, legal, and event risks.

The refocus on credit risk by both issuers and investors is likely to increase cross-border competition between financial intermediaries for bringing new issues to market, for "rating" new credits, and for allocating investment funds across the national markets. Competition is likely to involve non-European as well as European financial institutions and asset managers. Financial intermediaries from the United States—where investment houses and institutional investors have, respectively, specialized on the issuer and investor sides of these markets for decades—would appear to have a comparative and competitive advantage in supplying many of these services against all but the largest European financial intermediaries. Thus, the establishment of EMU is likely to contribute to the restructuring of the global business of investment banking and universal banking.

How far market desegmentation will go and how liquid the European sovereign debt market becomes will depend on how credit risks are priced. Several potential EMU member countries enjoy top ratings on debt denominated in domestic currencies and lower ratings on debt denominated in foreign currency (Table 50). There are several reasons for these differences. First, foreign currency debt cannot be repaid by printing domestic money and it has, therefore, higher default probabilities associated with it. Second, debt issued in domestic currency is mostly locally held so that governments, for political reasons, are more likely to continue to service domestic debt. Third, governments may find it easier to raise taxes or cut expenditures to repay domestic debt than to repay foreign investors. If these considerations are valid for euro-denominated debt issued by future EMU members, then interest rate spreads, and in particular credit spreads, could change to become more in line with those currently observed on the foreign-currency-denominated debt of these countries. This could amount to a downgrading of asset quality for those countries.[28] If EMU members redenominated all outstanding debt into euros, the share of foreign currency debt would then increase from current levels to 100 percent (Table 51). In this scenario, spreads could increase above those observed on the relatively small stocks of foreign currency debt presently outstanding.[29] Counteracting some of this pressure for spreads to rise would be the improved fiscal positions of several countries to meet the Maastricht criteria and the stability pact.

There are other factors that would influence credit spreads. Although the "no-bailout" clause in the

---

[28]Standard & Poor's has already indicated that it will initially award each country's euro-denominated debt the rating currently applied to foreign-currency-denominated debt and that European companies will be able to obtain ratings higher than those of their own governments; Moody's will adopt a case-by-case approach.

[29]See Drudi and Prati (1997).

Table 50. European Union: Ratings of Foreign and Local Currency Debt of Sovereign Governments, May 29, 1997

| | Foreign Currency | | | | | | Local Currency | | |
| | IBCA | | S&P | | Moody's | | IBCA | S&P | Moody's |
	Long-term	Short-term	Long-term	Short-term	Long-term	Short-term	long-term	long-term	long-term
European Union countries									
Austria	AAA	A1+	AAA	A-1+	Aaa	P-1	AAA	AAA	
Belgium	AA+	A1+	AA+	A-1+	Aa1	P-1	AAA	AAA	
Denmark	AA+	A1+	AA+	A-1+	Aa1	P-1	AAA	AAA	Aaa
Finland	AA+	A1+	AA	A-1+	Aa1	P-1	AAA	AAA	Aaa
France	AAA	A1+	AAA	A-1+	Aaa	P-1	AAA	AAA	Aaa
Germany	AAA	A1+	AAA	A-1+	Aaa	P-1	AAA	AAA	Aaa
Greece	BBB–	A3	BBB–	A-3	Baa1	P-2		A–	
Ireland	AA+	A1+	AA	A-1+	Aa1	P-1	AAA	AAA	Aaa
Italy	AA–	A1+	AA	A-1+	Aa3	P-1	AAA	AAA	Aa3
Luxembourg	AAA	A1+	AAA	A-1+	Aaa	P-1	AAA	AAA	
Netherlands	AAA	A1+	AAA	A-1+	Aaa	P-1	AAA	AAA	Aaa
Portugal	AA–	A1+	AA–	A-1+	Aa3	P-1	AAA	AAA	Aa2
Spain	AA	A1+	AA	A-1+	Aa2	P-1	AAA	AAA	Aa2
Sweden	AA–	A1+	AA+	A-1+	Aa3	P-1	AAA	AAA	
United Kingdom	AAA	A1+	AAA	A-1+	Aaa	P-1	AAA	AAA	Aaa
Memorandum items:									
North America									
Canada	AA	A1+	AA+	A-1+	Aa2	P-1	AAA	AAA	Aa1
Mexico	BB	B	BB	B	Ba2	NP		BBB+	
United States	AAA	A1+	AAA	A-1+	Aaa	P-1	AAA	AAA	Aaa
Japan	AAA	A1+	AAA	A-1+	Aaa	P-1	AAA	AAA	Aaa

Sources: Bloomberg Financial Markets L.P.; IBCA Ltd.; Moody's Investors Service; and Standard & Poor's.

Maastricht Treaty rules out the possibility of direct EU assistance to individual EMU member countries, it is unlikely that market participants will price sovereign debt as if it were corporate debt.[30] The mere size of public debt outstanding in any potential EMU member country relative to any single corporate issuer would imply significant systemic implications of an involuntary restructuring or an outright default by an EMU member country. This would increase the pressure to find alternative solutions.

From a pricing perspective, credit risk will become the most important risk and will make up the largest part of the remaining interest rate spreads among EMU issuers after the introduction of the euro. Unfortunately, there is no unambiguous guide to the likely levels or dispersion of sovereign credit spreads in EMU. One way of estimating credit spreads is to compare interest rates on sovereign debt issues that trade in a common currency. Among the potential EMU member countries that have issued dollar-denominated debt, as of June 1997, spreads between 10-year dollar

issues trading in domestic markets and comparable U.S. treasury issues ranged from a low of 23 basis points for Austria to a high of 30 basis points for Italy and Spain (Table 52).[31] Spreads on five-year issues ranged between a low of 6 basis points for Austria and a high of 12 basis points for Italy. Although it is difficult to assess whether these spreads are "high" or "low," it would appear that they are probably reflecting a good deal of market optimism about the prospects for a successful EMU and about the adjustments made in some countries.

Another rough benchmark of credit spreads is the pricing of debt issued by the separate legal entities making up the separate states of the United States and of the provinces of Canada. In the case of the United States, a sample of municipal bonds issued by traders over the period 1973–90 indicates that the largest spread during the 28-year period was 146 basis points; the mean of the spread was 32.4 basis points with a standard deviation of 24.8 basis points.[32] The sample also reveals that in December 1989, the last date in the sample, the maximum difference in spreads on 20-year general obligations issues of 41

---

[30]The "no-bailout" clause—Article 104b of the Maastricht Treaty—states that "the Community shall not be liable for or assume the commitments of Central Governments, regional or local authorities, public authorities, other bodies governed by public law, or public undertakings of any Member State, without prejudice to mutual financial guarantees for the joint execution of a specific project." The same provision applies to individual EU countries.

[31]One problem with using this method for estimating credit spreads is that the spreads may also reflect the market's assessment of other factors including liquidity, tax differences, name recognition, and investor preferences.

[32]See the analysis in Bayoumi, Goldstein, and Woglom (1995).

Table 51. European Union Countries, North America, and Japan: Foreign Currency Debt, 1996

(In percent of total government debt)

	Foreign Currency Debt	Year[1]
European Union countries		
Austria	17.5	1996
Belgium	11.4	1995
Denmark	14.9	1996
Finland	42.9	1996[2]
France	4.8	1995
Germany	0.1	1995
Greece	30.6	1996
Ireland	26.4	1996
Italy	6.1	1996
Luxembourg	3.5	1995
Netherlands	0.0	1996
Portugal	17.7	1996
Spain	7.3	1996
Sweden	28.2	1996
United Kingdom	4.6	1996
North America		
Canada	2.6	1996[3]
Mexico	89.0	1996
United States	0.0	1996
Japan	0.0	1996

Source: International Monetary Fund.
[1]Year for which the latest data are available.
[2]For central government.
[3]Data as of March 31, 1997, for the federal government.

U.S. states was 84 basis points. Regarding the Canadian provinces, a much more limited sample suggests that spreads over Canadian federal issues ranged from 36 basis points for Ontario to 78 basis points for Quebec (Table 53).[33]

Yet a third indication is the pricing of European corporate debt. If EMU member countries maintain their sovereign ratings of AAA, it is reasonable to expect that credit spreads between EMU member country issuers would be in the range of Standard & Poor's triple-A-rated corporate issuers. As of February 1997, spreads for five triple-A-rated corporate issues were in the range of between 10 and 45 basis points above their respective domestic benchmarks.[34]

Overall, it should be expected that there would be a convergence of interest rates on sovereign debt issued—and outstanding—by EMU member countries. Whether or not all of these issues trade at identical spreads will be determined by the market. To the extent that spreads remain, market segments will be identifiable. How much of an impact this will have on market liquidity remains to be seen.

The plan to introduce the euro has reopened the competition among European sovereign issuers for providing EMU with the *benchmark yield curve* for pricing other sovereign issues and private debt issues. This renewed competition is likely to increase the potential for further desegmentation of national debt markets. From an investor's point of view, the benchmark issue offers the highest return possible on what is deemed to be a "safe" investment. Such issues are usually high in volume, extremely liquid, and associated with various hedging instruments, with the added advantage of low bid-ask spreads. Benchmark issues are also used widely in repo markets and are typically usable as collateral for a wide range of other financial contracts. From the issuer's point of view, the key advantage is that the yield is the lowest possible for that particular market segment; the added liquidity also provides easy access to a wide investor base for issuance. Thus, the importance of benchmark status is that it provides access to the lowest-cost financing in a liquid market.

---

[33]See Salomon Brothers (1996).

[34]This range is from a sample of five Standard & Poor's triple-A-rated corporate issues with maturities in the 8- to 10-year range: Bayerische Vereinsbank in Germany (14 basis points), Rabobank in the Netherlands (19 basis points), British Telecom in the United Kingdom (42 basis points), Credit Local in France (45 basis points), and Unilever in the Netherlands (11 basis points).

Table 52. Estimates of Credit Spreads of EU Sovereigns, September 1996 and June 1997

(U.S. dollar spreads over treasuries in basis points)

	Three-Year Dollar Issues		Five-Year Dollar Issues		Ten-Year Dollar Issues	
	September 1996	June 1997	September 1996	June 1997	September 1996	June 1997
Austria	+4	−3	+10	+6	+24	+23
Belgium	+6	+5	+15	+9	+28	+26
Denmark	+6	+5	+13	+8	+27	+26
Finland	+6	+6	+16	+10	+30	+29
Ireland	+5	−6	+11	+9	+25	+25
Italy	+10	+9	+22	+12	+34	+30
Spain	+8	+8	+19	+11	+32	+30
Sweden	+8	+6	+17	+10	+27	+28

Source: Paribas, London.

Table 53. Interest Rate Spreads of Canadian Provinces

Province	Rating	Coupon (In percent)	Maturity	Indicative Bid-Side Spreads (In basis points) Dec. 30, 1996	May 23, 1997	Change
U.S. dollar issues						
Ontario	Aa3/AA−	6.000	Feb. 21, 2006	38	36	−2
Quebec	A2/A+	6.500	Jan. 17, 2006	58	58	0
Quebec	A2/A+	7.500	July 15, 2023	83	83	0
Saskatchewan	A3/A−	8.500	July 15, 2022	59	63	+4
				July 29, 1996		
Canadian dollar issues						
British Columbia	AA+/Aa1	. . .	5 years	6		
Newfoundland	Baa1	. . .	5 years	27		
Alberta	Aa2/AA	. . .	10 years	7		
Nova Scotia	A	. . .	10 years	28		

Sources: Goldman Sachs International, *Fixed Income Research: Corporate Bond Monthly* (June 1997), p. 41; and SBC Warburg (1996), p. 62.

The main candidates for benchmark status are German and French instruments, and it would appear that France possesses several technical advantages (Table 54).[35] First, the French sovereign market is widely seen to be very liquid because relatively larger issues are more evenly distributed across the maturity spectrum to generate a smooth yield curve. Second, French markets are supported by a transparent and liquid market for repurchase agreements; the bulk of deutsche mark repo trading is located offshore, mainly in London, mostly as a result of reserve requirements. These requirements have been lifted and so this French advantage will soon be lost. Third, France has already developed a strip market—which can be used to recalculate the exact value of each security on issue. Fourth, the French auction schedule has been for some time very regular and predictable, with the French Treasury announcing its plans at the beginning of the year. Finally, the French government has already announced its intentions to redenominate in euros the outstanding stock of debt on January 1, 1999. Although French paper is well placed to provide the benchmark yield curve for euro markets, all these advantages could be matched by other markets if measures are taken by other countries, and in particular by Germany, before the euro is introduced.

The "critical mass" approach requires that, starting in 1999, all new issues of government bonds and bills (at least those traded on the secondary market and expiring after the end of 2001) will have to be denominated in euros.[36] Countries have the option to redenominate their outstanding stock of debt in euros as of January 1, 1999. The coexistence of new euro-denominated bonds and old national currency bonds issued by the same government could segment the newly created euro market for government securities and reduce its relative liquidity. In addition to France, Belgium has also announced its intention to redenominate debt on January 1, 1999; Germany is in the process of deciding.[37]

Prospects for a European Corporate Bond Market

EU financial market legislation and the rapid development of the fund management industry have begun to chip away at long-standing regulatory and tax impediments to the development of European corporate debt markets. These markets have remained relatively small, however. Although outstanding debt securities issued by EU private entities totaled about $4 trillion (about 87 percent of the size of the U.S. corporate debt market), about 25 percent of this total was issued in international markets, of which about $268 billion were issued by nonfinancial entities. Domestic issuance in 1995 was also low compared with other, more highly developed markets: German firms issued only $0.142 billion and French firms only $6.4 billion, whereas U.K. firms issued $20.7 billion, Japanese firms $77.2 billion, and U.S. firms $154.3 billion (Table 55).[38]

---

[35]Another possibility is that the euro benchmark yield curve will be based on swap yields. Swap markets in EMU could become extremely liquid because all interest rate swap contracts, which are currently segmented by currency, will become perfectly fungible and will be unaffected by the credit standing of governments. If the ECB issues short-term paper, ECB "debt certificates," it is likely to become a benchmark for very short dated paper.

[36]See European Commission (1995).

[37]Debt redenomination creates a number of technical problems: not all public debt is dematerialized; there are different numerical trading and clearing conventions. Price display systems will have to adapt to show national currency and euro pricing for the same bonds. See Bank of England (1996) for a discussion of some of these technical problems.

[38]This figure for the United Kingdom refers to international bond issues as well because the domestic corporate bond market in the United Kingdom has become inseparable from the Euromarket.

Table 54. Euro Benchmark Yield Curve: Germany vs. France

Germany		France	
Instruments			
BUBILLs	Six-month maturity only; issue size is up to ECU 3.2 billion	BTFs	Maturities (every Thursday) up to one year; issue size averages ECU 2.8 billion
SCHATZ	Two-year maturity; first issue was ECU 5.2 billion	BTANs	Usually two- and five-year maturities; average size is ECU 8–11 billion
OBLs	Five-year maturity; issue size ECU 4.2–6.8 billion	OATs	Maturity of up to 30 years; average size issue is ECU 15.5–17 billion
Bunds	Ten- and 30-year maturity; issue size ECU 5.2–13 billion	TEC10	Floating-rate OAT
Treasury notes	Issuing ceased in mid-1995	Treasury bonds	No longer issued
Treuhand notes	Issued in 1993 and 1994 only; maturity was five years	Strips	Available every six months; available from 0 to 30 years

Issuing Procedure

The Federal Bond Consortium operates under the lead management of the Bundesbank. It has the characteristics of an underwriting and placing syndicate. Since 1992, membership has been open to foreign firms' legally dependent branches in Germany. At end-1995, there were 95 institutions in the consortium, including 48 foreign-owned banks.

Since August 1990 the majority of federal bonds have been issued by a combined method: one part via the syndicate and another by tender. In the case of Bunds and OBLs a portion of the issue amount is set aside for market management operations by the Bundesbank and subsequently sold in stages through the stock exchange.

An auction schedule is published roughly two weeks before the beginning of each quarter. The 2-year and 5-year bonds are now issued on a regular quarterly schedule. However, the issuing calendar 10-year and more so 30-year paper remains the focus for speculation. In addition, while issue size has been increased, liquidity across the yield curve varies considerably.

Primary dealer system, which numbers 20 members (7 foreigners). These are required to stimulate the secondary market, inform the French Treasury about market developments, and take active part in tenders. Any financial institution may apply for and receive primary dealer status after a brief period of observation as a reporting dealer. The advantages of becoming a primary dealer are (1) access to tenders; (2) noncompetitive bids, enabling the purchase of more securities at the marginal price at the tender; (3) the authorization to strip and reconstitute OATs; and (4) the ability to market their trading status to clients.

The French Treasury states its issuing plans in BTANs and OATs at the beginning of the year.

Almost all national negotiable debt is issued through tenders, Dutch style.

The issuing agenda is very regular: BTFs on Monday; OAT tenders on the first Thursday of each month, usually including a 10-year security; monthly BTAN tenders, usually on the 2-year and 5-year benchmarks. Issue amounts are set two days before the tender after consultation with the primary dealers.

Strips Market

On June 13, 1996, the Bundesbank announced plans to introduce the separation and separate trading of principal and interest for particular 10- and 30-year federal bonds during the course of 1997.

Since 1991, all OATs maturing on April 25 and October 25 (13 bonds in total) can be stripped. There is a principal certificate type for each strippable bond, but all coupon certificates with the same maturity are fungible, making it possible to rebuild OATs with coupons from another line. The amount that has been effectively stripped represents 17 percent of the strippable bond total and 4.75 percent of the total French franc debt (whereas U.S. strips are 25 percent and 4.35 percent respectively).

Repurchase Market

The deutsche mark repo market is hindered by two key factors: (1) the absence of a government-approved universal repo agreement; and (2) the fact that many domestic institutions do not make their bond holdings available for lending. This has meant the bulk of DM repos are traded offshore, mainly in London.

The French franc repo market, whose development has followed the model of the U.S., is by far the most sophisticated in Europe. The French Treasury initiated a legally binding repo agreement that forms the basis of the market's functioning. The market is very transparent and liquid, with 20 primary dealers being required to post prices on Reuters from which any institution can trade.

Source: Paribas.

The introduction of the euro is likely to accelerate the development of corporate bond markets, especially if the increased focus on credit risk in the EMU sovereign markets enhances the European institutions' expertise in assessing credit risk. First, as noted earlier, a single currency provides incentives for the creation of a much larger effective European institutional investor base. The increasingly yield-conscious be-

Table 55. Funds Raised in Capital Markets by Nonfinancial Enterprises in Selected Industrial Countries, 1990–95

(In percent of total)

	Bonds[1]	Shares	Others[2]	Total
European Union countries				
Italy	−0.68	25.55	75.13	100.00
Netherlands	1.17	42.19	56.65	100.00
Spain	1.71	29.27	69.02	100.00
Sweden	−0.88	33.73	67.15	100.00
Canada	7.14	27.91	64.95	100.00
United States	50.94	13.22	35.84	100.00
Japan	5.48	11.38	83.14	100.00

Source: Organization for Economic Cooperation and Development, *Financial Statistics, Part III: Nonfinancial Enterprises Financial Statements* (1995).

[1]Data for short-term bonds are not available for Italy, the Netherlands, and Japan.

[2]Residual including bank financing.

havior of European investors, and the coincident growth in fund management in Europe, has expanded the investor base for corporate debt securities—EU mutual funds now manage close to $1.4 trillion (see Table 48).

Although the credit risk culture has yet to take off in Europe the way it has in the United States, even a moderate shift will have a significant impact on international capital markets. For example, if the degree of disintermediation in EU countries was to close the securitization gap (adjusted for economic size) with the United States by 25 percent, this would unleash capital flows equal to roughly $2 trillion into international capital markets. This is roughly half the size of the entire market capitalization of EU or Japanese equity markets.

Second, EU firms have begun to show an increased desire to tap debt securities markets. An important factor spurring firms to issue debt securities is that European firms are beginning to adopt increasingly sophisticated, value-maximizing corporate financial policies. However, the underdevelopment of domestic corporate debt securities markets has presented an obstacle to firms wishing to issue debt securities. Although this obstacle has been circumvented to some degree by tapping the international securities markets, there are significant additional obstacles to accessing the international markets for all but the largest, "brand-name" firms.

While there are reasons for optimism about the development of a Europe-wide corporate debt market, it will most likely not occur quickly. The remaining impediments to the development of these markets fall into two categories: excessive regulation and the narrow institutional investor base. Excessive regulatory burdens have simply prevented these markets from

developing in some countries. For example, tax policy and issuance requirements prevented the development of commercial paper and bond markets in Germany until very recently. More generally, regulators in virtually all EU countries have discouraged issuance of lower-grade corporate debt securities. Regarding institutional investors, corporate debt securities are often highly heterogeneous across issuers as well as across issues (by the same issuer), so the costs involved in evaluating their currency risk, credit risk, and legal risk—contract terms, such as covenants—effectively means that these markets will be successful only if there is a large institutional investor base. Smaller issuers, small issues, and firms in smaller countries—in which currency risk figures more prominently for foreign investors—therefore may face a limited investor base.[39]

Equity Markets

The introduction of the euro is likely to accelerate the processes of competition, consolidation, and technological innovation that have characterized equity markets in recent years. In the second half of the 1980s, the London Stock Exchange attracted an increasing share of turnover in continental equities by creating a screen-based dealer market for non-U.K. stocks called SEAQ International (SEAQ-I) separate from the London dealer market. During this period, competition among the European exchanges was fierce. Since the early 1990s, continental exchanges have recouped a substantial share of trading with new electronic continuous auction markets, particularly the CAC in Paris and IBIS in Frankfurt, and SEAQ-I has declined in importance as an organized exchange. Nevertheless, London dealers are still the primary source of liquidity for large block transactions and for program trading in a significant number of continental stocks, even though they engage in considerably less customer dealing in continental equities, and considerably more brokering through the continental bourses.[40] Thus, since the introduction of continuous electronic trading on the continent, London dealers have taken a smaller proportion of orders on their own books and have worked orders mostly through the continental markets. As such, the activity of London dealers is reinforcing the liquidity of auction markets, and the London-based dealer market and the continental-based auction markets are simultaneously com-

---

[39]See Smith (1995). The importance of this heterogeneity of corporate debt securities is illustrated by the dominant role played by institutional investors in the most developed corporate debt securities market, the U.S. market: at end-1995, 72 percent of the stock of corporate bonds were held by domestic institutional investors, 7 percent by foreign investors, and 14 percent by households. Insurance companies were the largest single investor, holding 35 percent; public and private pension funds held 16 percent; and mutual funds, 8 percent.

[40]See Pagano (1996).

peting and interdependent. Currently, London is by far the dominant equity market in Europe in terms of companies listed, market capitalization, and turnover (Table 56). On the continent, Frankfurt and Paris have the largest exchanges, with a similar number of listed companies and capitalization. All other exchanges are significantly smaller.

Together with ongoing pressures from computerization and the implementation of the EU Investment Services Directive, the introduction of the euro will provide strong incentives for concentration among the European exchanges.[41] The euro will eliminate differences in the continental electronic trading systems and make them virtually identical. The most likely development is that a Europe-wide equity market for blue-chip stocks will emerge into a single electronic exchange with a screen-based automated order-driven trading system, like IBIS. This will be possible only if the trading costs of this system will remain competitive vis-à-vis those of proprietary trading systems. National bourses may survive by specializing in trading low-capitalization companies. While there are incentives for this kind of trading to concentrate in a pan-European electronic trading platform, local custody, settlement, and tax systems may allow for local trading to continue. Overall, EMU is likely to further increase cross-border equity trading and to enhance both the integration of national markets and overall market liquidity.

Also uncertain is EMU's impact on competition between auction and dealer systems. If EMU enhances market efficiency and reduces equilibrium equity prices and spurious price volatility, then execution risk will diminish and immediacy will become less important. This implies that dealer markets, where investors pay a premium for immediacy in terms of higher bid-ask spreads, will experience competitive pressures from auction-agency markets, where increased liquidity will reduce execution risk. In addition, to the extent that EMU will increase cross-border asset holding and trading, counterparty risk could increase or become more difficult to assess. This will also put dealer markets at a disadvantage, because dealers would have to raise bid-ask spreads to compensate for the higher counterparty risk. By contrast, auction-agency markets usually pool this risk.[42]

There are remaining impediments that could slow down consolidation. Some provisions of the Investment Services Directive—the concentration provision and the concept of "regulated market"—leave scope for "protectionism" on behalf of national stock ex-

changes (see the appendix at the end of this annex). Differences in accounting can also prevent institutional investors from purchasing stocks of certain countries. Finally, clearance and settlement procedures can affect equity trading by increasing transaction costs, which could be reduced through centralization of clearance and settlement services in a single European central securities depository (CSD), the so-called Euro-hub.[43]

Derivative Markets

The euro will affect derivative markets in two ways: several contracts will disappear or consolidate into a single contract; and a smaller number of contracts will increase the competition among European derivative exchanges. With the establishment of EMU and only euro interest rates, nearly 200 contracts involving 13 different currencies are likely to disappear. How the associated reduction in diversity will affect the 16 European futures and options exchanges is an open question. Initiatives are likely to emerge among the smaller exchanges to establish technical linkages and common settlement procedures. This will confine the race for post-EMU supremacy in derivative contracts to Europe's big three exchanges: the London International Financial Futures Exchange (LIFFE), Europe's biggest derivatives exchange, followed by the Deutsche Terminbörse (DTB), and Marché à Terme International de France (MATIF). In light of their specialization in interest rate contracts, LIFFE and MATIF are likely to be most affected by EMU.[44] Competition among the exchanges will also be affected by the development of electronic trading. DTB will be able to capitalize on its technological prominence with a fully electronic order-driven system with almost one-third of its members trading from workstations outside Germany. Both LIFFE and MATIF have maintained an open outcry structure. While LIFFE already has an electronic capability, MATIF is likely to be seriously handicapped by the failure in the summer of 1996 to finalize a link with DTB.

Other factors could also play a role. LIFFE's leading position may be damaged if the United Kingdom is not included in EMU and if access to TARGET and intraday liquidity is limited. DTB might gain a competitive edge from being located in Frankfurt. MATIF could benefit from the fact that the French govern-

---

[41]The ISD may facilitate cross-border branching of trading systems and remote trading. Article 15.4 favors remote membership: exchanges designated as "regulated markets" no longer require approval from EU states in which they want to establish as remote members.

[42]A dealer market might still be preferred because some traders may want to remain anonymous, which is usually not possible in the very transparent continental markets.

[43]There are five mechanisms for cross-border trades: (1) direct access to the home country CSD; (2) indirect access through local members; (3) indirect access through global custodians; (4) international CSDs; and (5) local-CSD-to-local CSD. The second and third methods are most widely used. See Giddy, Sauders, and Walter (1996).

[44]LIFFE derives half of its volume from short-term German Bund and interest rate futures and options, while 90 percent of trading on MATIF is in French notional bond and short-term interest rate contracts. Two-thirds of DTB's volume comes from stock index futures and options. Foreign exchange contracts are mainly traded in the highly liquid interbank market.

Table 56. European Union Countries, United States, and Japan: Equity Markets, 1996

| | Listed Companies (In units) | | Domestic Market Capitalization | | Annual Turnover | | | | | | Domestic (In percent of GDP) |
| | | | | | (In millions of ECUs) | | | (In percent of EU total) | | | |
	Domestic	Foreign	(In millions of ECUs)	(In percent of GDP)	Domestic	Foreign	Total	Domestic	Foreign	Total	
Markets in EU countries											
Amsterdam	217	216	302,452	96.10	149,587	653	150,241	8.96	0.11	6.58	47.53
Athens	217	0	18,988	19.64	5,695	0	5,695	0.34	0.00	0.25	5.89
Brussels	146	145	95,752	45.40	17,849	2,914	20,763	1.07	0.47	0.91	8.46
Copenhagen	237	12	57,281	41.46	29,111	698	29,810	1.74	0.11	1.31	21.07
Dublin	61	10	27,659	52.29	4,711	3	4,714	0.28	0.00	0.21	8.91
Germany	681	1290	531,553	28.34	621,454	18,778	640,231	37.22	3.06	28.04	33.13
Helsinki	71	0	49,444	50.41	17,538	0	17,538	1.05	0.00	0.77	17.88
Lisbon	158	0	19,706	23.40	5,658	0	5,658	0.34	0.00	0.25	6.72
London	557	833	1,368,000	153.61	335,644	580,777	916,421	20.10	94.59	40.13	37.69
Luxembourg	54	224·	25,910	164.53	604	17	620	0.04	0.00	0.03	3.83
Madrid	357	4	194,681	42.25	63,869	18	63,888	3.83	0.00	2.80	13.86
Milan	244	4	206,997	21.79	82,532	18	82,551	4.94	0.00	3.61	8.69
Paris	686	187	472,426	38.48	220,608	4,828	225,436	13.21	0.79	9.87	17.97
Stockholm	217	12	194,045	97.42	106,434	5,021	111,455	6.37	0.82	4.88	53.44
Vienna	94	35	25,719	14.16	8,265	281	8,546	0.50	0.05	0.37	4.55
EU total	3,997	2,972	3,590,614	52.83	1,669,560	614,006	2,283,566	100.00	100.00	100.00	24.56
Other markets											
New York	2,617	290	5,395,889	90.23	3,014,383	190,392	3,204,775	n.a.	n.a.	n.a.	50.41
NASDAQ	5,138	418	1,192,290	19.94	2,505,177	98,767	2,603,944	n.a.	n.a.	n.a.	41.89
Tokyo	1,766	67	2,374,733	64.88	738,711	1,214	739,925	n.a.	n.a.	n.a.	20.18

Sources: Federation of European Stock Exchanges; Federation of International Stock Exchanges; NASDAQ; New York Stock Exchange; and Tokyo Stock Exchange.

ment has been actively issuing ECU-denominated debt since 1989 and is the leading sovereign borrower in ECU. Experience in the ECU bond market suggests that where the active cash market resides, the futures business is likely to follow. In addition, some consider MATIF the best-placed exchange to trade the future euro benchmarks, since a smooth transition from the French franc to the euro could be ensured by enhancing the liquidity of existing contracts. Smaller exchanges in core euro countries (Belgium and the Netherlands) will be the first to see business decline, followed by the exchanges in peripheral countries (Italy and Spain). The likely outcome is that these exchanges will offer a smaller range of equity-based local contracts.

The most direct impact of EMU on the *structure of derivative contracts* will be the elimination of currency derivatives between the currencies of countries joining EMU. If EMU begins with core ERM countries, the negative impact on trading volumes will be muted, because trading in intra-core currency derivatives is relatively limited. Higher-volume contracts between core and non-core currencies will simply change into contracts between the euro and non-core currencies: for example, deutsche mark–lira contracts will simply become euro-lira contracts. The high-volume contracts between dollars, yen, and deutsche mark–bloc currencies will be little affected by the euro substituting for European currencies. If EMU enhances trading within, and capital flows to, the euro area, the demand for currency derivatives could increase. Activity in the European derivative markets may also increase during 1997–98 and 1999–2002 as foreign exchange and interest rate options are used to hedge risk in the transitional periods.

With the creation of EMU, the market for *interest rate swaps* will become larger and more liquid, as contracts of participating currencies become perfectly fungible. Enhanced liquidity is also likely to increase the use of swaps outside the banking sector. EMU will also boost the demand for options contracts on interest rate spreads and allow investors to hedge credit risk spreads between bonds of high-debt countries and the euro benchmark. Contracts based on interest rate spreads may also develop for private debt securities.

For *bond market futures,* it is difficult to know whether the market will demand a futures contract for each national bond, or whether a generic contract will emerge. The answer will depend on the volatility of credit spreads between the various national issues. If the spreads are stable, the low basis risk could lead the market to develop a single liquid 10-year futures contract similar to the U.S. treasury bond future. Otherwise, there could be a range of futures contracts with one for each national benchmark issue. The selection of deliverable bonds will also be crucial. If two or more national bonds are deliverable for a generic bond futures contract, the contract could favor the cheapest bond to deliver and create liquidity in that bond at the expense of higher-quality bonds. Basket-type euro futures contracts are unlikely to emerge because derivative exchanges would like to avoid repeating the experience of LIFFE with 10-year ECU futures contracts between 1990 and 1991. At that time, LIFFE's basket of deliverable bonds included ECU OATS, European Investment Bank bonds, U.K. gilts, and Italian government bonds. While all bonds in principle had the same rating, there was in practice always one that was cheaper to deliver. In effect, LIFFE's contract turned out to be an inadequate hedging tool.

Structural Implications for Banking Systems

EU Banking System

Combined, the banking systems of EU countries would form the largest banking system in the world, with more than 40 percent of world banking assets.[45] The total banking assets of France and Germany alone would be a third larger than those of the United States; those of the four larger countries (Germany, France, the United Kingdom, and Italy) would be two times larger; and those of all EU countries would be almost three times larger (Table 13).[46]

Reflecting the predominant role of bank-intermediated credit in continental Europe, the EU banking system would also be large in relation to the EU economy: in 1994, the ratio of banking assets to GDP was 176 percent in the EU against 69 percent in the United States. This ratio, in sharp contrast with the declining trends of the United States and Japan, has grown at an average rate of more than 3 percent a year in the period 1989–94.[47] Such growth suggests that in recent years the disintermediation trend in the European Union has not been as severe as the one in the United States. This is confirmed by the stable or growing ratio of households' deposits to personal disposable income observed since 1989 in the larger EU countries. (Among the 15 EU countries, in the period 1989–94, the ratio of banking assets to GDP has declined only in Denmark, Sweden, and Austria.) Moreover, in the larger countries, the share of deposits in total household financial assets has declined at a much slower pace than in the United States.[48]

In terms of employment, the EU banking sector is almost 50 percent larger than the U.S. sector, reaching

---

[45]See Barth, Nolle, and Rice (1997), Table 1.

[46]The United States is a valid benchmark because it has experienced a first wave of bank restructuring and technological innovations and because its GDP is only marginally smaller than that of the EU-15.

[47]See Kneeshaw (1995).

[48]See Bianco, Gerali, and Massaro (1996).

Figure 55. Labor Costs and Productivity in Banking, 1994

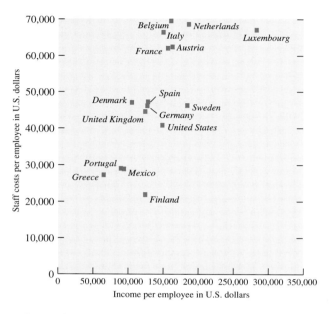

Source: Organization for Economic Cooperation and Development (OECD), *Bank Profitability: Financial Statements of Banks 1985–1995* (Paris: OECD, 1996).

a total of about 2.5 million employees. Although the larger banking sector of the EU could partly account for the higher employment, high staff costs per employee in relation to productivity suggest that many EU banking systems are overstaffed (Figure 55). Indeed, employment has already declined considerably since the late 1980s, especially in Nordic countries and the United Kingdom.[49]

Ownership and Types of Banks

The ownership structure of banks varies considerably across the European Union. The share of banking assets publicly owned ranges from zero in the United Kingdom to almost 60 percent in Italy.[50] Among the larger EU countries, public ownership is widespread in Germany (about 50 percent of banking assets), whereas it has considerably diminished in France (12 percent) after the wave of privatizations of the last decade. Among the smaller EU countries, ownership tends to be public in Greece and Portugal, and private in Belgium and the Netherlands.

---

[49]See BIS (1996a), p. 88.

[50]In Italy, state and local authorities controlled about 58 percent of banking assets at the beginning of 1997. This share is, however, bound to fall by an estimated 15 percent when the privatizations of Instituto Bancario San Paolo di Torino and Cariplo are completed.

In some countries, complicated public ownership structures are an additional obstacle to privatization and the restructuring of banking systems. In Germany, for example, savings banks (*Sparkassen*) carry as capital a guarantee from local municipalities, which makes it difficult for them to merge or be purchased by a shareholding company. In response to a complaint by private German banks, the European Union is currently considering whether German public-law banks (*Sparkassen* and *Landesbanken*) have an unfair competitive advantage deriving from subsidized public capital injections.

A complicated public ownership structure is also typical of the Italian banking system. Italian public banks became joint-stock corporations at the beginning of the 1990s, but many of them have remained controlled by nonprofit organizations (*fondazioni*), whose boards of trustees are appointed by local and central governments. The need to obtain the approval of both levels of government has often delayed privatization. Parliament is currently discussing a bill that introduces a number of incentives for *fondazioni* to sell off their assets, although it leaves a large degree of discretion regarding the timing and scope of the sale.

Market participants have problems monitoring and controlling banking institutions even in EU countries where private ownership prevails. This difficulty results from the lack of public disclosure on several financial activities of EU banks and from the lack of concentration of debt and equity claims, which is typical of most banking systems in the European Union. Weak corporate control is a source of concern because it may provide inadequate incentives to management and delay restructuring.[51]

There is also a considerable diversity of banking structures across the European Union in terms of domestic versus foreign ownership. Among the larger EU countries, the share of banking assets controlled by foreign banks ranges from 3.5 percent in Italy to 57 percent in the United Kingdom, and it is 14 percent in France, 4.5 percent in Germany, and 12 percent in Spain. Among the smaller EU countries, foreign banks have a particularly strong presence only in Luxembourg, Belgium, and Ireland.

The typology of EU banks varies considerably. Commercial banks prevail in Italy, France, Greece, Portugal, the United Kingdom, Belgium, and the Netherlands. Savings and cooperative banks play an important role in Germany, Italy, and Spain, and building societies have a large presence in the United Kingdom and Ireland. Whereas the number of banks in the latter categories has considerably declined over the last decade, the number of commercial banks has generally increased. The significance of these changes, however, should not be overemphasized be-

---

[51]See, for example, BIS (1996a).

Table 57. Bank Restructuring: Number of Institutions and Size Concentration[1]

		Number of Institutions			Concentration: Top Five		
		Peak (since 1980)					
	1995[2]		Year	Percent change[5]	1980[3]	1990	1995[4]
					(Percent share in total assets)		
European Union countries							
Belgium	150	163	1992	−8	64	58	59
Finland	352	631	1985	−44	63	65	74
France	593	1,033	1984	−43	57	52	47
Germany[6]	3,487	5,355	1980	−35			17
Italy	941	1,109	1987	−15	26	24	29
Netherlands	174	200	1980	−13	73	77	81
Spain[7]	318	378	1982	−16	38	38	49
Sweden	112	598	1980	−81	64	70	86
United Kingdom	560	796	1983	−30	63	58	57
United States[8]	23,854	35,875	1980	−34	9	9	13
Japan	571	618	1980	−8	25	30	27
Other countries							
Canada	1,030	1,671	1984	−38		55	65
Australia	370	812	1980	−54	62	65	67
Norway	148	346	1980	−57	63	68	58
Switzerland	415	499	1990	−17	45	45	50

Sources: Bank for International Settlements (1996a); British Bankers' Association; Building Societies Association; and national data.

[1]Deposit-taking institutions, generally including commercial, savings, and various types of mutual and cooperative banks; for Japan, excluding various types of credit cooperatives; and for Canada, excluding trust and loan companies (in 1994, 83 institutions).

[2]For Finland, Japan, and Sweden, 1994.

[3]For Finland and the Netherlands, 1985; France, 1986; Italy, 1983; and Switzerland, 1987.

[4]For Belgium, Japan, Switzerland, and the United Kingdom, 1994; and Finland, 1993.

[5]From peak to most recent observation where applicable.

[6]For number of institutions, western Germany only. Data for the whole of Germany: 1995, 3,784; percentage change, −30 percent.

[7]Concentration data for commercial and savings banks only.

[8]Excluding credit unions: 1995, 12,067; percentage change, −36 percent.

cause the operational differences between commercial banks and other types of institutions have been gradually diminishing.

In relation to North America and Japan, some continental European banks have had traditionally wider powers in terms of permissible activities and ownership ("universal" banks). The Second Banking Directive has recently created the conditions for extending similar powers to all EU banks, although the range of permissible activities across the EMU is far from being harmonized (see the first section of this annex). Following the implementation of the directive, banks have been allowed to enter the capital markets business in France, Italy, Spain, Greece, and Portugal. Moreover, in recent years, banks have considerably increased their presence in the insurance sector.[52] These trends, together with the expanding role of wholesale activities, have resulted in a growing ratio of noninterest income to gross income in almost all EU countries.

Financial Structure

EU financial markets are overbanked at the retail and local levels. Although the number of banking institutions in the European Union is substantially smaller than in the United States (Table 57), the number of branches is much larger, with an average population per branch in 1994 of 2,084 against 4,690 in the United States (Table 58). The population per branch ranges from 600 in Belgium to 8,384 in Greece and is below average in Germany, Spain, Austria, and Luxembourg. No uniform trend emerges across Europe except for the United Kingdom and some Nordic countries (Finland, Sweden, and Denmark), which have been reducing the density of their branches since 1985.

In recent years, the concentration of the banking system, measured by the share of total assets owned by the top 5 (or 10) institutions, has not shown a uniform trend in spite of an EU-wide reduction in the number of banks (Table 57). In the largest countries, with the exception of France, concentration has either remained unchanged or increased, suggesting an increase in EU-wide concentration. Nevertheless, Germany and Italy have a very large number of banks and

[52]There is still little evidence of securitization (see Jeanneau, 1996).

Table 58. European Union Countries, North America, and Japan: Population per Bank Branch

	1985	1992	1994	Change 1985–92 (In percent)	Change 1992–94 (In percent)
European Union countries					
Austria	. . .	1,695	1,715	. . .	1.18
Belgium	395	613	. . .	55.19	. . .
Denmark	1,534	2,096	2,316	36.64	10.50
Finland	1,670	2,106	2,784	26.11	32.19
France	. . .	. . .	2,212	. . .	. . .
Germany	1,569	2,050	1,832	30.66	−10.63
Greece	. . .	8,943	8,384	. . .	−6.25
Ireland	. . .	. . .	. . .	. . .	. . .
Italy	. . .	3,221	2,862	. . .	−11.15
Luxembourg	1,523	1,287	1,090	−15.50	−15.31
Netherlands	3,025	2,019	2,116	−33.26	4.80
Portugal	6,633	3,431	2,917	−48.27	−14.98
Spain	1,182	1,100	1,101	−6.94	0.09
Sweden	2,794	2,990	3,281	7.02	9.73
United Kingdom	4,163	4,937	5,272	18.59	6.79
North America					
Canada	. . .	. . .	. . .	. . .	. . .
Mexico	21,814	25,330	21,441	16.12	−15.35
United States	5,596	4,885	4,690	−12.71	−3.99
Japan	. . .	. . .	. . .	. . .	. . .

Source: Organization for Economic Cooperation and Development, *Bank Profitability: Financial Statements of Banks 1985–1994* (1996).

relatively low concentration. Moreover, consolidation in Europe has been much slower than in the United States, as indicated by the substantially smaller number and size of mergers and acquisitions (though the fact that the United States began the 1980s with a far more fragmented banking system than the European one can partly account for its faster consolidation process) (Table 59).

The absence of significant consolidation is difficult to explain against the background of strong competitive pressures and incentives for change. In recent years, local banking markets in Europe have experienced heightened competition associated with deregulation, the abolition of capital controls, and single market initiatives. These competitive pressures have lowered net interest margins (Table 60) and reduced bank profits (Table 61), overshadowing the effects of cyclical fluctuations.[53] Some banking systems have also had to increase provisions for nonperforming loans as real estate and property-related sectors weakened in the presence of declining or soft real estate prices. In most cases, European banks have been unable to counteract these trends with cost reductions and increased revenues in other areas of financial services. The resistance to consolidation can be attributed to a large extent to the remaining impediments to

cross-border competition in banking (see the appendix at the end of this annex) and to such factors as home currency advantage, extensive branch networks, and strong traditional and cultural relationships.

Single Market Initiatives and Cross-Border Activity

The Second Banking Directive (SBD, adopted in 1989 for implementation on January 1, 1993) introduced three key structural changes aimed at creating a single market (or "single passport") for banking services across the EU.[54] First, standards for prudential supervision were to be "harmonized" across the EU. Second, supervisory authorities "mutually recognized" the way in which these standards were applied in each EU country so that a single banking "license" or "passport" was needed to provide an agreed list of banking services throughout the EU (Table 45). Third,

---

[53]See OECD (1996).

[54]Not all countries respected the deadline of January 1, 1993. The SBD was implemented into national law in 1991 in Denmark; in 1992 in Germany, France, Ireland, Portugal, Greece, and the Netherlands; in 1993 in the United Kingdom, Italy, and Luxembourg; in 1994 in Belgium and Spain. Nine additional banking directives were introduced between 1986 and 1992: the Consolidated Accounts Directive (86/635), the Branch Establishment Directive (89/117), the Own Funds Directives (89/299 and 92/16), the Solvency Ratio Directives (89/647 and 91/31), the Money Laundering Directive (91/308), the Large Exposures Directive (92/121), and the Consolidated Surveillance Directive (92/30).

Table 59. Mergers and Acquisition Activity in Banking[1]

	Number of Mergers and Acquisitions				Value (in billions of U.S. dollars)			
	1989–90	1991–92	1993–94	1995–96[2]	1989–90	1991–92	1993–94	1995–96[2]
European Union countries								
Belgium	11	22	18	12	0.0	1.0	0.6	0.4
Finland	6	51	16	4	0.4	0.9	1.0	0.8
France	52	133	71	43	2.7	2.4	0.5	3.2
Germany	19	71	83	27	1.1	3.5	1.9	0.7
Italy	41	122	105	65	8.2	5.3	6.1	3.0
Netherlands	12	20	13	7	10.9	0.1	0.1	0.8
Spain	30	76	44	26	4.0	4.3	4.5	2.1
Sweden	10	38	23	8	2.0	1.1	0.4	0.1
United Kingdom	86	71	40	28	6.4	7.5	3.3	21.7
Other countries								
Australia	23	19	20	9	2.3	0.9	1.5	2.5
Canada	13	29	31	14	0.8	0.5	1.8	0.1
Japan	8	22	8	17	31.2	0.0	2.2	33.8
Norway	12	23	24	2	0.4	0.1	0.2	0.4
Switzerland	31	47	59	14	0.5	0.4	3.9	0.7
United States	1,501	1,354	1,477	1,176	37.8	56.8	55.3	82.5
Total	1,855	2,098	2,032	1,452	108.6	84.7	83.2	153.0
Memorandum item:								
Total nonbank financial	2,075	2,723	3,267	2,267	99.0	63.7	122.2	90.7

Sources: Bank for International Settlements (1996a); and Securities Data Company.
[1]Classified by the industry of the target; completed or pending deals; announcement date volumes.
[2]As of April 4, 1996.

home country regulators had primary regulatory responsibility for all banks based in the country even when the bank operated in another EU country.

Since the creation of a single market for banking services, cross-border activity has increased considerably in wholesale and investment banking and to a smaller extent in retail banking. According to a recent survey by Economic Research Europe (ERE96),[55] in the period 1992–95, the cost of supplying cross-border bank services has diminished. Moreover, cross-border trade has grown significantly in off-balance-sheet activities and investment management, but it has grown only "slightly" in retail and corporate activities. According to the same survey, EU banks carried out cross-border activity mainly through subsidiaries, by increasing sourcing of funds, and by acquiring controlling, or minority, interest in other EU financial institutions. Only to a smaller extent have EU banks opened cross-border branches and engaged in cross-border alliances, joint ventures, and mergers. Nevertheless, statistics collected by the EU Commission show a 58 percent increase in cross-border branches in the period 1992–95 (from 308 to 487, including 32 transformations of existing subsidiaries) with the United Kingdom, Germany, and France as the main

"home" countries, and Germany, the United Kingdom, and Italy as the main "host" countries. No recent data are available on cross-border alliances and joint ventures, but several alliances among banks have been reported, as well as several linkups between banks and insurance companies. Finally, although intra-EU mergers and acquisitions have been much fewer than domestic mergers and acquisitions, they increased in the late 1980s and early 1990s in Germany, France, Italy, and Spain.

Competitiveness, Efficiency, and Profitability

The single market program is expected to promote the competitiveness of the European banking system by reducing costs and increasing efficiency. Survey studies conducted at the end of the 1980s identified considerable scope for convergence of prices (defined as the margin between the interest rate charged on loans or paid on deposits and the money market rate) in the banking sector toward the lowest prevailing in the Community.[56] The decline in net interest margins reported in Table 60 seems to confirm this expectation. Furthermore, in the recent ERE96 survey, respondents agreed that competition intensified considerably in domestic retail and corporate markets during the period 1992–95. This survey also indicates that in all EU countries the margin between loan rates and

---

[55]The work, "A Study on the Effectiveness and Impact of Internal Market Integration on the Banking and Credit Sector" (hereafter ERE96), was commissioned by the European Commission and is not yet published. Minor changes could still be made before its expected publication in the second half of 1997.

[56]See Commission of the European Community (1988a, b).

Table 60. European Union: Net Interest Margins[1]

(In percent of average earning assets)

	1989	1990	1991	1992	1993	1994	1995	Change from High to 1995
European Union countries								
Austria	1.91	1.95	1.95	**2.13**	2.01	1.96	2.13	0.00
Belgium	**2.07**	2.04	1.84	1.85	2.06	1.98	1.76	−0.31
Denmark	2.18	2.47	2.28	**2.63**	2.40	2.37	2.10	−0.53
Finland	1.96	2.19	1.89	1.34	**2.90**	2.73	2.12	−0.78
France	3.20	2.89	**3.28**	3.18	2.49	2.51	2.21	−1.07
Germany	1.72	2.10	2.07	2.43	**3.35**	2.96	2.60	−0.75
Greece	**3.69**	2.73	1.26	0.12	−0.65	0.83	1.75	−1.94
Ireland			1.27	0.91	**2.92**	2.04	1.98	−0.94
Italy	3.62	3.71	3.38	3.41	**3.75**	2.97	3.06	−0.69
Luxembourg	0.46	0.50	0.46	0.88	**1.02**	1.01	0.93	−0.09
Netherlands	0.92	0.93	1.03	1.27	**2.72**	1.66	1.70	−1.02
Portugal		**6.32**	6.06	5.89	3.45	2.84	2.87	−3.45
Spain	4.93	**5.25**	4.85	4.18	5.12	3.98	3.23	−2.02
Sweden	2.17	2.72	**3.65**	2.15	1.62	−0.99	5.52	1.87
United Kingdom	0.35	0.48	0.68	1.67	**2.22**	1.68	1.66	−0.56
Memorandum items:								
North America								
Canada	2.40	**2.60**	2.43	2.29	2.10	1.81	1.93	−0.67
Mexico	1.21	5.21	6.53	**6.73**	3.54	2.27	3.10	−3.63
United States	3.25	3.32	3.43	**6.47**	4.39	3.40	2.77	−3.70
Japan	0.48	1.90	2.07	**3.53**	2.72	2.22	2.36	−1.17

Source: IBCA Ltd.

[1]Numbers in bold indicate the highest net interest margin for the 1989–95 period for each country.

money market rates has fallen in the period 1992–95 for all categories of loans: to a larger extent for corporate customer loans to both large and small firms, and to a smaller extent for retail customer loans and mortgages. The most substantial declines have taken place in France, Ireland, Spain, Denmark, and Greece. The same survey indicates a smaller reduction in deposit prices, again concentrated in France, Ireland, Spain, and Greece. In contrast, banking fees have not fallen and have even increased in some countries, in part because EU banks have tried to use fee income to compensate for shrinking interest income. This evidence notwithstanding, the convergence of banking prices in the EU is far from being completed. The ERE96 study shows that the highest price in the EU is often two (or more) times greater than the lowest one for almost all banking products, including commercial loans, mortgages, credit cards, checking accounts, personal equity transactions, and money transfer costs.

The single market program has not yet had a major impact on the efficiency of the EU banking system. In the period 1990–94, the EU-wide cost-to-income ratio remained approximately unchanged and there were few signs of convergence toward the EU average. Indeed, in each country, costs seem to have followed largely independent trends. In Germany, for example, the cost-to-income ratio has fallen from above the EU average to well below it, whereas in Italy, Spain, and Greece the same ratio has increased from below the average to well above it; at the same time, in the

United Kingdom and Ireland, costs have fallen farther below the average. In most countries, above-average staff costs seem to account for above-average cost-to-income ratios (Figure 55).

These persistent cost pressures have not been offset by substantial productivity gains. In the 1990s, greater competition has reduced net interest margins across the European Union for all categories and sizes of banks, except for savings banks and small banks, which have continued to enjoy higher margins. Countries with particularly high margins at the beginning of the 1990s—Spain, Portugal, and Greece—have experienced the largest declines. In the same period, the percentage of fee, commission, and other noninterest income over total gross income has grown in almost all EU countries, remaining well above the EU average in the United Kingdom, the Netherlands, Luxembourg, and Greece and well below it in Spain and Denmark.[57] The higher share of noninterest income has not allowed EU banks to maintain the profitability levels of the early 1990s. In 1994, the return on equity of all EU banks was half its 1990 level (5.5 percent against 10.9 percent) with the sharpest reductions in Italy and France, followed by Spain, Portugal, and

[57]The ERE96 study conducted an analysis of the productivity of the European banking system taking into account not only interest and noninterest income but also four different inputs. The conclusion was similar: "European banking markets do not appear to have become systematically more productive during the 1990s" (p. 97).

Table 61. European Union: Bank Profitability

	Pretax Profits[1]			Return on Assets[2]	
	1980–82[3]	1986–88	1992–94	1994	1995
	(In percent of assets)				
European Union countries					
Belgium	0.40	0.40	0.30	. . .	. . .
Denmark[4]	. . .	. . .	. . .	0.29	1.20
Finland[5]	0.50	0.50	–1.60	–0.69	–0.16
France	0.40	0.40	–0.10	0.17	0.27
Germany	0.50	0.70	0.50	0.52	0.56
Italy	0.70	1.00	0.80	. . .	. . .
Netherlands	0.30	0.70	0.60	0.69	0.72
Spain	0.70	1.10	0.60	0.70	0.79
Sweden	0.30	0.80	0.50	0.55	1.23
United Kingdom	1.10	1.00	0.70	1.22	1.27
Memorandum items:					
North America					
Canada[6]	0.50	1.00	1.10	1.12	1.16
United States	1.00	0.70	1.60	1.81	1.87
Other countries					
Japan[6]	0.50	0.60	0.20	–0.21[7]	–0.75[7]
Australia	0.90	1.20	0.70	1.60[6]	1.82[6]
Norway	0.60	0.00	0.20	1.31	1.81
Switzerland	0.60	0.70	0.60	0.63	0.52

Sources: IBCA Ltd; and Organization for Economic Cooperation and Development as adapted from Bank for International Settlements, *66th Annual Report* (1996).

[1]For Australia, Belgium, the Netherlands, and Switzerland, all banks; for others, commercial banks only (OECD data).

[2]Pretax profits of major banks (IBCA data).

[3]For Australia, Belgium, and France, 1981–82; and for Canada, 1982.

[4]The portfolio of securities is marked to market.

[5]The 1994 and 1995 reserves are not fully comparable because of a break in series.

[6]Fiscal years.

[7]The 1994 and 1995 data are combinations of half-year results at an annual rate and IBCA estimates.

Greece (where, however, the return on equity remains well above the EU average). Sizable improvements were recorded only in the United Kingdom, Ireland, and Luxembourg.

Single Currency and Restructuring of the EU Banking System

In EMU, the existence of larger and more liquid capital markets in Europe and the unavoidable reforms of European health, pension, and social security systems will create a large private pool of investable funds and will most likely expand the role of institutional investors and the demand for specialized asset management. This could open up each national market to cross-border competition. Continental banks will respond to this challenge by stepping up their current efforts to acquire, or merge with, specialized firms, and additionally to diversify their businesses against the risk of disintermediation by forming groups with institutional investors.

The creation of more liquid European capital markets—if not a Europe-wide capital market—is likely to encourage small and medium-sized corporations to access securities markets. Direct access to securities

markets will in turn affect the competitive position of banks and could start a gradual process of disintermediation. In this scenario, credit evaluation and local market underwriting skills will become extremely valuable. Thus, by creating incentives for the creation of broad, deep, and liquid private securities markets in Europe, the introduction of the euro and the establishment of EMU creates an *environment of competition* for shares of markets traditionally closely held and maintained by domestic universal banking institutions, both at the wholesale and retail level.

Wholesale Banking

At the wholesale level, with the removal of currencies and foreign exchange risk for intra-EMU cross-border transactions, there will be few remaining barriers to entry for the large global institutions. The commoditization of wholesale services and the cost of supplying them will determine customer relations. Competition in wholesale banking is driven by price, access to distribution networks, and geographical reach. Only a limited number of large financial institutions have the capital, resources, and geographical reach to compete globally in providing services to the top tier of multinational corporations and large and medium-sized companies with international operations.[58]

It is possible to identify several aspects of this competition and consolidation at the wholesale level that are related to the introduction of the euro. As noted earlier, the euro directly eliminates the "anchoring principle," advocated by many European central banks, which requires domestic financial institutions to lead-manage bond issues, creating cross-border competition for providing this investment banking service. This new competition could lead to consolidation and greater concentration through cross-border mergers and acquisitions. The euro also eliminates the 80 percent matching rule on foreign currency exposures of insurance companies and pension funds within Europe (see the appendix at the end of this annex). Under the existing rules, an EU insurance company, for example, cannot hold more than 20 percent of its assets in foreign currencies unless they are matched by liabilities denominated in the same currencies. The lifting of this restriction is likely to increase cross-border investment flows, and will open up this pool of investment funds to investment banks in EMU for providing underwriting, trading, brokerage, rating, and merger and acquisition advisory services. Banks strong in the above areas, with good placement power, are likely to see their franchises increase in value, and banks weak in these areas could be in the market for acquisitions of merchant banks and asset managers by continental European banks. Universal banks with strong investment banking franchises are also likely to benefit from EMU.

As a direct effect of a single currency, European banks will experience a substantial drop in banks' foreign exchange trading revenues on intra-EMU transactions. A single currency will eliminate revenues from intra-EMU exchange trading, sale of exchange rate and interest rate hedging instruments, commissions on cross-border money transfers, and government securities underwriting. These revenue losses will be permanent and are likely to be concentrated in wholesale banking with an expected reduction in profits between 10 and 15 percent. EMU is likely to affect credit institutions unevenly, reducing mostly revenues of those banks with a competitive edge in certain currencies or in the placing of assets denominated in such currencies. EMU is then expected to cause a sharp re-

duction in employment of foreign exchange traders and possibly a consolidation of firms specialized in the foreign exchange business.

The euro is also likely to have a number of indirect effects, all pointing in the direction of further consolidation in wholesale banking in Europe: lower profit margins through its general impact on competition; rationalization of foreign exchange and corporate and industrial treasury functions, which would reduce the demand for cash-management services provided by wholesale and investment banks; and reduction in the number of providers of regional and global payments processing services. This consolidation can only be hastened by the elimination of European currencies.

Competition is also likely to increase in correspondent banking as non-EMU banks reduce the number of correspondents they need inside the euro bloc. Consortia of banks providing basic electronic banking services, including payments to each other's customers in Europe, are also likely to emerge. The TARGET system will handle only large-value euro payments for central banks, large private banks, and very large companies, and smaller companies will have to go through banks' own payments systems and correspondent networks for low-value payments in euro. Competition in the market for wholesale money transmission services will also increase. As companies increase their cross-border activities, introduce more sophisticated treasury management, and concentrate their euro business in fewer banks, traditional home currency correspondent banks may be unable to compete with the global banks, which assure cost-effective and efficient payments services around the world through their own networks.

Retail Banking

At the retail level, there is a greater need for restructuring and consolidation. Several potential EMU countries have banking systems that are overstaffed, and staffs that are underemployed, relative to banks operating in more efficient banking systems. An open question is whether EMU will provide the impetus for change necessary for restructuring and consolidation of European retail banking. In the past, exchange rate stability has been associated with narrowing net interest margins among the core countries. One possible inference is that the euro might provide an added element of competition (see Table 60).[59] Additional pressures on interest rate margins would come from the

---

[58]There is now a consensus in the international financial markets that there is room for only about 10 large global players. The "names" most often mentioned, in industry magazines and by market participants, are ABN Amro, Barclays, Citicorp, Deutsche Bank, Goldman Sachs, J.P. Morgan, Merrill Lynch, Morgan Stanley, S.B.C. Warburg, and Union Bank of Switzerland. Others that are viewed as vying for a slot include Credit Suisse First Boston and Lazard Frères. The recent mergers of Chase and Chemical banks and of Morgan Stanley and Dean Witter are examples of what may occur in the coming years.

---

[59]The link between exchange rate stability and net interest margins is supported by the experience with Italian and U.K. spreads, both of which stopped converging during the 1992–93 period of extreme exchange rate turbulence. In addition, the independent role of exchange rate stability is supported by the significant convergence of margins before the introduction of single market initiatives in 1992.

emergence of EMU-wide securities markets, the harmonization of reserve requirements, and the greater transparency of financing terms and conditions associated with a single currency.

A single currency will also eliminate directly some of the remaining impediments to cross-border competition in banking discussed in the appendix. A single currency will make irrelevant, for example, the fact that in France some funds (SICAVs) are not allowed to engage in foreign exchange with non-French banks, as well as the laws in some countries precluding the inscription of mortgages in a currency other than the national currency. A single currency will also greatly reduce the importance of restrictions on accessing local capital markets, which are currently complicating the refinancing of mortgages.

EMU could also increase the likelihood of consolidation through cross-border bank mergers and alliances, as the more aggressive institutions position themselves to satisfy the increased demand for EMU-wide banking services that could come from greater cross-border trade and competition in European industry. While large European corporations are already requesting Europe-wide banking services, EMU could extend this demand to small and medium-sized firms that rely on retail banks for many of their needs. Households would also be likely to increase the demand for EMU-wide banking services. Competition in all of these areas is likely to increase between the stronger domestic and European financial institutions looking to increase market share and to penetrate markets in other EMU countries. Some competition could also come from large and fully vertically integrated financial institutions, including some global banks. In addition, some economic barriers to entry could be eroded by the introduction of the euro, although this is likely to occur indirectly through the euro's impact on securities markets and institutional investors and their impact on bank disintermediation. What all this implies is that EMU could make banking markets in Europe more "contestable" in the sense that the potential for competition from new entrants could act as a disciplining mechanism on incumbents and perhaps lead to more consolidation.

Given these pressures for change, how might restructuring take place within EMU? If the competitive pressures outlined above are allowed to exert their influence unconstrained, it would be reasonable to expect competition to lead to further mergers of small and medium-sized domestic institutions (some defensive, some offensive), cross-border mergers, significantly fewer institutions, more electronic branching, better and more efficiently provided services, and customer access to regional, international, and global markets. The number of institutions and branches would decline gradually, and the average size of institutions would increase as consolidation takes place. Staff levels would decline slowly through attrition.

Much of the adjustment could be internalized within the banking industry itself. In an environment in which regulations, union strength, and extensive public ownership make it difficult to close banks and to reduce costs through downsizing, the stronger institutions may be called upon to merge with poorly capitalized banks. In other instances, mergers will aim to boost profits without incurring the pain of cost cutting. Among the more successful or viable institutions, large banks will continue to purchase smaller banks (including savings institutions and community banks), in part to obtain access to relatively high-margin retail business and to diversify funding sources by expanding the branch network. Some of the more aggressive smaller banks would engage in defensive mergers or outright takeovers. Larger banks may also try to increase diversification and to acquire a hedge against disintermediation by establishing alliances with mutual funds and insurance companies. Computer technology will also aid in the consolidation process by allowing banks to concentrate back-office operations away from individual branches and to realize important economies of scale. The acquisition of technology may motivate some mergers, because it may allow some banks to gain access to the financial resources necessary to acquire and maintain competitive information technology infrastructures.

The euro will provide additional pressure for change but major progress will occur only after some structural issues are addressed. Obstacles have remained in place even after the introduction of the Second Banking Directive, and differences in taxation, regulations, and accounting and business practices, combined with the absence of an EU company law, impede cross-border entry (see the appendix).[60] Labor market laws will also continue to place limits on the potential efficiency gains from consolidation. Ownership structures in Europe are also likely to continue to prevent market forces from operating. Extensive state ownership delays both entry and exit from the banking system, resulting in a continued buildup of imbalances in troubled public institutions. In addition, institutions may continue to pay little attention to profitability because creditor and shareholder discipline is reduced by the fragmentation of debt and equity claims and by regulatory obstacles to takeovers.[61] Another factor is that European banking is still characterized by institutions with a national and often regional orientation. U.S. experience suggests that the inability to diversify across state boundaries was a major factor in the difficulties faced by several banking institutions. Finally,

---

[60]For example, a British bank that established operations and began to offer interest-bearing current accounts in France was forced to cease this practice on the grounds that French banks were prohibited from paying interest on such accounts and that the efficacy of monetary policy was threatened.

[61]See BIS (1996a).

in the United States, where labor market legislation provides significant scope for downsizing, the most important benefit of mergers was increased profitability from a better diversification of funding sources and loan portfolios—not cost savings.

The forms and extent of restructuring are likely to vary across the EMU. On the one hand, their different competitiveness levels imply that not all EU banking systems are in the same need of restructuring. On the other hand, the lack of harmonization of taxes, rules, and regulations, and the remaining impediments to cross-border activity, may distort competitive forces, accelerating the restructuring in some countries and delaying it in others.

The U.K. banking system is the most competitive in the European Union and the one in which restructuring is most advanced. U.K. banks have a high return on equity even though they operate in an environment with low net interest margins, few impediments to cross-border competition, and a highly developed financial market, which exposes them to the risk of disintermediation. Their performance is explained by a large and increasing share of noninterest income, below-average and falling cost-to-income ratios, a constant decline in the density of branches, and intense merger and acquisition activity. Only the Nordic countries and Ireland have also experienced some of the restructuring observed in the United Kingdom: although their banking systems are not as profitable, their costs tend to be relatively low and the density of their branch networks has been falling for several years.

In the large continental European banking systems of Germany, France, Italy, and Spain, restructuring is proceeding more slowly than in the United Kingdom. In some countries, branch networks have continued to expand and the number of banking institutions remains high. Low profitability prevails as net interest margins shrink rapidly without being offset by higher noninterest income. Moreover, costs in these countries—except Germany—tend to be above the EU average and privatizations are often delayed. A single currency is likely to intensify competitive pressures, but there is a risk that widespread public ownership and remaining impediments to cross-border activity will continue to reduce cross-border competition and delay restructuring, while the lack of harmonization of taxes, rules, and regulations will not allow a level playing field (see the appendix). Competition among EU banking systems might be impeded by the different scope for state intervention that each country will have depending on its fiscal position, and by the remaining differences in the regulatory and supervisory framework and in the deposit insurance schemes, whose importance will be enhanced by a single currency.

The experience of the United States and the Nordic countries, where banking crises occurred before restructuring took place, and the more recent experience

with resolving financial system problems in Japan, suggest that it is unlikely that Europe will be able to either grow out of its problems or resolve them entirely through private efforts unless there are further reforms. In addition, restructuring and consolidation in Europe are unlikely to be aided significantly by state interventions on a scale similar to the interventions that accompanied the restructuring of the European industry in the 1980s.[62] The funds available to bail out banks are likely to be limited, in the short run, by the commitments of EMU member countries to uphold the stability pact and to achieve further fiscal consolidation. In addition, any attempt to bail out troubled institutions might be prevented by EU regulations that guarantee fair competition and try to maintain a "level playing field" in the market for banking services.[63]

In summary, the introduction of a single currency is likely to provide additional competitive pressures that could potentially accelerate the desirable processes of restructuring and consolidation in European banking systems. Unless structural reforms are implemented across Europe, there is the risk that rigidities in labor markets, public ownership structures, and other policies affecting the adjustment in banking markets would delay the desirable effects of enhanced competition. This would allow financial problems in troubled institutions to build up to the point where crises might be unavoidable. If this occurs, the inconsistencies between EMU-wide plans for fiscal consolidation and existing financial sector policies will become glaring.

Financial Institutions

Overall, it is an open question which types of financial institutions will be able to take advantage of these opportunities and to deal better with the likely increase in bank disintermediation. Those firms that are better positioned to compensate for the decline in loan demand with noninterest income, for example, from placement services, will have an advantage. If the introduction of the euro leads to the creation of less segmented and more liquid securities markets, then it will encourage the development of financial intermediation based on direct access to securities markets. The predominance of this model of finance in the United States, the United Kingdom, and international markets reflects the market reality that, in the absence of strong regulations that create and protect a clear niche for banks, the business of taking deposits and providing loans—banking—has a role in finance as long as

---

[62]In that instance, several European governments smoothed the process by directly injecting funds, extending the scope of unemployment and welfare subsidies, and authorizing costly early retirement.

[63]Within the European Union, public funds have been injected into financial institutions in recent years in Finland, France, Italy, Norway, and Sweden.

the cost of borrowing directly (through private placements of the securities markets) exceeds the cost of borrowing indirectly through banks.[64] By making European capital markets more liquid and efficient, the introduction of the euro has the potential for encouraging further direct financing and for reducing the role of bank intermediation throughout Europe.

Another factor that could drive European entities toward more direct financing is the cost of acquiring information. It has been argued that financial intermediaries emerged because it is inefficient for many shareholders each to incur the cost of monitoring a firm's management.[65] To some extent, information costs explain the development and growth of universal banks in Europe, as their role as shareholder allows them to have an informational advantage over individual investors.[66] To the extent that EMU will increase the integration of European markets for goods and services, it will be easier for investors to assess the performance of firms as the need for detailed knowledge of each local market diminishes. If this occurs, the comparative advantage of universal banks is likely to diminish. As such, American investment firms would have a significant skill-based advantage, because they specialize in credit evaluation in the context of liquid securities markets.[67] The development of European capital markets could then be seen as a reduction in the barriers to entry for securities firms.

Only the largest of the European universal banks appear to be reasonably well positioned to counteract some of these advantages. First, they should have little problem in using their information-gathering advantage to move into credit valuation and bring an increasing number of firms to the bond and equity markets. In addition, their role as shareholders will be crucial in influencing the financing choices of corporations and preventing too rapid a shift toward equity and bond financing. When banks act as shareholders, they can distort the financing decisions of a firm to the point that the share of debt of the participating firm exceeds the level that maximizes the firm's value.[68] In this respect, a major penetration of American-style investment banks in the banking market of continental Europe would be possible only if a parallel shift in the prevailing form of corporate governance toward the securities model of financial intermediation were to be demanded by customers and to take place.[69] These counterbalancing factors suggest that any shift of financial activities away from the large European universal banks will be gradual. However, it is likely that the many small and medium-sized financial institutions within Europe that have tried to emulate the universal banking model will be vulnerable to competition from larger financial institutions and more efficient small and medium-sized intermediaries. One can also expect greater specialization among the middle-tier institutions.

Appendix
Remaining Impediments to Cross-Border Competition

Financial Services

A number of restrictions and regulatory obstacles to competition in financial services remain even after the full implementation of the Investment Services Directive (Table 62). The ISD itself leaves scope for independent interpretation of some articles that have the potential to hinder free cross-border trade in financial services. The main source of concern is the "concentration" principle, which could be implemented in a way that would allow national exchanges to retain some monopoly power. Article 14.3 of ISD authorizes, but does not require, EU countries to mandate that transactions in domestically traded securities be carried out only on "a regulated market." Other articles leave room for restrictive interpretations, such as those dealing with the regulated market (Article 1.13), transparency (Article 21), the ability of regulated markets to introduce screen trading in other EU countries (Article 15.4), and the prohibition of new markets (Article 15.5).

An uneven playing field in the market for financial services across the European Union persists also because of a number of restrictions hampering cross-border activities of institutional investors. Pension funds face several constraints on the composition of their portfolios that inhibit the freedom of capital movements and favor the funding of domestic governments and corporations (Table 63). The European Commission proposed a Pension Funds Directive to liberalize pension fund provisions, but it has never been adopted. Most countries set ceilings for the holdings of equities (Germany, Belgium, Denmark, Norway, Portugal, and Greece) and for foreign assets or assets denominated in foreign currency (Germany, France, Finland, Denmark, Sweden, Belgium, Portugal, and Austria). Furthermore, some countries require a minimum investment in government bonds (France and Belgium). Only the United Kingdom and the Netherlands impose few portfolio restrictions

Insurance companies face regulatory constraints set out in the Third EU Directive for the life insurance sector. Their asset allocation is subject to ceilings on their

---

[64]See Gurley and Shaw (1960).

[65]See Diamond (1984).

[66]A key feature of universal banks is that they hold equity shares large enough to monitor corporations. See Steinherr (1996).

[67]See Steinherr (1996).

[68]See Aoki (1984).

[69]The greater the liquidity of the secondary market, the more effective is the securities model of financial intermediation as a form of corporate governance based on the takeover mechanism. See Bolton and von Thadden (1996).

Table 62. Implementation of the European Union Capital Adequacy and Investment Services Directives

	Year	Laws and Regulations	Comments
Austria	1996	First Amendment of the Banking Act (November 1, 1996). Second Amendment of the Banking Act (January 1, 1997).	
Belgium	1995	Law of April 6, 1995, on "secondary markets, investment firms, intermediaries and advisers."	
Denmark	1995	Laws nos. 1071 and 1072 of December 20, 1995.	
Finland	1996	July 16, 1996, Act on Financial Services Firms (Sijoituspalveluyrityslaki); and Act amending the Securities Market Act (Arvopaperimarkkinalaki).	Both have been in effect since August 1, 1996.
France	1996	French Law no. 96-597 of July 2, 1996, "de modernisation des activities financières."	
Germany	1994	Law of July 26, 1994, "Wertpapierhandelsgesetz." Amendment of the Banking Act (January 22, 1996). Principles Concerning the Capital and Liquidity of Credit Institutions (October 2, 1996).	
Greece	n.a.		Implementation is expected.
Ireland	1995	Irish Investment Intermediaries Act 1995, dated July 1, 1995.	
Italy	1996	Legislative Decree no. 415 of July 23, 1996.	
Luxembourg	n.a.		Two bills were introduced in Parliament, one in July 1995, another in July 1996. They have not yet been adopted.
Netherlands	1995	Wet Toezicht effectenverkeer 1995.	
Portugal	1996	Bank of Portugal Notices ("Avicos") no. 7/96, 8/96, and Decree-Laws no. 232/96 of December 5, 1996, for Investment Services Directive and 9/96 of December 1996 for Capital Adequacy Directive.	
Spain	n.a.		Implementation is expected.
Sweden	1991	Securities Business Act, 1991, 981. Stock Exchange and Clearing Act, 1992, 543. Financial Supervisory Authority Regulation 1995: 40, 43, 45, and 59.	All these measures took effect on January 1, 1995.
United Kingdom	1986	Financial Services Act 1986, as amended.	

Sources: International Monetary Fund; and Wymeersch (1996).

holdings of equities (65 percent), real estate (40 percent), and loans (10 percent). Moreover, insurance companies must diversify equity holdings so that they do not hold more than 5 percent of the quoted shares of a single company or 0.5 percent of the shares in an unquoted company. Foreign currency investments are subject to "congruence" or matching rules, which require that liabilities in one currency be at least 80 percent matched by assets denominated in the same currency.

Mutual (investment) funds and portfolio management services are also subject to a number of regulatory barriers that obstruct cross-border trade. When the ISD is fully implemented, in principle no formal regulatory barriers should be left standing within the European Union. In practice, however, some obstacles to the distribution of funds across borders are bound to remain because of requirements on domestic legal forms and organizational structures (e.g., in the United Kingdom), disclosure and registration rules (e.g., in

Germany), and, above all, discriminatory tax treatment discouraging taxpayers from investing in foreign funds and providing incentives for investment in domestic equities or government paper. Additional hindrances are the different accounting practices, withholding taxes on dividends paid to foreigners, administrative burdens, performance measurement practices and requirements, and transaction charges.[70]

Under the provisions of ISD, fund management services offered by banks, insurance companies, investment dealers, or independent portfolio managers should face very few restrictions, since these services can be provided to other EU countries either through a permanent establishment or cross-border.

In almost all EU countries, bond issues are subject to the so-called anchoring principle according to which

---

[70]See OECD DAFFE/CMF(96)19/REV1.

Table 63. Regulatory Constraints on Portfolio Investment of Institutional Investors in Selected Industrial Countries

	Pension Funds	Insurance Companies	Mutual Funds
Austria	Minimum of 50 percent in bank deposits or bonds denominated in the Austrian currency. Ceiling on foreign financial assets (35 percent).	80 percent currency-matching rule.	None.
Belgium	Ceilings on foreign assets (50 percent); equities (65 percent); any single company (5 percent); property (40 percent); investment funds (30 percent); and business of the plan sponsor (15 percent).	80 percent currency-matching rule.	None.
Canada	A December 1991 law progressively raised the ceiling on foreign investment from 10 percent to 20 percent in 1994.	A June 1992 regulation removed ceilings on foreign investments but limits may be imposed based on prudential considerations.	Limit of 20 percent on foreign assets in the Registered Retirement Savings Plans (RRSP)–eligible funds.
Denmark	80 percent currency-matching rule. Maximum limit of 40 percent on "high-risk assets" (Danish and foreign equities, property loans, and unquoted investments).	80 percent currency-matching rule.	None.
Finland	80 percent currency-matching rule.	80 percent currency-matching rule.	None.
France	At least 34 percent of assets must be invested in securities guaranteed by the state. Ceilings on foreign assets (5 percent) and property (40 percent).	Investments are subject to the matching-assets rule; the location rule; and the allocation-of-assets rule. Ceilings on foreign assets (5 percent) and property (40 percent). Minimum share of public debt instruments (34 percent).	Subject to disclosure and asset-diversification rules. A fund may not hold more than 10 percent of any one category of securities of one issuer.
Germany	*Pensions Kassen:* 80 percent currency-matching rule. Ceilings on EU equities (30 percent); non-EU equities (6 percent); non-EU bonds (6 percent); and EU property (25 percent). *Spezialfonds:* Foreign fund manager is required to have a link with a German unit trust manager. *Book-Reserve System Funds:* No restrictions.	80 percent currency-matching rule.	None.
Greece	Ceilings on property and securitites listed in stock exchange (20 percent).	80 percent currency-matching rule.	None.
Italy	33.3 percent currency-matching rule (but assets denominated in ECU can be used to match liabilities in any currency). Ceiling on unlisted securities (50 percent if issued in OECD countries and 20 percent if issued by non-OECD countries). Ceilings of 20 percent on closed-end fund shares; 30 percent on securities issued by employer (20 percent if shares); 10 percent on securities issued by a single issuer (5 percent if unlisted); 10 percent on derivatives used for speculation.	80 percent currency-matching rule.	None.
Netherlands	"Prudent person" rule: an investment must be "solid." Limit on employer-related investment or self-investment; 5 percent in reserves and 10 percent in assets.	80 percent currency-matching rule.	None.
Norway	Ceilings on equities (20 percent) and foreign assets (30 percent).	80 percent currency-matching rule.	None.

Table 63 *(concluded)*

	Pension Funds	Insurance Companies	Mutual Funds
Portugal	Ceilings on foreign securities listed on OECD stock exchange (20 percent); unlisted bonds or on bonds listed on a non-OECD stock exchange or on commercial paper (10 percent); unlisted other securities or on other securities listed in a non-OECD stock exchange (5 percent), with the exception of money market instruments; property or mortgages (50 percent); single company (5 percent); companies belonging to the same group (20 percent); and single unit trust (20 percent).	80 percent currency-matching rule.	None.
Spain	Ceilings on assets other than bonds, equities, real estate, and bank deposits (10 percent).	80 percent currency-matching rule.	None.
Sweden	Foreign asset ceiling (5–10 percent) but generally restrictions not applicable since most pension funds are managed through the book reserve system.	80 percent currency-matching rule.	None.
United Kingdom	"Prudent person" rule. Self-investment restricted to 5 percent.	Subject to matching and localization rules, which require them roughly to balance liabilities expressed in a particular currency with assets in the currency. A company must ensure that its liabilities are covered by assets of appropriate safety, yield, and marketability, having regard to the classes of business carried on, that its investments are appropriately diversified and adequately spread, and that excessive reliance is not placed on investments of any particular category or description.	Collective investment schemes (unit trusts) are required to invest at least 90 percent of their assets in transferable securities in markets, selected by the fund manager in consultation with the trustees, that are regulated, recognized, operating regularly, and open to the public.
United States	Regulated by a special federal law— Employee Retirement Income Security Act (ERISA). Permissible investments subject to the "prudent expert" rule, which includes a requirement to give consideration to diversification and liquidity factors. Otherwise no explicit restrictions on holding foreign securities, including foreign equities and foreign-currency-denominated bonds.	U.S. state insurance regulations attempt "to prevent or correct undue concentration of investment by type and issue and unreasonable mismatching of maturities of assets and liabilities." These laws usually allow an unrestricted "basket" of investments for a certain amount of assets, which can be allocated to foreign securities in the range 0–10 percent of total assets.	Primarily regulated by the U.S. Securities and Exchange Commission (SEC) under federal laws. An open-ended fund may not hold more than 15 percent of its net assets in illiquid assets. Otherwise no explicit restrictions are imposed on investment in foreign securities.

Sources: International Monetary Fund; and Organization for Economic Cooperation and Development.

all bond issues in a national currency should be lead-managed by a bank, or bank branch, with a full-fledged new issues department domiciled in the country. The rationale behind this rule is that national central banks believe they can monitor and ensure compliance with their country's monetary legislation (like the ban on indexation in Germany) only if they have direct authority over the banks concerned at all times.[71] Simi-larly, most issuing states require primary dealers in government bonds to have a local presence and meet local supervisory standards.

Banking

The small increase in cross-border banking activity since 1992 is probably due to a number of remaining impediments to cross-border competition. Respondents to the ERE96 survey agreed that on average trade barriers in banking had declined "to some extent" over

---

[71]See Deutsche Bank Research (1996).

the period 1992–95 with the largest improvements in the wholesale area (corporate deposits and loans) and the smallest in the retail area (mortgages, insurance products, savings products, and consumer loans). But they believed that major barriers to operating in other EU countries remained. The cost of entering new geographical markets—in terms of establishing networks and acquiring information—was considered the most important barrier, followed by social barriers, legal hindrances, and national taxation regimes. By contrast, capital requirements, anticompetitive measures of domestic governments, and collusion between domestic banks were considered less important.

The ERE96 survey provides several examples of barriers in the banking sector that may discourage entry by foreign competitors. First, product restrictions persist in several countries: Greece, for example, prohibits real estate lending by foreign banks, Italy restricts the provision of payment instrument services by nonresidents, and France does not allow funds (SICAVs) to do foreign exchange business with non-French banks; furthermore, in France, the ban on interest-bearing check or cash deposit accounts effectively reduces the threat of foreign competition in the deposit market. Second, marketing financial services is more difficult in countries where door-to-door selling is prohibited or restricted (Denmark, France, Italy, and Spain). Finally, there are a number of obstacles in the field of mortgage credit. In several countries, foreigners face barriers in accessing local capital markets for refinancing: they are banned from issuing bonds in Greece, need a prior authorization in Belgium, Spain, France, and Italy, and cannot issue a bond payable in a foreign currency in Portugal. Other hurdles are the differences across EU countries in mortgage guarantees and taxes, as well as legislation precluding inscription of the mortgage in a currency other than a national currency.

Tax distortions in the allocation of savings across the European Union are due not only to the well-known lack of harmonization in the taxation of investment income but also to instances in which national tax systems effectively help to protect domestic financial sectors from foreign competition. In France and Belgium, for example, there are tax incentives to invest in domestic mutual funds (SICAVs). In France, tax-exempt saving accounts are available only from two French institutions (the French Post Office and the Caisse d'Epargne), and tax-exempt share savings plans are restricted to investing exclusively in French shares. In Italy and Portugal, the interest paid on loans from nonresidents is subject to a withholding tax, which practically excludes nonresidents from lending to domestic nonbanks. Finally, in some countries, insurance premiums are tax deductible only if the insurance contract is with a company having its headquarters in the national territory.

Differences in labor market and employment regulations can discourage foreign investors from buying domestic banking institutions, because European labor legislation is known to prevent a successful restructuring of the acquired banks. This type of labor-market legislation (e.g., in Germany, Italy, and the Netherlands) effectively protects the domestic banking sector from cross-border entry. Moreover, state subsidies and ownership may amount to protectionist distortions of trade in banking services, often difficult to detect. Furthermore, lax application of antitrust and competition policy can impede cross-border competition by allowing concentrations in banking and financial markets that can enhance—at least in the short run—the defensive potential of domestic institutions. In addition, a level playing field across the EU banking sector is unlikely to emerge with the existing differences in regulatory and supervisory frameworks, deposit insurance schemes, and until the start of EMU, reserve requirements. Finally, cross-border competition in financial markets will continue to be hampered by the "general good" opt-out clause accepted in the past by the European Court of Justice, which may be invoked by host states to ban products offered only by foreign banks if these threaten the general good of the citizens of the host country.[72]

---

[72]See ERE96, p. 113.

Annex V
Risk Management of Sovereign Liabilities

The integration of emerging market countries into the global economy and their greater access to external sources of financing have produced a corresponding increase in their exposure to swings in international asset prices. Developing county sovereign entities are especially exposed to international disturbances because of their large stock of unhedged foreign currency debt (relative to national income), and the fairly risky structure of their debt portfolios (currency composition and maturity profile). In a relatively unfamiliar, and at times volatile, international financial environment, the benefits earned by countries through prudent macroeconomic management and structural reforms can be severely compromised by losses due to unexpected changes in interest rates and exchange rates.[1]

The major multinational firms (both financial and nonfinancial) have adapted to similar risks by extensively using hedging techniques and derivative instruments to manage their risk exposures. The use of such techniques has been facilitated by important advances in financial technology in the last decade and by specialized risk management techniques developed by institutional funds managers. In contrast, many sovereign entities—some of them major players in international financial markets with large financial assets and liabilities—have lagged, by and large, behind the private sector in this respect. The recent experience of a small, but growing, number of sovereign borrowers that have reformed their liabilities management practices demonstrates that sound risk management can reduce the impact of external financial developments on debt portfolios, and potentially lower the cost of borrowing.

The existing literature on risk management is rich in its treatment of portfolio allocation problems, but it provides little guidance for sovereigns on how to manage the risk associated with sovereign debt exposures. By drawing on the experience and the well-established methodologies of large institutional investors and pension funds, and on the experience of sovereigns that have reformed their debt management policies, this annex examines three issues: (1) the risks involved for a government in carrying a large open foreign currency exposure; (2) the design of institutional arrangements that provide appropriate incentive structures for debt management; and (3) the establishment of benchmark portfolios embodying strategic preferences for incurring currency, interest rate, and credit risks, and the macroeconomic and institutional constraints on the country. These issues raise questions about the optimal currency exposure of a sovereign; the extent of interaction between debt management policy and monetary policy; and the degree of independence of debt management from political oversight. These issues are relevant for most countries—not just the emerging markets.

Foreign Currency Exposure of Sovereign Liabilities

The external exposure of developing countries' sovereign liabilities has increased steadily during the past two decades, from 7 percent of GDP in 1975 to about 30 percent in the mid-1990s (Figure 56). In 1995, the external debt held or guaranteed by developing country sovereigns was almost three times larger than their foreign currency reserves, exposing governments to a large net currency risk (Table 64). Foreign currency debt also exposed developing countries to foreign interest rate risk. Indeed, about half of developing countries' external debt was exposed to foreign interest rate risk, as 20 percent of the external debt was short term (under a one-year maturity) and 40 percent of the remaining long-term debt was at floating rates (mostly indexed to LIBOR).

Several developing countries have experienced the impact of adverse movements in foreign currencies and interest rates over the past twenty years. In the early 1980s, the debt-servicing burdens of countries in Southeast Asia, Latin America, and Africa were severely affected by the steep appreciation of the dollar, the worldwide increase in interest rates, and the sharp decline in commodity prices. This debt crisis resulted in output and employment losses, financial sector crises, and the exclusion of these countries from international financial markets for a decade.

In the first half of the 1990s, several Asian countries that had overcome the effects of the 1980s debt crisis through prudent fiscal policies experienced sig-

---
[1]This annex draws on the analysis in Cassard and Folkerts-Landau (forthcoming).

Figure 56. External Long-Term Public and Publicly Guaranteed Debt Outstanding
(In percent of GNP)

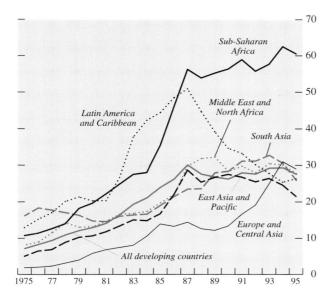

Source: World Bank, *Global Development Finance* database.
Note: The groupings are as shown in the source.

Table 64. Long-Term Public and Publicly Guaranteed External Debt Outstanding and Reserves Excluding Gold in Selected Developing Countries, 1995
(In billions of U.S. dollars)

	Long-Term Public and Publicly Guaranteed External Debt Outstanding	Total Reserves Excluding Gold
Asia		
China	94.7	75.4
India	79.7	17.9
Indonesia	65.3	13.7
Malaysia	15.9	23.8
Philippines	29.9	6.4
Thailand	17.2	36.0
Europe		
Czech Republic	9.6	13.8
Hungary	23.6	12.1
Poland	41.1	14.8
Russia	100.3	14.4
Turkey	50.1	12.4
Western Hemisphere		
Argentina	62.2	14.3
Brazil	96.6	49.7
Colombia	13.0	8.1
Mexico	94.0	16.8
Venezuela	28.5	6.3
Memorandum item:		
All developing countries[1]	1,448.6	538.4

Sources: International Monetary Fund, *International Financial Statistics* (June 1997); and World Bank, *Global Development Finance 1997.*

[1]World Bank data. International reserves include the country authorities' holding of SDRs, the reserve position in the IMF, foreign exchange holdings, and gold.

nificant increases in their debt burden due to their exposure to the Japanese yen. Between 1980 and 1994, East Asian and Pacific countries expanded their borrowing in Japanese yen from below 19 percent to 30 percent of total debt. Although the increase in yen-denominated borrowing was due partly to large concessional loans from Japan to Asian countries and the growing role of the yen in international trade and finance, it also reflected the desire of Asian borrowers to benefit from low interest rates on yen loans compared with U.S. dollar loans. Most of the countries did not hedge their yen exposure either in local currency or in the U.S. dollar, which accounts for a large part of their foreign currency revenues. As a result, the appreciation of the yen vis-à-vis the dollar and the Asian currencies in the 1990s led to a significant rise in the dollar value of their external liabilities (Table 65). The share of yen-denominated debt in total debt was subsequently reduced to 27 percent in 1995, and the share of yen-denominated foreign reserves enlarged.

In Indonesia, for example, a third of the increase in the dollar value of the external debt between 1993 and 1995 was due to cross-currency movements, primarily the appreciation of the yen. Indonesia's exposure to the yen has been especially costly as about 90 percent of its export revenues were denominated in dollars, while 37 percent of its external debt was denominated

in yen. In the Philippines, which has a third of its external debt denominated in yen, the appreciation of the yen accounted for about half of the rise in the dollar value of the external debt in 1995. In China, the appreciation of the yen is estimated to have increased the servicing costs of the public debt by about $5 billion. In Malaysia, the sharp appreciation of the yen in 1994 bumped up the dollar value of the external debt by 6 percent. In India, the external debt increased by almost 7 percent in 1995, almost exclusively on account of exchange rate changes.[2] The subsequent depreciation of the yen in 1996 offset some of the losses incurred by these countries.

The vulnerability of developing countries to external shocks is largely a function of the maturity profile of their foreign currency debt. A distinction needs to be made between a *short-maturity* foreign currency

[2]Changes in external debt are measured in dollar terms, as the latter is the main trade or invoice currency for Asian developing countries. The dollar is also the main currency against which Asian domestic currencies are managed (e.g., Indonesia, Philippines).

Table 65. External Debt Profile of Selected Asian Countries, 1995

	China	India	Indonesia	Malaysia	Philippines	Thailand
External debt (in U.S. dollars)	118.1	93.8	107.8	34.4	39.4	56.8
External debt (in percent of GNP)	17.2	28.2	56.9	42.6	51.5	34.9
External public debt (in percent of GNP)	13.8	24.0	34.5	19.7	39.1	10.6
External public debt/reserves (in percent)	1.2	3.5	4.4	0.6	3.9	0.5
Short-term debt (in percent of total debt)	18.9	5.4	20.7	21.2	13.4	32.2
Share of long-term debt at variable rates	29.6	24.4	48.1	57.3	39.2	62.8
Currency composition of long-term debt (in percent)						
U.S. dollars	57.9	53.3	21.5	45.1	31.5	26.6
Deutsche mark	1.7	6.5	4.9	1.1	1.5	2.3
Japanese yen	20.7	13.7	35.4	31.7	36.9	48.1
Other	19.7	26.5	38.2	22.1	30.1	23.0
Changes in debt stocks due to cross-currency valuations (1990–95)	6.8	6.8	12.7	3.2	4.4	5.5

Source: World Bank, *Global Development Finance 1997.*

debt and a *short-duration* foreign currency debt.[3] In the event of a currency crisis, a government with a short-maturity debt is exposed to both currency and interest rate risks, because both interest and principal payments have to be refinanced at the higher exchange and interest rates. A short-duration, long-maturity debt, however, exposes a sovereign only to interest rate risk, because the principal does not necessarily have to be refinanced during the crisis.

Events in Mexico during 1994–95 illustrate how reliance on short-term foreign currency debt can make a country vulnerable to liquidity crises, as the need to refinance a substantial volume of short-term debt in turbulent foreign exchange markets creates additional market pressure.[4] One of the lessons of the Mexican experience is that the external risk exposure of the government (currency composition, maturity profile, share of floating-rate debt, concentration of maturities) is as indicative as its debt leverage of its vulnerability to external shocks. Indeed, the Mexican crisis was partly attributable to financial markets' concerns about the currency composition and maturity of the public debt and not by its actual level, which was relatively low by OECD standards—51 percent compared with an OECD average of 71 percent.[5] The vulnerability of the Mexican economy to a financial crisis was exacerbated by the $29 billion of tesobonos maturing in 1995, with about $10 billion maturing in the first quarter, in light of the low level of foreign reserves ($6.3 billion) as of end-1994. Had the maturity of the tesobonos been longer and not bunched in the same quarter, the exchange rate crisis might not have turned into a debt-servicing crisis.

The large stock of foreign currency debt held by developing countries is a consequence of several historical and structural factors, including low domestic saving rates, the lack of domestic borrowing instruments, and reliance on official financing (multilateral and bilateral), which tends to be denominated in donor countries' currencies. Foreign currency debt may also be issued to signal the government's commitment to a policy of stable exchange rates or prices. In a game theory framework, the policymaker signals the time-consistency and credibility of policies to the public by raising the cost of reneging on the commitment. More recently, as emerging markets have regained access to international debt markets, the choice of currencies and the maturity structure of their external borrowing has often been driven by the lower risk premiums and coupon rates, and the corresponding initial budget savings.[6] Such unhedged debt strategies may be underestimating the risks associated with foreign currency borrowing for several reasons.

First, the capacity of governments to generate foreign currency revenues to repay their obligations is generally limited because government assets are predominantly the discounted value of future taxes denominated in the local currency. Governments have direct access to foreign currency revenues only when the economy is dominated by a public sector that derives most of its revenues from exports (e.g., oil, gold). Under those circumstances, foreign currency borrowing creates a natural hedge to the sovereign exposure. In a privatized and open economy, however, the government's currency exposure is limited to the

---

[3]The *duration* of a security differs from its *maturity* in that it takes into account the interest payments and amortization during the lifetime of the loan.

[4]See IMF (1995) for a discussion of the role of short-term foreign currency debt in the Mexican crisis.

[5]Calvo and Goldstein (1995).

[6]Several emerging market governments (e.g., Argentina, Colombia, Hungary, Mexico, and Turkey) have issued debt denominated in yen and deutsche mark in the past few years, without having a significant exposure to those currencies on the revenue side. Following the negative impact of the yen appreciation in 1994–95, a few of these countries (Colombia, Hungary, Mexico) began reducing or hedging their yen exposure.

sensitivity of its revenues to foreign currencies. Such sensitivity may be negligible if the private sector hedges its own currency risk exposure, which is the case in most industrial countries and many emerging markets.[7] In such instances, unless foreign currency borrowing accurately hedges the currency exposure of fiscal revenues, it exposes the sovereign to currency risk.

This representation of the scope of sovereign currency risk exposure may be criticized as too narrow on the grounds it does not include the financial exposure of various sectors of the economy (e.g., the banking system, the pension and social security funds, the energy sector) that have systemic risks that may spill over to the public sphere. But managing this broader definition of sovereign risk requires knowledge of the risk exposure of various sectors of the economy, of the correlations of risks among sectors, and of the extent to which the private sector hedges itself against those risks. In practice, governments rarely have access to such comprehensive information.

Second, it is unlikely that the output, welfare, and reputational costs that a developing country may suffer in the event of an adverse external shock are fully taken into account in emerging markets' external borrowing strategies. Although financial crises are low-probability events, their potential for disrupting the economy is substantial. Indeed, a net foreign exchange exposure exacerbates the impact of external shocks on the economy and limits the policy options of the authorities during a financial crisis. A sovereign with a large net foreign currency exposure would have difficulty pursuing an expansionary monetary policy to reflate the economy during a financial crisis, because it might cause a sharp decline in the domestic currency. A depreciation of the exchange rate would worsen the country's indebtedness and risk profile, and magnify, rather than dampen, the financial crisis. In the event of an adverse real exchange rate shock, a government may face the dual cost of a hike in its external-debt-servicing expense and a fall in the foreign currency value of its revenues.[8] In addition to the potential capital losses that a government may incur on its debt portfolio, its ability to access international markets to refinance its maturing debt is likely to be hindered.

Third, there is no conclusive empirical evidence that the diversification benefits of unhedged foreign currency borrowing outweigh the added risk from the effect of nominal and real exchange rate fluctuations on the debt portfolio.[9] By contrast, there are numerous studies of internationally diversified portfolios that show that investors can lower their risks without significant changes in returns by completely hedging their exposure to exchange rate movements, that is, purchasing power and interest rate parities do not hold.[10] During the 1980s, irrespective of investors' base currencies, the returns on currency-hedged foreign bond portfolios were less volatile than the returns on unhedged portfolios. Although such studies apply to portfolios held by institutional investors, sovereign entities are unlikely to predict the direction of exchange rates more accurately than they do.

In view of the risks associated with large, open foreign currency exposures and the existence of deep and liquid domestic capital markets, the governments of most industrial countries have limited their issuance of foreign currency debt. Among large advanced economies, Germany, Japan, and the United States do not issue foreign currency debt, while France and the United Kingdom issue only a small fraction of their debt in European currency units (ECUs). In Italy, foreign currency debt accounts for 6 percent of total government debt; in Canada, it represents about 3 percent of total public debt (reflecting debt accumulated in the past and debt issued to finance foreign reserves), and the budget deficit is funded entirely in domestic currency. In recent years, a number of small advanced economies, including Belgium and New Zealand, have stopped issuing foreign currency debt, except for replenishing their foreign reserves. In Ireland, gross foreign currency borrowing is limited to the level of maturing foreign currency debt. Spain and Sweden issue foreign currency debt, but hedge their currency risk through swaps or swap options (in Sweden only against the currency composition of the foreign currency benchmark, not against the exposure in kronor).

In developing countries, however, governments often need to access international debt markets to offset a shortage of local savings, lengthen the maturity of their debt, diversify their interest rate risk exposure across various asset markets, accumulate foreign exchange reserves, or develop benchmark instruments enabling domestic private entities to issue abroad.[11] When derivative markets (e.g., forward, futures, swap, options) in the domestic currency are available, governments can immediately hedge their foreign currency borrowing, thereby limiting their exposure to foreign exchange and interest rate movements. The

---

[7]There are definite benefits from estimating and hedging the exposure of fiscal revenues to foreign exchange rates—that is, estimating the impact of nominal and real exchange rates on export and import taxes, and on the taxation of exporters and multinationals' profits. Disentangling the effect of domestic and external factors on revenues, however, is likely to be difficult for an open economy with a diversified private sector.

[8]Dooley (1997).

[9]The overall risk of the portfolio may be reduced if the domestic currency cost of domestic debt is negatively correlated with the domestic currency cost of foreign currency debt.

[10]See for instance Perold and Schulman (1988), Eaker, Grant, and Woodard (1993), Glen and Jorion (1993), and Kritzman (1993).

[11]Global bonds, for instance, are a successful vehicle for countries (e.g., Italy, Argentina) to access a wide array of international investors.

foreign currency can be hedged into the domestic currency or into a currency closely correlated to the domestic currency that has liquid derivative markets. Issuing currency-hedged foreign debt would preclude a borrowing strategy solely targeted at reducing interest rate costs and softening internal budget constraints.

Almost all industrial countries and many emerging markets have access to derivative instruments to hedge their foreign exchange risk. Several emerging markets including Indonesia, Malaysia, Thailand, Brazil, and Chile have currency swap markets with maturities up to 5 or 10 years. In other emerging markets (e.g., Mexico, South Korea, Taiwan, and the Philippines), forward markets—the embryos of swap markets—are rapidly developing. World Bank borrowers may use a recently established scheme to improve their management of the currency and interest rate risks of their bank loans. Under the new World Bank scheme, borrowers can amend the terms of their existing currency-pool loans—currency composition and floating-rate/fixed-rate mix—to reflect their desired debt management strategy.[12] The scheme would allow eligible countries to restructure their external debt without using their swap credit lines with commercial banks, and at low transaction costs. The increasing sophistication of international derivative instruments expands considerably the ability of governments to hedge the risks associated with their foreign currency borrowing.[13] It also allows them to respond to opportunities to exploit market niches and expand their investor base—for example, to include Japanese or German retail investors—without bearing the cross yen-dollar exchange risk.

Reducing the currency risk exposure of emerging market sovereign debt and lengthening its maturity profile are medium-term strategies, and are contingent on the development of domestic capital markets and of hedging instruments denominated in the local currency. During the transition, the government's goal would be to manage its net foreign currency risk exposure effectively, so that its vulnerability to exchange rate and foreign interest rate fluctuations is bounded.

Institutional Framework

Efficient management of the external risk exposure of sovereign liabilities requires designing institutional arrangements that provide appropriate incentive structures for debt management, acquiring technical expertise and sophisticated information systems, and imposing strict internal management procedures. In most developing countries, it has proven difficult to create such incentive structures, attract qualified staff, acquire the technical expertise and systems, and develop the controls necessary to manage the overall sovereign risk exposure effectively.

Furthermore, in several developing countries, debt management policies lack transparency and accountability and are influenced by political considerations, rather than being guided by risk management practices. The lack of transparency and accountability allows debt managers to compromise the country's debt profile for short-term political gains by, for instance, issuing short-term debt solely because it demands lower interest rates, or borrowing in foreign currencies with low interest rates.[14] Although the budgetary cost can be reduced by these actions, the economic cost can be much higher and the sovereign's risk profile significantly worsened. Opaque institutional arrangements allow a policymaker with a short horizon to manipulate the structure of the public debt to his or her own benefit because the economic and political gains are immediate, while the potential costs (higher refinancing costs and higher expenditures) are transferred to the future. Investors' expectations that the risk of higher refinancing costs may lead to higher taxes or default rates, however, translate into a higher risk premium on the government debt.

The lack of transparency in debt management is further exacerbated by the fact that debt issuance is often not centralized within a single institution, but spread out among state, provincial, and local governments and parastatal institutions. In addition to confusing decision making and subjecting debt management to potential political pressures, such dispersion induces haphazard and uncoordinated borrowing, and hence an inefficient debt structure. Moreover, the exposure of the public debt to financial risks is unlikely to be assessed and hedged accurately under such a sprawling structure, thereby increasing its vulnerability to shocks.

Since the early 1990s there has been a heightened awareness among the governments of several OECD countries and some emerging markets of the importance of sovereign debt management, particularly in an environment of increasingly mobile and volatile capital flows and integrated capital markets. Several principles emerge from their experiences. First, it is preferable to separate debt management policy from monetary policy to preserve the integrity and indepen-

---

[12]World Bank (1996a). Currency-pool loans are multicurrency obligations, with the U.S. dollar, deutsche mark, and Japanese yen accounting for at least 90 percent of the dollar value of the currency pool. The currencies are targeted until 2001 in fixed currency ratios of 1 dollar for every 125 yen and 2 deutsche mark equivalent. All currency-pool loans are made at a variable rate reflecting World Bank cost of funding.

[13]The ability of governments to swap their foreign currency debt may also be constrained by their credit line limits with financial institutions, as swap transactions reduce such credit lines.

[14]Domestic debt mismanagement (excessive concentration of debt in short-term maturities, illiquid and costly debt issuance techniques, bunching of maturities) is widespread in a number of countries.

dence of the central bank. Second, it is desirable to shield debt management policy from political interference to ensure transparency and accountability in its conduct. Third, debt management can be improved if it is entrusted to portfolio managers with knowledge and experience in modern risk management techniques, and it is important to measure manager performance against a set of criteria defined by the ministry of finance. Finally, it is important to allocate sufficient resources for hiring highly qualified staff and for acquiring sophisticated systems to support them.

Separating Debt Management from Monetary Policy

In contrast to the integrated management of assets and liabilities by corporations, which manage financial risks by matching the currency composition and maturity of their assets with those of their liabilities, the management of sovereign assets and liabilities is usually not commingled. In the majority of countries, central banks are in operational charge of assets management, while ministries of finance maintain operational authority over liabilities management. Such separation of responsibilities in managing sovereign assets and liabilities is viewed as optimal by governments because it avoids the potential conflicts of interest between monetary policy and debt management, which might otherwise compromise the independence of the central bank. To illustrate: a central bank with a dual mandate to conduct monetary policy and debt management policy may be reluctant to raise interest rates to control inflationary pressures because such a move would adversely affect its domestic liability portfolio. Or it might be tempted to manipulate financial markets to reduce the interest rates at which government debt is issued or to inflate away some of the value of nominal debt. A central bank may also be tempted to inject liquidity in the market prior to debt refinancing, or to bias the maturity structure of the debt profile according to the stance of its monetary policy.

Conflicts of interest between debt policy and monetary policy may also arise if the central bank is in charge of managing the foreign currency debt portfolio of the government. For instance, the daily management of the liquidity of the foreign currency debt in the foreign exchange market—converting foreign bond proceeds into local currency, or converting local currency funds for foreign currency debt repayments—may conflict with the intervention policy of the central bank. The central bank's sales and purchases of securities to meet foreign currency debt requirements also could be perceived by the financial markets as having a signaling effect on its exchange rate policy, thereby undermining its effectiveness.

Although separating debt policy from monetary policy is necessary to preserve the integrity of the central bank, only close coordination between the ministry of finance and the central bank can ensure that debt management policy is consistent with monetary policy. Without proper coordination, the participation of the treasury in the foreign exchange market may have significant monetary implications, and may be at odds with the intervention policy of the central bank. Specifically, the central bank needs to be fully informed of the daily transactions of the agency in charge of debt management, so that it can adjust its day-to-day management of liquidity and intervention policies to offset the impact of these transactions on the market. This is particularly the case when the central bank has to meet the foreign currency needs of the treasury, such as exchanging the foreign currency proceeds of an external bond issue for local currency, or converting local currency funds into foreign currency for interest or principal repayments on foreign currency debt. Full cooperation between the two institutions also demands that the central bank inform the debt manager of the composition and maturity of its reserves portfolio, and update it on a regular basis, so that the debt manager can factor it into debt management policy.

Potential conflicts of interest between monetary policy and debt policy have induced several countries to separate the two functions. In *New Zealand,* all debt management functions carried out by the central bank, as agent of the debt office, have been conducted without reference to monetary policy considerations since 1988. The New Zealand debt office makes all pricing decisions on treasury bills and government bonds, and advises the Minister of Finance on the size and structure of the domestic borrowing program. The foreign reserves of the central bank are integrated in the debt office's asset and liability management process, however. Specifically, the debt office directly finances the central bank's foreign exchange reserves by maintaining foreign currency deposits at the central bank. Under this structure, the central bank manages its net foreign exchange exposure, while the debt office fully incorporates foreign reserves in its debt management.

In *Hungary,* the Ministry of Finance took over the cost of servicing the net national foreign currency debt in early 1997. While the National Bank of Hungary will remain formally responsible for the interest payments and amortization of the foreign loans issued under its name, it will receive transfers from the ministry broadly equivalent to the cost of servicing that part of external debt in excess of the foreign exchange reserves of the central bank at end-1996. The ministry will take full control of debt management in 1999, and the central bank will act only as the agent of the ministry. The shift of responsibilities from the central bank to the ministry was deemed necessary to ensure that the monetary policy objectives of the central bank did not interfere with any of its other functions or responsibilities.

In *South Africa,* the central bank has been until recently the government's agent for marketing its debt instruments, thereby exposing monetary and debt policies to the potential tensions described earlier. After a thorough review of debt policy, the South African authorities set out a new policy framework for debt management in 1996, delegating all policy issues related to state debt management to the Department of Finance. The central bank was made accountable to the department on all matters related to debt management, and funding activities undertaken by the central bank on behalf of the government were fenced off from monetary policy operations. A high-level body comprising representatives of the finance department and the central bank was established to coordinate monetary and fiscal policy objectives.

There are instances, however, where the central bank can be in charge of managing the foreign currency government debt and the foreign exchange reserves without creating conflicts of interests. This would apply to a government that issues foreign currency debt only to finance foreign reserves. *Denmark* provides a case in point. The Danish government decided in 1991 to regroup assets and liabilities management under the central bank's authority. The rationale behind the decision was to improve coordination of the management of the public debt and foreign reserves and to reduce the net exposure of the government to exchange rate risk.[15] Managing the net exposure of assets and liabilities was deemed to be more appropriate than managing their isolated exposures because of the limited use of foreign currency debt in funding budget deficits. Indeed, the Danish government issues foreign-currency-denominated debt to replenish foreign reserves only when they deviate from a desired level, while only kroner-denominated debt is used to finance the government deficit. Although the central bank is in charge of managing the net portfolio, the decision on the currency composition and the desirable maturity of the net portfolio is made jointly with the Ministry of Finance and the Ministry of Economic Affairs during quarterly meetings.

In most countries, however, foreign currency debt is not issued primarily to finance foreign reserves, but to finance the fiscal deficit and the current account deficit. Under those circumstances, it is preferable to forgo the efficiency of a single agency managing the sovereign's net risk exposure to avoid conflicts of interest.

Debt Management Framework

The separation of debt policy from monetary policy allows the central bank to fulfill its monetary objectives unfettered by debt policy objectives. In a similar vein, an efficient, transparent, and accountable debt management policy requires an organizational structure independent from political influence, with clearly defined objectives and performance criteria, and run by qualified staff, according to sound risk management principles. A number of countries (e.g., Austria, Belgium, Ireland, New Zealand, Portugal, and Sweden) have concluded that, to achieve such objectives, debt agencies with some degree of autonomy from the political sphere should be set up. Specifically, the formulation of debt policy (e.g., level of the debt, limits on domestic and foreign currency borrowing) is a political decision and, therefore, should rest in the hands of the government. The management of the sovereign debt, however, can be extracted from the political domain and assigned to a separate and autonomous debt management office (DMO). Under this arrangement, the ministry of finance defines the medium-term strategy for debt management—based on its objectives and risk preferences, and the macroeconomic and institutional constraints of the country—while the DMO implements that strategy and administers the issuance of the domestic and foreign currency debt.

Autonomous Debt Agencies

There are several advantages to a separate and autonomous debt management office. First, by recognizing that the structure of the sovereign debt portfolio is an integral part of public policy and deserves a distinct institutional presence, the authorities signal their commitment to a more transparent, evenhanded, and accountable debt management policy to financial markets and their political constituency. Second, an autonomous debt agency can be charged with a clearly defined objective, based on economic and market-based principles, and organized to achieve such an objective, without being hampered by either the management structure or pay scale of the public sector. In particular, an autonomous debt agency can maintain a flexible management and career path structure and link the pay scale of its personnel to that of private sector practitioners. Such a flexible pay structure would allow the DMO to attract staff qualified to manage increasingly complex financial instruments and markets. Third, a DMO perceived by investors as credibly independent from political decision making would contribute to lowering the country's risk premium and the government's borrowing costs, because it would be perceived as less likely to engage in risky strategies designed to maximize short-term political gains. The success of a DMO, however, hinges on the existence of an open and developed domestic financial system and an accountable structure within the public sector.

The main tasks of a debt agency are to manage the day-to-day risk exposure (liquidity risk, market risks)

---

[15] While the currency composition of the foreign debt and foreign reserves is matched, there is no immunization of interest risk.

of the sovereign debt portfolio and to ensure that the sovereign borrower has continuous and orderly access to international financial markets to meet its external obligations. In addition, the debt agency typically manages the domestic public debt portfolio. This entails managing liquidity risk by ensuring that future funding needs can always be met at the lowest cost and are smoothly spread over a number of years without significant repayments bunched in single periods. DMOs can also enhance the liquidity of the government securities market by increasing the transparency and predictability of debt issuance and creating liquid benchmark issues spread along the yield curve.[16] Greater transparency can be attained by planning and reporting in advance the financing requirements of the government, the maturity structure of future borrowing, and the auction dates of domestic debt issuance for the financial year. Greater predictability can be achieved by relying on regular and nondiscretionary debt issuance, primarily through auctions. By increasing liquidity and attracting a larger investor base, the DMO will help to reduce borrowing costs.

Sovereign risk exposure is not limited to government debt but characterizes debt contracted by all public and publicly guaranteed entities (provincial, state, or local governments, parastatals, and all other debt with a government's guarantee). Most governments, however, exclude publicly guaranteed debt from their debt management policies until the guarantees are invoked, and hence do not accurately reflect the risk profile of the sovereign. It is therefore important that all public debt be centralized under the management structure of the DMO and managed as a single portfolio.

Selected Examples of Debt Management Offices

Autonomous debt management offices have been established by law in a number of OECD countries, including Austria, Ireland, Portugal, and Sweden (Tables 66–69). Debt agencies were set up to improve the management of the public debt by hiring qualified portfolio managers, incorporating modern risk management techniques in debt strategies, and providing a greater incentive for the staff to lower borrowing costs. Although these DMOs report to their ministries of finance, they maintain a significant degree of autonomy from the latter, have their own boards of directors, follow specific investment guidelines against which their performance is evaluated, and remunerate their staff competitively. Denmark, Finland, and the Netherlands also grant their debt offices a degree of autonomy from the political process; Australia, New Zealand, and to a limited degree Denmark have spe-

cific performance criteria for their debt agencies.[17] Selected debt offices that have recently been established or reformed are surveyed below.

In *Ireland,* the government delegated in 1990 the borrowing and debt management functions of the department of finance and the domestic government bond market operations of the central bank to an autonomous debt agency, the National Treasury Management Agency (NTMA). The decision to establish the NTMA was justified on the grounds that it would be given clearly defined performance objectives and a degree of independence from other government objectives, and that the concentration of resources and expertise would result in better risk management and lower debt-servicing costs. The agency's main objective, which is cast with reference to a low-risk, medium-term benchmark portfolio, is to fund maturing government debt and annual borrowing requirements at a lower cost than that of the benchmark portfolio, while containing the volatility of annual fiscal debt-service costs.

In 1989, *Sweden's* National Debt Office (SNDO), which was founded in the eighteenth century, was transferred from the authority of the Parliament to that of the Ministry of Finance to improve debt management practices. The primary objective of the SNDO is to minimize the costs of borrowing within the limits imposed by monetary policy and to finance the day-to-day government budget deficit at the minimum possible long-term cost. The board of the SNDO—which is composed of, among others, the undersecretary of the Ministry of Finance and members of Parliament—establishes separate benchmark portfolios for the domestic and foreign currency debt and lays down the permitted deviations from the benchmark portfolios. Within these broad guidelines, the SNDO manages currency allocation and the maturity structure and market risk of the overall debt portfolio. The performance of the SNDO is evaluated by comparing the cost of the central government debt with that of the benchmark portfolio for the fiscal year.

The performance of the SNDO, which is reviewed by the board on a quarterly basis, has been remarkable over the past four years. Between July 1991 and June 1995, the overall savings on both the kronor debt and the foreign currency debt, relative to the benchmark portfolios, amounted to about 16 billion kronor. During that period, the SNDO also outperformed external managers, who are responsible for managing a small portion of the foreign currency debt on the same principles as those of the SNDO. Between January 1992 and July 1995, the funding costs of the external managers were 0.9 percentage point higher than the corre-

---

[16]When used in the context of domestic debt, a *benchmark* refers to a large and liquid debt security against which other debt securities (e.g., corporate, state enterprise) are measured and priced.

[17]Typically, performance criteria are attached only to how efficiently funding transactions are executed and do not cover other debt management functions (e.g., liquidity management, risk management).

Table 66.   Institutional Structure of Debt Offices in OECD Countries: Debt Offices Within the Treasury

	Australia	Belgium	Netherlands	New Zealand	Turkey
1.1 Position of debt management office (DMO) in government organizations.	Branch of treasury.	Treasury.	Agency in treasury.	Branch of the treasury.	General directorate in treasury.
1.2 Chief executive officer reports to:	Treasurer.	MoF.	Treasurer.	MoF.	The undersecretary and the minister.
1.3 Board of directors.	No.	No.	No.	Advisory board.	No.
1.4 Degree of independence from political power.	Highly independent.	Not independent.	Independent.	No specific independence.	Independent under normal circumstances.
2.1 Does the DMO have specific performance criteria?	Yes, both for long-term and operational performance.	No specific criteria.	General criteria for the maturity and the cost of borrowing.	Qualitative performance criteria relating to all services.	No.
2.2 Who evaluates the performance criteria?	DMO.	No specific evaluation.	Parliament.	Secretary of treasury.	...
2.3 Is there a penalty in case of a loss?	No.	No.	...	...	...
3.1 Is there a legal limit for domestic borrowing?	Yes, financial year budgetary need.	Yes, limit on the cost of borrowing.	Only an implicit limit (budgeted borrowing requirement).	No legal limit.	Only for government bonds; the limit is twice the budget deficit.
3.2 Who decides on the new limits?	DMO and the treasurer.	Parliament.	...	MoF may alter the program.	For government bonds, the parliament.
4.1 Who makes the final decision in an auction?	Treasury.	MoF.	Agent (chief executive of DMO).	DMO.	The undersecretary of treasury.
5.1 Involvement of DMO with cash management budget office.	Closely related.	Closely related.	Closely related.	Carried out by DMO. Closely related.	Direct involvement.

6.1 Duties other than debt management (in case of a crisis).	Political authority is needed for a direct offshore issuance.	In a foreign exchange market crisis, may implement special issues with suitable terms.	To suspend or withdraw an announced issue after consultation with treasurer.	None.	In consensus with monetary policy, may become an effective instrument to handle the crisis.
7.1 Comparative wage of a DMO officer.	Equivalent to civil servant, marginally lower than central bank officer.	Equivalent to civil servant, lower than private bank officer.	Equivalent to civil servant, lower than private bank officer.	Comparable to civil servant, comparable to bank officer.	Equivalent to civil servant, lower than private bank officer.
8.1 Fiscal agent.	Reserve Bank of Australia (central bank).	National Bank of Belgium and financial intermediaries.	Agency in treasury.	Registry, Reserve Bank of New Zealand (central bank).	Central bank.
8.2 Agency services.	…	Collecting the coupons and debiting the treasury account.	Handling the mechanics of sales.	Money collection, issuance, payments, and registration.	Handling auctions, bond sales on tap, redemptions and interest payments, and deposit account record keeping.
9.1 Size of book-entry form stock.	More than 90 pecent.	All treasury certificates and part of other public loans.	3 percent.	100 percent.	0 percent.
9.2 Number of track-keeping staff.	Five treasury officers for book-entry, 25 central bank staff for all areas of registry.	All treasury certificates and part of other public loans (17 persons).	One person.	Twenty-nine staff.	Twenty treasury officers.
10.1 Who handles the statistical followup and projection?	Debt management branch of the treasury.	Public debt office in the treasury.	Financial reporting and computer programming department of the agency.	…	Budget and domestic department provisions in treasury.
11.1 Basis of accounting.	Cash basis for budget accounts; accrual basis for financial statements.	…	Cash and accrual basis.	Cash accrual and marked-to-market basis.	Cash basis for budgetary purposes; accrual basis for following up the stock.

Source: Organization for Economic Cooperation and Development.
Note: DMO = debt management office; MoF = ministry of finance.

Table 67. Institutional Structure of Debt Offices in OECD Countries: Autonomous Debt Offices

		Austria	Ireland	Sweden
1.1	Position of debt management office (DMO) in government organizations.	Autonomous corporate body owned by MoF (AFFA).	Autonomous agency under the MoF.	Autonomous agency under the MoF.
1.2	Chief executive officer reports to:	MoF.	MoF.	. . .
1.3	Board of directors.	Yes.	Advisory committee.	Yes.
1.4	Degree of independence from political power.	Highly independent.	Independent in some broad guidelines drawn by MoF.	Independent except for volume of foreign currency borrowing.
2.1	Does the DMO have specific performance criteria?	No specific criteria.	Yes.	• For foreign exchange funding. • For domestic funding.
2.2	Who evaluates the performance criteria?	. . .	J.P. Morgan evaluates and reports to MoF.	Board of directors and MoF.
2.3	Is there a penalty in case of a loss?	. . .	No.	There is a limit only for foreign exchange funding.
3.1	Is there a legal limit for domestic borrowing?	Yes, the limit is set by the Financial Law.	No.	There is a limit only for foreign exchange funding.
3.2	Who decides on the new limits?	Parliament.	. . .	. . .
4.1	Who makes the final decision in an auction?	AFFA (DMO).	Officials in charge of market operations.	Officer in charge of auctions.
5.1	Involvement of DMO with cash management budget office.	Closely related.	Closely related. Takes the broad parameters.	Taken for granted.
6.1	Duties other than debt management (in case of a crisis).	On request of MoF, gives opinion on budget financing.	No special duties other than taking part in the advisory committee.	Must act parallel to the monetary policy (especially in foreign exchange crisis).
7.1	Comparative wage of a DMO officer.	Higher than civil servant, comparable to bank officer.	Higher than civil servant.	Higher than civil servant, lower than private bank officer.
8.1	Fiscal agent.	Postal savings bank. Also for cash management, other private banks.	Agency, except for the settlement of government bond transactions.	Swedish Central Securities Depository (VPC) in domestic currency.
8.2	Agency services.	. . .	. . .	Redemption of loans; payments of coupons.
9.1	Size of book-entry form stock.	73 percent.	100 percent.	100 percent till 1993.
9.2	Number of track-keeping staff.	Two officers.	Six officers and 15 central bank staff.	Swedish Central Securities and one person in debt office.
10.1	Who handles the statistical followup and projection?	MoF.	Department of finance.	Debt office.
11.1	Basis of accounting.	. . .	Cash basis for the most part; accrual basis for the administrative budget.	Cash basis supplemented by cost accounting.

Source: Organization for Economic Cooperation and Development (OECD).
Note: DMO = debt management office; MoF = ministry of finance.

Table 68.   Institutional Structure of Debt Offices in OECD Countries: Debt Offices Within the Central Bank

		Denmark	United Kingdom
1.1	Position of debt management office (DMO) in government organizations.	Denmarks Nationalbank (central bank).	Treasury and Bank of England.
1.2	Chief executive officer reports to:	MoF.	Treasury minister.
1.3	Board of directors.	No.	No.
1.4	Degree of independence from political power.	Borrowing program is approved by the MoF.	Independent within the limits set by the remit.
2.1	Does the DMO have specific performance criteria?	Only foreign currency portfolio is subject to evaluation.	Performance against the remit.
2.2	Who evaluates the performance criteria?	MoF.	Ministers.
2.3	Is there a penalty in case of a loss?	No.	…
3.1	Is there a legal limit for domestic borrowing?	Yes, limit on the level of debt outstanding.	Yes, limit by the funding remit.
3.2	Who decides on the new limits?	Parliament.	…
4.1	Who makes the final decision in the auction?	Denmarks Nationalbank.	Bank of England.
5.1	Involvement of DMO with cash management budget office.	Active involvement.	Closely related.
6.1	Duties other than debt management (in case of a crisis).	With the consensus of the bank and MoF, debt management may become an instrument in handling the crisis.	Money markets and foreign exchange and reserve management.
7.1	Comparative wage of a DMO officer.	Comparable to civil servant, lower than bank officer.	Comparable to civil servant, lower than private bank officer.
8.1	Fiscal agent.	Denmarks Nationalbank.	Bank of England.
8.2	Agency services.	…	Advising treasury in timing of sales, and deciding the acceptable price level of bids for stock.
9.1	Size of book-entry form stock.	Nearly 100 percent.	90 percent (optional).
9.2	Number of track-keeping staff.	Staff of 120 in Danish Securities Center (independent institution).	…
10.1	Who handles the statistical followup and projection?	Denmarks Nationalbank.	Treasury for projections; bank's Financial Statistical Division; government's Central Statistical Office.
11.1	Basis of accounting.	Cash basis.	Cash and accrual basis for calendar and fiscal year.

Source: Organization for Economic Cooperation and Development.
Note: DMO = debt management office; MoF = ministry of finance.

Table 69. Institutional Structure of Debt Offices in OECD Countries: Debt Offices Within the Ministry of Finance

	Canada	Germany	Greece	Japan	Mexico	Switzerland
1.1 Position of debt management office (DMO) in government organizations.	Department in MoF.	Directorate in MoF.	MoF.	Department in MoF.	Directorate in MoF.	Unit in MoF.
1.2 Chief executive officer reports to:	MoF.	MoF.	...	MoF, the government.	General director, MoF.	MoF.
1.3 Board of directors.	No.	No.	...	No.	No.	Monitoring committee.
1.4 Degree of independence from political power.	...	Independent except for important matters.	...	Dependent.	Independent within the broad objectives of the Development Plan.	Independent with some restrictions.
2.1 Does the DMO have specific performance criteria?	No.	No specific criteria.	...	No formal criteria.	A general (flexible) performance criterion.	No specific criteria.
2.2 Who evaluates the performance criteria?	...	...	...	...	Undersecretary.	...
2.3 Is there a penalty in case of a loss?	...	...	...	...	The director of public debt is responsible.	...
3.1 Is there a legal limit for domestic borrowing?	Yes, Borrowing Authority Act.	Yes, a limit is set by federal legislative authorizations (Budget Law).	No, except for the limit on treasury bill issues.	Yes, a limit is set by Budget Law.	Yes, a limit is set according to the federal budget.	No legal limit.
3.2 Who decides on the new limits?	Parliament.	Parliament.	Interest rates are set by MoF; amount is determined by subscription in the market.	The Diet (legislative branch of parliament).	Congress.	...
4.1 Who makes the final decision in an auction?	Department in MoF.	Division state secretary or MoF according to the implications.	...	Minister of finance.	General director and undersecretary.	Debt management unit.
5.1 Involvement of DMO with cash management budget office.	...	...	...	Related within the MoF.	Closely related.	Active involvement.

6.1 Duties other than debt management (in case of a crisis).	...	In situations with political implications may behave according to the decision of MoF in cooperation with Bundesbank or the cabinet.	...	None.	Government economic cabinet board decides what to do.	Management of assets, interest rates, and currency risk hedging.
7.1 Comparative wage of a DMO officer.	...	Equivalent to civil servant; difficult to compare with bank officer.	...	Equivalent to civil servant, lower than private bank officer.	Equivalent to civil servant, lower than private bank officer.	Equivalent to civil servant, lower than private bank officer.
8.1 Fiscal agent.	Bank of Canada.	German Bundesbank.	...	Bank of Japan (central bank).	Any private bank, usually Citibank.	Swiss National Bank.
8.2 Agency services.	Advising, recordkeeping, issuing, redeeming, international payment registration, and deposit accounts.	Lead manager in bond syndicate; tender procedures/auctions; support and smoothing operations in the secondary market.	...	Issuing, auction handling, redemption, international payment, registration.	Being counterparty in money market; functioning as custodians; handling auctions; collecting stamp duty.	
9.1 Size of book-entry form stock.	More than 90 percent.	Nearly 100 percent.	0 percent.	98 percent.	Approximately 40 percent.	2.5 percent of bonds and 96.5 percent of short-term papers.
9.2 Number of track-keeping staff.	CDS staff (privately owned nonprofit institution).	Staff of 235 in federal debt administration (independent institute).	...	Twenty-five staff.	Twelve staff.	Four people in accounts department of treasury.
10.1 Who handles the statistical followup and projecton?	Bank of Canada.	Division of federal government debt.	MoF.	Government debt division for statistical followup; budget bureau for projections.	(Domestic debt) director of public debt, general director of finance projections, treasury department, central bank general director of government accounting.	Financial plan and budget division and treasury back office.
11.1 Basis of accounting.	Cash basis.	Cash or accrual according to the statistical purpose.	...	Cash basis.	Real (cash basis).	Cash basis.

Source: Organization for Economic Cooperation and Development.
Note: CDS = Canadian depositories for securities; DMO = debt management office; MoF = ministry of finance.

sponding costs of the benchmark portfolio, whereas the SNDO's costs during the same period were 2.5 percentage points lower than those of the benchmark portfolio (Sweden, National Debt Office, 1995).

In *New Zealand,* the country's debt management strategy is implemented through the New Zealand Debt Management Office (NZDMO), which has been responsible for managing the public debt since debt management policy became disentangled from monetary policy objectives in 1988. Although the NZDMO has been placed in a division of the Treasury, it maintains some degree of autonomy from the rest of the government, and has its own advisory board. The board meets four times a year and includes, among others, a senior member of the Treasury and experts in risk management theory and practice. The role of the board is to provide advice and oversight across a broad range of strategic and operational risk management issues and to promote transparency in DMO decision making and supervision. The treasurer or head of the NZDMO recommends the strategic benchmark for the sovereign debt, in terms of currency mix and interest rate sensitivity, and the tactical trading limits imposed on the portfolio manager.[18] Both of these parameters have to be approved by the New Zealand Treasurer.

The objective of the NZDMO is "to identify a low risk portfolio of net liabilities consistent with the Government's aversion to risk, having regard for the expected costs of reducing risk, and to transact in an efficient manner to achieve and maintain that portfolio." In order to minimize its net risk exposure, the NZDMO has gradually set the duration and currency profile of its liabilities to match that of its assets. As most of the government assets are denominated in New Zealand dollars, this strategy has entailed a gradual elimination of the net public foreign currency debt—which was achieved in September 1996—and a lengthening of the duration of the domestic public debt. A significant change introduced by the NZDMO is the marking to market of all its financial liabilities on a daily basis; it has incorporated other private sector risk management practices in its debt management as well. The performance of the portfolio managers is measured on a daily basis by comparing the market value of the actual debt portfolio with the strategic benchmark portfolio.

In the past two years, a small number of emerging market countries have also reformed their debt management practices and introduced benchmarks for their external debt. In *Colombia,* the Ministry of Finance and Public Credit has implemented a series of measures to strengthen its liability management framework. The measures include increasing the staff in charge of managing and hedging its external debt

portfolio, modernizing the data systems supporting the staff, and consolidating the external borrowing strategies of the central government and the parastatal companies. Particular attention has been paid to attracting staff with the appropriate knowledge and experience in portfolio analysis and to offering competitive remuneration to retain them. The main reform introduced by the authorities is managing the sovereign liability portfolio with respect to a set of low-risk benchmark parameters specifying exchange rate, liquidity, and interest rate risks.

In *Hungary,* as noted earlier, the debt management office located in the Ministry of Finance has been charged with servicing the cost of the net sovereign foreign debt. The authorities have decided to align the currency composition of the foreign currency debt through hedging operations with that of the currency basket to which the national currency is pegged. Particular emphasis is being placed on lengthening the maturity of the debt, maintaining more than three-quarters of the debt in fixed-rate instruments, and evenly spreading debt redemptions to avoid rollover risks.

Although several other emerging market countries, including Argentina, Mexico, South Africa, and Turkey, are currently reviewing their debt management practices, in most developing countries debt offices are nonexistent, debt management objectives are cast in general terms, and there are no formal guidelines on the currency composition and maturity structure of the public debt.

Strategic Management of Sovereign Liabilities

Benchmarks for the Foreign Currency Debt Portfolio

A key building block in the institutional framework of sovereign risk management is the derivation of a benchmark or target portfolio for the external public debt.[19] A benchmark communicates the medium-term policy objectives of the policymaker to the portfolio manager and the framework within which he or she has to operate; it also provides a measure against which the performance of the manager can be evaluated. Devising a benchmark for the external public debt encourages policymakers to articulate and quantify their key objectives and cost/risk trade-offs, and to

---

[18]In view of the small amount of risk that the NDZMO is allowed to take, the position limits around the strategic benchmark portfolio are tightly defined.

[19]Benchmarks are most useful for the foreign currency debt portfolio. It is difficult to have a benchmark portfolio in the domestic market because the government is the largest borrower, and its securities act as benchmarks against which all other instruments are priced and measured. The government may have, however, a target domestic debt portfolio, specified in terms of duration; the target portfolio should serve as a reference point rather than as a benchmark to beat.

measure the currency, interest rate, liquidity, and credit risks that they are willing to tolerate on the portfolio. In essence, the establishment of a benchmark imposes discipline on the debt management policies of the sovereign borrower.

The selection of a benchmark for the external debt entails specifying the desired currency composition of the debt and, for each of the currencies, specifying the target duration, the maximum maturity, the breakdown between fixed- and floating-rate instruments, and the financial instruments permitted in the portfolio (e.g., bank loans, indexed-linked bonds, derivatives). Identifying and quantifying these factors is a challenging process, because they depend on the objectives and risk preferences of the policymaker and the macroeconomic and institutional constraints faced by the country. The composition of a benchmark is also strongly influenced by the numeraire in which costs are measured and the horizon over which such costs are estimated.

Objectives

Debt management objectives vary from one country to another, but in most instances they focus solely on lowering annual budget costs rather than on lowering the long-term economic cost of public debt. In recent years, however, a growing number of governments (e.g., Australia, Belgium, Sweden) have redefined their debt management objectives as minimizing the financial, long-term cost of public debt, not just budgetary costs.[20] In Belgium, the objective of public debt management is "to minimize the financial cost of the public debt, while maintaining market and operational risks at an acceptable level, taking into account the general objectives of budgetary and monetary policies." In Australia, the debt management objective is to minimize the long-term portfolio cost, defined as the time-weighted total debt cost (economic cost), subject to an acceptable level of risk, defined in terms of the annual debt-servicing costs (accounting measure of risk). Similarly, in Sweden, the overriding objective of the debt office is to minimize the costs of public debt within the limits imposed by monetary policy.

In setting such objectives, governments face a trade-off between minimizing the budget cost of the public debt and lowering the volatility of debt-servicing costs. The extent to which sovereign borrowers place greater emphasis on the first or second of these objectives has a significant impact on the target maturity of the benchmark and on the proportion of fixed- versus floating-rate instruments in the portfolio.

For instance, if the government's main objective is to lower debt-service costs, the target duration of the

benchmark portfolio would be short (assuming an upward yield curve) and biased toward issuing short-term or floating-rate instruments. A short-duration debt, however, has to be refinanced more frequently, thus exposing the portfolio to greater repricing risk (refinancing at a higher interest rate) or bunching risk (repayment of principal occurring within a short period). As mentioned earlier, the Mexican crisis illustrated the risks of a short-duration public debt.

If the government's main objective is to stabilize debt-servicing costs, the target duration of the benchmark would be longer and biased toward issuing long-term fixed-rate debt. In this case, although annual debt servicing volatility would be lower, the mark-to-market value of the debt would be more sensitive to interest rate movements. The Irish debt benchmark portfolio, for instance, has a long maturity profile, reflecting the government's bias toward debt-servicing stability. If the objective of the government is to minimize the volatility of the net present value of the debt on a year-to-year basis (a one-year time horizon), then a debt with a maturity of one year would minimize risk.

Risks

The key question to address when selecting the composition of the benchmark is the extent of risks (liquidity, market, credit) or losses that the policymaker is willing to tolerate. The risk tolerance of the sovereign may prove tricky to estimate, however, because there is no single measure of sovereign risk. Wheeler (forthcoming) recommends that the government align its risk preferences with those of the average or median citizen, who is typically risk averse. Indeed, since taxpayers cannot fully hedge or avoid the losses that the government incurs on its assets and liabilities portfolios, they would demand that the government follow a low-risk strategy. The risk preferences of a sovereign entity can also be approximated by taking those of institutions with a similar risk profile, such as pension funds, international financial institutions, life insurance companies, and long-term savings industries. A more systematic estimation of risk tolerance, however, would be to define it in terms of the maximum interest rate costs and excess volatility that can be sustained on the debt portfolio without jeopardizing the budget targets and medium-term objectives of the government. Any risk exceeding this tolerance level should be avoided.

The risk tolerance of a government ultimately depends on the size of the public debt, its currency composition, and its maturity. Any time the debt-service cost is an important element in government expenditures, its variation becomes a key element to watch, and the sovereign borrower is likely to be concerned with the volatility of its debt. This is particularly the case for governments that have a limited ability to

---

[20]The optimal level of the debt is a fiscal decision that is taken as given in the analysis.

generate foreign currency revenues or to access international markets. When the debt-to-GDP ratio is low, however, the sovereign has greater flexibility in terms of the choice of currencies in its portfolio and its duration. In particular, the sovereign borrower may diversify its portfolio to include currencies with lower yield, or shorten the maturity of its portfolio to reduce interest rate costs, knowing that its overall exposure to the higher risks is limited.

Macroeconomic Constraints

The two key macroeconomic policies that affect the currency composition and maturity profile of the external debt benchmark are the fiscal and monetary policies of the government. Budget targets, for instance, influence the desired duration of the benchmark. Budget targets may include maintaining the level of public debt to GDP below a certain percentage (e.g., to meet Maastricht criteria); reducing the government debt as a percentage of GDP over a certain horizon; or maintaining the public deficit below a certain percentage of GDP (e.g., stability pact after EMU). A cap on the debt-to-GDP ratio constrains the extent of volatility tolerated on the debt portfolio and biases the portfolio toward a longer duration. A cap on the budget deficit or on interest payments imposes a minimum average maturity on the portfolio, and constrains the proportion of floating-rate debt, thereby limiting the risks of interest rate and exchange rate shocks destabilizing the budget targets.

A monetary policy geared toward pegging the exchange rate to a currency or a basket of currencies (1) biases the choice of currencies in the benchmark portfolio toward the pegged currency (e.g., as in Hungary), and (2) limits the proportion of floating-rate and short-term domestic debt in the portfolio (e.g., as in Belgium), to allow the central bank greater flexibility in influencing short-term rates through open market operations. The incompatibility of a pegged exchange rate policy with a short-duration domestic debt was demonstrated during the 1992 ERM crisis. Several European central banks were constrained in their defense of their exchange rates during the crisis by the short duration of the public debt: both Italy and Spain had difficulty raising interest rates because of the short duration of their debt and the rapid impact of the higher rates on public expenditures. In countries in which a large portion of the debt is at floating rates, monetary policy would also be constrained by the pass-through of interest rate hikes to domestic borrowers (e.g., the United Kingdom during the ERM crisis).

The trade flows of a country may also influence the choice of currencies in the external public debt benchmark, particularly when trade flows dominate capital flows, or when a government's revenues are directly linked to the export of commodities denominated in foreign currencies (e.g., Colombia, Mexico, Saudi Arabia). In economies in which the exchange rate is determined by monetary policy and capital flows, rather than by trade flows, the latter need not determine the foreign currency composition of the benchmark. The governments of several industrial countries with debt benchmarks (e.g., Belgium, Denmark, Ireland) do not take trade flows into account when deciding on the target currency composition of their benchmarks; they expect currency hedging to be undertaken by private entities and corporations.

Institutional Constraints

An important institutional constraint that affects the target currency composition and duration of the benchmark is the extent of official borrowing (bilateral or multilateral) in the foreign currency debt portfolio, since official borrowing is generally denominated in the donors' currencies. Indeed, as more than half of developing countries' long-term debt is owed to official creditors, a significant part of the debt may be denominated in currencies that are not optimal from a risk management perspective. When developing countries have access to derivative markets or to the World Bank currency conversion scheme discussed earlier, they can hedge their exposure to some of these currencies.

Other institutional constraints that influence the composition benchmark include limiting the currency composition of the foreign debt to that of the foreign reserves portfolio (e.g., United Kingdom); maintaining a fixed percentage of foreign borrowing in a specific currency such as the ECU to develop the debt market of that currency (e.g., France, Italy); or partly aligning the currency composition of the external debt with that of the national foreign assets (e.g., oil stabilization fund in Colombia) to create a natural hedge. National assets are often designated for special purposes, however, and may not necessarily be at the disposal of the sovereign to service its foreign debt.

Numeraire and Horizon

The choice of a numeraire in which costs are measured is particularly important as it biases the currency composition of the portfolio toward that currency. Considering that the assets and revenues of most governments are denominated in the local currency, it would seem appropriate to measure the liabilities and interest payments of the government in the same currency; the risk-neutral numeraire for a sovereign portfolio is therefore the local currency.[21] The local cur-

---

[21]Belgium, Denmark, Ireland, and New Zealand, among others, use their local currency as the numeraire for their foreign currency debt. In Colombia, the dollar is used as numeraire, as the closest substitute to the peso, owing to its importance in trade and capital flows and exchange rate management.

rency could be taken as the numeraire even when a country pegs its exchange rate to another currency or to a basket of currencies. Taking the pegged exchange rate as the numeraire would give the sovereign only a nominal hedge against currency risk, because there is always a risk that the currency will be devalued or the peg abandoned.

To avoid frequent changes in its composition and maintain its neutrality from political considerations (budget cycle) a benchmark needs to be defined over a medium-term horizon (e.g., three to five years).

Analytical Framework

Having identified its objectives, risk preferences, and constraints, the policymaker then has to choose an appropriate analytical framework to model the stochastic properties of the variables involved and derive the benchmark debt portfolio. There is no unique methodology that can be used to derive a benchmark portfolio. Efficiency frontier models, which estimate the cost/risk characteristics of various currencies and interest rates in a portfolio, have been used by a number of countries (e.g., Belgium, Ireland, and New Zealand) to derive their benchmarks. Drawing the most efficient combination of expected costs, variances, and correlations for the different currencies and interest rates, the analyst obtains an efficiency frontier—representing a set of portfolios that offer the lowest expected cost for a given level of risk.[22] The most conservative approach is to choose, among these portfolios, the minimum variance portfolio—the portfolio that yields the lowest costs at the minimum level of risk—as the benchmark portfolio.

The success of a benchmark as a risk management tool is closely linked to its robustness to changes in its underlying assumptions, including various financial market outcomes or interest rates and exchange rate scenarios. Robustness can be assessed by comparing the performance of the benchmark under various price movements—for example, lower and higher interest rates, a flattening or a steepening of the yield curve, and an appreciation or depreciation of the domestic currency vis-à-vis the foreign currencies included in the portfolio. Given that debt management includes managing the exposure of the sovereign borrower to low-probability, high-risk events, the robustness of the benchmark to extreme market conditions (tail events) also has to be tested. This can be done by simulating the effect of market collapses, sharp changes in exchange rates (the ERM crisis, the Mexican crisis), in-

terest rates, or commodity prices (oil shock) on the benchmark.[23] The benchmark would be robust if, under all scenarios, its risk-adjusted cost performance is superior to all other portfolios. Depending on the results of the tests, the benchmark may have to be readjusted to reflect the risk tolerance of the sovereign to catastrophic events.

A benchmark is especially effective as a disciplinary tool when its composition and the performance of the debt manager relative to the benchmark are made public. Such public disclosure is essential for creating a transparent and accountable debt management policy. In order to be used by policymakers to monitor the performance of their debt managers, a benchmark portfolio needs to be easily replicated in the marketplace as a low-cost passive strategy and structured to track available bond and money market indices (e.g., the J.P. Morgan or Salomon Brothers Money Market and Government Bond indices). A benchmark that includes complex currency or interest rate hedging strategies may be difficult and costly to replicate by the portfolio manager because of a lack of information on the instruments or high transaction costs. Finally, the composition of the benchmark needs to be reviewed regularly to incorporate important changes in the objectives and risk preferences of the government.

Selected Examples of Debt Benchmarks

A number of countries have developed benchmarks for their public debt. In *Ireland,* the benchmark is designed to be consistent with the annual debt-service budget within which the NTMA has to operate. As such, the review of the benchmark is annual and matches the budget cycle. The NTMA attempts to beat the benchmark both by funding at different dates than the benchmark, in order to take advantage of favorable market opportunities, and by issuing at different maturities. The NTMA chooses its maturities subject to a limit on the amount of debt it is permitted to issue and subject to guidelines on the proportions of foreign currency and floating-rate debt. The performance of the DMO is evaluated by comparing the difference between the actual and benchmark portfolios at the end of the year, both of which are marked-to-market and net present valued in local currency. Although the currency composition and duration of the Irish benchmark are not made public, the deviations of the actual portfolio from the benchmark tend to be small. According to the NTMA, as of December 1996, the foreign currency composition of the Irish debt was as follows: 29 percent in deutsche mark, Dutch guilders,

---

[22]Expected returns are implied from forward exchange rates, swap curves, and the interest rate term structure, whereas variances and correlations are derived from historical data. In order to be risk-neutral, benchmarks should rely on expectations derived from market prices rather than on the government's forecasts of foreign currencies and interest rates.

[23]Stress tests can be simulated by adding standard deviation shifts to the parameters used in estimating the portfolio (e.g., adding one or two deviations to the currency and interest forward or swap rates), or by assigning probabilities to future market scenarios.

and Swiss francs, 43 percent in pounds sterling and French francs, 20 percent in U.S. dollars, 3 percent in ECUs, and 5 percent in Japanese yen and other currencies.

In *Sweden,* the benchmark serves as the limit within which the foreign currency debt may be exposed to currency and interest rate risks. Within the risk limits laid down by its board, the SNDO takes positions in the foreign exchange and bond markets to bring the long-term cost of the debt below that of the benchmark portfolio. As of December 1996, the currency composition of the Swedish benchmark was 25 percent deutsche mark, 16 percent French francs, 12 percent U.S. dollars, 10 percent pounds sterling, 6 percent Japanese yen, and the rest in ECUs and ECU-basket currencies. The currency composition of the benchmark primarily matches the weights of the currencies in the ECU basket (82 percent), while the U.S. dollar and Japanese yen are included in the portfolio for diversification. The duration of the foreign currency debt portfolio is around 2.2 years. The interest rate structure of the benchmark is based on diversified borrowing along the yield curve to reduce shocks to specific parts of the yield curve and to reduce bunching risk over a certain year.

In *Colombia,* the recently established external debt benchmark includes a higher portion of dollar debt than currently (80–85 percent instead of the current 72 percent), in line with the currency exposure of government revenues. The rest of the portfolio is to be divided between deutsche marks (around 12 percent) and Japanese yen (around 3 percent). The selection of the benchmark reflects the structure of currency flows into the country and the risk tolerance of the government. The benchmark portfolio has a longer maturity profile and a smaller share of floating-rate debt than the actual external debt portfolio.

In *Hungary,* the currency benchmark for the foreign currency debt (foreign and domestic) that is now serviced by the Ministry of Finance matches the composition of the basket to which the national currency is pegged (70 percent deutsche mark, 30 percent U.S. dollar). The composition of the remaining foreign currency debt held by the central bank, however, matches that of the foreign exchange reserves. These examples notwithstanding, in most developing countries, benchmarks for the external public debt remain nonexistent.

Deviations from the Benchmark Portfolio

Sound risk management would necessarily require that, at times, the debt manager moves the actual debt portfolio away from the benchmark portfolio to adjust to changes in market conditions or incorporate new expectations about market developments. As any divergence from the strategic benchmark portfolio introduces currency and interest rate risks, however, the ministry of finance would need to cap those risks by imposing strict guidelines on the maximum permissible deviation from the benchmark and the extent to which the sovereign portfolio may be exposed to market risks.

The discretion of debt managers over the management of the sovereign debt varies from one country to another, depending on the risk preferences of the sovereign borrower, the size of the debt, and the expertise of portfolio managers. A government burdened with a large debt-service cost relative to its budgetary expenditure would necessarily limit the extent to which debt managers can deviate from the benchmark portfolio, because of the large fiscal consequences of a risky strategy. This would apply, for example, to a country that wants to join EMU and thus has to abide by Maastricht criteria. In such instances, the debt manager would follow a passive investment strategy, ensuring that the actual debt portfolio follows the benchmark portfolio closely. Governments with a small debt burden and the means to acquire sophisticated risk management systems and experienced portfolio managers have greater flexibility in allowing their debt managers to pursue an active debt management strategy. For instance, debt managers may be encouraged to outperform the benchmark by deviating from the benchmark's currency weights and duration by a certain percentage, according to their expectations of future market movements. Active debt management may also involve taking advantage of arbitrage opportunities and irregularities in the market, through liquidity or credit transformation transactions.

In Denmark, the maximum level of deviation from the benchmark has been set at DKr 2.5 billion in each country. In Sweden, the SNDO may deviate from the currency composition of the debt benchmark portfolio by 3 percentage points, and by 0.5 percentage point from the duration of the benchmark. In Belgium, the government has opted to pursue a passive debt management strategy because of the high operational costs of active management. Canada has also renounced an active debt management policy and focuses only on minimizing refunding risks.

Conclusion

In a world of mobile capital flows and integrated capital markets, governments holding large and unhedged foreign currency liabilities may be exposed to risks that they are not always fully equipped to manage properly. In the current environment, the sound management of sovereign liabilities has become an important element of a country's ability to safeguard its exposure to external risks.

An important step toward reducing the vulnerability of emerging markets to external shocks is to reform the institutional arrangement governing debt policy, so that it promotes a professional, transparent, and publicly accountable incentive structure. The experience of the governments that have already reformed their debt management practices suggests that such objectives are best achieved if debt management is assigned to a separate debt agency with a degree of autonomy from political influence. Under such an arrangement, the ministry of finance formulates and publicly announces its debt strategy, while the debt agency implements that strategy and manages the day-to-day exposure of the debt portfolio according to the investment guidelines of the ministry of finance.

Regrouping liabilities management under a separate and autonomous agency improves the assessment and management of the risk exposure of the country and shields the debt agency from political pressures. It also enables the authorities to charge the agency with a clearly defined objective and to organize it to achieve that objective, without being hampered by either the management structure or pay scale of the public sector. Furthermore, assigning debt management to an autonomous debt agency enables a clear separation of responsibilities between debt management and monetary policy, thereby avoiding the conflicts of interest that arise when a central bank is in charge of both functions.

An appropriate and transparent vehicle for communicating the objectives and preferences of the ministry of finance to the debt office is the establishment of benchmarks for the foreign currency debt portfolio. The benchmark portfolios, which can be derived using portfolio optimization techniques, specify the currency composition, the maturity structure, and the permissible instruments of the sovereign debt portfolio. To cap the exposure of the portfolio to market risks, the ministry of finance may impose strict limits on the margin of deviation of the portfolio manager from the benchmark. A key element of this framework is to disclose to the public on a regular basis both the benchmark portfolio and the performance of the debt manager relative to the benchmark. Such public disclosure is essential for creating a transparent and accountable debt management policy.

Annex VI

Capital Flows to Emerging Markets— A Historical Perspective

In early 1989, the secondary market price of the external bank debt of the initial Brady plan countries stood at only 40 cents on the dollar, and private capital flows were largely limited to concerted lending or arrears. Indeed, some observers argued that the heavily indebted emerging market countries might not be able to regain access to private international financial markets for a generation. Instead, the 1990s have witnessed a movement of capital to emerging markets on a scale (when measured relative to their GDPs) not seen since the gold standard era of the late 1800s and early 1900s. This growing integration of emerging markets into the international financial system is viewed by a number of observers as reestablishing the type of relationships between capital-importing and capital-exporting countries that existed in earlier periods of high mobility, such as 1880–1914 and the 1920s.[1]

Clearly, close international linkages offer benefits associated with directing capital to its most productive uses and providing investors with improved opportunities for portfolio diversification. However, the past two and a half decades have demonstrated that integration carries risks as well: access to international markets can be lost abruptly or exchange rate arrangements can be subject to speculative attacks, especially if there are doubts about the sustainability of a country's macroeconomic policies.[2]

These considerations raise two questions: how does the cyclical nature of capital flows to emerging markets since 1973 compare with that of earlier periods of high capital mobility, and why has there been such a strong renewal of private capital flows to emerging markets in the 1990s, given the dismal experience of the 1980s?[3]

This annex examines these questions, putting the recent flow of capital to emerging markets in historical perspective. It starts by comparing the nature and scale of capital flows to emerging market countries in the past two decades with those experienced in two earlier periods of high capital mobility: the gold standard period (1870–1914) and the 1920s. In these historical periods divergent macroeconomic developments in capital-exporting and capital-importing countries often generated a boom-bust pattern of flows that was sometimes accentuated by crises in capital-importing countries. Next, the factors that have influenced the scale, composition, and geographic distribution of the capital flows to emerging market countries since the mid-1970s are examined and the recent attempts at identifying the key developments in both emerging market and industrial countries, as well as the changes responsible for the resurgence of flows in the 1990s, are reviewed.

Earlier Periods of High Capital Mobility

The classical gold standard era, which lasted from roughly 1870 to 1914, is typically regarded as the longest period of high capital mobility between a set of major capital-exporting countries, the United Kingdom and to a lesser extent France and Germany, and a set of "emerging markets."[4] The key features of global capital markets during this period were as follows:

- The scale of total capital flows, as measured by the average of the absolute values of current account deficits relative to GDP for the major capital-exporting and capital-importing countries, was higher during 1870–1930 than it has been in subsequent decades (Figure 57). This index averaged 3.3 percent over 1870–1914 and has as yet reached only 2.6 percent in the 1990s.

---

[1]See, for example, Obstfeld and Taylor (1997).

[2]Appendices 1 and 2 to this annex examine the recent theoretical and empirical literature on the determinants of balance of payments and banking crises that often accompany reversals in capital inflows and speculative attacks on exchange rate arrangements.

[3]We focus on the period after 1973 because between 1945 and 1972 flows among industrialized countries dominated international capital movements; the volume of capital flowing to emerging markets was marginal.

[4]There were two major capital importing-country groups. One group, consisting of the countries in North America, Latin America (principally Argentina, Brazil, and Mexico), and Oceania (Australia), received capital primarily from the United Kingdom and used it in large part for development finance. The other group, consisting of countries in Eastern and Central Europe, Scandinavia, the Middle East, and Africa, was provided finance mainly by France and Germany, often of a nondevelopmental nature to cover fiscal gaps. See Bayoumi (1989) and Taylor (1996) for statistical evidence on high capital mobility in the late 1800s and early 1900s.

Figure 57. Capital Mobility Index[1]
(In percent of GDP)

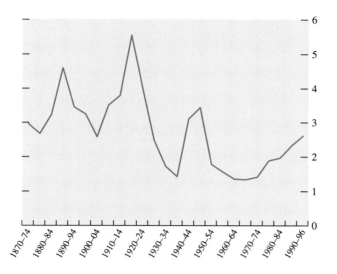

Source: Taylor (1996).

[1]The index is defined as the average of the absolute values of current accounts relative to GDP for major capital-importing and capital-exporting countries. The countries include Argentina, Australia, Canada, Denmark, France, Germany, Italy, Japan, Norway, Sweden, the United Kingdom, and the United States.

- When measured relative to GDP, private capital flows of the earlier era were at least as large as in the 1990–96 period and in many instances considerably larger. The main capital exporter, the United Kingdom, saw annual capital outflows averaging almost 5 percent of GDP over 1880–1914, with levels at times reaching 7 percent and even 9 percent in the years before World War I. France and Germany saw smaller flows relative to GDP that, on average, were about 3 and 2 percent, respectively, over the same period (Figure 58). Among capital importers, between 1881 and 1890 annual inflows to Australia averaged 9.5 percent of GDP and about 2.5 percent of GDP in the next decade; Canada had annual inflows amounting to over 6 percent of GDP in the 1880s, about 4.5 percent in the 1890s, 7 percent in the first decade of the twentieth century, and over 14 percent between 1910 and 1913 (Figure 59).
- Foreign capital was an important source of finance for investment in the 1870–1914 period—for example, it financed over a third of domestic investment in New Zealand and Canada and about a quarter of that in Australia and Sweden (Figure 60). In comparison, capital inflows have amounted to about 10 percent of domestic investment in emerging markets during the 1990s.

Figure 58. Net Capital Outflows, 1880–1913
(In percent of GDP)

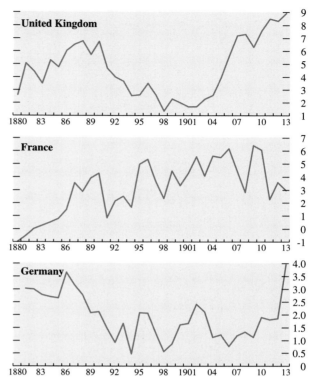

Source: Bloomfield (1968).

- Portfolio investments were far more important than direct investment. In the 1870–1914 period direct investment represented about 10 percent of the United Kingdom's foreign investments.[5] By contrast, foreign direct investment has accounted for 39 percent of net private capital flows to emerging markets in the 1990s.
- Some capital-importing countries accumulated a part of the inflows as official reserves (gold and foreign exchange). Available estimates indicate that international reserves quadrupled in Russia and Belgium, doubled in India and Sweden, and increased substantially in the United States during 1870–1914.[6] As mentioned in Annex I, emerging market reserve accumulation amounted to almost half of total net flows during 1990–96

[5]In 1913, the three main creditors, the United Kingdom, France, and Germany, held 80 percent of the US$35 billion stock of securities issued by capital-importing countries. This was six times larger than their holdings in 1874 and indicates a net capital outflow of some US$30 billion (Bloomfield, 1968; United Nations, 1949).

[6]Bloomfield (1963).

Figure 59. Net Capital Inflows, 1880–1913
(In percent of GDP)

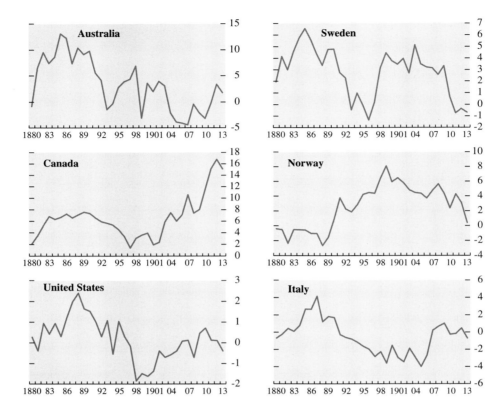

Source: Bloomfield (1968).

and as a consequence reserve holdings more than tripled over the period.

• Although lending was mostly financed by private sources, the bulk of international borrowing for investment depended directly or indirectly on government action. Most of the borrowing was undertaken by governments, primarily for railway construction, utilities, and public works. The private borrowing was largely done by railroad companies with the assistance of government guarantees.

A combination of push and pull factors explains the movement of capital during 1870–1914. An important institutional feature was the role of investment banks in providing a stimulus to global flows. Given the high fees and commission, it was in the interest of merchant and investment banks to provide information about the profitability of ventures in the newly developing areas and persuade representatives of foreign governments and railroads to issue bonds. The financial intermediaries had considerable bargaining power vis-à-vis both bondholders and the borrowers because

of their advantage in collecting and processing information and their ability to raise vast sums of money. In general, investors earned relatively high returns on their portfolio investment. After adjusting for losses due to defaults, Edelstein (1982) estimates that investors earned returns between 160 and 390 basis points over domestic portfolio investments in relatively safe instruments.

The period from 1870 to 1914 was characterized by high variability in capital flows between capital-exporting and capital-importing countries. Investment flows from the United Kingdom were buoyant in the early 1870s, most of the 1880s, the early 1890s, and then again in the years before World War I. It is widely accepted that capital flows from the United Kingdom were countercyclical in nature.[7] A decline in investment demand and thereby interest rates in the United Kingdom would stimulate a capital outflow as investors sought higher returns abroad. This outflow

_____
[7]Cairncross (1953), Cardoso and Dornbusch (1989), Dunning (1970), Thomas (1967), Kindleberger (1982), Vos (1994).

Figure 60. Contributions of Capital Flows to Investment, 1870–1914 versus 1980–90s

(Ratio of capital flows to investment)

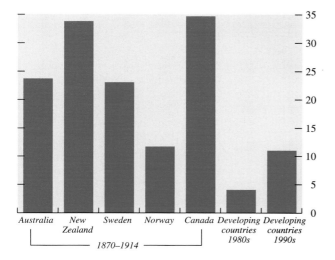

Sources: Bloomfield (1968); and International Monetary Fund, *World Economic Outlook.*

most often took the form of purchases of bonds issued by borrowers in the capital-importing countries. These funds were used to finance various types of investments, including the expansion of export-related industries. At some point, a recovery in the United Kingdom and/or an increase in the discount rate by the Bank of England to stem its loss of gold reserves would lead to higher interest rates in the United Kingdom and hence a reduced capital outflow. The balance of payments positions of the capital-importing countries would not necessarily deteriorate, however, if the investments funded by earlier inflows led to increased exports to a buoyant United Kingdom economy. The higher export revenues would then offset the decline in capital inflows.

Two factors would at times disrupt this counter-cyclical interaction between trade and capital flows. First, as capital outflows from the United Kingdom declined, in some cases the export-related projects in borrowing countries were incomplete or otherwise incapable of producing enough exports to offset the decline in capital inflows. Second, even if borrowing countries were in a position to increase their exports, the rise in interest rates in the United Kingdom sometimes led British companies to sell off or otherwise reduce their inventories of imported goods. This would often lead to a sharp decline in the terms of trade of the capital-importing countries at the same time that capital inflows were declining. In some cases, the combination of slowing capital inflows and stagnant or falling export receipts would lead to slower economic growth and, as a result, stagnant or falling do-

mestic revenues and expanding fiscal deficits. Occasionally, this situation would not be corrected quickly enough, and the borrower would have to suspend debt-service payments or abandon its gold standard commitment or both (Table 70). At times, such turning points were accompanied by institutional failures, including banking crises, in the capital-importing and (less frequently) in the capital-exporting countries.

Reaction to failures in contractual obligations depended on the motivation for the lending. When borrowers of development finance did default, assistance was given at the same time as some "conditionality" or accommodation was imposed by the creditors. While it was in the interest of the newly developing countries to have access to the London capital market and the political and economic dominance of Britain assured that international debt contracts were honored, it is worth noting that the British government generally followed a policy of laissez-faire and the capital market operated virtually free of any intervention. As Fishlow puts it, "The government offered friendly offices but no intervention, diplomatic or more forceful, on behalf of bondholders."[8] By contrast, the reaction of capital-exporting nations to defaults on sovereign loans raised to close fiscal gaps was, at times, quite drastic. It could involve direct intervention to restructure public finance and its administration.

High capital mobility after World War I lasted only until the advent of the Great Depression and represented an attempt to reestablish the capital market relationships that had existed before the war. But three major shifts had changed the environment: (1) the United States had become a major capital-exporting country; (2) the United Kingdom's lending had become more focused on its colonies, while the United States took up the role of major purchaser of bonds issued by Latin American and European borrowers; and (3) a much greater share of international lending went to finance public sector nondevelopment expenditures rather than investments.

The United States saw its holdings of foreign assets rise from $6.5 billion in 1919 to $14.8 billion in 1929. External investment by the United States was, on average, 1 percent of GNP in the 1920s, while that of the United Kingdom, which had been 4 to 5 percent of GNP in the first half of the 1920s, fell to below 2 percent in the second half. The limited information available about the distribution of capital among individual capital-importing countries suggests that some countries were more affected than others by the changes in the international environment. In Canada, external debt payments exceeded capital inflows between 1923 and 1926, but there were net inflows amounting to 2 percent of GNP in the late 1920s. By comparison, in

[8]Fishlow (1985), p. 398.

237

Table 70. Selected Crises, 1870–1914

	Description	Cause
Turkey (1875)	Debt default	Fiscal deficits were funded by foreign borrowing that eventually could not be sustained.
Peru (1876)	Debt default	Falling guano exports and stagnation of other revenues combined with increasing fiscal deficits to generate a crisis.
Egypt (1876)	Debt default	Increased foreign borrowing to finance consumption led to unsustainable debt growth.
Argentina (1890)	Debt crisis and institutional failure	Argentina's inability to meet debt-service payments led to the bailout of Baring Bros.
United States (1873)	Financial crisis	Bank runs and failures and fears about U.S. commitment to gold parity followed a stock market crash.
Greece (1893)	Debt default	Increased borrowing to finance consumption led to unsustainable debt growth.
United States (1894–96)	Speculative attack	Speculation against the U.S. gold standard parity followed the Sherman Act (1890) and increasing fiscal deficits.
Brazil (1898)	Debt default	A decline of 64 percent in coffee prices over the preceding five years generated an external crisis.
United States (1907)	Financial crisis	Banking panic and suspension of cash payments followed interest rate hikes and bank failures.
Canada (1907)	Speculative attack/banking crisis	High interest rates in Canada (in response to hikes in the United States) led to excessive credit expansion that generated speculation against the Canadian dollar.
Brazil (1914)	Debt default	A sharp decline in coffee prices in the preceding two years generated a debt crisis.

Sources: Fishlow (1985); Bordo and Schwartz (1996); and Rich (1989).

Argentina net capital inflows were around 3 percent of GNP, only slightly below those in the gold standard era.

Of crucial importance was the fact that, in contrast to the earlier classical gold standard era, the capital flows of the 1920s were procyclical rather than countercyclical and made the system far less stable and more prone to crisis. Increases in domestic investment in the United States coincided with increases in capital exports.[9] This procyclicality in foreign lending was in part associated with the fact that an upswing in investment in the United States was typically accompanied by a sharp rise in domestic savings as well. In addition, the capital outflows also occurred during periods of rising commodity prices, which increased the perceived creditworthiness of the capital-importing countries. On the upswing, increased creditworthiness of capital importers coincided with greater availability of capital. On the downswing, reduced capital flows combined with declining export demand, as the United States economy slowed, reinforced the spiral. To make matters more difficult for the emerging markets of the time, while the United Kingdom had financed countries that produced goods that it imported, U.S. capital exports were directed to countries that produced goods that competed with its exports. And, whereas the United Kingdom's policy during the period 1870–1914 was generally one of laissez-faire and free trade, the United States followed a more protectionist policy in the 1920s.

The experience in 1870–1914 and 1919–30 highlights three key features: (1) in both periods the flow of capital to emerging markets was highly variable, with sharp increases in flows regularly followed by sharp downturns; (2) in both periods the downturns in capital flows often involved some combination of divergent macroeconomic conditions between the major capital-exporting countries and the larger capital-importing countries and economic or political crises in individual capital-importing countries; and (3) both periods of high capital mobility were ended by major economic or political events (i.e., World War I and the Great Depression, respectively).

International Capital Flows After the First Oil Shock

While it is clear that there have been enormous structural changes in the international financial system and the global economy, the cyclical pattern of capital flows between emerging markets and the international financial centers in recent times does have similarities

[9]Vos (1994).

Table 71. External Financial Resources to Developing Countries

(Percent shares)

	1960–61	1970–72
Aid	56	47
Bilateral	54	37
Multilateral[1]	2	10
Other official flows	13	9
Private flows	31	44
Direct investment	19	17
Bank sector	6	16
Bonds	n.a.	2
Private export credits	6	9
Total flows	100	100
Memorandum item:		
Total flows (in billions of U.S. dollars; 1983 prices)	34.8	53.6

Source: Vos (1994).
[1]Includes grants by private voluntary agencies.

with earlier periods, especially regarding the role of divergent macroeconomic and structural developments between lenders and borrowers in producing sharp changes in capital flows.

Capital Flows in 1973–89

The renewal of private capital flows to emerging markets that began in the early 1970s followed a nearly 40-year hiatus. The segmentation of capital markets between mature and emerging market countries reflected both the disruptions associated with the Great Depression and World War II as well as the maintenance of comprehensive systems of capital controls in many countries throughout the 1950s and 1960s. As a result, official capital flows and foreign direct investment dominated the limited flows of financial resources between mature and emerging market countries (Table 71).

In contrast to the limited flows in the 1950s and 1960s, the period since 1973 has witnessed net private capital flows to emerging markets amounting to nearly US$1.32 trillion. Nonetheless, the pattern of flows has been highly uneven, with an initial surge of inflows in the 1973–82 period ($163 billion), followed by a collapse of flows during the rest of the 1980s ($103 billion), and then a renewed surge in the 1990s.

The capital flows that took place between the first oil crisis of 1973 and 1982 were closely associated with the recycling of oil revenues. Bank loans were the principal instruments for intermediating these flows, and balance of payments data suggest that such loans (including trade credits) accounted for 57 percent of total flows. Geographically, the movement of capital was concentrated on borrowers in Asia and Latin America.

In many ways, the second recycling effort, in the late 1970s, initially seemed less problematic than that following the earlier shock of 1973–74. In part, this reflected the view that the international financial system had played an important role in facilitating the first recycling. The optimism, however, was not borne out by events. According to James (1996), the problems that arose as a result of the second wave of recycling were related to the global imbalances that developed in the aftermath of the second oil price shock. After the first oil price shock, many countries, concerned about the fragility of their economies, had attempted to postpone adjustment and maintained a relaxed monetary stance. The inflationary consequences of such policies had undermined stability even further. After the second oil price shock, most countries tightened monetary policy but many were still unwilling to make the necessary but painful fiscal adjustments. As a result, real interest rates rose and borrowing became expensive and more difficult to service.

The emergence of debt-servicing difficulties in many heavily indebted emerging market countries in mid-1982 brought to an abrupt halt the inflow of private capital. Net private inflows fell from a peak of nearly $49 billion in 1981 and $19 billion in 1982 to only a $9 billion inflow in 1983 and a $5 billion outflow in 1984. This abrupt slowdown in lending, and in some cases reversal of capital transfers, were even more dramatic for heavily indebted emerging markets in the Western Hemisphere, which together saw net private inflows decline, from a peak of $46 billion in 1981 and $16 billion in 1982, and then reverse, to outflows of $9 billion and $2 billion in 1983 and 1994, respectively. While net private inflows to all emerging markets recovered modestly in the 1986 to 1989 period (averaging roughly $20 billion a year), the Western Hemisphere experienced virtually no net private inflow during that four-year period.

In a number of respects, the sharp rise in capital flows to emerging market countries in the 1970s followed by the subsequent crash in the early 1980s was similar to the pattern of lending booms in the 1880s and the 1920s and the bust in the 1890s and 1930s. However, the international lending of the 1970s differed from that of earlier periods in the extent to which banks were directly exposed. By the end of 1981, it was calculated that the exposure of U.S. banks to Latin American debt amounted to 97 percent of capital and in many individual cases well above 100 percent. The combined exposure of U.S. banks to Mexico alone amounted to 34 percent of their capital.

The debt crisis that started in 1982 has been attributed to developments in the highly indebted countries and to changes in their external environment. First, a number of emerging markets pursued unsustainable macroeconomic and financial policies during the late 1970s and early 1980s. External borrowing was used to finance large fiscal imbalances, producing strong inflationary pressures. In addition, some countries followed exchange-rate-based stabilization policies and liberalized their financial systems without setting up an appropriate prudential regulatory and supervisory framework, which led to lending and consumption booms that ended up in banking and balance-of-payments crises (see Appendix 1 at the end of this annex). In other countries, distortions in domestic financial markets, often a byproduct of restrictions on financial activities and on the payment of market-related interest rates, created strong incentives for the residents of some countries to place funds in offshore markets that offered more attractive financial returns and a more stable financial environment. Indeed, various estimates suggest that the large-scale capital inflows to the public sector in many of the heavily indebted emerging markets were matched to a large degree by corresponding private sector capital outflows.[10]

Second, the external environment facing many emerging market countries deteriorated at the beginning of the 1980s. Growth in the mature markets slowed sharply in the late 1970s, declining from an average rate of growth of 4 percent in 1978 to slightly more than 1 percent in 1981. This prolonged sluggishness of activity in the mature markets contributed to a decline in the growth of exports and a deterioration in the terms of trade for many non-oil emerging market countries. For that group, the volume of exports, which had expanded at 9 percent a year from 1976 to 1979, decelerated to 5½ percent in 1980 and 4 percent in 1981. The deterioration in the terms of trade initially arose from the oil price increases during 1979 and 1980 but was extended through 1981 by cyclical weakness in primary product prices. For the net oil importers as a group, the cumulative deterioration of the terms of trade from 1977 to 1981 exceeded 15 percent—equivalent to some $45 billion to $50 billion in terms of 1981 trade values. At the same time, as part of efforts to curb inflationary pressures in the mature markets, interest rates in major financial markets and in major offshore centers rose sharply from the late 1970s through 1981. For example, the three-month London interbank offered rate (LIBOR) on U.S. dollar deposits rose from an average annual rate of 9 percent in 1978 to nearly 17 percent in 1981. Since many of the syndicated loans that were made to emerging market borrowers carried interest rates that were tied directly to LIBOR, these countries experienced a sharp rise in their debt-servicing payments.

The decline in net private capital inflows in the 1980s was accompanied by a sharp deterioration in the macroeconomic performance of many emerging market economies. For example, the average rate of growth for all emerging markets fell from roughly 4¼ percent in 1977–81 to approximately 1½ percent in 1982 and 1983. Moreover, those emerging markets that experienced debt-servicing difficulties saw their rate of growth fall from roughly 4 percent a year during 1977–81 to a decline of 1 percent a year in 1982 and 1983. In addition, inflation accelerated in countries that experienced debt-servicing difficulties, from approximately 35 percent a year in 1977–81 to 58 percent in 1982–84. While it is generally recognized that the growth rates of the late 1970s were often supported by unsustainable fiscal deficits and financial policies, the worsening of macroeconomic performance and more rapid inflation further reduced the perceived debt-servicing capacity of the heavily indebted countries. On top of this, the external debt position of many of the heavily indebted emerging market countries deteriorated sharply compared with the early 1970s. For example, the ratio of external debt to exports of goods and services for heavily indebted emerging market countries with debt-servicing difficulties shot up from 182 percent in 1981 to 236 percent at the end of 1983 and to 375 percent in 1986. Also, the ratio of external debt service payments to exports of goods and services for these countries rose from 32 percent in 1981 to 44 percent by 1986.

The economic situation confronting the heavily indebted emerging market countries at the beginning of the 1990s created considerable skepticism about how rapidly these countries would be able to reestablish their access to international financial markets. Some observers argued that it could take a substantial time before access was restored, despite several years of adjustment effort and concerted lending.[11]

This pessimism reflected in part a perception at the time that the macroeconomic performance of the heavily indebted emerging market countries that had experienced debt-servicing difficulties was deteriorating again. While this group had seen a modest recovery in its economic growth in the period from 1984 to 1986 (averaging 3.5 percent a year), the rate of growth slowed to 1.5 percent in 1988–89. Inflation at the same time rose sharply, from an average rate of 69 percent a year in 1984–86 to 190 percent in 1988–89. Fiscal imbalances also remained in the range of 6 to 7 percent of GDP and the external debt position of these countries showed little improvement. The average ratio of debt-service payments to exports of goods and services for this group of countries in 1988–89 (35.9 percent) was virtually identical with that in 1982 (35.5 percent). In addition, the ratio of external debt to exports increased from 218 percent in 1982 to an average of 338 percent in 1988–89.

---

[10]See, among others, Dooley (1986), Mathieson and Rojas-Suarez (1993), Reisen and Yeches (1993), and Rojas-Suarez (1991).

[11]See United States, Senate (1990).

Capital Flows in the 1990s

Despite this pessimism at the start of the decade, total net private capital flows to emerging markets in the 1990–96 period soared to $1,055 billion, more than seven times the amount they received in the 1973–81 period. Moreover, net private flows during 1990–96 were over nine times as large as net external borrowing from official creditors (see Table 13). Geographically, the distribution of these flows has been quite uneven. Asia received the largest proportion, 40 percent, and Western Hemisphere countries secured the next largest chunk at 30 percent. By contrast, only 8 percent of the flows went to economies in transition and around 5 percent to African countries. The composition of the net flows also changed dramatically from the 1978–82 period. While the syndicated bank loan was the dominant instrument associated with capital flows during 1978–82, portfolio investment (particularly bonds) and foreign direct investment have been the most important instruments since 1990. The share of foreign direct investment reached 40 percent of total net private capital flows during the period 1990–96 and portfolio flows accounted for 39 percent. Perhaps the most significant change has been in portfolio equity flows, which rose from $1 billion (3 percent of total net private capital flows) in 1990 to $16 billion (7 percent of total net private flows) in 1996. In total, inflows of private capital rose from the equivalent of 3 percent of domestic investment in emerging market countries in 1990 to 13 percent in 1996.

The 1990s also witnessed an expanding participation of emerging market institutions in major financial centers, in part related to the more active management of the growing foreign exchange reserves of these countries. The scale of these holdings and its implications are discussed in Annex I.

Another aspect of the increasing activities of emerging market residents in global financial markets has been the growing importance of capital flows among emerging markets themselves. Since the capital account reporting systems of these markets typically provide relatively limited information about the country of origin of most capital flows, much of the evidence is still anecdotal. One example of growing intraregional flows has been increased investment abroad by Chilean firms. Foreign acquisitions by Chilean companies in 1996 are estimated to have been worth $2.3 billion. Most of the purchases were of state-owned assets being privatized in Argentina, Brazil, Colombia, and Peru, and many of these acquisitions were financed with foreign borrowing in the form of bank loans and through bond issuance. Asia has also seen expanding intraregional flows. Outside of Japan, Hong Kong, China, remains the largest capital exporter in Asia and the single largest outward investor among emerging markets. In the period 1990–95, Hong Kong companies invested a total of $78 billion overseas, of which 65 percent went to China. While China remains a net importer of capital, its firms are beginning to invest abroad, with the financial services sector attracting the largest share of these foreign investments. Already, China is the largest investor in Hong Kong; and, by end-1995, Chinese firms had invested $450 million in Singapore and an estimated total of $462 million in Malaysia, Thailand, Indonesia, and the Philippines. More generally, in 1995, intraregional flows were estimated by some observers to account for about 40 percent of total foreign direct investment (FDI) in Southeast Asia, up from 25 percent in 1990. As an example of this trend, Malaysian firms accounted for 75 percent of the roughly $2 million received by Cambodia in 1995.

Factors Stimulating Capital Flows and Renewed Market Access in the 1990s

The large-scale capital flows to emerging markets in the 1990s stimulated a number of empirical studies that sought to identify the key factors driving them. These studies have typically divided the factors influencing capital flows into so-called push and pull factors.[12] *Push* factors encompass both structural and cyclical developments in international (mainly mature) financial markets that have led investors to diversify their portfolios internationally and seek higher yields in emerging markets. *Pull* factors refer to the macroeconomic and structural policies in emerging markets, as well as other political and noneconomic developments, that have increased their perceived creditworthiness.

Structural Changes

The scale and composition of the capital flows to emerging markets in the 1990s have been influenced by a series of ongoing structural changes in international financial markets. Clearly, the most important change has been the growing liberalization of domestic financial markets and capital account transactions in both mature and emerging market economies. While the removal of capital controls in mature markets in the 1980s and 1990s is well documented, there has also been considerable opening of emerging market economies. Box 9, using an index of capital account restrictions, illustrates the weakening of capital controls in developing countries.

---

[12]Calvo, Leiderman, and Reinhart (1996), Fernandez-Arias (1996), and World Bank (1997) examine the causes and provide an empirical perspective on private capital flows in the 1990s. Agénor (1996) is a recent theoretical analysis of push versus pull factors.

Box 9. Liberalization of Capital Controls in Emerging Markets

The figure plots an index of capital controls in emerging markets. This index is based on information on 163 countries obtained from the IMF's annual survey of Exchange Arrangements and Exchange Restrictions and constructed using the methodology of Bartolini and Drazen (1997). Three dummy variables for each country for each year were constructed corresponding to whether a country restricted capital account transactions, used multiple exchange rate practices, or enforced surrender requirements for export proceeds. An index for each country for each year is obtained by summing its dummy variables and dividing by three. It varies between zero and one, with zero representing a complete lack of controls and one the existence of all the restrictions mentioned above. The aggregate capital control index shown is the mean of the country indices for each year.

The loosening of capital controls in emerging markets since the mid-1980s is clearly brought out by the index. The figure also suggests that the decline in capital account restrictions may have contributed to the recent boom in capital flows to emerging markets. The correlation between the index and capital inflows is –0.3 over the period shown and provides some simple corroboration for the claim that liberalization of external transactions has been instrumental in attracting foreign capital.

Capital Controls in and Flows to Emerging Markets

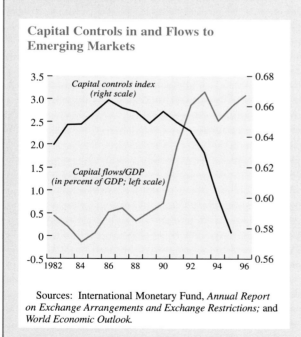

Sources: International Monetary Fund, *Annual Report on Exchange Arrangements and Exchange Restrictions;* and *World Economic Outlook.*

cial system, the process is at an early stage.[13] Recent empirical studies provide a similar picture: there is a growing degree of de facto integration of domestic and international financial markets, in the sense that it is becoming increasingly difficult to keep domestic financial market conditions isolated from developments in international markets.[14]

The growing importance of portfolio flows (both bond and equity) in the 1990s has reflected two other fundamental structural changes in international financial markets, namely, the growing role of institutional investors and securitization. Institutional investors, including mutual funds, insurance companies, pension funds, and, more recently, hedge funds, have become increasingly important purchasers of emerging market securities. To an important degree, their participation in such markets has been driven by the desire both to increase the overall return on their portfolios and to diversify the risks associated with these portfolios. Although these institutional investors typically allocate only a relatively small proportion of their total portfolios to emerging market assets, their sheer size has contributed to the rising tide of capital flowing to emerging markets.

Securitization has involved a greater use of direct debt and equity markets—in which the lender or investor holds a tradable direct claim on the borrower or firm—and a shift away from indirect finance—in which an intermediary holds a nontraded loan asset and the saver holds a liability (which may be tradable) on the intermediary. Another form of securitization has involved the creation of exchange-traded futures and options contracts. In this case, a certain type of risk, usually one associated with price volatility, is securitized. While the substitution of direct for indirect instruments has been driven in part by the lower relative cost of borrowing on securities markets by the more creditworthy borrowers (who often have a higher credit rating than banks), the growing importance of both exchange-traded and over-the-counter (OTC) derivative products has been strongly affected by the desire of portfolio managers (particularly from large institutional investors) to either hedge or increase their exposure to certain types of asset-price risks.

A final "structural" factor that has been especially important for the pricing of derivative products has

[13]The World Bank (1997) index, based on country risk ratings by *Institutional Investor* magazine, combines a measure of a country's ability to attract different forms of private flows (with portfolio capital given a weight of five, commercial bank flows a weight of three, and foreign direct investment a weight of one), and a measure of the diversification of a country's source of finance (with countries receiving funds from diverse sources being regarded as more highly integrated). According to this index, the number of emerging markets classified as highly integrated increased from 2 in 1985–87 to 13 in 1992–94, whereas the number of countries classified as highly or moderately integrated increased from 26 to 39.

[14]See, for example, Dooley, Mathieson, and Rojas-Suarez (1996), Haque and Montiel (1991), and Reisen and Yeches (1993).

An index of integration developed by the World Bank shows that while many more emerging markets are now better integrated into the international finan-

been the development of an academic literature on how to price options—the Black-Scholes (1973) pricing model and its refinements. Although options have been traded for centuries, it was only in 1973 that the Chicago Board of Trade founded the Chicago Options Exchange to create a centralized market for trading options on listed securities. While options have always been priced by the markets, the Black-Scholes technique and subsequent improvements have added a significant degree of precision to such pricing and greatly facilitated the management and trading of financial risks.

A facilitating factor has been the revolution in information technologies, which has increased the ability of investors and creditors to better manage their portfolios and to undertake more robust analyses of credit and market risks. The increased computing power has fundamentally transformed the way information is processed by financial institutions, enlarged the databases that can be managed, and facilitated the pricing of complex derivative products. Improvements in telecommunication technology have complemented changes in computer technologies by allowing for both more rapid transmission of information across markets and better control over geographically dispersed financial operations. These technological changes have affected flows to emerging markets by increasing the efficiency of global securities markets in processing and managing the issuance of bond and equity issues, by facilitating the syndication of bank loans, and by providing emerging market borrowers and investors with derivative products with which to manage exchange rate, interest rate, and credit risks.

Taken together, the structural changes have implied that capital flows to emerging markets in the 1990s have occurred in a fundamentally different environment from that of the 1970s. The globalization of international bond and equity markets, as well as the growing role of institutional investors, has facilitated a shift from indirect finance (syndicated bank lending) to direct (bond and equity) finance. The advances in information technologies have also allowed international banks and investors to manage the risks associated with internationally diversified portfolios more easily. The management of the interest rate, exchange rate, and, more recently, credit risks associated with these portfolios has also been facilitated by the emergence of a variety of new derivative products. These structural developments have thus created incentives for international investors, especially institutional investors, to deal in an increasingly broad range of instruments issued by public and private borrowers from an expanding set of emerging markets.

Macroeconomic Pull and Push Factors

While structural changes in international financial markets have increased the role of institutional in-

vestors and improved the access of emerging market borrowers, recent empirical studies of the determinants of capital flows to emerging markets in the 1990s have also highlighted the roles played by macroeconomic policies and cyclical developments. The performance of emerging market economies during the 1990s stands in sharp contrast with that in the period between the emergence of the debt crisis in 1982 and the initiation of the Brady plan in 1989.[15] Fiscal deficits for emerging market countries that experienced debt-servicing difficulties fell from an average of 6 percent of GDP in 1983–89 to 3 percent of GDP in 1990–96. Although less progress was initially made in containing inflation, with the average rate of inflation for countries with debt-servicing difficulties rising from 77 percent a year in 1979–89 to 177 percent a year in 1990–95, the rate of this group fell to 36 percent in 1995 and 19 percent in 1996. By contrast, the real rate of output growth for the countries with debt-servicing difficulties rose from 2.2 percent a year in the period 1979–89 to over 6 percent in the period 1990–96. Similarly, exports of goods and services of this group of countries, which had grown at 6 percent a year in the 1983–89 period, expanded at an average annual rate of nearly 11 percent during the 1990–96 period. This surge of exports allowed for a decline in the ratio of external debt service payments to exports of countries with debt-servicing problems from 162 percent in 1990 to 128 percent in 1996 despite the rapid growth that had taken place in their external debt. Moreover, the ratio of external debt to GDP fell from 54 percent in 1990 to 37 percent in 1996.

The improving economic performance of many emerging market countries has played a key role in improving their access to international financial markets (see Figures 12 and 13 in the report and the discussion in Annex I). Indeed, between end-1989 and the first quarter of 1997, the number of emerging market countries with a Moody's credit rating almost quintupled, rising from 11 to 52 (Table 72). And, since the beginning of 1996, there have been many more upgrades than negative actions by major credit rating agencies.

In addition to the improvement in macroeconomic performance of emerging market countries, recent studies have stressed the key role played by the extensive privatizations undertaken by this group of countries, and more generally, by the switch to a strategy of opening their economies to international trade and capital flows.

Empirical studies have also emphasized the impact of changes in the global macroeconomic environment during the 1990s. Inflation in the major industrial countries has continually declined between 1990 and

---

[15]The recent evolution of the macroeconomic performance of emerging market economies has been examined in detail in various IMF *World Economic Outlook* reports issued during the 1990s.

Table 72. Moody's Initial Ratings of Emerging Market Countries

	1989 and Before	1990	1991	1992	1993	1994	1995	1996	1997:Q1
Rated countries									
Yearly total	11	1	0	1	5	8	5	16	5
Cumulative total	11	12	12	13	18	26	31	47	52
Africa									
Mauritius								Baa2	
South Africa						Baa3			
Tunisia							Baa3		
Asia									
China	A3								
Hong Kong, China	A2								
India	A2								
Indonesia						Baa3			
Korea	A2								
Malaysia	Baa1								
Pakistan						Ba3			
Philippines					Ba3				
Singapore	Aa3								
Taiwan Province of China						Aa3			
Thailand	A2								
Europe									
Bulgaria								B3	
Czech Republic					Baa3				
Croatia									Baa3
Cyprus								A2	
Hungary	Baa2								
Kazakhstan								Ba3	
Malta						A2			
Lithuania								Ba2	
Moldova									Ba2
Poland							Baa3		
Romania								Ba3	
Russia								Ba2	
Slovak Republic							Baa3		
Slovenia								A3	
Turkey				Ba3					
Middle East									
Bahrain								Ba1	
Egypt								Ba2	
Israel							A3		
Jordan							Ba3		
Kuwait								Baa1	
Lebanon									B1
Oman								Baa2	
Qatar								Ba1	
Saudi Arabia								Baa3	
United Arab Emirates								Baa1	
Western Hemisphere									
Argentina	Ba3								
Bahamas									A3
Barbados						Ba2			
Bermuda						Aa1			
Brazil	Ba1								
Chile						Baa2			
Colombia					Ba1				
Mexico		Ba2							Baa1
Panama									
Peru								B2	
Trinidad and Tobago					Ba2				
Uruguay					Ba1				
Venezuela	Ba3								

Note: Moody's rating:
   Investment grade—Aaa, Aa, A, Baa
   Noninvestment grade—Ba, B
   Default grade—Caa, Ca, C, D
   In addition, numbers from 1 (highest) to 3 are often attached to differentiate borrowers within a given grade.

1996, with the average annual rate of inflation for this group of countries falling from slightly above 4 percent to less than 2 percent. As a consequence, their nominal short- and long-term interest rates have fallen: short-term rates from an average of 7.3 percent in 1987–90 to 4.3 percent in 1994–96, and long-term rates from 8 percent to 6.3 percent during the same periods. Many observers argue that these declines in nominal interest rates in industrial countries have been a crucial influence on the amount of capital flowing to emerging markets.

Recent research seems to indicate that economic fundamentals and profitable opportunities in recipient countries combined with changes in international interest rates influence flows to emerging markets. The weight of evidence does not seem to favor the view, expounded in earlier research (for example, Calvo, Leiderman, and Reinhart, 1993; Fernandez-Arias, 1996), that movements in international interest rates are the most important factor influencing the magnitude of flows. An update of the Calvo and others (1993) analysis in World Bank (1997) indicates (1) the degree of co-movement of flows to emerging markets was much lower in the 1993–96 period relative to the 1990–93 period; (2) the correlation between U.S. interest rates and total flows to emerging markets, which was negative over the 1990–93 period, is close to zero over the period 1990–96. The lower correlation between *total* flows to emerging markets and U.S./industrial country interest rates can be explained by the fact that foreign direct investment, which is largely unresponsive to (moderate) changes in international interest rates, has increased as a proportion of total capital flows to developing economies. The role of bank lending has declined and FDI flows have gradually increased to become the largest component, rising from 26 percent of total flows in 1991–92 to 45 percent in 1995–96.

Appendix 1
Determinants of Balance of Payments and Banking Crises

Reversals in capital inflows have been associated with balance of payments and banking crises. Recent research has focused on identifying a set of macroeconomic and financial indicators that appear to be the main determinants of such events and could possibly be useful as a set of early warning indicators of a country's vulnerability to crises.

Balance of Payments Crises

Empirical studies of the determinants of balance of payments crises utilize variables that play a key role in theoretical models of speculative attacks.

Theoretical Models

The early theoretical models argued that balance of payments crises occurred when deteriorating macroeconomic fundamentals became inconsistent with a fixed exchange rate regime. Krugman (1979) and Flood and Garber (1984a, b), for example, developed models in which excessive domestic credit expansion led to a gradual loss of international reserves and ultimately to a speculative attack on the domestic currency that forced the authorities to abandon the fixed parity and adopt a flexible exchange rate regime. Excessive domestic credit expansion could arise as a result of the need to finance a government budget deficit or to provide financial assistance to a weak banking system or both. Moreover, the credit creation could also spill over to domestic goods markets, leading to an increase in the relative price of nontraded goods, and thereby a real exchange rate appreciation that would contribute to a trade deficit or smaller trade surplus. Furthermore, if there was uncertainty about the domestic credit policy or the level of reserves that the authorities were willing to commit to defend the exchange rate, domestic interest rates would gradually increase as the crisis became more likely.[16]

More recent theoretical models of balance of payments crises argue that a fixed exchange rate regime can be maintained only as long as it is compatible with other policies. These theories imply that a crisis can arise even if there is no deterioration of economic fundamentals (Obstfeld, 1994). For example, a government may be forced to abandon a fixed exchange rate if defending the parity involves increases in interest rates that unduly increase the costs of servicing the domestic debt or seriously weaken the banking system.

A key feature of the more recent analyses is that macroeconomic policies are not regarded as predetermined but are taken as responding to the expectations of agents. This interdependence creates the possibility of self-fulfilling crises—crises arising without obvious policy inconsistencies—that are difficult to predict. However, the new theories do not assert that exchange rates can be attacked irrespective of economic fundamentals. Rather, they suggest it is necessary to consider a broader set of fundamentals that affect the government's and market participants' incentives and constraints when examining the determinants of balance of payments crises. More important, recent models show that the ability of a sudden change in expectations to trigger an attack is bounded by the position of fundamentals, such as the amount of short-term debt that the government has to roll over (Obstfeld, 1994; Calvo, 1995; and Cole and Kehoe, 1996), the desired degree of sterilized intervention (Flood and Marion,

---

[16]For an extensive review of the early speculative attack literature see Agénor, Bhandari, and Flood (1992).

1996), or the access to international liquidity from private sources or other central banks (Lall, 1997).

Empirical Evidence

A number of studies have attempted to estimate the probability of a devaluation on the basis of fundamentals implied by various theoretical models of balance of payments crises. In an early study of devaluations in Mexico, Blanco and Garber (1986) estimated the probability of a devaluation occurring in the next quarter by comparing a "shadow" exchange rate—determined by a set of fundamentals that included the evolution of real income and money demand, as well as domestic credit creation—and the official fixed parity. They estimated probabilities of devaluation that increased to peaks of 20 percent just prior to the major devaluations of 1976 and 1982 and fell to low levels immediately after the devaluations. Cumby and van Wijnbergen (1989) applied the speculative attack model to the Argentine crawling peg of 1979–81 and found that the probability of an attack was driven mostly by domestic credit creation and that it reached a level of roughly 80 percent just before the actual devaluation. In another application of the model to Mexico's experience in the 1980s, Goldberg (1994) found that the probability of a devaluation over a one-month forecast horizon reached nearly 100 percent just before the crisis and that domestic credit creation—rather than external credit constraints or deviations from purchasing power parity—was the main driving force of the speculative attacks.

In an attempt to characterize the nature of balance of payments crises across a broad range of emerging markets, Frankel and Rose (1996) studied a panel of annual data from 1971 through 1992 for over a hundred emerging market countries. The authors classified the potential determinants of currency crashes into four categories: (1) domestic macroeconomic indicators, such as monetary (credit) and fiscal shocks; (2) external variables, such as real exchange rate appreciation, the size of the current account imbalances, and the level of external indebtedness; (3) foreign variables, such as OECD output growth and world interest rates; and (4) the maturity and ownership composition of the external debt. The study confirmed previous results: balance of payments crises tend to occur when domestic credit growth is high, and when international reserves and output growth are low. Such crises also tend to be associated with increases in world interest rates, real exchange rate appreciations, and a fall in FDI inflows. Interestingly, neither current account nor government deficits appear to have a statistically significant effect on a typical balance of payments crisis. However, high ratios of short-term external debt, of concessional debt, and of public debt to total external debt appear to increase the probability of a balance of payments crisis in the next year.

The Mexican crisis of 1994–95 and its impact on other emerging markets—the so-called Tequila effect—stimulated a number of recent studies. For example, Sachs, Tornell, and Velasco (1996) identified three major factors that determined whether a country was vulnerable to a financial crisis: a low level of international reserves relative to broad money; a large appreciation of the real exchange rate; and a weak banking system. These three factors explain around 70 percent of the variability of a "crisis index" for a sample of 20 emerging markets in the period November 1994–June 1995. Other factors, such as the size of a country's current account deficit, the scale of capital inflows, and the fiscal position during the period 1990–94, did not help predict the occurrence of a balance of payments crisis.

Kaminsky, Lizondo, and Reinhart (1997) propose a new methodology for the design of an early warning system for balance of payments crises. Examining a group of earlier empirical studies, the authors attempt to identify those indicators found to be most useful in predicting crises. These earlier empirial studies include some that focus on estimating the probability of a crisis—as discussed above—as well as others in which the behavior of the indicators in the precrisis period was systematically compared with its behavior in a control group (consisting of either noncrisis countries or the same country in "tranquil" times). A summary of those indicators is provided in the first two columns of Table 73. The authors conclude that an effective warning system should consider a broad variety of indicators because currency crises seem to be preceded by multiple economic, and sometimes political, problems. Variables regarded as the most useful indicators of currency crises include international reserves, domestic credit expansion, credit to the public sector, the real exchange rate, and domestic inflation. In addition, output growth, the trade balance, export performance, and the fiscal deficit have shown some usefulness as predictors of crises. The structure of the external debt and the current account balance were not regarded as useful indicators.

Based on their review, Kaminsky, Lizondo, and Reinhart (1997) propose a "signals" early warning system and they use this approach to analyze 76 currency crises that occurred in 15 developing countries and 5 industrial countries during 1970–95. The authors define a crisis as a period in which an index of "exchange market pressure" (comprising a weighted average of monthly percentage changes in the exchange rate and in gross international reserves) is above its sample mean by more than three standard deviations. An indicator signals a crisis when the deviation from its mean crosses a threshold level, which is defined using the tail-ends of the distribution of the indicator over the sample period. The approach allows the authors to measure how often an indicator gives good signals—that is, when the signal was indeed fol-

Table 73. Performance of Crises Indicators

Indicators	Regression Studies[1]		"Signals" Approach (Percentage of crises called)	
	Number of studies considered	Statistically significant results	Balance of payments crises	Banking crises
Capital account				
International reserves	13	12	75*	81
Short-term capital flows	2	1	n.a.	n.a.
Domestic-foreign interest differential	2	1	86	100*
Other	2	1	n.a.	n.a.
Debt profile				
Share of short-term debt	2	0	n.a.	n.a.
Other	7	2	n.a.	n.a.
Current account				
Real exchange rate	12	10	57**	58**
Current account balance	6	2	n.a.	n.a.
Trade balance	3	2	n.a.	n.a.
Exports	3	2	85**	84*
Imports	2	1	54	60
Terms of trade	2	1	79	95
Other	3	0	n.a.	n.a.
International				
Foreign interest rates	3	1	n.a.	n.a.
Foreign price level	2	1	n.a.	n.a.
Foreign real GDP growth	1	0	n.a.	n.a.
Financial				
Credit growth	7	5	56*	50
Money multiplier	1	1	73*	71**
Real interest rates	1	1	89	100*
Lending/deposit rates	1	0	67	69
Money supply-demand gap	1	1	61*	39
Change in bank deposits	1	0	49	64
M2/reserves	2	2	80**	77
Money	3	2	n.a.	n.a.
Inflation	5	5	n.a.	n.a.
Other	4	4	n.a.	n.a.
Real sector				
Real GDP growth or level	8	5	77*	89*
Unemployment	3	2	n.a.	n.a.
Change in stock prices	1	1	64**	80**
Other	1	1	n.a.	n.a.
Fiscal				
Fiscal deficit	5	3	n.a.	n.a.
Credit to public sector	3	3	n.a.	n.a.
Government consumption	1	1	n.a.	n.a.
Institutional/structural				
Exchange/capital controls	2	1	n.a.	n.a.
Financial liberalization	2	1	n.a.	n.a.
Other	7	4	n.a.	n.a.
Political	4	3	n.a.	n.a.

Sources: Based on Kaminsky and Reinhart (1996); and Kaminsky, Lizondo, and Reinhart (1997).
Notes: *means that the indicator has a noise-to-signal ratio of less than 75 percent.
    **means that the indicator has a noise-to-signal ratio of less than 50 percent.
    n.a. indicates variable was not considered in the cited sources.
[1]Balance of payment crises.

lowed by a crisis in the next 24 months—as well as how often it gives a false signal ("noise")—that is, it is not followed by a crisis in the next 24 months. The third column in Table 73 shows that virtually every indicator correctly identified a crisis in at least half of their respective samples. The authors then argue that the noise-to-signal ratio can be used to decide which indicators to drop from the list of possible indicators.

An increase in the ratio of lending to deposit rates and a sudden fall in bank deposits—indicators of solvency and liquidity problems in the banking system, together with rapid import growth, were eliminated on these grounds. A considerable real exchange rate appreciation, a slowdown in export growth, a fall in stock market prices, and an increase in the ratio of M2 to reserves are the most efficient indicators of a currency crisis. A low level of international reserves, excess credit growth, and a recession also give fairly accurate signals of a potential balance of payments crisis.

Balance of Payments and Banking Crises

Several recent studies have attempted to identify the linkages between balance of payments crises and banking crises, where the latter are defined to encompass situations in which many banks suffer severe liquidity or solvency problems or both. Banking systems in emerging markets have been viewed as more vulnerable to crises than those in mature markets (Mishkin, 1996). First, emerging markets are often subject to large and volatile swings in the terms of trade that can adversely affect the debt-servicing capacity of a country's export- and import-competing industries and thereby weaken domestic banks' balance sheets. Second, unanticipated devaluations can severely damage balance-sheet positions, especially when banks and nonfinancial firms have issued large amounts of foreign-currency-denominated debt during periods of protracted real exchange rate appreciation. Third, when deregulation of the financial system leads to rapid credit expansion, a sharp increase in nonperforming loans is likely, especially when banks have weak credit evaluation systems and there is inadequate bank supervision (Goldstein and Turner, 1996; Honohan, 1997).

There have been far fewer cross-country studies of the determinants of banking crises than of balance of payments crises, reflecting in part the fact that it is difficult to obtain reliable and comparable balance-sheet data for banks.[17] Kaminsky and Reinhart (1996) apply the "signals" approach to 26 banking crises during the period 1970–95. The main results of that study are presented in the last column of Table 73. Recessions and large corrections in the stock market preceded over 80 percent of the banking crises. High real interest rates were associated with all of the 20 crises for which interest rate data were available. Large terms of trade deteriorations over the preceding 24 months foreshadowed a banking crisis in 95 percent of the cases studied. However, the terms of trade indicator did not have much predictive success, as it crossed the threshold in a large number of episodes in which a crisis did not result (having a noise-signal ratio of approximately 1).[18] The evidence from credit growth seems to confirm that the effects of lending booms have been mixed (Goldstein and Turner, 1996; Caprio and Klingebiel, 1997). While rapid growth in financial intermediation, as measured by the growth of the money multiplier, quite accurately signals a future crisis in more than 70 percent of the cases, the same is not true for the indicator on credit growth (Table 73). Finally, the appreciation of the real exchange rate is as good a signal for banking crises as it is for balance of payments crises, and is also quite accurate.

Theoretical Analyses

A key question addressed in recent studies is the direction of causation between balance of payment crises and banking crises. Indeed, one difficulty is that both crises may have common roots in domestic and external macroeconomic developments.

Most studies assume that there are two ways in which a balance of payments crisis could lead to a banking crisis. First, a large loss in international reserves that leads to the abandonment of the fixed parity could, if not sterilized, produce a sharp decline in credit availability that may lead to increased bankruptcies of nonfinancial firms and consequently a banking crisis. Indeed, if depositors participate in the run against central bank reserves, they may force the commercial banks to suspend the convertibility of deposits (as was the case in the U.S. financial panic of 1893 (Miller, 1996)) or to reduce lending abruptly and force the liquidation of profitable investments. Second, a devaluation could create insolvencies among banks that had taken large foreign exchange exposures.[19] Even if the foreign exchange position of the banks is small, a large number of loans to nontradable sectors (such as the real estate sector) could lead to a large number of nonbank insolvencies that, in turn, could weaken the banks' positions.

A banking crisis could give rise to a balance of payments crisis if the central bank allowed an excessive expansion of domestic credit to finance the bailout of the banks or the depositors or both under an explicit or implicit deposit insurance scheme. Velasco (1987)

---

[17]Most studies analyze specific cases of banking crises, with an emphasis on the macroeconomic determinants of the crises (see Sundararajan and Baliño (1991) and Lindgren, Garcia, and Saal (1996)). Caprio and Klingebiel (1997) also stress microeconomic determinants of banking crises, such as poor supervision and regulation, deficient bank management, and political interference in lending decisions.

[18]Using a larger sample of banking crises, Caprio and Klingebiel (1997) found that, in 75 percent of the cases, the terms of trade fell by more than 10 percent in the years preceding the episode, with an average fall of 17 percent.

[19]That over-the-counter derivatives and other investment vehicles facilitate the avoidance of prudential bank regulations—in particular, with respect to foreign exchange exposures—was demonstrated in the Mexican crisis of 1994–95 (Garber, 1996).

shows that a government with otherwise prudent financial policies could be forced to expand domestic credit in order to support the banking system and thereby generate a balance of payments crisis. Alternatively, if the government finances the bailout by issuing large amounts of domestic debt, market participants may perceive that the authorities have incentives to reduce the burden of the debt through inflation or currency devaluation and this may lead to a self-fulfilling crisis.

Another possibility is that both balance of payments and banking crises are the result of common macro-economic developments. Especially important in this regard are large swings in world interest rates that influence business conditions in emerging markets and at the same time the volume of capital flows, which in such markets are often intermediated by the banking system (Calvo, Leiderman, and Reinhart, 1993; IMF, 1995). The growing integration of world capital markets in the 1990s has dramatically increased the opportunities for investors to diversify risks. It has been argued, however, that highly diversified investors may not have the incentive to learn about individual countries because each constitutes a small share of the portfolio, and this situation could make capital flows highly sensitive to new information (Calvo, 1995). A large capital outflow could produce a sharp reduction in banks' domestic deposits, and, unless offset by central bank actions, this could magnify the response of foreign investors and cause both a balance of payments and a banking crisis (Goldfajn and Valdés, 1997).

Empirical Evidence

In their study of 76 balance of payments and 26 banking crises, Kaminsky and Reinhart (1996) note that there was no apparent link between both types of crises during the 1970s, when financial markets were highly regulated and banking crises were rare events. In the 1980s and 1990s, however, balance of payments and banking crises became much more closely linked following the widespread deregulation of financial markets. Indeed, the authors find that banking crises precede—and help predict—balance of payments crises, while the converse is not true. More than half of the banking crises studied were followed by a balance of payment crisis within three years and about one quarter of the banking crises began a year (or less) before a currency crisis. The crises in the southern cone of Latin America in the early 1980s (Argentina, Chile, and Uruguay in 1981–82), those in the Nordic countries (Finland, Norway, and Sweden in 1991–92) as well as those in Brazil (1987), Colombia (1983), Mexico (1984), Peru (1985), Thailand (1983), Turkey (1994), and Venezuela (1994) were among the cases in which financial crises began before the turmoil in foreign exchange markets. Although the authors found

statistical evidence that banking crises help predict balance of payments crises, they concluded that both crises were the result of common financial developments, which included either financial liberalization or improved access to international capital markets that is accompanied by a boom-bust cycle in asset prices and economic activity.

Kaminsky and Reinhart (1996) also conclude that since most of the crises are preceded by a deterioration in fundamentals, it would be difficult to characterize them as a result of self-fulfilling changes in market expectations. As noted in Table 73, both types of crisis are preceded by recessions, in part due to a worsening of the terms of trade, an overvalued exchange rate, and steep increases in real interest rates. The rapid increase in financial intermediation, reflected in the growth of the money multiplier and the M2/reserves ratio, also increases the financial vulnerability of economies to a reversal of capital flows or steep declines in asset prices.

Appendix 2

Speculative Attacks in the 1990s: Have Economic Models Got It Right Yet?

The speculative attacks that forced devaluations in Europe in 1992–93 and the devaluation and subsequent floating of the peso in Mexico in 1994 were dramatic events that stimulated a large body of research intended to evaluate the lessons learned from the attacks. That new research builds off a base that originates in the rational expectations revolution of the 1970s and 80s. The use of forward-looking expectations spawned a theory of speculative attacks that allowed economists to view such attacks on fixed exchange rate regimes as infrequently observed but completely standard events rather than pathologies.

The first generation of papers, published around 1980, modeled speculative attacks as the market's attempt to profit from dismantling inconsistent government policies through the money markets.[20] In these models, speculators fully understand the market and realize that fiscally required excessive money creation combined with a fixed exchange rate are inconsistent policies over the longer run. Printing money allows countries to finance fiscal deficits but leads to an excess supply of domestic money, to be cashed in for international reserves. Speculators realize that eventually reserves will be exhausted and policy adjusted—either the printing presses will stop or the currency will be devalued.

---

[20]See Salant and Henderson (1978), Krugman (1979), and Flood and Garber (1984b). Agénor, Bhandari, and Flood (1992) survey this literature.

The insight of the first-generation models rested on the prediction that the attacked currency's interest rates jump upward after the attack. This could be expected, it was argued, if the attacked exchange rate were allowed to float after a successful attack. The idea is that after the attack, the currency will depreciate, reflecting continued excessive domestic money printing. Domestic currency interest rates jump upward after the attack to compensate for expected currency depreciation. Higher domestic currency interest rates induce portfolio holders to shift wealth out of interest-rate-controlled assets like currency.

Normally, such a portfolio reallocation is accompanied by a price change—here a depreciation of the domestic currency reflecting the size of the portfolio reallocation. Anticipating this price change, speculators rush to the central bank to exchange domestic money for international reserves, hoping for a capital gain. This portfolio speculation is the attack. Foreign-currency-denominated assets move from public to private portfolios, and domestic currency assets from private to public portfolios. The asset shift matches the demand shift that set it in motion. Usually, the larger is the attack, the smaller is the price change required to rebalance portfolios.

As an extreme example, imagine a speculative attack foreseen perfectly by speculators. Here speculators can be expected to compete away foreseen riskless profits so that the exchange rate does not jump at all at the time of the attack. To find out when the speculative attack takes place, find the point in time when remaining international reserves at the domestic central bank, which are slowly being depleted, precisely match the portfolio reallocation indicated by the post-attack interest rate shift. At this instant, remaining reserves are sold to speculators precisely fulfilling shifted private demand. This simple scenario, which has been extended widely, provides the first insight into interpreting a speculative attack as a market's response to inconsistent policies.

This story worked well in helping to interpret speculative attacks in developing countries such as Argentina in 1981 and Mexico in 1982.[21] It ran into at least three problems, however, with the attacks in the 1990s. First, in the 1992–93 European attacks, month-to-month reserve changes did not tell the entire story of government commitments in the exchange markets. Second, in the recent European and the Mexican episodes, the speculative attacks were largely sterilized and therefore not allowed to disturb domestic money supplies. Third, while underlying money growth (fiscal finance) in the first generation was excessive, policy in some countries, France for example, seems not to have been overly expansionary.

The first problem is the easiest to deal with. The first-generation models were quite explicitly set up to mimic small countries whose capitulation to an attack involves allowing the exchange rate to float and whose actions do little to influence large partners. The European crises involved large countries that devalue in crisis (not float) and had entered into borrowing arrangements with each other and with the anchor country, Germany. With devaluation rather than flotation, the first-generation models allow for reserve losses prior to devaluation, but then predict an *equally large inflow after the devaluation,* which may occur too quickly to be picked up from monthly reserve observations. Speculation against a country's currency peg to the anchor is speculation against both the country's reserve stock and against that country's borrowing arrangements. In the event of the attack, the borrowing arrangements broke down. Fulfilling the borrowing arrangements would have compromised German monetary policy. Seeing the collapse of their credit lines, countries such as the United Kingdom took discretion to be the better part of valor and devalued. This is entirely consistent with the first-generation models, albeit in an expanded multicountry version.

The second problem is a bit harder to solve. The hallmark of the first-generation models is the final attack on international reserves that results in an equal decline of the domestic money supply. In the recent attacks, reserve losses were sterilized, insulating the money supply against the speculative attack.[22] The insulation is secured by the monetary authorities who, at the instant of the speculative attack, expand the domestic component of the monetary base to offset the effect of reserve losses on the money supply. The domestic part of the base is normally expanded by an open market purchase of domestic government securities and in this case the open market operation is precisely the size of the speculative attack. Thus, sterilization moves the portfolio-adjustment part of the speculative attack from the money market into the bond market.

This switch of markets in no way changes the basic principles of the attack, but it complicates the story and puts it on much less firm footing. When moved to the bond markets, the first-generation speculative attack scenario requires that changes in the stocks of bonds available to the private sector influence interest rate spreads. The attack scenario must rely, therefore, on *risk aversion,* the economic property that is relevant for determining the effectiveness of sterilized intervention. If bond market participants are risk averse—at least in the short run—then sterilized intervention may be effective and the attack scenario is basically unaltered except for the interpretation of a few parameters. If risk aversion is not present, however,

---

[21]See Cumby and van Wijnbergen (1989) on Argentina and Blanco and Garber (1986) on Mexico.

[22]See Flood, Garber, and Kramer (1996).

then sterilized intervention is ineffective—even in the short run—and we simply have to look elsewhere for a speculative attack model. Presently, our empirical understanding of risk aversion in exchange markets is minimal. Traces of it show up regularly, usually as statistical demonstrations that market participants almost certainly are not risk neutral. Yet simple aggregate models of risk aversion, including those based on privately available bond stocks, perform poorly.

The third problem involves the observation that in the 1990s attacks, particularly in Europe, some governments' policies were not overly expansionary and need not have caused a crisis. Instead of having an expansive government as the root cause of the attack, government reactions to private expectations become the important element in triggering the crises. In these models, the private expectation of currency depreciation can put the government in a bind that it can escape from only by depreciating the currency. In this sense, currency crises can be self-fulfilling events. Expecting the crisis can make it more likely to happen. Research like this is called *second generation.*[23]

Private expectations can impose pressures on government. A private sector may expect currency depreciation, for example, and that will be built into interest rates (raising them), labor contracts (raising wages), and other pricing decisions (causing seemingly unwarranted inflation). A government with other problems—a fragile banking system, voters with floating-rate mortgages, unemployed workers at a low point in the business cycle—may attempt to reduce these pressures by fulfilling private expectations. The idea is that once satisfied, these expectations will abate, at least for a while, so interest rates will fall and labor market difficulties will be eased. Following this logic, the expectation of depreciation can cause a depreciation in a self-fulfilling way. If the private sector expects depreciation, a well-meaning government may need to depreciate, but if the private sector does not expect depreciation, then none may be needed. There may be *multiple equilibria,* and which one is chosen depends entirely on expectations.

Were such multiple equilibria present in the 1992–93 European attacks or the 1994 Mexican episode? The empirical verdict is still out. This approach matches up well with the lack of excessive expansion in fundamentals before the crisis in some European countries, but since this was the observation that initiated the approach, it cannot be regarded as independent confirmation. The currency depreciations proposed in this approach do not exist in a vacuum, however. Other nominal magnitudes or policies have to be adjusted after the depreciation, and these fail to show up consistently in the empirical work. For example, little postattack expansion occurred in France, but there was some easing in Germany and the United Kingdom. Thus, current research suggests while self-fulfilling crises are not the norm, they cannot always be ruled out.[24]

---

[23]See Flood and Garber (1984a), and Obstfeld (1997).

[24]See Eichengreen, Rose, and Wyploz (1995).

Statistical Appendix

Table A1. Merrill Lynch Global Investor Survey[1]

Currency Exposure	Heavily Overweight	Moderately Overweight	Neutral Weight	Moderately Underweight	Heavily Underweight	Net Exposure Index[1]
U.S. dollar						
Dec. 3, 1992	24	47	20	5	4	70.50
Dec. 2, 1993	19	36	27	11	7	62.25
Dec. 1, 1994	8	33	29	22	8	52.75
Feb. 21, 1995	12	32	26	23	7	54.75
May 26, 1995	8	36	26	21	9	53.25
Aug. 17, 1995	20	42	24	8	6	65.50
Nov. 21, 1995	10	52	22	12	4	63.00
Feb. 22, 1996	9	58	23	7	3	65.75
May 23, 1996	16	51	19	12	2	66.75
Aug. 21, 1996	10	46	22	19	3	60.25
Nov. 27, 1996	13	39	21	21	6	58.00
Feb. 26, 1997	20	58	12	8	2	71.50
Japanese yen						
Dec. 3, 1992	11	13	42	11	23	44.50
Dec. 2, 1993	1	6	35	35	23	31.75
Dec. 1, 1994	3	18	31	21	27	37.25
Feb. 21, 1995	4	5	35	22	34	30.75
May 26, 1995	7	17	33	20	23	41.25
Aug. 17, 1995	2	9	24	23	42	26.50
Nov. 21, 1995	3	6	24	21	46	24.75
Feb. 22, 1996	2	2	25	39	32	25.75
May 23, 1996	2	9	33	34	22	33.75
Aug. 21, 1996	4	7	41	26	22	36.25
Nov. 27, 1996	7	8	28	28	29	34.00
Feb. 26, 1997	0	8	27	30	35	27.00
Pound sterling						
Dec. 3, 1992	0	4	22	34	40	22.50
Dec. 2, 1993	6	31	47	9	7	55.00
Dec. 1, 1994	15	29	28	16	12	54.75
Feb. 21, 1995	4	17	36	22	21	40.25
May 26, 1995	4	9	50	19	18	40.50
Aug. 17, 1995	5	20	50	16	9	49.00
Nov. 21, 1995	1	25	46	16	12	46.75
Feb. 22, 1996	4	29	44	12	11	50.75
May 23, 1996	6	27	41	16	10	50.75
Aug. 21, 1996	3	32	46	8	11	52.00
Nov. 27, 1996	17	37	34	7	5	63.50
Feb. 26, 1997	12	32	39	12	5	58.50
Deutsche mark, Netherlands guilder, and Swiss franc						
Dec. 3, 1992	13	19	27	25	16	47.00
Dec. 2, 1993	7	25	25	32	11	46.25
Dec. 1, 1994	8	33	30	18	11	52.25
Feb. 21, 1995	23	24	28	14	11	58.50
May 26, 1995	21	30	26	16	7	60.50
Aug. 17, 1995	14	25	21	29	11	50.50
Nov. 21, 1995	20	45	17	13	5	65.50
Feb. 22, 1996	12	38	22	22	6	57.00

Table A1 *(concluded)*

Currency Exposure	Heavily Overweight	Moderately Overweight	Neutral Weight	Moderately Underweight	Heavily Underweight	Net Exposure Index[1]
May 23, 1996	8	20	25	34	13	44.00
Aug. 21, 1996	11	38	18	26	7	55.00
Nov. 27, 1996	12	16	34	25	13	47.25
Feb. 26, 1997	4	15	35	27	19	39.50
French franc, Belgian franc, Danish krone, and ECU						
Dec. 3, 1992	4	19	28	29	20	39.50
Dec. 2, 1993	4	14	37	26	19	39.50
Dec. 1, 1994	2	9	35	34	20	34.75
Feb. 21, 1995	5	16	29	30	20	39.00
May 26, 1995	1	25	40	23	11	45.50
Aug. 17, 1995	0	29	41	20	10	47.25
Nov. 21, 1995	4	19	38	27	12	44.00
Feb. 22, 1996	4	11	38	34	13	39.75
May 23, 1996	1	9	35	33	22	33.50
Aug. 21, 1996	0	8	47	22	23	35.00
Nov. 27, 1996	2	5	39	32	22	33.25
Feb. 26, 1997	2	5	38	33	22	33.00
Italian lira, Spanish peseta, and Swedish krona						
Dec. 3, 1992	4	19	28	29	20	39.50
Dec. 2, 1993	4	14	37	26	19	39.50
Dec. 1, 1994	5	17	27	21	30	36.50
Feb. 21, 1995	5	8	30	30	27	33.50
May 26, 1995	5	11	37	17	30	36.00
Aug. 17, 1995	9	29	31	12	19	49.25
Nov. 21, 1995	8	18	44	10	20	46.00
Feb. 22, 1996	6	20	39	13	22	43.75
May 23, 1996	11	28	34	12	15	52.00
Aug. 21, 1996	4	16	40	24	16	42.00
Nov. 27, 1996	7	27	31	21	14	48.00
Feb. 26, 1997	6	22	40	21	11	47.75

Source: Merrill Lynch Global Investor Survey.

[1]The Merrill Lynch Global Investor Survey is a regular survey of 100 international fund managers. The net exposure index as shown in the sixth column is a weighted average of the first five columns, with weights of 1.00, 0.75, 0.50, 0.25, and 0, respectively.

Table A2. Net Foreign Purchases of U.S. Bonds
(In millions of U.S. dollars)

	Marketable Treasury Bonds and Notes	Bonds of U.S. Government Corporations and Federally Sponsored Agencies	Corporate Bonds
1972	3,316	. . .	1,881
1973	305	. . .	1,961
1974	−472	. . .	1,039
1975	1,995	. . .	766
1976	8,096	. . .	1,202
1977	22,843	2,712	1,617
1978	4,710	1,273	1,024
1979	2,863	545	733
1980	4,898	2,557	2,879
1981	15,054	1,566	3,467
1982	17,319	−358	1,809
1983	5,427	−15	918
1984	21,499	1,175	11,721
1985	29,208	4,340	39,792
1986	19,388	6,976	43,672
1987	25,587	5,047	22,497
1988	48,832	6,740	21,224
1989	54,203	15,094	17,296
1990	17,918	6,267	9,672
1991	19,865	10,244	16,915
1992	39,288	18,291	20,789
1993	23,552	35,428	30,572
1994	78,801	21,680	37,992
1995	134,115	28,729	57,853
Of which:			
Europe	49,976	21,209	49,109
Of which:			
Germany	6,136	1,073	4,865
France	482	230	913
Italy	603	360	−302
United Kingdom	34,754	17,126	40,465
Spain	−3,881	−39	80
Asia	32,467	4,934	2,594
Of which:			
Japan	16,979	1,069	1,181
Singapore	8,875	268	−258
People's Republic of China	703	855	14
Taiwan Province of China	−3,405	−495	−63
Hong Kong, China	4,919	−58	956
1996	244,725	48,960	77,978
Of which:			
Europe	118,345	18,803	56,194
Of which:			
Germany	17,647	1,650	3,514
France	2,624	243	4,931
Italy	1,960	−84	−78
United Kingdom	65,381	10,942	43,702
Spain	18,414	7	462
Asia	98,001	14,596	9,806
Of which:			
Japan	41,390	7,595	6,099
Singapore	7,802	1,341	1,095
People's Republic of China	14,453	2,756	257
Taiwan Province of China	4,608	−1,129	8
Hong Kong, China	14,366	915	1,737

Source: U.S. Department of Treasury, *Treasury Bulletin*.

Table A3. Net Purchases of Securities in Major Industrial Countries

(In billions of U.S. dollars)

	Bonds						Equities				
	United States	Japan	Germany	France	United Kingdom	Canada	United States	Japan	Germany	France	Canada
Net purchases of domestic securities by nonresidents											
1986	70.04	16.30	27.07	. . .	3.21	16.23	18.72	−15.76	6.82	. . .	1.35
1987	53.13	36.76	19.30	. . .	7.33	5.68	16.27	−42.84	−0.79	. . .	5.01
1988	76.80	13.49	1.24	. . .	1.50	12.64	−2.00	6.81	3.00	. . .	−1.93
1989	86.59	78.15	11.96	. . .	−3.10	14.78	9.87	7.00	12.11	. . .	3.34
1990	33.86	47.93	13.77	36.93	−7.97	12.33	−15.09	−13.28	−2.09	6.00	−1.48
1991	47.02	68.50	35.80	21.25	10.47	22.98	11.16	46.78	1.92	7.75	−0.87
1992	78.37	−0.56	79.79	48.30	4.10	14.54	−5.14	8.73	−2.03	5.65	0.77
1993	89.55	−31.07	126.44	19.94	20.82	21.70	21.54	19.99	4.89	13.64	9.23
1994	138.47	−13.72	14.62	−36.15	1.85	10.83	2.17	48.78	0.70	4.88	4.74
1995	220.70	−8.46	60.73	2.84	5.26	21.78	11.24	50.70	−0.78	6.82	−3.08
1996	371.66	25.27	64.97	−31.29	15.75	13.58	13.23	49.42	14.14	12.12	5.71
Q1	70.56	3.03	18.28	−20.22	5.05	0.26	3.63	24.86	0.60	3.12	1.22
Q2	64.48	10.18	9.75	−13.37	3.74	4.32	6.77	19.40	9.73	6.10	3.26
Q3	110.53	10.59	18.72	3.98	2.57	1.14	−0.54	1.16	−0.08	−1.28	0.05
Q4	126.09	1.46	18.23	−1.68	4.38	7.86	3.37	4.00	3.89	4.18	1.17
Net purchases of foreign securities by residents											
1986	3.69	94.93	7.47	. . .	. . .	0.13	1.89	7.05	2.25	. . .	1.49
1987	7.95	70.88	13.83	. . .	. . .	0.66	−1.08	16.87	−0.35	. . .	0.81
1988	7.43	83.96	38.71	. . .	. . .	0.09	1.94	2.99	2.77	. . .	2.36
1989	5.94	95.29	25.11	. . .	. . .	1.34	13.12	17.89	1.65	. . .	2.05
1990	22.32	33.43	14.60	8.03	. . .	0.05	8.95	6.26	−0.39	−0.51	1.91
1991	15.65	70.68	14.50	9.41	. . .	0.99	31.39	3.63	1.15	2.90	4.76
1992	18.60	37.37	43.35	18.04	. . .	0.51	32.21	−3.01	0.75	1.57	5.16
1993	62.74	36.34	20.02	27.62	. . .	3.08	63.36	15.33	4.90	2.57	6.74
1994	11.58	69.55	30.93	23.41	. . .	0.17	47.13	14.06	7.01	2.10	6.28
1995	48.29	93.76	17.32	17.86	. . .	0.64	50.28	−0.16	−1.59	−1.60	3.30
1996	45.22	93.87	17.60	44.05	. . .	1.37	57.88	8.17	10.08	2.27	12.12
Q1	11.95	4.50	7.10	11.76	. . .	−0.31	22.48	−4.29	3.85	0.02	3.17
Q2	2.80	27.06	4.09	9.83	. . .	−0.89	17.40	8.60	−0.69	4.40	2.15
Q3	13.04	22.11	3.96	7.98	. . .	1.57	8.07	0.68	0.48	0.82	2.58
Q4	17.43	40.20	2.46	14.48	. . .	1.01	9.92	3.17	6.44	−2.97	4.23

Source: BZW Securities Limited, *Global Economic Digest* (April 1997); and U.S. Department of Treasury, *Treasury Bulletin*.

Table A4. External Positions of Banks in Individual Reporting Countries
(In billions of U.S. dollars)

| | Amounts Outstanding | | | | | Estimated Exchange-Rate-Adjusted Changes | | | | | |
| | | | | 1994 | 1995 | 1996 | | | | | |
	1994	1995	1996			Total	Q1	Q2	Q3	Q4
Assets										
All countries	7,116.7	8,072.6	8,289.9	274.9	680.0	496.6	75.0	57.3	163.9	200.5
European countries	3,842.4	4,398.5	4,635.4	95.7	377.3	403.6	117.9	52.5	137.9	95.2
Austria	65.2	77.0	76.1	1.7	8.9	2.8	2.4	0.9	−0.9	0.5
Belgium	230.8	260.3	259.8	11.1	23.2	11.1	15.1	−8.0	17.6	−13.6
Denmark	46.4	52.2	57.7	−11.0	3.0	8.0	0.9	3.0	3.0	1.1
Finland	12.7	15.3	18.9	−0.3	2.2	4.0	1.3	1.0	0.5	1.2
France	541.4	623.7	583.7	−19.5	62.8	−14.7	3.1	−14.4	16.1	−19.5
Germany	469.2	563.7	597.1	−12.8	71.5	63.1	0.9	13.2	6.8	42.2
Ireland	28.3	43.0	65.2	3.9	14.2	22.8	6.2	4.2	6.2	6.2
Italy	136.6	162.4	214.5	−20.6	21.2	52.0	−2.4	14.2	8.4	31.8
Luxembourg	390.7	423.9	429.8	45.6	12.5	28.4	18.5	1.0	1.9	7.1
Netherlands	175.1	201.0	204.3	−7.4	19.8	12.4	22.6	4.6	14.2	−28.9
Norway	6.5	5.9	7.8	−0.3	−0.7	2.0	1.8	. . .	−0.2	0.5
Spain	110.6	145.8	130.1	−11.8	30.1	−9.7	−5.0	−7.9	3.1	0.2
Sweden	24.7	36.2	44.7	−2.8	10.2	9.9	7.8	2.6	4.8	−5.3
Switzerland	404.3	437.6	485.6	22.2	13.2	68.5	18.0	17.6	8.2	24.7
United Kingdom	1,199.8	1,350.3	1,460.0	97.7	85.2	142.9	26.9	20.6	48.3	47.1
Other industrial countries	1,595.3	1,884.2	1,871.0	19.2	188.6	65.7	−33.6	11.5	0.1	87.7
Canada	55.8	65.6	80.3	14.0	9.5	14.9	1.6	5.0	−0.9	9.1
Japan	1,007.6	1,217.9	1,123.5	22.3	110.0	−20.1	−31.1	−2.3	−10.4	23.7
Japanese offshore market	573.7	667.7	573.0	26.5	111.8	−45.1	−35.3	−5.3	−13.0	8.6
Others	433.9	550.2	550.5	−4.2	−1.8	24.9	4.2	3.0	2.6	15.1
United States	531.8	600.7	667.1	−17.0	69.1	71.0	−4.1	8.8	11.4	54.8
International banking facilities	246.3	254.9	261.0	4.3	9.2	9.5	−7.8	−3.3	−2.5	23.1
Others	285.5	345.8	406.2	−21.4	59.9	61.4	3.6	12.1	13.9	31.7
Other reporting countries	1,679.0	1,790.0	1,783.5	159.9	114.1	27.4	−9.4	−6.7	25.9	17.6
Bahamas	194.2	188.5	192.7	26.1	−6.5	4.9	1.4	−11.8	14.5	0.9
Bahrain	61.0	60.0	63.4	4.3	−1.2	3.8	−1.5	−0.2	5.5	−0.1
Cayman Islands	437.5	457.7	460.5	40.6	19.0	4.6	−6.4	7.0	−6.2	10.2
Hong Kong, China	614.8	655.2	608.6	75.8	44.2	−22.8	−6.4	−11.6	−0.2	−4.6
Singapore	362.9	420.0	444.3	12.5	58.8	30.5	−1.5	9.5	11.6	11.0
Other[1]	8.7	8.7	14.1	0.6	−0.2	6.4	5.0	0.5	0.7	0.1

Table A4 *(concluded)*

| | Amounts Outstanding | | | Estimated Exchange-Rate-Adjusted Changes | | | | | | |
| | | | | | | 1996 | | | | |
	1994	1995	1996	1994	1995	Total	Q1	Q2	Q3	Q4
Liabilities										
All countries	7,154.4	7,827.5	8,066.5	572.6	475.1	498.0	134.1	45.9	127.3	190.7
European countries	3,891.0	4,402.9	4,673.6	303.7	307.1	436.8	177.7	54.5	104.7	99.9
Austria	73.7	84.4	89.7	2.4	7.1	10.2	5.3	0.2	4.2	0.5
Belgium	234.4	272.5	266.4	20.5	29.6	6.2	17.2	−7.8	8.4	−11.5
Denmark	28.7	31.9	38.8	1.0	1.6	8.2	1.3	3.5	3.6	−0.2
Finland	20.3	20.5	16.2	−3.1	−0.4	−3.7	−1.8	−1.5	0.3	−0.6
France	560.4	612.9	617.0	32.2	29.1	28.8	32.0	−9.5	19.5	−13.1
Germany	411.9	539.2	570.6	84.7	109.0	60.4	18.5	17.2	−4.0	28.7
Ireland	28.9	45.7	64.2	3.6	16.2	18.8	6.0	2.5	5.2	5.2
Italy	235.0	230.9	247.7	1.9	−13.9	21.0	10.1	4.7	1.3	4.9
Luxembourg	347.3	382.4	383.6	26.6	14.1	22.0	9.1	1.0	5.5	6.3
Netherlands	167.8	198.9	217.9	1.7	24.0	28.5	19.7	12.2	10.7	−14.0
Norway	6.9	8.2	17.9	−2.2	1.2	9.7	3.1	1.8	−0.2	5.0
Spain	103.2	112.2	128.0	9.8	0.9	20.5	3.3	6.2	6.7	4.4
Sweden	50.9	55.1	56.7	−1.9	1.8	3.3	7.5	−0.7	−0.3	−3.3
Switzerland	338.3	366.6	404.0	33.7	12.5	53.0	11.7	7.9	6.3	27.2
United Kingdom	1,283.3	1,441.5	1,554.9	92.7	74.2	149.8	34.8	16.9	37.5	60.5
Other industrial countries	1,626.9	1,690.3	1,660.3	115.8	61.0	11.5	−37.4	−6.3	−6.7	61.8
Canada	82.5	81.8	93.6	14.6	−1.3	12.0	−2.2	1.8	−0.4	12.9
Japan	723.7	738.3	695.8	3.0	14.4	−7.5	−13.1	−17.9	0.5	22.9
Japanese offshore market	291.8	306.6	294.4	5.3	17.8	−1.2	0.2	−11.6	4.9	5.3
Others	431.9	431.7	401.4	−2.2	−3.4	−6.3	−13.2	−6.3	−4.4	17.6
United States	820.7	870.2	870.9	98.1	47.9	7.0	−22.0	9.8	−6.7	25.9
International banking facilities	423.5	455.3	424.6	39.9	31.3	−25.8	−8.0	−7.8	−17.1	7.2
Others	397.2	414.9	446.3	58.2	16.7	32.7	−14.1	17.7	10.4	18.7
Other reporting countries	1,636.4	1,734.3	1,732.7	153.2	107.0	49.8	−6.2	−2.4	29.3	29.1
Bahamas	202.9	193.6	196.2	29.1	−9.9	3.2	−0.7	−13.4	14.5	2.7
Bahrain	57.7	55.6	58.7	5.4	−2.2	3.4	−1.2	−0.9	5.4	0.1
Cayman Islands	430.3	444.6	445.8	39.2	12.2	3.6	−7.0	7.7	−6.4	9.3
Hong Kong, China	582.3	620.3	579.9	74.2	47.3	−6.1	−3.5	−4.6	1.1	0.8
Singapore	357.3	413.4	441.4	6.7	58.7	41.2	2.6	8.4	14.1	16.0
Other[1]	5.8	6.7	10.7	−1.3	0.8	4.5	3.6	0.3	0.5	0.1

Source: Bank for International Settlements, *International Banking and Financial Market Developments*.
[1]Includes the Netherlands Antilles and the offshore branches of U.S. banks in Panama.

Table A5. Annual Turnover in Derivative Financial Instruments Traded on Organized Exchanges Worldwide

(In millions of contracts traded)

	1986	1987	1988	1989	1990	1991	1992	1993	1994	1995	1996
Interest rate futures	91.0	145.7	156.3	201.0	219.1	230.9	330.1	427.1	628.6	561.0	612.2
Futures on short-term instruments	16.3	29.4	33.7	70.2	76.0	87.3	144.9	180.0	282.3	266.5	283.6
Three-month Eurodollar[1]	12.4	23.7	25.2	46.8	39.4	41.7	66.9	70.2	113.6	104.2	97.1
Three-month Euroyen[2]	0.0	0.0	0.0	4.7	15.2	16.2	17.4	26.9	44.2	42.9	37.7
Three-month Euro-deutsche mark[3]	0.0	0.0	0.0	1.6	3.1	4.8	12.2	21.4	29.5	25.7	36.2
Three-month PIBOR futures[4]	0.0	0.0	0.5	2.3	1.9	3.0	6.4	11.9	13.2	15.5	14.1
Futures on long-term instruments	74.7	116.4	122.6	130.8	143.1	143.6	185.2	247.1	346.3	294.5	328.6
U.S. Treasury bond[5]	54.6	69.4	73.8	72.8	78.2	69.9	71.7	80.7	101.5	87.8	86.0
Notional French government bond[4]	1.1	11.9	12.4	15.0	16.0	21.1	31.1	36.8	50.2	33.6	35.3
Ten-year Japanese government bond[6]	9.4	18.4	18.9	19.1	16.4	12.9	12.1	15.6	14.1	15.2	13.6
German government bond[7]	0.0	0.0	0.3	5.3	9.6	12.4	18.9	27.7	51.2	44.8	56.3
Interest rate options[8]	22.3	29.3	30.5	39.5	52.0	50.8	64.8	82.9	116.6	225.5	151.1
Currency futures	19.9	21.2	22.5	28.2	29.7	30.0	31.3	39.0	69.7	99.6	73.7
Currency options[8]	13.0	18.3	18.2	20.7	18.9	22.9	23.4	23.8	21.3	23.2	26.3
Stock market index futures	28.4	36.1	29.6	30.1	39.4	54.6	52.0	71.2	109.0	114.8	119.9
Stock market index options[8]	140.4	139.1	79.1	101.7	119.1	121.4	133.9	144.1	197.5	187.3	178.7
Total	315.0	389.6	336.3	421.2	478.3	510.5	635.6	788.0	1,142.9	1,211.5	1,161.9
North America	288.7	318.3	252.2	287.9	312.3	302.7	341.4	382.3	513.5	455.0	428.2
Europe	10.3	35.9	40.8	64.4	83.0	110.5	185.0	263.5	398.0	354.7	425.8
Asia-Pacific	14.4	30.0	34.4	63.6	79.1	85.8	82.8	98.4	131.9	126.4	115.2
Other	1.6	5.5	8.9	5.3	3.9	11.6	26.3	43.7	99.4	275.4	192.7

Source: Bank for International Settlements.

[1]Traded on the Chicago Mercantile Exchange-International Monetary Market (CME-IMM), Singapore International Monetary Exchange (SIMEX), London International Financial Futures Exchange (LIFFE), Tokyo International Financial Futures Exchange (TIFFE), and Sydney Futures Exchange (SFE).

[2]Traded on the TIFFE and SIMEX.

[3]Traded on the Marché à Terme International de France (MATIF) and LIFFE.

[4]Traded on the MATIF.

[5]Traded on the Chicago Board of Trade (CBOT), LIFFE, Mid-America Commodity Exchange (MIDAM), New York Futures Exchange (NYFE), and Tokyo Stock Exchange (TSE).

[6]Traded on the TSE, LIFFE, and CBOT.

[7]Traded on the LIFFE and the Deutsche Terminbörse (DTB).

[8]Calls plus puts.

Table A6. New Interest Rate and Currency Swaps

(In billions of U.S. dollars)

	1987	1988	1989	1990	1991	1992	1993	1994	1995
Interest rate swaps									
All counterparties	387.8	568.1	833.6	1,264.3	1,621.8	2,822.6	4,104.7	6,240.9	8,698.8
Interbank (ISDA member)	125.9	193.1	318.0	484.5	761.7	1,336.4	2,003.9	3,199.5	4,989.8
Other (end user and brokered)	261.9	375.0	515.5	779.7	860.0	1,486.2	2,100.8	3,041.4	3,709.0
End user	257.0	371.4	503.4	705.3	844.7	1,436.7	2,000.6	2,962.4	3,709.0
Financial institutions	168.7	238.1	317.9	420.1	492.4	853.9	1,115.7	1,632.5	2,292.9
Governments[1]	21.7	32.9	39.6	74.7	79.0	148.9	198.6	178.8	232.4
Corporations[2]	62.6	98.2	139.5	210.6	273.3	434.0	678.0	1,150.9	1,183.7
Unallocated	4.1	2.3	6.5	0	0	0	8.3	0.1	0
Brokered	4.9	3.5	12.1	74.4	15.3	49.5	100.2	79.0	0
Currency swaps									
All counterparties	172.8	248.5	356.3	425.5	656.8	603.7	590.4	758.6	910.2
(Adjusted for reporting of both sides)	(86.3)	(124.2)	(178.2)	(212.7)	(328.4)	(301.9)	(295.2)	(379.3)	(455.1)
Interbank (ISDA member)	35.8	58.7	101.3	122.6	208.0	132.4	110.9	162.3	307.6
Other (end user and brokered)	136.9	189.8	255.0	302.9	448.8	471.3	479.5	596.3	602.6
End user[3]	67.8	93.9	127.1	150.7	219.1	234.7	239.0	296.7	301.3
Financial institutions	31.9	43.5	52.2	51.4	98.6	78.9	77.2	107.6	143.8
Governments[1]	13.9	19.3	23.0	23.4	30.7	42.1	52.7	54.3	49.0
Corporations[2]	21.5	29.1	46.2	75.9	89.7	113.7	109.0	134.7	108.5
Unallocated	0.6	2.0	5.7	0	0	0	0	0.1	0
Brokered	1.2	2.1	1.0	1.6	10.7	1.9	1.5	3.0	0
Total (interest rate and currency swaps for all counterparties)	474.1	692.3	1,011.8	1,477.0	1,950.2	3,124.5	4,399.9	6,620.2	9,153.9

Sources: Bank for International Settlements, *International Banking and Financial Market Development*; and International Swaps and Derivatives Association, Inc. (ISDA).

[1]Including international institutions.

[2]Including others.

[3]Adjusted for double counting because each currency swap involves two currencies.

Table A7. Currency Composition of Notional Principal Value of Outstanding Interest Rate and Currency Swaps

(In billions of U.S. dollars)

	1987	1988	1989	1990	1991	1992	1993	1994	1995	June 1996
Interest rate swaps										
All counterparties	682.9	1,010.2	1,502.6	2,311.5	3,065.1	3,850.8	6,177.3	8,815.6	12,810.7	15,584.2
U.S. dollar	541.5	728.2	993.7	1,272.7	1,506.0	1,760.2	2,457.0	3,230.1	4,371.7	4,993.9
Japanese yen	40.5	78.5	128.0	231.9	478.9	706.0	1,247.4	1,987.4	2,895.9	3,853.7
Deutsche mark	31.6	56.5	84.6	193.4	263.4	344.4	629.7	911.7	1,438.9	2,128.0
Pound sterling	29.7	52.3	100.4	242.1	253.5	294.8	437.1	674.0	854.0	856.3
Other	39.5	94.8	195.8	371.5	563.3	745.4	1,406.1	2,012.4	3,250.2	3,752.3
Interbank (ISDA members)	206.6	341.3	547.1	909.5	1,342.3	1,880.8	2,967.9	4,533.9	7,100.6	...
U.S. dollar	161.6	243.9	371.1	492.8	675.0	853.9	1,008.4	1,459.8	2,287.3	...
Japanese yen	19.5	43.0	61.1	126.1	264.9	441.3	820.8	1,344.8	1,928.5	...
Deutsche mark	7.9	17.2	32.6	78.4	111.2	175.6	356.1	514.5	831.0	...
Pound sterling	10.4	17.6	40.0	100.1	106.3	137.2	215.2	315.4	477.7	...
Other	7.1	19.6	42.2	112.1	184.9	272.8	567.4	899.4	1,576.1	...
End user and brokered	476.2	668.9	955.5	1,402.0	1,722.8	1,970.1	3,209.4	4,281.7	5,710.1	...
U.S. dollar	379.9	484.3	622.6	779.9	831.0	906.3	1,448.6	1,770.3	2,084.3	...
Japanese yen	21.0	35.5	66.9	105.8	214.0	264.7	426.7	642.5	967.4	...
Deutsche mark	23.7	39.3	52.0	115.0	152.2	168.8	273.7	397.1	607.8	...
Pound sterling	19.3	34.7	60.4	142.0	147.3	157.6	222.0	358.7	376.2	...
Other	32.4	75.2	153.6	259.4	378.3	472.7	838.4	1,113.1	1,674.4	...
Currency swaps[1]										
All counterparties	182.8	319.6	449.1	577.5	807.2	860.4	899.6	914.8	1,197.4	1,294.7
U.S. dollar	81.3	134.7	177.1	214.2	292.2	309.0	320.1	321.6	418.9	473.2
Japanese yen	29.9	65.5	100.6	122.4	180.1	154.3	158.8	170.0	200.0	263.9
Deutsche mark	10.7	17.0	26.9	36.2	47.6	53.4	69.7	77.0	119.0	105.9
Pound sterling	5.3	8.9	16.7	24.5	37.4	40.1	44.2	43.0	45.8	46.5
Other	55.7	93.5	127.8	180.3	250.0	303.7	306.9	303.4	413.8	405.2
Interbank (ISDA members)	35.5	82.6	115.1	155.1	224.9	238.9	218.5	211.3	310.0	...
U.S. dollar	16.7	34.1	48.2	59.7	86.8	90.9	82.3	80.4	114.3	...
Japanese yen	7.2	18.6	28.3	37.4	60.9	53.9	53.3	49.3	58.0	...
Deutsche mark	1.6	3.0	5.4	7.6	9.4	12.6	12.9	12.0	21.1	...
Pound sterling	1.1	1.6	4.3	6.2	8.4	10.4	7.1	6.5	6.9	...
Other	9.0	25.4	28.8	44.1	59.5	71.1	63.0	63.1	109.8	...
End user and brokered	147.3	237.0	334.1	422.5	582.3	621.6	681.1	703.6	887.5	...
U.S. dollar	64.6	100.7	128.9	154.5	205.3	218.2	237.7	241.2	304.7	...
Japanese yen	22.7	47.0	72.2	85.0	119.2	100.4	105.6	120.6	142.1	...
Deutsche mark	9.1	14.0	21.5	28.5	38.2	40.8	56.9	65.0	98.0	...
Pound sterling	4.2	7.3	12.4	18.3	29.1	29.7	37.0	36.6	38.9	...
Other	46.7	68.1	99.0	136.2	190.6	232.6	244.0	240.4	303.9	...

Sources: Bank for International Settlements, *International Banking and Financial Market Developments;* and International Swaps and Derivatives Association, Inc. (ISDA).

[1]Adjusted for double counting because each currency swap involves two currencies.

References

Agénor, Pierre-Richard, 1996, "The Surge in Capital Flows: Analysis of 'Pull' and 'Push' Factors" (unpublished; International Monetary Fund) (forthcoming in *International Journal of Finance and Economics*).

———, Jagdeep Bhandari, and Robert P. Flood, 1992, "Speculative Attacks and Models of Balance of Payments Crises," *Staff Papers,* Vol. 39 (Washington: International Monetary Fund, June), pp. 357–94.

Aoki, Masahiko, ed., 1984, *The Economic Analysis of the Japanese Firm* (NewYork: North-Holland).

Artis, Michael J., and Mark P. Taylor, 1990, "Abolishing Exchange Control: The U.K. Experience," in *Private Behaviour and Government Policy in Interdependent Economies,* ed. by Anthony S. Courakis and Mark P. Taylor (Oxford: Clarendon Press).

———, 1994, "The Stabilizing Effect of ERM on Exchange Rates and Interest Rates: Some Nonparametric Tests," *Staff Papers,* International Monetary Fund, Vol. 41 (March), pp. 123–48.

Bank for International Settlements, 1996a, *Annual Report* (Basle).

———, 1996b, 1997, *International Banking and Financial Market Developments* (Basle).

———, 1996c, "Financial Market Volatility: Measurement, Causes, and Consequences," Conference Paper No. 1. (Basle).

———, 1996d, *Settlement Risk in Foreign Exchange Transactions,* Committee on Payment and Settlement Systems No. 17 (Basle).

Bank of England, 1996, *Practical Issues Arising from the Introduction of the Euro,* Issues 1–3 (London, April).

Barth, James R., Daniel E. Nolle, and Tara N. Rice, 1997, "Commercial Banking Structure, Regulation, and Performance: An International Comparison," Economics Working Paper 97-6, Office of the Comptroller of the Currency (Washington).

Bartolini, Leonardo, and Allan Drazen, 1997, "When Liberal Policies Reflect External Shocks, What Do We Learn?" *Journal of International Economics,* Vol. 42 (May), pp. 249–73.

Basle Committee on Banking Supervision, 1997, *Core Principles for Effective Banking Supervision* (Basle: Bank for International Settlements, April).

Bayoumi, Tamim, 1989, "Saving-Investment Correlations: Immobile Capital, Government Policy, or Endogenous Behavior?" IMF Working Paper 89/66 (Washington: International Monetary Fund).

———, Morris Goldstein, and Geoffrey Woglom, 1995, "Do Credit Markets Discipline Sovereign Borrowers? Evidence from U.S. States," *Journal of Money, Credit, and Banking,* Vol. 27, Pt. I (November), pp. 1046–59.

Berger, Allen N., and David B. Humphrey, 1997, "Efficiency of Financial Institutions: International Survey and Directions for Future Research," Finance and Economics Discussion Series No. 1997–11 (Washington: Board of Governors of the Federal Reserve System).

Bergsten, C. Fred, 1997, "The Impact of the Euro on Exchange Rates and International Policy Cooperation," in *EMU and the International Monetary System,* ed. by P. Masson, T. Krueger, and B. Turtleboom (Washington: International Monetary Fund).

Bianco, Magda, Andrea Gerali, and Riccardo Massaro, 1996, "Financial Systems Across 'Developed Economies': Convergence or Path Dependence?" (unpublished; Rome: Bank of Italy).

Bishop, Graham, 1997, "The European Central Bank and the Prudential Regulation of the Financial System," paper presented at a conference on the "Monetary, Fiscal and Financial Implications of European Monetary Union," European University Institute, Florence, June 1997.

Black, Fischer, and Myron J. Scholes, 1973, "The Pricing of Options and Corporate Liabilities," *Journal of Political Economy,* Vol. 81 (May/June), pp. 637–54.

Blanco, Herminio, and Peter M. Garber, 1986, "Recurrent Devaluation and Speculative Attacks on the Mexican Peso," *Journal of Political Economy,* Vol. 94 (February), pp. 148–66.

Bloomberg Business News, 1997, "U.S. Economy: Greenspan Says U.S. Stocks 'Not Unreasonable,' " March 5.

Bloomfield, Arthur I., 1963, "Short-Term Capital Movements Under the Pre-1914 Gold Standard," Princeton Studies in International Finance, No. 11 (Princeton, New Jersey).

———, 1968, "Patterns of Fluctuation in International Investment Before 1914," Princeton Studies in International Finance, No. 21 (Princeton, New Jersey).

Board of Governors of the Federal Reserve System, 1984, "The Federal Reserve Position on Restructuring of Financial Regulation Responsibilities," *Federal Reserve Bulletin* (Washington, July), pp. 548–57.

———, 1997, "Family Finances in the United States: Recent Evidence from the Survey of Consumer Finances," *Federal Reserve Bulletin* (Washington, January).

Bodart,Vincent, and Paul Reding, 1996, "Exchange Rate Regime, Volatility, and International Correlations on Bond and Stock Markets" (unpublished; Namur, Belgium: Department of Economics, University of Namur).

Bolton, Patrick, and Ernst-Ludwig von Thadden, 1996, "Blocks, Liquidity, and Corporate Control," London School of Economics Financial Markets Group Discussion Paper No. 249 (October).

Bordo, Michael, and Anna J. Schwartz, 1996, "Why Clashes Between Internal and External Stability Goals End in

Currency Crises, 1797–1994," NBER Working Paper No. 5710 (Cambridge, Massachusetts: National Bureau of Economic Research).

Borio, Claudio, 1997, "Monetary Policy Operating Procedures in Industrial Countries," BIS Conference Paper No. 3 (Basle: Bank for International Settlements).

Bridgewater Associates, 1997a, "Turning Apples into Oranges—Unlocking the Mystery of Market Segmentation of Bradys and Euros," *Bridgewater Daily Observations,* January 20.

———, 1997b, "Earnings Expectations for U.S. Equities," *Bridgewater Daily Observations,* March 11.

———, 1997c, "Equity Mutual Fund Activity," *Bridgewater Daily Observations,* April 16.

BZW Securities Limited, 1997, *Global Markets Digest Q1 1997* (London, January).

Cairncross, Alec K., 1953, *Home and Foreign Investment 1870–1913: Studies in Capital Accumulation* (London: Cambridge University Press).

Calvo, Guillermo A., 1995, "Varieties of Capital-Market Crises," IMF Seminar Series, No. 1995–03 (Washington: International Monetary Fund).

———, Leonardo Leiderman, and Carmen M. Reinhart, 1993, "Capital Inflows and Real Exchange Rate Appreciation in Latin America: The Role of External Factors," *Staff Papers,* International Monetary Fund, Vol. 40 (March), pp. 108–51.

———, 1996, "Inflows of Capital to Developing Countries in the 1990s," *Journal of Economic Perspectives,* Vol. 10 (Spring), pp. 123–39.

———, and Morris Goldstein, 1996, "What Role for the Official Sector?" in *Private Capital Flows to Emerging Markets After the Mexican Crisis,* ed. by G.A. Calvo, M. Goldstein, and E. Hochreiter (Washington: Institute of International Economics).

Caprio, Gerard, and Daniela Klingebiel, 1997, "Bank Insolvency: Bad Luck, Bad Policy, or Bad Banking?" in *Annual World Bank Conference on Development Economics 1996,* ed. by M. Bruno and B. Pleskovic (Washington), pp. 79–104.

Cardoso, Eliana, and Rudiger Dornbusch, 1989, "Foreign Private Capital Flows," in *Handbook of Development Economics,* Vol. 2, ed. by Hollis Chenery and T.N. Srinivasan (Amsterdam; New York: North Holland).

Cassard, Marcel, and David Folkerts-Landau, forthcoming, "Risk Management of Sovereign Assets and Liabilities," IMF Working Paper (Washington: International Monetary Fund).

Christoffersen, Peter, Guay Lim, and Garry Schinasi, 1997, "Using Asset Prices to Assess Inflationary Pressures: Constructing a Broad-Based Price Measure for Japan, 1970–96" (unpublished; Washington: Research Department, International Monetary Fund).

Claessens, Stijn, Michael P. Dooley, and Andrew Warner, 1995, "Portfolio Capital Flows: Hot or Cold?" *World Bank Economic Review,* Vol. 9 (January), pp. 153–74.

Cole, Harold L., and Timothy J. Kehoe, 1996, "A Self-Fulfilling Model of Mexico's 1994–95 Debt Crisis," *Journal of International Economics,* Vol. 41 (November), pp. 309–30.

Commission of the European Communities, 1988a, "The Economics of 1992," *European Economy,* Vol. 35 (March), pp. 86–95, 171–97.

———, 1988b, "Annual Economic Report 1988–1989," *European Economy,* Vol. 38 (November), pp. 7–9, 137–41.

Cumby, Robert E., and Sweder van Wijnbergen, 1989, "Financial Policy and Speculative Runs with a Crawling Peg: Argentina 1979–81," *Journal of International Economics,* Vol. 27 (August), pp. 111–27.

Deutsche Bank Research, 1996, "EMU and Financial Markets—Some Issues and Prospects," *EMU Watch,* No. 22, December 9.

Deutsche Bundesbank, *Kapital Markt Statistik* (Frankfurt, various issues).

Diamond, Douglas W., 1984, "Financial Intermediation and Delegated Monitoring," *Review of Economic Studies,* Vol. 51 (July), pp. 393–414.

Dooley, Michael P., 1986, "Country-Specific Risk Premiums, Capital Flight and Net Investment Income Payments in Selected Developing Countries," DM/86/17 (Washington: International Monetary Fund).

———, 1997, "Profitable Speculation and Monetary Unions," paper presented at a conference on the "Monetary, Fiscal, and Financial Implications of European Monetary Union," European University Institute, Florence, June.

———, forthcoming, "Governments' Debt and Asset Management and Financial Crises: Sellers Beware," in *Risk Management for Sovereign Countries* (Washington: International Monetary Fund).

———, Donald J. Mathieson, and Liliana Rojas-Suárez, 1996, "Capital Mobility and Exchange Market Intervention in Developing Countries," WP/96/131 (Washington: International Monetary Fund).

Drudi, Francesco, and Alessandro Prati, 1997, "Differences and Analogies Between Index-Linked and Foreign-Currency Bonds: A Theoretical and Empirical Analysis," in *Managing Public Debt: Index-Linked Bonds in Theory and Practice,* ed. by Marcello De Cecco, Lorenzo Pecchi, and Gustavo Piga (Cheltenham, United Kingdom; Brookfield, Vermont: Edward Elgar), pp. 195–216.

Dunning, John H., 1970, *Studies in International Investment* (London: Allen & Unwin).

Eaker, Mark, Dwight Grant, and Nelson Woodard, 1993, "A Multinational Examination of International Equity and Bond Investment with Currency Hedging," *Journal of Futures Markets,* Vol. 13, (May), pp. 313–24.

Edelstein, Michael, 1982, *Overseas Investment in the Age of High Imperialism: The United Kingdom, 1850–1914* (New York: Columbia University Press).

Eichengreen, Barry, Andrew Rose, and Charles Wyplosz, 1995, "Exchange Market Mayhem: The Antecedents and Aftermath of Speculative Attacks" *Economic Policy,* Vol. 21 (October), pp. 249–312.

Eijffinger, Sylvester, C.W. Lemmen, and Jan J.G. Lemmen, 1995, "Money Market Integration in Europe," *Swiss Journal of Economics and Statistics,* Vol. 131 (March), pp. 3–37.

Elstein, Aaron, 1997, "1996 Activity Slowed Down, But Deals Should Heat Up," *American Banker,* January 31, pp. 2A–9A.

Emerging Markets Traders Association, 1997, *Debt Trading Volume Survey 1996* (March 17).

Emmons, William, 1997, "A Tale of Two Cycles," *Monetary Trends,* Federal Reserve Bank of St. Louis (April).

ERE (Economic Research Europe), forthcoming, "A Study on the Effectiveness and Impact of Internal Market Integration on the Banking and Credit Sector" (unpublished; Economic Research Europe and Public and Corporate Economic Consultants (PACEC) Ltd., Cambridge, England).

Euromoney, 1997, "Exotics Enter the Mainstream" (March), pp. 127–30.

European Commission, 1995, *Green Paper on the Practical Arrangements for the Introduction of the Single Currency* (Luxembourg: Office for Official Publications of the European Community).

European Monetary Institute, 1996, "First Progress Report on the TARGET Project" (Frankfurt, August).

———, 1997, *The Single Monetary Policy in Stage Three: Specification of the Operational Framework* (Frankfurt, January).

Feldstein, Martin, and Charles Horioka, 1980, "Domestic Saving and International Capital Flows," *Economic Journal,* Vol. 90 (June), pp. 314–29.

Fernandez-Arias, Eduardo, 1996, "The New Wave of Private Capital Flows: Push or Pull?" *Journal of Development Economics,* Vol. 48 (March), pp. 389–418.

Fishlow, Albert, 1985, "Lessons from the Past: Capital Markets During the Nineteenth Century and the Interwar Period," *International Organization,* Vol. 39, pp. 383–439.

Flood, Robert P., and Peter M. Garber, 1984a, "Gold Monetization and Gold Discipline," *Journal of Political Economy,* Vol. 92 (February), pp. 90–107.

———, 1984b, "Collapsing Exchange Rate Regimes: Some Linear Examples," *Journal of International Economics,* Vol. 17 (August), pp. 1–13.

———, and Charles Kramer, 1996, "Collapsing Exchange Rate Regimes: Another Linear Example," *Journal of International Economics,* Vol. 41 (November), pp. 223–34.

Flood, Robert P., and Nancy P. Marion, 1996, "Speculative Attacks: Fundamentals and Self-Fulfilling Prophecies," NBER Working Paper 5789 (Cambridge, Massachusetts: National Bureau of Economic Research).

Flood, Robert P., and Andrew K. Rose, 1995, "Fixing Exchange Rates: A Virtual Quest for Fundamentals," *Journal of Monetary Economics,* Vol. 36 (August), pp. 3–37.

Folkerts-Landau, David, and Peter Garber, 1992, "The European Central Bank: A Bank or a Monetary Policy Rule," NBER Working Paper No. 4016 (Cambridge, Massachusetts: National Bureau of Economic Research), pp. 1–33.

Frankel, Jeffrey A., 1996, "Exchange Rates and the Single Currency," in *The European Equity Markets: The State of the Union and an Agenda for the Millennium,* ed. by Benn Steil (Copenhagen: European Capital Markets Institute).

———, and Andrew K. Rose, 1996, "Currency Crashes in Emerging Markets: An Empirical Treatment," *Journal of International Economics,* Vol. 41 (November), pp. 351–68.

Frankel, Jeffrey A., Steven Phillips, and Menzie Chinn, 1993, "Financial and Currency Integration in the European Monetary System: The Statistical Record," in *Adjustment and Growth in the European Monetary Union,* ed. by Francisco Torres and Francesco Giavazzi (New York: Cambridge University Press).

Fratianni, Michele, and Juergen von Hagen, 1990, "The European Monetary System Ten Years After," Carnegie Rochester Conference Series on Public Policy, Vol. 32, pp. 173–242.

Garber, Peter M., 1996, "Managing Risks to Financial Markets from Volatile Capital Flows: The Role of Prudential Regulation," *International Journal of Finance and Economics,* Vol. 1 (July), pp. 183–95.

———, 1997, "Notes on the Role of TARGET in a Stage III Crisis" (unpublished; Brown University).

Giddy, Ian, Anthony Saunders, and Ingo Walter, 1996, "Clearance and Settlement," in *The European Equity Markets: The State of the Union and an Agenda for the Millennium,* ed. by Benn Steil (Copenhagen: European Capital Markets Institute), pp. 321–54.

Glen, Jack D., and Philippe Jorion, 1993, "Currency Hedging for International Portfolios," *Journal of Finance,* Vol. 48 (December), pp. 1865–86.

Goldberg, Linda S., 1994, "Predicting Exchange Rate Crises: Mexico Revisited," *Journal of International Economics,* Vol. 36 (May), pp. 413–30.

Goldfajn, Ilan, and Rodrigo O. Valdés, 1997, "Capital Flows and the Twin Crises: The Role of Liquidity," IMF Working Paper 97/87 (Washington: International Monetary Fund).

Goldman Sachs International, 1997a, "Are BTPs Too Expensive?" *Italian Economics Analyst,* Issue No. 97/01 (February).

———, 1997b, "The Equity Risk Premium and the Brave New Business Cycle," *U.S. Economics Analyst,* Issue No. 97/08 (February).

Goldstein, Morris, 1997, "The Case for an International Banking Standard," Policy Analyses in International Economics No. 47 (Washington: Institute for International Economics).

———, and Michael Mussa, 1993, "The Integration of World Capital Markets," IMF Working Paper 93/95 (Washington: International Monetary Fund).

Goldstein, Morris, and Philip Turner, 1996, "Banking Crises in Emerging Economies: Origins and Policy Options," BIS Economic Paper No. 46 (Basle: Bank for International Settlements).

Goodhart, Charles, and Dirk Schoenmaker, 1995, "Monetary Policy and Banking Supervision," *Oxford Economic Papers,* Vol. 47 (October), pp. 539–60.

Greenspan, Alan, 1997, remarks at the Conference on Bank Structure and Competition at the Federal Reserve Bank of Chicago, January 5, 1997, *BIS Review,* No. 50 (May 29), pp. 1–7.

Group of Ten, 1997, *Financial Stability in Emerging Market Economies* (Basle: Bank for International Settlements, April).

Gurley, John G., and Edward S. Shaw, 1960, *Money in a Theory of Finance* (Washington: Brookings Institution).

Haque, Nadeem U., and Peter J. Montiel, 1991, "Capital Mobility in Developing Countries: Some Empirical Tests," *World Development,* Vol. 19 (October), pp. 1391–98.

Honohan, Patrick, 1997, "Banking System Failures in Developing and Transition Countries: Diagnosis and Prediction," BIS Working Paper No. 39 (Basle: Bank for International Settlements).

Howell, Michael J., 1993, "Institutional Investors and Emerging Stock Markets," in *Portfolio Investment in Developing Countries,* ed. by Stijn Claessens and Sudarshan Gooptu, World Bank Discussion Paper No. 228 (Washington: World Bank), pp. 78–87.

International Monetary Fund, 1994, 1995, 1996, *International Capital Markets: Developments, Prospects, and Policy Issues,* World Economic and Financial Surveys (Washington: International Monetary Fund).

———, 1997, *World Economic Outlook, May 1997: A Survey by the Staff of the International Monetary Fund,* World Economic and Financial Surveys (Washington).

Ireland, National Treasury Management Agency, 1996, *Report and Accounts for the Year Ended December 31, 1995.*

James, Harold, 1996, *International Monetary Cooperation Since Bretton Woods* (Washington: International Monetary Fund; New York: Oxford University Press).

Jeanneau, S., 1996, "The Market for International Asset-Backed Securities," *International Banking and Financial Market Developments* (Basle: Bank for International Settlements, November), pp. 36–46.

Jones Lang Wootton, 1997, *Quarterly Investment Report: The European Property Market* (London).

J.P. Morgan, 1996, "The Euro, FX Reserves and Vehicle Currencies: Some Unusual Findings," Morgan Guaranty Trust Company, Foreign Exchange Research (September 13).

———, 1997a, "European Economic Outlook" (January/February).

———, 1997b, "Bearish on the Nikkei" (February 28).

———, 1997c, "What Happens If EMU Is Delayed?" (March 21).

Kaminsky, Graciela L., and Carmen M. Reinhart, 1996, "The Twin Crises: The Causes of Banking and Balance-of-Payments Problems," IMF Seminar Series, No. 1996–12, pp. 1–26.

Kaminsky, Graciela. L., Saul Lizondo, and Carmen M. Reinhart, 1997, "Leading Indicators of Currency Crises," IMF Working Paper 97/79 (Washington: International Monetary Fund).

Kenen, Peter B., 1997, "Monetary Policy in Stage Three: A Review of the Framework Proposed by the European Monetary Institute," paper presented at a conference on the "Monetary, Fiscal, and Financial Implications of European Monetary Union," European University Institute, Florence, June.

Kindleberger, Charles P., 1965, *Balance of Payments Deficits and the International Market for Liquidity,* Princeton Essays in International Finance No. 46 (Princeton, New Jersey).

———, 1982, "The Cyclical Pattern of Long-Term Lending," in *The Theory and Experience of Economic Development: Essays in Honour of Sir W. Arthur Lewis,* ed. by Mark Gersovitz and others (London: Allen & Unwin).

Kneeshaw, J.T., 1995, "A Survey of Non-financial Sector Balance Sheets in Industrialized Countries: Implications for the Monetary Policy Transmission Mechanism," BIS Working Paper No. 25 (Basle: Bank for International Settlements).

Kritzman, Mark, 1993, "Optimal Currency Hedging Policy with Biased Forward Rates," *Journal of Portfolio Management,* Vol. 19, No. 4, pp. 94–100.

Krugman, Paul, 1979, "A Model of Balance-of-Payments Crises," *Journal of Money, Credit, and Banking,* Vol. 11 (August), pp. 311–25.

Lall, Subir, 1997, "Speculative Attacks, Forward Market Intervention, and the Classic Bear Squeeze" (unpublished; Washington: International Monetary Fund).

Lauterbach, Beni, and Uri Ben-Tsiyon, 1993, "Stock Market Crashes and the Performance of Circuit Breakers: Empirical Evidence," *Journal of Finance,* Vol. 48 (December), pp. 1909–25.

Lee, Charles, Mark Ready, and Paul Seguin, 1994, "Volume, Volatility, and the New York Stock Exchange Trading Halts," *Journal of Finance,* Vol. 49 (March), pp. 183–214.

Lindgren, Carl-Johan, Gillian Garcia, and Matthew I. Saal, 1996, *Bank Soundness and Macroeconomic Policy* (Washington: International Monetary Fund).

Masson, Paul R., and Bart G. Turtelboom, 1997, "Characteristics of the Euro, the Demand for Reserves, and Policy Coordination Under EMU," in *EMU and the International Monetary System,* ed. by Paul R. Masson, Thomas H. Krueger, and Bart G. Turtelboom (Washington: International Monetary Fund).

Masson, Paul R., Thomas H. Krueger, and Bart G. Turtelboom, eds., 1997, *EMU and the International Monetary System* (Washington: International Monetary Fund).

Mathieson, Donald J., and Liliana Rojas-Suárez, 1993, *Liberalization of the Capital Account: Experiences and Issues,* IMF Occasional Paper No. 103 (Washington: International Monetary Fund).

Melick, William R., and Charles P. Thomas, 1997, "Recovering an Asset's Implied PDF from Option Prices: An Application to Crude Oil During the Gulf Crisis," *Journal of Financial and Quantitative Analysis,* Vol. 32, No. 1, pp. 91–115.

Miller, Victoria, 1996, "Speculative Currency Attacks with Endogenously Induced Commercial Bank Crises," *Journal of International Money and Finance,* Vol. 15 (June), pp. 383–403.

Mishkin, Frederic S., 1996, "Asymmetric Information and Financial Crises: A Developing Country Perspective," IMF Seminar Series, No. 1996–11.

"Mixed Reactions to US Regulatory Changes," 1997, *International Financing Review,* Issue No. 1169, February 8, p. 99.

Mussa, Michael, 1988, Commentary on Charles Goodhart, "The International Transmission of Asset Price Volatility," in *Financial Market Volatility,* Federal Reserve Bank of Kansas City Symposium Series, pp. 127–32.

Obstfeld, Maurice, 1994, "The Logic of Currency Crises," NBER Working Paper No. 4640 (Cambridge, Massachusetts: National Bureau of Economic Research).

———, 1997, "Destabilizing Effects of Exchange-Rate Escape Clauses," *Journal of International Economics,* Vol. 43 (August), pp. 61–78.

———, and Alan M. Taylor, 1997, "The Great Depression as a Watershed: International Capital Mobility over the Long Run," NBER Working Paper No. 5960 (Cambridge, Massachusetts: National Bureau of Economic Research).

O'Keefe, John P., 1996, "Banking Industry Consolidation: Financial Attributes of Merging Banks," *FDIC Banking Review,* Vol. 9 (December).

Organization for Economic Cooperation and Development, *OECD Financial Statistics, Part III, Non-financial Enterprises Financial Statements,* various issues (Paris: OECD).

————, 1996, *Bank Profitability: Financial Statements of Banks, 1985–1995* (Paris).

Pagano, Marco, 1996, "The Cost of Trading in European Equity Markets," London School of Economics Financial Markets Group Special Paper Series No. 83, pp. 1–22.

Paribas Capital Markets, 1996, "EMU Countdown," *International Research* (London: Banque Paribas), September 9.

————, 1997, "EMU Countdown," *International Research* (London), various issues.

Perold, Andre F., and Evan C. Schulman, 1988, "The Free Lunch in Currency Hedging: Implications for Investment Policy and Performance Standards," *Financial Analysts Journal*, Vol. 44 (May–June), pp. 45–50.

Prati, Alessandro, and Garry Schinasi, 1997, "European Monetary Union and International Capital Markets: Structural Implications and Risks," IMF Working Paper 97/62 (Washington: International Monetary Fund).

Reisen, Helmut, and Helene Yeches, 1993, "Time-Varying Estimates on the Openness of the Capital Account in Korea and Taiwan," *Journal of Development Economics*, Vol. 41 (August), pp. 285–305.

Rich, Georg, 1989, "Canadian Banks, Gold, and the Crisis of 1907," *Explorations in Economic History*, Vol. 26 (April), pp. 135–60.

Rojas-Suárez, Liliana, 1991, "Risk and Capital Flight in Developing Countries," in *Determinants and Systemic Consequences of International Capital Flows*, by Morris Goldstein and others, Occasional Paper No. 77 (Washington: International Monetary Fund).

Sachs, Jeffrey D., Aaron Tornell, and Andrés Velasco, 1996, "Financial Crises in Emerging Markets: The Lessons from 1995," *Brookings Papers on Economic Activity: 1*, Brookings Institution, pp.147–215.

Salant, Stephen W., and Dale W. Henderson, 1978, "Market Anticipations of Government Policies and the Price of Gold," *Journal of Political Economy*, Vol. 86 (August), pp. 627–48.

Salomon Brothers, 1996, "Managing Convergence," *Prospects for Financial Markets* (December).

————, 1997a, *Chilean Bank Reference Guide: December 1996* (New York, March).

————, 1997b, *Argentine Bank Reference Guide: December 1996* (New York, April).

SBC Warburg, 1996, *EMU: Opportunity or Threat?* (December).

Smith, R. Todd, 1995, "Markets for Corporate Debt Securities," IMF Working Paper 95/67 (Washington: International Monetary Fund).

Söderlind, Paul, and Lars E.O. Svensson, 1997, "New Techniques to Extract Market Expectations from Financial Instruments," NBER Working Paper No. 5877 (Cambridge, Massachusetts: National Bureauu of Economic Research) (forthcoming in *Journal of Economic Research*).

Standard & Poor's, 1996, "Brady Bonds Still Top Asset Class in Emerging Markets," *Credit Week* (May 9).

Steinherr, Alfred, 1996, "Universal vs. Specialized Banks," Economic Studies Working Paper No. 20 (Washington: American Institute for Contemporary German Studies, The Johns Hopkins University, December).

Sundararajan, Vasudevan, and Tomás J.T. Baliño, eds., 1991, *Banking Crises: Cases and Issues* (Washington: International Monetary Fund).

Sweden, National Debt Office, 1996, *Annual Report for Fiscal Year 1994/95.*

Taylor, Alan M., 1996, "International Capital Mobility in History: The Saving-Investment Relationship," NBER Working Paper No. 5943 (Cambridge, Massachusetts: National Bureau of Economic Research).

Thomas, Brinley, 1967, "The Historical Record of International Capital Movements to 1913," in *Capital Movements and Economic Development*, ed. by John A. Adler (New York: St. Martin's Press).

Triffin, Robert, 1966, *The Balance of Payments and the Foreign Investment Position of the United States*, Princeton Essays in International Finance No. 55 (Princeton, New Jersey).

United Nations, 1949, *International Capital Movements During the Interwar Period* (New York: United Nations).

United States, Department of Commerce, *Survey of Current Business*, various issues.

————, Department of the Treasury, *Treasury Bulletin*, various issues.

————, Office of the Comptroller of the Currency, 1996, *Quarterly Derivatives Fact Sheet*, 4th quarter.

————, Senate, 1990, "Implementation of the Brady Plan," Hearing Before the Subcommittee on International Debt of the Committee on Finance (March 2).

Velasco, Andrés, 1987, "Financial Crises and Balance of Payment Crises: A Simple Model of the Southern Cone Experience," *Journal of Development Economics*, Vol. 27 (October), pp. 263–83.

Vos, Rob, 1994, *Debt and Adjustment in the World Economy: Structural Asymmetries in North-South Interactions* (New York: St. Martin's Press).

Wheeler, Graeme, forthcoming, "New Zealand Experience with Autonomous Sovereign Debt Management," in *Risk Management for Sovereign Countries* (Washington: International Monetary Fund).

World Bank, 1996a, "Offer of Currency Choice for Existing Currency Pool Loans," *IBRD Financial Products.*

————, 1996b, *World Debt Tables 1994–95* (Washington).

————, 1997, *Private Capital Flows to Developing Countries: The Road to Financial Integration* (New York: Oxford University Press).

Wymeersch, Eddy, 1996, "The Implementation of the ISD and CAD in the National Legal System," paper presented at a conference of the University of Genoa, "European Investment Markets: Implementation of the ISD and National Law Reforms," Genoa, November.

265

World Economic and Financial Surveys

This series (ISSN 0258-7440) contains biannual, annual, and periodic studies covering monetary and financial issues of importance to the global economy. The core elements of the series are the *World Economic Outlook* report, usually published in May and October, and the annual report on *International Capital Markets*. Other studies assess international trade policy, private market and official financing for developing countries, exchange and payments systems, export credit policies, and issues discussed in the *World Economic Outlook*.

World Economic Outlook: A Survey by the Staff of the International Monetary Fund

The *World Economic Outlook*, published twice a year in English, French, Spanish, and Arabic, presents IMF staff economists' analyses of global economic developments during the near and medium term. Chapters give an overview of the world economy; consider issues affecting industrial countries, developing countries, and economies in transition to the market; and address topics of pressing current interest.
ISSN 0256-6877.
$35.00 (academic rate: $24.00; paper)

1997 (Oct.). ISBN 1-55775-610-4. **Stock #WEO-297.**
1997 (May). ISBN 1-55775-648-1. **Stock #WEO-197.**
1996 (Oct.). ISBN 1-55775-610-4. **Stock #WEO-296.**
1996 (May). ISBN 1-55775-567-1. **Stock #WEO-196.**

International Capital Markets: Developments, Prospects, and Key Policy Issues
by an IMF staff team led by David Folkerts-Landau with Donald J. Mathieson and Garry J. Schinasi

This year's capital markets report provides a comprehensive survey of recent developments and trends in the mature and emerging capital markets, including equities, bonds, foreign exchange, and derivatives, and banking systems. The report focuses on two major international policy challenges: the implications of European Economic and Monetary Union (EMU) for financial markets and the management of external liabilities of emerging market countries.
$20.00 (academic rate: $12.00; paper).

1997. ISBN 1-55775-686-4. **Stock #WEO-697.**
1996. ISBN 1-55775-609-0. **Stock #WEO-696.**
1995. ISBN 1-55775-516-7. **Stock #WEO-695.**

Staff Studies for the World Economic Outlook
by the IMF's Research Department

These studies, supporting analyses and scenarios of the *World Economic Outlook*, provide a detailed examination of theory and evidence on major issues currently affecting the global economy.
$20.00 (academic rate: $12.00; paper).
1995. ISBN 1-55775-499-3. **Stock #WEO-395.**
1993. ISBN 1-55775-337-7. **Stock #WEO-393.**

Issues in International Exchange and Payments Systems
by a staff team from the IMF's Monetary and Exchange Affairs Department

The global trend toward liberalization in countries' international exchange and payments systems has been widespread in both industrial and developing countries and most dramatic in Central and Eastern Europe. Countries in general have brought their exchange systems more in line with market principles and moved toward more flexible exchange rate arrangements in recent years.
$20.00 (academic rate: $12.00; paper).
1995. ISBN 1-55775-480-2. **Stock #WEO-895.**

Private Market Financing for Developing Countries
by a staff team from the IMF's Policy Development and Review Department under the direction of Steven Dunaway

The latest study surveys recent trends in flows to developing countries through banking and securities markets. It also analyzes the institutional and regulatory framework for developing country finance; institutional investor behavior and pricing of developing country stocks; and progress in commercial bank debt restructuring in low-income countries.
$20.00 (academic rate: $12.00; paper).
1995. ISBN 1-55775-526-4. **Stock #WEO-1595.**
1995. ISBN 1-55775-456-X. **Stock #WEO-995.**

International Trade Policies
by a staff team led by Naheed Kirmani

The study reviews major issues and developments in trade and their implications for the work of the IMF. Volume I, *The Uruguay Round and Beyond: Principal Issues*, gives an overview of the principal issues and developments in the world trading system. Volume II, *The Uruguay Round and Beyond: Background Papers*, presents detailed background papers on selected trade and trade-related issues. This study updates previous studies published under the title *Issues and Developments in International Trade Policy*.
$20.00 (academic rate: $12.00; paper).

1994. *Volume I. The Uruguay Round and Beyond: Principal Issues*
ISBN 1-55775-469-1. **Stock #WEO-1094.**
1994. *Volume II. The Uruguay Round and Beyond: Background Papers*
ISBN 1-55775-457-8. **Stock #WEO-1494.**
1992. ISBN 1-55775-311-1. **Stock #WEO-1092.**

Official Financing for Developing Countries
by a staff team from the IMF's Policy Development and Review Department under the direction of Anthony R. Boote

This study provides information on official financing for developing countries, with the focus on low- and lower-middle-income countries. It updates and replaces *Multilateral Official Debt Rescheduling: Recent Experience* and reviews developments in direct financing by official and multilateral sources.
$20.00 (academic rate: $12.00; paper)
1995. ISBN 1-55775-527-2. **Stock #WEO-1395.**
1994. ISBN 1-55775-378-4. **Stock #WEO-1394.**

Officially Supported Export Credits: Recent Developments and Prospects
by Michael G. Kuhn, Balazs Horvath, Christopher J. Jarvis

This study examines export credit and cover policies in major industrial countries.
$20.00 (academic rate: $12.00; paper).
1995. ISBN 1-55775-448-9. **Stock #WEO-595.**

Available by series subscription or single title (including back issues); academic rate available only to full-time university faculty and students.

Please send orders and inquiries to:
International Monetary Fund, Publication Services, 700 19th Street, N.W.
Washington, D.C. 20431, U.S.A.
Tel.: (202) 623-7430   Telefax: (202) 623-7201
E-mail: publications@imf.org
Internet: http://www.imf.org